Readings on
Reading Instruction

Readings on Reading Instruction

EDITED BY

Albert J. Harris

and

Edward R. Sipay

SECOND EDITION

DAVID McKAY COMPANY, INC.
New York

Contributors

Charlotte Agrast, Teacher of Grade 6, Coventry School, Cleveland Heights, Ohio

May Hill Arbuthnot, Late Professor of Education and Author, Western Reserve University, Cleveland, Ohio

A. Sterl Artley, Director, Child Study Clinic, University of Missouri, Columbia, Missouri

Alden W. Badal, Associate Superintendent—Planning, Research and Evaluation, Oakland Public Schools, Oakland, California

Jack Bagford, Professor of Education, University of Iowa, Iowa City, Iowa

Joan C. Baratz, Project Director, Education Study Center, Washington, D.C.

Emmett A. Betts, Research Professor, Reading Research Laboratory, University of Miami, Coral Gables, Florida

Emery P. Bliesmer, Professor of Education and Director, Clinical Reading Service, Pennsylvania State University, State College, Pennsylvania

Marguerite B. Bougere, Associate Professor, Tulane University, New Orleans, Louisiana

Lou E. Burmeister, Professor of Curriculum & Instruction, University of Texas at El Paso, El Paso, Texas

Dorothy Burrus, Assistant Professor and Coordinator of Laboratory Experiences, University of Maryland, College Park, Maryland

Allen D. Calvin, Chairman of the Board, Behavioral Research Laboratories, Palo Alto, California

John B. Carroll, Senior Research Psychologist, Educational Testing Service, Princeton, New Jersey

Jeanne Chall, Professor of Education and Director, Reading Laboratory, Harvard University, Cambridge, Massachusetts

Marie B. Clark, Elementary Supervisor, Vincennes Community Schools, Vincennes, Indiana

Theodore Clymer, Professor of Education, University of Minnesota, Minneapolis, Minnesota

Martha Dallmann, Professor of Elementary Education, St. Cloud State College, St. Cloud, Minnesota

Mary Ann Daniel, Secondary Reading Coordinator, Upper Dublin School District, Fort Washington, Pennsylvania

Amo De Bernardis, President, Portland Community College, Portland, Oregon

Lee C. Deighton, Formerly President, The Macmillan Company, New York, New York

Edward W. Dolch, Late Professor Emeritus of Education, University of Illinois, Champaign, Illinois

Dolores Durkin, Professor of Education, University of Illinois, Urbana, Illinois

Robert Dykstra, Professor of Education, University of Minnesota, Minneapolis, Minnesota

Dorothy Ebert, Principal, Ortega Elementary School, Austin, Texas

Joan T. Feeley, Instructor, William Paterson College, Wayne, New Jersey

Muriel Fisch, Formerly Teacher of Grade 6, Board of Education, New York, New York

Herman M. Frankel, M.D., Director, Prescriptive Education Program, Portland (Oregon) Public Schools, Clinical Instructor, Dept. of Pediatrics, University of Oregon Medical School

Marianne Frostig, Executive Director, Marianne Frostig Center of Educational Therapy, Los Angeles, California

John I. Goodlad, Dean, Graduate School of Education, University of California, Los Angeles, California

Kenneth S. Goodman, Professor, Wayne State University, Detroit, Michigan

Yetta M. Goodman, Associate Professor of Education, University of Michigan at Dearborn, Dearborn, Michigan

William S. Gray, Late Professor Emeritus of Education and Director of Research in Reading, University of Chicago, Chicago, Illinois

Albert J. Harris, Professor Emeritus, Office of Teacher Education, City University of New York, New York, New York

Gertrude Hildreth, Professor of Education and Psychology, Voorhees College, Denmark, South Carolina

J. Kendall Hoggard, Associate Professor of Education and Director, Reading Center, State College of Arkansas, Conway, Arkansas

Lyman C. Hunt, Jr., Director, Reading Center, University of Vermont, Burlington, Vermont

Helen Huus, Professor of Education, University of Missouri-Kansas City, Kansas City, Missouri

Joseph P. Kender, Director, Reading and Study Clinic, Lehigh University, Bethlehem, Pennsylvania

Jack W. Kriege, Reading Specialist, Bonita Unified School District, San Dimas, California

James L. Laffey, Associate Professor of Education and Director, ERIC/CRIER, Indiana University, Bloomington, Indiana

Mary Louise Lake, Associate Professor of Education, University of Tampa, Tampa, Florida

John H. Langer, Chief, Preventive Program Division, Bureau of Narcotics and Dangerous Drugs, Formerly Associate Professor of Education, Indiana University, Southeast Campus, New Albany, Indiana

Margaret La Pray, Professor of Education and Director, Learning Difficulties Center, San Diego State College, San Diego, California

Nancy Larrick, Author, Editor, and Associate Professor, Lehigh University, Bethlehem, Pennsylvania

Edwin P. Larsen, Supervisor of Research and Group Testing, Oakland Public Schools, Oakland, California

Beatrice Lieben, Consulting Child Psychologist and Director, The Community School, Englewood, New Jersey

Sara W. Lundsteen, Associate Professor, University of California at Irvine, Irvine, California

Ruth Martin, Supervisor, More Able Child Program, Castro Valley School District, Castro Valley, California

Robert A. McCracken, Coordinator of Elementary Education and Director, Reading Center, Western Washington State College, Bellingham, Washington

Constance M. McCullough, Professor of Education, San Francisco State College, San Francisco, California

Mary Meighen, late author and general supervisor, Escanaba Public Schools, Michigan

Amelia Melnik, Associate Professor of Education, University of Arizona, Tucson, Arizona

Donald Merryman, Coordinator of Elementary Education, Baltimore County, Maryland

Edith F. Miller, English Teacher Grades 5 and 6, Glen Ridge Middle School, Glen Ridge, New Jersey

Helen F. O'Leary, Associate Professor of Education and Co-Director of Reading Clinic, University of Massachusetts, Amherst, Massachusetts

Lillian Orme, Principal, Chester A. Franklin Elementary School, Kansas City, Missouri

Martha Thompson Orr, Formerly Elementary Supervisor, Avonworth Union School District, Bon Avon, Pittsburgh, Pennsylvania

Riva R. Reich, Faculty, Graduate Programs, Bank Street College of Education, New York, New York

Ramon Ross, Professor of Education, San Diego State College, San Diego, California

David H. Russell, Late Professor of Education, University of California, Berkeley, California

Harry W. Sartain, Professor of Education and Director of Falk Laboratory School, University of Pittsburgh, Pittsburgh, Pennsylvania

William D. Sheldon, Professor of Reading Education and Director of the Reading and Language Arts Center, Syracuse University, Syracuse, New York

Harry Singer, Professor of Education, University of California, Riverside, California

Edward R. Sipay, Professor of Education and Director of Reading Clinics, State University of New York at Albany, Albany, New York

Nila B. Smith, Distinguished Service Professor of Education, University of Southern California, Los Angeles, California

Floyd Sucher, Professor of Education and Coordinator—Graduate Elementary Education, Brigham Young University, Provo, Utah

Stanford E. Taylor, President, Taylor Associates, Lloyd Harbor, New York

Miles A. Tinker, Consulting Psychologist, Santa Barbara, California; Profesor Emeritus of Psychology, University of Minnesota, Minneapolis, Minnesota

Ronald Wardhaugh, Director, English Language Institute, University of Michigan, Ann Arbor, Michigan

Olivia R. Way, Media Specialist and Librarian, Ridge Elementary School, Ridgewood, New Jersey

Martha Gesling Weber, Professor of Education, Bowling Green State University, Bowling Green, Ohio

Kathleen Wise, Retired, formerly educational consultant, Lyons and Carnahan.

Paul A. Witty, Professor Emeritus of Education, Northwestern University, Evanston, Illinois

L. Jean York, Associate Professor of Education, University of Texas at Austin, Austin, Texas

Contents

Chapter		Page
I	**Perspectives on Reading**	1
	1. What Is "Reading"?: Some Current Concepts—Theodore Clymer	1
	2. Key Factors in a Successful Reading Program—Albert J. Harris	7
	3. Reading Research That Makes a Difference—David H. Russell	15
	4. Research That Should Have Made a Difference—Harry Singer	18
	5. Reading: Seventy-five Years of Progress—Nila Banton Smith	27
II	**The Psychology and Psycholinguistics of Reading**	35
	6. Some Principles of Learning Applied to Reading—Gertrude Hildreth	35
	7. Child Development and Reading—Albert J. Harris	41
	8. A Psycholinguistic Analysis of Reading Behavior—John B. Carroll	47
	9. Reading: A Psycholinguistic Guessing Game—Kenneth S. Goodman	54
	10. Linguistics—Reading Dialogue—Ronald Wardhaugh	62
III	**Reading Readiness**	71
	11. Readiness Is the Best Prevention—J. Kendall Hoggard	71
	12. Developing Reading Readiness—Helen Huus	76
	13. Building Readiness for Reading in First-Grade Children through Special Instruction—Lillian Orme	79
	14. Evaluating Reading Readiness Tests—Albert J. Harris	82
	15. What Does Research Say About the Time to Begin Reading Instruction?—Dolores Durkin	88
IV	**Beginning Reading**	96
	16. Basal Reading Approaches—William D. Sheldon	96
	17. Innovations in Beginning Reading—Jeanne Chall	102
	18. The Effectiveness of Code- and Meaning-Emphasis Beginning Reading Programs—Robert Dykstra	110
	19. Interpreting the USOE Cooperative Reading Studies—Edward R. Sipay	116
	20. Vital Principles in Need of Application—Constance M. McCullough	122
V	**Measuring Reading Outcomes and Determining Needs**	130
	21. Areas of Concern in Evaluation—Albert J. Harris	130
	22. Understanding Test Scores—Alden W. Badal and Edwin P. Larsen	140
	23. The Graded Word List: Quick Gauge of Reading Ability—Margaret La Pray and Ramon Ross	145

24. Informal Inventories—Emmett Albert Betts   147
25. Using an Informal Reading Inventory to Affect Instruction—
    Robert A. McCracken   151
26. Informal Reading Inventories—Joseph P. Kender   156

VI   Grouping for Effective Reading Instruction   159

27. The Structured Reading Program—Theodore Clymer   159
28. You Can Systematize Your Reading Program—Jack W. Kriege   164
29. Independent Reading Activities—Constance M. McCullough   172
30. "Reading Levels" Replace Grades in the Non-Graded Plan—John
    I. Goodlad, Fred E. Brooks, Irene M. Larson, Neal Neff   176
31. Grouping Helps Children Succeed in the Intermediate Grades—
    Marie B. Clark   180

VII   Individualized Reading   184

32. Philosophy of Individualized Reading—Lyman C. Hunt, Jr.   184
33. You Can Individualize Your Reading Program Too—Mary Ann
    Daniel   187
34. Record Keeping for Individualized Reading—Muriel Fisch   190
35. The Place of Individualized Reading in a Well-Planned Program—
    Harry W. Sartain   193
36. Individualized Reading: Theory and Practice—Edward R. Sipay   199

VIII   Word Recognition and Word Analysis   206

37. Sensation and Perception: The Complexity of Word Perception—
    Stanford E. Taylor   206
38. The Role of Phonics in Teaching Reading—Jack Bagford   214
39. Phonics: Consonants—Emmett Albert Betts   218
40. Development of Vowel Sounds—Mary Meighen and Marjorie Pratt   221
41. Recognition of Long Words—E. W. Dolch   224
42. Content of a Phonics Program—Lou E. Burmeister   228
43. Using Children's Reading Miscues for New Teaching Strategies—
    Yetta M. Goodman   234

IX   Development of Vocabulary   238

44. Vocabulary and Concept Development—John H. Langer   238
45. Vocabulary Development in the Primary Grades—Marguerite B.
    Bougere   244
46. Activities for Increasing Hearing and Speaking Vocabularies—
    Kathleen Wise   249
47. First Aid for Vocabularies—Mary Louise Lake   252
48. Vocabulary Development in the Classroom—Lee C. Deighton   254
49. Stimulate Reading . . . with a Dictionary—Edith F. Miller   257

X   Reading Comprehension   261

50. Levels of Discussion in Reading—Nila Banton Smith   261
51. Questions: An Instructional-Diagnostic Tool—Amelia Melnik   265

52. Procedures for Teaching Critical Reading and Listening—Sara W. Lundsteen   270
53. Teach Them to Read Between the Lines—Charlotte Agrast   277
54. Developing Critical and Creative Thinking Skills Using the Newspaper—Dorothy Burrus   280

XI   Reading in Content Areas   284
55. Effective Study—Its Nature and Nurture—A. Sterl Artley   284
56. The Development of Locational Skills—Martha Dallman   294
57. Stimulate Reading with Individual Research Projects—Edith F. Miller   299
58. The Demon of Arithmetic—Reading Word Problems—Martha Gesling Weber   302
59. Five Steps to Reading Success in Science—Metropolitan School Study Council   306

XII   Recreational Reading   311
60. Reading Interests—Helen Huus   311
61. Developing Life Values Through Reading—May Hill Arbuthnot   318
62. Making Books Come Alive for Children—Nancy Larrick   325
63. How Elementary School Teachers and Librarians Work Together— Olivia R. Way   329

XIII Materials for the Reading Program   334
64. Preserve the Basic Reading Program—Helen F. O'Leary   334
65. The Purposes of Workbooks and Teachers' Guides—Martha Thompson Orr   339
66. Developing Classroom Reading Centers—Floyd Sucher   342
67. Audio-Visual Reading Tools—Amo De Bernardis   347
68. How to Teach with Programmed Textbooks—Allen D. Calvin   351

XIV   Some Special Issues in Reading Instruction   356
69. Characteristics of Effective Oral Reading—William S. Gray   356
70. Toward More Purposeful Oral Reading—Emery P. Bliesmer   360
71. Research on Some Aspects of Comprehension: Rate, Flexibility, and Study Skills—Albert J. Harris   364
72. Devices to Improve Speed of Reading—Miles A. Tinker   371
73. Parents Are Needed in a Good Reading Program—Nancy Larrick   375

XV   Reading for the Gifted   383
74. A Balanced Reading Program for the Gifted—Paul A. Witty   383
75. Enrichment Activities for the Superior Child in the Reading Program—Ruth Martin   390
76. Using Trade Books with Superior Children—Donald Merryman   393
77. Accelerating the Reading Speed of Sixth-Grade Gifted Children— Robert A. McCracken   396

XVI Helping the Retarded Reader 399

78. The Diagnosis of Reading Disabilities—Albert J. Harris 399
79. Five Suggestions: An Approach to the Identification and Management of Children with Learning Disabilities—Herman M. Frankel, M.D. 404
80. More Than Remedial Reading—Riva R. Reich 409
81. Corrective Reading in the Classroom—Marianne Frostig 413
82. Attitudes, Platitudes, and Conferences in Teacher-Parent Relations Involving the Child with a Reading Problem—Beatrice Lieben 420

XVII Reading Instruction for the Disadvantaged 428

83. Reading and Disadvantaged Children: Psychological and Sociological Factors—Albert J. Harris 428
84. Selected Language Research and Its Implications for Teaching Reading to the Disadvantaged—James L. Laffey 437
85. Linguistic and Cultural Factors in Teaching Reading to Ghetto Children—Joan C. Baratz 443
86. Implications for Teachers—Primary Level: Grades 1–3—L. Jean York and Dorothy Ebert 448
87. Teaching Non-English Speaking First-Graders to Read—Joan T. Feeley 454

Index 463

List of Figures

Figure	*Page*
Major components of reading (Gray)	6
Understanding test scores	141
Interpretation of grade equivalent scores	142
Interpretation of percentile scores	143
Distribution of reading test scores for School "X"	144

List of Tables

Table	*Page*
Means, Standard Deviations, and Intercorrelations of Pretests and Final Tests	85
Intercorrelations among Pretests and Final Tests, 1963–64 Study, for Total Population and Control Group	86
Classification of Reading Programs Used in the Cooperative Research Study According to Publisher, Common Label, and Certain Instructional Variables	111
Reading and Spelling Achievement of Pupils in Code-Emphasis and Meaning-Emphasis Reading Programs	113
Shoe Size of 28 Third-Grade Children in September	152
Book Size of 28 Third-Grade Children in September	153

Preface to
the Second Edition

In selecting the articles for this revised edition, we adopted as a main guiding principle the requirement that each contribution should have meaning and value for the reading teacher and teacher-to-be. Among the qualities we looked for were: representation of current and forward-looking viewpoints; interpretation of theory into practical consequences; relevance to today's teachers of reading; and clarity of style. As compared to the First Edition, there are fewer reports of specific research studies, but more papers that interpret the research in a particular area. We have sought for variety of points of view. Inclusion of a paper means that we think it effectively presents a significant position—with which we may or may not agree.

We anticipate that this book's major use will be as a supplementary reading in courses on the teaching of reading. Even in a well-stocked teacher-education library there is likely to be only one copy of the journal or other publication in which one of the articles originally appeared. It is ordinarily unwise to assign the reading of a periodical article to a class in order to have group discussion about it later; the one library copy soon disappears. Inclusion in a book of readings makes it possible for all to read the same articles. Excessive reliance on a single textbook is less likely to result, and the students have the opportunity to become acquainted with the writings of many of the leaders in the field of reading.

Numerous changes will be noted by those who have used the First Edition. Almost two-thirds of the 87 articles are new. More than half of the articles have been published since 1965, and more than three-quarters in the past decade. A few of the articles in the First Edition have been retained because we have not found a more recent treatment that we liked better. By and large, the new articles reflect the important developments that have taken place in reading instruction since the First Edition was published. Although the number of articles is slightly smaller, the average length of the articles has increased.

No chapter remains the same. The majority of the chapters retain only one "old" article, and in all but three chapters the "new" articles outnumber the "old." The chapter on oral reading has been deleted, the topic being covered in a new chapter on "Special Issues." Another new chapter, "Reading Instruction for the Disadvantaged," has been added.

A special note of thanks is due to Barbara M. Steger for her most able assistance in locating articles and her opinions about their value to teachers of reading.

We are, of course, greatly indebted to all of the authors and publishers of the articles included, for without their cooperation this book could not have been completed. A list of the authors, giving their present positions, precedes the Contents. Specific acknowledgment to author and source is given in a footnote at the beginning of each article.

ALBERT J. HARRIS
EDWARD R. SIPAY
December, 1971

I

Perspectives on Reading

It seems appropriate to begin a book concerned with reading instruction by seeking some answers to the as yet unanswered question "What is reading?", for as Clymer points out, "A teacher's definition of reading influences every action he takes in the classroom." Therefore, the first article summarizes various and differing definitions of reading, and presents one comprehensive model. This is followed by Harris's article, which offers guidelines for evaluating a reading program.

In the third article, Russell reviews ten studies that in his opinion have influenced reading instruction. Singer's article gives assent to Russell's selection of relevant research but cites "other studies that should have made a difference, but did not."

Finally, Smith presents a historical review of reading instruction in the United States since 1910, and makes some prediction about its future. Re-reading this article before reading Chapter IV, "Beginning Reading," might be interesting in determining the novelty of "new" approaches.

1. What Is "Reading"?: Some Current Concepts *

THEODORE CLYMER

Introduction

DURING the last two decades, increased attention has been given to definitions and explanations of reading. The influence of these definitions and explanations on in-structional procedures in the classroom may not be immediately apparent, but an examination of a few definitions in action will serve to indicate the impact of prevailing descriptions of reading on how and what we teach and on how we assess

* From Theodore Clymer, "What Is 'Reading?: Some Current Concepts," in Helen M. Robinson (ed.), *Innovation and Change in Reading Instruction,* Ch. I, Sixty-Seventh Yearbook of the National Society for the Study of Education, Part II (Chicago: University of Chicago Press, 1968), pp. 7–11, 23–27. Reprinted by permission of the author, the National Society for the Study of Education, and The University of Chicago Press.

what our pupils have learned in reading.

Recently a mother accosted an intermediate-grade teacher with this question: "Why haven't you let my girl read this week?" The bewildered teacher thought through the busy school schedule and, while he could not immediately recall all of the activities in his classroom that week, he knew that the girl had been reading and working on an independent project. At this point the mother provided a clue to her concept of reading by adding, "She hasn't read to you once this week!" It was now clear that this parent's definition of reading was an incomplete one so far as the teacher's program was concerned. To this mother, "reading" was oral reading. So narrow a concept of reading would result in an instructional program which neglects many of the desirable outcomes of a modern program.

In an interview with a capable boy who was having reading problems, the author asked, "Why do you think you have trouble reading?" Without hesitation, this bright child of ten responded, "Oh, I read all right, it's just the words that bother me." His diagnosis was a good one. He was a bright, perceptive child with a fairly good stock of sight words and an excellent technique of gaining general significance from his reading, but he had no word-analysis skills. His definition of reading was getting the gist of the author's message, and this he could do; but he lacked some other abilities which might be involved in a broader definition of reading. His concept of reading prevented him from seeing clearly his shortcomings as an effective reader.

Definitions of reading which give a unique or limited emphasis or focus to the reading program are not restricted to pupils or to their parents. The statement from Flesch, "I don't understand it; I just read it," presents in capsule form one of the real controversies in the definition of reading. Does reading involve only the translation of printed symbols to the spoken word, or does reading involve understanding of those words as well? If concern for understanding is eliminated from our definition of reading, obvious and sweeping changes are mandatory in our instructional programs and in the ways we evaluate our success in instruction. Instructional programs which deal with "nonsense" words, pay little attention to backgrounds for understanding, and spend the major portion of time on word-analysis skills are logical outcomes of reading defined as translation of printed symbols to the spoken word.

These brief and selective illustrations of the impact of the definition of reading on instructional procedures will have served their purpose if the reader is alerted to carefully assess the material which follows for its implications on reading instruction. A clear concept of reading is not just an "academic" concern. A teacher's definition of reading influences every action he takes in the classroom.

The difficulty in formulating a comprehensive and satisfactory definition of reading is also apparent. The areas of perception, psychology of learning, linguistics, social psychology, and language learning are a few of the fields contributing to an understanding of the reading process and the reading program.

Some Current Definitions

As Spache points out, a clear definition of reading is essential to planning the goals of the instructional program.[1] The lack of attention in reading textbooks to a definition of reading is, therefore, sur-

---

[1] George D. Spache, *Reading in the Elementary School* (Boston: Allyn & Bacon, 1964), p. 4.

prising. It is the unusual text which devotes much attention to the definition of reading. An examination of all types of professional literature reveals few systematic attempts to define the reading process in any comprehensive fashion.

Some Partial Definitions

Walcutt presents a simplified and assured definition of reading.[2] The title of his article seems to imply that anyone who disagrees with him is using a nonprofessional definition. And who could admit to that? His definition is three-pronged: (*a*) Reading is "decoding the printed visual symbol into a spoken word." (*b*) Reading is "understanding language." (*c*) Reading is appreciation of great literature and the cultural heritage it represents. From his discussion, it is clear that he believes the reading program has special responsibilities in the areas of decoding symbols and appreciation, but that "understanding language" is not really within the province of the reading program. He makes this clear when he states that understanding language "is not really reading at all."

Thus, to Walcutt, reading is decoding and literary appreciation in the highest and finest sense. How the child is helped to bridge the gap between these two important goals of the curriculum is not indicated.

The linguists have been active in defining reading in terms of their concern for oral language. To some linguists, reading is "talk written down," as Tinker and McCullough point out.[3] The impact of such a description on instruction, if it is accepted as a total definition, is clear: the major job of the reading program will be the teaching of "decoding skills."

Reed raises a serious objection to what he calls extreme statements of the primacy of speech over writing.[4] He notes that the newer grammars move from syntax to speech and writing rather than vice versa. He also questions the defining of writing as a secondary representation of speech, for to do so would render us unable to explain deaf-mutes who read or skilled readers who read with far greater speed than the most rapid speaker can speak.

In some cases, this primacy-of-speech concept impels the linguist to specify the type of word-analysis program which should be provided. Here the writer sometimes feels like the graduate student who said, "I can understand what they say. It's just the material that comes after the 'therefore' that troubles me." Fries indicates that, while reading is not a simple process, it can be summed up in a simple statement. "One can 'read' insofar as he can respond to the language signals represented by graphic shapes as fully as he has learned to respond to the same language signals of his code represented by patterns of auditory shapes."[5] The crucial word here is "respond." Evidently, triggering the oral response which is represented by the print produces reading.

The type of word recognition typically associated with the linguistic approach is that which is based on the regular consistency of letter and sound. Fries carries the matter further and places emphasis upon "spelling patterns" or, in other

---

[2] Charles C. Walcutt, "Reading—a Professional Definition," *Elementary School Journal*, LXVII (April, 1967), 363–65.

[3] Miles A. Tinker and Constance M. McCullough, *Teaching Elementary Reading* (New York: Appleton-Century-Crofts, 1962), p. 11.

[4] David W. Reed, "A Theory of Language, Speech and Writing," *Elementary English*, XLII (December, 1965), 845–51.

[5] Charles C. Fries, *Linguistics and Reading* (New York: Holt, Rinehart & Winston, Inc., 1963), p. 131.

words, upon larger visual units. His basic approach, however, is the same as that of Bloomfield, who states that the child should be presented with carefully programed material in teaching the orthographic-phonic regularities of English.[6]

This consistency approach is challenged by interpretations of research completed by Levin and his co-workers.[7] The results of Levin's work suggest that beginning a task with a list of words containing variable grapheme-phoneme relationships creates an expectation of variability of correspondences which transfers to a second situation and facilitates learning. A "set for diversity" may, therefore, be a valuable aid in the transfer of learned relationships to new situations. If this evidence is verified in other settings, the consistency theory is clearly challenged.

Gibson is representative of the experimental child psychologists who have taken an interest in reading. Gibson's research in the perception of children has led her naturally to some of the initial problems of visual discrimination in the prereading period. Her work also reflects the work of the Cornell group, including Hockett and Levin. She characterizes reading behavior as (a) receiving communication, (b) making discriminative responses to graphic symbols, (c) decoding graphic symbols to speech, and (d) obtaining meaning from the printed page.[8]

Gibson does not concern herself with the communication aspects of reading, because she believes the child has mastered this by the time he begins to learn to read. Reading instruction, then, includes attention only to the other three aspects of reading behavior listed in the preceding paragraph.

Unfortunately, Gibson's discussion of her research is restricted almost entirely to material on making discriminations and on decoding. Obtaining meaning is given little attention in her widely quoted article.

Betts and a number of his students have defined reading as a thinking process.[9] Admittedly, thinking is involved in even the narrowest definition of reading, but such a definition seems to provide no real avenue to understanding, for as Robinson points out, the nature of thought is complex and obscure.[10] There is undoubtedly value in considering thinking as one aspect of the reading process if such a position emphasizes the need for broader goals of a reading program. . . .

A Comprehensive Skills Model: Gray and Robinson

Few comprehensive models of reading have appeared in the literature. The most detailed model was presented by Gray [11]

---

[6] Leonard Bloomfield, "Teaching Children To Read," in Leonard Bloomfield and Clarence L. Barnhart, *Let's Read: A Linguistic Approach* (Detroit: Wayne State University Press, 1961).

[7] Harry Levin and J. Watson, "The Learning of Variable Grapheme-to-Phoneme Correspondence," in *A Basic Research Program on Reading* (Cornell University Cooperative Research Project No. 639 [Ithaca, N.Y., 1963]).

[8] Eleanor J. Gibson, "Learning To Read," *Science,* CXLVIII (May 21, 1965), 1066–72.

[9] Emmett A. Betts, "Reading: Psychological and Linguistic Bases," *Education,* LXXVI (April, 1966), 454–58.

[10] Helen M. Robinson, "The Major Aspects of Reading," in H. Alan Robinson (ed.), *Reading: Seventy-Five Years of Progress* ("Supplementary Educational Monographs," No. 96 [Chicago: University of Chicago Press, 1966]), pp. 22–32.

[11] William S. Gray, "The Major Aspects of Reading," in Helen M. Robinson (ed.), *Sequential Development of Reading Abilities* ("Supplementary Educational Monographs,"

and has been updated and amplified by Robinson.[12] In the material which follows, the model presented by Gray and Robinson is summarized and evaluated.

The Gray-Robinson model is essentially a skills model. While Gray gives some attention to the process of reading, his model is primarily a catalog of skills required for the various aspects of reading. He gives some (rather incomplete) attention to the process of reading. Gray stated that an analysis of the evidence available showed that the understandings, skills, and attitudes common to most reading activities can be classified under four headings. These headings are:

1. Word perception, including pronunciation and meaning
2. Comprehension, which includes a "clear grasp of what is read"
3. Reaction to and evaluation of ideas the author presents
4. Assimilation of what is read, through fusion of old ideas and information obtained through reading

While each of these aspects is discussed separately, Gray makes it abundantly clear that these aspects operate simultaneously and that reading must be considered a "unitary act."

The four major aspects of reading were illustrated and their relationships revealed by Gray's diagram (Fig. 1). Word perception is at the center of the diagram, for, without the skills for this aspect of reading, communication cannot take place. The first concentric band represents "comprehension." Gray's definition of comprehension includes three levels or types of understandings. The first of these is "literal" comprehension, which involves a "clear grasp of what is read." The second level is determining implied

meanings. The third level focuses on the implications and significance of the author's ideas beyond those things actually stated. In popular terms, these three levels are described by Gray as "ability to read the lines, to read between the lines, and to read beyond the lines." [13]

The second concentric band, identified as "reaction," seems to be what many authors have called "critical reading." This aspect of reading, according to Gray, involves an inquiring attitude, standards or criteria of judgment, reaching conclusions, and emotional responses to content. How some of the skills involved in reaction differ from the third level of comprehension is not made clear by Gray.

Assimilation or fusion of ideas, represented by the outer band, comes about, according to Gray, through the exercise of critical judgment, of creative thinking, and of combining information secured from reading with one's previous experiences. Again Gray does not clearly demonstrate how the skills involved in this aspect of reading are differentiated from the skills involved in his other aspects—reaction, for example. The differences appear to be of degree rather than of kind.

Gray provided four elaborate diagrams, each explaining to some extent one of the four aspects of reading. In addition, he attempted to describe how these four major aspects operated in a diagram entitled "Composite View of the Reading Act." Gray attempted also to show how each of the four aspects of reading is involved in reading in the content field and in reading for different purposes. These diagrams are not reproduced here, for Gray did not provide a

---

No. 90 [Chicago: University of Chicago Press, 1960]), pp. 8–24.

[12] Robinson, *op. cit.,* pp. 22–32.

[13] His quoted words are a paraphrase of an earlier statement by Edgar Dale in "The Art of Reading," *News Letter* (Ohio State University), XI (February, 1946), 1.

FIGURE 1.—Major components of reading (Gray).

complete explanation of his visual representations. In addition, his paper represented a first version of a model which undoubtedly he would have revised and extended.

Robinson, in a thoughtful analysis of Gray's model, drew upon the research literature in an attempt to validate the major aspects of reading.[14] Included in Robinson's discussion are evaluations of "substrata-factor theory" research, several theoretical models of reading, and a number of relevant experimental analyses of the reading act. Robinson carefully indicated that her concern was with the skills dimension of reading, not with the process of reading or the techniques of reading instruction.

Robinson retained the four major as-

pects as given by Gray—word perception, comprehension, reaction, and fusion. The design of her diagram differs, however. Two reasons are presented for this change: accommodation of a fifth aspect, rates of reading, and demonstration of the limitless opportunities for growth in the four aspects.

In her descriptions of the aspects of reading, Robinson sharpens the definitions of each of the first three aspects. She sees word perception as composed of word-recognition skills and word meanings. Comprehension, the second aspect, is divided into literal and implied meanings. Intellectual judgments and emotional responses are given as the two divisions of reaction. Unfortunately, Robinson does not supply a new description of assimilation, which might have more clearly differentiated this aspect

[14] Robinson, *op. cit.*, pp. 22–28.

from reaction and from comprehension.

Speed or rate is an important aspect of Robinson's revised model. She notes that rate of reading must be flexible and adjusted to the reader's purpose and the nature of the material. She illustrates the use of various rates in meeting different demands and conditions and thereby shows the close relationship of rate to the other major aspects of reading.

The Gray-Robinson model is a useful tool for examining some of our current concepts concerning reading. The comments below summarize some of the major observations which can be made about the model:

1. The emphasizing of the need to clearly differentiate *skills, processes,* and *instructional procedures* is a major contribution of the model. While these three factors are related and interdependent, a distinction among these factors is essential for thoughtful and productive analysis of reading.
2. Robinson has properly centered her attention on the skills as the area most likely at present to produce fruitful results.
3. A careful analysis of process is vital to further understanding of reading, but, at present, the analysis might better be made on a part of the process, such as word

perception or one type of comprehension, rather than on the total process of reading. Gray's attempts to depict the total process with all its interrelationships resulted in such elaborate systems of representation that his work is perhaps most useful for stimulating further analysis of certain parts of the process. There is no question, however, of the major value of Gray's first efforts to catalogue the reading process and its function.

4. Robinson's refinement of the model has clarified word perception and comprehension; but, to this writer, further delineation and description of the skills in assimilation and reaction are important future developments which probably must await additional evidence from basic and applied research.
5. The model, especially as refined by Robinson, clearly recognizes the interrelationships among the major aspects of reading, while at the same time it attempts to determine the specific details of the four aspects: word perception, comprehension, assimilation, and reaction. Reading can be viewed as a totally unified or global trait which denies analysis. Reading can also be defined as a long list of independent skills. The model as revised by Robinson steers a reasonable middle course between these two points of view.
6. The model will be a useful tool for stimulating further discussion, writing, and research. . . .

2. Key Factors in a Successful Reading Program *

ALBERT J. HARRIS

FOR many years, study skills experts have been advising that it is desirable to turn

* From Albert J. Harris, "Key Factors in a Successful Reading Program," *Elementary English*, 46 (January, 1969), 69–76. Reprinted by permission of the National Council of Teachers of English.

headings into questions and then to focus on the facts and ideas that provide answers to the questions. I am going to follow this advice: in talking about key factors in a successful reading program, I will really consider key questions which can guide us in evaluating a reading program and deciding whether or not everything is being done that can make a reading program effective. How many key questions there are is somewhat arbitrary, but I shall attempt to consider ten.

1. *Are we giving every child a successful start in reading?*

The concept of reading readiness has had its ups and downs. Originally it was a highly desirable corrective for a situation in which 20 to 40 percent of young children, plunged abruptly into the beginning of reading instruction, failed to make enough progress to be promoted. In providing for a more gradual and sometimes delayed start on formal reading instruction, some school systems went to the opposite extreme of delaying children who were ready along with those who needed a readiness period and program. Recent evidence indicates that a readiness program may be a sheer waste of time for children who are mature when they enter the first grade. On the other hand, the child who shows specific weakness in certain areas of readiness is likely to benefit when readiness instruction is designed specifically to overcome these weaknesses. For the most part, readiness weaknesses fall in four main areas: general language patterns, vocabulary and concepts, visual perception, and auditory perception. An effective readiness program should make use of readiness tests that can locate areas of weakness and should provide specific learning sequences in each area in which a weakness is found.

Another factor in a successful start is the increasingly recognized fact that children vary in the modes of learning that are most natural for them. For some children a predominantly visual approach succeeds well. For a minority, a method in which auditory perception and phonics are stressed may be highly desirable. A still smaller minority have difficulty with both visual and auditory avenues to learning, and for them a reliance on tracing and writing procedures may allow successful learning to go forward.

Still another important factor in a successful start is the pace of instruction. A program which is too slow for many children may cause boredom and disinterest. One which is too fast leaves many members of the group floundering and frustrated. An alert awareness of the way in which the children are reacting to the instruction, day by day, helps an effective first-grade teacher to keep the pace of the program in line with the learning abilities of the children.

2. *How well are we helping children to become independent in word recognition?*

The question of whether or not to teach phonics is a long-dead issue that continues to be dug up from time to time by crusaders ignorant of what is going on in our schools. There is a legitimate difference of opinion in this area, but it is not concerned with whether or not to teach phonics. Everyone agrees that children need to be taught the techniques for independence in word recognition and to become quick and accurate in word recognition.

The differences of opinion are concerned with a number of specific questions. Should reading activity be meaningful from the beginning, or is it efficient to start with nonsense syllables or words in lists? What is the best sequence in which to introduce phonic elements? Is it better to teach phonetically irregular words from the beginning, or is it best to start only with regular words and introduce the exceptions much later? Is it advisable to start with an artificial alphabet in which each symbol represents a unique sound and transfer to the regular alphabet later, or is it better to work with the regular alphabet from the beginning? How valuable is it to use a different color for each sound, particularly vowel sounds? On these and other related questions research has not yet provided definite answers.

For three years (1964–67) I was involved in a study of reading methodology in the first, second, and third grades.[1] One of the things that turned up is that the number of minutes per day spent in actual reading instruction is a crucially important factor in the outcomes. Teachers who spend major portions of their time on direct reading instruction tended, in general, to get better results than teachers who spent the major part of their language arts time on what may be described as supportive activities. Within each of the four teaching methods we compared there are certain activities that seem to have high pay-off value and others that seem to be noncontributory.

In most published research on beginning reading, the experimenters have told the teachers how much time to spend on reading instruction and have assumed that this is what took place. We had our teachers keep daily time records on a systematic schedule. We found that, despite instructions, there were wide variations within each method both in the total amount of time spent per day and in the time spent on specific phases of reading and the language arts. I have therefore come to the conclusion that much of our available research on first-

[1] A. J. Harris, C. Morrison, Blanche L. Serwer, and L. Gold. *A Continuation of the CRAFT Project: Comparing Reading Approaches with Disadvantaged Urban Negro Children in the Primary Grades*. Final Report, Project 5-0570-2-12-1 (New York: Selected Academic Readings, 630 Fifth Ave., 1968). See also summaries in *The Reading Teacher,* May, 1966; May, 1967; and January, 1969.

grade reading is inconclusive because we do not have the facts to separate the effects of teaching methods from those of instructional time.

Independence in word recognition is not merely a learning of basic phonics. It includes a variety of techniques, including efficient forming of inferences from context clues, the use of principles of structural analysis of words into roots, prefixes, and suffixes, and a flexible approach that moves from one alternative to another until the word is successfully solved. In the middle grades we need to add effective dictionary skills, including speed in locating the word in the dictionary and guided practice in the proper use of the key to pronunciation.

3. *Are we stimulating vocabulary growth sufficiently?*

The high correlation that is nearly always found between meaningful vocabulary and reading comprehension indicates that vocabulary development must be one of our most important areas of concern. Children understand the meaning of a word only when they have had enough experience out of which to develop an appropriate concept for the word. In the past few years we have become much more vividly aware of the limitations in background of experience, in concept development, and in meaningful vocabulary that handicap thousands of children in their progress in school. Vocabulary deficiencies are especially significant among children who come to school with educational and cultural disadvantages. It has been shown that many disadvantaged children have less than half of the meaningful vocabulary possessed by typical middle-class children.

To stimulate vocabulary growth, a number of different kinds of efforts are necessary. One of these is to provide real experiences in which new words and their meanings are absorbed easily and quickly. When real experience cannot be brought into the classroom, or the pupils cannot be taken out of the classroom to the experience, substitute or vicarious experience can frequently be provided.

Each area of the curriculum has certain basic concepts whose meanings need to be understood accurately and fully. Teachers need to take time to provide abundant illustrations of these concepts and to check and recheck the children's understandings of them.

A third avenue to vocabulary development is through the medium of wide independent reading. Once one gets beyond the vocabulary of the primary grade basal readers, any new word is likely to come up so seldom in a particular teaching sequence that it takes the reading of millions of running words in order to find most of the words in the vocabulary of an educated and intelligent adult. Providing the materials, time, and encouragement for independent reading is one way in which the school can build vocabulary.

A fourth aspect of vocabulary growth is teaching the efficient use of the dictionary. Most of us learned to use dictionaries by trial and error and have never become really skillful at it. Today we have better dictionaries than ever before, and they start at first-grade level. Guided practice in the correct use of dictionaries should be built into our comprehensive reading program.

A final important factor in vocabulary development is the stimulation of an interest in words and their meanings. Here, contests and games of various kinds can be harnessed to vocabulary learning to good effect. Children can become sensitized, through competitive games, to the meanings of new words they come across and to the varied meanings which most of our common words can carry.

4. *Are we making effective use of audio-visual aids for reading instruction?*

For years, there has been a dispute among reading specialists over the value of what have generally been described as "reading machines." These are devices for projecting words or phrases quickly or for controlling the rate at which a particular reading selection is presented. Some of them have been on the market for years and have sold thousands of units. In general, however, research in the upper grades and secondary school has failed to show any significant advantage for a machine over a non-machine instructional procedure. What advantages the machine may have seem to lie more in the area of novelty and motivation than in promoting learning efficiency.

During the three years of the CRAFT Project, my staff explored the use of a variety of audio-visual procedures in beginning reading. Our teachers tried overhead projectors, tape recorders, filmstrip projectors, listening corners, and show-and-tell devices combining a record with a filmstrip; they took cameras along on field trips in order to record what was seen for later illustration and discussion. Our results indicate that for the teachers who had good training in how to utilize this kind of equipment, large amounts of time spent with such procedures were beneficial to reading skills. However, for teachers who had not been carefully trained in audio-visual teaching, the more time spent with audio-visual procedures, the worse the reading test results.

This suggests a word of caution to those districts that have been spending money on a wide variety of audio-visual equipment and supplies. Supervision and training in the use of audio-visual procedures is essential if this equipment is to repay its cost, and, if such training is not provided, a profusion of such equipment may actually interfere with the instructional program.

5. *Are we meeting the problem of individual differences effectively?*

In order to provide effectively for individual differences in learning to read, the first essential is an adequate diagnostic program. Such a program provides the teacher with information on such essentials as the correct level of difficulty for the materials the child should be reading, the specific skills he has mastered, and the specific skills in which he needs further help. When there are severe or persistent problems, diagnosis needs to go beyond this to explore the possible handicaps that may be preventing the child from making progress.

Another minimum essential for effective individualization is a collection of materials that can provide for the wide variety of levels of competence to be found in almost any reading class. The past few years have seen a tremendous increase in the production of materials that are adaptable to individual progress and individual rates of learning. As such materials become more widely known, and as their content is improved, it will become increasingly possible to allow each child to proceed at his own best rate of speed.

6. *Are we providing a rich and varied reading diet?*

A child who ate nothing but rich, sweet desserts would soon become a medical case of malnutrition. Similarly, a one-sided reading diet may produce unbalanced reading skills, interest, and attitudes. Children need a balanced reading diet as much as they require balanced food intake.

One form of reading malnutrition is based upon the assumption that reading can be learned entirely from basal readers. It is true that something like 95 percent of the classrooms in this country employ basal readers as the core of instruction in reading. But unless there is considerable reading diet beyond the contents of the basal program, the children must be regarded as being on a bare subsistence level so far as reading nutrition is concerned. Wide reading beyond the confines of any one set of books is necessary if we are to develop the reading skills needed for the future.

When there are classroom libraries, school libraries, and well-stocked children's rooms in nearby public libraries, a balanced, varied, and nutritious reading diet becomes possible. I have at times expressed the opinion that the best way to evaluate a library is in terms of the number of books reported as lost or damaged. The higher this number, the more effective the library in promoting reading among children. When I visit a library and see shelves full of neat and shining books, my first guess is that this is a room that makes it hard for children to get at the collection.

The promotion of independent reading requires cooperation between teacher and parent. The hours devoted to television, which have averaged nearly three hours a day for elementary children over the past twenty years, absorb much of the quiet indoor time that used to be available mainly for recreational reading. Unless parents cooperate by limiting TV viewing time and by encouraging and fostering reading as a leisure time activity, the efforts of the school in this direction are likely to fall short of their desired goals.

7. *Are we giving sufficient training in the careful analysis of difficult material?*

In the early grades we quite often

hear the complaint that the language of the children is richer and more varied than that employed in their reading materials. By the time children reach the intermediate grades, the complaint more frequently is that the language of the book is far more complex and difficult than the language to which the child is accustomed. This is far more true for children from educationally limited backgrounds than it is for children whose parents are college graduates. For all children, however, increasing complexity of writing style becomes a major problem to be surmounted as children move into the content and reference books of the middle grades and secondary school.

Recently there has been renewed attention to the desirability of providing guided practice in functional sentence analysis. Without necessarily using the terminology of formal grammar, it is possible to provide a scheme for checking understanding of the basic meaning of a sentence. Who or what did something? What happened? To whom or to what? How? When? Where? Why? The systematic application of these questions makes it possible for a child to locate the key ideas within a sentence and to unravel the meaning of long and difficult sentences.

In a fifth-grade selection about the first Continental Congress, I found this sentence: "They declared that they did not ask for freedom from England but only that they be given certain rights which all Englishmen should enjoy."

A teacher who had the misfortune of having to teach with such a poorly written textbook could take off some of the curse by asking some questions and teaching children how to find the answers. For example, what is the antecedent of "they?" How many things did they declare? What does "they be given"

mean? What does it mean to *enjoy* a right?

Quite a few years ago a whole book was written on the subject of how to read a page.[2] Without going into that much detail, it seems evident that we can make far more of an effort than we have done in the past to help children learn to cope with the complexities of scholarly writing. In doing so, we need to use subject matter taken from the content subjects and to provide for the systematic development of a wide range of study skills. These range from simple skills like learning alphabetical order and how to use an index to the very complex ones of learning how to outline and to write summaries of difficult and challenging selections.

8. *Are we making it fun to read?*

Survey after survey has revealed disappointing facts about the reading habits of adults.[3] Disappointment applies not only to the adult population in general but also to those who are college graduates. It even extends to the reading habits of teachers. Even among those who do read regularly and frequently, the reading diet is all too often confined exclusively to light fiction. Magazine readers greatly outnumber book readers, and book readers who regularly read thought-provoking books or works of genuine literary excellence form a regrettably small minority.

[2] I. A. Richards, *How to Read a Page* (New York: W. W. Norton and Co., 1942).

[3] Naomi C. Chase, "Lifetime Reading Habits," pp. 43–48 in Dorothy M. Deitrich and Virginia H. Mathews (eds.), *Development of Lifetime Reading Habits,* Joint Committee on Reading Development of the American Book Publishers Council and the International Reading Association (Newark, Del.: International Reading Association, 1968).

If a person becomes a reading addict, his love of reading causes him to find the time to read regardless of other activities. Our most avid readers do go to movies, do have social lives, and do watch television. They do have friends and do participate in outdoor sports and activities. But somehow or other they always find time for reading. Our problem is to learn how to make such an addiction to reading more widespread.

It is clearly evident that adult leadership is very important in the development of the habit of reading for pleasure. The model provided by the parents is very influential. In addition, contagious enthusiasm for reading displayed by teachers can be extremely effective in promoting independent reading. A good reading teacher is a good book salesman.

9. *Are we evaluating all the important aspects of growth in reading?*

I referred earlier to the importance of testing procedures that provide the classroom teacher with diagnostic information necessary to make correct decisions in deciding the level of difficulty at which individual children are ready to read and to locate specific skills in which they need additional help. Standardized tests of reading ability are especially valuable for making comparisons among pupil populations and for tracing growth in research studies. Because they show how a child compares with other children rather than exactly what he can do with specific kinds of reading materials, standardized tests are somewhat less useful for instructional guidance than has often been assumed. To find out if a child is ready for a particular book, or in other words whether the book fits the child, it is necessary to try the book on for size. If the book is too difficult, the child experiences frustration and failure and learns little or nothing useful from his exposure to it. If the book is too easy and too limited, the child experiences boredom and discomfort and becomes less interested in reading than he was before. Taking the time to try the book on for size is an important feature of an effective reading program. The teacher who neglects to do this assigns many children to the wrong materials and then is disappointed by the way in which they respond.

We need wider use of tests that can pinpoint specific weaknesses in word recognition, comprehension, vocabulary, and study skills. Developing better group tests in these areas is a task for the future.

Besides the areas of reading which can today be measured with objectivity, there are some areas that are more subjective and harder to evaluate. We need to emphasize the importance of reading interests and attitudes. We need to encourage teachers to judge the taste and discrimination that children display in their reactions to different kinds of reading materials. We need to emphasize the importance of varying the rate of reading in accordance with the requirements of the material and the purpose for reading. And finally, we need to put far greater emphasis upon sensitivity to the child's ability to read with critical judgment.

10. *Are we making adequate provisions for the retarded reader?*

Essentially, we have two kinds of retarded readers. The smaller group consists of children who are already reading at an average or even slightly above average level, but who are so bright that their reading skills should be far higher than their present competence. These children are properly called underachievers in reading. They are frequently overlooked because they are not failing, but the gap that they show between potential reading ability and attained reading ability is sometimes distressingly large. Locating such pupils through a comparison of intelligence and reading scores is one of the values of a testing program.

The children whose reading skills are inadequate in terms of the normal expectation for their age and grade placement divide broadly into three groups. The largest of these groups is that of children who are generally slow in their intellectual development and whose reading is on a par with, and sometimes even a little above, their level of competence in other areas of intellectual functioning. Such pupils need a reading program which is adapted to their limited abilities, rather than a corrective or remedial program.

The next largest group consists of those children who are moderately below average for their grade. These children can usually be taught successfully in the classroom when the teacher groups them appropriately and provides learning materials and activities appropriate to their level.

The third group of retarded readers includes those with genuine and severe disabilities in reading. These children need more intensive individualized study and diagnosis and usually do not begin to respond well to instruction until they receive help in small groups or on a completely individualized basis. Sometimes even that is ineffectual, and a careful, comprehensive, clinical diagnosis by representatives of a variety of professions may be necessary. Such facilities for clinical study may be found in a special reading clinic connected with a college, university, or large school system, or in a child guidance clinic under public or private auspices. The recognition that a particular child needs intensive diagnostic study is the first step toward providing for his needs. Those who have worked with such disabled readers are vividly aware that this is a vitally important activity, and one that is richly rewarding when it succeeds. I recently glowed with pride when I learned that one of my former disability cases is now an outstanding sculptor; some of you may have had similar success stories. Let us hope that the bright, disabled reader who goes unrecognized and is considered to be mentally retarded is rapidly becoming a thing of the past.

In summary, asking the right questions helps us to set appropriate goals for the reading program, and to develop a well-rounded program which does not concentrate on a few desirable outcomes to the neglect of others. A successful reading program should pay attention to at least ten areas of concern: beginning reading, independence in word recognition, vocabulary development, use of audio-visual aids, provisions for individual differences, richness and variety of materials, training in study-type reading, fostering of interest in reading, evaluating all important areas of reading, and providing for retarded readers.

3. Reading Research That Makes a Difference *

DAVID H. RUSSELL

It is a peculiarly American custom to select "the best ten" or "one hundred best" individuals or products. This article selects the "best ten" examples of reading research, not because they are most valuable in all situations, but in response to the challenge of a superintendent of schools who said to me, "You university people are always talking about ways research should influence teaching. . . . When did research ever influence the teaching of reading?"

At the time, my answer to the skeptical superintendent was not as complete as I should have liked, so as a result of thinking over his challenge, I list here more fully ten studies which have widely influenced reading instruction over the years. Because most of the researches are well known, I describe their methods and results only briefly.

The first of the classic studies is the series of investigations by G. T. Buswell and C. H. Judd, made at the University of Chicago around 1920. These are examples of "basic" research in education —studies which may be regarded as "pure," as discovery of knowledge for its own sake, but studies which had great influence in showing the advantages of silent over oral reading and which illus-

trated the differential nature of the reading act.

The analyses destroyed the notion that reading is a unitary activity. Instead, they suggested that reading skills differ with different purposes and materials. Accordingly, wise teachers began to help the child learn to read for a variety of purposes and to use different kinds of printed matter.

A second memorable study was the investigation of errors in paragraph comprehension made by E. L. Thorndike in 1917. This was an example of applied research. In an area which took oral teaching of reading for granted, Thorndike clearly showed differences between mouthing words and understanding meaning. He likened the process of reading a paragraph to that of solving a problem or combining dispersed ideas into a related whole.

By illustrating the wide variety of errors children made in the comprehension of a relatively simple paragraph, Thorndike demonstrated the need for instruction in getting meaning from the printed page. He also raised the issue of causes of misunderstanding and attributed it in part to the overpotency of certain words, thus foreshadowing some recent psychological work on individual perceptions.

A third classic publication, related to Thorndike's study, was a teaching study which helped provide teachers with concrete materials they could use in place of the common oral attack of that day. This was the investigation described in A. I. Gates's *New Methods in Primary Reading*.

* From David H. Russell, "Reading Research That Makes a Difference," *Education Digest*, XXVI (April, 1961), 28–31; reported from *Elementary English*, XXXVIII (February, 1961), 74–78. Reprinted by permission of Mrs. David H. Russell, *Education Digest*, and the National Council of Teachers of English.

In this study, Gates did not toss phonics out the window, as sometimes claimed, but he did show the importance of visual techniques and a method he called "intrinsic" in getting meanings of words and sentences. Such a study led directly to a revolution in teaching materials and in methods which combined a variety of ways for children to recognize words.

Like his study of primary methods and materials, Gates's *The Improvement of Reading* is a report of a number of experiments with diagnostic material. It represents not only a fresh concept in the scientific study of reading but was among the first major investigations in a long list of researches on diagnostic and remedial activities.

The point of view in *The Improvement of Reading* is that most reading retardation and disability are not explained by vague, blanket terms, such as "laziness" or "low intelligence" or "bad attitude," but are the result of a group or syndrome of specific, related factors which must be diagnosed exactly.

The Improvement of Reading contained a battery of diagnostic tests which have been extended by different authors in numerous books and articles on diagnostic and remedial activities. The present-day reading clinic is one example of the diagnostic approach to educational problems, a concept exemplified in Gates's pioneer work.

Reading Interests

A fifth classic in the field of reading investigation was the book on children's reading interests prepared by L. M. Terman and Margaret Lima. *Children's Reading,* reinforced by some of the educational theories of the day, helped provide a basis for the concept of developmental reading. Terman and Lima discovered the typical interests of boys and girls at various age levels and showed how these changed from preschool through early adolescent years. Accordingly, they not only provided some basis for the selection of children's literature at various ages, but they also helped evolve a dynamic concept of children's reading.

The sixth study is an example of the historical method of research. Nila B. Smith's *American Reading Instruction* illustrates the long gradual development of methods and practice which are a basis for what teachers do in classrooms today.

For nearly 300 years, and dating back at least to the alphabet method and theological content of the *New England Primer,* devoted teachers have worked to help their students read accurately and efficiently. Smith's historical survey has given considerable confidence to all persons concerned with reading instruction in what they do and what they advocate.

The methods and materials in use today are not based on the personal opinion of some textbook author or school principal, nor on the whim of an individual teacher. Rather, they are the result of generations of trial in classrooms from colonial to modern times. Smith's study, which should be extended into the last 25 years, can and does provide a background against which current criticisms of teaching can be measured and a basis established for continued research in methods and materials.

A seventh study opened up a new field for evaluation of reading materials rather than influencing classroom teaching methods. This was W. S. Gray and Bernice Leary's *What Makes a Book Readable.* Their formula for measuring the level of difficulty of printed materials has since been simplified by Lorge and other useful formulas developed by Dale-Chall, Flesch, and Spache. Such work still requires extension into measures of concept difficulty and density. It is influencing the writing of textbooks and other materials and makes possible some matching of pupil ability and reading materials to challenge it.

Phonics Research

The role of phonics in reading instruction suggests that research on the topic should be included in any list of "best ten." Unfortunately, no investigation in this area can be labeled "definitive." One of several worthy of mention is the D. C. Agnew study made in 1939, not because it answered all questions about phonics, but because it combined several methods of attack and because it attempted to solve a complex instructional problem, one that some researchers, prophets, and charlatans have attempted to oversimplify ever since.

In general, the Agnew study suggests that there are both advantages and disadvantages in emphasizing phonics methods. It is included as a representative of a group of studies which gave careful leads to the use of phonics.

The ninth study on the list was selected only after much difficult deliberation. In terms of impact, however, the vote goes to Ruth Strang for a series of studies and publications which clearly pointed to the need for developmental reading instruction in secondary schools and colleges. The first edition of *Problems in the Improvement of Reading in High School and College* collated the scattered work in the field up to 1937 and *Explorations in Reading Patterns* extended the interest in reading habits from adolescence into adulthood.

Strang's work helped develop the strong current interest in reading in the post-elementary years and began some study of the relationships of reading interest to other patterns of response to reading materials, an area in which the research is only beginning.

The last study in the "ten best" list is easy to select, not because its impact has yet been great, but because it points the way to important future developments. It is W. S. Gray's *The Teaching of Reading and Writing*. This is a survey done for UNESCO in 1956 of methods of instruction in reading and writing around the world. Our methods of study in comparative education are not well developed, but the Gray description points to worldwide problems in literacy, in types of language, and in adaptation of instruction to the nature of the language.

It is worth noting that each of the mentioned studies was closely connected to the problems of its day. For example, the laboratory studies by Buswell and Judd gave basic data about a little-known process in the days psychology was beginning as a science. The impact of the Thorndike and Gates studies can be understood only when one realizes that reading instruction of that day was almost completely oral. The Terman study coincided with some phases of the Progressive Education movement. The Agnew study dealt with a problem which is still concerning primary and intermediate-grade teachers; and the Gray survey, whose impact is still to be felt, came in a day when the United States was beginning to take an interest in the social and educational welfare of the underdeveloped nations of the world.

Each of these ten studies had impact because they were closely related to the context in which they were made. As we look to the future we must also ask: What is relevant and pressing?

Research in reading has influenced, and will influence, practice. Research can "make a difference."

4. Research That Should Have Made a Difference *

HARRY SINGER

SOME research in reading has made a difference in reading instruction. In the judgment of Russell (1961), the ten "best" or widely influential studies had the following consequences: (1) a change in the definition and consequent teaching of reading from a process of just sounding out words to getting meaning from the printed page through reasoning or problem-solving processes (Thorndike, 1917); (2) a shift in emphasis from oral to silent reading and use of different kinds of materials to teach children to read for a variety of purposes (Buswell, 1920; Judd and Buswell, 1922); (3) development and use of concrete materials and techniques for teaching various ways of recognizing words in silent reading (Gates, 1928); (4) construction and value of tests for diagnosing reading, providing the basis for the eventual establishment of reading clinics (Gates, 1927); (5) selection of children's literature according to developmental changes in children's interests (Terman and Lima, 1929); (6) appreciation of the evolution of current reading methods and ma-

* From Harry Singer, "Research That Should Have Made a Difference," *Elementary English,* 47 (January, 1970), 27–34. Copyright © 1970 by the National Council of Teachers of English. Reprinted by permission of the author and the National Council of Teachers of English. Travel funds for presenting this invitational paper at the Second World Congress on Reading, Copenhagen, Denmark, August 1–3, 1968, were provided by the Research Committee of the Academic Senate of the University of California, Riverside.

terials (Smith, 1934); (7) objective measurement of levels of difficulty of reading materials (Gray and Leary, 1935); (8) insight into some advantages and disadvantages of phonics instruction (Agnew, 1939); (9) the foundation of and concern for post-elementary instruction in reading (Strang, 1938; 1942); and (10) establishment of the need for adapting reading instruction to the language of a country and appraisal of world wide problems in literacy (Gray, 1956).

However, there are other studies that should have made a difference, but did not. From the studies which fit into this category, I have selected a handful for review. Undoubtedly other researchers in reading might select another set. However, the studies I have selected have significant implications for objectives, evaluation of teaching and research, reading readiness, word recognition training, and the round-robin or reading-circle type of instruction.

Review of Research

In 1921, Gates (1921) administered a battery of tests to assess oral and silent reading (speed and comprehension), vocabulary knowledge, and intelligence (group and individual) in grades 3 through 8. From analysis of the resulting correlation matrix, he concluded that "the results do not justify the conclusion that we have, in reading, a group of functions bound by some general factor." Furthermore, he found that there is a "useful distinction between 'ability to comprehend' and 'rate of reading.'"

Although these conclusions led Gates to construct his *Reading Survey Test for Grades 3 to 8* to assess separately speed and level of comprehension, his study did not have any widespread effect upon objectives or evaluation of reading instruction. Even today schools do not attempt systematically to develop or to assess both speed and comprehension, particularly at the elementary level, perhaps because of a primary concern with development of accuracy in reading, but, I also suspect because of a lack of awareness of the importance of or a need to develop speed of reading. Although, under present instructional procedures, individuals do improve their subabilities and processes for attaining speed of reading as they progress through the grades (Singer, 1965), systematic instruction might accelerate the rate of development of speed of reading. Since there are some factors common to speed and comprehension or power of reading, improvement in speed of reading is also likely to have salutory effects upon power of reading. Elsewhere, I have suggested that:

. . . individuals . . . need to mobilize some different subsystems as they shift from Speed to Power, and vice-versa. Perhaps these subsystems may be developed more effectively by alternating instruction from accuracy to speed of response. For example, after an individual has been taught by an analytical method to arrive at an accurate recognition of a word, he can be given practice in a variety of ways for perceiving the word accurately *and* quickly. An individual could, therefore, learn to be *effective and efficient* in solving his reading tasks. Analogous to the rate, accuracy, and processes necessary for mature development in arithmetic (Brownell, 1961), an individual by alternately developing subsystems necessary for speed and power of reading could make progress towards maturity in both reading components. Thus, the curriculum would emphasize the necessary subsystems

in the context of appropriate purposes in order to promote individuals' developments of speed and power of reading to their highest potential (Singer, 1965).

Corroborating Gates's conclusions that reading is not a general, unitary factor, McCullough (1957) found that the intercorrelations of comprehension scores for tests of main ideas, details, sequence, and creative reading at the second-grade level were low, ranging from .26 to .50 with a median of .45. Second graders could, therefore, score high on one type of comprehension and low on another, and vice versa. Hence, if a single type of comprehension measure were used and teachers did not teach for this type of comprehension, the results might be misleading. Although this pitfall in assessing comprehension could be avoided by selecting or constructing tests that are relevant to the curriculum, we find that in practice the criterion of curricular validity for tests does not tend to be satisfied.

Because of the high degree of pupil and teacher mobility in the United States, not only from one state to another but also within the state, curricular validity for standardized tests is difficult to obtain. For example, California, a state with a high mobility index, has been receiving about 1,000 arrivals from other states each day for the past 20 years. Also, one of four of its residents is estimated to move each year, mostly within the state. Furthermore, one third of its teachers have been trained and have taught in other states (Stone and Hempstead, 1968). Teachers new to a school district are, of course, unfamiliar with its curriculum, and pupils who transfer into a school district from out of state or from another school district within the state are likely to have experienced a different curriculum. Under these conditions, it is understandable why California is encountering difficulties in adopting a standardized test, particularly for the primary grades, that would be valid for all of its locally controlled school districts.

The relative specificity of different kinds of comprehension tasks in the primary grades also has implications for methodological studies. For example, in the Research Program in First Grade Reading Instruction, only one test of reading comprehension was utilized for comparing the 27 methodological studies, probably for the same reason that schools limit their testing program to a single test —lack of time. Consequently, the result that "Wide differences in mean achievement of classrooms were found for all the programs" (Bond and Dykstra, 1967) may, in part, be due to degree of congruency between types of comprehension questions in the reading achievement test and those types stressed in the various classrooms.

Whether or not a particular variable is predictive of reading achievement, especially at the end of the first year of instruction, depends to some degree upon the common elements among the predictor variable, the evaluation instruments, *and* the method of instruction. This conclusion was reached by Gates, Bond, and Russell (1939) who assessed four average first-grade classes in New York City on 62 variables at the beginning of the year and then correlated these variables with the Gates and Stanford Reading Achievement Tests at three periods during the year. They found that at the top of the list of predictive measures were tests of word and letter recognition and phonic combinations.

Because variations in correlations accompanied methodological differences, they recommended:

Reading readiness tests, therefore, must be chosen to fit the teaching method. In other words one should test the reading abilities which the teaching program will attempt to develop in order to determine the needs of each pupil before instruction is begun and to predict the pupil's likelihood of becoming a successful reader.

However, the Gates, Bond, and Russell study did not have a wide influence on reading instruction because, as Chall (1967) explains, the study with its environmental emphasis went against the "conventional wisdom" of its day, which Durkin (1968) points out had a maturational bias.

Instead, a study which had a significant and long lasting effect, but shouldn't have, was the study by Morphett and Washburne (1931). They recommended that "a child would gain considerably in speed of learning if beginning reading was postponed until the child had attained a mental age of six years and six months" on the Detroit First Grade Intelligence Test or *seven years and six months* on the Stanford Binet Test of Intelligence. Their recommendation was based on the finding that of the children who had attained a mental age of six years and six months on the Detroit Test, 78 percent made satisfactory general progress, that is, progressed through at least 13 steps of the Winnetka program and had learned a minimum of 37 sight words by February. Even though the Morphett and Washburne recommendation was based upon a particular test of intelligence and a particular method of instruction, "conventional wisdom" generalized their recommendation to all tests of intelligence, programs of instruction, and evaluation instruments. Instead, perhaps in consonance with the conventional wisdom of our day, with its emphasis on not just *matching* instruction to individual capacities but on designing curricula to *stimulate* the development of such capacities, we have recommended that "since children are at various stages of readiness for instruction in reading during kindergarten . . . that provision should be made for such individual differences by adapting the teaching strategy of a differential curriculum" (Singer, Balow, and Dahms, 1968).

The widespread impact of Cattell's study (1886) was also not justifiable since his conclusions based on adult readers were applied to instruction of beginning readers. Cattell adduced evidence that adults or *mature* readers could perceive meaningful sentences or words more rapidly than unrelated groups of letters or words. This finding, along with other experimental data (Erdmann and Dodge, 1898), was interpreted as indicating that readers perceived whole words by means of their configuration. Perhaps unaware of developmental changes in perception as individuals learned to read, the whole word method with its emphasis on word configuration as a primary cue for word recognition was used for teaching *beginning* readers how to read. Even after Buswell (1922) had demonstrated that readers on the average took two fixations per word in the *initial* stages of learning to read, progressed through developmental changes in word perception, and at *maturity* in reading perceived on the average one and a quarter words per fixation, children were still taught to use configuration as a cue.

Even if configuration cues were appropriate for beginning readers, word frequency control with selection and presentation of high frequency words that are uniformly similar in appearance would tend to preclude use of such cues in the initial stages of reading. Yet, as Chall (1967) has pointed out, basal readers in the early 1960's had actually increased the use of word frequency control over previous basal readers and were still advocating teaching beginning readers the whole word method as "the prime means of word recognition" and to utilize configuration as a cue to perceive them (Chall, 1967).

The finding in the Gates, Bond, and Russell (1939) study that perception of printed words and letters is among the best predictors of subsequent reading achievement is consistent with reports over the past 40 years. Some time ago, Gates (1926) found that perception is not a unitary function because the intercorrelations among perception of numbers, geometric symbols, and printed words were quite low; the average intercorrelation correlation among these stimuli for grades 1 through 6 was only .35. Because of the specificity of perception, he suggested that "differences in reading ability may depend considerably upon the specific skills pupils have of perceiving a certain kind of material, namely, *printed words. . . .*" Balow (1963) and Barrett (1965) have also found that perception of visual representations of verbal stimuli, not ability to respond accurately to pictures or geometric objects, is the best predictor in a reading readiness battery for subsequent achievement at the end of first grade. Moreover, discrimination training given on printed words, particularly those that will be met later in the reading program, is likely to lead to positive transfer for recognition of these words (Staats, Staats, and Schutz, 1962). The implication from these studies appears to be that perceptual training on materials other than printed words is not as likely to develop the ability to perceive printed words nor is such training as likely to be related to reading achievement. Despite the implication, we still find materials produced and instructional programs pursued which purport to prepare children for reading with such titles as *We Read Pictures* and *We Read More Pictures* (Gray, Monroe, and Artley, 1956) or which claim to remedy word perception difficulties by training pupils to perceive non-verbal stimuli (Frostig and Horne, 1964) or by having them engage in motor exercises designed to correct their laterality (Delacato, 1959). Instead, the research evidence implies that to the extent that perceptual improvement is needed in reading readiness or in remedial reading programs, emphasis should be on visual perception and discrimination of printed words. If these printed words occur in close temporal and spatial contiguity to referent objects and actions, it would be possible to develop not only perceptual but also conceptual responses to printed words (Singer, 1966).

A device which purports to improve speed and span of perception and hence increase speed of reading is the tachistoscope. Advertisements for the tachistoscope appeal to American values of efficiency and economy of time. Moreover, in consonance with the spirit of the Industrial Revolution, there is ready acceptance, among educational decision-makers, of machines as a way of reducing costs of education. With the increased availability of funds, particularly federal funds, school districts have purchased abundant amounts of equipment, such as tachistoscopes.

However, the evidence indicates that there is only a correlation of about .06 between the tachistoscopic speed of perception and rate of reading easy prose. To determine why the relationship is low, Gilbert (1959a, b, c, and d) conducted a series of studies of speed of processing visual stimuli. Using college students and a motion picture technique for separating and measuring the components of duration of fixation or pause time, he was able to demonstrate that the average adult fixation time of a quarter of a second could be separated into three parts. The parts, each about two-twenty

fourths of a second in duration, consisted of seeing time, central processing time, and eye movement stabilizing time. Gilbert's results seem to explain why students who improve their speed of perception in tachistoscopic training fail to transfer their improved perceptual speed to normal reading. The explanation appears to be that tachistoscopic training is aimed at only *one* of the three components of the fixation pause, seeing time. But, in normal reading, eye movement stabilizing time occurs and is a necessary source of interference in speed of perception (Holmes and Singer, 1964). One implication from Gilbert's studies is that evaluation of improvement in speed of reading necessitates measurement of all three components of the fixation pause. It is possible that reduction in one of the components, such as seeing time, may be compensated by an increase in another component, such as processing time or eye movement stabilizing time.

Translating Research Results into Classroom Practices

Obstacles

If we ask why the studies reviewed in this paper have not yet had widespread impact upon teaching reading, we would give several major reasons, some of which have already been cited in the text. On this list would be inattention or even ideological resistance to research results (Moynihan, 1968), findings contrary to "conventional wisdom" (Chall, 1967), acceptability of only those research findings that are in accord with the prevailing maturational-environmental bias (Durkin, 1958), susceptibilities of educational decision makers to commercial propaganda, and variation in adequacy of dissemination of findings (Chall, 1967).

Strategy

To the above I would add one more reason, gleaned from an experience I had in translating basic research results into classroom practice: for basic research findings to make a difference in classroom practice, they have to go through several developmental steps before they are in a form that can be used in the classroom. In this translation experience, I used a study reported by Gilbert (1940) on the disruption of eye movement behavior in reading that occurs when a poor reader is trying to follow the oral reading of a good reader, and vice-versa. Essentially, the poor reader is frustrated in trying to keep up with the good reader; in turn, the good reader is annoyed in having to adapt to the poor reader's pattern of reading behavior. Although this study was done about thirty years ago, primary grade teachers still follow the practice of having pupils learn to read by taking turns reading aloud while the rest of the group with their eyes locked into step with the pupil reading aloud tries to follow along, reading silently. The learning theory for such instruction is that each pupil in the group who sees the word and hears the correct or corrected response is having his own silent or oral response to the stimulus word reinforced. However, observation of such instruction reveals that the children do not have their eye movements locked into step. The good reader might be reading ahead when he is supposed to be following the poor reader, while the poor reader, in turn, might lag behind the good reader or do something else, such as look out the window. Since this behavior is apparent to teachers, why don't they do something else? Spache (1964) believes that teachers find that this mode of instruction is the easiest to use, but another answer is possible: teachers do not have an alternate method.

To provide an alternative to what I have called the "lock-eyed" strategy for teaching reading, I suggested that the teacher have one pupil read aloud while the other pupils close their books or not even have books and just listen to the pupil who is reading aloud. An experienced and competent teacher in one of my advanced courses in teaching reading decided to try this alternative out on her class of first-grade pupils. She informed me that the strategy seemed to work, but the pupils who were listening appeared to be bored. I then suggested that she make the listening purposeful by giving them questions about the story or that she develop *active* listeners by having the pupils learn to formulate their *own* questions about the story and listen for answers as each pupil read aloud in turn. As a result of this modification, the teaching strategy was quite effective: children in the reading group were an attentive audience; they could not use the "vulture technique" of raising their hands to be called upon by the teacher as soon as the oral reader made an error in reading, and the teacher did not have to use conformity procedures to keep all eyes locked in step.[1]

Although I heartily recommend the stepwise procedure described above for translating basic research findings into classroom practice, I am not advocating that teachers should limit themselves to the use of a purposeful listening strategy for teaching reading. However, I believe that teachers should understand the

[1] Mrs. Shirley Cronin, Moreno Valley Unified School District, Moreno Valley, California, participated in working out this active listener strategy and later demonstrated, via video tape, all three instructional procedures (the traditional "lock-eyed" procedure, listening *without* a purpose to oral reading and listening *with* a purpose to oral reading).

effects of various instructional procedures, such as the "lock-eyed" *vs.* the "purposeful listening" strategy, and that teachers should have a variety of methods and techniques in their repertoire. They are then more able and more likely to adapt teaching methods and modes to instructional needs of their pupils and to use their teaching methods and strategies to solve instructional problems and enhance reading achievement.

Conclusion

In the past some research has not had the impact upon practice that it should have. However, in the future, translation of basic research findings into classroom practice is more likely to occur and in a more systematic way. New educational institutions have been organized by the U.S. Office of Education, such as the research and development centers in universities, computer storage and retrieval of educational information centers, regional laboratories, supplementary instructional centers in public schools, and institutes for teachers. As these institutions begin to mesh with each other and with established educational institutions, such as school systems and teacher education and research programs in universities and colleges, and as school districts employ more specialized personnel, which they are already beginning to do, the probability will be greater that research which should make a difference, will.

References

1. AGNEW, DONALD C. *The Effect of Varied Amounts of Phonic Drill on Primary Reading.* Durham, N.C.: Duke University Press, 1939.
2. BALOW, IRVING H. "Sex Differences in First-Grade Reading," *Elementary English,* 40 (1963), 303–306; 320.
3. BARRETT, THOMAS C. "The Relationship Between Measures of Prereading Visual Discrimination and First-Grade Reading Achievement: A Review of the Literature," *Reading Research Quarterly,* 1 (1965), 51–76.
4. BOND, GUY L., and DYKSTRA, ROBERT. "The Cooperative Research Program in First-Grade Reading Instruction," *Reading Research Quarterly,* 2 (1967), 5–142.
5. BROWNELL, WILLIAM A. "Rate, Accuracy, and Processes in Learning." Abridged by T. L. Harris and W. E. Schwahn (eds.), *Selected Readings on the Learning Process.* New York: Oxford University Press, 1961. Pp. 388–400.
6. BUSWELL, GUY T. "An Experimental Study of the Eye-Voice Span in Reading," *Supplementary Educational Monographs,* No. 17. Chicago: University of Chicago Press, 1920.
7. ———. "Fundamental Reading Habits: A Study of Their Development," *Supplementary Educational Monographs,* No. 21. Chicago: University of Chicago Press, 1922.
8. CATTELL, JAMES McKEEN. "The Time it Takes to See and Name Objects," *Mind,* 11 (1886), 63–65.
9. CHALL, JEANNE. *Learning to Read.* New York: McGraw-Hill, 1967.
10. DELACATO, CARL H. *The Treatment and Prevention of Reading Problems.* Springfield, Illinois: Charles C. Thomas, 1959.
11. DURKIN, DOLORES. "When Should

Children Begin to Read." *Innovation and Change in Reading Instruction,* Helen M. Robinson (ed.). The Sixty-Seventh Yearbook of the National Society for the Study of Education, Part II. Chicago: University of Chicago Press, 1968. Pp. 30–71.

12. ERDMANN, B., and DODGE, R. *Psychologische Untersuchungen über dos Lesen und Experimenteller Grundlage.* Halle: Neimeyer, 1898. Reviewed in Irving H. Anderson and Walter F. Dearborn (eds.), *The Psychology of Reading.* New York: Ronald Press, 1952.

13. FROSTIG, MARIANNE, and HORNE, DAVID. *The Frostig Program for the Development of Visual Perception.* Chicago: Follett, 1964.

14. GATES, ARTHUR I. "An Experimental and Statistical Study of Reading and Reading Tests," *Journal of Educational Psychology,* 12 (1921), 303–14.

15. ———. "A Study of the Role of Visual Perception, Intelligence and Certain Associative Processes in Reading and Spelling," *Journal of Educational Psychology,* 17 (1926), 433–45.

16. ———. *The Improvement of Reading.* New York: Macmillan, 1927.

17. ———. *New Methods in Primary Reading.* New York: Bureau of Publications, Teachers College, Columbia University, 1928.

18. ———, BOND, G. L., and RUSSELL, D. H. *Methods of Determining Reading Readiness.* New York: Bureau of Publications, Teachers College, Columbia University, 1939.

19. GILBERT, LUTHER C. "The Effect on Silent Reading of Attempting to Follow Oral Reading," *Elementary School Journal,* 40 (1940), 614–21.

20. ———. "Genetic Study of Eye Movements in Reading," *Elementary School Journal,* 59 (1959), 328–35. (a)

21. ———. "Influence of Interfering Stimuli on Perception of Meaningful Material," *California Journal of Educational Research,* 10 (1959), 15–23. (b)

22. ———. "Saccadic Movements as a Factor in Visual Perception in Reading," *Journal of Educational Psychology,* 50 (1959), 15–19. (c)

23. ———. "Speed of Processing Visual Stimuli and Its Relation to Reading," *Journal of Educational Psychology,* 50 (1959), 8–14. (d)

24. GRAY, WILLIAM S. *The Teaching of Reading and Writing.* An International Survey, UNESCO. Chicago: Scott, Foresman, 1956.

25. ———, and LEARY, BERNICE. *What Makes a Book Readable.* Chicago: University of Chicago Press, 1935.

26. ———, MONROE, MARION, and ARTLEY, A. STERL. *We Read Pictures, We Read More Pictures,* and *Before We Read.* Chicago: Scott, Foresman, 1956.

27. HOLMES, JACK A., and SINGER, HARRY. "Theoretical Models and Trends Toward More Basic Research in Reading," *Review of Educational Research,* 34 (1964), 127–55.

28. JUDD, CHARLES H., and GUY T. BUSWELL. *Silent Reading: A Study of the Various Types,* Supplementary Educational Monographs, No. 23. Chicago: University of Chicago Press, 1922.

29. McCULLOUGH, CONSTANCE M. "Responses of Elementary School Children to Common Types of Reading Comprehension Questions," *Journal of Educational Research,* 51 (1957), 65–70.

30. MORPHETT, MABEL, and WASHBURNE, CARLTON. "When Should Children

Begin to Read," *Elementary School Journal,* 31 (1931), 496–503.

31. MOYNIHAN, DANIEL P. "Sources of Resistance to the Coleman Report," *Harvard Educational Review,* 38 (1968), 23–36.

32. RUSSELL, DAVID G. "Reading Research That Makes a Difference," *Elementary English,* 38 (1961), 74–78.

33. SINGER, HARRY. "A Developmental Model for Speed of Reading in Grades Three Through Six," *Reading Research Quarterly,* 1 (1965), 29–49.

34. ———."An Instructional Strategy for Developing Conceptual Responses in Reading Readiness." *Vistas in Reading,* J. A. Figurel (ed.). Proceedings of the Eleventh Annual Convention, International Reading Association, 11 Part I (1966), 425–31.

35. ———, BALOW, IRVING H., and DAHMS, PATRICIA. "A Continuum of Teaching Strategies for Developing Readiness at the Kindergarten Level." *Forging Ahead in Reading,* J. A. Figurel (ed.). Proceedings of the Twelfth Annual Convention of the International Reading Association, 12 (1968), 463–68.

36. SMITH, NILA B. *American Reading Instruction.* New Jersey: Silver Burdett, 1934.

37. SPACHE, GEORGE S. *Reading in the Elementary School.* Boston: Allyn and Bacon, 1964.

38. STAATS, CAROLYN K., STAATS, ARTHUR W., and SCHUTZ, RICHARD E. "The Effects of Discrimination Pretraining on Textual Behavior," *Journal of Educational Psychology,* 53 (1962), 32–37.

39. STONE, JAMES C., and HEMPSTEAD, R. ROSS. *California Education Today.* New York: Thomas Y. Crowell, 1968.

40. STRANG, RUTH. *Problems in the Improvement of Reading in High School and College.* Lancaster, Pa.: The Science Press, 1938.

41. ———. *Explorations in Reading Patterns.* Chicago: University of Chicago Press, 1942.

42. TERMAN, L. M., and MARGARET LIMA. *Children's Reading.* New York: Appleton, 1929.

43. THORNDIKE, EDWARD. "Reading as Reasoning: A Study of Mistakes in Paragraph Reading," *Journal of Educational Psychology,* 8 (1917), 323–32.

5. Reading: Seventy-five Years of Progress *

NILA BANTON SMITH

Reading Progress: 1891 to 1910

SEVENTY-FIVE years takes us back to 1891. We will pick up the march of progress in reading at that date and trace it through to 1966. As we roll back the curtain of time to observe the reading scene during the years elapsing between 1891 and 1910, we see a colorful pageant of events and an ever-quickening pace of developments.

Perhaps of first importance in this march of progress was the budding of research in reading that occurred in the United States during this period (1,2,3,4).† The studies conducted were preponderantly of the laboratory type and were few in number, but they must be recognized as the beginning of an interest which burgeoned during succeeding periods.

Interest in the scientific study of reading began in Europe about the middle of the nineteenth century. Most of the early studies were conducted in France and Germany. A few investigations, however, were made in the United States by Amer-

icans who had been stimulated by reports from abroad. By 1910 thirty-four studies had been reported by investigators in England and the United States. Although these studies were not sufficient in number or practical enough in application to have an impact upon classroom instruction, they are historically important because they were firsts in reading research.

Another first in this period was the attention given to reading disability. Men in the medical profession preceded all others in the study of children who had difficulty in learning to read. These men attributed the cause of reading retardation to "congenital alexia" or "word blindness." Many reports on this subject were published between 1900 and 1910.

The first professional book on reading appeared in 1908. The subject had attained sufficient status and content by that time to move one individual to write a book about it. This individual was Edmund Burke Huey, and the title of his book was *The Psychology and Pedagogy of Reading* (4).

As for methods and materials, three developments are worthy of mention. One of these was the development of new phonetic alphabets similar to the Augmented Roman Alphabet of today. The Shearer System, which appeared in 1892, made use of such an alphabet (5), and ten years later the first reader of the Standard Reading Series was printed in another phonetic alphabet, the Scientific Alphabet (6). At first glance, a page in the first reader resembles very closely a page in one of the current books printed in I.T.A., as the Augmented Roman Al-

* From Nila Banton Smith, "Reading: Seventy-five Years of Progress," in H. Alan Robinson (ed.), *Reading: Seventy-five Years of Progress,* Supplementary Educational Monographs, No. 96, December, 1966, pp. 3–12. Reprinted by permission of the author and The University of Chicago Press.

† This paper is based upon facts presented in the writer's book *American Reading Instruction* (Newark, Del.: International Reading Association, 1965), where interested readers may find a detailed bibliography. A brief bibliography has been provided at the end of this paper, however, and references are made to it throughout by number.

phabet is popularly called, except that the former has a few diacritical markings. Neither of these early alphabets was accepted for wide usage. Their development, however, did indicate that even at this time some Americans were striving to invent easier ways of teaching reading.

Two other types of methods and their accompanying materials were developed during this period and used widely throughout the country. One of these was the extremely synthetic and highly organized phonic method, which arose as an answer to criticisms of the word method previously in use. By this method, children spent several weeks working with the sounds of the letters before they began to read. The "family" idea of attaching consonant sounds to common phonograms was also developed at this time. According to this idea, children memorized groups of words such as *ball, call, fall, mall, pall, tall,* and *wall,* and then read readers whose content had been contrived to give practice on these "family" words. Several series of readers based on this method were published and widely used.

Quite the opposite to the synthetic phonic method was the sentence-story method, which was advocated by several educators and which placed heavy emphasis upon literature. This approach was an outgrowth and an expansion of the word method. The essential steps of this method were as follows: first, the teacher told a story or rhyme to the children until they had memorized it or, at least, had become very familiar with it; the selection was then read and analyzed into separate words and phrases; and eventually phonics was applied, although greatly subordinated. The several reading series that were published to implement this plan made use of literature for the most part.

Reading Progress: 1910 to 1925

This was the most exciting period of progress that had ever taken place in reading. It was also the period in which the University of Chicago emerged as an institution of leadership in reading research and in the development of reading as an area of professional specialization.

The dramatic period beginning in 1910 contained the first truly great breakthrough in American reading instruction. This era in the history of reading was marked by the birth of the scientific movement in education. In 1909 Thorndike made the initial presentation of his handwriting scale to a meeting of the American Association for the Advancement of Science, and in 1910 the scale was published. Generally speaking, the publication of the Thorndike scale is recognized as the beginning of the contemporary movement for the scientific measurement of educational products. In the immediately ensuing years, scales and tests appeared rapidly; among these was a reading test—*The Gray Standardized Oral Reading Paragraphs,* devised by William S. Gray at the University of Chicago. This test was published in 1915. Other reading tests, mostly involving silent reading, followed shortly.

With the advent of tests there was an enormous spurt in scientific investigation (3,4,8,9). As previously stated, only thirty-four studies in reading had been reported in the English language up to 1910. From 1910 to 1924, a total of four hundred thirty-six accounts of reading studies were published by investigators in the United States alone.

Although the great preponderance of studies was conducted with the use of the new tests, there were also some very significant laboratory studies. Foremost among these were several studies conducted by Charles H. Judd and Guy T. Buswell at the University of Chicago and reported in monographs published during the years 1918 to 1922 (10,11,12,13).

The first doctoral dissertations in reading which came to my attention were written at the University of Chicago in 1917: "Studies of Elementary School Reading through Standardized Tests," by William S. Gray; "Types of Reading Ability as Exhibited through Tests and Laboratory Experiments," by C. T. Gray; and "An Experimental Study of the Psychology of Reading," by William Anton Schmidt. Between 1917 and 1924 thirteen additional doctoral dissertations on reading were completed. So it was that a newly emerging and far-reaching educational discipline, namely the scientific study of reading, burst like a bombshell into our slumbers during this short but exciting period.

Remedial reading had a phenomenal development at this time. Interest in it now extended far beyond the medical profession. Beginning about 1910, some psychologists began to concern themselves with reading deficiency, and in the twenties, personnel in the public schools joined in the new movement to help children who were having difficulty in learning to read.

Two outstanding pioneers in developing diagnostic and remedial techniques were William S. Gray and Arthur I. Gates. Both published articles and prepared monographs on this subject in the early twenties. Two of the most notable monographs released by them at this time were Gray's *Remedial Cases in Reading: Their Diagnosis and Treatment* ("Supplemental Educational Monographs," No. 22; Chicago: University of Chicago, 1922); and Gates's *The Psychology of Reading and Spelling: With Special Reference to Disability* ("Contributions to Education," No. 129; New York: Teachers College, Columbia University, 1922). These two giant contributors to reading progress began their important research and writing in this auspicious period and continued to make significant contributions in the many years ahead.

Other innovations introduced during the period were experience charts, individual instruction in reading patterned after the Winnetka and Dalton plans, and the singling out of speed as a reading skill that could be developed through practice.

As for method, the teaching of reading underwent the most drastic change that had ever taken place. From the beginning of reading instruction, oral reading had maintained its supreme and undisputed claim over classroom methods. In marked contrast to the traditional practice, we find a period of years, approximately between 1918 and 1925, in which there was an exaggerated and, in some cases, almost exclusive emphasis upon silent reading procedures. At no time in reading history has a new methodology taken hold so rapidly and been extended so widely.

All of these things happened in the short span of fifteen years. It was a great day when the scientific movement in education began to operate in the field of reading. Even though researchers only scratched the surface during this initial period, it was a momentous epoch in history of reading. It truly marked our first great breakthrough in the improvement of reading instruction.

Reading Progress: 1925 to 1935

Progress during this next period may be characterized largely as extension and application rather than initiation and innovation. The years between 1925 and 1935 were remarkable in productivity of reading research (7,8,9,14). From July 1,

1924, to June 30, 1935, a total of 654 studies dealing with an extraordinarily wide variety of topics and problems were published, and thirty-five doctoral dissertations in reading were completed.

Throughout these years there were major developments in the diagnosis and remediation of children with reading disabilities. In fact, remedial reading was the chief subject of study during this period. Two new theories were much discussed. Samuel T. Orton associated causes of reading deficiency with left or mixed laterality—handedness, eyedness, and footedness (15). Grace M. Fernald attracted much attention with her kinesthetic method, which placed emphasis upon tracing words and letters (16). The terms "reading disability" and "reading deficiency" continued to be used, especially in psychological studies. "Remedial reading," however, came into more general use in connection with reading improvement in schools.

The outstanding innovation of this period was the application of the reading readiness concept. In 1926 the International Kindergarten Union, in co-operation with the U.S. Bureau of Education, conducted an investigation of pupils' readiness for reading instruction in first grade (17). This study brought reading readiness problems sharply to the attention of teachers in widespread areas.

It was in 1927 that Mary Maud Reed's research revealed the startling data that one in every six children failed at the end of the first semester in first grade and that one in every eight failed at the end of the second semester in first grade (18). Educators everywhere began to see the need for preparing children to learn to read. The fire once kindled soon became a conflagration that finally enveloped the vast majority of public schools in the country.

The program for teaching reading be-came much broader during this period than at any time in the past. Part I of the Twenty-Fourth Yearbook of the National Society for the Study of Education recommended new and broad objectives in reading (19). The increasingly rapid flow of research revealed new skills, interests, and needs, with the result that the new programs came to encompass both oral and silent reading, both literary and factual material, and much more detailed and explicit plans for teaching skills than formerly.

There was, however, a division in the philosophy of teaching reading during this period. One group believed that children should be given carefully planned sequential practice in skills. These educators continued to use basic readers. The readers no longer placed major emphasis on silent reading, however, but embodied the broader objectives mentioned above.

The other group was convinced that learning took place best when the child was permitted to arrive at and carry out his own purposes—meeting and solving attendant problems within the context of his own experiences and needs. This teaching philosophy was given application under the general title "the activity program." In such programs the children worked freely and spontaneously and actively, following their own interests; and the teachers were intrigued with the new "game" of trying to get all of their subject matter across through "units of work."

The activity program continued into the next period of history. At present we hear no more about teaching reading according to this plan. The short-lived application of the philosophy behind this method, however, had its good effects. The activity program was first to bring quantities of library and reference books into the classroom. It was first to use cooperatively prepared materials other than experience charts. And it was first to point out the practical possibilities of teaching reading in the content areas.

One other mark of progress that occurred during this period should be mentioned. The practice of appointing general elementary supervisors increased rapidly between 1920 to 1928. And by 1930, Detroit and a few other large cities had taken an additional step. They had replaced their general supervisors with special supervisors in each of the basic school subjects—arithmetic, language, spelling, and reading. Thus it was at this point that the special supervisor of reading entered the scene in American schools.

Reading Progress: 1935 to 1950

The entire period from 1935 to 1950 was marked by national and international unrest eventuating in and including another war. Probably the most obvious effect of these circumstances on reading instruction was a reduction in output of research and instructional materials (7,8, 9,14,20). Whereas published research had previously numbered over one hundred reports per year, during the war year 1943–44 only fifty-four appeared. Recovery in numbers was not achieved until the fifties. The number of doctoral dissertations completed was also drastically reduced during this period.

The number of new series of basal readers published between 1935 and 1950 decreased sharply. Whereas sixteen basal series had been listed as new in the preceding period, only four series were published before the war, and during the last two years of the forties two more got under way by publishing their primary programs.

The content of basal reading series did not change drastically. Even in this distressing period, however, there were some evidences of progress. The worldwide tension that was felt at this time caused a few forward-looking educators to start fresh views on the uses of reading in our complex society. These people set up a new aim for teaching reading—the equipment of individuals with skills they need to live effectually in a world seething with problems. The social effects and uses of reading became matters of concern and were reflected in articles in periodicals and increasing numbers of studies. These emerging and significant viewpoints and concerns about reading were direct outgrowths of social and political stresses.

Interest in reading disability increased rapidly. The multiple-causation theory was developed; informal diagnosis was used for the first time; mechanical aids to reading appeared; and there was the beginning of a trend toward the development of clinics in public school systems.

Advances in method included utilization of the interrelationships of reading and the other language arts, the addition of context clues and structural analysis in word attack, and the extension of comprehension and work-study skills.

Developments in reading supervision also took place. During this period a number of school systems appointed a special person for supervisory service in reading, and the term "reading consultant" made its initial appearance in educational literature. And so reading, in its buoyancy, continued to give evidence of progress even in a period of international conflict.

Reading Progress: 1950 to 1966

In pursuing the progress of reading through three-quarters of a century, we have at last arrived at the era in which we are now living—a stimulating but terror-filled era in human existence, an era of unparalleled activity and unprecedented change.

The vast accumulation of knowledge and the technological revolution have brought problems to our civilization. Other problems have arisen from threats to our democratic way of life from competing nations who would establish world communism. Arising from the recognition of these problems are governmental plans for improving the social and economic lives of our people. The key solution proposed for implementing these plans is education, and since education cannot proceed without reading, there is a compelling motive to increase literacy. Liberal funds are being made available by the government to finance reading research, to buy more reading materials, to equip remedial reading centers, to establish institutes for those wishing to improve their teaching of reading, and to provide fellowships for those wishing to specialize in reading.

Never in the history of our country has reading been the subject of such high interest. Never have opportunities to learn to read been extended to so many individuals at all age levels, in school and out. Truly, reading instruction has grown to entirely new dimensions in the enlarged and important role it has to play in achieving national goals. Without a doubt, the national recognition and support given reading instruction by the government constitute the most salutary and conspicuous mark of progress in the history of American reading instruction.

As a result of these stimulating influences, authors of basal reading series are enlarging their programs with multiple-texts and other methods reflecting the most recent research and trends. Many new approaches to beginning reading are being published. New reading materials are being prepared for teaching those who are illiterate or functionally illiterate. Interest in reading disability is expanding, and increased use is being made of contributions from other disciplines. The demand for well-trained reading specialists is greater than the supply. Several states are now setting up special reading requirements for pre-service and post-service preparation, and several others require certification for reading specialists. Research, the common denominator of *all* progress in reading, is now at an unprecedented high in both quantity and quality (7,9,20,21,22,23,24).

Reading Progress in the Future

It is not difficult to describe reading progress in the past. The fact that we have records printed in word symbols and that we are able to read these symbols makes it possible for us to review the past whenever we desired. The future is different, of course, since no records have been written and pathways are uncharted. In spite of these handicaps I shall venture a few forecasts.

Undoubtedly, audio-visual materials will play a major role in the teaching of reading in the future—particularly such automated devices as television, films, recorders, computers, and others yet to be invented.

There are some who say that practically all learning in the future will take place through the use of programed material administered by computers. Much experimentation in the teaching of reading by computer is now under way. Computers can, no doubt, be helpful in establishing certain elements of skill that require practice. But to teach other essential processes of reading, such as getting meanings from word symbols arranged in sentences, interpretation, critical reading, and appreciation, which do not lend themselves to predetermined answers, oral dialogue, mental interaction, and exchange of thoughts are required. The teacher will always be essential in teaching the kind of reading skills that will be necessary in our future civilization.

Provisions for meeting individual needs will receive a significant emphasis in the teaching of reading. There will be drastic advances in the preparation of instructional materials that show greater ingenuity and adaptability in coping with individual differences. Since children have different styles of learning, we will find ways of ascertaining these styles early in a child's reading life and in using the materials appropriate to each style.

Teachers will be much better prepared to teach reading, and each class or group will have available several teachers with different special talents that may be called into use. Designs for more flexible scheduling will permit better time distribution to accommodate the gifted readers, the ordinary readers, and those requiring corrective or remedial instruction.

Clinics will be established in connection with practically all public schools. In college clinics, the facilities will be used largely for research and teacher preparation rather than as a service station for improving the reading of individual students, as is so often the case at present.

There are other possibilities for the future that could be discussed. Within the limits of this paper, however, I will mention only one more—the potential of reading research. We have made tremendous strides in investigation during the last half-century, but perhaps we have only scratched the surface of topics to study and experimental techniques to develop. We shall need fresh, piercing insights to ascertain hitherto unexplored areas for research; we shall need unique experimental designs and new statistical techniques; and withal, we shall need great ingenuity to shape reading methods and materials in the image of our findings.

Such unprecedented progress has been made during the past seventy-five years that we may wonder whether there could ever be another period so productive of reading advancement. There still are many new worlds to conquer, however, and many new contributions to make in this fascinating field. May each of us who is living in the present thrilling age of reading contribute his share to the quickening pace of progress.

References

1. GRAY, WILLIAM S. *Summary of Investigations Relating to Reading,* Supplementary Educational Monographs, No. 28. Chicago: University of Chicago Press, 1925.

2. DEARBORN, WALTER F. "The Psychology of Reading," *Archives of Philosophy, Psychology and Scientific Methods,* I, No. 4 (March, 1906).

3. ———. "Professor Cattell's Studies of Reading and Perception," *Archives of Psychology,* IV, No. 30 (April, 1914).

4. HUEY, EDMUND BURKE. *The Psychology and Pedagogy of Reading.* New York: Macmillan Co., 1908 (revised 1912, 1915).

5. SHEARER, JAMES W. *Combination Speller.* St. Louis, 1894.

6. FUNK, ISAAC KAUFMAN, and MONTROSE, MOSE I. *Standard Reading Series, First Reader.* New York: Funk & Wagnall's Co., 1902.

7. GRAY, WILLIAM S. "Summary of Investigations Relating to Reading," *Elementary School Journal* (1925–32); and *Journal of Educational Research* (1933–60).

8. U. S. Library of Congress Catalog

Division, *American Doctoral Dissertations.* Washington, D. C.: Government Printing Office, 1913–40.

9. GOOD, CARTER V., LYDA, MARY LOUISE, JENSON, GLENN, BROWN, STANLEY, ANDERSON, HAROLD, MAPES, JOSEPH, ELAM, STANLEY, and others, *Research Studies in Education.* Bloomington, Ind.: Phi Delta Kappa, Inc., 1923–65.

10. JUDD, CHARLES H. *Reading: Its Nature and Development,* Supplemental Educational Monographs, No. 10. Chicago: University of Chicago Press, 1922.

11. JUDD, CHARLES H., and BUSWELL, GUY T. *Silent Reading: A Study of the Various Types,* Supplemental Educational Monographs, No. 23. Chicago: University of Chicago Press, 1922.

12. BUSWELL, GUY T. *An Experimental Study of the Eye-Voice Span in Reading,* Supplemental Educational Monographs, No. 17. Chicago: University of Chicago Press, 1920.

13. ———. *Fundamental Reading Habits: A Study of Their Development,* Supplemental Educational Monographs, No. 21. Chicago: University of Chicago Press, 1922.

14. BETTS, EMMETT ALBERT, and BETTS, THELMA MARSHALL. *An Index to Professional Literature on Reading and Related Topics.* New York: American Book Co., 1945.

15. ORTON, SAMUEL T. "Specific Reading Disability—Strephosymbolia," *Journal of American Medical Association,* XC (April 7, 1928), 1095–99.

16. FERNALD, GRACE M. *Remedial Techniques in Basic School Subjects.* New York: McGraw-Hill Book Co., 1943.

17. *Pupils' Readiness for Reading Instruction upon Entrance to First Grade,* City School Leaflet No. 23.

Washington, D. C.: Bureau of Education, U. S. Department of the Interior, 1926.

18. REED, MARY MAUD. *An Investigation of Practices in First Grade Admission and Promotion.* New York: Teachers College, Columbia University, 1927.

19. *Report of the National Committee on Reading.* The Twenty-Fourth Yearbook of the National Society for the Study of Education, Part I. Bloomington, Ill.: Public School Publishing Co., 1925.

20. Dissertation Abstracts. Ann Arbor: University Microfilms, 1938–65.

21. ROBINSON, HELEN M. "Summary of Investigations Relating to Reading," *Journal of Educational Research,* LIV (February, 1961).

22. ———. "Summary of Investigations Relating to Reading," *Reading Teacher,* XV, XVI, XVII (January, 1962; January, 1963; February, 1964).

23. ———, WEINTRAUB, SAMUEL, and HOSTETTER, CAROL A. "Summary of Investigations Relating to Reading, July 1, 1963, to June 30, 1964," *Reading Teacher,* XVIII (February, 1965), 331–428.

24. ———, ———, and SMITH, HELEN K. "Summary of Investigations Relating to Reading," *Reading Research Quarterly,* I (Winter, 1966).

25. HARRIS, THEODORE L. "Summary of Investigations Relating to Reading," *Journal of Educational Research,* LV, LVI, LVII, LVIII (February, 1962 through 1965).

26. ———, OTTO, WAYNE, and BARRETT, THOMAS C. "Summary and Review of Investigations Relating to Reading, July 1, 1964, to June 30, 1965," *Journal of Educational Research,* LIX (February, 1966), 243–68.

II

The Psychology and Psycholinguistics of Reading

Knowledge of the learning process, child development, and the psycholinguistic nature of reading is essential for the teacher planning and conducting an effectual reading program. The articles in this chapter provide a broad view of these highly complex concepts. Hildreth's opening article indicates how some basic learning principles may be applied to reading instruction. This is followed by Harris's summary of the literature dealing with the relationship of child development and reading.

The last three articles present psycholinguistic and linguistic viewpoints of reading behavior. Carroll states that the activity of reading can be analyzed into two processes—speech reconstruction and the apprehension of meaning—even though they may occur simultaneously. Goodman goes on to suggest that reading is not a precise process, but rather a "psycholinguistic guessing game" by which the efficient reader selects the "fewest, most productive areas necessary to produce guesses which are right the first time." Wardhaugh's discussion of the relationship of reading and linguistic principles closes the chapter.

6. Some Principles of Learning Applied to Reading *

GERTRUDE HILDRETH

EVERY teacher is concerned about giving children the tool of reading which will unlock for them a wide world of new ex-

* From Gertrude Hildreth, "Some Principles of Learning Applied to Reading." Reprinted from the May 1954 issue of *Education*, pp. 544–49. Copyright © 1954 by The Bobbs-Merrill Co., Inc., Indianapolis, Ind.

perience. Whether the children learn this tool easily, or slowly and ineffectively will depend in large part upon the teacher's understanding of the learning process as it relates to reading instruction.

This article will summarize the basic principles of learning applied to reading and show how they relate to teaching.

These principles give clues to techniques of instruction, to classroom management of learners, to the use and construction of appropriate reading materials. Violation of any of the basic learning principles usually results in ineffective learning if not outright failure. These principles have application to other skills learned at school as well as to symbol learning and habit formation in general.

The reading process is highly complex because it requires discrimination of word forms both visually and with the ear, the two processes operating simultaneously. At the same time reading requires thinking and anticipating meanings expressed in words, essentially a puzzle-solving process.

Purposing and Motivation

It is a well-known fact that you cannot teach a child anything that he does not want to learn. If he genuinely wants to learn he is halfway there before he starts. What a child is forced to learn as a school task won't help the learning process along very much. Children show different degrees of interest in beginning reading. As one teacher commented about a slow learner, "His self-starter seemed to be missing." In both the beginning stages and later on, a genuine interest in learning helps to make reading achievement possible. The teacher must be careful not to confuse lack of interest in learning or will to learn with lack of ability or immaturity that inhibits learning. Lack of interest contributes to lack of attention, a condition that lies at the root of the slow progress made by restless children.

Too often the anxious parent demands of the teacher, "You've got to make my boy learn." "Leave it to me," replies the teacher. "We'll see that he does." But high pressuring an unready or reluctant learner is apt to have the opposite effect.

Instead of becoming interested, the child "goes sour" and refuses even to try. Furthermore, he not only comes to hate reading but to dislike the teacher.

The teacher who understands this fundamental learning principle makes certain that at all times the pupils, whether reading alone or to an audience, read for genuine purposes related to their own concerns. At the same time that children are learning to read we want them to learn to love to read. It is shortsighted for the teacher to try to teach reading without considering whether the materials used for instruction interest the pupils.

One slow boy's chief interest was in raising pigeons. The teacher suggested that he go to the library and inquire whether the librarian had anything easy to read on this subject. Sure enough, a book was found for him that he read, though not too easily. But he kept on trying and was soon back demanding more material on his hobby.

Learning with Understanding: Reading for Meaning

In reading, getting the meaning is all that counts. Everything in the learning process must contribute to eventual grasp of meanings, to reading with full understanding. This principle has a number of important implications for learning and instruction. Every exercise in which a child engages, e.g., matching words, seeing the separate parts in words, saying the words on sight of the flash cards, must lead to comprehension of the printed page. All that counts in learning the ABC's or phonics as aids to reading is the *application* of word-recognition skills to the interpretation of print.

As a matter of fact children of even ordinary caliber use all the intelligence they have to make sense out of what they are learning. After drilling on the ABC's for days on end, one beginner finally asked at home, "Mother, what's an L–M–N–O–P?" There are some children who have gone along learning to read even as far as fourth grade without realizing that there is more to reading than word calling.

One reason that readiness is so important is because it insures sufficient maturity for beginners to learn meaningfully from the outset of school instruction. Reading is always easier for the beginner or for the advanced student if he has learned to think meanings on sight of the context and has learned to derive meanings of puzzling words through context clues, so far as possible, e.g., "The word must be *mosquito* because that's probably what the man was bitten by." Reading is easier if you can think what comes next. This principle explains why extensive practice in reading silently to get meanings or to find answers to questions is desirable at all grade levels.

Experiential Background
Basic to Learning to Read

A principle related to the foregoing is that for the learner to have a background of experience which ties in with reading context helps to insure learning with understanding. The child is most apt to learn to read with understanding who has had a rich background of relevant experience, whereas the child from an impoverished background may lack experiences that would aid interpretation of context.

Strange as it may seem, free play activities in kindergarten and the primary grades build and sustain reading readiness because they bring the child into intimate contact with his environment, broadening and sharpening his perceptions, and developing his use of language. Children who lack this experiential readiness must be given experiences related to the context used in teaching reading.

A good rule is always to start reading with the things the child knows about, talks and asks about, with material that is related to things he can actually pick up, touch and examine; things he likes to work with, situations that interest him here and now because they are within his level of understanding.

A slow learning class had a rabbit presented to them which they kept for a time in the classroom. They were excited over this event and every day told stories and wrote down things about their new pet. They put him in numerous stories; even wrote him a letter. Net result: before long all the children, even the slowest, were catching on to the reading trick, seeing the relation between talk and writing and reading, learning to absorb a growing vocabulary of common, everyday words.

A slow boy who was keen about sports made better progress when his reading lessons centered about his hobby. Here is one story he learned to read easily.

> We play baseball.
> Bob bats the ball.
> I am the catcher.
> We play ball in the park.

Reading and Spoken Language

Because reading deals entirely with spoken word symbols recorded in graphic form, the skill is properly classified as but one phase of the language arts. As one child expressed it, "Readin's just talk wrote down." Language is the tool through which ideas are stored in memory. For these reasons oral language is the basis of interpreting print. As a general rule, anything children have difficulty saying cannot be easily read. There is usually a close relationship between a child's growth in oral language and his progress in reading. It is a wise precaution for the teacher to check each child's "linguability" before predicting the rate at which he will probably learn to read and before planning lessons for the pupils.

The Child Must Do His Own Learning

Learning to read is no exception to the general rule that the best learners always show active effort to learn: they stay with the task until it is accomplished. The child must do his own learning. No one can do it for him. Too often teaching is considered an external process, something done to the child to "make him learn," instead of the mental reactions the child must make on his own account. The child who learns best experiments with the print before him. He asks and responds to questions; he works as hard as he would in trying to solve a puzzle. The good teacher demands that the child think for himself, and work at the task as his own responsibility.

Learning to Read Requires Forming Habits

Catching on to the reading trick, the essential technique the adult uses whenever he wants to get the latest news from the evening paper, is a matter of forming habits which result in synchronizing a set of regimented, arbitrary eye movements (the motor part of the task), with perception and interpretation (the thinking part). This requires hours of practice over a period of years, first to "catch the trick," then to perfect it. The reading technique, like piano playing or certain workbench skills, isn't of much use unless it functions swiftly and smoothly when a new task confronts the performer. Some children never do get off the plateau where their reading skills have become

fixed at a low level of performance, a level too low to be of any practical use in school or life. All of the basic principles of habit formation apply to the task of learning to read.

Learning by Association

Learning to read requires essentially learning to attach meanings already known through conversation to groups of arbitrary letters representing words. The task of the child is first to realize that every word is composed of a relatively small number of letters (the alphabet); then to learn to recognize at sight (spot recognition) as many of these commoner recurring words as possible; and finally to become skillful in using techniques that aid in distinguishing between confusing word forms. The process is not unlike the teacher's task of learning to connect the name of each new student with his face in a class of 30.

How do children learn to fix words in mind? How do mature readers recognize familiar words, and the less familiar or unknown word symbols? We know that children and adults alike have learned to respond to clues of many sorts, features of word structure, visual-sound associations, and others that help to recall the meaning of the observed words. A general rule is that a word is easier to recall when some meaningful association can be established between the word, its form or sound, and the ideas it represents. It is harder to remember words, that is, to build meaningful associations that serve as clues to recognition, if the words stand for abstract ideas rather than for concrete objects. This explains why such words as *which, because, these, outside, every* are difficult for children to learn in any language. When teachers appreciate these facts, they have more patience with children's difficulties in word recognition.

The Role of Perception in Learning to Read

Perception is the mind's response to sensations received from the outside world. Without the capacity to perceive, the human mind would be unable to form associations with symbols and their meanings or to store up memories of word forms, to discover similarities and differences in word forms, a skill that is fundamental in reading and in learning to read. In reading, the visual and auditory perception of word forms must operate smoothly, swiftly, simultaneously. Since all the words printed in English are but longer or shorter combinations of only 26 different letter forms (actually only about 22 of these are frequently used, and several of these are confusing, e.g., "a," "e," "o," "c,"), learning to distinguish among confusing word symbols becomes a formidable task for any child.

Many a child's troubles with reading stem from the inevitable confusions he experiences because many words which look alike mean quite different things, e.g., *quick* and *quit*, *bright* and *brick*, and so on. Furthermore, the very same word can have different meanings in sentences. One reason slow learners fail to get off a low level plateau is that they are unable to advance in word discrimination because of the rush of new words that soon surrounds them.

The implication of this principle for teaching is that plenty of practice should be given in distinguishing word forms visually and aurally. Children must be trained to look and listen with the intent of learning the distinctions in word forms. Learning to see and hear the distinctions between confusing common words should occupy a considerable part of a child's reading practice time. The teacher should be cautious about keeping·the vocabulary simple enough to insure steady growth in word perception and avoid introducing confusing words too near together in the child's reading experience.

The Role of Practice.

No one ever did learn anything so complex as the English reading without steady practice extending over a period of years. Practice can be mechanical or it can be productive. In the first case, it may result merely in stamping in errors; in the latter, practice is meaningful. As a result there is steady gain in speed and efficiency because errors are eliminated and correct responses take their place. Trial and error is still a usable concept in considering childhood learning of language skills if we mean by this term that the child, through his continual experimental trials in attacking reading materials, solves his reading puzzles correctly, with the teacher's aid, and on that account is more successful the next time he tries. Under conditions of effective practice there is steady improvement in word recognition and in grasp of the ideas back of the words. Eventually, as a result of fruitful practice, the child reads with a feeling of familiarity and comparative ease.

The fact that words are of unequal difficulty was pointed out above. The teacher who recognizes which words are relatively difficult for most children as well as for an individual pupil makes sure that more practice is given to the "demon items." At times there should be reading practice with material for beginners or slow learners that contain no new word difficulties, an assimilation period so that children can feel fully at home with the words they are learning. There should be frequent vocabulary review (1) with words in normal reading context and (2) words separately out of context.

The Role of Attitudes and the Emotions in Learning to Read

Extensive research has shown that children often have difficulty in learning when disturbing emotional conditions and unfavorable attitudes stand in their way. Children with behavior problems, those who show poor control, are overactive, distractable, unusually aggressive and destructive, babyish and irresponsible, usually have trouble learning to read. There is evidence that the child's fantasies, obsessions, and inhibitions may make it difficult for him to learn certain words.

Discouragement from failure in the early learning stages is apt to have disastrous consequences, because fear and anxiety tend to inhibit efforts to learn. The slow child, particularly, falls a prey to fear and anxiety when he sees those around him making better progress than himself, or when an unsympathetic teacher scolds, shames, or ridicules his efforts before others. What can be this child's feelings when he hears his mother say to the teacher, "He's pretty dumb, but you've got to make him learn, or what will the neighbors think?" Threats and sarcasm slow a child down by causing him to stumble and make errors. Feelings of success are essential to motivate any child to keep on trying. He must see that his efforts count for something; he must have the teacher's approval if he has honestly tried. He should feel happy as the result of his effort to learn. This doesn't mean that teachers should avoid telling a child when he has made an error, but rather that unreasoned punishment of errors may stop the learning process altogether. The teacher's attitude of encouragement, helpfulness, patience, understanding of the child's feelings will accomplish far more than harsh discipline.

Individual Differences

Individual differences show up whenever human beings at any stage of maturity set out to learn the same thing. These differences in learning merely reflect the biological law of human variability. Teachers must recognize differences in the capacities of children the same age and of similar background in learning to read. Where one repetition of a word will suffice for a certain child, another pupil may require ten repetitions and still be uncertain of the word. In general there is a tendency on the part of teachers to underestimate the amount of repetition required by slow learners to fix facts in mind.

Day in, day out the workers in reading clinics hear the same plea, "Can't you bring my child up to grade so he can pass?" Now what would we rather have the child do, waste his valuable time in a vain effort to "come up to grade" or receive some well-planned instruction that will keep him progressing steadily? Once more we must remind ourselves that trying to keep all the children up to some arbitrary, uniform grade standard is wholly unrealistic, even more so today than formerly when "straight promotions" were not so much in vogue. Let our slogan be: each child progressing at his level, with feelings of accomplishment and satisfaction with his efforts.

To adjust the program to individual differences we must ask with respect to every pupil (1) What is his readability level, in other words, how well can he now read? (2) What is the readability level of the material we have here for him to read? Now let's try the books on for size and make sure of a good fit.

Providing for individual differences in ability to read becomes particularly serious in today's crowded classrooms. In a group larger than 25 pupils, slow learners cannot receive the amount of individual attention they need for building good reading habits. There should be much more experimentation with multiple group work, with subgroups no larger than 6 to 10 slow learners.

The transition points from the end of Grade 1 and Grade 2 to the beginning of the next grade offer hazards for many young children because they usually pass to a new teacher who assumes that most of the class have made standard progress during the preceding year. To obviate this hazard two procedures are recommended. (1) Every teacher should pass on to the next teacher an individual report for each child indicating exactly how far he has progressed during the past year, and (2) in some cases it is wise for the teacher to go ahead with the group for another year so that no sharp breaks in learning will occur.

There is no question that the best learners of reading had good teachers who patiently helped them over the hurdles and obstacles, who demonstrated efficient techniques, and at the same time helped the children keep up their interest in getting ahead with the task.

7. Child Development and Reading *

ALBERT J. HARRIS

Reading Readiness

IT seems even more true today that chronological age in itself has no significant relationship to success in learning to read; that age is a dimension in which both maturation and learning take place. In 1961 Bruner stated: "any subject can be taught effectively in some intellectually honest form to any child at any stage of development" (4). While this is an extreme statement of an antireadiness position and was probably not intended to be taken literally, it has been quite influential in stimulating exploration of the

* From Albert J. Harris, "Child Development and Reading," in Marion D. Jenkinson (ed.), *Reading Instruction: An International Forum,* First World Congress on Reading, Paris, 1966. (Newark, Del.: International Reading Association, 1967), pp. 336–49. Reprinted by permission of the International Reading Association.

learning ability of very young children. This was soon followed by O. K. Moore's reports of success in teaching reading to children at the ages of two to four with an automated typewriter (19), and Durkin's reports on children who learned how to read before entering school, without apparent harm (9). Holmes has offered a reasonable hypothesis linking the ability of young children to learn reading to the pupil-teacher ratio. "Other things being equal the earliest age at which a child can be taught to read is a function of the amount of time or help the teacher can give the pupil" (13). His summary of the available research showed a desirable class size of fewer than 10 children per teacher, if reading is to be successfully taught below the age of five. The younger the child, the more individual instruction is necessary.

The fact that some children are ready to learn to read at an early age should not deflect attention from the fact that other children are lacking in reading readiness when instruction normally begins. One of the recent studies supported by the U.S. Office of Education sheds a clear light on this issue. Spache and his co-workers tested the effects of readiness programs in eight Florida counties in parallel white and Negro schools. Pupils in the top quarter were started on reading in September. The second quarter started reading in November, the third quarter in January, and the lowest quarter in March. Specific materials to develop visual and auditory perception skills were used flexibly in the readiness groups. The effectiveness of the readiness program appeared to increase as the ability levels of the pupils decreased. In the two lowest Negro quartiles, the experimental children who started reading late in the year scored higher on reading tests than the control Negro children who had several more months of reading instruction (20).

It seems evident that children vary widely in their readiness for reading instruction, and that those who are lacking in specific aspects of readiness can benefit from instructional efforts designed to build up deficient readiness skills. On the other hand, there is no discernible benefit in delaying the start of reading for those who are ready. Current research suggests a flexible age for beginning reading rather than a fixed age, whether the latter be five, six, or seven.

Intellectual Development

During the past few years additional strength has been given to the viewpoint that early experiences have a profound influence on the degree to which an individual develops his intellectual potential. Two books in particular have focused attention on the importance of early en-vironmental conditions and on the opportunities to improve the conditions for the mental growth of children. J. McVicker Hunt marshalled evidence from a wide variety of sources to show, first, that impoverishment of experience can slow mental development; and second, to argue that better utilization of the learning potential of young children could bring about a "substantially faster rate of intellectual development and a substantially higher adult level of intellectual capacity" (14). Bloom gave particular attention to the evidence that as children get older the I.Q. becomes less variable, concluding that the best opportunities for improving the mental functioning of children are in the first four years (3). These writers have been influential in the pressure building up, now clearly evident in the United States, to move public education down into the preschool years.

Additional evidence has accumulated that the relation between intelligence and reading is low to moderate at the beginning level, but increases as children get older. For example, in Durkin's group of early readers the correlation between I.Q. and reading achievement was only .40 at the beginning of the first grade, but was .79 at the end of the fifth grade (9). As the nature of the reading task becomes more one of comprehension and interpretation, intelligence becomes a stronger determining factor.

The use of intelligence tests has recently come under fire because such tests are unfair to some children. Wechsler has recently answered this argument. He stated: "When it is asserted that intelligence tests are unfair to the disadvantaged and minorities, one must be mindful of the fact that they are simply recording the unfairness of life. . . . The culprits are poor housing, broken homes, a lack of basic opportunities, etc., etc. If the various pressure groups succeed in eliminating these problems, the I.Q.'s of the disadvantaged will take care of themselves" (23).

It is still true that group intelligence tests that present the child with printed questions are unfair to the retarded reader, and that nonverbal tests are not good measures of the abilities required for success in reading. A verbal individual intelligence scale, such as the *Revised Stanford-Binet* or the *Wechsler Verbal I.Q.*, is still the best basis for estimating the level at which a child should be able to read with comprehension.

Language Development

The tempo of language development in children seems to have increased in recent years. Strickland found that the sentence patterns used by children in their oral communications were considerably more varied than the sentence patterns used in early reading materials (21). Ames devised a new test to estimate size of vocabulary and came to the conclusion that in his first-grade population, which had a mean I.Q. of 112, the median score corresponded to a listening vocabulary of about 12,000 words (1). It would seem that with the stimulation of television and other influences that were missing from the childhood lives of their grandparents, today's children tend to develop mastery over their spoken language somewhat earlier than former generations. By the age of six, the majority of today's children have listening and speaking abilities that range far beyond the language used in beginning reading instruction.

This conclusion, however, does not apply to the children who have come to be described as educationally disadvantaged. In a noteworthy study to which wide attention has been given, Deutsch studied the language abilities of white and Negro children of varied social class groupings, at first-grade and fifth-grade levels. The children of low socioeconomic status were at a disadvantage on 22 measures, and the combination of Negro race and low socioeconomic status was related to lower scores on an additional 2 measures in the first grade, and 12 measures in the fifth grade. Deutsch concluded that inadequate patterns of linguistic development become an increasing handicap in school learning between the first and fifth grades for disadvantaged children. His results suggest that the lack of language stimulation in early home life and in early school years may make it increasingly difficult for the disadvantaged child to keep up with educational expectations as he gets older (8).

Perceptual Development

Considerable attention has been paid in the past few years to the relationship between perceptual development and reading, both in regard to success in beginning reading and in studies of reading disability.

The perceptual aspects of reading are very complicated, because discriminations must be made not just on discrete stimuli, but rather on a succession of stimulus conditions in which both spatial and temporal patterns must be distinguished. As I have previously stated, "Reading is a continuing cycle of excitation and reaction in which each moment of perception produces a feedback effect which sets the person for the following perception. In this rapidly repeating cycle the sequential perceptions are apprehended as forming linguistic sequences that convey large units of meaning" (11).

The significance of visual perception for reading was discussed in great detail by Vernon (22). Since then additional evidence has accumulated which reinforces the conclusion that several aspects of visual perception are significant in the early stages of learning to read. Goins (10) found that good readers in first grade were those who were able to hold in mind a total configuration at the same time as they attended to significant parts. Either a vaguely global perception or exclusive attention to parts could cause difficulty. Malmquist reported from Sweden that visual perception tests which used groups of letters or digits showed significant correlations with first-grade reading, while tests which involve geometrical shapes or meaningful pictures had very low correlations with reading (16).

Preliminary data on an analytic test of five aspects of visual perception by Frostig suggest that the test may be useful in detecting children who need special training to improve their visual perception skills (17).[1] A number of other perceptual tests are in process of development or validation at present.

Information is meager as yet concerning the effectiveness of training procedures designed to improve the visual perception of young children. According to Spache, two months of visual perception training in first grade produced as much growth on perception tests as took place in four to six months of regular reading instruction (20). However, only in the lower half of the population did stress on perceptual training seem to result in improved learning of reading.

Aspects of visual perception that await better tests are the ability to achieve closure of incomplete or interrupted figures, and ability to clearly distinguish figure from background.

Auditory perception is also important in beginning reading. The simple ability

[1] However, recent research indicates that correlations between the Frostig subtests and corresponding aspects of reading skills are not high. (Eds.)

to tell whether or not two pronounced words are exactly alike, as measured by the *Wepman Auditory Discrimination Test,* has been shown to be difficult both for poor readers (6,21) and for disadvantaged children (7). Poor auditory discrimination is likely to be accompanied by indistinct or faulty speech articulation as well as by difficulty in establishing correct associations between printed symbols and the sounds they represent. Another aspect of auditory perception that is significant for reading is the ability mentally to fuse, blend, or synthesize the sounds of word parts into whole words. Chall (5) has reported evidence that a simple test of auditory blending had a substantial relationship to success in early reading.

There is little evidence as yet on the value of training programs designed to improve auditory perception. Spache's results indicated that growth in this area was not significantly better for those given an experimental readiness program than for those given regular reading instruction, except for older Negro boys (20). Whether this area of ability is more resistant to training, or whether better training programs are needed, is not clear; the latter possibility seems reasonable.

Since reading involves the association of sounds with visual symbols, it is not surprising that recent studies have shown poor readers to be slower and less accurate than normal readers in tasks involving rapid change from visual to auditory or from auditory to visual stimuli (15). . . .

Sociocultural Factors and Reading

The strong interrelationship between social class and progress in reading was most strikingly shown by Barton (2). As part of the Columbia-Carnegie Study of Reading Research and Its Communication, data were collected from 1,500 classrooms in the United States. He summarized his results in part as follows:

. . . The gist of these findings is that the norm for upper middle-class children is a year ahead of "grade level," from the end of first grade on; while the norm for lower working-class children (the poorer and more culturally deprived part of the working class) is to fall back until they are a year or more behind by the time they reach the fourth and fifth grade. We have looked into these findings further, introducing two more sociological variables—community size and class size.

The effect of socioeconomic class is still the most striking single feature. It remains even when we control for the fact that working-class children are more often in large cities, and in large classes.

But we can also see that the working-class children do notably better in the small communities, under 10,000. What is there about small communities which has the effect of moderating the influence of social background on reading?

Further, we can see that class size appears to make a difference—but that this is much greater for middle-class children, and in communities smaller than 100,000. Why is this? We have other data, incidentally, which show that better facilities usually benefit those who are better off to start with; this suggests how difficult it is to try to compensate for poor home background by the usual kinds of school facilities.

The studies by Deutsch and Spache, referred to earlier in the discussion of reading readiness, have improved our understanding of the ways in which the disadvantaged child is handicapped in coping with the tasks of beginning reading. Systematic research on ways of improving the reading progress of educationally disadvantaged children is very recent, and major studies are continuing at present. In my own study, in which four ways of teaching reading to Negro children in New York City are being com-

pared, we still have a year to go before final analysis of results (12).[2] A recent publication of the International Reading Association has described a number of the interesting programs recently developed in the United States in the effort to diminish the reading retardation of disadvantaged children (24). Most of these have not yet been subjected to research evaluation.

Personality Development and Reading

While research on the personality traits correlated with reading success and failure has continued, the general conclusions stated in 1961 do not require change.

An absorbing interest in reading may be one phase of a richly varied, healthy adjustment, or it may provide a way of avoiding social contacts and evading reality. Failure in reading can be a result of emotional difficulties that were well established before the child entered school, or it can be a continuing source of frustration to which the child must erect defenses of one sort or another. While reading failure is found in a high proportion of the emotionally disturbed and of delinquents, the causal relationships are many and varied.

Similarly, attempts to find differences distinguishing the personality of poor readers from that of good readers generally fail because of the wide variety of personalities to be found within the reading disability group.

The value of psychotherapy as a method of treatment for reading disabil-

[2] The final results of the CRAFT Project showed a lack of statistically significant differences among the average third-grade reading scores of those taught with basal readers, basal readers plus phonics, language-experience, and language-experience with audio-visual supplementation. (Eds.)

ity has been under discussion for years. I am inclined to agree with the conclusions stated by Rabinovitch, as follows: "For those children with a mild reading retardation secondary to emotional problems, psychotherapy is indicated. For those with the primary or dyslexic syndrome the need is for intensive, long-term remedial therapy" (18). . . .

References

1. AMES, WILBUR S. "The Understanding Vocabulary of First-Grade Pupils," *Elementary English*, 41 (1964), 64–68.

2. BARTON, ALLEN H. "Reading Research and Its Communication: The Columbia-Carnegie Project." *Reading as an Intellectual Activity*, J. Allen Figurel (ed.). International Reading Association Conference Proceedings, 8 (1963), 247.

3. BLOOM, BENJAMIN S. *Stability and Change in Human Characteristics*. New York: Wiley, 1964. P. 237.

4. BRUNER, JEROME S. *The Process of Education*. Cambridge: Harvard University Press, 1961. P. 33.

5. CHALL, JEANNE, ROSWELL, FLORENCE G., and BLUMENTHAL, SUSAN H. "Auditory Blending Ability: A Factor in Success in Beginning Reading," *Reading Teacher*, 17 (November, 1963), 113–18.

6. CHRISTINE, DOROTHY, and CHRISTINE, CHARLES. "The Relation of Auditory Discrimination to Articulatory Defects and Reading Retardation," *Elementary School Journal*, 65 (November, 1964), 97–100.

7. DEUTSCH, CYNTHIA P. "Auditory Discrimination and Learning: Social Factors," *Merrill-Palmer Quarterly of Behavior and Development*, 10 (July, 1964), 277–96.

8. DEUTSCH, MARTIN. "The Role of Social Class in Language Development and Cognition," *American Journal of Orthopsychiatry*, 35 (January, 1965), 78–88.

9. DURKIN, DOLORES. "A Fifth-Year Report on the Achievement of Early Readers," *Elementary School Journal*, 65 (1964), 76–80.

10. GOINS, JEAN T. *Visual Perceptual Abilities and Early Reading Progress*. Supplementary Educational Monographs, No. 87. Chicago: University of Chicago Press, 1958.

11. HARRIS, ALBERT J. "Perceptual Difficulties in Reading Disability." *Changing Concepts of Reading Instruction*, J. Allen Figurel (ed.). International Reading Association Conference Proceedings, 6 (1961), 283.

12. HARRIS, ALBERT J., and SERWER, BLANCHE L. "Comparing Reading Approaches in First-Grade Teaching with Disadvantaged Children," *Reading Teacher*, 19 (May, 1966), 631–35.

13. HOLMES, JACK A. "When Should and Could Johnny Learn to Read?" *Challenge and Experiment in Reading*, J. Allen Figurel (ed.). International Reading Association Conference Proceedings, 7 (1962), 237–41.

14. HUNT, J. MCVICKER. *Intelligence and Experience*. New York: Ronald Press Co., 1961. P. 363.

15. KATZ, PHYLLIS A., and DEUTSCH, MARTIN. "Relation of Auditory-Visual Shifting to Reading Achieve-

ment," *Perceptual and Motor Skills,* 17 (October, 1963), 327–32.

16. MALMQUIST, EVE. *Factors Related to Reading Disabilities in the First Grade of the Elementary School.* Stockholm: Almqvist & Wiksell, 1958.

17. MASLOW, PHYLLIS, FROSTIG, M., LEFEVRE, D. W., and WHITTLESEY, J. R. B. "The Marianne Frostig Developmental Test of Visual Perception, 1963 Standardization," *Perceptual and Motor Skills,* 19 (October, 1964), 463–99.

18. RABINOWITZ, RALPH. "Dyslexia: Psychiatric Considerations." *Reading Disability: Progress and Research Needs in Dyslexia,* John Money (ed.). Baltimore: The Johns Hopkins Press, 1962. Pp. 73–80.

19. ROWAN, HELEN. "Tis Time He Should Begin to Read," *Carnegie Corporation of New York Quarterly,* IX, No. 2 (1961), 1–3.

20. SPACHE, GEORGE D., *et al. A Study of a Longitudinal First-Grade Readiness Program.* Cooperative Research Project No. 2742. Tallahassee, Fla.: Florida State Department of Education, 1965.

21. STRICKLAND, RUTH G. *Language of Elementary School Children: Its Relationship to the Language of Reading Textbooks and the Quality of Reading of Selected Children.* Bloomington, Indiana: Bulletin of the School of Education, Indiana University, VI, No. 4 (July, 1962).

22. VERNON, M. D. *Backwardness in Reading.* Cambridge: Cambridge University Press, 1957.

23. WECHSLER, DAVID. "The I.Q. Is an Intelligence Test," *The New York Times Magazine,* June 26, 1966, p. 66.

24. WHIPPLE, GERTRUDE, and BLACK, MILLARD, compilers. *Reading for Children Without—Our Disadvantaged Youth.* Newark, Del.: International Reading Association, 1966.

8. A Psycholinguistic Analysis of Reading Behavior *

JOHN B. CARROLL

DESPITE the large amount of research and expository writing in the field of reading, the nature of reading as behavior has still not yet been accurately described in the light of knowledge from the two most relevant disciplines, psychology and linguistics. For it is not psychological theory alone that is needed for fruitful analysis of a field of instruction, but also knowledge and principles from other relevant disciplines, most obviously those related to the subject matter of instruction.

* From John B. Carroll, "A Psycholinguistic Analysis of Reading Behavior," *English Teaching Forum,* 4 (Spring, 1966), 2–7. Reprinted by permission of the author, the United States Information Agency, and the National Society for the Study of Education. For a more complete version of this article, please refer to: John B. Carroll, "The Analysis of Reading Instruction: Perspectives from Psychology and Linguistics," in E. R. Hilgard (ed.), *Theories of Learning and Instruction,* Sixty-Third Yearbook of the National Society for the Study of Education, Part I (Chicago: The University of Chicago Press, 1964), pp. 336–53.

This brief article presents a fairly detailed analysis, from both psychological and linguistic viewpoints, of the behavior we call reading.

Language, Speech, and Reading

Reading behavior, even though not completely understood in all its aspects, is descriptively not as complex as it has sometimes been depicted. Reading must be defined in the context of a proper understanding of the nature of language and its actualization in spoken or written messages in a particular language or dialect.

I have defined language as "a structured system of arbitrary vocal sounds which is used, or can be used, in interpersonal communication by an aggregation of human beings, and which rather exhaustively catalogues the things, events, and processes in the human environment." [1] The system inherent in a language derives essentially and primarily from the sequence of articulated, heard sounds in *spoken* utterances or messages.

The speech communities of many languages have developed conventional systems whereby spoken messages can be recorded in written, visual form. Not all the features of spoken messages are normally represented in the writing system (although special transcription systems can be devised to represent all the meaning-bearing elements of spoken messages), but enough of them are symbolized to permit competent speakers of the language (who can also read) to reconstruct the spoken form of a written message in most of its important features. Writing systems usually contain elements of their own which do not correspond explicitly to anything in spoken messages—for example, paragraphing, punctuation, capitalization, and different ways of writing items which are phonemically identical (as *hair—hare*). Many written messages are composed, transmitted, and read with very little involvement of overt speech, but *construction of a spoken form is always possible.*

The behavior we call *reading* may be described as the perception and comprehension of written messages in a manner paralleling that of the corresponding spoken messages. That is to say, just as speakers of a language can comprehend spoken messages, persons who have learned to read can comprehend written messages. Comprehension of spoken messages and comprehension of written messages are not entirely independent processes, however. Save for the case of an individual who learns to read a foreign language before he learns to understand it—and there is considerable doubt about what "reading" can mean in such a case—learning to read a language depends not only upon the ability to understand the spoken form of a language but also upon the ability to reconstruct the spoken forms of written messages. In "reading aloud," it is evident that the individual can make this reconstruction. In "silent reading"—even at very high rates and without detectable subvocal activity—it is reasonable to assume that comprehension occurs in response to some kind of internal representation, however abbreviated or fragmentary, of a spoken message. The reader does not respond solely to visual symbols; he also responds to some sort of reconstruction of a spoken message which he derives from the written message. In interpreting the comprehension of written messages, we must draw upon whatever we can find out about the comprehension of spoken messages.

[1] John B. Carroll, *The Study of Language* (Cambridge, Mass.: Harvard University Press, 1953), p. 10.

The activity of reading can, therefore, be analyzed into two processes: (a) on the basis of the written message, the construction or reconstruction of a spoken message or of some internal representation of it; and (b) the comprehension of messages so constructed. It is of the greatest importance to consider these processes separately, even though typically they may occur virtually simultaneously, for different psychological and linguistic problems are involved in each of them.

Nevertheless, nothing said here should be taken to imply that these two processes —speech reconstruction and the apprehension of meaning—should be separated in procedures of teaching. There is evidence, in fact, that the teaching of the mechanics of speech reconstruction (techniques of word recognition) is best done with materials which are maximally meaningful to the learner—for example, words that are labels for things of interest to the learner or very simple sentences that convey an interesting or useful message.

The Speech Repertory

In what follows, we shall be concerned solely with the processes by which a child learns to read the written form of his native language. The teacher of English as a second language will recognize aspects of these processes that apply to their teaching of reading in English.

The reconstruction of spoken messages from written messages depends upon the development of the speech repertory as a whole and particularly on the ability to recognize features of the spoken language system that correspond in some way with features of the writing system. By the age of beginning school, the normal child has acquired, largely out of awareness, most of the basic phonology and grammar of his language, as well as a substantial vo-cabulary. In other words: (a) He can discriminate (respond differentially) to all or nearly all of the phonemes of his language, and (usually) produce these phonemes with fair accuracy. (b) He can understand and produce all the major sentence types of his language; in fact, his sentences are often more varied and complex than those found in the usual primer. (c) His vocabulary is numbered well into the thousands.[2]

At the same time, it must be recognized that children vary widely in their speech repertories. Children who have difficulty with the discrimination or the production of phonemes will generally experience difficulty in learning to read until these handicaps are no longer present. Some children have learned a dialect of English which is markedly substandard or at variance with the dialect of the teacher, so that they do not make the same phonological or grammatical distinctions as the teacher. Some children have limited vocabularies because they come from intellectually impoverished environments.

Phonemics, Graphemics, and Phonics

If reading as a subject matter has a "content," that content is the relation between the structure of spoken messages and the system of marks or symbols used to represent these messages. Strangely enough, this content is rarely discussed (save in the most general terms) in textbooks on the teaching of reading and its psychology. There is no comprehensive compendium or description of the relationship, although large parts of it are

[2] Nevertheless, children's vocabularies have sometimes been overestimated. See Irving Lorge and Jeanne Chall, "Estimating the Size of Vocabularies of Children and Adults: An Analysis of Methodological Issues," *Journal of Experimental Education*, 32 (1963), 147–57.

now available.[3] To make matters worse, writers on the teaching of reading have often failed to make appropriate distinctions or to use proper terminology when discussing the writing system of English, which they characterize as "unphonetic." Linguistic scientists, who are the authorities in these matters, reserve the term *phonetics* for the study of the purely acoustic and articulatory aspects of speech sounds in languages. *Phonemics* is their term for the study of the ways in which certain classes of sounds are distinctive sound units (*phonemes*) in particular languages. Just as phonemes are the minimal sound units in a language, *graphemes* are the minimal visual symbolic units in a writing system. And just as phonemes may occur in certain ranges of free or conditional variation in actual utterances, graphemes (alphabetic letters, digits, punctuation marks, and the like) may appear in variant forms (upper and lower case, different type faces, different handwritten shapes, and so on). English orthography utilizes an alphabetic principle whereby the relationship between speech and writing can be most easily described in terms of correspondences between graphemes and phonemes.

These correspondences, in English, are more regular than irregular, contrary to the impression often given. It may be estimated that a computing machine could be programed to "translate" a printed text into phonemes with better than 95 percent accuracy even without building into the computer program information about irregularly spelled words. The program would simply incorporate a large number of rules for translating graphemes in conjunction with other graphemes in their immediate environ-

ments. Now, the number of such rules might be much larger than the number it would be feasible to embody in a procedure for teaching reading to children, but many of them are of considerable power. There is evidence, in fact, that mature readers behave as if they had acquired a large number of these rules.[4]

These considerations allow us to give an intermediate criterion of reading behavior: An important stage in the development of reading behavior is reached when the learner has mastered the important grapheme-phoneme correspondences which help in the reconstruction of spoken from written messages. At this stage, the learner may be said to have "broken the code" of English orthography. Further development in reading involves increasing facility in the use of this code.

Word Recognition As Problem-Solving

Let us focus attention on that phase of the reading process which we have described as the reconstruction of spoken messages. For a variety of reasons, the natural unit for this process of reconstruction is the *word;* that is, messages are in general reconstructed word by word even though skilled readers are able to apprehend and reconstruct groups of words simultaneously.

In the fullest sense of the term, recognition of a printed word is the reconstruction of the corresponding spoken word (or some internal surrogate thereof) and the apprehension of whatever meaning would be contained in the spoken word (or the particular meaning conveyed by a particular spelling).

[3] Eleanor M. Higginbottom, "A Study of the Representation of English Vowel Phonemes in the Orthography," *Language and Speech,* V (April-June 1962), 67–117.

[4] Eleanor J. Gibson, J. J. Gibson, Anne Danielson, H. Osser, and Marcia Hammond, "The Role of Grapheme-Phoneme Correspondence in Word Perception," *American Journal of Psychology,* LXXV (December 1962), 554–70.

In the mature reader, word recognition occurs extremely rapidly and unhesitatingly. This process of rapid recognition is not well understood. Research evidence suggests that frequency of past experience is an important factor in speed of recognition, but this does not guarantee that word recognition is not based on a highly speeded recognition of higher-order grapheme-phoneme correspondences. In any case, the goal of reading instruction should be to produce rapid recognition facility for as many words as possible. In the mature reader, it is perhaps true, astounding as it may seem, that reading is based upon a capability of instantly recognizing thousands or even tens of thousands of individual word patterns, almost as if words were Chinese characters not structured by an alphabetic principle.

Nevertheless, it must be emphasized that whole-word perception is dependent upon perceptions of parts—even rather small details of a pattern. One may guess that differences between such easily confused pairs as *unclear* and *nuclear* can be reliably perceived at tachistoscopic speeds not very far from normal thresholds for words of similar length and frequency. There is little evidence that mature readers use "word-shape" (the general outlines of a word) as a cue for word recognition; it is doubtful that use of this cue should be an objective of the teaching of reading. Rather, beginners need to learn to perceive individual letters as details of word patterns.

When the beginning reader meets a word with which he is unfamiliar, that is, one that he cannot recognize instantly, the process of word recognition may be regarded as a case of problem-solving. Various cues are available to him; sometimes certain cues will very quickly allow him to arrive at a proper reconstruction of a word; at other times, cues must be used to suggest a series of possibilities. In this case, the learner must essentially go into a "search-routine," testing out each one of the possibilities until a satisfactory one is found. The case will vary, of course, depending upon whether the spoken word and its meaning happen to be in the child's speech repertory. It will also vary depending upon what kind of information is available to allow the child to confirm his guess—whether, for example, there is sufficient context to test the correctness of a guess.

This analysis suggests that the process of learning to read involves the building up in the learner of a "set" to expect not only variety in the kinds of word recognition problems he will meet but also (and particularly) ambiguity in the cues available to him. For example, letter-shapes in handwriting (and sometimes in print) are often ambiguous; grapheme-phoneme correspondences are in some cases highly ambiguous (for example, initial *ge-* or *gi-* yield "hard" or "soft" *g* with about equal frequencies); whole words are sometimes ambiguous, as when they are homographs [for example, *read* = /riyd/ (or, with a variant vowel symbol, /rid/), to rhyme with *bleed;* and, also, *read* = /red/ (or /rɛd/), to rhyme with *bed*]; and context may yield only partially reliable information.

Some suggestions may be made toward the further specification of cues available for word-recognition. For the present purposes, it seems useful to discuss four classes of cues, forming successive levels of a hierarchy.

Letters (*graphemes*).—The weight of experimental evidence suggests that a pattern can be more easily recognized when the individual has learned to recognize the distinctive parts of the pattern. The distinctive parts of printed words are, of course, the letters composing them. The beginning reader must be able to discriminate and recognize the graphemes commonly found in texts. The variant forms of each grapheme (for example, upper- and lower-case forms, printed and cursive forms, and so on) must be recognized as belonging to a single class. The ability to say the names of graphemes should be a goal of instruction, not only because this affords a method of testing recognition but also because the names are useful in other phases of instruction. At the same time, the learner must understand that the names of graphemes are not in every case useful cues for the letter-sound correspondences, to be discussed next.

Letter-sound correspondences (*"phonic cues"*).—Because of the alphabetic principle underlying English orthography, letters or combinations of letters standing in printed words can be cues to the phonemic constituents of the corresponding spoken words. For convenience, let us call these "phonic cues." In learning to make use of them, the beginning reader must become aware [5] that a spoken word is a sequence of sounds and that the left-right order of letters in writing corresponds to this temporal sequence, though not always in a one-to-one match. He should also become aware of the structure of syllables, the general pattern being $[C] V [C]$, where C stands for a consonant or consonant cluster, and V for a vowel or diphthong, and where the brackets denote that the element enclosed may or may not be present. With regard to the actual use of phonic cues, the *goal* is *not* to have the learner acquire formally

[5] In speaking of the learner's "becoming aware" of such a fact, we do not mean that he needs to be taught the formal verbal statements we use here; we are describing things which we believe normally even a young child can become aware of in the sense of coming to have his perceptions organized or structured in a certain way.

stated rules concerning letter-sound correspondence but to teach habits of responding to letters and letter-combinations in terms of those correspondences which occur with sufficient frequency in English orthography to make them fairly reliable cues. Because the correspondences quite frequently are different for the initial consonantal material and for the remainder of a syllable, it is useful to deal with these components separately. (In fact, it may often be useful to deal with the second component, the $-V [C]$ material of a syllable, in terms of pattern recognition; examples of high-frequency patterns are *-am, -ame, -ain*, with transfer to similar patterns *-at, -ate, -ait*.)

Intra-word context cues.—In dealing with polysyllabic words, it is often possible for the beginning reader to reconstruct the word by parts; commonly occurring syllables like *un-, -cept-,* and *-ty* will come to be recognized instantly and supply a kind of context for suggesting the possibilities to be tested for the rest of the word.

Larger-context cues.—The context of a given word consists of the other parts of the total message in which it stands. Normally, this context is verbal, but it may also be pictorial or graphic. Context may place certain limitations upon the range of possibilities which may occur in the place of the given word. The limitations are partly of a grammatical and partly of a semantic nature. For example, the context may enhance the probability that a certain word in a sentence is a noun and the name of a fruit ("He picked a _____ off the tree and ate it"). The learner must be taught to use the context to suggest the range of possibilities within which he organizes the "search-routine" mentioned earlier, but he must also be taught to select only those possibilities which conform to the phonic cues also available. He must become aware that there are certain cases in which the context is diacritical for the proper reconstruction of the spoken counterpart of a word. For example, to reconstruct the spoken form of "He made a bow," more context is needed than is given. (This could mean "He made a bow before the audience" [6] or "He made a bow and arrow." [7])

The Reading Task Beyond Word Recognition

Even if the reader properly reconstructs the spoken counterpart of each word in a printed text, he may not necessarily comprehend the total message. He may "call off" the words as if they stood in a list and fail to apprehend the manner in which the message would normally be uttered with its linguistic features of stress, intonation, and juncture. There is a "set" or "attitude" to be taught, to the effect that printed texts correspond to spoken utterances and that part of the task of reading is to infer the most probable spoken utterance pattern for each sentence. The child must be taught the skill of putting the separate words together as a total utterance. He must learn not only to read aloud, with acceptable spoken utterance patterns, but also to read silently, with the normal overt utterance being represented in a kind of inner speech. His silent-reading speed must be accelerated as much as may be consistent with comprehension and the nature of a particular reading task (reading for details, skimming, searching for information, etc.). Further, the reader must learn the significance of such "paragraphemic" features of printed texts as punctuation, paragraphing, change of type font, tabular arrangement, and so forth.

Reading Comprehension

Comprehension, whether of speech or writing, is a process not completely understood and difficult to describe briefly, in any case. It can be described linguistically as a process of comprehending morphemes (minimal meaning units) and the grammatical constructions in which they occur. The lexical meanings of morphemes can be stated in terms of objective referents and their attributes and relationships; the meanings of grammatical constructions can be described in terms of structural relationships among persons, things, and/or events in spatial and temporal configurations. The native speaker of a language normally acquires a wide range of both lexical and grammatical meanings without their having been explained to him. Problems of reading comprehension appear to arise mainly when texts contain lexical, grammatical, or ideational materials which happen to be outside the reader's repertory.

It is sometimes said that reading is a process of apprehending thought. This can also be well said of listening; there is no difference in principle between speech and writing with respect to the intellectual demands they make.

We shall have to leave the analysis of reading behavior at this point, recognizing that there are further aspects of reading behavior which need to be provided for in the curriculum: critical judgments, evaluation of argumentation, literary appreciation, and so on. For now, it will have to stand as an article of faith that these aspects can be specified in behavioral terms, at least to the extent of identifying the classes of stimuli (for example, types of reading material) which might be expected to evoke certain kinds of responses.

[6] Here *bow* is pronounced /baw/ (or /bau/), to rhyme with *now* and *cow*.

[7] Here *bow* is pronounced /bow/ (or /bo/), to rhyme with *no* and *know*.

9. Reading: A Psycholinguistic Guessing Game *

KENNETH S. GOODMAN

As scientific understanding develops in any field of study, pre-existing, naive, common sense notions must give way. Such outmoded beliefs clutter the literature dealing with the process of reading. They interfere with the application of modern scientific concepts of language and thought to research in reading. They confuse the attempts at application of such concepts to solution of problems involved in the teaching and learning of reading. The very fact that such naive beliefs are based on common sense explains their persistent and recurrent nature. To the casual and unsophisticated observer they appear to explain, even predict, a set of phenomena in reading. This paper will deal with one such key misconception and offer a more viable scientific alternative.

Simply stated, the common sense notion I seek here to refute is this:

"Reading is a precise process. It involves exact, detailed, sequential perception and identification of letters, words, spelling patterns and larger language units."

In phonic-centered approaches to reading, the preoccupation is with precise letter identification. In word-centered approaches, the focus is on word identification. Known words are sight words, precisely named in any setting.

This is not to say that those who have worked diligently in the field of reading are not aware that reading is more than precise, sequential identification. But, the common sense notion, though not adequate, continues to permeate thinking about reading.

Spache presents a word version of this common sense view: "Thus, in its simplest form, reading may be considered a series of word perceptions." [1]

The teacher's manual of the Lippincott *Basic Reading* incorporates a letter by letter variant in the justification of its reading approach: "In short, following this program the child learns from the beginning to see words exactly as the most skillful readers see them . . . as whole images of complete words with all their letters." [2]

In place of this misconspection, I offer this: "Reading is a selective process. It involves partial use of available minimal language cues selected from perceptual input on the basis of the reader's expectation. As this partial information is processed, tentative decisions are made to be confirmed, rejected or refined as reading progresses."

More simply stated, reading is a psycholinguistic guessing game. It involves an interaction between thought and language. Efficient reading does not result from precise perception and identification of all elements, but from skill in selecting

* From Kenneth S. Goodman, "Reading: A Psycholinguistic Guessing Game," *Journal of the Reading Specialist,* 6 (May, 1967), 126–35. Reprinted by permission of the author and the College Reading Association.

[1] George Spache, *Reading in the Elementary School* (Boston: Allyn and Bacon, Inc., 1964), p. 12.

[2] Glenn McCracken and Charles C. Walcutt, *Basic Reading,* Teacher's Edition for the Pre-Primer and Primer (Philadelphia: J. B. Lippincott Co., 1963), p. vii.

the fewest, most productive cues necessary to produce guesses which are right the first time. The ability to anticipate that which has not been seen, of course, is vital in reading, just as the ability to anticipate what has not yet been heard is vital in listening.

Consider this actual sample of a relatively proficient child reading orally. The reader is a fourth-grade child reading the opening paragraphs of a story from a sixth-grade basal reader.

"If it bothers you to think of it as baby sitting," my father said, "then don't think of it as baby sitting. Think of it as homework. Part of your education. You just happen to do your studying in the room where the baby brother is sleeping, that's all." He helped my mother with her coat, and then they were gone.

So education it was! I opened the dictionary and picked out a word that

sounded good. "Phil/oso/phi/cal!" I yelled. Might as well study word meanings

1. Phizo   2. Phiso/soophical first. "Philosophical: showing calmness

and courage in the face of ill fortune."

2. future   3. futshion
I mean I really yelled it. I guess a fellow

has to work off steam once in a while.[3]

He has not seen the story before. It is, by intention, slightly difficult for him. The insights into his reading process come primarily from his errors, which I choose to call miscues in order to avoid value implications. His expected responses mask the process of their attainment, but his unexpected responses have been achieved through the same process, albeit less successfully applied. The ways that they deviate from the expected reveal this process.

In the common sense view that I am rejecting, all deviations must be treated as errors. Furthermore, it must be assumed in this view that an error either indicates that the reader does not know something or that he has been "careless" in the application of his knowledge.

For example, his substitution of *the* for *your* in the first paragraph of the sample must mean that he was careless, since he has already read *your* and *the* correctly in the very same sentence. The implication is that we must teach him to be more careful, that is to be more precise in identifying each word or letter.

But now let's take the view that I have suggested. What sort of information could have led to tentatively deciding on *the* in this situation and not rejecting or refining this decision? There obviously is no graphic relationship between *your* and *the*. It may be of course, that he picked up *the* in the periphery of his visual field. But, there is an important non-graphic relationship between *the* and *your*. They both have the same grammatical function: They are, in my terminology, noun markers. Either the reader anticipated a noun marker and supplied one paying no attention to graphic information or he used *your* as a grammati-

[3] William D. Hayes, "My Brother Is a Genius," in Emmett A. Betts and Carolyn M. Welch (eds.), *Adventures Now and Then*, Book 6, Betts Basic Readers, Third Edition (New York: American Book Company, 1963), p. 246.

cal signal ignoring its graphic shape. Since the tentative choice *the* disturbs neither the meaning nor the grammar of the passage, there is no reason to reject and correct it. This explanation appears to be confirmed by two similar miscues in the next paragraph. *A* and *his* are both substituted for *the*. Neither is corrected. Though the substitution of *his* changes the meaning, the peculiar idiom used in this dictionary definition, "in the face of ill fortune," apparently has little meaning to this reader anyway.

The conclusion this time is that he is using noun markers for grammatical, as well as graphic, information in reaching his tentative conclusions. All together in reading this ten-page story, he made twenty noun marker substitutions, six omissions, and two insertions. He corrected four of his substitutions and one omission. Similar miscues involved other function words (auxiliary verbs and prepositions, for example). These miscues appear to have little effect on the meaning of what he is reading. In spite of their frequency, their elimination would not substantially improve the child's reading. Insistence on more precise identification of each word might cause this reader to stop seeking grammatical information and use only graphic information.

The substitution of *hoped* for *opened* could again be regarded as careless or imprecise identification of letters. But, if we dig beyond this common sense explanation, we find (a) both are verbs and (b) the words have *key* graphic similarities. Further, there may be evidence of the reader's bilingual French-Canadian background here, as there is in subsequent miscues (*harms* for *arms, shuckled* for *chuckled, shoose* for *choose, shair* for *chair*). The correction of this miscue may involve an immediate rejection of the tentative choice made on the basis of a review of the graphic stimulus, or it may result

from recognizing that it cannot lead to the rest of the sentence, "I hoped a dictionary . . ." does not make sense. (It isn't decodable.) In any case, the reader has demonstrated the process by which he constantly tests his guesses, or tentative choices, if you prefer.

Sound*s* is substituted for sound*ed,* but the two differ in ending only. Common sense might lead to the conclusion that the child does not pay attention to word endings, slurs the ends or is otherwise careless. But, there is no consistent similar occurrence in other word endings. Actually, the child has substituted one inflectional ending for another. In doing so he has revealed (a) his ability to separate base and inflectional suffix, and (b) his use of inflectional endings as grammatical signals or markers. Again he has not corrected a miscue that is both grammatically and semantically acceptable.

He for *I* is a pronoun for pronoun substitution that results in a meaning change, though the antecedent is a bit vague, and the inconsistency of meaning is not easily apparent.

When we examine what the reader did with the sentence *"Might as well study word meanings first,"* we see how poorly the model of precise sequential identification fits the reading process. Essentially this reader has decoded graphic input for meaning and then encoded meaning in oral output with transformed grammar and changed vocabulary, but with the basic meaning retained. Perhaps as he encoded his output, he was already working at the list word which followed, but the tentative choice was good enough and was not corrected.

There are two examples, in this sample, of the reader working at unknown words. He reveals a fair picture of his strategies and abilities in these miscues, though in neither is he successful. In his several attempts at *philosophical,* his first attempt comes closest. Incidentally, he reveals here that he can use a phonic letter-sound strategy when he wants to. In subsequent attempts he moves away from this sounding out, trying other possibilities, as if trying to find something which at least will sound familiar. Interestingly, here he has a definition of sorts, but no context to work with. *Philosophical* occurs as a list word a number of times in the story. In subsequent attempts, the child tried *physica, physicacol, physical, philosovigul, phizzlesovigul, phizzo sorigul, philazophgul.* He appears to move in concentric circles around the phonic information he has, trying deviations and variations. His three unsuccessful attempts at *fortune* illustrate this same process. Both words are apparently unknown to the reader. He can never really identify a word he has not heard. In such cases, unless the context or contexts sufficiently delimit the word's meaning, the reader is not able to get meaning from the words. In some instances, of course, the reader may form a fairly accurate definition of the word, even if he never recognizes it (that is matches it with a known oral equivalent) or pronounces it correctly. This reader achieved that with the word *typical* which occurred many times in the story. Throughout his reading he said *topical.* When he finished reading a check of his comprehension indicated that he knew quite well the meaning of the word. This phenomenon is familiar to any adult reader. Each of us has many well-defined words in our reading vocabulary which we either mispronounce or do not use orally.

I've used the example of this youngster's oral reading not because what he's done is typical of all readers or even of readers his age, but because his miscues suggest how he carries out the psycholinguistic guessing game in reading. The miscues of other readers show similarities and differences, but all point to a selective, tentative, anticipatory process quite unlike the process of precise, sequential identification commonly assumed.

Let's take a closer look now at the components the reader manipulates in this psycholinguistic guessing game.

At any point in time, of course, the reader has available to him and brings to his reading the sum total of his experience and his language and thought development. This self-evident fact needs to be stated because what appears to be intuitive in any guessing is actually the result of knowledge so well learned that the process of its application requires little conscious effort. Most language use has reached this automatic, intuitive level. Most of us are quite unable to describe the use we make of grammar in encoding and decoding speech, yet all language users demonstrate a high degree of skill and mastery over the syntax of language even in our humblest and most informal uses of speech.

Chomsky has suggested this model of sentence production by speakers of a language: [4]

Thus, in Chomsky's view, encoding of speech reaches a more or less precise level and the signal which results is fully formed. But in decoding, a sampling process aims at approximating the message and any matching or coded signal which results is a kind of by-product.

In oral reading, the reader must perform two tasks at the same time. He must produce an oral language equivalent of the graphic input which is the *signal* in reading, and he must also reconstruct the meaning of what he is reading. The matching in Chomsky's interpretation model is largely what I prefer

---

[4] Noam Chomsky, lecture at Project Literacy, Cornell University, June 18, 1965.

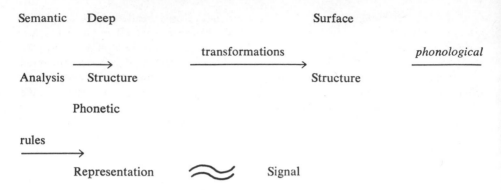

A model structure of the listener's sentence interpretation, according to Chomsky, is:

to call a recoding operation. The reader recodes the coded graphic input as phonological or oral output. Meaning is not normally involved to any extent. This recoding can even be learned by someone who doesn't speak the language at all, for example, the bar-mitzvah boy may learn to recode Hebrew script as chanted oral Hebrew with no ability to understand what he is chanting; but when the reader engages in semantic analysis to reconstruct the meaning of the writer, only then is he decoding.

In oral reading there are three logical possible arrangements of these two operations. The reader may recode graphic input as oral language and then decode it. He may recode and decode simultaneously. Or, he may decode first and then encode the meaning as oral output.

On the basis of my research to date, it appears that readers who have achieved some degree of proficiency decode directly from the graphic stimulus in a process similar to Chomsky's sampling model and then encode from the deep structure, as illustrated in Chomsky's model of sentence production. Their oral output is not directly related to the graphic stimulus and may involve transformation in vocabulary and syntax, even if meaning is retained. If their comprehension is inaccurate, they will encode this changed or incomplete meaning as oral output.

The common misconception is that graphic input is precisely and sequentially recoded as phonological input and then decoded bit by bit. Meaning is cumulative, built up a piece at a time, in this view. This view appears to be supported by studies of visual perception that indicate that only a very narrow span of print on either side of the point of fixation is in sharp focus at any time. We might dub this the "end of the nose" view, since it assumes that input in reading is that which lies in sharp focus in a straight line from the end of the nose. Speed and efficiency are assumed to come from widening the span taken in on either side of the nose, moving the nose more rapidly or avoiding backward movements of the eyes and nose, which of course must cut down on efficiency.

This view cannot possibly explain the speed with which the average adult reads, or a myriad of other constantly occurring phenomena in reading. How can it explain, for example, a highly proficient adult reader reading and rereading a paper he's written and always missing the same misprints. Or how can it explain our fourth-grader seeing "study word meanings first" and saying "study what it means?"

No, the "end of the nose" view of reading will not work. The reader is not confined to information he receives from a half inch of print in clear focus. Studies, in fact, indicate that children with severe visual handicaps are able to learn to read as well as normal children. Readers utilize not one, but three kinds of information simultaneously. Certainly without graphic input there would be no reading. But, the reader uses syntactic and semantic information as well. He predicts and anticipates on the basis of this information, sampling from the print just enough to confirm his guess of what's coming, to cue more semantic and syntactic information. Redundancy and sequential constraints in language, which the reader reacts to, make this prediction possible. Even the blurred and shadowy images he picks up in the peripheral area of his visual field may help to trigger or confirm guesses.

Skill in reading involves not greater precision, but more accurate first guesses based on better sampling techniques, greater control over language structure, broadened experiences and increased conceptual development. As the child develops reading skill and speed, he uses increasingly fewer graphic cues. Silent reading can then become a more rapid and efficient process than oral reading,

for two reasons: (1) the reader's attention is not divided between decoding and recoding or encoding as oral output, and (2) his speed is not restricted to the speed of speech production. Reading becomes a more efficient and rapid process than listening, in fact, since listening is normally limited to the speed of the speaker.

Recent studies with speeded up electronic recordings where distortion of pitch is avoided have demonstrated that listening can be made more rapid without impairing comprehension too.

Though the beginning reader obviously needs more graphic information in decoding and, therefore, needs to be more precise than skilled readers, evidence from a study of first graders by Yetta Goodman [5] indicates that they begin to sample and draw on syntactic and semantic information almost from the beginning, if they are reading material which is fully formed language.

Here are excerpts from two primer stories as they were read by a first-grade child at the same session. Ostensibly (and by intent of the authors) the first, from a second preprimer, should be much easier than the second, from a third preprimer. Yet she encountered problems to the point of total confusion with the first and was able to handle exactly the same elements in the second.

Note, for example, the confusion of *come* and *here* in "Ride In." This represents a habitual association in evidence in early reading of this child. Both *come* and *here* as graphic shapes are likely to be identified as *come* or *here*. In "Stop and Go," the difficulty does not occur

[5] Yetta M. Goodman, College of Education, Wayne State University, Doctoral Study of Development of Reading in First Grade Children.

See article no. 43 in this book, p. 234–37.

RIDE IN

Run
~~Ride~~ in, Sue.
Run
~~Ride~~ in here.
Come here
~~Here~~ I ~~come~~, Jimmy.
Can Come
~~And here~~ I (stop)⁶

STOP AND GO

Jimmy said, "Come here, Sue,
    too
Look at my ~~toy~~ (train.)

See it go.
      toy
Look at my lit/tle ~~train~~ go."
        toy
    Sue said, Stop the ~~train~~.
    Come
Stop it ~~here~~, Jimmy."
        toy
    Jimmy said, "I can stop the ~~train~~.
    toy
See the ~~train~~ stop."
        too.
    Sue said, "Look at my ~~toy~~.
    toy.
It is in the ~~train~~.
      too
See my little red ~~toy~~, Jimmy.
      toy
It can ride in the ~~train~~."
        toy
    Jimmy said, "See the ~~train~~ go.
Look at it go."
    Suzie   too
    ~~Sue~~ said, "Look at my little red ~~toy~~.
      toy
See it go for a ~~train~~ ride."
    Suzie   too
    ~~Sue~~ said, "My little red ~~toy~~!
    said   too
© Jimmy, my ~~toy~~ is not here.
        toy
It is not in the ~~train~~.
      toy
Stop the ~~train~~, Jimmy.
        too
Stop it and look for my ~~toy~~."⁷

⁶ Emmett A. Betts and Carolyn M. Welch, "Ride In," *Time to Play,* Second Pre-Primer, Betts Basic Readers, 3rd Edition, Language Arts Series (New York: American Book Company, 1963).

⁷ Emmett A. Betts and Carolyn M. Welch, "Stop and Go," *All In A Day,* Third Pre-Primer, Betts Basic Readers (New York: American Book Company, 1963).

when the words are sequential. She also substitutes *can* for *and* in the first story, but encounters no problem with either later. *Stop* stops her completely in "Ride In," a difficulty that she doesn't seem to know she has when she reads "Stop and Go" a few minutes later. Similarly, she calls (ride) run in the first story, but gets it right in the latter one.

Though there are miscues in the second story, there is a very important difference. In the first story she seems to be playing a game of name the word. She is recoding graphic shapes as phonological ones. Each word is apparently a separate problem. But in "Stop and Go" what she says, including her miscues, in almost all instances makes sense and is grammatically acceptable. Notice that as *Sue* becomes better known she becomes *Suzie* to our now confident reader.

A semantic association exists between *train* and *toy*. Though the child makes the same substitution many times, nothing causes her to reject her guess. It works well each time. Having called (train) *toy*, she calls (toy) *too* (actually it's an airplane in the pictures), not once, but consistently throughout the story. That doesn't seem to make sense. That's what the researcher thought too, until the child spoke of a "little red *too*" later in retelling the story. "What's a 'little red too,'" asked the researcher. "An airplane," she replied calmly. So a train is *toy* and a plane is a *too*. Why not? But, notice that when *toy* occurred preceding *train*, she could attempt nothing for *train*. There appears to be a problem for many first graders when nouns are used as adjectives.

Common sense says go back and drill her on *come, here, can, stop, ride, and;* don't let her go to the next book which she is obviously not ready to read.

But the more advanced story, with its stronger syntax, more fully formed language and increased load of meaning makes it possible for the child to use her graphic cues more effectively and supplement them with semantic and syntactic information. Teaching for more precise perception with lists and phonics charts may actually impede this child's reading development. Please notice, before we leave the passage, the effect of immediate experience on anticipation. Every one of the paragraphs in the sample starts with "Jimmy said" or "Sue said." When the reader comes to a line starting *Jimmy*, she assumes that it will be followed by *said* and it is not until her expectation is contradicted by subsequent input that she regresses and corrects her miscue.

Since they must learn to play the psycholinguistic guessing game as they develop reading ability, effective methods and materials, used by teachers who understand the rules of the game, must help them to select the most productive cues, to use their knowledge of language structure, to draw on their experiences and concepts. They must be helped to discriminate between more and less useful available information. Fortunately, this parallels the processees they have used in developing the ability to comprehend spoken language. George Miller has suggested ". . . psycholinguists should try to formulate performance models that will incorporate, . . . hypothetical information storage and information processing components that can simulate the actual behavior of language users." [8]

I'd like to present now my model of this psycholinguistic guessing game we call reading English. Please understand that the steps do not necessarily take place in the sequential or stretched out form they are shown here.

[8] George A. Miller, "Some Preliminaries to Psycholinguistics," *American Psychologist*, 20 (1965), 18.

1. The reader scans along a line of print from left to right and down the page, line by line.
2. He fixes at a point to permit eye focus. Some print will be central and in focus, some will be peripheral; perhaps his perceptual field is a flattened circle.
3. Now begins the selection process. He picks up graphic cues, guided by constraints set up through prior choices, his language knowledge, his cognitive styles and strategies he has learned.
4. He forms a perceptual image using these cues and his anticipated cues. This image then is partly what he sees and partly what he expected to see.
5. Now he searches his memory for related syntactic, semantic and phonological cues. This may lead to selection of more graphic cues and to reforming the perceptual image.
6. At this point, he makes a guess or tentative choice consistent with graphic cues. Semantic analysis leads to partial decoding as far as possible. This meaning is stored in short-term memory as he proceeds.
7. If no guess is possible, he checks the recalled perceptual input and tries again. If a guess is still not possible, he takes another look at the text to gather more graphic cues.
8. If he can make a decodable choice, he tests it for semantic and grammatical acceptability in the context developed by prior choices and decoding.
9. If the tentative choice is not acceptable semantically or syntactically, then he regresses, scanning from right to left along the line and up the page to locate a point of semantic or syntactic inconsistency. When such a point is found, he starts over at that point. If no inconsistency can be identified, he reads on seeking some cue which will make it possible to reconcile the anamolous situation.
10. If the choice is acceptable, decoding is extended, meaning is assimilated with prior meaning and prior meaning is accommodated, if necessary. Expectations are formed about input and meaning that lies ahead.
11. Then the cycle continues.

Throughout the process there is constant use of long and short term memory.

I offer no apologies for the complexity of this model. Its faults lie, not in its complexity, but in the fact that it is not yet complex enough to fully account for the complex phenomena in the actual behavior of readers. But such is man's destiny in his quest for knowledge. Simplistic folklore must give way to complexity as we come to know.

10. Linguistics—Reading Dialogue *

RONALD WARDHAUGH

IN recent years there has been considerable discussion of the relationship of linguistics to reading and of the possible application of the findings of linguistic research to the teaching of reading. Quite recently, several summaries of this dis-

* From Ronald Wardhaugh, "Linguistics—Reading Dialogue," *Reading Teacher,* 21 (February, 1968), 432–41, 489. Reprinted by permission of the author and the International Reading Association.

cussion have appeared and certain conclusions have been drawn. In one such summary Carroll (1964), a psychologist with a longstanding interest in linguistics, criticizes reading researchers for their failure to incorporate linguistic findings into the procedures which they have chosen to examine in their research and points out that though much reading research has been methodologically sound, it has been rather inconclusive because of its deficiencies in content. On the other hand, in another summary, Betts (1966) points out some of the relationships he perceives between reading and linguistics and criticizes linguists for dabbling in reading and for adopting a rather naive approach to the psychological and pedagogical problems in reading. In an attempt to summarize the whole reading-linguistics dialogue, Devine (1966) points out that although the dialogue has been characterized by statements of opinion rather than by statements of fact, it gives one good reason to be optimistic that the findings of linguistic research will prove to be of use to reading specialists.

Linguistics and Reading

The linguistics-reading dialogue so far has been one in which a particular view of linguistics has prevailed. In this view the main findings of linguistics which have application to the teaching of reading and to reading research may be summarized as follows: (a) language is speech and writing is a recodification of speech so that English graphemes and punctuation marks are representations, often imperfect, of phonemes and intonation patterns; (b) language is patterned, that is, grammatical; (c) language is spoken in dialects of which Standard English is one, albeit an important one; and (d) linguists prefer descriptions of linguistic data to prescription and to any kind of

mentalistic introspection. Although many linguists would agree with these statements, nevertheless they characterize but one part of current linguistic thought and omit the most significant concerns of linguists today. It should be noted too that even if they were comprehensive, current reading procedures lag sadly behind them and this linguistic "lag" itself deserves more than a passing comment.

Linguists agree that speech and writing may be considered to be different codes but insist that the speech code is in some way basic to the written code. Consequently, they insist that it is necessary always to make a clear differentiation between comments about the sounds of speech and comments about the symbols of writing. However, in spite of the work of Bloomfield and Barnhart in *Let's Read* (1961) and of Fries in *Linguistics and Reading* (1963) even these very basic facts have not been taken into consideration in the majority of texts on reading. Fries, for example, insists on careful use of the terms *phonics, phonetics,* and *phonemics* and such careful use must be recognized as crucial if there is to be any really worthwhile discussion of these topics by reading specialists. However, except for what is on the whole a sound book by Cordts, *Phonics for the Reading Teacher* (1965), books on reading still continue to confuse statements about phonology with statements about orthography and to use the terms phonics, phonetics, and phonemics almost in free variation. A linguist cannot help but regard Heilman's *Phonics in Proper Perspective* (1964) as an example of just this type of confusion and wonder what kind of success such a perspective could possibly guarantee. Furthermore, a recent series of articles in *The Reading Teacher* by Clymer (1963), Bailey (1967), and Emans (1967) on phonic generalizations would have benefited from a much closer attention to linguistic data than any of the authors chose to give, for here is a good example of the type of investigation of which Carroll speaks in which adequate methodology is dissipated on material which is often linguistically indefensible.

While this criticism of phonics is deserved, the linguists themselves mentioned above, Bloomfield and Fries, are not above criticism for their views. Both overstress the importance of the phoneme-grapheme relationship and both oversimplify the process of reading. Learning to read means more than acquiring high-speed recognition responses to various letter patterns as Fries would have it. However, many of the teaching procedures he advocates, such as the use of contrast, the stress on vowels, the insistence on whole word patterns, and the separation of reading and writing, seem to be excellent both linguistically and pedagogically.

Phoneme and Grapheme

Reading teachers and particularly reading researchers must make themselves aware of the phoneme-grapheme correspondence, the clear distinctions among phonics, phonetics, and phonemics, and the difference between statements about speech and statements about writing. Fortunately, there is much linguistic research available on these topics. Current work in linguistics does, however, indicate that a word of caution is required on the subject of the phoneme. The majority of linguists have always viewed the phoneme as a convenient linguistic fiction, and a hard to define one at that, rather than as an absolute linguistic fact. Today many linguists manage to do without phonemes at all because such linguists believe that a distinct phonemic level is not required in describing a language. More important to

them than the phonemic level is a level of representation which is sometimes called the morphophonemic. For example, instead of singling out the broad phonetic differences among the endings of *cats, dogs,* and *judges,* the [s], [z] and [ez], and calling these differences phonemic differences because of certain contrasts elsewhere in the language, as in *sip* and *zip,* such linguists point out that English plural formation is characterized by a morphophonemic sibilant, which is quite predictably realized in various phonetic shapes according to environment as [s], [z] or [ez]. This sibilant is therefore well represented by the English *s* spelling. Likewise, they stress the importance of what they call the morphophonemic connection in English between such pairs of words as *produce* and *production, nation* and *national,* and *long* and *longer.* In each case it seems that a phonemic spelling and an insistence on "traditional" phonemicization conceals rather than reveals the linguistic facts. It might even be said that English spelling in many cases is a good (or at least better than previously acknowledged) representation of the phonological facts of English. What this means for reading specialists is that there is reason to have serious doubts that a child beginning to read is well served by a strict insistence on a one-to-one phoneme-grapheme correspondence when current linguistic research suggests first of all that the phoneme neither exists nor is always a particularly useful fiction and, secondly, that rules for pronouncing are dependent in part on grammatical and lexical information.

That there is really nothing new in what has just been said is readily apparent if one comes across an interesting paper by Edward Sapir (1963) which first appeared over thirty years ago entitled "The Psychological Reality of Phonemes." Although Sapir claimed in this paper that phonemes have a psychological reality, a close examination of what he says shows that what he was talking about were morphophonemes rather than phonemes. He also seems to have been hinting at a distinction between linguistic facts, that is, linguistic reality, and linguistic data, that is, the observable characteristics of language, and this fact-data distinction is one which is extremely important in current linguistic thinking.

Linguistics: the Dialogue Within

From approximately 1930 to 1960 linguistic research was largely concerned with data, that is, with making observations of linguistic events and with procedures for classifying these observations. Out of this work came considerable development and clarification of such concepts as the phoneme, the morpheme, the sentence pattern, the intonation contour, the linguistic level, the slot and its fillers, and so on. In fact this is exactly the kind of linguistic research that is referred to in most discussions of linguistics by reading experts. Lefevre's book, *Linguistics and the Teaching of Reading* (1964), is a good example of this type of linguistic endeavor and a good application of it to reading. However, it would not be unfair to say that there are severe shortcomings in this kind of linguistics and that linguistics surely has more to offer reading than Lefevre offers.

Classifications of collections of English utterances do not reveal a great deal about English. It seems fair to say that they do not, for example, account for a speaker's ability to relate some of the sentences to others within a corpus. They do not account for an ability to distinguish between sentences and nonsentences. They do not account for a speaker's feelings that some sentences are confused, or deviant, or ambiguous. They do not allow

one in some principled way to predict possible English sentences which might occur in the future. And so on. A grammar accounting for the facts of English will be very different from the grammar presented by Lefevre and will not just present data. Instead, such a grammar will attempt to get behind the data and classifications of the data into the facts and into explanations of linguistic abilities.

Books and articles relating linguistics to reading have favored the data rather than the fact approach. For this reason they find it difficult to demonstrate an insightful and economical relationship between sound and symbol. Similarly, statements that writing is speech put down on paper are not as adequate as they should be. Raw speech is not language in any significant sense for the data of linguistic performance are not the facts of linguistic competence and the data of written performance are something else again. Speech performance is characterized by pauses, repetitions, syntactic shifts, and so on, whereas almost all the reading material presented to children is written in well-controlled sentences, a very different type of performance. The same basic competence apparently underlies performance in both speech and writing but the performances of speech and writing are not easily related to each other. The data are different, they are not easily convertible, and they are not at all convertible if a superficial view of linguistics is accepted.

It would be true to say that linguistics has not been the same since 1957, the year of the appearance of Noam Chomsky's *Syntactic Structures* (1957). In this book and since then (1965), Chomsky has put forward a theory of language which has revolutionized linguistics but which appears hardly to have touched the reading researcher. Perhaps this is not surprising for the theory is not easy to explain and any simple explanation is very likely to be distorted and misunderstood. The theory stresses the fact that a good explanatory grammar of a language requires a set of explicit syntactic rules which generate sentences of that language together with grammatical descriptions of the generated sentences and such a set of rules will reveal sentences to have deep structures on which semantic rules operate and surface representations which are mapped out by phonological rules. The phonological and graphemic surface features of sentences are automatic and superficial and contribute nothing to the understanding of sentences. Sentences may be understood correctly only if the listener or reader knows the deep underlying elements and only if he understands the deep relationships among these elements.

Comprehension: the Syntactic Basis

The importance of such a linguistic theory for an understanding of comprehension surely cannot be overestimated. Adequate comprehension of any sentence, spoken or written, requires more than just high-speed recognition, as for Fries, or left-to-right linear decoding, as in a stochastic model of the reading process, or recognition of surface patterns. In order to fully comprehend a sentence a listener, or reader, must be able to relate the correct deep structure to the surface structure of the sentence and to project a consistent semantic reading on the individual words. A reaction to the surface structure alone, that is, a recognition of individual sounds, letters, words or superficial syntactic patterns, is insufficient for comprehension, since comprehension requires that each sentence be given both syntactic and semantic interpretations in depth.

The following sentences offer illustrations, deliberately oversimplified for the purposes of the argument, of a few major syntactic problems that appear to be of interest in an understanding of comprehension.

1. The boy took the pen.
2. The pen was taken.
3. Who took the pen?
4. What did the boy take?
5. What was taken?

Sentence one requires the comprehender to assign a deep reading which will show that *The boy* is the deep subject of the sentence, *took the pen* the predicate, and *the pen* the deep object.

i   The boy took the pen

Sentence two differs from the first in that different elements and different relationships are present. The deep subject is an unspecified *SOMEONE* and the deep object is *the pen*.

ii   SOMEONE took the pen (Passive).

This deep structure accounts for the fact that a correct interpretation of *The pen was taken* requires an understanding that an unspecified person did the taking and this unspecified person took the pen, *the pen* being the underlying or deep object of the sentence though the superficial or grammatical subject.

The deep structures of sentences three, four, and five may be represented as follows:

iii   (Question) SOMEONE took the pen.

iv   (Question) The boy took SOMETHING.

v   (Question) SOMEONE took SOMETHING (Passive).

Still another group of sentences illustrates the need for the comprehender to understand exactly what is in the deep structure and what is not there.

6. The dog amazed the boy.
7. The boy was amazed by the dog.
8. The boy was amazed.
9. The dog's strength amazed the boy.

10. Who was amazed by the dog's strength?

These sentences have deep structures which may be represented as follows.

vi The dog amazed the boy.

vii The dog amazed the boy (Passive).

viii SOMENOUN amazed the boy (Passive).

ix SOMETHING [The dog was strong] amazed the boy.

x (Question) SOMETHING [The dog was strong] amazed SOMEONE (Passive).

In order to comprehend the above sentences it is necessary to be aware that an unspecified *SOMENOUN* is the deep subject "causing" the amazement in eight, that *SOMETHING* is "causing" the amazement in both nine and ten, and that this *SOMETHING* is the fact that *The dog was strong*, the only plausible interpretation of *The dog's strength*.

The type of analysis just illustrated could be carried much further into ambiguous sentences, complement structures, complex sentences, pronominal substitutions and various kinds of noun and verb classes. Here it serves the purpose of illustrating the interest that linguists are now taking in accounting for how sentences are understood, particularly in specifying what there must be in sentences and in speakers to make communication possible. A transformational-generative grammar offers an explicit characterization of the grammatical elements in sentences, a characterization which strives for completeness and which clearly distinguishes what is important about the underlying facts of language from what is involved in actual performance. The theory says nothing about performance, that is, about how a human being actually generates or interprets sentences. *It does say though that anyone who wants to understand how a human being does either such task must recog-nize the facts just presented and that anyone who does not cannot hope to discover anything very revealing about actual sentence production and interpretation. An adequate model of the comprehension process must also in some way encompass the linguistic facts just presented.*

Comprehension: the Semantic Basis

Interest in transformational-generative grammars has also fostered some intriguing work in semantics, particularly that of Katz and Fodor (1963). Katz and Fodor have proposed a semantic theory which relates closely to Chomsky's syntactic theory. How that theory might apply to basic language competency in reading may be characterized as follows. The comprehension of a sentence requires that that sentence be given a reading of its deep grammatical structure together with a reading of its semantic content. This latter reading requires that the lexical items, or words, in a sentence be interpreted in a manner consistent with each other and that inconsistent readings be rejected. The ability to give a consistent reading would imply that sentence production and interpretation requires in producers and interpreters some sense of a semantic norm and that this norm can be explicitly characterized.

Some illustrations, based on suggestions from Nida (1964), may serve to clarify these basic concepts.

11. The man sat in the chair.

12. The man died in the chair.

In sentence eleven a correct interpretation of the meaning of *chair* would be one which marked this occurrence of *chair* for such characteristics as "object," "human use" and perhaps "harmless." Sentence twelve might arouse a suspicion that a "harmless" rather than "harmful" distinction cannot be guaranteed because the verb *died* appears in the sentence.

Sentence twelve is consequently more likely to pose an interpretation problem than sentence eleven. In sentences thirteen and fourteen the ambiguity of twelve is resolved. "Harmful" replaces "harmless" as a characteristic of *chair*.

13. He died in the electric chair.

14. He died in the chair for his crime.

Electric in thirteen and *for his crime* in fourteen require that *chair* be given a different reading from *chair* in eleven and illuminate some of the difficulties encountered in twelve. In sentences fifteen and sixteen a similar meaning for *chair* to that in eleven seems to be required.

15. He took the chair.

16. He accepted the chair.

However, the addition of *at the meeting* to fifteen would require a "role" rather than "object" characteristic for *chair* just as would the addition of *at the university* to sixteen. Furthermore, *chair* in fifteen would now require an additional "judicial" characteristic just as *chair* in sixteen would require an additional "academic" characteristic.

The Language of Poetry

A general ability to recognize the correct syntactic and semantic interpretations of sentences is also basic to any kind of specific ability to recognize that a particular sentence is incapable of a syntactic or semantic interpretation, that is, it is either ungrammatical or nonsensical. It is also basic to an ability to interpret deviant sentences, particularly the deviant sentences of figurative and poetic language. Sentences seventeen to twenty-one are examples of such sentences.

17. My dog passed away yesterday.

18. Salt is eating away my car's fenders.

19. All nature sleeps.

20. He sat in black despair.

21. The king was a lion in battle.

Normally only human beings pass away, only certain animates eat and sleep, only concrete things are capable of color, and lions are non-human whereas kings are human. These sentences deviate from the English norm but not far enough so that they cannot be given interpretations which relate them to that norm. Because such interpretations can be achieved the sentences can be understood and it is possible to account for the "human-ness" of *dog* in seventeen, the animism of *salt* in eighteen and *nature* in nineteen, the metaphoric blackness of *despair* in twenty and the animal attributes of *king* in twenty-one. Anyone with an interest in poetry can see how that interest and linguistic knowledge come together at this point. Linguists are indeed conducting research which is relevant to an understanding of poetic and literary style and some of this research is proving to be most revealing. Again the basic distinctions between competence and performance and between grammars accounting for facts and grammars accounting for data provide the insights.

The Dialect Problem

In writing about linguistics and reading it is appropriate to mention the dialect work that is being conducted in several large cities, for example by Labov in New York (1966), by Stewart in Washington, D. C. (1965), and by McDavid in Chicago (1965). These investigations are producing descriptions of the English spoken in such cities which will be invaluable for teachers of English and reading. The language of many children in these cities is very different from that of their teachers and of their textbooks. The dialect studies tell us what the main phonological and grammatical differences are and the findings suggest that teachers should clearly differentiate the teaching of the language habits of any kind of standard spoken English from the teaching of reading. It is possible to read standard written English in almost any dialect and a standard printed text can be associated with dialects which show considerable phonological and grammatical variation from what might be considered the standard spoken dialect of a particular city or region. There are several reports in the literature of children reading the standard written forms in nonstandard spoken forms which are the dialect equivalents of the standard forms only to be told that the readings are "incorrect" by the teachers. In each instance the child understood what was on the page, understood it in fact so well that he gave the printed words the "correct" phonetic realizations in his own dialect and in each case the teacher revealed her confusion between teaching the child to read and teaching him to speak a different dialect. Likewise, the problem of teaching a child to say *with* not *wif* or to distinguish *den* and *then* is in most cases a dialect problem not a reading problem and almost never is it a speech correction problem in the usual sense of that term. Again a little linguistic knowledge can go a long way in helping teachers to arrive at sensible attitudes and procedures in teaching spoken and written English to such children.

Concluding Observations

It will be apparent that no definition of reading has been offered in this paper but at least one has been rejected, reading as high-speed recognition. Reading is much more complicated a process than mere recognition and it is in no sense a passive process. It requires effort to get meaning from the printed page. It requires perceptual skills not required in oral communication, particularly, of course, visual skills. A written text is also a special type of linguistic performance; it is not just speech written down. In addition, most of us read and comprehend far faster than we can listen and comprehend and this fact must be explained somewhere in a theory of reading which incorporates the view of language advanced here. However, no matter what definition of reading is finally agreed to, certain basic linguistic principles must be recognized in such a definition.

The first principle is that a clear understanding of any kind of language use can be based only on discovering answers to the questions of what language is and how language works. Transformational-generative theory gives clues to the answers to these questions. The second principle is that there is an important distinction between competence and performance. In teaching, the concern is with the former for it is competence which allows one to produce and understand new sentences. Performance, on the other hand, is but a record of those particular sentences that were produced along with the imperfections that occurred in their production. Performance acts, of course, at the same time as a kind of screen through which we must investigate all competence. The final principle is that most, if not all, language behavior is rule governed behavior and this fact must be taken into account if one is to seek to reinforce or change existing behavior. These three principles must be taken into account in any theory of reading which aims to provide reading teachers and reading researchers with the kind of explanatory power that linguists themselves are now attempting to require of linguistic theory.

References

1. BAILEY, MILDRED H. "The Utility of Phonic Generalizations in Grades One Through Six," *The Reading Teacher, 20* (1967), 413–18.
2. BETTS, E. A. "Linguistics and Reading," *Education, 86* (1966), 454–58.
3. BLOOMFIELD, L., and BARNHART, C. L. *Let's Read.* Detroit: Wayne State University Press, 1961.
4. CARROLL, J. B. "The Analysis of Reading Instruction: Perspectives from Psychology and Linguistics," *Theories of Learning and Instruction.* E. R. Hilgard (ed.). Sixty-Third Yearbook of the National Society for the Study of Education, Part I. Chicago: University of Chicago Press, 1964.
5. CHOMSKY, N. *Syntactic Structures.* The Hague: Mouton, 1957.
6. ———. *Aspects of the Theory of Syntax.* Cambridge, Mass.: M.I.T. Press, 1965.
7. CLYMER, T. "The Utility of Phonic Generalizations in the Primary Grades," *The Reading Teacher, 16* (1963), 252–58.
8. CORDTS, ANNA D. *Phonics for the Reading Teacher.* New York: Holt, Rinehart & Winston, 1965.
9. DEVINE, T. G. "Linguistic Research and the Teaching of Reading," *Journal of Reading, 9* (1966), 273–77.
10. EMANS, R. "The Usefulness of Phonic Generalizations above the Primary Grades," *The Reading Teacher, 20* (1967), 419–25.
11. FRIES, C. C. *Linguistics in Reading.* New York: Holt, Rinehart & Winston, 1963.
12. HEILMAN, A. W. *Phonics in Proper Perspective.* Columbus, Ohio: Charles E. Merrill, 1964.
13. KATZ, J. J., and FODOR, J. A. "The Structure of a Semantic Theory. *Language, 39* (1963), 170–210.
14. LABOV, W. *The Social Stratification of English in New York City.* Washington, D. C.: Center for Applied Linguistics, 1966.
15. LEFEVRE, C. A. *Linguistics and the Teaching of Reading.* New York: McGraw-Hill, 1964.
16. McDAVID, R. I., JR. "Social Dialects: Cause or Symptom of Social Maladjustment," *Social Dialects and Language Learning.* Roger W. Shuy (ed.). Champaign, Illinois: National Council of Teachers of English, 1965.
17. NIDA, E. A. *Toward a Science of Translating.* Leiden: E. J. Brill, 1964.
18. SAPIR, E. "The Psychological Reality of Phonemes," *Selected Writings of Edward Sapir.* D. G. Mandelbaum (ed.). Berkeley and Los Angeles: University of California Press, 1963.
19. STEWART, W. A. "Urban Negro Speech: Socio-Linguistic Factors Affecting English Teaching," *Social Dialects and Language Learning.* Roger W. Shuy (ed.). Champaign, Illinois: National Council of Teachers of English, 1965.

III

Reading Readiness

Reading readiness is a complex state influenced by a number of interacting factors, some of which are amenable to instruction. Hoggard opens this chapter by suggesting ways the home and school might work together to help achieve readiness and thus prevent failure in learning to read. Huus then discusses some important readiness factors and how they might be developed; and Orme reports a successful experiment in which a special readiness program was developed to identify and satisfy the special reading needs of first-grade pupils.

These are followed by two articles dealing with the measurement and concept of reading readiness. The uses and limitations of reading readiness tests are discussed by Harris. Finally, Durkin, who reviews the changing concept of reading readiness and some research, points out a possibility that should be kept in mind when reading the next chapter: a child's success in learning to read may well depend not only on the child's own abilities (his readiness) but also on the kind and quality of instruction given.

11. Readiness Is the Best Prevention *

J. KENDALL HOGGARD

"TEACHER, teacher, I can count to a hundred!" six-year-old Kaye announced the first time she could get her teacher's at-

* From J. Kendall Hoggard, "Readiness Is the Best Prevention." Reprinted from the May 1957 issue of *Education*, pp. 523–27. Copyright © 1957 by the Bobbs-Merrill Company Inc., Indianapolis, Ind.

tention. It was Kaye's first day in school, and she was eager to get started.

She not only could count to a hundred, but in the days to follow her teacher noted that Kaye knew what numbers meant and that she had an excellent speaking vocabulary on a variety of subjects. Kaye recognized many words such as her name, mother, school, car, boy, girl, children, and book when she saw them. She had traveled, and she had a rich background of information drawn from books her parents had read to her. The teacher knew that, without a doubt, Kaye and the four or five other children in her room with the same type of background would have little trouble learning to read.

In this same room, however, was a small group which represented the other extreme. Gale was one of these. Gale was full of life, was well adjusted, talked at length concerning her home, and showed every indication of being alert and intelligent. Yet, Gale had no concept of numbers, her experience with books and stories was very limited, and she did not know her address or telephone number.

On the third day of school Gale was observed at noon buying candy. She had selected six cents worth and had offered the clerk one cent for full payment. Obviously, Gale—for the first time—was up against the stark reality of the value of money.

An investigation of the home background of these two children revealed no marked differences from an economic standpoint. The children were approximately the same age, both healthy, neither had any physical defects, and vision and hearing were normal. From all that could be observed both were very intelligent, and yet, Kaye and her group were ready to read while Gale and her group were not.

The above situation is repeated over and over in almost every first-grade room in America each year. In studying this illustration three problems immediately present themselves: First, is there anything the home can do to help the preschool child get ready for school? Second, what can the school do for children like Gale in order to prevent them from developing into reading problems? Third,

how can the school and home more effectively work together at the preschool and first-grade level in order to insure better adjustment of all first-grade children?

Is There Anything the Home Can Do to Help the Preschool Child Get Ready for School?

There certainly are many things that parents can do in order to get their children ready for school. The school needs to help the parent realize this fact. Furthermore, the school needs to recommend specific activities to the parents of preschool children. Vague generalities are not enough.

In the first place, every person interested in children should know that reading is only one phase of the language development process. Contrary to popular opinion, learning to read does not begin at the age of six or seven, it begins with birth and continues throughout the life of the individual. Before a person can read he needs a wealth of experience so that words have meaning and association with persons, objects, and events. These experiences are the first stage in language development and they are the foundation upon which the other stages depend.

As the child grows and develops, he enters the second stage, which is called hearing comprehension. At this point, he learns that certain words which he hears others speak represent certain things. As his hearing vocabulary is increased, the child attempts to speak, and, as time goes on and his experience with sounds increases, he is able to enter the third stage, which is speech production. Now he can talk and make others understand him.

For most children the age of six to seven is the time at which initial experiences with the fourth stage, formal reading, take place. In this stage the child must learn to associate sound and meaning with the words he sees. A large part of his first years in school will be devoted to teaching him to make these associations. Simultaneously, he will enter the fifth stage, writing. Learning to write should be delayed, in the opinion of most authorities, until the child has a reading vocabulary of from three to four hundred words.[1]

This brief description of the stages in language development is intended to show that a large part of that development takes place before the child enters school. The parents who know and understand these stages will give attention to the experience, hearing comprehension, and speech production aspects of language development in their preschool children.

Almost without exception, every home in America can see to it that its children have the rich experiences that preschool children should have before entering school. Family excursions to the park, to the zoo, to the open country for city children and to the city for rural children, will contribute greatly to the knowledge of the child. Family picnics, fishing trips, Sunday drives in the family car, trips on the train and bus, visits to museums, the airport, the beach, the mountains and rivers are experiences which will enable the child to grow into reading.

Books should be introduced into the life of the child between the age of one and two. Many homes make a practice of reading together at bedtime which is an excellent way of sharing experiences and extending horizons. Parents can draw heavily on the great store of books that are now available in every supermarket, drugstore, and newsstand in America. Literally hundreds of different titles are available for as little as 25 cents to as much as one wishes to pay.

[1] This statement is less true now than when it was written. (Eds.)

There should be a balance between the modern and new stories of the times and the golden ones which have delighted children in the past.

Public libraries are full of books that tell the story of the American heritage, and the librarian will be delighted to help the parent select books that are appropriate to be read to the three-, four-, or five-year-old.

Television also offers an excellent opportunity to children if it is properly used. Parents should make every effort to watch television with their children so that they may know what concepts and ideas they are being exposed to. Programs should be well selected and those that may be harmful should be avoided. When necessary, parents should give the child help in understanding and assimilating material so as to avoid confusion.

Broadened experiences, a wise introduction to the world of books, and constant selectivity and supervision in materials are valuable contributions that any home may make in helping the preschool child get ready for that eventful first year in school.

What Can the School Do for Children Like Gale in Order to Prevent Them from Developing into Reading Problems?

The first grade, without a doubt, is one of the most critical periods in the life of the child. Here for the first time the six-year-old leaves the shelter and close associations of the home and steps out into a strange new world. This world will make many new demands, and the child will be confronted with an array of new experiences to which he must try to adjust. For some this adjustment will be accomplished with little difficulty. For others it will be the beginning of years of frustration and anxiety for they are destined to become known as reading problems. Yet, with the exception of 5 percent of all children who go to school, most reading disability can be prevented. Prevention starts at home, but it must be continued and extended by the school if it is to be effective.

One of the chief causes of reading failure is rushing children into the initial reading program before they are ready. Gale is not ready. In far too many instances, however, children with Gale's language deficiency will enroll in schools where the teacher's chief concern is to get them started on reading without giving any attention to readiness.

Recently, the writer made a survey of 72 schools for the purpose of finding out practices in regard to reading readiness. It was alarming to find that 27 schools started all first graders in the preprimer during the first or second week in school. It was more alarming to learn that four school systems started all first graders in the primer. The explanation was made that since the primer contains all the vocabulary to be found in the preprimer, the program simply starts with the primer in order to save time.

Such a policy illustrates well the fact that far too many teachers and parents still expect beginners to read soon after school starts in September. In these situations some children are under so much pressure that learning to read becomes an unbearable task. The classroom is filled with fear and tension which serves to aggravate the language deficiency of children like Gale.

Reading authorities are in agreement that reading readiness is the very foundation of prevention. More, not less, attention needs to be given to reading readiness at all levels of learning, but especially at the first-grade level.

Under proper leadership, first-grade teachers should be anxious to take care of the readiness needs of all the children

in their room. The question they most often ask is, "Where can I get help?"

It cannot be emphasized too strongly that all acceptable reading programs now available to schools have marvelous readiness programs. With these programs, teachers' manuals are offered in which the author sets forth his philosophy and outlines his plan for carrying out the program.

In addition to offering specific suggestions, the manual outlines the plan of organization the author recommends. The example of Kaye and Gale illustrates the fact that children vary widely in their readiness for reading. This means that in the early part of the year most teachers will need two groups—those who are ready for reading and those who are not. The children in the latter group may require weeks or months of help in language development before they are ready to read. Some of this group, however, will develop faster than others, so as the year progresses other reading groups are formed by the teacher as needs arise. These groups must always be flexible. In addition, many activities such as music, art, science, and playtime require different groupings.

The author's plan for organizing these activities deserves the most careful study by the teacher. There are no short cuts, and the school that gives little or no attention to the readiness program is creating reading problems in children like Gale.

Can the School and the Home More Effectively Work Together at the Preschool and First-Grade Level in Order to Insure Better Adjustment of All First-Grade Children?

Yes, indeed, and the school must lead the way. One community has found a very effective way to outline to parents the preschool and first-grade needs of the child.

This school system is in a town of 25,000 people and has twelve elementary schools. Through the use of a continuous census, the school has the name and address of the parents of most preschool children.

In February and March a series of conferences are planned in each elementary school for parents who will have children entering the first grade the following September. Written invitations are sent to every known parent in the district while others are reached through the press, radio, and T.V. The announcements carry an outline of the program and a list of specific questions to be discussed. Questions like the following are included: What can I, as a parent, do now in order to get my child ready for school in September? Does failure to learn to read during the first few months of school mean that my child has a low I.Q.? Will my child be taught phonics? What is included in the process of learning to read? Should I teach my child to count? My child is trying to write; what should I do? What is reading readiness?

As a rule, these conferences are well attended. In one school with an anticipated first-grade enrollment of 100, 81 parents attended.

The principal of each school is in charge of the program. The meeting usually starts with a thirty-minute talk by the Director of Instruction in which the school's philosophy is outlined. Many of the questions mentioned above are covered in this talk. At the end of the speech, the principal of the school acts as moderator and the parents are encouraged to ask questions. The first-grade teachers with the Director of Instruction act as a panel to whom questions are directed.

For years this school system has produced a parents' handbook, "Ready for First Grade." These are distributed and explained. Included in the 24-page handbook is information on reading readiness. The handbook also contains specific suggestions as to what the preschool child should be taught, recommended summertime activities and a list of 100 appropriate books from which the parent may choose the ones he wishes to read to the child. Books written by reading specialists for parents' use are also suggested.

After the handbooks are distributed, plans for two additional conferences, which occur after school starts in September, are announced. The first meeting comes at the end of the fifth week of school—usually the first week in October. During this week, all first-grade children are dismissed at noon. Starting at 1 P.M. on Monday and continuing through Friday, individual parent-teacher conferences take place. Each conference is scheduled with the parent ahead of time and lasts approximately thirty minutes.

The second conference, which is held between Thanksgiving and the Christmas holidays, is another one to which all first-grade parents are invited. At this final conference, explanation is given as to why one group is reading while another is still in reading readiness. Time is allowed at the meeting for parents to ask further questions concerning their child's progress.

It would be hard, indeed, to overemphasize the excellent accomplishments of these conferences. Complaints from first-grade parents to school authorities have almost ceased. Parents and teachers alike have nothing but praise for the plan, and home and school have gone a long way toward understanding each other.

The number of parents who are trying to teach their own children formal reading have almost disappeared. Few parents need ask, "What can I do to help my child?" They know, and they are ready to follow suggestions that are given.

Parents and teachers in this system are proud of their Kayes, Gales, Jims, and Johns. They are all different and their individuality must be accepted and cher-

ished. Any school program which is worth its salt will provide for these needs through a program centered around a philosophy of prevention. The home can help and it wants to help, but the school must lead the way.

12. Developing Reading Readiness *

HELEN HUUS

THE term "reading readiness" came into the vocabulary of most primary teachers with the publication of Harrison's book in 1936 (1). Until very recently, the basic considerations presented in that volume had not been challenged. However, the advent of television, the academic pressures following in the wake of Sputnik I, subsequent "new" curriculums for elementary schools, and recent studies of children who come to school already reading have influenced thoughtful teachers to reevaluate the role of readiness in the total program of teaching children to read.

Prerequisites for Reading

Some prerequisites for reading are common to all learning—such factors as health, mental alertness, emotional adjustment, and having parents who give love and support. However, the discussion here is limited to aspects more specifically related to the act of reading itself.

Visual factors—It stands to reason that if a child's vision is impaired, he is likely

* From Helen Huus, "Developing Reading Readiness," from *Instructor*, 74 (March, 1965), 59–60. Copyright © 1965 Instructor Publications, Inc. Reprinted by permission of the author also.

to have difficulty in differentiating between symbols that are similar in shape and detail. Those of you with faulty vision can understand this, for if you try to read without your glasses, you soon realize the strain and guesswork that result. Consider, too, that you have had experience with reading and even a faint outline can give you a clue.

Adequate checks must be made of children's vision—more than just the Snellen test at twenty feet. Tests at reading distance and checks on muscle balance and visual fusion are also needed. Even with vision corrected, some children have problems of recognizing differences between o, c, and e; b, d, p, and q; or u, n, and m. Until children see such symbols as different, they are not ready to read. Activities such as fitting puzzles together, matching pictures or symbols with successively finer differentiations, locating like and different letters in groups, and matching two like words in a set of three, give children practice.

Some newer methods for beginning reading emphasize teaching first the letters of the alphabet, both lower case and capitals. Other methods emphasize the importance of combining initial teaching of reading with the child's writing of the words. In both instances, one of the purposes is to call the child's attention to the distinctive features of letters. This visual discrimination requires not only the ability to "see" differences and likenesses, but also to recognize and remember them.

Auditory factors—Before children come to school, most of them have learned to speak the language they will be reading. In learning this language, they repeat what they hear others around them say. Although a child's hearing may be good, he may say "chimley," "breakthast," or "wiver," partly because he has not listened to finer distinctions and partly because he has not learned to say some sounds in certain positions.

He must hear differences between such like words as *pig, dig, wig; than, that; white, wight;* and *which, witch.*[1] Saying words that begin or end the same way, *Peter Piper,* for example, and noting alliteration in Mother Goose rhymes, finding rhyming words, then thinking of additional ones, help to establish auditory distinctions.

Children delight in the sound of words, and they will, without invitation, chime in on the refrain of "hundreds of cats, thousands of cats, millions and billions and trillions of cats" (2). So capitalize upon this and let them say poetry together without the formality of labeling it "choral speaking." Singing, too, helps develop auditory discrimination, and it is always a wonder that some children who cannot speak words correctly seem to have little difficulty when singing. Perhaps you may play a game where sounds like pouring water or sharpening a pencil are made behind a screen, with the children trying to figure out what is happen-

ing. In any case, point out to them sounds that need careful attention.

Language factors—Facility with language is one indication of readiness for reading. Just as the child's pronunciation indicates his ability to hear and mimic, so do his vocabulary range and sentence structure indicate his level of maturity. Compare the language of a child who says, "Me go too," with one who asks, "If you go to the library, may I go with you?" The difference is obvious, but teachers need to know the various levels of language development so that they recognize sophisticated and immature patterns.

Teachers can provide a speech model for children to emulate; they can engage children in conversation—really listen to them, answer their questions, and encourage them to speak freely. "Show and Tell" has become so firmly entrenched in primary grades that traveling fathers are on the lookout for appropriate objects to bring back for Junior. Still, the exercise does provide children a means to present ideas and to discuss.

Retelling stories, particularly folktales with their definite sequence, telling original stories, or engaging in dramatic play are other activities that encourage children to talk. Sometimes a picture or a series of related pictures serves as the stimulus; sometimes the naming and classifying of objects; and sometimes the playing of a game such as "I went to Denver and took my _____," with each child in turn adding his bit.

Experience factors—One of the most striking characteristics of children with preschool years barren of ordinary childhood experiences, and meager exposure to language and books, is deficient language development. In fact, such children usually lack many of the very qualities that make for readiness to read: speaking and understanding language, the ability to form concepts, visual and audi-

[1] For children in whose environment /w/ often replaces /hw/, so that *which* is pronounced /wich/, such fine differentiations should not be stressed for beginning readers. (Eds.)

tory discrimination, attention and memory, motor coordination, good relationship to adults, order in living, and self and group image (3). The provision of interesting experiences during the readiness period aids in bridging this gap, for these not only will provide children with the content of what to say, but will build the vocabulary with which to say it.

Take a trip around the school if you cannot get a bus or make other arrangements to take the children off the school grounds. Let the principal or supervisor tell what he does, what he thinks the school should do, and how the children can cooperate. Visit the librarian, the custodian, or another class, or take a walk around the grounds. Be alert to possibilities for extending the children's vocabulary: Talk about the maple tree, the oak, the elm, rather than just "trees," or say "corridor" instead of "hall," and notice how quickly the children follow suit.

When you are back in the classroom, make a chart of each visit, using these later to call attention to such details as the first sentence, "Mary's sentence," to capital letters and their uses, to letters that look alike, to words that are identical or similar, and to the elements that make a story interesting. Illustrate the chart by drawing or making models.

The activity of making the chart lets the children see the language arts as an integrated whole, for they *tell* the story, the teacher *writes* it down, someone *reads* what it says, and the rest *listen*. Reading becomes a part of the day's activities, and children come to understand, like the six-year-old reported by Monroe, that it is "just *talk* wrote down!" (4).

Children's books—those wonderfully illustrated stories, enchanting tales, and singing verses—provide endless pleasure besides being instructive. Think of the concepts gained from Jack and Jill "fetching" water, from Dr. Foster going to Gloucester, or from the ride to Banbury Cross. Add the sensory images of the fairy tales, the humor of Dr. Seuss, and the warm relationships of Little Bear and his family and friends, and you get a glimpse of what books can do.

When to Start Teaching Reading

One of the pressing questions of the moment is when to start reading instruction. The pat answer is, of course, "When children are *ready.*" The word itself connotes a certain tentativeness, for when a child has acquired the abilities that send him into reading, its usefulness is outlived, only to spring forth again at a higher level as readiness for the new task. Needlessly prolonging the stage of readiness is as foolish as ignoring it altogether, for some fives are advanced socially, physically, and mentally over some six-year-olds.

A sensible and realistic approach includes a recognition of learning as a continuum and of reading as having its own sequence. Since each child progresses at a pace that is his own, teachers who know the sequence of teaching reading can accept these children and accommodate to them. It may mean letting some who are in kindergarten go "up" to first grade for their reading; it may mean letting some use their ability by reading to others in the kindergarten and then giving them individual help on their own reading needs; it may mean letting kindergarten teachers keep a group two or three years in order that children can make an easy transition into reading without paying much attention to grade designations.

And so teachers provide environmental experiences through trips and excursions; fact and fancy through stories and poetry; skills and habits through lessons in discrimination; and opportunities for expression through art, music, and the manipulation of materials. While children are enjoying these interesting, varied activities, they are all the while readying themselves for learning that which most of them came to school to do—learn to read for themselves.

References

1. HARRISON, M. LUCILE. *Reading Readiness.* Boston: Houghton Mifflin Co., 1936.
2. GAG, WANDA. *Millions of Cats.* New York: Coward-McCann, 1928.
3. CLARK, KENNETH. "Discrimination and the Disadvantaged," *College Admissions 7: The Search for Talent.* New York: College Entrance Examination Board, 1960. Pp. 12–18.
4. MONROE, MARION. *Growing Into Reading.* Chicago: Scott, Foresman and Co., 1951. P. 68.

13. Building Readiness for Reading in First-Grade Children through Special Instruction *

LILLIAN ORME

ELEMENTARY-SCHOOL educators know that much of pupil nonpromotion occurs in the first grade, that inability to read is a leading reason for nonpromotion, and that many nonpromotions represent a failure of the school rather than of the pupil. Placing responsibility on the schools is justified after viewing the success of later remedial instruction which is adjusted to the abilities and interests of children. This outcome suggests that

* From Lillian Orme, "Building Readiness for Reading in First-Grade Children through Special Instruction," Thirty-Fourth Yearbook, *National Elementary Principal,* XXXV (September, 1955), 43–46. Copyright © 1955 by National Association of Elementary School Principals, National Education Association. All rights reserved. Reprinted by permission of the author and *National Elementary Principal.*

many children might have succeeded from the beginning had their initial instruction been as well adjusted to their needs as the remedial teaching.

With this knowledge in mind we experimented with a special program of initial instruction at the W. W. Yates School in Kansas City, Missouri. Our specific purposes were: (a) to develop a special readiness program with emphasis on the reading needs of first-grade pupils, (b) to test the value of readiness materials, and (c) to determine the degree of success of this program.

Experimental Procedure

The matched group technic was used. Entering first-grade pupils were divided into two groups, one control group and one experimental, each group having the same distribution of intelligence test scores as determined by the *Revised Stanford-Binet Scale*.[1] Two rooms of first-graders taught by two regular teachers made up the control group. One room, taught by the writer, made up the experimental group.

During the first month in school, all the first-graders were given the *Metropolitan Readiness Tests*.[2] The scores showed that slightly more than 78 percent of all the children were not ready for formal instruction in reading: 77 percent of the experimental group, 82 percent of one control group, and 76 percent of the second control group.

Materials and Methods

The materials and methods used with the experimental group differed appreciably from those used with the control groups. The experimental group used reading readiness and preparatory books, pupil workbooks accompanying the basic readers, supplementary materials such as picture cards, phonetic cards, charts, tests, and other books and related content.

Materials for reading in the control groups were not designated by the experimenter. They were allowed to proceed with their reading instruction in nearly complete freedom of choice of materials and technics. Principal materials used in the control groups were the basal reading series, supplementary texts, preprimers, flash cards, charts, and similar ones. The absence of direction of procedures and technics for the control groups was to establish or to maintain as nearly as possible the conventional or normal practice of reading instruction. The only restriction was that reading readiness books were to be used only by the experimental group.

For the experimental group a longer time was allowed for the readiness period before beginning teaching the reading skills. The length of the readiness period depended upon the developmental level of the individual child, his adjustment, and progress. The program of special instruction was designed to include: (a) the city-adopted course of study, (b) activities to meet specific needs, and (c) provisions for the varying rates of progress of pupils.

The room of the experimental group was arranged in seven centers of interest with appropriate materials.

Results at End of the First Year

At the end of the first year, all the children were given the *Gates Primary Reading Tests*.[3] The scores of the children of the experimental group were above those of the children in both control groups. A gain of two months on the average was made by the experimental group over the first control group and three months over the second control group.

Results at End of the Second Year

The pupils entered the second grade in the normal enrollment process. Since each class remained fairly intact, there was opportunity for further study of the effects of the readiness program. The writer did not teach the pupils in the second grade. Although no special instruction was provided during the second year, the probability of permanence of

[1] Louis M. Terman and Maud A. Merrill, Revised Stanford-Binet Scale (Boston: Houghton Mifflin Co., 1937).

[2] Gertrude H. Hildreth and Nellie L. Griffiths, *Metropolitan Readiness Tests* (New York: World Book Co., 1950).

[3] Arthur I. Gates, *Gates Primary Reading Tests* (New York: Teachers College, Columbia University, 1939).

Center of Interest	*Purpose*
Reading Center	
Reading table, chairs, bookcase, bulletin board, reading easel, readiness books, charts, *Our Big Book,* basic readers, workbooks, pictures, word phrases and sentence cards, phonetic cards, chalkboards, pocket card holder	Children work directly with the teacher for development of reading readiness and of reading.
Library Corner	
Reading table and chairs, picture and story books, preprimers and primers, mounted pictures and picture cards, scrapbooks, picture dictionary	Free reading by the children
Play Corner	
Playhouse equipment, dolls, toys	Dramatic play and social experiences
Science Center	
Tables, shelves of specimens and exhibits, magnet, aquarium	Interest and observation
Arithmetic Center	
Abacus, beads, bottles (half pint, pint, and quart), buttons, clock dial, play money, ruler, yardstick, splints, calendar, geometric forms	To help develop number readiness and build number concepts
Painting Center	
Easel, newspapers, cloths, tempera paints, large brushes, jars	Medium for self-expression and development of physical dexterity
Sharing Center	
Games, puzzles, toys, things children bring from home, class projects	Child interest in and sharing with others

the earlier instruction was indicated by the results of the *Gates Advanced Primary Reading Tests* [4] which were given to the pupils at the end of that year. The children who had been in the experimental group maintained superiority in all areas of the tests. The predictive value of the reading readiness tests used before beginning reading was shown by the fact that those pupils who reached or exceeded the norm on the readiness tests

invariably succeeded with reading, and conversely, the poor risks remained poor risks except for the few who received the adjusted program of instruction in the experimental group.

Implications for School Programs

Children of the first grade who are found to have deficiencies in readiness should neither be excluded from the first grade and put with younger children in the kindergarten nor forced into a beginning reading program for which they are not ready. They should be given a definite

[4] Arthur I. Gates, *Gates Advanced Primary Reading Tests* (New York: Teachers College, Columbia University, 1943).

program of readiness training which offers them a chance to succeed, with methods and materials adjusted especially to meet their needs and abilities.

At all times the first-grade program must be planned for the continual development of the skills necessary for reading progress. By presenting a varied and rich reading readiness program the first-grade teacher is assured of guiding a maximum number of pupils to success in reading.

14. Evaluating Reading Readiness Tests *

ALBERT J. HARRIS

READING readiness tests were first developed in the 1930's, and by the close of that decade there were at least eight readiness tests available, three of which are still fairly widely used. The manuals of these early readiness tests recommended them for use for a variety of purposes, such as the following: (1) to identify immature children, quite lacking in readiness, who are likely to do very poorly in first-grade reading unless given special help; (2) to provide an objective measure as a check on teacher judgment; (3) to locate specific strengths and weaknesses which would help the teacher to formulate an appropriate instructional program; (4) to determine how nearly ready various groups of children are for the beginnings of formal reading instruction; (5) to provide a basis for equalizing groups in experimental studies of beginning reading instruction.

From the beginning, it became evident that convenience and ease of administration would be major factors in determining which readiness tests would survive and which would not. For example, two of the early tests required completely individual administration. While these tests were used to some extent in clinics, they never became tools for the classroom teacher. Similarly, tests which required a combination of group testing and individual testing, or which required a series of test sessions over more than three days, never achieved any degree of popularity. There has been a general preference for tests with between three and six subtests, allowing some detection of specific strengths or weaknesses, but reasonably easy to administer and to score.

The major factor in the evaluation of readiness tests should be the evidence concerning their validity. The validity of a test may be defined as the degree to which the test measures what it is supposed to measure. In achievement tests, content or face validity is quite important; this is the degree to which the content of the test parallels or samples the knowledge which the test is intended to cover. In a social studies test, or an arithmetic test, an experienced teacher can judge fairly well whether or not the test provides a reasonable sample of the

* From Albert J. Harris, "Evaluating Reading Readiness Tests," in Coleman Morrison (ed.), *Problem Areas in Reading—Some Observations and Recommendations,* Rhode Island College Reading Conference Proceedings (Providence, R.I.: Oxford Press, 1965), pp. 9–16. Reprinted by permission of Dr. Coleman Morrison.

knowledge, concepts, and problem-solving abilities that are important in that particular area of the curriculum. For a readiness test, or for any test whose purpose is to predict future performance, the main question about validity is how well the test can predict future achievement. For a reading readiness test, the question is how well the readiness test, given before the children are started in formal reading instruction, will predict achievement when their reading ability is tested after a suitable period of instruction.

Validity is usually stated in terms of the coefficient of correlation between scores on the readiness test and scores on a reading achievement test given at a later time. It would be easy if we could simply compare the coefficients of correlation obtained with different readiness tests, and on the basis of these correlations determine the one best readiness test. Unfortunately, it is not that simple, because these correlations are influenced by a number of factors besides the readiness test itself.

One of these factors is the range of differences among pupils. The wider the differences among the children, the higher the correlations are likely to be between readiness tests and achievement tests. A second influence is the degree to which reading instruction is individualized; the more successful the teacher is in helping each child according to his needs and at an appropriate rate of learning for him, the higher the correlations are likely to be. A third factor is the pace of the program as a whole. When this is too slow, the children high in readiness are unlikely to learn as well as expected. On the other hand, if the pace is fast for the whole class, the percentage of failure is likely to be higher than anticipated. Related to this, also, is the factor of class size, which limits the degree to which the

program can be fitted to the needs of individuals and small groups (7).

Another very important factor influencing the predictive effectiveness of various kinds of readiness tests is the nature of the instructional program. It is no accident that during the period in which the look-and-say method of instruction was paramount and phonic teaching was slighted, the readiness tests tended to emphasize visual perception and paid very little attention to auditory perception. In the large-scale study conducted by Durrell and his students several years ago, in which considerable stress was placed upon early learning of the alphabet and on functional phonics, it is not surprising that knowledge of the alphabet before instruction in school had the highest predictive ability (6).

In general, correlations between reading readiness tests and reading achievement scores at the end of the first grade, second grade, or third grade tend to fall in the range between .30 and .60 (3,5, 11,14,17). Correlations of this size are usually described as substantial rather than high. They provide fairly good indicators of the expected average performance of a group, but when the correlation is within this range there are always quite a few individual exceptions. The exceptions include both low-scoring children who learn to read well, and high-scoring children whose achievement in reading is disappointing. For this reason, scores on readiness tests must be regarded as providing only part of the information about children that is necessary in order to make suitable instructional provisions for them in the first grade (9).

Current reading readiness tests tend to include three or more of the following kinds of measures:

1. Visual perception: matching of pictures, geometrical forms, letters, and words.
2. Verbal comprehension, including vocabu-

lary and concepts, sentence comprehension, and following directions.

3. Auditory perception, including recognizing whether whole words are the same or different, recognizing rhyming sounds, or finding words with similar initial consonant sounds (4,6).

4. Ability to identify letters of the alphabet and digits.

5. Sample lessons, in which a small number of words are taught by a specified procedure for a specified length of time, and then ability to recognize the words is tested (6).

6. Rating scales for teachers to rate the children on characteristics which are not tested in the objective subtests (4).

7. Ability to draw or to copy a drawing (12).

Each of the seven kinds of abilities just mentioned has some relevance in the total picture of readiness for learning to read. There has been little or no consistency in the research as to which of these are the most vital or most essential. As new tests of a particular kind are developed, the usefulness of that kind of test may be found to have increased. For example, there has been considerable recent research interest in tests of auditory perception and visual perception, including new types of tests which require individual administration (4,12,16).

As an example of the kinds of fluctuations one gets in validity studies with reading readiness tests, I will comment briefly on Table I and Table II of a research study just completed (10). Table I gives the intercorrelations among twelve variables, including the *Pintner-Cunningham Primary Mental Test,* three scores based on the *Lee-Clark Reading Readiness Test,* the *Bender Visual-Motor Gestalt Test, Wepman Auditory Discrimination Test,* an experimental motor ability test, four subtests of the *Metropolitan Achievement Test,* and the *Metropolitan Average Reading* score. As is characteristic of most such studies, the correlations

between the various pretests and average reading at the end of the first-grade range between .36 and .51. With the exception of tests six and seven, differences in the sizes of the correlations are of doubtful statistical significance.

Table II shows the correlations obtained in a second year of the same study. Two scores based upon parts of the *Gates Reading Readiness Test* were substituted for the *Lee-Clark,* the *Bender* was retained, and two new measures were tried out, an experimental group visual-motor test and a teacher rating scale. The method of instruction in both years was highly individualized. In the second year twenty of the children were singled out for instruction with methods other than the predominantly visual method, and correlations are given both for the total group and for the forty-two children whose instruction in word recognition was predominantly visual. The correlations with *Metropolitan Average Reading* were above .60 for both the *Gates Visual Perception* score and the *Pintner-Cunningham* I.Q. The *Teacher Rating Scale* was only slightly lower, and the *Rhyming Test* also had substantial validity. Two visual-motor tests came out lowest in this particular study.

It seems quite probable that the superiority of the visual perception measure over the rhyming or auditory perception, and the visual-motor tests, is due to the fact that the method of instruction for these children stressed a visual approach. Had the approach been one stressing phonics, a quite different table of correlations might have been obtained.

I have used this illustration to show that a test does not have a single validity, but that its validity changes according to the circumstances in which it is used. Validity depends partly upon the method of instruction employed, partly on the

TABLE I

Means, Standard Deviations and Intercorrelations of Pretests and Final Tests

Variable	Mean	S.D.	Intercorrelations										
			2	3	4	5	6	7	8	9	10	11	12
1. Pintner-Cunningham I.Q.	109.78	15.96	.477	.566	.539	.491	.379	.403	.380	.445	.460	.508	.490
2. Lee-Clark Visual Pcpt.	34.04	7.58	—	.571	.980	.470	.408	.419	.358	.444	.432	.576	.470
3. Lee-Clark Vocabulary	17.61	2.18		—	.723	.482	.394	.481	.411	.473	.386	.584	.465
4. Lee-Clark Total	51.65	9.01			—	.513	.439	.469	.401	.488	.457	.626	.508
5. Bender Visual-Motor	10.17	3.73				—	.345	.544	.294	.429	.320	.462	.418
6. Wepman Auditory Discr.	29.42	7.77					—	.314	.280	.373	.294	.368	.362
7. Queens College Motor Test ...	14.69	3.35						—	.267	.380	.306	.290	.363
8. MAT Word Knowledge*	49.05	10.24							—	.774	.686	.569	.825
9. MAT Word Discrimination ...	51.57	11.15								—	.815	.635	.963
10. MAT Reading	49.59	8.42									—	.684	.914
11. MAT Arithmetic	48.95	7.63										—	.690
12. MAT Average Reading	50.29	9.27											—

NOTE: N = 100, omitting the 10 experimental children and those with incomplete data.
* MAT standard scores

TABLE II

Intercorrelations Among Pretests and Final Tests. 1963–64 Study, for Total Populations and Control Group

	1	2	3	4	5	6	7	8	9	10	11
1. GATES VISUAL PCP …		.455	−.233	.457	.575	.601	.565	.618	.611	.637	−.013
2. GATES RHYMING ……	.553		−.140	.503	.508	.389	.299	.423	.410	.403	.181
3. BENDER ……………	.208	.150		−.517	−.369	−.406	−.189	−.262	−.201	−.182	−.204
4. QUEENS V-M ………	.510	.350	−.508		.462	.559	.419	.390	.384	.425	.189
5. RATING SCALE ……	.568	.507	−.321	.371		.604	.476	.552	.606	.586	−.065
6. PINTNER-CUNN IQ …	.589	.367	−.389	.523	.563		.543	.551	.610	.614	−.266
7. MAT WORD KNOW. …	.644	.333	−.153	.397	.434	.563		.771	.816	.929	−.169
8. MAT WORD DISC. ……	.629	.541	−.322	.400	.587	.577	.747		.826	.816	−.183
9. MAT READING ……	.612	.510	−.182	.373	.590	.624	.773	.829		.967	−.189
10. MAT AVERAGE ……	.672	.592	−.171	.423	.578	.624	.894	.746	.948		−.199
11. AGE IN MONTHS ……	.146	.231	−.231	.235	−.040	−.201	−.140	−.108	−.127	−.120	

NOTE: Correlations in upper part are based on the Total Population of 62 children; r's in the lower part are based on the Control Group of 42 children.

learning of the children, partly on the efficiency of the teacher.

However, a suitable combination of a number of measures, none of which has high validity, may produce a combination which has considerably better predictive ability than any of its components. Four of the tests listed in Table II were combined into a total score according to a multiple regression equation. The resulting composite score has a correlation with average reading of .775, substantially higher than that of any of the single tests. Determining the best possible weights for the separate tests, however, is a statistical problem well beyond the statistical resources of nearly all teachers. If a school system is to get the best possible accuracy out of its readiness testing program, it needs the services of someone who can apply appropriate statistical techniques.

In summary, performance on objective tests of mental ability and on tests devised specifically to measure readiness for reading is useful in the evaluation of readiness. All such tests are limited in what they cover and are never perfect predictors. Observations and judgments by teachers provide the only available evidence about some aspects of readiness, and can be improved by using an appropriate kind of rating scale and by being alert to the implications of children's day-to-day behavior and performance. The combined use of teacher ratings with appropriately selected tests is superior to either tests alone or teacher judgment alone.

References

1. BALOW, IRVING. "Sex Differences in First-Grade Reading," *Elementary English,* 40 (March, 1963), 303–12.
2. BRAZZIEL, WM. F., and TERRELL, MARY. "An Experiment in the Development of Readiness in a Culturally Disadvantaged Group of First-Grade Children," *Journal of Negro Education,* 31 (Winter, 1962), 4–7.
3. BRYAN, QUENTIN R. "Relative Importance of Intelligence and Visual Perception on Predicting Reading Achievement," *California Journal of Educational Research,* 15 (January, 1964), 44–48.
4. CHALL, JEANNE, ROSWELL, FLORENCE G., and BLUMENTHAL, SUSAN H. "Auditory Blending Ability: a Factor in Success in Beginning Reading," *The Reading Teacher,* 17, no. 2 (November, 1963), 113–18.
5. DODSON, JAMES C., and HOPKINS, KENNETH D. "The Reliability and Predictive Validity of the Lee-Clark Reading Readiness Test," *Journal of Developmental Reading,* 6 (Summer, 1963), 278–81.
6. DURRELL, DONALD D. "First-Grade Success Study: A Summary," *Journal of Education,* 140 (February, 1958), 2–6.
7. FRYMIER, JACK R. "The Effect of Class Size upon Reading Achievement in First Grade," *The Reading Teacher,* 18, no. 2 (November, 1964), 90–93.
8. GATES, ARTHUR I. "The Necessary Mental Age for Beginning Reading," *Elementary School Journal,* 37 (1937), 497–508.
9. HARRIS, ALBERT J., and SIPAY, EDWARD R. *Effective Teaching of Reading* 2nd ed., New York:

David McKay Company, 1972, p. 43.

10. HARRIS, ALBERT J. *Individualizing First-Grade Reading According to Specific Learning Aptitudes.* New York: Office of Research and Evaluation, Division of Teacher Education, The City University of New York, 1965. Pp. 1–12 (Mimeographed).

11. KINGSTON, ALBERT H., JR. "The Relationship of First-Grade Readiness to Third- and Fourth-Grade Achievement," *Journal of Educational Research,* 56 (October, 1962), 61–67.

12. KOPPITZ, ELIZABETH M., MARDIS, V., and STEPHENS, T. "A Note on Screening School Beginners with the Bender Gestalt Test," *Journal of Educational Psychology,* 52 (April, 1962), 80–81.

13. MATTICK, WM. E. "Predicting Success in the First Grade," *Elementary School Journal,* 63 (February, 1963), 273–76.

14. MITCHELL, BLYTHE C. "The Metropolitan Reading Tests as Predicters of First-Grade Achievement," *Educational and Psychological Measurement,* 22 (Winter, 1962), 765–72.

15. MORRISON, IDA E. "The Relation of Reading Readiness to Certain Language Factors," *Challenge and Experiment in Reading.* Proceedings of the Seventh Annual Conference of the International Reading Association, New York: Scholastic Magazines, 7 (1962), 119–21

16. SMITH, CAROL E., and KEOGH, BARBARA K. "The Group Bender Gestalt as a Reading Readiness Screening Instrument," *Perceptual and Motor Skills,* 15 (December, 1962), 639–45.

17. ZINGLE, HARVEY W., and HOHOL, A. E. "Predictive Validity of the Metropolitan Readiness Tests," *Alberta Journal of Educational Research,* 10 (June, 1964), 99–104.

15. What Does Research Say About the Time to Begin Reading Instruction? *

DOLORES DURKIN

QUESTIONS about the time to begin reading instruction are invariably bound up with the concept "reading readiness." Consequently, how they are answered directly reflects how this concept is interpreted.

When the term "reading readiness"

* From Dolores Durkin, "What Does Research Say About the Time to Begin Reading Instruction?" *Journal of Educational Research,* 64 (October, 1970), 52–56. Reprinted by permission of the author and the *Journal of Educational Research.*

was first used in the 1920's, the common interpretation was that readiness is the product of maturation; more specifically, of a certain stage in the child's development which equips him with the requirements for success in learning to read. Because this interpretation was generally accepted over four decades and, secondly, because it directly affected the readiness research that was done during the same 40 years, an understanding of why it was both proposed and accepted is important.

Although proposed in the 1920's, the

initially assigned meaning stemmed from psychological ideas that were popular at the start of the century. One way to describe them is to describe some of the beliefs of G. Stanley Hall, for it was his teachings that dominated the psychological world at that time.

One teaching was that genetic factors determine the characteristics and abilities of each individual. With this as the accepted assumption, it was natural for the early years of the century to give attention to hereditary rather than environmental factors, and to the maturation process rather than to learning and practice.

Another of Hall's influential beliefs was rooted in his acceptance of the doctrine of recapitulation, a doctrine defined briefly but clearly by Hall himself in a 1904 publication:

The most general formulation of all the facts of development that we yet possess is contained in the law of recapitulation. This law declares that the individual, in his development, passes through stages similar through which the race has passed, and in the same order (14).

Hall's acceptance of the recapitulation theory led him to support this view of man: (a) Each individual, as he grows and develops, passes through certain stages, and (b) these stages follow each other in an inevitable, predetermined order. Because the learning process was being assigned only secondary importance, progress through these "inevitable stages" was explained with a reference to maturation.

Later, the special importance assigned to maturation was continued in the writings of Arnold Gesell, a student of Hall's who gave sustained support to his teacher's beliefs. As Gesell offered his explanation of development, he referred to processes like "intrinsic growth," "neural ripening," and "unfolding behavior" (9,

10,11). Whatever the language, however, the contention was the same: Growth and development proceed in stages; progress from one to another is dependent upon spontaneous maturation or, put more simply, the passing of time. Such a contention met with little criticism during the 1920's, and, as a result, during this time "reading readiness" first entered the educator's professional vocabulary. This accounts not only for the original interpretation but also for the quickness with which it was accepted.

Why "reading readiness" became part of the educator's vocabulary in the 1920's can be explained with a reference to the Measurement and Testing Movement, which permeated both education and psychology by 1920 (22). Among other things, its concern for objective measurement led to an abundance of national surveys designed to uncover what and how much children were learning in school. Common among the findings was that the rate of nonpromotion for first-graders was considerably higher than for children at other levels and, secondly, that inadequate achievement in reading generally was the cause of retentions (5, 6,20). What subsequently became as frequent as the reports of the two findings was the question: *Why* are first-graders not succeeding with reading?

It would seem, at least in retrospect, that a multifactor explanation would be offered that might reasonably include problems related to—too large classes, too few materials, inadequate teacher preparation, wrong methodology, unmotivated children, and so on. This, however, was not the case. Because the 1920's were permeated by the ideas of Hall and Gesell, the *one* explanation that was both proposed and accepted placed the blame on the children's lack of readiness when reading instruction began. Or, in Hall-Gesell terminology, the children were having difficulty because at the time instruction was initiated, they had not yet reached that stage of development which would allow them to be successful. The solution? Within the Hall-Gesell framework, the obvious one was to have the schools postpone instruction until the children matured and became ready for it.

Mental Age Description

Once the "doctrine of postponement" was accepted, efforts were made to define that stage of development which equips children with the prerequisites for success in reading, and to define it in such a way that it could be measured and thus identified. Because of the new availability of group intelligence tests—another product of the Measurement and Testing Movement—the earliest of these efforts sought out a mental-age level that might define it. While other researchers were involved, the one whose findings were to be quoted for an unusually long amount of time was Carleton Washburne, a well-known leader in the then popular Progressive Education Movement. In a research report written by himself and Mabel Morphett in 1931, it was proposed that a child is ready to read when he has a mental age of 6.5 years, and it is only then that he should be introduced to reading (19).

Of interest is the fact that just a few years later Arthur Gates and his associates published a series of research articles in which the reported data went contrary to the Morphett-Washburne proposal. The findings of one study, for instance, led Gates to observe:

Reading is begun by very different materials, methods, and general procedures, some of which a pupil can master at the mental age of five with reasonable ease, others of which would give him difficulty at the mental age of seven (7).

Because conflicting findings were being reported, it was only natural to wonder why the Morphett-Washburne data from a study of one teaching method in one school system (Winnetka, Illinois) were so readily accepted as being applicable to all children. I believe a combination of factors suggests an answer. For one thing, the Morphett-Washburne proposal fit in perfectly with the temper of the times in which it was made. It gave support to the doctrine of postponement because most children entering first grade have not yet reached the mental age of 6.5 years. It also supported the notion that development proceeds in stages, and it honored the Measurement and Testing Movement by being precise and objective. Finally, any attempt to explain the unusual influence of the mental-age concept of readiness must take into account the prominence of Carleton Washburne. He was not only superintendent of the Winnetka schools—widely admired and copied in the 1930's—but also one of the most prestigious leaders of the Progressive Education Movement. As a result, what Washburne said was listened to—and not only in reading. Even earlier than 1931, for instance, he had made very specific proposals about what was to be taught in arithmetic and at which mental-age level (23).

With all these facts in mind, neither his mental-age description of reading readiness nor the influence it wielded should come as any great surprise. In fact, they simply demonstrate what still continues to be true of research: the quality and general applicability of a study are not always what determines the influence of its findings.

Reading Readiness Tests

While some researchers were pursuing a mental-age description of readiness, others were initiating studies designed to measure combinations of abilities which might also add up to readiness. These attempts to construct and evaluate reading readiness tests began in the late 1920's and have been continued right up to the present (2,18).

Early forms of the tests, like many currently in use, typically included subtests said to evaluate vocabulary development and auditory and visual discrimination abilities. The most noticeable difference, when earlier editions are compared with the most current ones, lies in the visual discrimination subtest. Now the trend is to use letters and words; earlier, simple pictures and geometrical forms were the usual stimuli. It was, in fact, this use of stimuli other than letters and words that often resulted in low coefficients of correlation for readiness test scores and subsequent achievement in reading. Gates, this time in 1939, was one of the first to make this point when he reported on a very comprehensive study of readiness scores as predictors of success with reading (8). The general conclusion of that report was phrased this way:

It should be noted that among the tests of little or no predictive value are many tests and ratings widely recommended in books and articles on reading readiness testing and teaching (8).

Once again, Gates and other researchers who also found a reason in their data to question the predictive value of readiness tests were generally ignored. In fact, during the 1930's, the 1940's, and even into the 1950's, the typical school practice was to use composite readiness scores, sometimes along with MA data, for making decisions about when to start teaching reading. Such a practice, it must be noted, in no way violated either the doctrine of postponement or the high esteem accorded the maturation process. Still assumed was that entering first-graders are too immature to learn to read and would start the year by participating in a readiness program. It was only after such participation that administrators and teachers would begin to consider, with the help of readiness test scores, when reading instruction should begin.

The 1960's

Certainly there is no need now to explain with any detail why the 1960's are referred to as a revolutionary period for early childhood education. Suffice it to say that these years became an era in which unprecedented attention went to the young child; in particular, to the unique importance of the early years for his eventual intellectual development (3, 16). It was also an era in which the productivity of learning opportunities was stressed, with very little explicit attention going to the maturation process. Thus, at least for early childhood education, it was a time that contrasted sharply with the four prior decades.

With the sharp changes it was only natural to have questions raised about the traditional interpretation and use of the readiness concept. After all, an era which assigns critical importance to learning opportunities during the pre-first-grade period is not likely to be patient with school practices that postpone reading instruction beyond the start of the first-grade year and assume the passing of time will insure a readiness for it.

As the years have shown, the typical response to the impatience was neither complicated nor imaginative. For the most part, schools simply altered the timing of traditional practices. Readiness tests were administered earlier, often in kindergarten where readiness workbooks could be found too. In first grade, reading instruction usually was started sooner than was typical for the earlier decades—although readiness programs still could be found in some first-grade classrooms, especially in school districts that had no kindergartens. In a few places the change in timing was more radical: they introduced reading in kindergarten. In other areas, however, opposition to this was as great and vocal as it had been in years gone by.

With such changes as these occurring in the 1960's, what was learned about readiness, and thus about the optimum time to begin reading instruction? Not much, and for a variety of reasons.

To begin with, the decade gave very little attention to the basic nature of readiness. In fact, some who were urging that reading be started even before the kindergarten year seemed either to ignore the factor of readiness or to take it for granted that all children are ready before the ages of 5 and 6. Those who did deal with the concept merely stressed that many aspects of readiness are learned and therefore can be taught.

Some of the learned and thus teachable aspects were like what was being evaluated in readiness tests; so, with some alterations, they continued to be used in great quantities throughout the 1960's. As was mentioned earlier, one common change in the visual discrimination subtests was the use of letters and words in place of pictures and geometrical forms. A change of more recent origin is the inclusion of a letter-naming subtest. Although this change has been explained with a reference to studies that show a significant correlation between letter-naming ability and later achievement in reading (4), it does not take into account the likelihood that the prereader's ability to name letters was the result of much more than something that might be labeled "readiness." More specifically, to assume that a young child's letter-naming ability

in and of itself leads to success in reading is to overlook the strong likelihood that the research referred to measured an ability that was one product of an out-of-school environment that will always be contributing to the child's success in school.

This particular use of research is singled out here because it helps to underscore what has always been a serious flaw in readiness research. Here I refer to its unfortunate tendency over the years to present correlation data as if they indicated cause-effect relationships and, secondly, to omit attention to possible reasons for the reported correlations. In fact, the customary procedure has been one in which researchers collect readiness scores at one point in time and reading scores at another. Correlation coefficients for the two sets of data are then reported—and that is it.

Although, in more recent years, this type of research has decreased, it has been replaced only by equally nonproductive studies. For example, it is now common to find reports in which the researcher simply takes for granted the validity of some readiness test as he uses it to assess the value of the variable under study for preparing children to be successful with reading. Thus, in recent years readiness test scores have been used as the criterion measure for evaluating such things as the use of teacher aides, special science materials, a pre-first-grade summer program, Frostig workbooks, and Delacato's crawling prescriptions (1,13,17,21,25). At other times they have been used to establish the relative value of attending kindergarten and not attending, of having mothers involved in a program and not having them, of one type of maternal behavior *vs.* some other type, and so on (12,15,24). Underlying all the reports is the implicit assumption that readiness scores really do tell how well or poorly a child will perform when reading instruction gets underway.

While one can understand the desire of researchers to use instruments that will yield "objective" data than can be statistically analyzed—how else can one get "significant" findings?—one cannot help but be disapppointed with their failure to point out the possible flaws in an instrument. In fact, if researchers continue to act as if the validity of readiness tests is unquestionable, then we can hardly expect school personnel to rise above traditional practices which should have been seriously questioned right from the start. Because the most important reason for questioning both the practices and the research on which they are based still exists, it will be dealt with now in some detail.

Wrong Question

For as long as the reading readiness concept has been with us—and this is true whether maturation or learning or some combination of the two is given credit for readiness—the assessment question posed by both educators and researchers has been, "Is the child ready?" Unfortunately, such a question is the wrong one to ask because it is incomplete. It focuses only on the child, thus omitting attention to an equally important variable; namely, the reading instruction that will be available.

Another way of making this same point is to say that the traditional way of asking the question neglects the *relational* aspect of readiness. It fails to recognize that whether or not a child is ready— that is, whether or not he will be successful in learning to read—depends not only on his own abilities but also on the kind and quality of instruction that is offered. Realistically, this means that a child might be very ready if one type of instruction can be made available, but unready if another is offered.

Since different kinds of instruction make different demands of the learner, this relational dimension also points out that readiness should not be equated with a single collection of abilities, as has been the traditional practice. Instead, we should be thinking in terms of readiness in the sense that one collection of abilities makes a child ready for one kind of instruction, while a somewhat different collection might make him ready to cope with another.

A Second Major Flaw

Still another flaw exists in the kind of thinking and questioning that have been typical when readiness is the concern. This is the failure to realize that the process of learning to read does not require children to be ready to learn everything at once. All of the pieces that comprise "reading ability" are not taught at once; therefore, they need not be learned all at once. Yet, as questions about a child's readiness to read have been considered in the past, answers seem to assume that he must be able to do everything—and right away. Such an assumption needs to be replaced by one which recognizes that a child learns to read, a step at a time; and that the important readiness requirement is that he is able to learn the first step. Fortunately, success with that first step often prepares him to be ready for the second.

Implications for Future Research

If the two flaws which have been mentioned are valid criticisms of the way educators and researchers have traditionally thought about readiness, then certain implications follow.

For example, if readiness is dependent

both on the child's abilities and, as Ausubel has phrased it, on *"the demands of the learning task,"* then future research efforts ought to go in the direction of (a) assessing more successfully than has been done up to now the relevant abilities of each child; (b) identifying the possible methodologies for reading as well as the learning demands of each; and (c) helping teachers match children in terms of their abilities, with methodology in terms of what it requires of the learner. It must also be emphasized that, once these basic tasks have been done, it is only *longitudinal* studies that will be able to pass judgment on their success.

If, in what seems like a staggering task, it is also kept in mind that a child does not learn to read "all at once," then what will also come to the forefront is the realization that those who make decisions related to readiness need only be concerned with the question, "Is this child ready to read, given the fact that such-and-such will be the first learning requirement?"

Admittedly, the suggestion of a more complicated picture of readiness than has been traditionally inferred in the question, "Is the child ready?" also suggests the need for more complex research than has been undertaken up to now. However, to let a wrong question guide research is to inevitably end up with wrong and meaningless answers. And, we have enough of them already.

References

1. AYERS, JERRY B., MASON, GEORGE E. "Differential Effects of Science: A Process Approach upon Change in Metropolitan Readiness Test Scores Among Kindergarten Children," *Reading Teacher,* 22 (February, 1969), 435–49.

2. BERRY, FRANCIS M. "The Baltimore Reading Readiness Test," *Childhood Education,* 3 (January, 1927), 222–23.

3. BLOOM, BENJAMIN S. *Stability and Change in Human Characteristics.* New York: John Wiley and Sons, 1964.

4. CHALL, JEANNE. *Learning to Read: The Great Debate.* New York: McGraw-Hill Book Company, 1967.

5. DICKSON, VIRGIL E. *Mental Tests and the Classroom Teacher.* New York: World Book Company, 1923.

6. Editorial, "Educational News and Editorial Comment," *Elementary School Journal,* 33 (May, 1933), 641–55.

7. GATES, ARTHUR I. "The Necessary Mental Age for Beginning Reading," *Elementary School Journal,* 37 (March, 1937), 497–508.

8. ———, BOND, G. L., RUSSELL, D. H. *Methods of Determining Reading Readiness.* New York: Bureau of Publications, Teachers College, Columbia University, 1939.

9. GESELL, ARNOLD L. *The Mental Growth of the Preschool Child.* New York: The Macmillan Company, 1935.

10. ———. *Infancy and Human Growth.* New York: The Macmillan Company, 1928.

11. ———. *The First Five Years of Life.* New York: Harper and Brothers, 1940.

12. GIL, MOHINDRA. "Relationship Between Junior Kindergarten Experi-

ence and Readiness," *Ontario Journal of Educational Research,* 10 (Autumn, 1967), 57–66.

13. GORALSKI, PATRICIA J., and KERL, JOYCE M. "Kindergarten Teacher Aides and Reading Readiness," *Journal of Experimental Education,* 37 (Winter, 1968), 34–38.

14. HALL, G. STANLEY. *The Psychology of Adolescence.* New York: D. Appleton and Company, 1904.

15. HESS, ROBERT. "Maternal Behavior and the Development of Reading Readiness in Urban Negro Children," *Self and Society, Yearbook of the Claremont Reading Conference,* 32 (1968), 83–99.

16. HUNT, J. MCVICKER. *Intelligence and Experience.* New York: The Ronald Press Company, 1961.

17. JACOBS, JAMES N., WIRTHLIN, LENORE D., MILLER, CHARLES B. "A Follow-Up Evaluation of the Frostig Visual-Perceptual Training Program," *Educational Leadership,* 26 (November, 1968), 169–75.

18. JOHNSON, ROGER E. "The Validity of the Clymer-Barrett Prereading Battery," *Reading Teacher,* 22 (April, 1969), 609–14.

19. MORPHETT, M. V., and WASHBURNE, C. "When Should Children Begin to Read?" *Elementary School Journal,* 31 (March, 1931), 496–508.

20. REED, MARY M. *An Investigation of Practices in First-Grade Admission and Promotion,* New York: Bureau of Publications, Teachers College, Columbia University, 1927.

21. STONE, MARK, and PIELSTICK, N. L. "Effectiveness of Delacato Treatment with Kindergarten Children," *Psychology in the Schools,* 6 (January, 1969), 63–68.

22. THORNDIKE, ROBERT L., and HAGEN, ELIZABETH. *Measurement and Evaluation in Psychology and Education.* New York: John Wiley and Sons, 1969.

23. WASHBURNE, CARLETON. "The Work of the Committee of Seven on Grade-Placement in Arithmetic," *Child Development and The Curriculum,* Chapter 16, Thirty-Eighth Yearbook of the National Society for the Study of Education, Part I. Bloomington, Ill.: Public School Publishing Company, 1939.

24. WILLMON, BETTY. "Parent Participation as a Factor in the Effectiveness of Head Start Programs," *Journal of Educational Research,* 62 (May–June, 1969), 406–10.

25. WINGERT, ROGER C. "Evaluation of a Readiness Training Program," *Reading Teacher,* 22 (January, 1969), 325–28.

IV

Beginning Reading

Beginning reading instruction is critically important. Failure in the initial exposure to reading instruction may negatively color the child's attitude toward himself, reading, and school. Therefore, concerned efforts should be made to assure success in learning to read during the initial stages. One of the factors that may influence success is the approach employed to teach the child to read.

A number of different beginning reading approaches are now available. Many of these are described by Sheldon and Chall in the first two articles. The third article cites some findings of the Cooperative Research Studies for First-Grade Reading Instruction. When reading Dykstra's conclusions concerning the relative effectiveness of code- and meaning-emphasis approaches, be certain to read the last paragraph carefully. Sipay presents limitations that should be considered in interpreting the Cooperative Reading Studies, while McCullough reviews "Vital Principles in Need of Application" in her wide-ranging examination of the problems of teaching beginning readers.

16. Basal Reading Approaches *

WILLIAM D. SHELDON

BASAL reading instruction is concerned with the development of those fundamental habits, attitudes, and skills essential to effective silent and oral reading.

* From William D. Sheldon, "Basal Reading Approaches," in James F. Kerfoot (ed.), *First Grade Reading Programs,* Perspectives in Reading, No. 5 (Newark, Del.: International Reading Association, 1965), pp. 28–35. Reprinted by permission of the International Reading Association and the author.

Rationale of the Program

The program rests on the assumption that a set of essential and fundamental skills are generally known and that these are of such a nature that a series of books, workbooks, and manuals which present these skills in a sequential order are essential to their development.

Proponents of the use of basal readers suggest that an adequate basal reading program provides the essential prerequisites to successful growth in word comprehension, interpretation, and all aspects of mature reading. However, it is recognized that the basic skills are brought to full use when children are led to utilize these skills in reading of library books and the texts used in the various content areas.

Some basal reading experts suggest that the programs they have designed afford the springboard for successful application of reading skills in all of the life-long reading tasks of each individual.

The reading specialists who subscribed to Conant's *Learning to Read,* A Report of Conference of Reading Experts, supported the following statement:

By and large, the child learns precisely what he is led to learn in response to the content and structure of the teaching materials. As applied to the teaching of reading, this means that effective teaching depends upon the careful programming of reading materials in terms of (a) the sound values of letters and letter combinations, (b) practice in recognition of words as wholes, (c) the apprehension of meaning both of single words and large units such as phrases, sentences, and paragraphs, and (d) the development of suitable habits of adjusting one's approach to reading in the light of one's purpose for reading.

The rationale of the basal reading approach, as suggested by Chall rests partly on research, partly on experience and partly on belief. The rationale has been and will be modified to adjust to new research and new experiences which lead to new beliefs about the most successful ways in which basal reading approaches can aid pupils to read most successfully.

Description of the Program

Method

The one word which seems most descriptive of basal reading approaches is *eclectic.* The procedures are eclectic in terms of the development of readiness, vocabulary, word recognition and word perception, comprehension skills and a love of literature.

The method of teaching involves certain common procedures which accompany each lesson. These procedures involve motivating children to read by various introductory devices, developing concepts basic to each lesson, teaching of certain word-analysis skills, reviewing of known words and the development of an understanding of new meanings of these known words, introducing new words and their meanings, emphasizing the comprehension of what is to be read, what is read, and what has been read.

Other aspects include the encouragement of critical thinking and developing a love of and taste for the best in reading material. At higher grade levels the basal program encourages the development of an ability to read the varied content material with understanding, the adjustment of rate of reading to purpose for reading, the mastery of such study skills as skimming, summarizing, and reviewing, and developing ability to use those locational skills which are necessary for all information seeking.

Teachers using basal readers ordinarily teach children in small groups and provide for acceleration or deceleration of the pace of instruction according to the individual child's ability to progress.

The method stresses continuity, sequence, and integration and is most successful when these three basic ideas, first stated by W. S. Gray, are supported by instructional practice.

Material

It hardly seems necessary to discuss the basal materials usually presented for first-grade pupils but because of current misunderstandings we shall present the various items in some detail. The material consists of the following:

Several picture readiness books
Three or four preprimers, a primer, and a first reader

Readiness tests, diagnostic in nature, are supplied before the preprimers are used. These follow the use of readiness materials of a formal and informal nature. Some series include an achievement testing program with tests designed to measure how well pupils master the program of vocabulary, word analysis, and comprehension skills development presented at each book level.

Every series has some sort of activity or workbook designed to provide review or new material related to each story taught. At the first-grade level these workbooks are saturated with word attack and vocabulary review exercises and limited comprehension lessons. While they are designed more or less for independent use by pupils, many of the exercises require teacher supervision.

A few programs have related filmstrips and recordings designed to give practice in phonics.

Supplementary readers are also provided in some of the basal programs. These are intended to give children practice in the new words they have learned and to aid them to develop fluent silent reading in easy materials based on a vocabulary already learned in the basal preprimers, primers and first readers.

One such supplementary book is a hard covered preprimer which reviews all the words and skills learned in the paperbacked preprimers. Other supplementary books are either paperbacked or hardcovered and present known words and concepts in new story form.

The base of the program is the teachers manual or guidebook. While pupils do not use the manuals, they are actually the most important part of any series. The manuals present the author's philosophy, a step-by-step pattern of lessons, sources of supplementary materials, vocabulary lists, diagnostic tests, and hundreds of ideas which teachers can use in developing additional word and comprehension building exercises.

At the present time most of the negative comments made about basal readers focus on the preprimers and the limited content of these reading materials. Many critics read a few lines from the first preprimer and evoke laughter by clever parodies. Jokes related to the first-grade teacher who finds her car stuck in the snow or mud, or wedged between two other cars, make the point. The teacher, allegedly brainwashed by the materials used to teach first-grade pupils, on seeing her car, shouts

"Oh, Oh, Oh,
Look, Look, Look,
Damn, Damn, Damn."

In our discussion of organization we will present some of the specific aspects of the content of basal readers.

The strength of the basal material lies in the careful development of vocabulary and word analysis skills in colorfully illustrated stories. The weakness of the material seems to be partly a lack of visibility in the way in which the vocabulary, word analysis, and comprehension skills are developed.

Organization

The basal reading program is organized horizontally and vertically. The horizontal organization involves the coordinated use of reader, workbook, and manual and the correlated use of word cards, phonics charts, supplementary exercises presented in manuals, and other resource materials related to specific lessons.

An example of horizontal organization is taken from a first reader story, *Garden Spiders*. The story is presented in seven well-illustrated pages near the middle of the first reader.

Prior to reading the story the teacher reads the manual and learns something about garden spiders. The manual offers suggestions related to the identification of probably known and possibly unknown concepts related to garden spiders and the story. It is suggested that pictures of spiders, bees, flies, and caterpillars be presented and that a discussion of spiders, guided by certain questions, ensue.

Words previously presented and reappearing in *Garden Spiders,* with perhaps different meanings, are reviewed in context. New vocabulary is developed, both in context and in lessons developing phonic and structural analysis. Phrase-reading exercises are presented.

The story is then read silently with key questions guiding this first reading. The illustrations are referred to when they lend to the meaning of the story.

After the story is read silently once, the children are directed to reread it in order to be able to tell the life story of the spider in sequence.

At this point the teacher can introduce two activity book lessons. The first lesson is done independently while the second is presented by the teacher. One of these is designed to develop the ability to recall and interpret facts and ideas presented in the story. The other tests the visual and auditory mastery of the 46 words introduced in the unit in which *Garden Spiders* appears.

Comprehension and vocabulary building exercises are recommended in the manual which the teacher can present on the chalk board, through discussion, or on duplicated sheets.

Supplementary pages related to the story are found in prepared pads and can be used to further strengthen word analysis skills, build comprehension, and help firm up the study skills of outlining and summarization related to this story.

Related to the introductory phonics lessons are certain examples presented in the phonics charts. The charts are used to pinpoint the skills of consonant substitution, rhyming endings, and the identification of vowel sounds with written letters in words.

Enrichment activities are recommended which can either extend the science background of the pupils or enrich their knowledge of geography by a study of maps showing where spiders live.

Other enrichment-type activities include reference to easy-to-read stories of spiders found in other basal readers and in a variety of library books. The teacher may read poems about spiders such as Howlitt's "The Spider and the Fly" or A. P. Herbert's "The Spider." Recordings, films, and filmstrips which expand knowledge of the spider and his life are also recommended in the manual, while filmstrips and recordings developing the auditory-visual aspects of phonic development are also available.

It is this complex of concepts, word analysis skills, interesting silent reading, comprehension development, discussion, and all the related corollary activities that are overlooked by some critics and assumed to be unnecessary by others. The aim in this horizontally enriched lesson is to produce not only a person who knows words and how to analyze them but to develop a clear appreciation of the rich offerings reading has for him and the fact that reading is related to the broader aspects of life.

The vertical organization of basal readers, even at the first-grade level, would take chapters to describe. However, in brief, we can describe the elements in the following four phases of vertical development:

1. Social organization
2. Vocabulary
3. Word-analysis skills
4. Comprehension

Social Organization. The spiral of social organization is based on the home and the family. The immediate family life of one or two children is presented in readiness materials. Pictures depict the family in dozens of lifelike situations.

Preprimer story activities continue with the family and present a gradual broadening of activities beyond the home and into the school.

The primer centers its stories around the school, introduces pets, many new adults, the farm, and other special places, such as stores and the airport.

The first reader expands horizons by introducing children to the town or city at large with its helpers, zoos, rodeos, the library and again extends the characters to include a wide variety of individuals.

By the time the child has completed basal materials of the first grade he has increased the scope of his social interaction in ever widening circles, gradually increasing the distance traveled from home and his range of experiences and acquaintances.

Vocabulary. Vocabulary is introduced carefully and reviewed continuously. The new vocabulary is carefully controlled and presented according to the expert's consideration of the number of words which can be learned at a time by the average first-grade child and the number of repetitions needed. The words presented are usually the high service words of the English language, and ordinarily word lists, supplemented by the special vocabulary needed in each story, supply the vocabulary. Studies have indicated that certain words are commonly presented

in most basal programs while the need for certain words in particular causes the differences found in the vocabulary presented in the readers of different series. While there is a rather wide difference in the number of new words presented in various basal readers—and this difference may become greater because of new interest in increasing the vocabulary range of basal readers—the average number of words presented in preprimers is 60, in the primer 110, and the first reader 175. This number, of course, is smaller than the actual number of words learned by pupils in a grade one basal program, but there is no way of knowing how many words first-grade pupils learn in addition to the 345 words which are mastered. An educated guess suggests that average pupils learn at least a thousand words if the 345 words taught directly are combined with words gradually acquired through analytic and contextual skills.

Word-analysis Skills. The leading basal programs present word-analysis skills in chart form. One such chart suggests four general areas of word-analysis skills presented in the grade one program: auditory discrimination, visual discrimination, and visual-auditory discrimination provided for phonic and structural analysis. . . .

Briefly, at the readiness level, auditory discrimination is developed by:

1. Recognizing and discriminating among common sounds, similar sounds, rhyming elements
2. Recognizing the initial consonants
3. Developing sensitivity to inflectional variants

Again, at the readiness level, visual discrimination is developed by a recognition of differences in configuration of:

1. Forms and shapes of objects
2. Letter forms
3. Word forms
4. Sentence forms

Incidentally the charge of configurationism leveled by a certain anti-basal reader group apparently does not consider the value of prereading visual discrimination training involving a variety of forms.

At the preprimer level pupils are taught a 60–70 word basic sight vocabulary through a visual and auditory discrimination of common sounds and forms, rhyming elements, initial consonants, and combine a knowledge of configuration clues, picture and context clues, and capital and lower-case letters with skill in recognizing inflectional endings added to nouns and verbs.

At the primer level the emphasis shifts from auditory and visual discrimination to visual-auditory discrimination which opens the way for intensive instruction in phonics and structural analysis based on a mastered vocabulary learned at the preprimer level.

During the primer lessons the visual discrimination clues learned previously are extended while certain aspects of phonic analysis, i.e., initial consonants, initial consonant substitutions and the rhyming elements are introduced and reviewed until a mastery level is achieved. Structural skills are reviewed and compound words are presented and studied.

The first reader lessons extend all the skills learned previously and add to the study of rhyming elements. Final consonants are studied and final consonant substitution is practiced while initial consonant blends are introduced and their substitution practiced. Initial consonant digraphs are developed. Added structural analysis skills include certain inflectional endings and the use of contractions.

Some basal programs have included an emphasis on vowels at the first-grade level while other programs develop the identification of vowels through their context in words. An emphasis on learning the alphabet and letter names has also developed recently even though several studies seem to indicate that most children enter the reading program with a rather broad knowledge of letter names, upper and lower case, and a singsong, often nonsensical knowledge of the alphabet.

Comprehension. The sequence of comprehension skill development is harder to pinpoint than the more easily identifiable word analysis program. However, the following comprehension skills are developed almost simultaneously in the first-grade basal reading program:

1. Identifying the main idea
2. Noting significant details and their relationships to one another and to the main ideas
3. Making inferences and drawing logical conclusions
4. Recognizing the motives, moods, and emotional reactions of story characters
5. Recalling the sequence of story development
6. Classifying related ideas and making generalizations
7. Following directions

The subtlety with which comprehension skills are introduced in the manual lessons often leads casual observers to doubt whether such skills are actually developed at the first-grade level at all. While developing tests of comprehension for pupils who had completed preprimers, primers, and first readers, it was certainly apparent to the writer that while these comprehension skills are elusive and difficult to test, pupils could identify main ideas and important details, recall material in correct sequence, and follow directions. Less evident were skills related to 3, 4, and 6 above. . . .

17. Innovations in Beginning Reading *

JEANNE CHALL

INNOVATION in reading is not new. It has gone on for several hundred years. However, from about 1930 on, a certain consensus about beginning reading appears to have prevailed. Most methods textbooks and published reading programs for children have agreed on these basic points:

1. Reading is given a broad definition. It includes as major goals, *right from the start,* word recognition, comprehension, interpretation, appreciation, and application of the facts to the study of personal and social problems.
2. Children start with "meaningful reading" of whole words, sentences, and stories as closely geared to their own experiences and interests as possible. From the start, silent reading is a preferred mode.
3. After the child recognizes "at sight" about 50 words (some authors call for more, some less), he begins, through a process of analysis of words "learned as wholes," a study of the relationship between the sounds in spoken words

* From Jeanne Chall, "Innovations in Beginning Reading," *Instructor,* 74 (March, 1965), 67, 91–96. Copyright © 1965 Instructor Publications, Inc. Reprinted by permission of the author also. The complete report on which this article is based has been published as: Jeanne Chall, *Learning to Read: The Great Debate* (New York: McGraw-Hill, 1967), hardback and paperback. This article comes from data gathered for The City College—Carnegie Reading Study. It was made possible by a grant from the Carnegie Corporation of New York. The author wishes to acknowledge the assistance of Mrs. Mildred Bloomfield in analyzing the various programs.

(phonemes) and the letters representing them (graphemes), that is, phonics. However, even before phonic instruction is begun, and then along with phonic instruction, the child is encouraged to identify new words by the other means of word analysis—picture and meaning clues and structural analysis.

4. Instruction in phonics and other word-analysis skills is spread over the six years of the elementary school. Phonic instruction usually starts slowly in grade 1, and picks up momentum in grades 2 and 3.
5. Phonics is not to be drilled or practiced in "isolation," but is to be "integrated" with the "meaningful' connected reading. In addition, the sounds are not to be isolated and blended to form words.
6. The vocabulary of the basal readers for grades 1, 2, and 3 is repeated often and is carefully controlled on a meaning-frequency principle, using words that are the most frequent in general reading matter and judged by the author to be within the child's understanding.
7. A readiness or preparatory period, followed by a slow and easy start in first grade, is recommended for all children. A longer readiness period is recommended for those judged "not ready" for formal reading instruction.

The above principles, based partly on research, partly on theory, partly on experience, and partly on belief, have become, since about 1930, the "conventional wisdom" of beginning reading instruction. Since the middle 1950's, however, one after another aspect of this conventional wisdom has been vehemently challenged. Out of these challenges have come new programs and approaches, some resembling rather closely the older programs discarded for the "modern" programs of the 1930's. As in the past, most current innovators claim that theirs is "the new," "the natural," "the logical," and "the true." One additional claim has been added—that theirs is "the most scientific."

Are we heading for a new wave of change, only to be disappointed again 10 or 20 years from now?

It was this question that prompted us, more than two years ago, to look into the state of affairs in beginning reading instruction. With support from the Carnegie Corporation of New York, we have reviewed the relevant research, analyzed published reading programs representing "conventional" and "new" approaches, interviewed proponents of these programs, observed classes using them, and talked informally with teachers and administrators (I.R.A. *Proceedings,* Vol. 8, 1963, pp. 250–54).

This is not the time or place to report our findings, which will be published in their entirety elsewhere. However, one point must be made now. All of us who have worked on this problem have come away with a profound sense of humility. We have been struck with the extreme difficulty of being objective in this area where emotional, professional, and financial involvement runs so high. The best of us can be easily ensnared by too hasty conclusions from limited evidence.

Any evaluation of new or conventional programs will therefore have to await the publication of our full report. Instead, we present below brief descriptions of some of the new programs—with the hope that teachers and administrators may gain from the descriptions a clearer understanding of the principles underlying both the conventional and the new. They will be presented in what we believe is the historical order of their impact as challenges to conventional programs.

Phonic Innovations: Partial Reading Programs

Even predating Flesch's *Why Johnny Can't Read,* in 1955, some school systems were using more concentrated and separate phonics programs—*Reading with Phonics* (Hay-Wingo; J. B. Lippincott Co.); *Phonetic Keys to Reading* (Sloop, Garrison, and Creekmore; The Economy Co.); *The Phonovisual Method* (Schoolfield and Timberlake; Phonovisual Products). However, since 1955, many more phonics programs have appeared, only a few of which can be mentioned here: Sister Mary Caroline's *Breaking the Sound Barrier* (The Macmillan Co.); Spalding's *The Writing Road to Reading* (Whiteside, Inc., and Wm. Morrow & Co.); and most recently, Gattegno's *Words in Color* (Encyclopaedia Britannica Press).

These programs vary, but most of them have these characteristics in common when compared with the phonics programs in conventional basal reading series: they teach phonics more directly, they teach it earlier, and they cover more ground. Some are frankly synthetic—teaching letters representing certain sounds that are then blended to form words. Some combine phonics with writing and spelling, while others teach phonics combined with little stories to be "read for meaning." Some insist on the mastery of a considerable amount of phonic knowledge before connected reading is begun, while others follow the conventional pattern of teaching phonics by a process of analysis, only after a sight vocabulary has been mastered.

Significantly, none of these separate phonics systems claims to teach the beginner all that is needed in beginning reading. All are designed to be used with existing materials—particularly the conventional basal readers which supply practice in sight and meaningful reading.

In principle, most of the authors and proponents of these separate phonics programs accept the broad definition of beginning reading of the prevailing view. Their major disagreement with conventional basal series is that the phonics taught in these reading programs is "too little and too late."

Phonic Innovations: Total Reading Programs

Within the past two years, two basal reading programs based on a heavier phonics emphasis have been published. Both series start the young learner off on letters and sounds, but the *Open Court Series* (Trace and McQueen; Open Court Publishing Co.) delays the reading of stories until a considerable amount of phonic knowledge is mastered. The *Basic Reading Series* (McCracken and Walcutt; J. B. Lippincott Co.) introduces story reading early, in conjunction with phonic instruction.

Both series also have a significantly heavier vocabulary load, especially in the readers for the first, second, and third grades. The *Open Court Readers,* in addition, concentrate on literature—folk and fairy tales—as early as the first grade.

Two older total reading programs, also with a heavier and earlier phonics emphasis, are the Carden materials (*Carden Method*), published privately by the author, and Daniels and Diack's *Royal Road Readers* (Chatto and Windrus), published in England. The Carden method has been in existence a long time but has received new popularity since 1955. Mae Carden makes a special point about the *exclusion* of pictures in her readers and the fact that hers is a total language program, teaching comprehension and literary appreciation as well as phonics.

The *Royal Road Readers,* based on a "phonic-word" approach, control vocabulary on a spelling regularity principle. Although the "meaning of the letters" is taught through a process of analysis similar to the pattern in conventional basal series, the use of regularly spelled words for the beginning materials, according to the authors, aids the child in *discovering for himself* the relationship between the sounds and the symbols. This is the same theoretical assumption made by many linguists who also suggest that beginning materials control vocabulary on spelling regularity.

Linguistic Innovations

As early as 1942, Leonard Bloomfield, a distinguished linguistic scholar, questioned the "meaning" emphasis in beginning reading and called instead for the first step to be the learning of the "code," or "the alphabetic principle" (*Elementary English Review,* Vol. 19, 1942, pp. 125–30 and 183–86). Meaning, considered so important by authors of conventional programs, he stated, comes naturally as the "alphabetic code" is broken, since the meaning of the word is already known to the child from his speech and listening.

How is the child to be taught the code? Not as do the conventional basal reading programs, by teaching first such high-frequency words as *look, come, go, to* (the *o's* in these words represent four different sounds). Such words only frustrate the beginner's attempts at learning "the code." Instead, we should teach the beginner, first, those words that are spelled regularly, from which he can *dis-*

cover for himself the relationship between the sounds and the letters, *e.g., Nan, Dan, fan, man.* To facilitate such learning, oral rather than silent reading should be stressed at the beginning, and use of context and picture clues discouraged. The Bloomfield materials contain no illustrations.

Bloomfield's articles were veritably ignored when they were first published. Ironically, it was Flesch who revived them in 1955 to support his call for a return to phonics, although Bloomfield expressly stated that he was just as opposed to a "phonic" as he was to a "sight" method. Ironically, too, it was only after Flesch that the Bloomfield teaching materials, co-authored by Clarence Barnhart, were published (*Let's Read: A Linguistic Approach;* Wayne State University Press), although they had been in existence and used experimentally for some time. Recently, a more childlike edition, with a teacher's manual, has been issued (*Let's Read: Experimental Edition;* C. L. Barnhart, Inc.).

It is to be emphasized that Bloomfield was opposed to sounding and blending. He insisted that words always be read as wholes, although the shapes and names of the letters should be mastered before word reading is started. According to Bloomfield, when a new word is taught or when a child fails to recognize a word, he is to spell it (say the letters), not sound it.

More recently, C. C. Fries in his book, *Linguistics and Reading* (Holt, Rinehart & Winston), has presented an account of modern linguistic knowledge, an analysis of the reading process in light of that knowledge, and suggestions for a "linguistically sound approach" to the teaching of reading, especially in the beginning stages.

Similarly to Bloomfield, Fries takes issue with the broad definition of beginning reading of the prevailing view—with its stress on meaning, appreciation, and application. Instead, he divides the reading process into three stages. The beginning, or "transfer" stage, is the time for concentrating on the learning of the "visual signs" for the language which the child has already mastered through listening and speech.

Fries' "transfer" stage is similar to Bloomfield's "code." It is effected best, according to Fries, by having the child practice the reading of words grouped by contrasting spelling patterns—such as, *can, came; rat, rate*—with the most common and consistent spelling patterns presented first.

Like Bloomfield, Fries is opposed to sounding and blending. He also relies on the child's discovering for himself the relationship between sounds and symbols. When a child misses a word, he is encouraged to spell it, not sound it.

A reading program based on the Fries linguistic principles has been issued recently (*A Basic Reading Series Developed upon Linguistic Principles [Preliminary and Experimental]*; Fries Publications, Ann Arbor, Mich.).[1]

Other reading programs based on linguistic principles are in print. Three pre-primers by Stratemeyer and Smith (*The Linguistic Science Readers;* Harper & Row) also control vocabulary on a spelling regularity principle. But they introduce another feature—one that has nothing to do with linguistics but no doubt involves the authors' conception of child interest. The main characters in the Stratemeyer-Smith preprimers are animals, rather than the conventional brother-sister-baby threesome, their pets, and friends. Unlike the Bloomfield and Fries

[1] Now published as the *Merrill Linguistic Readers,* C. C. Fries *et al.* (Columbus, Ohio: Charles E. Merrill Co., 1966). (Eds.)

programs, these preprimers have color illustrations and a story line.

A linguistic approach for teaching reading to preschool and primary-grade children has been developed recently by Robert and Virginia Allen (*Read Along with Me;* Bur. of Pub., T.C., Columbia University). Contrary to the Bloomfield and Fries approaches, this program encourages sounding and blending.

Still another linguistic approach has been suggested by Carl Lefevre in his book *Linguistics and the Teaching of Reading* (McGraw-Hill). Lefevre has not yet produced a reading program. However, it appears, to this reviewer at least, that such a program would resemble more the older "sentence" and "experience" approaches than the previously cited linguistic approaches.

Another beginning reading program that may be classified are linguistic is the Richards-Gibson *Language for Learning Series* (Washington Square Press). The major control is on sentence patterns, although there is some control of letters as well. There is no teaching of sound-letter relations.

From the above, we see there is no one approved "linguistic" approach. Different linguistic scholars make different interpretations of the relevance of linguistics (the scientific study of the nature of language) to beginning reading, and come out with different reading programs. However, the most current linguistic innovations agree on at least one point— they take issue with the broad definition of beginning reading of conventional programs. With the exception of perhaps Lefevre and Richards-Gibson, they propose that the "decoding" aspects of reading be the first emphasis, to be followed later by the broader aspects of meaning, appreciation, and application.

In many respects, the linguistic innovations are similar to the phonic innovations, although most linguistic scholars are just as strongly opposed to the phonic innovations as they are to conventional programs. More recently, however, there appears to be a rapprochement between the two. In fact, it is hard to classify some programs. The Allen and Daniels-Diack programs may be classified as either phonic or linguistic. Gattegno makes a point of being both.

ITA—The Initial Teaching Alphabet

Like many linguistic programs, ITA, devised by Sir James Pitman, has its roots in dissatisfaction with acquisition of the "code" by conventional approaches. However, unlike the linguists who accept English spelling as it is, introducing it to the child *as if* it were spelled regularly, then gradually letting him in on "the awful truth," Pitman has augmented our alphabet to 44 characters, closely corresponding to the phonemes (sounds) in our language.

The Initial Teaching Alphabet is to be used only for the beginning stage in reading. After the child has learned to read in ITA with some degree of fluency, he transfers to "traditional orthography"— our conventional spelling.

It is important to note that ITA as originally devised and experimented with in England did not propose change in method. The only change was in the medium—the use of 44 characters, all in lower case. In fact, it was hypothesized that ITA would prove beneficial for either a sight or a phonic emphasis in beginning reading when compared to traditional orthography. The *Janet and John* series (English version of *Alice and Jerry*) used by ITA in the English experiment incorporates the principles cited earlier for conventional basal reading programs.

The American ITA demonstration currently underway in Bethlehem, Pa., uses a new reading series by Mazurkiewicz and Tanyzer (*Early-to-Read: ITA Program;* ITA Publications). This series makes some changes in method as well as in medium—putting greater stress on early learning of the alphabet and phonics, writing, and a higher vocabulary load.

O.K. Moore's Responsive Environment

O.K. Moore has for the past few years made the popular press with dramatic stories of three- and four-year-olds learning to read by use of automated typewriters (*Carnegie Corporation of New York Quarterly,* Vol. IX, No. 2, April 1961). The major purpose behind his work is not to demonstrate what has been known for a long time—that young children can learn to read—but that early reading is beneficial for a child's general intellectual development.

Methods and materials used by Moore depart significantly from conventional approaches. The child starts by learning letters; then he proceeds to words and sentences. As he explores and strikes a key, the automated typewriter calls out the name of the letter or symbol that was struck. This goes on until the child learns the names of the letters. Then gradually a teacher, called by Moore a "booth-girl," takes him through a series of steps in which he reproduces on an electric typewriter the letter that is presented to him on a televisionlike screen. Later the child types words and sentences. He also reads from various books, including basal readers, and writers words, sentences, and stories.

Like Bloomfield and Fries, Moore separates the reading process into several stages, the first stage being the acquisition of the code or the alphabetic principle. Later the stress is on meaning, application, and appreciation. Sound-letter connections are not taught. Instead, the child "spells out" the words when he first learns them and as a means of recall and attack.

Individualized Reading and the Language-Experience Approach

A different line of innovation is concerned with classroom organizational patterns, pacing, motivation, and subject-matter content of reading materials. Essentially, individualized-reading proponents accept the broad definition of reading of the conventional view, but propose the use of a large variety of reading materials—trade books, magazines, newspapers, textbooks—from which each child selects his own reading instructional material (self-selection) and proceeds at his own pace (self-pacing). Because the child selects his own books it is claimed that they satisfy his vital interests and are of an appropriate difficulty level—neither too easy nor too difficult.

There is much variation in individualized reading programs. Some teachers make no use of group instruction from basal readers—self-selection of trade books is focal. Others make only some use of group instruction from basal readers and workbooks for "skills instruction." And still others who say they have an individualized reading program give daily basal reading instruction in groups with some time devoted to the reading of trade books or other materials selected by the children. The same program may be labeled either conventional basal reader or individualized reading, depending upon who labels it.

Similarly to the other innovations, the basic features of individualized reading have been known and practiced for a long time, often under a different label. In the 1920's individualized reading was known as "free reading."

Language-Experience Approach

The Language-Experience approach of R. Van Allen incorporates much of the basic philosophy of individualized reading. But it also includes one essential feature from the linguistic and phonic innovations—early acquisition of the code.

From individualized reading, it borrows the importance of unique interests and needs of each child. But it makes the first step in reading not self-selection of books written by others, but reading of the child's own writings, which according to L-E proponents veritably guarantees vital interest.

The child's first stories are encouraged through his own artistic productions and are recorded by his teacher. Later, the child writes his own captions and stories, aided by some "formal" instruction in the writing and spelling of common words. The child's stories are "edited" by the teacher, who, while correcting his misspellings, teaches him the connection between sounds and letters (phonics). As with individualized reading, a child is encouraged to proceed at his own pace.

Language-Experience programs also vary considerably from teacher to teacher. In San Diego, some teachers supplemented the L-E program with daily reading in groups from conventional basal readers, while others never used basal readers, relying only on child-written materials and trade books.

Montessori

The current interest in the Montessori Method is another example of an innovation that is a rediscovery of the old. Dr. Maria Montessori's method enjoyed a great but short popularity in the United States from 1909 to 1917. The present rediscovery of Montessori may be attributed to two basic features of her method—emphasis on early learning (from ages three to six) and self-pacing of learning in a "prepared environment."

As a first step in learning to read Italian (which is spelled more regularly than English), Montessori started the young child off by teaching him to recognize, name, write, and sound the letters of the alphabet. Later, he learned to blend the sounds into words, and then combine the words into meaningful sentences. The steps for teaching each of these aspects of reading and writing are described so beautifully in a recent translated book of Montessori's selected writings (*The Montessori Method;* Schocken Books), that I cannot recommend it too highly.

Programmed Learning

The major innovation of programmed learning has been in the format of reading materials that permits better individualization of instruction. Instead of the basal readers and workbooks that are designed primarily to be used under the guidance of a teacher, the reading tasks are presented in small units largely under the child's direction.

Theoretically, any approach to beginning reading may be "programmed"—sight, sentence, meaning, phonic, or linguistic. However, it is interesting to note that two recently published "programmed" beginning reading courses—McGraw-Hill's *Programmed Reading* (Buchanan, Sullivan Associates) and Grolier's *First Steps in Reading* (TMI, Grolier, Teaching Machine Course TM-002)—rely heavily on a phonic-linguistic approach. The content (subject matter) of both the McGraw-Hill and the Grolier programs also differs from conventional materials, consisting largely of discrete words and sentences, with humorous illustrations, but no definite story line.

Other Basal-Reader Innovations

In addition to the two new basal reading series described above under Phonic Innovations, we must mention the new integrated series published by Follett, the preprimers of which are now available (*The Detroit Series;* Follett Publishing Co.).[2] Produced by The Detroit Writers' Committee of the Great Cities School Improvement Program, this is probably the first attempt to have both Negro and white children and adults as the main characters in a basal reading series.

The first three preprimers of the Follett series contain about half the number of different words in the usual three preprimers of conventional basal series. In general, all other aspects of the prevailing view appear to be accepted: a slow easy start, a meaning and appreciation emphasis from the start, sight words first, vocabularly controlled on a meaning-frequency principle, phonics and other word analysis skills introduced later and taught primarily from an analysis of known sight words.

Summary

The above innovations are admittedly only a sample of the many new published programs. Still others are in manuscript form awaiting a favorable verdict from

[2] Now complete through the third grade. (Eds.)

the editorial departments of educational publishers. The profusion indicates that we are indeed in a state of flux in beginning reading.

Generally, three major lines of innovation in the new reading programs seem to be apparent:

1. Innovations to bring about earlier acquisition of the alphabetic principle.

2. Innovations to bring about greater individualization of instruction.

3. Innovations to bring about changes in content, either by making it more vital, realistic, and imaginative, or by underplaying the story content altogether.

Some of the new programs make changes only in one, some in two, and some in all three. All of them continue to incorporate some aspects of conventional programs. When new programs are tried in schools, changes not directly related to the new approach itself often occur—lifting ceilings on readers, devoting more time to reading, missionary zeal of parents and teachers, providing more library books—thus making it difficult to evaluate the special effects of the changes in the approach.

However, our analysis of the research in beginning reading seems to indicate that some approaches to beginning reading do lead to better results than others, at least through the third grade. Our final report will present this information, with full documentation, together with fuller analyses of conventional and new programs.

18. The Effectiveness of Code- and Meaning-Emphasis Beginning Reading Programs *

ROBERT DYKSTRA

IN her recent book, Chall (1967) concluded that code-emphasis reading programs tend to produce better overall reading achievement, at least in the initial stages of instruction, than do meaning-emphasis programs. She defined code-emphasis programs as those which aim at the beginning to teach the pupil mastery of the alphabetic code rather than expecting from him a mature reading performance. Meaning-emphasis programs, according to Chall, are those which emphasize from the very beginning the necessity of reading for meaning, undoubtedly a more mature skill than mere code-breaking. The typical basal reading series belongs to the meaning-emphasis category. Many current programs, however, are characterized by an early concentrated emphasis on learning the alphabetic code which characterizes printed English. This is especially true of a number of recently published "linguistic" programs.

The Cooperative Research Program in First-Grade Instruction provided considerable data with which to test Chall's conclusion. Many of the projects which participated in this research venture compared the relative effectiveness of basal programs and certain innovative instructional programs, a number of which belong to Chall's code-emphasis category.

* From Robert Dykstra, "The Effectiveness of Code- and Meaning-Emphasis Beginning Reading Programs," *Reading Teacher,* 22 (October, 1968), 17–23. Reprinted by permission of the International Reading Association and the author.

The Coordinating Center at the University of Minnesota reported, in two separate volumes, the results of the combined analysis of the data which compared basal and various other programs at the end of grades one and two (Bond and Dykstra, 1967; Dykstra, 1967). The present report draws together specific data from the Cooperative Research Program pertinent to the issue of the relative effectiveness of code-emphasis programs in initial reading instruction.

Programs

Information about three relevant types of reading programs evaluated in the first-grade reading studies is presented in Table 1. Programs are categorized as conventional basal, linguistic, and phonics-first basal in accordance with Chall's classification scheme. The Programmed Reading Series was not labeled "linguistic" by Chall, but because of its claim to be linguistically based and its similarity in many respects to linguistic materials it has been placed in that category for purposes of this report.

Certain of the instructional variables which differentiate the three types of programs are presented in Table 1. More complete descriptions of these variables are found in Appendix A of Chall's book. It is apparent that conventional basal, linguistic, and phonics-first basal programs are differentiated by a number of instructional variables such as vocabulary load, type of vocabulary control, phonics load, and initial response modes.

TABLE 1

Classification of Reading Programs Used in the Cooperative Research Study According to Publisher, Common Label, and Certain Instructional Variables.

Variables	Conventional Basal			Linguistic Approaches				Phonics— First Basal
	1*	2	3	1**	2	3	4	1***
Goals of Beginning Instruction: Reading for *Meaning* (M) or Learning the *Code* (C)	M	M	M	C	C	C	C	C
Motiv. Appeal at Beginning: *Content* (C) or *Process* (P) of Learning to Read	C	C	C	P	P	P	P	P/C
Major Criterion For Selecting Words: *Meaning Freq.* (MF) or *Spelling Regularity* (SR)	MF	MF	MF	SR	SR	SR	SR	SR
Vocabulary Load: First Year	LOW	LOW	LOW	HIGH	HIGH	HIGH	HIGH	HIGH
Phonics Instruction: *Analytic* (A) or *Synthetic* (S)	A	A	A	A	A	S	S	S
Phonic Load: First Year	LOW	LOW	LOW	HIGH	HIGH	HIGH	HIGH	HIGH
Cues to Use: *Structural* (S) or *Meaning* (M)	M	M	M	S	S	S	S	S
"Set" for *Regularity* (R) or *Diversity* (D)	D	D	D	R	R	R	R	R
Structural Clues Employed: *Sounding and Blending* (SB), *Visual Analysis and Substitutions* (VAS), or *Spelling* (SP)	VAS	VAS	VAS	SP	SP	SB	SB	SB
Response Modes: *Whole Words* (WW) or *Letters First* (LET)	WW	WW	WW	LET	LET	LET	LET	LET

1*	Scott, Foresman—The New Basic Readers	
2	Ginn—Ginn Basic Readers	
3	Allyn and Bacon—Sheldon Basic Readers	
1**	Barnhart—Let's Read	
2	Merrill—Basic Reading Series Developed on Linguistic Principles	
3	Singer—Structural Reading Series	
4	McGraw-Hill—Programmed Reading	
1***	J. B. Lippincott—Basic Reading	

The first row of the table indicates that conventional basal programs are characterized by an early emphasis on meaning, while the various linguistic programs and the phonics-first basal program belong to the code-emphasis group. It was possible, therefore, to make certain comparisons of the relative effectiveness of meaning-emphasis and code-emphasis instructional materials in beginning reading.

The experimental design utilized by the Coordinating Center enabled comparisons between basal and linguistic materials and between conventional basal programs and phonics-first basal series. The rationale underlying the analysis is presented in detail in other reports of the Cooperative Research Program (Bond and Dykstra, 1967; Dykstra, 1967). The analysis conducted by the Coordinating Center utilized data collected from various projects participating in the research program, thereby giving information about the relative effectiveness of various types of materials across a number of projects.

Achievement was measured in the Cooperative Research Study by means of a number of instruments. Oral word pronunciation was measured by the word list from the *Gates-McKillop Reading Diagnostic Test* and the Fry Phonetically-Regular Word List which was developed specifically for the research program. Accuracy of connected oral reading and rate of reading were assessed by the *Gilmore Oral Reading Test*. The *Stanford Achievement Test* was used to evaluate spelling, silent reading, word recognition, and silent paragraph comprehension.

Findings

The findings of the analysis comparing basal and linguistic programs are reported in Table 2. Relative performance of basal (meaning-emphasis) and linguistic (code-emphasis) pupils on the various measures is reported for both the end of grade one and the end of grade two. At the end of first grade, 1,357 pupils were used to evaluate spelling and silent reading ability. This number dropped to 959 by the end of the second grade. Approximately 250 pupils were used at both testing points to analyze oral word pronunciation, accuracy of oral reading, and reading rate.

Linguistic pupils were better in oral word pronunciation and silent reading word recognition at the ends of both grades one and two. Pupils in the code-emphasis linguistic programs were also better spellers at the end of grade two, although the reverse was true at the end of the first grade. Therefore, it is apparent that early emphasis on learning the alphabetic code resulted in superior ability at decoding words in isolation as well as superior ability at encoding spoken words by the end of the second grade. It should be emphasized, however, that not all of the differences favoring either linguistic or basal pupils were statistically significant. The analysis was very complex because of the number of projects involved and in many cases it was impossible to come up with a simple, straightforward comprehensive test of the relative effectiveness of the two treatments for this reason, the data presented in this article may best be used to illustrate trends. Details concerning the significance of observed differences are presented elsewhere (Bond and Dykstra, 1967; Dykstra, 1967).

Differences in accuracy of reading a connected passage orally and in understanding paragraphs read silently favored the basal pupils at both testing points. This finding lends some support to the view expressed by many reading authorities that concentrated early emphasis on learning the code to the virtual exclusion

TABLE 2

Reading and Spelling Achievement of Pupils in Code-Emphasis and Meaning-Emphasis Reading Programs.

Achievement variables	Programs compared	
	Conventional Basal (Meaning Emphasis) vs. Linguistic (Code Emphasis)	Conventional Basal (Meaning Emphasis) vs. Phonic/First Basal (Code Emphasis)
Oral Word Pronunciation		
Grade 1	CODE	CODE
Grade 2	CODE	———
Accuracy of Oral Reading		
Grade 1	MEANING	CODE
Grade 2	MEANING	———
Spelling		
Grade 1	MEANING	CODE
Grade 2	CODE	CODE
Silent Reading Word Recognition		
Grade 1	CODE	CODE
Grade 2	CODE	CODE
Silent Reading Comprehension		
Grade 1	MEANING	CODE
Grade 2	MEANING	CODE
Rate of Reading		
Grade 1	MEANING	CODE
Grade 2	CODE	———

of reading for meaning may have a negative effect on comprehension. However, the differences favoring basal pupils on the second-grade comprehension test were negligible (Dykstra, 1967, p. 105). The evidence concerning reading rate is less clearcut. Basal pupils were faster readers at the end of grade one, but pupils whose initial instruction had been in linguistic materials were reading at a higher rate by the end of the second grade. Therefore, it does not appear that an early emphasis on learning the alphabetic code necessarily produces halting word-by-word reading at least through the second grade.

The Cooperative Research Study also evaluated the relative effectiveness of conventional basal materials and the phonics-first reading series. Chall's analysis of this series indicated that it differs from conventional basal materials primarily in its approach to teaching and practicing new words. In other aspects of the instructional program, however, Chall found that the phonics-first basal system did not differ greatly from conventional basal readers.

The comparative effectiveness of these programs in terms of first-grade and second-grade reading and spelling achievement was evaluated. All of the performance measures at either testing point favored the code-emphasis phonics-first program. Code-emphasis pupils were superior in the word recognition and comprehension skills involved in silent reading after one year and two years of instruction. They were also better spellers at both testing points. Information regarding reading rate, oral word pronunciation, and accuracy of oral reading is available only at the end of the first grade, where all differences favored the phonics-first code-emphasis group. Furthermore, practically all of the differences reported for this particular comparison of code-emphasis and meaning-emphasis programs were statistically significant (Bond and Dykstra, 1967; Dykstra, 1967). Pupils comprising the sample for the first-grade reading measures numbered 191, while the sample used for evaluating first- and second-grade silent reading and spelling totaled 1,013 and 441 respectively.

Discussion

Data from the Cooperative Research Program in First-Grade Reading Instruction tended to support Chall's conclusion that code-emphasis programs produce better overall primary-grade reading and spelling achievement than meaning-emphasis programs. This superiority is especially marked with respect to pronouncing words orally in isolation, spelling words from dictation, and identifying words in isolation on a silent reading test. It is apparent that concentrated teaching of the alphabetic code is associated with improved initial ability to encode and decode words. This evidence reinforces the view that pupils can be helped to learn sound-symbol relationships.

It is difficult to make conclusions about the relative effectiveness of analytic and synthetic phonics programs. The relatively successful code-emphasis programs utilized both types of instruction. Evidence

is also inconclusive about the relative effectiveness of unlocking a new word by sounding out the word and blending it together versus spelling the word letter-by-letter as advocated by the Bloomfield-Barnhart and Fries materials. The code-emphasis programs differed on this point, yet were relatively successful as a group in producing pupils with above-average word recognition skills. For further information on this point it would be well to look at individual studies which evaluated separately each of the types of code-emphasis programs or which compared two or more code-emphasis programs (Schneyer, 1967; Sheldon, 1967; Ruddell, 1967; Tanyzer, 1966; Hayes, 1967).

The relative effectiveness of code-emphasis and meaning-emphasis programs in influencing ability in reading comprehension is still somewhat ambiguous. Taken as a group pupils who learned to read by means of conventional basal readers were slightly superior in silent reading comprehension to pupils whose initial instruction had been in linguistic materials. However, this finding was reversed in the comparison of conventional basals with phonics-first basal materials. In this latter comparison all differences favored the code-emphasis phonics-first basal program.

It should be noted that Chall in her analysis of various types of instructional programs found the phonics-first program to differ little from conventional basals in its emphasis on comprehension, follow-up activities for a lesson, teacher guidance in reading, and similar variables. Perhaps this indicates that it is essential to direct the beginners' attention to a variety of reading tasks and to stress understanding of what is read in addition to developing the ability to decode words. Evidence seems to indicate that some direct early instruction in the more mature aspects of reading behavior may be helpful.

Conclusions regarding the influence of code-emphasis and meaning-emphasis programs on rate of reading are likewise ambiguous. At the end of the first grade pupils in linguistic programs were slower oral readers than pupils in basal programs. By the end of grade two, however, this finding was reversed. Pupils in the phonics-first code-emphasis program read at a higher rate than conventional pupils at the end of grade one, but no evaluation of rate of pupils in these programs was reported at the end of grade two. On the basis of the limited information available, there appears to be little reason for concern that first-grade and second-grade pupils in code-emphasis programs become slow, halting readers. Longitudinal data are necessary to test the long-range consequences of the two types of programs.

Similar problems exist in drawing conclusions from the data on accuracy of connected oral reading. Basal pupils read more accurately than linguistic pupils at both testing points. However, phonics-first basal pupils read more accurately than conventional basal pupils at the end of grade one. Here again the evidence can best be termed conflicting. It is likely that other variables peculiar to certain code-emphasis programs account for the lack of unanimity in the findings.

Needed Clarification

Although the study supports, in general, Chall's conclusions concerning the superiority of code-emphasis programs in beginning reading, a note of caution is in order. There is no clear evidence that the early emphasis on code per se is the *only* or even the *primary* reason for the relative effectiveness of the code-emphasis programs. The major types of programs which were compared differed in a number of respects in addition to the varying emphases on code and meaning. The possibility exists that some other characteristic of these programs (higher expectations of pupil achievement, for example) may be a more crucial element in determining pupil achievement than the emphasis on code-breaking. It is also possible that some particular combination of factors within the code-emphasis programs accounted for their effectiveness. There is some evidence for this conjecture in that the various code-emphasis programs did not appear to be equally effective. Unfortunately, studies of the nature discussed in this report compare *one complex* of instructional factors with *another complex* of instructional factors, thereby making it impossible to isolate the single characteristic (if indeed there is one) which makes one program more effective than another. Researchers interested in this question will likely have to turn to laboratory investigations.

References

1. BOND, G. L., and DYKSTRA, R. *Final Report of the Coordinating Center for First-Grade Reading Instruction.* (USOE Project X-001) Minneapolis: University of Minnesota, 1967.

2. BOND, G. L., and DYKSTRA, R. "The Cooperative Research Study in First-Grade Reading Instruction," *Reading Research Quarterly,* 2, no. 4 (1967), 9–142.

3. CHALL, JEANNE. *Learning to Read.* New York: McGraw-Hill, 1967. P. 137.

4. DYKSTRA, R. *Final Report of the Continuation of the Coordinating Center for First-Grade Reading Instruction Programs.* (USOE Project 6-1651) Minneapolis: University of Minnesota, 1967.

5. HAYES, R. B., and WUEST, R. C. "I.t.a. and Three Other Approaches to Reading in the First Grade—Extended into Second Grade," *The Reading Teacher,* 20, no. 8 (1967), 694–97, 703.

6. RUDDELL, R. "Reading Instruction in First Grade with Varying Emphasis on the Regularity of Grapheme-Phoneme Correspondences and the Relation of Language Structure to Meaning—Extended into Second Grade,"

The Reading Teacher, 20, no. 8 (1967), 730–36.

7. SHELDON, W. D., NICHOLS, NANCY, and LASHINGER, D. R. "Effect of First-Grade Instruction using Basal Readers, Modified Linguistic Materials, and Linguistic Readers—Extended into Second Grade," *The Reading Teacher,* 20, no. 8 (1967), 720–25.

8. SCHNEYER, J. W. "Reading Achievement of First-Grade Children Taught by a Linguistic Approach and a Basal Readers Approach—Extended into Second Grade," *The Reading Teacher,* 20, no. 8 (1967), 704–10.

9. TANYZER, H. J., and ALPERT, H. "Three Different Basal Reading Systems and First-Grade Reading Achievement," *The Reading Teacher,* 19, no. 8 (1966), 636–42.

19. Interpreting the USOE Cooperative Reading Studies *

EDWARD R. SIPAY

THERE is always the danger of accepting without question the findings of any published study. However, the temptation to do so may be increased when a number of studies were conducted cooperatively and sponsored by the USOE. In addition, such widely publicized and long awaited studies are bound to be quoted, not always correctly, by various individuals and groups for a variety of purposes. Therefore, the discerning professional should read carefully at least the accounts

* From Edward R. Sipay, "Interpreting the USOE Cooperative Reading Studies," *Reading Teacher,* 22 (October, 1968), 10–16, 35. Reprinted by permission of the International Reading Association.

of these studies which appear in the journals, and then judge each study on its own merits. The purpose of this article is to assist the reader by pointing out some of the limitations which should be considered when interpreting the findings of the Cooperative Studies of Reading Instruction.

Since the topic is "limitations," it seems appropriate to list the limitations of this article. First, except for the Coordinating Center final reports, the comments are based primarily on journal articles rather than on the complete reports of the individual projects. It is not always possible to include as much data as desired in an article; however, the journal articles were used because they are the most accessible to the general public. Second, every limitation cited does not pertain to every study, nor even to a majority of the studies. Third, some of the limitations would have been difficult, if not impossible, to overcome. Finally, it should be noted that some investigators, particularly Bond and Dykstra, acknowledged the limitations of their studies.

The following points, as well as others should be considered when interpreting the findings of the USOE reading studies, especially those concerning the relative effectiveness of instructional methods.

Implementation of Method

Although based on a limited number of observations, Chall's findings (1966) revealed that teachers using a given method varied in their implementation of that method. It therefore seems important to control or adequately to account for the implementation of the methods under comparison. Not only may the ways in which the methods are employed have a significant effect on the achievement of the pupils; but also, if teachers deviate to any extent from the labeled method(s), one may not really be comparing what he thinks is being compared. Therefore, if implementation is not controlled, any conclusions drawn from the data regarding the relative effectiveness of particular methods are open to question.

The manner in which and the extent to which implementation of methods was controlled varied greatly from study to study. In some studies, teachers kept logs; it should be noted that Chall's study (1966) found a discrepancy between what teachers said they did in first-grade reading and what they were observed to do in their classrooms. In other projects, teachers were observed by various personnel on a very limited basis; and, many studies did not report any attempt to control or to account for implementation of methods.

Neither was the amount of instructional time devoted to the teaching of reading held constant from one study to the next. In fact, it is difficult to determine if equal time was given to treatments within many projects. It is realized that low correlations were found between instructional time and some final measures; and, that how the time was used is more important than the amount of time allocated.

Generalizing from the Results

Not only were uncommonly used methods often not clearly defined; but also, differences existed in instructional programs labeled similarly. Stauffer (1966) reported that after attempts to coordinate three studies on a common language arts basis, the directors concluded the approaches were similar but not the same. Likewise, at least five different basal series, two linguistic programs, three phonic programs, and even two i.t.a. programs were employed in the studies. Basal reader programs differ (Mason, 1963), and an inspection of the materials will reveal differences among programs in other "methods." In addition, all of the possible programs (e.g., there are more than five commonly used basal series and many more than two phonics-first programs) were not employed. The possibility therefore exists that not *all* programs of one type will produce initially better results than will *all* programs of another type. In short, results concerning a "method" cannot be generalized to all programs having the same general label.

Nor can the results of the projects be generalized to all children. The populations varied from study to study. Some studies were conducted in large urban areas, others in rural areas, and some in suburbia. These children differed in cultural, socioeconomic, and even language backgrounds. More importantly, no one method proved to be superior for all children in all aspects of reading as measured by the tests employed.

Even when legitimate statistically significant differences were found between or among treatments, it should be remembered that the differences were based on group averages. It is likely that although one treatment produced a higher average score, some individuals in that treatment scored lower than some individuals in the other treatments. This presents the possibility that although one treatment group has a higher mean, another treatment program may have been more effective for a particular group of children.

On the basis of present knowledge one cannot predict with great accuracy if a particular program will be more effective than others for a given child, nor know what aspects of a program work best for which child. The USOE studies did little to add further knowledge regarding these points.

Teacher and Instruction Setting Variables

In addition to the limitations imposed by differences in the implementation of the methods, factors concerning the teachers themselves may have influenced the results of the studies. Teacher variables must have been operative for as Fry (1966, p. 668) pointed out: "The variation between classrooms [within a method] was much greater than the variation between methods. What this means is that some factor, such as possible better teaching, influenced the class reading achievement scores much more than the methods used."

Although they reported only slight but positive correlations between teacher characteristics and reading achievement when all studies were included, when Bond and Dykstra (1967) compared the five highest-ranking projects with the five lowest-ranking projects the following teacher characteristics were found to be significantly different: superior ratings of class structure, class participation, awareness of and attention to individual needs, and overall teacher competence.

As for the effect of instructional setting, Dykstra (1967) reported that:

In general, projects appeared to have a greater influence on the reading ability of pupils than did the particular instructional method or materials utilized. Specific programs were relatively effective in one project, relatively ineffective in other projects. On the other hand, all programs used in the same project were found to be quite similar in effectiveness. This would indicate that the entire instructional setting is involved in the effectiveness of an instructional program in reading. Differences in method or materials alone do not alter, to any great extent, the reading growth of pupils (p. 164).

Thus, it would appear that teacher characteristics and/or the instructional setting may have greatly influenced the outcomes of the studies. Few projects, however, reported any attempt to control for the effect of such variables.

Assignment to Treatments

It is possible that in certain studies, treatment groups were not "equal," thereby giving an advantage to a particular treatment. In their Coordinating Center report, Bond and Dykstra (1967) wrote,

. . . there was evidence of nonrandom assignment of pupils to treatments in certain projects. In some cases there were substantial differences in pupil performance on premeasures for the experimental treatments.

The analysis of covariance was used to adjust for pre-measure differences but there is a question of how adequately this statistical technique adjusts for differences in capabilities between groups (p. 152).

The manner by which children, or classes, or teachers were assigned to treatments frequently was not reported. When reported, a variety of practices became evident. In one study (Spencer 1966), pupils were assigned to classes by a random method, but teachers were assigned by individual preference for an approach. In another instance (Tanyzer, 1966), the teachers were selected at random from volunteers and nine first-grade classes randomly selected from two districts whereas another district contributed its entire first-grade population. In a third study (Harris, 1966, p. 632), "There was random assignment of four methods to schools, two methods to each school; random assignment of teachers to the two methods within the school; and finally random assignment of pupils within each school to the two methods."

Attrition of Subjects

The attrition rate of subjects was fairly high in some studies. For example, in one study (Reid, 1966) complete data were available for only 73 percent of the original 424 subjects. It is conceivable that such losses could have influenced the final results of any study. Indeed, there is some evidence to substantiate this possibility. Dykstra (1967) reported:

For some reason, non-persist pupils in one treatment were better achievers in first grade than were non-persist pupils in the other treatment while the reverse was true for pupils who persisted. This nonrepresentative retention may be a factor influencing the results. Furthermore, in almost every instance, the pupils who persisted through the second grade were significantly superior in

first-grade achievement than were pupils lost during the second-grade phase of the study. Therefore, pupils on whom results are reported in this study are superior to pupils from the participating projects in general (p. 166).

At the risk of oversimplification, what this all means is that a particular treatment or treatments may have achieved higher scores because their "better" subjects were left to take the tests.

Experimental Variable

Because the individual rather than the class was used as the experimental unit in most of the individual projects, many of the conclusions based on the obtained statistically significant differences may not be valid. If the appropriate experimental unit had been used, statistically significant differences may not have occurred. In short, there might have been little or no "proof" that one method produced better results than other methods.

In addition to Stauffer's general comment (1967) concerning possible limitations of the tests employed in the studies, there is some evidence that the instruments were of doubtful validity for certain project populations. The Spanish-speaking first-graders in one study (Horn, 1966) attained a large number of zero scores on the instruments, and similar results (Chall, 1966) were reported for culturally disadvantaged children. Moreover, it is impossible to assess exactly what effect high numbers of zero scores and restricted ranges of scores had upon the reported findings.

There also is some indication that the tests employed may have had a bearing on the results obtained. According to Reid (1967, p. 603), "All of the midyear test results showed a definite tendency for children to score higher in those tests which measured the skills in which they

had received direct training. The closer
the test resembled the learning situation,
the more likely a significant difference
was found between two methods, favoring the method with closer learning-test
resemblance."

Schneyer (1966, p. 651) made a somewhat similar observation, "One conclusion that might be drawn from the data
. . . is that pupils tend to obtain better
results on criterion measures that employ
vocabulary similar to the vocabulary to
which they are accustomed."

In short, if different measures had been
employed, the possibility exists that different results might have been obtained.

Hawthorne Effect

Some directors of the individual studies, such as Mazurkiewicz (1967), Ruddell (1966), and Vilscek (1966), attempted to control for the Hawthorne
effect. Yet, as Bond and Dykstra (1967)
pointed out,

Another limitation which might influence the
results is that there appeared to be differences among projects in the extent to which
the Hawthorne effect was controlled. It is
likely that the newer programs profited from
the increased motivation, the greater teacher
and parental interest, the awareness on the
part of pupils and teachers that experimentation was going on, and similar factors usually associated with new methodological
techniques. The extent to which these ex-
traneous factors were controlled in the
various projects undoubtedly influenced the
results. In this regard, it is likely that the
less traditional instructional projects profited
from whatever Hawthorne effect was present in the investigation (pp. 152–53).

Reporting of Findings

Although in the strictest sense they
are not limitations of the studies per se,

the reader should examine carefully the
data reported and the conclusions drawn
from these data.

In at least three tables (Reid, 1966;
Mazurkiewicz, 1966; Mazurkiewicz,
1967) are errors in the data reported.
These may be typographical errors; nevertheless the information is inaccurate.

The need to understand what a test
actually measures is illustrated by the
study (Mazurkiewicz, 1966) which compared the instructional levels attained by
two treatment groups. The reader should
realize that the test employed, the *Botel
Reading Inventory,* measures the ability
to pronounce words in isolation; and does
not involve comprehension of connected
discourse. The instructional level is determined by correct pronunciation of
70–90 percent of the twenty words at a
particular reader level in the Word Recognition test.

Other project reports illustrated the
need for reading carefully. One study
(Spencer, 1966), reported that, "After
ten days of instruction the individualized
class (IR) knew significantly (.01 level)
more letter names and phonemes than the
basal reader class." However, if both
treatment groups did not receive such
instruction, and there was no indication
that they did, the results are not too surprising especially in light of the previous
comments in this paper regarding
the possible influence of the tests employed.

As for the conclusions which were
drawn, perhaps the most paradoxical is
the one in which the investigator (Morrell, 1966) concluded that one method
allowed her to provide better supervisory
service, despite the fact that the only statistically significant differences found favored the other method.

In summary, the following points
should be considered when interpreting
the USOE reading studies:

Summary

1. The manner in which a program was implemented probably varied within and among projects, thereby affecting the obtained results.
2. Programs often were not clearly defined: differences existed in programs labeled as being the same method, and all available programs were not employed. Therefore, it is impossible to generalize the results to *all* programs.
3. No one program proved to be superior for all children in every aspect of reading measured. Therefore it is impossible to generalize the results to *all* children.
4. The program and materials alone did not account for the growth in reading. Teacher variables and instructional setting probably were just as influential, if not more so.
5. Treatment groups may not have been "equal" because of the way in which pupils and teachers were assigned to treatments.
6. The attrition of subjects may have influenced the results.
7. The appropriate experimental unit, the class, was not used in most of the individual projects. Therefore the obtained results may not be valid.
8. The tests employed may have had a bearing on the obtained results.
9. The long-range effects of the program are yet to be determined.
10. The innovative programs probably profited from whatever Hawthorne effect was operative.
11. The reported findings and conclusions are not always accurate and may be misleading.

References

1. BOND, G. L., and DYKSTRA, R. *Coordinating Center for First-Grade Reading Instruction Programs*. Minneapolis, Minn.: University of Minnesota, 1967.
2. CHALL, JEANNE, and FELDMANN, SHIRLEY. "First-Grade Reading: An Analysis of the Interactions of Professed Methods, Teacher Implementation, and Child Background," *The Reading Teacher, 19* (1966), 569–75.
3. DYKSTRA, R. *Continuation of the Coordinating Center for First-Grade Reading Instruction Programs*. Minneapolis, Minn.: University of Minnesota, 1967.
4. FRY, E. B. "First-Grade Reading Instruction Using Diacritical Marking System, Initial Teaching Alphabet, and Basal Reading System," *The Reading Teacher, 19* (1966), 666–69.
5. HARRIS, A. J., and SERWER, BLANCHE L. "Comparing Reading Approaches in First-Grade Teaching with Disadvantaged Children," *The Reading Teacher, 19* (1966), 631–35; 642.
6. HORN, T. D. "Three Methods of Developing Reading Readiness in Spanish-Speaking Children in First Grade," *The Reading Teacher, 20* (1966), 38–42.
7. MASON, G. "An Analysis and Comparison of Programs for Teaching Word-Recognition in Basal Reading Series and Phonics Materials." Unpublished Doctoral Dissertation. Syracuse University, 1963.
8. MAZURKIEWICZ, A. J. "I.t.a. and t.o.

Reading Achievement When Methodology Is Controlled," *The Reading Teacher, 19* (1966), 606–10.

9. ———. "I.t.a. and t.o. Reading Achievement When Methodology Is Controlled—Extended into Second Grade," *The Reading Teacher, 20* (1967), 726–29.

10. MORRELL, KATHERINE. "A Comparison of Two Methods of Reading Supervision," *The Reading Teacher, 19* (1966), 617–21.

11. REID, H. C., and BELTRAMO, LOUISE. "Teaching Reading to the Low Group in the First Grade," *The Reading Teacher, 19* (1966), 601–5.

12. RUDDELL, R. B. "Reading Instruction in First Grade with Varying Emphasis on the Regularity of Grapheme-Phoneme Correspondence and the Relation of Language Structure to Meaning," *The Reading Teacher, 19* (1966), 653–60.

13. SCHNEYER, J. W. "Reading Achievement of First-Grade Children Taught by a Linguistic Approach and a Basal Reader Approach," *The Reading Teacher, 19* (1966), 647–52.

14. SPENCER, DORIS U. "Individualized First-Grade Reading Versus a Basal Reader Program in Rural Communities," *The Reading Teacher, 19* (1966), 595–600.

15. STAUFFER, R. G. "The Verdict: Speculative Controversy," *The Reading Teacher, 19* (1966), 563–64; 575.

16. TANYZER, H. J., and ALPERT, H. "Three Different Basal Reading Systems and First-Grade Reading Achievement," *The Reading Teacher, 19* (1966), 636–42.

17. VILSCEK, ELAINE, MORGAN, LORRAINE, and CLELAND, D. "Coordinating and Integrating Language Arts Instruction in First Grade," *The Reading Teacher, 20* (1966), 31–37.

20. Vital Principles in Need of Application *

CONSTANCE M. MC CULLOUGH

THE contributions of the science of linguistics to the field of reading instruction are chiefly in the areas of decoding symbols into sound and structure, and decoding sound and structure into meaning. These are two of the four major areas

* From Constance M. McCullough, "Vital Principles in Need of Application," in Elaine C. Vilscek (ed.), *A Decade of Innovation: Approaches to Beginning Reading,* Proceedings of the Twelfth Annual Convention, 12, Part 3 (Newark, Del.: International Reading Association, 1968), 180–91. Reprinted by permission of the International Reading Association and the author.

recognized in the reading process, two additional ones being the interpretation of meanings and their application to or integration with other ideas.

Because these contributions affect directly only two parts of the four-part process, one of the first facts we must observe is that these linguistic contributions are a part, not the whole, of our concern in teaching reading. And because they are only a part of these two parts, we should further modify our consideration of them. In other words, if we drop everything we have ever done about teaching reading and do nothing but what the science of linguistics suggests, again we sin in the direction of an extreme; and it is perhaps by extremes as much as by our mistakes that we do less well than we might in teaching children to read.

At the outset let us admit that children are reading better now than their parents did at their ages, better than their older brothers and sisters. The norms of reading tests are having to be revised because the average child in a particular grade level now is getting a higher raw score than his predecessor did a few years ago.

At the same time, we must not be overcome by vanity in this achievement. We are only one possible factor in it. Another tremendous factor is the greater stimulation of the modern environment, the greater opportunity to develop concepts, which are the *sine qua non* of reading comprehension.

The twenty-seven cooperative studies of different beginning reading programs showed that the quality of teaching made more difference than the method used, a finding widely viewed as proof that no one method is the best answer. But a little more thought brings still another conclusion: that perhaps each program in its individual way misses perfection by the same degree though not in the same respect; all hit the target, but none hits the bull's-eye. This is a sorry thought but not unexpected, since we are still pioneering in the reading field, still fitting pieces of the jigsaw puzzle together, still agreeing or disagreeing on interpretations of insufficient data.

In applying linguistic knowledge to the teaching of reading, we must distinguish between linguistic knowledge and methods used by linguists in teaching language. It is a temptation to adopt both the knowledge and the methods; yet it must be said in all honesty that while linguistic knowledge is a product of rigorous scholarly endeavor, methods of teaching language range from ancient to modern, reflecting more of logic than of psychological soundness.

We are fortunate that some linguists have departed from their major role of information-getters, to become material-producers; but we must not forget that, while we are not in a position to view their knowledge critically, we are in a position to assess the wisdom of their teaching procedures and sequences, and perhaps to improve upon them.

We should distinguish also between methods of teaching the spoken language and methods of teaching the reading of that language. Imitation and memorization are important in the acquisition of speech patterns. The reading process involves retrieval of these acquisitions and keen observation of relationships, to recapture the author's thought and reflect upon it. Thus, while speaking and reading may share the same language, they are not identical processes. What is good for one is not necessarily good for the other.

Our objective is to teach "book English." We have to add spoken book English to the child's speech patterns and sounds before we can expect the child to read and understand book English. This is not to say a little; it is to say a great deal; for every child in our society is to some extent a foreigner to book English. Since there is some research to support the idea that the age of seven is an optimal age at which to add a language, we should probably press forward in kindergarten and first grade, if not before, to prepare the child for this addition. And since the characteristics of the child's home language, which make the learning of book English difficult, are different for different children, diagnosis of the differences between the home language and the book English sounds and patterns must take place prior to instruction and, in some respects, along with it. Otherwise, we shall continue to build a superstructure upon a foundation which cannot support it.

Language experience charts are one of the approaches to reading which can preface and accompany a reading program. If the child says, "Wannagome" for "I want to go home," some teachers faithfully reproduce this language on a chart, following the imperative that the child must feel his language is respected, and that he must see his language written exactly as it is said. If, however, another principle is added, that the child should be taught book English as efficiently as possible, teachers may wish to delay dictated charts until these can be useful models of reading materials.

Probably the most important of all principles to teach children is the relativity of language. Consider the relativity of sounds: the *b* in *battle* as compared with the *b* in *cab;* the *o* in *not* as compared with the *o* in *note;* the *th* in *this* as compared with the *th* in *think.* One has to inspect the word as a whole before one knows whether the *th* is voiced or unvoiced, and then he knows only because he has heard these words before— if, indeed, he has. Consider the effect of context on the word *bear,* the possible meanings of *"Now you've done it."* The sounds assigned to words and letters and the meanings of words and larger units of composition are modified by their environment. To learn them in isolation is to learn them only in part; is, in fact, to misrepresent the task of reading them.

Children need to learn both the fact that letters are assigned certain sounds according to their positions in a pattern and that some letters are assigned variable sounds within the same or a different framework. The *c*'s in *circus* are controlled by the vowels which follow them, to yield the *s* or *k* sound. The *tear* we

shed and the *tear* in a garment have no structural reason for their difference, only a meaning reason. C. C. Fries has suggested that children should see what different words they can produce by putting different vowel sounds between consonants. The p-l patterns become pal, pel, pil, pol, pul; pale (pail), peel (peal), pile, pole (poll), pule; powl, paul, poil, pull, pool. This can be a creative exercise for the child, not a ready-made teacher-patterned ritual. Variations in spelling for the same sound can become an impressive discovery.

Phonics and Blending

Phonics, as we know it, was suitable in the last century because we did not have the linguistic knowledge to warrant a different procedure. We taught that letters said a certain sound, in spite of the fact that most of our letters are either variable in sound or unpronounceable alone.

In some languages each consonant letter is a pronounceable unit, carrying a vowel sound with it. In Hindi, for instance, the letter *m* is actually an *m* plus a schwa sound (*muh*) unless a separate vowel is attached to change that condition. So, in Hindi, it is perfectly proper and possible to sound consonants separately. But in English this is not the case.

The vowels in English are produced in a flow of air. The consonants initiate or interrupt that flow and are not audible without it. Thus the vowels *a, o* and *i* are the only letters that appear as single words in our language. When we require children to say or even whisper the consonant alone, we are misrepresenting the language to them. So we must decide to what extent we can afford to misrepresent these conditions in initial instruction, or whether it is wise at all to do so. Certainly we take a good deal of trouble to avoid misrepresentation of mathematical truths in beginning arithmetic, and science truths in beginning science. What if we should decide not to misrepresent the language in initial instruction in reading? It could be done, but not by i.t.a. as it is now taught, or by some of the other systems in which we have invested funds and loyalties.

Because we have had a letter approach to sounding words, we have invented a blending problem. Children learn the sounds to associate with certain letters, according to our instruction, but have trouble putting them together into a pronounceable whole. In fact, many good and poor readers alike prefer to discover the identity of strange words by other means.

At recurring points in our history we have insisted that *c-a-t* should be blended as *c-at,* at other times, as *ca-t.* Thus we have produced *cuh-at* and *ca-tuh,* neither of which has ever been known to sit on a fence and howl.

Now we need to look at the facts of our language. The vowel in *cat* affects both the *c* and the *t.* (The word *car,* with its *r*-controlled *a* shows such relationships even more clearly.) The child who would attack this word successfully must know that the *a* gives the *c* the sound usually associated with *k,* and that a vowel between two consonants in the same syllable is usually short. So he derives a short *a* from the *a* of the word. He raises the back of his tongue against the soft palate to produce the initial *k* position, and immediately switches to the flattened tongue, short *a* position; then finishes by bringing the tip of his tongue to the final *t* position against the gums behind the upper front teeth if he has any. If he hasn't lost all of his wind, he has produced *cat;* and he has done it without the addition of a schwa sound prior to the short *a.* Readiness activities for sounding out *cat* include aural and oral practice in hearing and saying the short *a* sound in varying combinations.

Future generations of teachers may know that the blending problems of the twentieth century and earlier were due to faulty pedagogy, but not unless we change what we are doing. Probably many defensive arguments will be raised for the old way, to maintain the comfort of the customary instead of the customer; but in the end we may have a sounder sound system.

Attention and Confusion in Language Learning

And speaking of faulty pedagogy, we frequently have violated the principle that learning is most effective when attention is greatest. When we teach the association of a sound with a letter, the point of greatest attention should be the point at which this association is observed. But frequently we have *told* the child the sound, and have merely asked him to find that letter in other words and pronounce them with that sound in them. He can go through these motions with any sound we give him, but that is no assurance that he will remember which sound he made for which exercise. If we want to impress the child with the association, *his* pride in discovery and *his* attention should be invested, not just ours in telling him what we know. If, further, he keeps his own record of what he has discovered, he will not only remember it better but will have it to refer to for review. Typically, the only record is in the teacher's head.

A favorite habit of language teachers is to group together things that are much alike: letters, words, and sounds. *M* and *n* are so much alike, teach them together, they say; the same with the words *take* and *bring,* because of their common burden; and *t-h-e-r-e* and *t-h-e-i-r,* because of their common sound. Speech therapists know better than this. They establish one learning and after that, another;

and only after both are well known are they brought together, with reduced chance of confusion. In beginning reading instruction, words grossly different in form, sound, or meaning can be more easily learned together. And we are fortunate that the natural language of children contains many grossly different words and varied sentence forms.

The Reading Process: The Decoding of Symbols into Sounds

Now let us turn to the reading process itself, to see what insights we can gain for a beginning reading program. Suppose the author wants to convey these simple thoughts:

> The deer met the bear.
> The deer had antlers.
> The deer lowered his antlers.

These sentences are of the type N V N (noun, verb, noun), have a common subject, and make pretty dull reading. The author combines these ideas into one sentence, and he does it in such a way as to give importance to the *way* the deer met the bear.

The deer met the bear with lowered antlers.

The phrase *with lowered antlers* is in a typical position of an adverbial expression. With luck, it will be no reflection on the bear.

The decoding of symbols into sound involves the following if the words are not known as sight words: The child must choose the voiced form of *th* in *the;* and, seeing the consonant beginning the next word, give the final *e* the schwa sound. In *deer* he must realize that *ee* yields a long *e* sound modified by the presence of the final *r*—the hooked long *e,* as Webster calls it—the *e* with the second heroin shot. *Met* is the closed syllable, short *e* situation. The *ea* in *bear* could produce *beer, bare, burr,* or *bar.*

Nothing but the realization that this is the fur-bearing bear, and an auditory memory of its name, can save the reader here. *With* has the short *i* of the closed syllable. Its *th* is voiced or unvoiced, depending on the part of the country it is voiced in. The *ow* in *lowered* could be long *o* or *ou.* If *er-ed* are recognized as variant endings, the *low* is stressed, and the *er-ed* becomes *er'd,* not *ert* or *ered.*

Antlers contains two syllables, having two vowels. The first vowel in the closed syllable is short, and the second is modified by *r.* The *s* in the final position following *r* has the sound associated with *z.* The stress is penultimate, and the child may luckily guess this, mistaking *-er* as a variant ending.

Of course, if the child knows some words by sight, or recognizes some parts, such as *low, ant,* and the *s, er,* and *ed* endings, he shortens the process of decoding. One purpose of the controlled vocabulary is to reduce the burden of decoding symbols into sounds; another is to make a few words very familiar to the point of rapid recognition; and a third is to help the memorization of words which are not regularly spelled.

The Reading Process: The Decoding of Symbols and Sounds into Structures (Syntax)

While the reader decodes the symbols into sounds, he is also noting the structure of the sentence and the role of each word, phrase, or clause in it. If there were more than one sentence, he would be noticing the relationship of one sentence to another, in the presence of pronoun referents and structure words.

In the sentence we are using as an example, *The* is a noun determiner. *Deer* could be an adjective, but *met,* followed by another *the,* suggests that *deer* is the subject and *met* is the verb. *Deer* can be singular or plural, and *met* does not give a clue as it might in present tense: *deer meet, deer meets.* You can imagine what *deer meet* would do to a bad speller in this situation.

If the child knows that *met* is past tense, he knows that the sentence refers to a completed act. The *bear* must be another noun, the thing acted upon, because it follows *the* and is followed by a function word, *with.* The *ed* ending of *lowered* suggests a verb form, and, after the preposition *with,* must be an adjective. *Antlers,* with its *s* ending, following an adjective and preposition, must be a noun, a plural.

A child who knows the English language represented by this sentence can catch the clues to order (the typical N V N pattern), the noun determiners (*the—the*), the suggestion of time (*met*) (*lowered*), and number (*antlers*). A child who does not know any English that uses articles and variant endings in an expected order needs a great deal of support from the listening and speaking areas of the curriculum before he is ready to read a sentence like this. Even with a good English background, a child could not tell whether *deer* was singular or plural. He would have to seek a clue elsewhere in the composition.

The Reading Process: The Decoding of Meaning

Besides being able to decode the symbols into sounds, and into expected word groupings, the reader must decode the meaning of what he is sounding out. When the author writes *THE deer,* the reader must, as Lee Deighton has said, "hold in abeyance" his decision about the number of deer until he gets a further clue. *Met* looks simple but may refer to action or stance. Does it mean that the deer *faced* the bear, *approached* him, *reacted to* the sight of him, *touched* him or *rammed* him? The bear is the one that

got the action, from one or more deer, some time in the past.

If the reader does not know what a deer is, what a bear is, what their attitude toward each other is, what their weapons are, what their food is, he cannot sense the situation. It may as well be *The icks met the oiks.* You see the tremendous role of concepts and the wisdom of dealing as much as possible with familiar concepts in beginning reading, when the struggle with symbols is so great.

We sophisticated readers take *with* for granted, but *with* has different meanings. To fight *with* enemies is to fight *against* them. To part *with* them is to part *from* them. So *with* is a word to watch. The position of *with* after *bear* may suggest that it introduces something characteristic of the bear (the bear with the bad foot), or the way he is doing something (with caution), or something he has (with the honey), or a reference to time (with no delay). But here is a bear with lowered something: eyes? paws? self-concept? No, antlers.

If the reader knows who is wearing antlers this season, he knows that the *with* expression refers back to the singular or plural deer at the first of the sentence. And because the sentence order was not *The deer with lowered antlers met the bear,* the reader suspects that with lowered antlers isn't the normally jaunty way the deer wear antlers these days, but a special stance in honor of the bear.

Coming back to the meaning of *met,* let us suppose that a sentence preceding the one we have analyzed said:

The bear and deer approached each other slowly.

In this case, *met* suggests action. But suppose the preceding sentence said, instead:

As the deer started to raise its head from the salt-lick, it saw a bear approaching.

Now, the *met* is stance. The antlers are already low. Suppose the sentence was:

The picture showed a bear and a deer in a meadow.

Now both animals are stationary, and there is no time difference or movement.

The Reading Process: Interpretation and Application

Surrounding sentences give added dimensions to sentence meaning, requiring some awareness of the thought patterns the author is following. The deer lowered his antlers *because* of the approaching bear. We have a cause and effect relationship without benefit of a clue to the reader in the form of a word like *because*. Or, in the description of the picture our preceding sentence *describes* the situation (a picture), and the second sentence tells a *detail* of it. One might expect an additional sentence offering another detail.

In any case, the reader has to go beyond what he has sounded out and structured out, and what he knows of the meaning of what he has read to interpret and apply what he has gathered. Why would a deer lower its antlers on sight of a bear? Does the reader generalize *threat* from *stance,* and see that the deer is a threat to the bear and the bear to the deer? Both are now motivated by fear. Perhaps they just happened upon each other and have reacted in surprise. What will happen next? Why?

A good reader anticipates beyond the sentence he is reading. Furthermore, he applies the information in some ways, and perhaps philosophizes. Would a deer ever attack a bear? Or vice versa? Am I sometimes afraid when I need not be? Mike McClintock's *A Fly Went By* is a good follow-up for this matter of unwarranted fear.

The Reading Process versus Logic

The reading act is not a logically sequential act of first decoding sound, then structure, then meaning, then interpretation, and then use of integration; it is rather an act of interplay among all of these. We don't sound the whole sentence before we utilize clues to structure, sense some possible clues to meaning and relationship, formulate hunches about the total meaning, and see possible applications of this meaning to past and future ideas. Only linguistic analysis uses such logical sequence. What is good for the analyst is not necessarily good or normal for the reader.

A baby is lucky that it has no teeth. Otherwise an analyst would come along with chewing exercises, forbidding the flow of saliva until chewing had been perfected; then with salivating without chewing or swallowing, and finally swallowing without chewing or salivating; all this without benefit of something worth chewing, salivating, and swallowing.

Does this sound like the program that first teaches sounds associated with letters until all are memorized, then patterns of letters within words until the child can manipulate them, then one sentence pattern at a time until all patterns are mastered, and finally something in the natural language? Does it sound like the program which first teaches sentence reading, then whole words, and finally the letter-sound associations?

Does it sound like the program which teaches all regularly spelled words first, and only later the ones which defy phonic solution?

We have all been using one or another type of logical approach—fragmented approach—in attempting to teach something that does not behave that way. Because we have discovered components, we have ordered them unnaturally and are serving them to children in unnatural sequences. So it was that some reader series served consonants in the first-grade books and vowels in the second, causing the child to wait a whole year before he could sound out a whole word, and causing parents to panic. The most useful consonant-vowel combinations could have been presented first, but this did not occur to the logicians who designed the program.

An important principle to recognize is that logical organization is something to be *achieved* by a learner, not *imposed* upon him. The linguist loves his field partly because he can make discoveries about its logical relationships and its vagaries. The child should have this same privilege of discovery.

Logically, some linguists believe that the child's initial reading material should contain only regularly spelled words. Other linguists believe that the child's natural language should be used. Unfortunately these two ideas are incompatible. But it is possible to use the child's natural language and to have a parallel program of exercises using some of the same words and emphasizing form and nonsense.

Again, logically, some of us have thought that word analysis had to be based upon words which the child had in his sight vocabulary. This meant that sight vocabulary had to precede analysis. Others disagreed: letter sounds should be learned first, then words. But neither really had to precede the other. All that was required was for the child to be told what two words said, so that he could hear their common sound and find by sight the letter making that sound.

All of the elements in the reading process, and all of the skills and understandings and attitudes required in these elements, must be present in the initial reading program, unless we wish deliberately to misrepresent the reading act and establish habits which must be broken. And even though we do not value the completeness of the reading act at every level, surely we must consider the children who are disturbed if they have to learn sentences or words entirely as wholes, or children who do not have the auditory discrimination to approach reading successfully through the phonic mode.

Final statement

We are in a stage of transition. Perhaps we always shall be, as long as we and the language live. But I believe there is great hope for a better reading program, a greatly improved one, if we try to put together in a mutually beneficial relationship some of the ideas which have divided us.

Why should a child read a whole year before he can sound out a word? Why should he have to sound out everything? Why should all of his beginning reading be nonsense? Why should it start with mimicry? Why should it be entirely his own language? Why should it rhyme as nothing in English literature rhymes, to the distress of comprehension? Why should a child learn initially, in the same lesson, words which are confusing in form? Why should consonants precede vowels or vowels consonants? Why should we blend when we can bend?

The answer is that we have all been viewing the reading process from different angles and letting logic and custom blind us to the natural conditions for effective learning.

Now we have the new linguistic evidence. We have much information on the ways in which learning takes place. We have the language of children all around us, and a wealth of children's literature. Something better than we have ever achieved is just ahead.

V

Measuring Reading Outcomes and Determining Needs

Almost every school administers reading tests, yet little use is made of the test results. It's as though the procedure involved is: test-score-file-forget.

Harris lists and discusses twelve purposes for giving tests, as well as suggesting how tests might be selected and test results utilized. Badal and Larsen's article should help test users to understand standardized test scores.

Use also should be made of informal tests for various purposes. For example, because there is a high correlation between word recognition and reading ability, a quick assessment of reading ability may be obtained by administering a graded word list such as the one by LaPray and Ross. Informal reading inventories are covered in the last three articles. Betts presents definitions and procedures; McCracken discusses their use to affect instruction; and Kender describes their limitations.

21. Areas of Concern in Evaluation *

ALBERT J. HARRIS

To be unable to evaluate what teachers are doing and what children are doing is to be lost in the forest with no compass.

* From Albert J. Harris, "Areas of Concern in Evaluation," *Significant Issues in Reading,* Proceedings of the Twenty-Third Annual Reading Institute at Temple University, 4, 1966. (Philadelphia: Reading Clinic, Temple University, 1968) 62–72. Reprinted by permission of Temple University.

Evaluation, then, is an essential topic for the person working in the field of reading. One must not only understand some of the technicalities about how to give tests and how to score them and look up norms, but also try to discover the inner purposes of the tests—what are the tests for, and at what times evaluative procedures other than tests are needed. There are many areas of evaluation in reading where there are no satisfactory tests, and it becomes necessary to improvise.

Purposes of Tests

The first question is, "Why do we give tests? What purposes do they serve?" There must be more than twelve different purposes for giving tests in the area of reading, but a list of just twelve should be sufficiently suggestive of the total breadth.

The first use is that of comparing the results of one group of pupils with other groups of pupils, as in a large-scale survey. The comparison may be between a class and other classes, or a school and other schools within a community, or a whole community as compared to other communities. In these kinds of comparisons, it is usually considered enough to use a test which has one overall score, or at most a very small number of parts. The concern is generally more with the question of norms than with the question of the instructional application of the results.

A second purpose is the prediction of the probable success or failure of individual pupils. Here, of course, from the end of kindergarten or beginning of first grade with readiness tests and on up through the grades, the assumption is made that what the children have done so far helps to predict what they are likely to do in the future. A report of a recent study in New York City indicates that the reading test results obtained at the end of the second grade predicted eighth-grade performance better than any intelligence measure they had utilized for the same purpose, and almost as well as any reading test given in between those grades. If this is true (and it may not be true in other communities, but it is worth checking), then it would seem to indicate that what happens in the first two grades

is of crucial importance, and would point to the need for careful step-by-step checking on what beginning readers learn, before nonlearning can go too far.

A third purpose is for classification of pupils into groups for reading instruction. In some schools, reading tests are used to classify children into so-called homogeneous groups for all instruction. This is particularly prevalent in junior high schools where, very often, the results of a survey-type reading test are used to set up seventh-grade classes in numerical order from one (for brightest or best readers) to seventh or eighteenth (which are the ones reading below fourth-grade level). Of course, the term "homogeneous" cannot be used with any real accuracy. It would be preferable to call them "less heterogeneous" classes rather than "homogeneous" classes. Grouping in this way restricts the range somewhat, but anyone who has worked with so-called "homogeneous" classes has found out there are still plenty of individual differences left, no matter what is used to slice up the total population.

A fourth and somewhat related use is for the selection of pupils for special reading courses or remedial programs. Here, it seems, the reading tests that are used are usually reasonable for the purpose; but many crimes are committed in the use of tests to determine whether or not the children are capable of improving. Group I.Q. tests are often used, and a child who scores less than 90 on a group I.Q. test is often barred from the remedial program. This is in conflict with the well-established fact that, on the most widely used upper-grade and secondary school I.Q. tests, it is impossible for a poor reader to score above 90 I.Q. because he cannot read the questions. If he cannot read the questions, it is not an I.Q. test for him. It is just another reading test. Therefore, in the selection of pupils for special reading courses or remedial programs, extreme care must be exercised in what is used as a measure of reading potentiality; much more care with that than with the reading tests themselves.

A fifth use is for the measurement of specific sub-skills as a guide to group and individual instruction. Here most teachers rely on their own testing procedures, or on the use of published exercises as tests.

A sixth possible use is as a basis for the choice of instructional materials according to difficulty. Ever since Dr. Betts first published the idea of using the Informal Reading Inventory (a collection of book samples), there has been a lively argument as to the relative accuracy of standardized tests versus the book sample technique as a way of gauging the instructional materials most likely to fit the needs of individual youngsters.

A seventh use is the measurement of reading performance at intervals during an instructional program to check on the outcomes of the teaching of specific skills, or at the end of specific instructional periods as a kind of final test or check-up.

An eighth use is to compare the results of one experimental procedure with the results of other experimental procedures. In most of these research studies an appropriate battery of pre-tests is given before the teaching program is started. Then another battery of tests is given at the end of the experimental teaching period and the amounts of gain as a result of the different procedures are compared.

A ninth use is to provide diagnostic information that is useful in the analysis of both the causation and the instructional needs of children with reading problems.

A tenth use is as part of the admission requirement to certain schools or to special programs. In New York City, for example, a minimum reading test score of 7.0 is one of the entrance requirements for many of the senior high school programs. In some private schools, a reading grade of one year above the national norm is a minimum requirement for admission.

Number eleven is used as one of the requirements for pupil promotion or graduation. Many school systems still insist that in order to be allowed to enter the second grade, a first grader must score 2.0 or higher by the end of the first grade. This always seems like a echo from the dark ages, because it evidences the fact that they have no confidence in the ability of their second-grade teachers to pick up children where they are and carry them forward from there; or no interest in doing this. They are still committed to a doctrine of giving mass instruction and ignoring individual differences.

The twelfth use is to measure teacher effectiveness. This is where teachers have a very strong personal interest. "Why is the administration asking us to give the test, and what are they going to do with the scores after they get them?"

There are probably many more than these twelve kinds of uses, but these seem to be the most frequent and the most important uses of testing in the field of reading. Some of them are proper. Some of them are improper. Some of them are just misguided in the way in which they are applied. Putting the impact on teachers at the end of the list leads to the second major question—what impact does a testing program have upon the teachers and upon the children?

Impact of Tests

All classroom teachers know that when a testing program is inflicted from above it tends to engender resentment. It seems like time taken away from teaching; it involves dreary moments of just standing, watching, and waiting while the children are using up the time limit. Very often teachers resent being asked to score the tests and they show it in the way in which they do the scoring.

In a large-scale first-grade reading experiment, which was one of the 27 recipients of federal funds to take part in a cooperative, nationwide effort, all the tests were given that the central committee decided upon. The children were from twelve of the lowest achieving schools in New York City, located in Central Harlem, Bedford-Stuyvesant, and South Jamaica. The administration of ten separate pre-tests was a disastrous experience for both teachers and children. First of all, most of the tests were much too hard for the children, and over and over again they ran into frustration as they tried to do what they were asked to do. Secondly, the teachers were inexpert in administering tests. Thirdly, anyone who has tried to give standardized tests according to standardized instructions to little five- and six-year-olds who have never been in a classroom before, and have been subjected to little or no disciplinary training at home before they arrive in September, will appreciate some of the problems of administering reading readiness tests to non-kindergarten-trained children with this kind of background. By the time the testing program was over, the morale level was down close to zero. When the teachers were told, "Well, that's over; you can now begin to teach," you could almost hear a sigh of relief coming up from all of the schools and all the teachers, and morale gradually built up. A testing program can be deleterious to the morale of children and of teachers if it is too long, and particularly, if the tests chosen are so difficult that a large number of the children experience little but frustration in taking them.

Consider some other factors. What influence does the time of year have? Standardized tests are usually given at one of two times in the year—usually in the late spring around May, but sometimes early in the year, even during the first week.

When end-of-year testing is done, the purposes are usually of three types:

(1) to provide information on which decisions concerning pupil classification for the following year will be made: decisions about promotion, about grouping, and even sometimes, decisions related to what materials to order for next year's classes; (2) to compare class with class within the school, school with school within the district, district with district within the city, and the city as a whole with other comparable cities, or if it is a small community, with similar communities elsewhere; and (3) to draw some conclusions about the effectiveness of the teacher.

As was mentioned before, this last is a tricky business. What the children learn depends partly on what they have learned in previous years. As a matter of fact, the higher up in the grades the testing is done, the more the percentage of what they do seems to be based upon what they have brought to the class at the beginning of the year, and the less it seems to depend upon what this specific teacher has been able to do during the year. If one does not take into consideration where the children were at the beginning, the judging is not of just one teacher, but of the composite effects of all the teachers the children have had.

When an attempt is made to take into account where the children were at the beginning of the year, there are many technical complications. Not only what they have learned in the past, but also what seems to be their potential for learning in the future must be considered. I.Q. as well as previous reading level has a bearing on this. In judging the effectiveness of teachers, is it sensible to judge the beginning first-grade teacher on the same scale as the teacher who has been in that grade for fifteen years, or should allowances be made for the teacher's previous background and experience?

There are all sorts of complications here. It is not at all surprising that teachers as a total group have a deep, dark suspicion of any attempt to rate their effectiveness in teaching on the basis of achievement tests given to their children. Yet in any other occupation, the practitioner's effectiveness is judged by his results; the baseball or football player is being judged by thousands of people any time he does anything. The actor, actress, musician, dancer, and so on—all are subjected to merciless evaluation every time they appear in public. Lawyers are judged by whether they win or lose cases; doctors by whether they lose a high proportion of their patients.

It is a real, professional obligation to work out some way of evaluating teacher effectiveness. If the effective teacher cannot be distinguished from the ineffective, how can the general level of performance improve? . . . This problem must be solved, in spite of its many technical complications and its intimate relationship with teacher morale.

One of the possible effects of the year-end testing program is that the teacher feels that this is a way of spying on her. As a result, some teachers are motivated to resort to defensive behavior. "It is too late for me to make any use of these results in teaching the children I have now, so this test doesn't do me any good. Therefore, I'm not really interested in whether it's accurate or inaccurate." Some teachers learn in advance which form of which test is going to be given,

and teach the specific answers to specific items on the test, a very illegitimate procedure which ruins the test as a standardized test. Other teachers resort to somewhat lesser forms of sabotage such as forgetting to stop the children at the end of the time limit, or walking around the room and giving hints to children who seem puzzled. Finally, when such tests are corrected by the teacher of the children, it is surprising how few of their mistakes lower the score and how many of them raise the score. This could be a completely unconscious form of error, but nevertheless, one can understand the motivation for it.

What happens on the other hand, if instead of testing in May, the job is done in September or October? First of all, the teacher has the idea, "I didn't teach these children last year; therefore, the test can't possibly be used to evaluate what I did. They evaluate what some other teacher did with these children." She does not have the same feeling of being under scrutiny, or subjected to a form of spying. Second, she certainly ought to have the feeling, "I have almost a whole year ahead of me. If I can interpret these test results in a way that helps me improve my own planning of what to teach, what materials to use and how to use them, then the test is for my benefit more than it is for the benefit of the administration."

Now it happens that the administrator, if he is really intent upon evaluating someone, can attempt to draw some conclusions from these results about the effectiveness of last year's teacher, if he has kept the classes together as class units or if he is willing to go to the trouble of reconstructing last year's classes by collecting scores from a variety of new classes. Actually it is not often done, and when testing programs are carried out in the fall, the improvement of instruction is usually the primary and sometimes the only purpose. For this reason, fall testing programs seem definitely preferable to spring testing programs. They have far greater potential for benefiting the children and the teachers and impose far less of a threat upon anybody.

What are some of the effects of testing on learning? Pupils in general, and particularly bright pupils who are interested in getting good marks, do their best to learn what they expect to be tested on. One major difference between Phi Beta Kappa and ordinary college students is that the students who fairly consistently get A's spend a lot of time and effort trying to guess what the final examination questions are going to be. They set up lists of such possible questions and then prepare model answers for them which they then proceed to commit to memory. If they know the test is going to be an objective-type test with anywhere from one hundred to three hundred questions, they expect that a lot of these questions will be on the fine details that are contained in the footnotes in the textbook and in the charts and tables. So they pay extra attention to those. If, on the other hand, they know that the professor is addicted to using a small number of rather broad essay questions, they go over their recollection of everything he has talked about in his own lectures during the semester, trying to decide what he is most interested in and, therefore, what he is most likely to ask about. If the university keeps a file of previous exams, they will go over the exams of the past five years in that course and chart the relative probability of any one question's recurring. It is true at the college level. Very likely it is true also at the high school level and at the elementary school level.

In New York City high schools, the teachers know (at least at the junior and senior levels, or at the terminal levels in one-year courses like American History) that at the end of the course, the children are going to have to take a uniform state-wide examination. The result is that the last four to six weeks of the school year are spent reviewing the recent state-wide tests and making sure that every question that was asked in them has been thoroughly taken up and reviewed in class. This may or may not be effective in secondary school teaching. It happens to be true in practically every senior high school classroom in New York State, in every subject in which there is a state-wide test. If New York State can be used as a guinea pig, it can be predicted with confidence that as soon as the nature of the nationwide test is known, teachers will begin to teach for good performance on that test.

A second corollary is that teachers tend to neglect outcomes that are not going to be evaluated. This, it would appear, is even more serious and potentially far more deleterious. It does not mean that teachers will neglect everything that is not tested on standardized tests given once a year. However, unless the teacher has worked out ways of evaluating the outcomes that she considers significant in her own teaching, she is going to neglect some areas that should be important, or she is never going to find out how effective her work was in promoting those particular objectives. This is especially true in those areas that are relatively more difficult to evaluate —in the development of literary appreciation, in the development of high-level and broad-ranging reading interests, in the development of critical reading skills, etc. These areas, which are the hardest to evaluate, therefore tend over and over again to be neglected by the teacher who is very much concerned about how her children are going to do on the formal testing program.

Needed Developments in Testing

Recreational Reading

In the area of recreational reading there are only primitive measuring instruments, and there are many technicalities and problems in attempting to set up measuring instruments. For example, many teachers are utilizing one or another kind of individualized recreational reading program and they have all kinds of record keeping systems. Some of them are naive enough to be satisfied with the child's simply counting the number of books he has read, and they set certain arbitrary standards. Those who complete a certain number of books by such and such a date get their names on a special list or a gold star or some other mark of recognition. The inevitable result seems to be that those children who are reward-minded look for the thinnest books with the least amount of print per page and they go through them one a day. At the end of a month, they have perhaps twenty or more such books to their credit, but the total amount of actual reading might not be more than that of a child who, disregarding this reward system entirely, has plowed his way through two mature, demanding, and thick books. Simply counting the number of books read is not very effective.

The next level of operation is usually to check on the number of pages read in the book. Again it is a counting procedure. Perhaps in a remedial program where the teacher is working with small enough groups so she knows what books these are based on, and can move a child gradually to more and more mature books, this is a fully justified procedure. However, in a classroom where it is very difficult to keep track of the quality of the reading done by 20, 30, or more children, it is an incomplete way of evaluating recreational reading and needs to be supplemented by other ways of judging the quality and even the amount of reading done.

Whatever scheme is set up, there are some children who are going to find an illegitimate way to beat it. If, for example, the children's word is taken for whether they have read a book or not, without checking in some way on whether they show any signs of having read it, some children are going to be tempted to claim credit for books that they have not even opened. Other children are going to try to find out how much of the book they have to go through in order to be able to beat the teacher when she tries to check up on them. That leaves a limited number of alternatives. One is to cultivate, in the children, the belief that the teacher's evaluation is not nearly as important as what the pupil gains out of what he does. Therefore, a child who cheats the system is only fooling himself —he is not gaining from the program what will benefit him, cause him to become a better and more mature reader, or help him out in the future.

If this concept is developed, there need not be such great concern for trying to cross-check on the cheaters. However, if this attitude is not adopted by the children and the child who claims false credit is rewarded more than the child who reports honestly exactly what he did, more and more children get tempted to cheat. This is the result of an ineffective honor system at any level of school. What one rewards and what one does not reward has a tremendous effect upon the children's reaction to the reading program and specifically to recreational reading. Improper sets of rewards have worked havoc in many an otherwise well-designed recreational reading program.

Study Skills

In the area of study skills, the problem is usually the lack of any attempt to evaluate what children are learning, and, as a result, a relative neglect of the teaching of *how* to study as compared to teaching what to study. More effort should be devoted in the content areas to teaching children how to tackle the material they should master. This would eliminate the need to spend so much time drilling the learned outcomes. It would be more likely to generate self-reliant and self-motivated students who will go ahead to learn not just what they expect the teacher to check up on, but well beyond it. The main point is that the way in which the evaluation program is set up has far greater effects on what pupils learn and how they learn it than most teachers have recognized in the past. Because of its tremendous impact on what students learn, the program of evaluation deserves careful and prolonged thought and planning.

Test Selection

One recurring problem is that of choosing a reading test. Each of the publishers has a very persuasive salesman and very enticing publicity. How does one decide which test to use? On intelligence tests, aptitude tests and even reading readiness and achievement tests, the manual, published research, and reviews in the *Mental Measurement Yearbooks*—the sixth of which has been published—contain very helpful ideas about what tests are good for, and what research has discovered about them. Every school should have access to the *Mental Measurements Yearbook* when it comes to test selections. Since it very often happens that there are two or three reviews given and they do

not agree completely with one another, whoever is responsible for the final decision in test selection, whether it is an individual or committee, needs to have some personal sophistication in judging and evaluating tests. It is not a job for the typical classroom teacher. They are not trained for it and it is unfair to ask them to do this.

A number of things must be considered when looking over a standardized test. Are the skills being tested relevant to what has been taught? How good are the individual items used? Is the content such that it seems reasonably fair to the different groups of children who will be taking it? Can several adults agree perfectly as to what are the right answers?

The appropriateness of the scoring procedure needs to be studied. Particularly in the primary grades, a test that does not correct for guessing is open to the possibility that some children will go down the page marking items at random and then get a spurious score which is based mostly on sheer guesswork. In a four-choice multiple-choice item, the chances of tossing a set of dice and getting the answer right are one out of four. So, on a forty-item four-choice answer, a score of ten equals zero. And if in the table of norms it corresponds to a grade score of 2.0, there is something wrong with the test. Total nonreaders quite often score 2.0 or higher on widely used first- and second-grade reading tests.

The range of difficulty should, of course, be appropriate for all the children to be tested. This is met in tests with very easy items at one end and very hard items at the other, and many items of middle difficulty in between.

The norms should be looked over carefully and whatever impartial evidence is available about the norms should be looked up. In one study several nationally used achievement tests were utilized on the same group of children. Two of the three standardized tests agreed very well with each other in terms of the average level and also in terms of the scores of individual pupils, but the third came out with grade scores practically a whole grade higher than the other two.

Norms on new revisions may differ from those on previous editions. It appears that the new version of the *Pintner-Cunningham* gives children I.Q.'s roughly seven points lower than did the previous version. The new *Stanford Primary I* seems to give reading scores that run three to five months lower than the scores on the most recent previous *Stanford Primary I*. Unless such facts about tests are known, interpretation of their results cannot be correct. The test may reflect the fact that children around the country are doing better in reading than they did ten years ago. As a result, it takes more right answers to get an average score. That is what this change in norms means. Children are doing better on both intelligence tests and reading tests. As a result, one must take this into account in evaluating local results or make some fantastic errors of interpretation.

The reliability of standardized tests is usually high enough so that the slightly higher reliability of one test over another is of practically no significance. But on teacher-made tests, this is a most important problem. This is true in tests which employ book samples. Recently reading difficulty formulas were run on three to four samples of every selection in a new basal reader. The following ideas were evident in the result:

1. The first page of any new selection tends to be harder than any subsequent page in the selection. Sometimes it is two whole grades harder according to the formula, because several of the terms that are going to be used throughout the story appear on that first page;

2. While the sections of the book go up in steady order from the beginning of the book to the end of the book, there is considerable fluctuation among the selections in any one chapter. This is almost inevitable. If the author is trying to provide a variety of content, generally the fiction selections are easier than the factual ones.

Picking one hundred or two hundred word selections out of a book and then thinking a gauge of the pupils' ability to read the whole book has been attained is not realistic. On a few more samples the children will very likely fluctuate up and down, because the problem of the reliability of the single sample from a long book is a very serious one. If quite a large number of samples from the book are tried out on the same pupil, and a sample selected which gives the most representative results for the whole group of samples, it provides fairly safe ground. Picking just one sample and relying on that is likely to lead to quite a large number of misjudgments.

Ease and convenience of administration and scoring are, of course, very tempting bait. Wide use is now being made of a relatively new test-scoring machine called the IBM 1230. The 1230 is a machine that relies on photosensitive cells to read the answers. A pile of test answer sheets goes in at one end, and punched cards with the scores on them come out of the other end, all ready to put into the computer. No human hand has to have anything to do with the scoring, or counting the scores, or recording them. Movement is from pupil answer to answer sheet to machine to another machine to tables of results. Once in a while the machine goes haywire, but as compared to human capacity for errors it is comparatively error free.

The most effective way of scoring for large-scale testing programs is obviously to eliminate human error as much as possible. The speed of the whole process is also fantastic. The machine can score roughly 20 papers in the time it takes a human being to score one. Modern technology will be a tremendous assist in large-scale testing programs.

This technology is of little or no help to the individual teacher who gives a test to her own class and then wants to find out for herself what it means. Even here, however, tests in which the authors have taken the trouble to work out arrangements of item answers so that a cardboard sheet with holes in it can be put over the page and the right answers counted, are more trouble free than those that demand comparing one list of answers on a scoring key with the list of answers on the pupil's page.

In choosing among competitive tests, there are all kinds of things to consider. The choice should usually be up to people who have some knowledge and training in this field. Then the test should be tried out on your local population, and, if it does not seem to work well, a new one or a different one should be tried.

Diagnostic Testing

Another major problem in the area of evaluation of reading is the scarcity of diagnostic tests for group administration. For years, psychologists and remedial specialists have had reasonably satisfactory means of diagnosing the disabled reader in a clinical situation where there is one child at a time and relatively unlimited time in which to study him. The classroom teacher with thirty youngsters has a different set of problems when it comes to diagnosis. Because there have been no very effective tests for class diagnosis, very little class diagnosis is done except on a very informal teacher-impression basis, which in the hands of some teachers works excellently, but in the hands of many teachers, does not work at all.

The tests prevalent in the 20's and early 30's, were tests like the *Sangren-Woody* and the *Iowa Silent Reading Test*. These had from seven to ten parts. After interpreting the results for a reasonably large number of children and comparing the information about their classroom performance, very meaningful interpretations could be made of the children's silent reading performance from the pattern of high and low scores on these tests. Oh, yes, they had faults. The reliabilities of individual subtests were below 90. The tests were perhaps too heavily weighted with speed, and tended to handicap a child who was a slow but very careful reader. There were certain other problems. . . .

At the primary level, some of the big test batteries are beginning to incorporate tests of word attack skills, and this is a step in the right direction. But the tests give an overall score. To find which children failed on which item, one must pore over the blanks themselves, tally the results, and then remember what was established years ago—that unless there are at least three items to test one skill, the passes and failures are too much dependent upon chance and cannot be relied upon as really diagnostic.

There are practically no usable tests in certain areas in which outcomes of instructional programs should be evaluated. The area of critical reading is the one in which diagnostic testing is needed most urgently. If there is anything a democracy must develop in its schools, it is the ability to read critically and intelligently; to have criteria for judging when the printed material is reliable or is likely to be unreliable. If this is not done, both our children and our country are shortchanged. However, until there are good tests for measuring the outcomes, teachers are not going to know whether their efforts to teach critical reading skills are really working, except by their own relatively crude procedures, which are the best available at present. Test construction in this area is a top priority job.

A second area of need is that of literary appreciation. Test constructors tend to measure what is easiest to measure—level of comprehension—and easiest to sell. They have been dodging the difficult problems in test construction in the whole area of reading. In areas in which there is greatest need to develop more effective teaching techniques, there are no satisfactory evaluation instruments to judge results.

One area of evaluation in which many schools are still lagging far behind is in the measurement of the health factors that are related to success in the reading program. The archaic Snellen Chart test used to test vision is thirty years behind the times. Anyone who has read the research on what visual factors are related to success and failure in reading knows that the Snellen test does not pick them out. There are relatively quick screening tests that can be given to children at the rate of one every four minutes by teachers or school nurses. The lack of pressure on schools by reading specialists to install such vision testing programs is inexcusable.

One final point—in recent years there has been a tendency to neglect or ignore rate of reading as one of the factors that ought to be evaluated. As a result, in secondary schools in particular, where more ought to be done about rate of reading, it is often true that teachers do not even know which children are extremely slow readers. Therefore, nothing can be done to help them.

Conclusions

Those objectives of the reading program which are not evaluated tend to be neglected. Reading specialists and the curriculum specialists in each school system can make long lists of the specific reading objectives that teachers are supposed to be trying to implement. However, anything that is not evaluated does not improve.

22. Understanding Test Scores *

ALDEN W. BADAL AND EDWIN P. LARSEN

A. Three Key Questions in Interpreting Test Results

THERE are three key questions which should be kept in mind when studying the scores of a single student or the score

averages of a group of students (See Figure 1).

What skills are being measured or tested? For example, just what does a student need to know in order to get a high score on a certain reading test?

* From Alden W. Badal and Edwin P. Larsen, "On Reporting Test Results to Community Groups: Types of Test Scores," *NCME Measurement in Education,* 1, no. 4 (May, 1970), 3–6. Reprinted by permission of the authors and the National Council on Measurement in Education.

With whom are pupils being compared? All test scores are basically a comparison of a pupil's performance with some other pupils'—usually a group of the same age. It is important to keep in mind who these "other" pupils are.

What type of score is being used? Pupils may be compared using a number of different types of scores. What do grade equivalents and percentile scores mean?

1. What skills are measured?

—Reading

—Arithmetic

—Language skills

—Spelling

—Scholastic aptitude (intelligence)

2. With whom are pupils being compared?

—Typical pupils across the nation (national norms)

—Pupils throughout the state (state norms)

—Pupils throughout the city (local norms)

3. What type of score is being used?

—Grade placements

—Percentile ranks

FIGURE 1.—Understanding test scores.

In helping parents understand test scores, as much time may be spent in attempting to develop background concepts as in talking about the actual test score statistics.

B. Types of Tests Given in the Schools.

There are two main types of tests which are given to children in the elementary schools:

Achievement tests. These tests are made up of questions on types of materials and understandings which are commonly taught in the schools throughout the country. For example, in a reading test children are asked to read short paragraphs similar to those found in textbooks and to answer questions to show how well they have understood what has been read. Arithmetic or mathematics tests contain addition, subtraction, multiplication, and division problems. Also, they often contain questions to show how well students can solve word problems. A writing test usually asks pupils to determine whether or not a sentence has proper punctuation, capital letters, and spelling. Pupils are also asked to select sentences which express an idea most clearly.

Scholastic aptitude tests. This is the second type of test most often administered in the schools. These tests are sometimes loosely referred to as intelligence or "IQ" tests. The test makers themselves prefer to consider these tests as measuring school abilities. Tests of this type are intended to give an estimate of the level of achievement test performance which may be "expected" of a given pupil or group of pupils. These scholastic aptitude tests attempt to measure a student's background of understandings which are learned from both in-school and out-of-school experiences. Scholastic aptitude tests are more general in nature than achievement tests, but they must not be considered to measure innate or un-changing aspects of "intelligence." They merely give a reasonable estimate of the background or tool skills of a pupil at the present time and, therefore, how well we may expect him to perform in read-ing, reason with numbers, and use the English language in written work. . . .

C. Test Norms or Comparison Groups.

The most common types of standard-ized test scores are those which compare a pupil's performance with a "national norms group." The publisher of a test carefully selects a sample of children from all parts of the nation in order to estimate what is the average or normal level of performance of children at a given grade level. This procedure is much like that used by opinion polls. The in-formation obtained from this sample be-comes the publisher's "national norms," and we can determine how a child or group of children compares to this norm. Since these norms are based on only a sample of children, it is occasionally found that these norms are not com-pletely accurate. They may be "too easy" or "too hard."

In California at certain grade levels a pupil's scores can also be compared to other children in the same grade through-out the state. The state score patterns and averages based on testing all children in the state at selected grade levels are used as "state norms," to tell, for example, how a sixth-grader ranks in reading abil-ity in comparison to other sixth graders throughout the state.

The score averages of the city provide yet another comparison in evaluating local school results. The question here is, "How well does a pupil or school rank within the city?"

One can see that it is important to keep in mind the group with which pupils are being compared.

D. Types of Scores

We have discussed the skills which the tests measure and the group with whom pupils are being compared. The next question is what type of score is used to make these comparisons. There are two types of scores which we will use in our discussion.

Grade equivalent scores. Grade equiv-alents, sometimes called grade placement or just grade scores, are often used be-cause the number of correct answers on a test has little meaning in itself. Publish-ers administer the test to children in dif-ferent grade levels during a given school month. The average of a grade level is assigned a grade equivalent value such as 1.9, 2.9, 3.9 (See Figure 2). With these grade equivalent values determined, the test authors then estimate the in-be-tween values. We can, therefore, compare

Number Correct	Grade Equivalent	Interpretation
20	4.3	Score earned by "av-erage" 3rd grader in ninth month of grade 3.
19	4.1	
18	3.9	
17	3.7	
16	3.5	
15	3.3	Score earned by "aver-age" 2nd grader in ninth month of grade 2.
14	3.1	
13	2.9	
12	2.7	
11	2.5	
10	2.3	Score earned by "aver-age" 1st grader in ninth month of grade 1.
9	2.1	
8	1.9	
7	1.8	
6	1.7	
5	1.6	
4	1.5	
3	1.4	
2	1.3	
1	1.2	
0	1.1	

FIGURE 2.—Interpretation of grade equiva-lent scores.

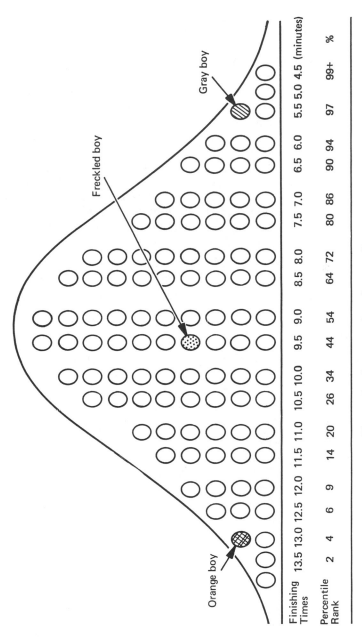

FIGURE 3.—Interpretation of percentile scores

a pupil's raw score with other children. One will note scores such as 1.3, 5.6, and so on. In Figure 2 "1.3" refers to the score earned by an "average" first grader at the 3rd month of the school year; and "5.6" means a score level which is typical at the 6th month of grade five.

Percentiles. Percentiles are a type of test score which is also useful in comparing the test performance of children. A percentile is not the same as percent correct which is often seen on such teacher-made tests as spelling or arithmetic. A percentile is a pupil's rank within a theoretical group of 100 pupils who represent the patterns of ability or skill across the country, school district, or other normative group.

Students differ widely in their abilities and performance. If we were to select a hundred "typical" youngsters from all parts of the nation and ask them to run a one-mile race, we would soon find differences in running skills. Figure 3 indicates the possible results of that race. Let us say, for example, that almost all children run more rapidly than the "orange" boy. The "freckled" boy is fairly average; about half of the children are ahead and half are behind. And very few are as fast as the "gray" boy. We can rank these children using the percentile system.

In Figure 3 the orange boy ranks at the 4th percentile—4 out of 100 run as fast or more slowly than this boy; 96 out of 100 are faster. The freckled boy

Number Correct	Number of Students		
20	/		
19	//		
18	/		
17	///		
16	//		
15	~~////~~ /		
14	~~////~~		
13	~~////~~ ///	Q_3	¾ or 75% at or below a score of 13.
12	~~////~~ ~~////~~ //		
11	~~////~~ ~~////~~ /	Mdn	½ or 50% at or below a score of 11.
10	~~////~~ ///		
9	~~////~~ ~~////~~		
8	~~////~~	Q_1	¼ or 25% at or below a score of 8.
7	~~////~~ //		
6	~~////~~		
5	///		
4	///		
3	/		
2	//		
1			
0	/		
Total Students	96		

FIGURE 4.—Distribution of reading test scores for School "X."

falls in the middle area where most children fall with his percentile rank of 44. This means that 44 out of every one hundred pupils run as fast or slower; 56% run faster. Finally, the gray boy receives a score at the 97th percentile, meaning that 97 out of one hundred run this fast or slower; only 3 out of one hundred run more rapidly. This same ranking system is used to describe scholastic ability and achievement test scores. Percentiles tell how many children out of every one hundred in the state or nation score at or below a certain score level. By subtracting a percentile value from 100, the number scoring higher can be determined.

The 50th percentile is considered to be right "on the grade level" or right at the average of the norm group. Pupils may vary somewhat either above or below this value and still be considered within the "average range." In general the percentile range of 25 through 75 is considered to be the average range so that pupils who are a few points above or below the 50th percentile are considered to be essentially average. Students above and below the 25 to 75 range are clearly above or below average.

E. Summary Statistics

When tests are administered to groups of pupils, there will be quite a range of scores—some pupils may get nearly all questions correct; others, very few correct. The distribution of scores on a reading test shown in Figure 4 will illustrate this fact. In order to summarize this array of scores, median and quartile statistics are used.

- Q_1 indicates the score at or below which ¼ or 25% of the pupils fell. Three-fourths of the pupils scored higher.
- The median indicates the middle point in the score range. One-half of the students are above and one-half are below this point. This is important to keep in mind. A median obviously does not reflect the scores of all children—many pupils are somewhat higher; many are somewhat lower.
- Q_3 indicates the score at or below which ¾ or 75% of the children have scored. One-fourth have scored higher.

If the size of a school is fairly small— 50 or fewer pupils—caution must be used in interpreting medians and quartiles. A change in the score of one pupil may cause the average to change several points. . . .

23. The Graded Word List:
Quick Gauge of Reading Ability *

MARGARET LA PRAY AND RAMON ROSS

THE San Diego Quick Assessment is a quick way to gauge a student's reading ability. It is a graded word list, formed by drawing words randomly from basal reader glossaries, and from the Thorndike list. Words initially were assigned

*From Margaret LaPray and Ramon Ross, "The Graded Word List: Quick Gauge of Reading Ability," *Journal of Reading,* 12 (January, 1969), 305–7. Reprinted by permission of the International Reading Association and the authors.

levels according to these sources, with some shifting on the basis of students' responses.

The graded word list has two uses: (1) to determine a reading level; (2) to detect errors in word analysis. One can use the test information to group students for corrective practice or to select appropriate reading materials for those students.

The list is remarkably accurate when used for these purposes. During the last two years we have had students in our undergraduate reading classes give this test to children in our campus laboratory school. Following testing, we asked them to recommend appropriate reading levels for these children. In all but four cases out of more than one hundred, their recommendations coincided with those of the classroom teachers who had been working with these children for a large portion of the year.

The list, like other instruments, is not appropriate for all students. Among high school and adult groups, we find it most effective for those who have poor decoding skills. Junior high students need not be so disabled for this to be an effective instrument.

Administration

1. Type out each list of ten words on an index card.
2. Begin with a card that is at least two years below the student's grade-level assignment.
3. Ask the student to read the words aloud to you. If he misreads any on the list, drop to easier lists until he makes no errors. This indicates the base level.
4. Write down all incorrect responses, or use diacritical marks on your copy of the test. For example, *lonely* might be read and recorded as *lovely*. *Apparatus* might be recorded as *a per' a tus*.
5. Encourage the student to read words he does not know so that you can identify

the techniques he uses for word identification.
6. Have the student read from increasingly difficult lists until he misses at least three words.

PP	Primer	1
see	you	road
play	come	live
me	not	thank
at	with	when
run	jump	bigger
go	help	how
and	is	always
look	work	night
can	are	spring
here	this	today

2	3	4
our	city	decided
please	middle	served
myself	moment	amazed
town	frightened	silent
early	exclaimed	wrecked
send	several	improved
wide	lonely	certainly
believe	drew	entered
quietly	since	realized
carefully	straight	interrupted

5	6	7
scanty	bridge	amber
certainly	commercial	dominion
develop	abolish	sundry
considered	trucker	capillary
discussed	apparatus	impetuous
behaved	elementary	blight
splendid	comment	wrest
acquainted	necessity	enumerate
escaped	gallery	daunted
grim	relativity	condescend

8	9	10
capacious	conscientious	zany
limitation	isolation	jerkin
pretext	molecule	nausea
intrigue	ritual	gratuitous
delusion	momentous	linear
immaculate	vulnerable	inept
ascent	kinship	legality
acrid	conservatism	aspen
binocular	jaunty	amnesty
embankment	inventive	barometer

11
galore
rotunda
capitalism
prevaricate
risible
exonerate
superannuate
luxuriate
piebald
crunch

Analysis

1. The list in which a student misses no more than one of the ten words is the

Error	*Example*
reversal	*ton* for *not*
consonant	*now* for *how*
consonant clusters	*state* for *straight*
short vowel	*cane* for *can*
long vowel	*wid* for *wide*
prefix	*inproved* for *improved*
suffix	*improve* for *improved*
miscellaneous	(accent, omission of syllables, etc.)

level at which he can read independently. Two errors indicate his instructional level. Three or more errors identify the level at which reading material will be too difficult for him.

2. An analysis of a student's errors is useful. Among those which occur with greatest frequency are the examples below:

3. As with other reading tasks, teacher observation of student behavior is essential. Such things as posture, facial expression, and voice quality may signal restlessness, lack of assurance, or frustration while reading.[1]

24. Informal Inventories *

EMMETT ALBERT BETTS

SYSTEMATIC guidance in reading is, first of all, differentiated guidance. One of the first steps in systematic guidance is to estimate levels of the individual learners in the class. Until this is done, discussions of word analysis, semantic analysis, critical reading, concept development, group dynamics, and bibliotherapy deteriorate to the patter of faddists.

* From Emmett Albert Betts, "Informal Inventories," in *Handbook on Corrective Reading for the American Adventure Series* (New York: Harper & Row, 1952), pp. 3–8. Reprinted by permission of the author and Harper & Row, Publishers, Inc.

Basic Information

To put reading instruction on a systematic basis, two questions must be answered. First, what is the highest level at which the child can read "on his own"? This is usually called the *independent* reading level. Second, what is the highest level at which the child can read under

[1] Since the Graded Word List procedure does not attempt to measure either knowledge of word meanings or comprehension of connected material, it may overestimate the reading levels of children who have special weaknesses in comprehension. (Eds.)

teacher supervision? This is usually called the *instructional* reading level.

Merits

An informal reading inventory has several merits. First, the teacher is given direct evidence on achievement and needs in terms of available instructional material. Second, the teacher is provided with a technique for detecting everyday needs in the classroom. Third, the child is convinced of his needs and sees how to improve his skill. The procedure is sound, understandable, and practicable.

To promote general language competence, the teacher guides her pupils in terms of their reading levels. Wholesome attitudes toward reading are fostered.

Achievement Levels

Basal Level

With the exception of nonreaders, a learner usually can read material at some level of readability without *symptoms* of frustration, such as lip movement, finger pointing, word-by-word reading, tension movements, high-pitched voice, reversal errors, lack of attention to punctuation, and low comprehension. At this level he can pronounce all of the words without hesitation.

The highest readability level at which the individual can read without symptoms of frustration is the basal level. Often this is also the independent reading level. As succeeding levels of reading ability are attempted, two things happen. First, the number of symptoms increases. Second, each symptom becomes intensified.

Independent Level

The independent reading level is the highest level at which the learner can read with full understanding and freedom

from frustration. The reading is done without tension movements, lip movement, finger pointing, and other evidences of difficulty. Silent reading is characterized by a relatively fast rate of comprehension and absence of vocalization. Oral re-reading is characterized by rhythm, accurate interpretation of punctuation, accurate pronunciation of more than 99 percent of the words, and a conversational tone. At the independent level, the reading is fluent. The learner practices good reading habits.

Instructional Level

The instructional level is the highest level at which the learner can read satisfactorily under teacher supervision in a group situation. For normal progress, this reading has the same characteristics as independent reading, with one exception. The child may require help on the recognition of words, but never more than 5 percent. If he must have help on more than one word in twenty, his comprehension bogs down. He becomes frustrated.

At a level just above the independent reading level, word recognition and/or comprehension needs may appear. If this is the only problem, the instructional level may be at this point.

Frustration Level

Above the instructional level, symptoms of frustration usually increase rapidly. For example, at the next higher level, the rhythm of oral reading may tend to break and silent lip movement may be evidenced. At succeeding levels, there may be finger pointing, tension movements, a high-pitched voice, and other symptoms of frustration. This tendency to lip movement deteriorates to whispering and then to mumbling over unknown words.

Materials for Inventory

The materials used for an informal inventory are those found in a classroom equipped to meet the wide range of reading levels therein. They may be graded textbooks, graded current events materials, or other instructional materials graded in reading difficulty.

In order to guide reading development systematically, the teacher needs to have two types of information: (1) the reading achievement levels of each individual in the class, (2) the relative reading difficulty (readability) of each book used. THE AMERICAN ADVENTURE SERIES is graded in readability. Hence, the teacher who uses this series needs only to determine the starting level book for her group.

For an individual inventory, a series of graded materials is used. Short selections are read, beginning at a low level of readability and continuing until the individual's independent reading level is identified. Symptoms of difficulty are used as indicators of lack of achievement. . . .

Procedure for Inventory

The informal inventory is one of the most direct and effective means of appraising reading levels and needs. By using a graded series of reading materials, the teacher or clinician may observe responses in a reading situation. It is possible to estimate reading achievement levels in a well-motivated situation. In addition, specific needs may be evaluated in terms of related needs and background skills.

An informal inventory is easily administered. It is simply the observation of an individual as he reads at successively higher levels of readability. He starts at a low level, which causes no difficulty, and continues until the desired information on reading achievement is obtained.

An informal reading inventory situation may embrace an individual or a group. In a class of twenty to thirty-five pupils, there may be two or three who should be studied individually. However, the chief advantage of this no-cost inventory is that the teacher is provided with a technique for estimating reading levels and needs in *all* reading activities everyday. It is as valuable in a group situation as in an individual situation.

Group Inventories

Reading achievement may be assessed in two types of group situations. First, during each directed reading activity, the teacher notes both reading levels and needs. For some of the pupils, the material may be too difficult; for others, the material may be too easy. Since the teacher's obligation is to challenge all learners in a class, she uses some system of grouping.

Second, a group inventory may be administered in the same way as an individual inventory. The teacher explains to the group the purpose of the inventory and interests the pupils in finding out about themselves. She also encourages the group to note the differences in reading difficulty of the materials used for the inventory. Then each individual is given an opportunity to read in a motivated situation. This is continued with increasingly higher level materials until some members show signs of frustration.

In general, the first procedure is more satisfactory. Since modern schools use a cumulative guidance folder for each learner, the teacher usually has the benefit of the previous teacher's observations. The data is used to form tentative groups. Reassignment to groups is based on observations during directed reading activities, supplemented by an occasional individual inventory.

Individual Inventories

In some instances there is a need for learning more about the reading level and needs of an individual than can be learned from a group inventory. About 10 percent of the learners in a regular classroom may profit from an individual inventory. In a corrective group, even more of the learners need to be studied in this manner. Since only five to fifteen minutes are required for each inventory, the time is well spent.

Establishing Rapport

One of the chief values of an informal inventory is the understanding it gives the learner regarding his own needs. He proves to himself that he *can read* at some level. He develops self-confidence and interest.

A few minutes used for explaining the purpose and procedure of an informal inventory are well spent. How well one reads depends considerably upon the emotional climate of the situation. An understanding of what is expected is essential to rapport between the teacher and the learner.

General Procedure

At each readability level, three steps are taken:

1. Oral reading at sight of a page or less.
2. Silent reading of a succeeding section of the material.
3. Oral re-reading of the material read silently.

Evaluating Comprehension

Following each of the first two steps, the examiner tests the reader's comprehension. For step 3, the examiner requests the individual to read orally the parts that answer specific questions.

Different types of questions are asked in order to evaluate the reader's ability to:

1. Recall facts.
2. Associate an appropriate meaning with a term.
3. Identify a sequence of events.
4. Draw conclusions.
5. Apply information.

Estimating Starting Level

In order to give the learner a running start, begin with a very easy book, e.g., *Friday—the Arapaho Indian.* Usually, this starting level can be estimated from a word recognition test and general observation.

Oral Reading At Sight

This procedure is never used in a directed reading activity. However, it has many merits in a testing situation.

The learner is told that he is to begin reading aloud and that he will be asked questions about what he has read. He is then given a quick preview of the selection and some general questions to answer.

During the oral reading, the examiner notes hesitations, speed, rhythm, word pronunciation errors, interpretation of punctuation, and tension movements. Oral reading at sight induces difficulties. It brings to light pronunciation and comprehension needs.

Silent Reading

This is standard procedure in a directed reading activity. Generally speaking, the first reading of a selection is always done silently.

After the findings on the oral reading at sight are recorded, the examiner asks the learner to continue with silent reading. One selection is read orally at sight; a succeeding selection is read silently. This silent reading is guided by sequential questions about the short selection. The learner reads silently until he finds the correct answer. He either gives the answer in his own words or re-reads orally the correct answer, depending upon what the examiner wishes to observe.

During the silent reading, the examiner notes speed, lip movement, tension movements, head movement, and other evidences of confusion or frustration. A record is kept of unknown words, comprehension scores, and other relevant information.

Oral Re-reading

At and below the instructional level, the oral re-reading usually is much more fluent than oral reading at sight. At the independent reading level, the oral re-reading is done without hesitation and without symptoms of need for additional help.

There are at least two ways to approach oral re-reading. First, it may be done as a check on answers to silent reading questions. The learner merely reads answers to questions he locates by reading silently.

Second, the oral reading may be done following the completion of the silent reading activities. The learner may read orally the answers to different types of questions. Or he may re-read orally the whole selection for some specific purpose.

25. Using an Informal Reading Inventory to Affect Instruction *

ROBERT A. MC CRACKEN

IN one third grade in a traditional school, basal reading was the adopted program. It was September. Mrs. Smith was the teacher. She had taught fifteen years but she was new to teaching third grade. She asked the reading consultant

* From Robert A. McCracken, "The Informal Reading Inventory as a Means of Improving Instruction," in Thomas C. Barrett (ed.), *The Evaluation of Children's Reading Achievement*, Perspectives in Reading, No. 8 (Newark, Del.: International Reading Association, 1967), pp. 90–95. Reprinted by permission of the International Reading Association and the author.

for help because the children in her reading groups were not responding well. She had inherited three reading groups from the second grade and had shifted one child.

Her top group had six children reading from a 3–2 level basal reader and doing the accompanying workbook exercises. The children were a joy but always finished their reading seat-work before the teacher had another activity ready. Her middle group had fourteen children reading from a 3–1 level and doing a good job. Her bottom group had eight children trying to read from a 3–1 level basal reader. They could not work independently even after instruction. They had trouble with silent reading, needed constant help when reading orally around the circle, and rarely got better than 50 percent the first time they did their workbook exercises. The teacher was using the same techniques with each group, techniques which seemed to work only with the middle group.

The reading consultant administered an informal reading inventory. The reason for Mrs. Smith's difficulties was apparent from the results. All six pupils in the top group were independent at level 3–2. All fourteen pupils in the middle group needed instruction at third reader level. All eight pupils in the bottom group were frustrated with 3–1 level material. Mrs. Smith and the second-grade teacher had recognized individual differences, knew how to conduct informal testing without realizing it, but did not know how to record or evaluate the results.

Mrs. Smith saw the implications, but she was worried. The children would not like to be treated differently. The low group would be embarrassed by an easy book. They had read the 2–2 book last year!

The reading consultant made a chart, reproduced in Table 1. Each child took off his shoe and read his shoe size.

Each child was asked, "Why do you wear that particular shoe size?"

Pupils answered consistently, "Because it fits."

"Why don't you wear a bigger shoe? Don't you want your foot to grow faster?"

"That's crazy," a pupil said. "If my shoe didn't fit, it would hurt my foot or fall off when I run."

The reading consultant and the children talked about shoe sizes and the sequence of numerals indicating sizes. They talked about the impossibility of feet growing to be size 6 without having first been size 5 or size 4. They agreed that feet grow gradually from size 1 to 2, from 2 to 3 to 4, etc., not suddenly. They talked about book size and developed the concept that the numerals on basal readers are sizes, not grade level. They

TABLE 1

Shoe Size of 28 Third Grade Children in September

Size		Number of Pupils
7 - 8		1
5 - 6		5
4		4
3		5
2		6
1		6
12		1

developed the concept that children learn to read book 2 after mastering book 1, book 3 after mastering book 2, etc.

The reading consultant made another chart, reproduced in Table 2. He told the children that he had measured their book sizes just as a shoe salesman might measure their foot sizes. He asked the pupils what their book sizes meant. From the top group came responses such as, "I need a harder book. Our reader is too easy. I've got a big book size." From the bottom group came responses such as, "I knew that book was too hard. I need an easy book. No wonder reading is hard."

Mrs. Smith told the children that many of them were going to shift into different books for reading instruction, that they would work in these books for one week, and that she would then ask them if their books fit. She explained that after the shoe salesman fits the shoe to your foot, he asks you to walk around a bit to see how it feels. After a week's instruction Mrs. Smith was going to ask, "How does your book fit?"

For a week the top group worked in book 4 and was assigned to choose library books for independent reading. The middle group continued reading from 3–1 level. The bottom group worked from a reader bridging 1–2 and 2–1 levels. The methods of instruction shifted slightly during this first week primarily because the children in the bottom group did not need constant attention.

At the end of the week one boy asked to change. He was the poorest reader in the middle group. He wanted to work in the bottom group. Two of the top group children said that book 4 was "Awful easy, but better than 3–2."

Some things stand out in this story:

1. *Children recognize and accept individual differences.* Teachers project adult fears when thinking that children are embarrassed by our recognizing that they are *poor* readers. The use of the word *poor* reflects this attitude. No one speaks of a

TABLE 2

Book Size of 28 Third Grade Children in September

Book Size		Number of Pupils
6 and above	📖📖	2
5	📖📖	2
4	📖📖	2
3^2	📖📖📖📖📖📖	6
3^1	📖📖📖📖📖📖📖📖	8
2	📖📖📖📖📖	5
1	📖📖📖	3

poor shoe size. Children frequently are relieved when the teacher recognizes their difficulties. In the same way, adults are relieved when a doctor says, "You have *mal-and-sicitis*. It will take awhile but we can cure it." Compare reactions to this statement and to one in which the doctor says, "I don't think there is anything wrong with you. Just try a little harder to think that you're well."

2. *Children can understand the need for grouping and individual attention.* They accept book size as a concept, and they accept instruction whenever they can succeed. *Poor* readers do not object to *easy, baby* reading books if they are successful in them. *Poor* readers don't want to fail in *easy* materials. If they are going to fail, they want to fail something respectable. Failure at grade level is respectable. It is this reaction to failure in *easy* books which has led teachers to conclude that pupils reject *easy* materials.

3. *A low reading group can work independently much of the time.* The material has to be at their instructional level.

Mrs. Smith had a worry. Won't the children in group one miss the skill program? Obviously not. The children already had mastery of the skill program. Mrs. Smith had another worry. Won't the low reading group be retarded by the lack of challenge? One can infer the answer by observing the top group. The top group came to third grade with mastery of the third-grade reading program without ever having been taught from a reader harder than 2–2. Perhaps these children would have been more advanced had they had instruction at higher levels. But one cannot, on the basis of observations of top reading groups, conclude that *challenging* children makes them successful. Our most successful groups are those which have never been challenged much by reading group work. Working at an easy level with high success seems more important than challenge.

This story does not end with three groups in basal readers. The top group expanded into individualized reading without the teacher's being aware of it. Much of the reading instruction shifted to social studies and science. The success of the top group in self-selection led to the middle and bottom groups' having the same privilege. The classroom library was greatly expanded with plenty of easy picture books.

The informal testing led to a closer analysis of individual needs. Mrs. Smith assumed responsibility for continuous diagnostic observation. When a child had difficulty at instructional level, Mrs. Smith could see the difficulty because it was not shrouded with the maze of troubles which abound at frustration level. The able readers moved into projects which occasionally frustrated them, but more often just highlighted instructional needs; inefficient study skills and inefficient, ineffective note-taking stood out.

Mrs. Smith developed a sensitivity to standards of performance so that her instruction took its cue from pupils' performances, not from grade-level expectancies. The stumbling of the poor reader group no longer sounded right because that was the way the poor reading groups always sounded. The fluency of the top reading group no longer sounded right when it reflected complete independence with the material. Both Mrs. Smith and the pupils were affected by the use of the informal reading inventory, and so was the teacher of grade four the following year when the pupils did not want to be in the same book and told the teacher why. But that is another story.

The description of another class, a fifth grade with 37 pupils, follows. Mr. Baron wanted to improve his social studies teaching. He had 40 copies of one text, as mandated by the district curriculum. He was doing the best job he could, but found that discipline sometimes was a problem. When discipline was not a problem, the children were apathetic and he had trouble covering the work. Mr. Baron knew about informal testing, although he had never really used it much. With 37 pupils he said he didn't have time to test each child. He already had the grades for the first six weeks of work in social studies: 5 A's, 11 B's, 15 C's, 4 D's, and 2 F's. Mr. Baron said they had tried projects and grouping but it didn't work. He had reverted to reading the text around the room. "At least I know that they have covered the material that way," he said.

Mr. Baron sounds like a teacher you and I don't want in our school. But he is not a poor teacher. He is frustrated. This is the classic syndrome of frustration in reading; the child and the teacher are equally frustrated.

The reading consultant visited Mr. Baron's social studies class for one day and listened to the reading circle. He noted the names of the pupils who were obviously frustrated, those who found the material to be at their independent level, and those who read with instructional competence. The consultant compared his results with Mr. Baron's grades. Much to Mr. Baron's surprise the reading consultant had identified the D and F pupils as frustrated and identified the A students as independent. The reading consultant had rated five others very close to frustration. Mr. Baron admitted that they were really D pupils but he had too many already. Mr. Baron had done his informal testing, although he did not realize it. But what to do?

Space does not permit describing the intervening steps. They are apparent from the results. The informal reading inventory, however, was discussed in a manner similar to that in Mrs. Smith's class.

Two months later Mr. Baron still had 40 basic social studies texts. Mr. Baron worked with his whole class to set purpose. He then read this basic text quickly, precisely, with added but not overwhelming explanation to those students who wanted to listen while 22 other pupils worked with 46 other books and two sets of encyclopedias. Most of the 46 other books were social studies texts. There were only single copies of 35 of them. Each book had been numbered to tell the book size. Each of the 22 children used the index or table of contents, working out page references which augmented the content of the *basic text*.

Two days later the pupils were all reading. The former F students were looking at pictures and reading captions and were reading some of the material from a social studies book labeled with a numeral one. Some A pupils were working in an adult encyclopedia, some with junior and senior high texts, and one pupil was tackling a college text. The pupils were fitting themselves to book levels. Study guides were developed jointly with Mr. Baron from the basic text material. For two days to two weeks pupils read, discussed in groups, collated and wrote, and finally summarized and tested.

Again some things stand out:

1. Pupils willingly accept individual differences and individual treatment.
2. A teacher was unaware that he had even given an I.R.I. and he was therefore unaware of the implications.
3. Poor readers can read independently in content areas.

One problem developed in both of these classes. The pupils soon asked, "Why do we all have the same spelling list? Why are we all at the same place in our arithmetic book?" But these are the problems which teachers know how to solve.

26. Informal Reading Inventories *

JOSEPH P. KENDER

BOTH informal reading inventories and standardized reading tests have a place in providing effective instruction for children, but when a teacher wants to know which book best fits a child, informal measures offer the better solution. Studies by Rosner (1963), Sipay (1963), and Davis (1964), among others, show that standardized tests of reading are not accurate in placing children in materials for instruction.

Criteria Studies

One of the earliest references to informal reading inventories was made by Durrell (1940); however, the most comprehensive discussion of the subject was presented by Betts (1946). His criteria of 95 percent word recognition and 75 percent comprehension are almost universally regarded as acceptable standards for reading at what is commonly called the "instructional level."

It is interesting to note that the familiar 95 percent criterion is the result of a study by Killgallon (1942) in which he examined forty-one fourth graders on an informal reading inventory. He set up *a priori* criteria for the establishment of instructional level, tested his subjects, and found that the most suitable percentage of accuracy for acceptable pronunciation of words was 95 percent.

* From Joseph P. Kender, "Informal Reading Inventories," *Reading Teacher,* 24 (November, 1970), 165, 167. Reprinted by permission of the International Reading Association and the author.

The much quoted 75 percent comprehension criterion has even less experimental validity. Bormuth (1969) reports that it can be attributed to E. L. Thorndike who obtained it from classroom teachers. The ultimate source of the criterion seems to be oral tradition.

Cooper (1952), too, attempted to establish suitable criteria for scoring informal reading inventories. Having hypothesized that there is a direct relationship between the ratio of word perception error and gains in reading, he tested 1000 elementary children and found that those who made the fewest number of word perception errors made the greatest gains in reading. He analyzed the performance of the children and established scoring criteria. Despite his more scientific approach to the problem, his criteria have been virtually ignored.

Other investigations have examined criteria for evaluating the performance of children on informal reading inventories. For example, Daniel (1962) and Kender (1966) studied the effectiveness of applying varying criteria and procedures for placing pupils in books for instruction. A most recent study by Packman (1970) analyzed some commonly used criteria for evaluating the reading ability of some thirty fourth graders whom she placed into six groups on their ability to comprehend written material. She reported that certain criteria such as word recognition scores, rate of oral reading, and quality of intonation were beneficial in appropriately placing children in reading material while other criteria such as rate of silent reading, vocalizing, head movement, and finger pointing had little value.

Validation Studies

McCracken (1964) and Botel (1969) conducted research in order to validate their own respective tests. Using standards prescribed by Betts, McCracken based the validity of his test, *The Standard Reading Inventory,* on the vocabulary of three basal readers and tested the validity of his passages by using well-known readability formulas. He further corroborated the results by administering the test to 664 pupils in grades one through six and using the ratings of twenty-five reading authorities.

Botel proposed a design for determining the validity of informal reading inventories by cross validating reading tests and readability measures through the use of correlational and matching procedures. The correlations among all the tests and readability measures were unusually high. The matchings indicated the lack of any perfect combination of tests and readability estimates. Despite this fact, the matches between certain tests—among them the *Botel Reading Inventory*—and certain readability estimates were superior to the matches between other combinations.

Summary

Informal reading inventories have been established as useful instruments for evaluating the reading of children. In many instances, however, criteria for using these instruments are more pragmatic than scientific. More research is needed especially in defining more precisely acceptable levels for oral reading fluency and comprehension. Despite these shortcomings informal reading inventories are among the best tools of evaluation we have.

References

1. BETTS, E. A. *Foundations of Reading Instruction.* New York: American Book, 1946.
2. BORMUTH, J. R. *Development of Readability Analysis.* (Report of Project No. 7-0052) Washington, D.C.: United States Department of Health, Education, and Welfare, 1969.
3. BOTEL, M. "The Validity of Informal Reading Testing." Paper read at the Fourteenth Annual Convention, International Reading Association, Kansas City, May, 1969.
4. COOPER, J. L. "The Effect of Adjustment of Basal Reading Achievement." Unpublished Doctoral Dissertation. Boston University, 1952.
5. DANIEL, J. E. "The Effectiveness of Various Procedures in Reading Level Placement," *Elementary English, 39* (1962), 590–600.
6. DAVIS, SR. M. C., RSM. "The Relative Effectiveness of Certain Evaluative Criteria for Determining Reading Levels." Unpublished Doctoral Dissertation. Temple University, 1964.
7. DURRELL, D. D. *Improvement of Basic Reading Abilities.* New York: World Book, 1940.
8. KENDER, J. P. "An Analysis of Factors Associated with Informal Reading Tests at the Eighth-Grade Level." Unpublished Doctoral Dissertation. University of Pennsylvania, 1966.

9. KILLGALLON, P. A. "A Study of Relationships among Certain Pupil Adjustments in Language Situations." Unpublished Doctoral Dissertation. Pennsylvania State College, 1942.

10. McCRACKEN, R. A. "The Development and Validation of the *Standard Reading Inventory* for the Appraisal of Reading Performance from Grades One Through Six. Improvement of Reading Through Classroom Practice." *Proceedings of The International Reading Association Annual Convention, 9* (1964), 310–13.

11. PACKMAN, L. A. "Relationships Between Selected Measures of Behavior and Levels of Reading Comprehension for Good, Average, and Poor Readers." Unpublished Doctoral Dissertation. University of Pennsylvania, 1970.

12. ROSNER, S. A. "Some Notes on Standardized and Informal Tests with Clinical Cases," *Delaware Valley Reading Bulletin, 3* (1963), 1.

13. SIPAY, E. R. "A Comparison of Standardized Reading Scores and Functional Reading Levels." Unpublished Doctoral Dissertation. University of Connecticut, 1963.

VI

Grouping for Effective Reading Instruction

The effective teacher of reading knows when to employ whole class, group, and individual instruction. Since, however, most instruction is probably done with groups, this chapter is concerned with grouping practices.

Clymer starts by presenting the characteristics of an effective structured program but also considers the possible dangers in using such a program. Kriege's article offers nine steps that can help to systematize a reading program. This is followed by McCullough's practical suggestions for handling individual differences through the use of independent reading activities. Next, Goodland discusses an alternative to organizing schools by grade levels. Finally, Clark argues strongly for the need to group beyond the primary grades.

27. The Structured Reading Program *

THEODORE CLYMER

IN principle no informed person can be opposed to a reading program which adjusts to individual differences, just as no one who understands children and

* From Theodore Clymer, "The Structured Reading Program," in *Controversial Issues in Reading and Promising Solutions,* Supplementary Education Monographs, No. 91, compiled and edited by Helen M. Robinson (December, 1961), pp. 75–80. Reprinted by permission of the author and The University of Chicago Press.

how they learn can object to a program which is organized or structured. However, when we speak of *the* individualized method and *the* structured method, we pass beyond general principles and go on to spell out specific procedures on which there can be a clear and careful evaluation based on research, classroom practice, expert opinion, and logical analysis. In other words, when we progress from principle to practice, we can see, compare, and perhaps resolve differences.

In the space available four questions will be treated in turn. They are: What are the characteristics of an effective, structured reading program? What are the major dangers in a structured program? What are the problems in an individualized program? And finally, what does research reveal about these two approaches? [1]

What Are the Characteristics of an Effective, Structured Program?

Three carefully developed teaching tools form the foundation of an effective program. These tools are the end product of a careful application of research in child development, reading methods, learning theory, and children's interests.

The basic reader. The basic or basal reader is designed with a careful control and gradual introduction of vocabulary, concepts, and mechanical features which research has demonstrated create learning problems for the pupil as he develops reading skill. In addition, the content of the basal reader is carefully selected to meet the standards of both child interest and literary quality. Except for some obvious problems at the preprimer level where vocabulary is limited, the stories of well-designed basal series fulfill the criteria of good literature.

The value systems and social customs portrayed in primary basal readers have been criticized as "middle class" and therefore not in harmony with the background many children bring to school. To these critics we may ask, "What is wrong with middle class values?" Is working diligently, helping with a family project, caring for pets, treating neighbors, friend, and family with kindness and respect a poor set of values to de-

velop? We may also ask these critics, "What value systems shall we substitute?"

The teacher's manual. The teacher's manual or guide is a second essential tool in a structured reading program. If full use is to be made of the basal reader, the teacher's manual must play an important role. It is only by consulting the manual that we learn the word-recognition skills, concepts, and comprehension abilities the author intended a particular selection to develop. The sequence of skills and abilities the program is designed to develop is revealed through the teacher's manual. The manual is not a recipe book—and it should not be used as one. You cannot add thirty-five children, fold in one teacher, slowly blend eight units from a basal reader, and get good reading by the end of the year. A manual is a rich source of ideas and suggestions. In no way does it circumscribe teaching; in no way can a manual replace an intelligent, alert teacher who is professionally prepared to teach reading. The manual suggests; it does not bind; it enriches, not limits. Any teacher who uses a modern teacher's guide knows that a selective adaptation of the ideas presented must be made because there is just too much in the manual for time to permit the use of all the suggestions presented.

A crisp, new-looking manual with a sparklingly clean cover leaves me depressed. Unless such a manual has just been requisitioned, it is serving little purpose other than to decorate the teacher's desk. My preference is a dog-eared, well-worn manual with clippings inserted, notes for additional questions and activities liberally sprinkled in the margins, with underlining and comments throughout. Such a manual is serving the purpose the authors intended.

One additional suggestion for effective use of manuals: One copy for the classroom and one for home is ideal if the

---

[1] In this shortened version, Dr. Clymer's discussion of the third and fourth questions has been omitted. (Eds.)

budget will permit it. Such a plan effectively solves the problem of your being where the manual isn't. More than once I carried the manuals home for careful study, made my selections and additions of questions and activities, then arrived at school the next day and discovered that I'd left my homework at home. Two manuals help to solve this problem.

From these comments you can see that my view is that a manual serves as a guideline, not a navigation chart. Intelligent selection, adaptation, and additions by a professionally trained teacher are prerequisites for effective use of the manual. Use of a manual is not the mark of a poorly prepared instructor—rather, its use indicates a teacher who understands the reading process and the importance of sequence in developing reading skills.

The workbook. First of all, we are not discussing workbooks in general but the workbook that *accompanies the basal reader* the children are using. In this workbook we have the third of our essential tools, but perhaps the tool which must be used with the most discretion. The workbook usually provides a follow-up on the skills taught through the basic reader lesson. In certain series the workbook serves as a preparatory activity to reading selections from the reader. In either case, construction of the workbook is such that it provides additional practice on vocabulary, word-recognition skills, and comprehension abilities which are congruent with the sequence and scope of the reading program.

Selection and adaptation are keynotes to use of the workbook. Certain children, or groups of children, may not need further practice in the skill presented on certain pages of the workbook. A lesson on initial consonants, for example, may be omitted when a group is already proficient in this skill. Conversely, additional exercises must be provided on certain abilities for some children when they fail to achieve proficiency upon completion of the exercises provided by the workbook. No author can even hope to prepare a program which will be a "perfect fit" for every child. Here again, the teacher's professional judgment to supplement, to adapt, and to reject is required. Workbooks can and have been misused. Such misuses are not inherent in this third tool of the program. Our problem is not to eliminate the workbook but to be intelligent in its use.

Correction of workbook exercises is essential for good teaching. These exercises cannot be completed and then forgotten. Both the pupil and the teacher must be aware of problems and strengths which are revealed by performance on these exercises. Children often should have the opportunity to locate and correct their own errors. Research in learning reveals that immediate knowledge of success or lack of success is closely related to growth. Applying this psychological principle requires that the pupil be informed—the sooner the better—of the results of his efforts.

To summarize our discussion on the use of the basal reader, teacher's manual, and workbook of the basal reader, we can say that these tools, when used intelligently, critically, and professionally, offer a program for instruction with sequence and scope which is unparalleled by other approaches.

Time provisions. The program described to this point is not accomplished in a few minutes stolen from a crowded curriculum. At all grade levels—including the high school—we must take a firm stand and provide time for teaching reading. Schools with successful programs provide generous time allotments for reading instruction. Primary teachers somehow find the time. Intermediate grade teachers put up a valiant battle to find time for reading instruction. Unfortunately they don't always win the struggle. In the junior and senior high organization, reading is often lost in a welter of scheduling problems and activities. The answer to the time problem is to list in order of importance the objectives of the curriculum. If such an approach is taken, reading can easily claim its rightful proportion of the time available in the school day. Fifty to sixty minutes daily is certainly not excessive in the intermediate grades. One period a day for at least one semester per year is not an unrealistic demand in the junior and senior high school. There *is* time in the school day. Our job is simply to take what is needed for reading.

Grouping within the class. Two years ago this Conference [2] considered the problems of grouping practices in adjusting to individual differences. The proceedings of the conference suggest that the final solution for individual differences must be found in the instructional practices of the teacher. Grouping plans, no matter how intricate, cannot produce groups of pupils who can be given uniform instruction. Since differences in reading ability within classes are here to stay, we must adjust our instructional program to these differences through grouping within the classroom.

Providing appropriate organizational routine, worthwhile independent work, and instruction for three or perhaps more groups is a topic of great concern to all of us, but this topic is unfortunately beyond the scope of our presentation in this session. Two comments are pertinent here. First, accomplishing this task is not easy. Careful planning, skill, and hard work are blended together in generous

[2] Annual Reading Conference, University of Chicago.

proportions to achieve the goal of good group instruction. The second comment is one of simple mechanics of instruction: as the number of instructional groups increases, the amount of the teacher's time available for any one group decreases. Sixty minutes of instruction with three groups allows the teacher to spend twenty minutes with each group. The same instruction time would allow ten minutes per group if six groups are used. Thirty groups (an individualized approach) would permit two minutes per group in a sixty-minute period. A little speculation reveals that the advantage of greater homogeneity of instructional groups is soon offset by the smaller amount of time available for teaching a group.

Provisions for organization. A major contribution of a structured program is the organization provided in reading instruction. This organization is apparent in a number of ways. Consider first the provision for introduction of vocabulary, background, and concepts when a small group uses the same material. In this setting it is possible for the teacher to prepare the pupils to read the selection with understanding and without undue problems because of unanticipated vocabulary. If each member of the class is reading a different selection or book, such preparation is obviously impossible.

A second way in which the structured program provides organization is through a thorough comprehension program. Purposes for reading should be varied and carefully selected so that all the major comprehension skills are given a balanced emphasis. Such balance and organization is not likely to result from a happenstance selection of purposes. The manual, by providing a full range of purposes for reading, insures that effective comprehension abilities are developed.

A third way in which a basic program

provides organization is in a carefully developed and sequential program of word recognition. In actual practice an effective and broad word-recognition program may be one of the most difficult aspects of reading to manage without aid from a basic system. How can we insure that our students have been (1) exposed to all appropriate aspects of word-recognition and word-analysis skills, (2) introduced to these in the most effective sequence, and (3) developed in a balanced manner so that neither over- nor underdependence upon any one technique occurs?

Use of a basic program is no guarantee of perfect performance in word-recognition skills. Yet it seems clear that the probability of a broad, effective program is greatly enhanced when carefully prepared materials are used.

Topical and personal reading. With all its aids, organization, and careful development of skills, the basic program will fail dismally if it does not do one more thing. It must stimulate reading beyond the basic text. The basic program is only the "how to read" aspect of a total reading curriculum. Simply "knowing how" is not enough to develop effective reading ability. Once the skills are taught they must be practiced in a variety of situations in which students read on topics of concern to class enterprises—whether related to the content of the reader, the social studies, or science curriculum. In addition to reading related to class projects, problems, and other assignments, personal reading must form an important part of the total reading curriculum. By re-emphasizing the importance of personal reading, the "individualized reading program" has performed a real service for it has made us sensitive to the contribution which the child's free-time reading can make to reading growth. A reading curriculum which neglects

topically organized reading and fails to provide a well-selected collection of good books for personal reading—and time for reading them—will not achieve the goals we hold for a modern reading program.

What Are the Major Dangers in a Structured Reading Program?

There are certain dangers in the use of basal reading programs. The recognition of these dangers and proper planning can do much to avoid these problems. Three major dangers are discussed below.

Uniform application. Because the basic program is so well organized and so much aid is given the teacher in providing exercises, activities, and directions, it may be tempting for a teacher to administer a uniform program of instruction to all children regardless of need. This problem may be one of in-service education for the school systems. It may also mean that the teacher-training institutions have failed to show the teacher how to organize his class for differentiated instruction. Whatever its origin, the problem is real and should be acknowledged.

The text as the total program. As was pointed out earlier, the basic text cannot be considered the entire reading curriculum. Programs which stop with the basal reader have failed to provide sufficient experiences with other worthwhile materials and cannot fully develop reading skills. An effective program will extend throughout the day, touching on all content areas and will stimulate reading of a wide range of materials.

Failure to apply insight. Because they respect the research and scholarship of the authors of basic reading series, teachers may be hesitant to deviate from the suggestions in the manual or to alter directions for workbook pages, or in other ways apply professional insight in the use of basal materials. But no author claims to have designed a program to meet all needs and to be suitable for every situation. The effective use of basal readers involves professional insight to meet special needs of children. Professional judgments are still the province of the teacher and must remain so, if our programs are to be truly effective.

28. You Can Systematize Your Reading Program *

JACK W. KRIEGE

WHAT teacher doesn't try constantly to bring system to her reading program? And what teacher doesn't run into problems the moment she begins making up the first chart or progress form?

Oh sure, there are elaborate systems available from many producers of educational materials. But most of these are tied to a particular basal reading program —and, therefore, little use to the teacher who is individualizing her reading instruction. And the others are costly—too costly, often, for the teacher with limited discretionary funds.

Give it up? No. You can systematize your reading program effectively by concentrating on the *method* behind any systematic approach to teaching reading. Doing so is hardly as easy as 1-2-3. It takes a lot of hard work, plus a determination to see it through. But the effort pays off—in dividends to you and your students. The following nine steps illustrate how a systematized reading program might be developed—in this case, for a typical third grade:

1. *Take inventory*. Instead of sitting back and wishing you could order certain materials, find out what is already available in your school. One item you're almost certain to find will be the basal reader; however, don't forget that in most third-grade classes there are students who read above and below that level. So play it safe and obtain copies of the basal reader from the second- and fourth-grade teachers, too.

The teacher's manuals for most basal programs contain valuable exercises which relate to the stories, and which fall generally under the categories of comprehension and vocabulary development. Although these exercises are frequently overlooked or incompletely utilized, they can be included in a systematized program.

Other classroom items which belong in your inventory include paperback books for independent reading, context skill development booklets on the third- through fifth-grade levels, reading games (both commercial and self-made), and any perceptual development materials—such as puzzles and pegboards—which you may have on hand.

Most schools also have many items which, upon a teacher's request, are available for use on a revolving basis.

These are the items which, unfortunately, are frequently not put to good use simply because a definite schedule is not imposed. Make it your business, then, to find out not only what items are available, but also when you can use them. Then put down in your inventory something like this: SRA Reading Laboratory, three days per week; EDL Controlled Reader, two days per week; tape recorder and listening station, two days per week; Language Master, one day per week.

As far as your tape recorder lessons are concerned, you can create them specifically for your own class, or you can join forces with other teachers at your grade level.

2. *Organize the materials in sequence.* The secret of using materials effectively is to arrange them in a sequence which will get low students to work at their own level and also increase their skill in gradual steps. Many items, such as the basal reader selections, the SRA Reading Laboratory, and the Controlled Reader filmstrips, are already arranged in sequence. The others —independent reading books and reading games, for example—should be sequentially arranged by you and marked according to their difficulty level so that they may be easily recognized and selected by the students.

Once the materials are arranged in this manner, you may find it helpful to construct a chart, such as the one shown on page 170 listing the levels of the materials, their availability and the number of students that can use them simultaneously.

3. *Design an efficient room.* The use of a variety of materials simultaneously for 25 or 30 students is an invitation to pure chaos, unless you take the time and trouble to organize different areas of the classroom for small-group study. The sketch on page 168 shows how a classroom might be arranged to allow for efficient use of the materials.

Some of the items in the diagram, of course, are not absolutely required for the arrangement; others may simply not be available. The rug, for example, is an added benefit, but is certainly not essential to the design of the program; and if sufficient chairs are not on hand, they can be transported from area to area by the children.

4. *Determine reading levels.* After the materials have been arranged sequentially by grade level, the next step is to determine at what grade level each student is reading, so that he may begin working with materials commensurate with his ability.

The ratings *high, average,* and *low,* so often assigned to children in reading group situations are really not adequate for placement in specifically graded reading materials. A more definite reading-grade placement must be determined.

Don't rely on the scores from standardized achievement tests to help you out. In the first place, the results are usually obtained too late in the year to be of assistance; secondly, the scores are frequently invalid, particularly in the case of poor readers who, through random guessing, often register scores far above their actual capability. . . .

5. *Assign appropriate materials.* Once the reading levels are determined, you'll be able to start your youngsters working with the available materials. Wherever possible, have them begin with materials a year lower than their test score indicates. There's nothing like a little success right at the outset to

Schedule of reading activities

Time blocks	GROUP IA		GROUP IB		GROUP IIA		GROUP IIB		GROUP III	
	Activity	Area	Activity	Area	Activity	Area	Activity	Area	Activity	Area
MONDAY 1	Context booklet	B	Listening exercise	E	Independent reading			B	Group reading*	D
MONDAY 2	Listening exercise	E	Independent reading	B	Group reading*			D	Comprehension exercise	B
MONDAY 3	Independent reading	B			Comprehension exercise			B	Listening exercise	E
TUESDAY 1	Group reading*	D			Listening exercise	E	Power Builders	B	Chalkboard / Perceptual ex.	G / F
TUESDAY 2	Comprehension exercise	B			Independent reading	B			Correct comprehension exercise*	D
TUESDAY 3	Independent reading	B					Listening exercise	E	Vocabulary exercise	B

WEDNESDAY

Period				
1	B — Power Builders	D — Correct comprehension exercise*	E — Language Master	F — Perceptual ex.
			E — Reading games	F — Perceptual ex.
2	D — Correct comprehension exercise*	B — Power Builders	E — Reading games	E — Language Master
			E — Reading games	E — Language Master
3	B — Vocabulary exercise	B — Power Builders		F — Perceptual ex.

THURSDAY

Period				
1	F — Controlled Reader	B — Context booklet	B — Vocabulary exercise	D — Correct vocabulary exercise*
2	B — Independent reading	D — Controlled Reader	F — Correct vocabulary exercise*	B — Independent reading
			E — Reading games	D — Controlled Reader
3		B — Independent reading	F — Controlled Reader	

FRIDAY

Period				
1	B — Context booklet	D — Correct vocabulary exercise*	F — Controlled Reader	E — Reading games
				G — Chalkboard
2	F — Controlled Reader	B — Power Builders	F — Independent reading	E — Power Builders (begin)*
3	B — Context booklet	F — Controlled Reader	B — Reading games	B — Power Builders (continue)

* Total attention of teacher required.

167

Classroom arrangement

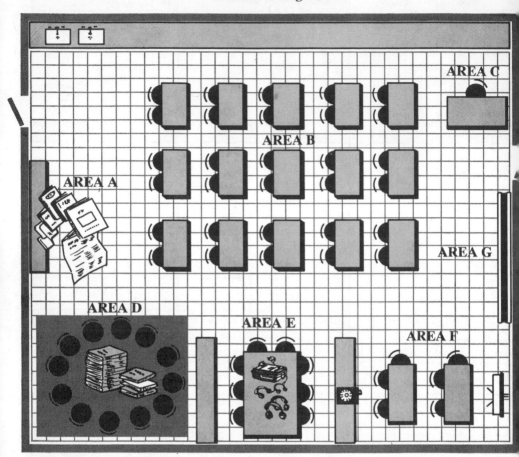

Area	Furnishings	Materials and Equipment	Activities
A	8' shelves.	Independent reading books; SRA Reading Laboratories; other graded independent reading materials.	Selection of independent reading materials.
B	15 2-place desks; 30 chairs.		Independent reading and writing exercises.
C	Teacher's desk.		Individual consultation.
D	8'x10' rug; 12-14 chairs.	Basal readers.	Group oral reading and discussion.
E	4'x6' table and 8 chairs; 2 6' shelves.	Tape recorder and listening station; reading games.	Listening activities; independent reading activities.
F	2 2'x4' tables and 6 chairs; projection screen.	Controlled Reader; puzzles, pegboards and other perceptual development materials.	Projected reading exercises; perceptual development activities.
G	Chalkboard.		Chalkboard exercises.

boost a child's confidence and enthusiasm.

Remember, though, you're working with materials that are available at your school—not with a well-equipped, neatly packaged reading program. The materials you have at your disposal may not cover all your students or they may be available for only limited periods of time.

If that's the case, you'll just have to play it by ear. For example, if you don't have Controlled Reader filmstrips below the second-grade level, skip this activity with children who score considerably below the third-grade level. And if the Language Master at your school is available just one day each week, limit its use to the eight or nine students who can benefit most from it.

6. *Group the students according to level and need.* Grouping, if done arbitrarily, can result in the students becoming locked in position, without allowance for individual differences within the group. And yet grouping is necessary to insure effective use both of the materials and of the teacher's time. The solution is to make the groups flexible and varied according to the needs of the students and the requirements of the materials.

What this means in terms of dividing your class into groups is this: First, you'll have to make that basic division into groups that read at fourth-, third- and second-grade levels. Once that's done, you'll have to subdivide into smaller groups, because such items as the Controlled Reader, booklets, reading games and perceptual development materials are suitable for use by only six to eight students at a time.

Let's say you have a class of 30 third-graders. After determining reading levels, you might end up with these basic groupings: Group I, fourth reader, 10 students; Group II, third reader, 14 students, and Group III, second reader, six students.

Incidentally, it's best to subdivide as evenly as possible. Why overload the listening station if you don't have to? Thus, your subdivision of the above three groups would look like this: Group IA, five students; Group IB, five students; Group IIA, seven students, and Group IIB, seven students. Obviously, you won't have to subdivide Group III since it has only six students.

One last word about grouping: The students in each group should be working with materials of the same level *only* when necessary, such as with the Controlled Reader,[1] listening station and basal reader selections. When using individualized materials —the context skill booklets, SRA Reading Laboratory, independent reading book and so on—each child in the group should be working at his own level.

7. *Construct a schedule.* One glance at page 166 should be enough to convince you that drawing up a schedule of reading activities is not something you can knock off in a spare hour or two. After all, you'll probably be juggling five or six groups of children, six classroom areas and as many items of material as you've been able to collect from around the school.

And if that's not problem enough, you'll also have your own schedule to worry about. A few of the activities —such as group reading and correcting vocabulary exercises—require the total attention of the teacher. You

[1] The teacher also should be sure that the rate at which the material is shown is appropriate for each child in the group. (Eds.)

won't be able to schedule these activities in the same time slot unless you've mastered the trick of being in several places at once.

Nevertheless, a schedule—for all the headaches it will give you—is an absolute must. Fail to draw one up and you won't have a systematic reading program . . . you'll have an hour of complete confusion.

The schedule on page 166 assumes that one hour is being set aside for reading. The hour is divided into three 20-minute blocks of time. It is a weekly schedule, which will probably prove the most workable for you.

Once you have the schedule made up, copy it and post it on the bulletin board. Then, if a large diagram of the room arrangement is also posted, your youngsters will know exactly where they are to go and what they are to do at any given time.

Oh yes, about that business of scheduling those activities which require your total attention. Try to schedule them for the first two time blocks of each day. That way you can save the final time block for individual help.

8. *Keep track of progress.* It will be necessary to keep up-to-date, individual

Material Sequence and Availability Chart

Item	Reading Level					Days Available					Simultaneous Student Use
	1	2	3	4	5	M	T	W	T	F	
Basal reading program											
Texts		X	X	X		X	X	X	X	X	15
Comprehension exercises		X	X	X		X	X	X	X	X	15
Vocabulary exercises		X	X	X		X	X	X	X	X	15
SRA Reading Laboratory											
Power Builders	X	X	X	X	X		X	X		X	15
Listening Skill Builders		X	X				X	X			8
Controlled Reader		X	X	X					X	X	6–8
Context skill booklets		X	X	X	X	X	X	X	X	X	7
Language Master	X	X	X						X		2–3
Tape recorder and listening station						X	X				8
Paperback books	X	X	X	X	X	X	X	X	X	X	15
Reading games	X	X	X			X	X	X	X	X	10
Perceptual development materials											
Puzzles	X	X				X	X	X	X	X	5
Pegboards	X	X				X	X	X	X	X	8
Templates	X	X				X	X	X	X	X	3–4

A list of materials like this can come in handy when you start matching up children and the reading tools available to your classroom.

records on each student, but make it easy on yourself. Let each child record his own progress.

Whenever possible, a child's achievement should be noted down in percentage scores. This makes it easy for the student and the teacher to tell at a glance how successful the work has been, and whether it's time to advance to a higher level.

Other activities may need no more than a simple notation of the numbers of items completed. But be sure the child lists them so that he can keep track of those he has completed and thus maintain the proper sequence.

9. *Evaluate each student's progress frequently.* Each child should have his progress evaluated every two or three weeks so that necessary alterations can be made in his reading program. Here's an easy way to do it: If a student has achieved 100 percent five or six times in succession on a particular activity, move him to the next higher level of that activity. If he is consistently getting scores below 70 percent, he should probably be moved to the next lower level.

The nonindividualized group activities will probably pose a little more difficulty when it comes to evaluation and alteration, but approximately the same guidelines may be used for the group as for the individual. And if one member of the group achieves consistently above or below the level of the group as a whole, he should be moved to another group—even if it means disrupting that delicate balance you've achieved between children and available material.

At the end of each quarter or each semester you should again administer some test like the Wide Range Achievement Test to determine the progress of each student.[2]

We've been assuming all along that you're a third-grade teacher and you're probably not. Nevertheless, the nine steps outlined above still apply. For another grade level, or even another third-grade class, the materials, groups, and schedule will be different. But the *method of development* will remain the same. In short, any teacher of any grade level with any materials can develop a systematic reading program— providing they have the will, determination, and energy. And that leaves it strictly up to you.

[2] Depending upon what the teacher has attempted to teach, other measures (e.g., comprehension or auditory discrimination) may be more appropriate. (Eds.)

29. Independent Reading Activities *

CONSTANCE M. MC CULLOUGH

THE responsibility of providing independent learning activities stems directly from a basic instructional problem—the handling of individual differences. Every day the teacher must be ready to provide a number of worthwhile activities which her pupils may carry on independently while she works with small groups of children who have abilities and needs in common.

Although independent reading activities have long been an essential part of a good instructional program, the general acceptance of modern methods of grouping increased their importance. It is inevitable that when a teacher works with groups, some pupils will be left without her direct guidance. Once it was thought adequate just to keep these children busy, and meaningless sedentary activities— often labeled "seatwork"—were devised to occupy their time. But increasingly teachers realized that in a class with several groups, some children were working without guidance for rather large portions of reading time. Consequently they began to plan their work more carefully in order that every pupil might engage in a variety of useful endeavors. They prepared genuine teaching materials and found other published materials as well. The term "seatwork," odious to many teachers because of its association with

meaningless activity, was replaced by the term independent learning activities.

The practice of using groups in reading makes it possible to divide a class so that each group reads a book appropriate to the general level of the children in that group. The children in each group read the same book as the core of their systematic reading program, discuss and react to the selections, and learn reading techniques together.

The grouping system does not, of course, imply complete segregation of groups of children. Far from it! Children from various groups are brought together through additional types of grouping. For example,

a. interest grouping, in which children interested in cowboys, read about cowboys and report their findings as a group
b. research grouping, in which children seek out information through reference books and factual and story material and summarize their findings
c. special needs grouping, in which a few children who need extra help in a certain reading skill are given it as a group until the need is fulfilled
d. team grouping, in which two children needing the same practice are teamed together occasionally
e. grouping in which a child from one reading group helps a child from another reading group

Furthermore, the whole class may engage in a reading club, in which children who have read and liked books outside the reader series report their impressions to the entire class. The class may also en-

* From Constance M. McCullough, "Independent Reading Activities," in *Contributions in Reading*, no. 10, pp. 1–6. Copyright © 1952. Reprinted by permission of the author and Ginn and Co., Waltham, Mass.

gage in choral reading of a poem or a prose selection that all like and can read, may listen to a story, or may watch a presentation by one reading group as the culmination of a story or a unit of stories in their reader. In any one class many groups will be operating.

The teacher decides which child belongs in which group

a. by studying what the previous teacher has to say about his reading
b. by noting the books he is able to read successfully
c. by observing some of his casual book choices
d. by noting his daily performance in reading with other children in the class
e. by examining the results of reading tests which show the level of material he is able to read successfully and the skills in which he needs training.

Sometimes when still in doubt about a child, the teacher has him read aloud brief selections from preprimer, primer, first reader, and so on through a series until his reading becomes halting and meaningless. The teacher tries to place him, then, with a reader which he can read successfully under her direction and guidance and which has a manual and workbook that present the skills he next needs.

Of course the teacher may make some mistakes, but these can be promptly corrected. Grouping should be flexible, so that a child remains in a group only as long as his progress warrants. What about the child's embarrassment in being placed in a particular group? Few children will be embarrassed if the teacher shows as much pleasure in working with one group as in working with another, if the teacher shows respect for and interest in good work at whatever level it is performed, and if the teacher does a good job of parent education in regard to the importance of placement at a congenial level.

Some children will have to work hard to keep up with their groups. The teacher should see that they have material that is easy for them to read in some of their activities. Other children will find their group work simple. The teacher should see that in their other reading activities these children are provided with material that is challenging to them in difficulty, something "their size." Thus all children will be acquiring fluency and power in reading, and all will be benefiting from group experiences. . . .

Children Need Physical Variety in Activities

Independent learning activities do not necessarily keep the children at their desks. They may also take them to the reading table where they may find books to read, to the cloakroom, hall, or rear of the classroom where they may plan or engage in a dramatization or committee work, or to the blackboard where they may write or draw.

Certainly life is more serene when every pair of trousers and every little skirt are anchored at their own desks. But restless young bodies cannot take long stretches of immobility. It is easier for a teacher to put physical variety into her children's activities than to handle the disciplinary problems which arise if Nature is defied.

The necessity for physical variety clearly indicates the fallacy of always giving the children all the equipment they require for their independent work period. After they have finished the major task set them, they may better go one by one to the nearby cupboard or shelf for their art paper, to the library table for their books, or to the shelf of games for their games, rather than sit wiggling miserably for the whole time.

You may say, "But they get into trouble

when they wander around the room." Yes, they do, unless we prepare them by helping them to set standards of conduct for those occasions which will prevent trouble, such as:

We go quietly.
We waste no time getting our material.
We do not disturb other people.
We go the shortest way.

It is important, too, that we hold frequent evaluation periods in which we discuss how well our rules are working and what we can do about them. Wise planning on the part of the teacher in the placement of children and materials reduces the frequency and magnitude of crises. At the same time it helps the child to develop a spirit of cooperation and of responsibility for his own progress.

How to Give Directions

Independent activities practically always involve some verbal directions from the teacher. When directions are written on the blackboard, they should be read orally by the children as proof that they can read them. There should also be an explanation by the children of just what they are going to do so that the teacher will know that they really comprehend the task.

Some hectographed or workbook materials, or questions at the ends of stories in a reader series may be sufficiently self-explanatory. If the teacher has any doubt of the children's understanding, however, it is better to have them take time to tell what they are going to do than to have them interrupt the reading group or each other by asking questions later. With hectographed or workbook material it is usually safe to have the children work the first item on the page under guidance, then do the remainder themselves.

When the teacher has several groups in a class, prior to working with the first group, she will have to give directions to the other groups to get them started on their independent activities. Adhering to a few simple word patterns is always a good idea, for it avoids the danger that the children will be troubled by complicated directions which divert their attention and obscure the reading skill that is being developed. Moreover, if there is more than one type of response to be made—such as circling a word, crossing out a word, writing in a word, underlining a sentence, finishing a rhyme, and the like—giving directions may be time-consuming. Furthermore, children readily forget the second direction by the time they must use it. Therefore, it seems sensible to keep to a minimum the types of response in an exercise or write reminders on the blackboard.

At the conclusion of a meeting with one group, the teacher gives the pupils directions for their independent work. Thus her system is to give prior directions to groups which will work independently, teach one group, and give those pupils directions for their independent work before leaving them.

Adapting the Task to the Group

Each group of children is reading at a different level of difficulty. Perhaps in one class one group is reading preprimers, another primers, another first readers. The independent activities will have as their purpose, of course, the improvement of reading at these different levels. The work of the preprimer group will involve reading of the preprimers and activities using the vocabulary of that level. The difficulty of the work can be controlled in part by seeing to it that the tasks are within the vocabulary limits of the book concerned.

Another method of control is to introduce the task clearly and fully to the group, allowing time for the children to engage briefly in the activity while the teacher is still working with them. Thus they are ready for the type of thought involved and simply have to apply it to many examples. In other words, the work will be more successful if the children are familiar with the task and practice individually the learning activities which have already been initiated in group work.

The Teachers' Manuals which accompany basic readers offer many suggestions for independent activities. These Manuals were made to help the teacher provide activities suitable to the stage of reading development which the child has reached.

Learning activities must be selected or prepared with care. If the task is too hard for some children, they will give up in despair and may think of disastrous ways of occupying themselves. If it is too easy, the children will finish it too quickly, and the same problem will arise. There are two major cures for both these diseases. One is to have some elasticity in the assignment—a latter portion which includes such an activity as writing one's reaction, making up a story, drawing a picture or a series of pictures. This method gives the child the satisfaction of finishing the earlier, specific-response type of work, yet makes it possible for him to work creatively on related reading activities.

A second suggestion is that the class have in mind certain activities which may be carried on after all work is done —reading a book, playing a game, writing or drawing on the blackboard—something connected with reading and promoting reading skill and appreciation. Some teachers in the lower grades make charts portraying the kinds of activities which are useful and legitimate and agreed upon by the class. A child at a loss for activity has only to look at the chart to see the possibilities. In higher grades teachers list these possibilities on a chart or blackboard. Thus it becomes the individual's

recognized responsibility to take care of himself. As one teacher said, "Everybody in my room knows that school is not a place just to sit."

Independent reading activities should yield a definite result: something written, something drawn, questions answered, a dramatization ready for presentation. A definite result leaves no room for, "I did it but I forget now," and makes more certain the efficient use of time. It makes a child feel that his effort has culminated in real achievement; he knows a job is done.

Suggestions for Kinds of Materials

We should not feel limited, as we sometimes do, in the materials available for independent reading activities. Actually they are numerous. Workbooks, hectographed exercises, and games made by mounting materials on cardboard serve many skills-development purposes. The games can be classified and kept in a certain place, so that a child needing help of a certain type, say initial-consonant attack, can go to the proper shelf for a game which will give him practice in that skill.

Pupil-made picture dictionaries such as large card files with a picture on one side of the card and its corresponding word on the other, can be built and used in the independent work period. Art and writing materials for the purpose of expressing ideas about the things read are also necessary equipment. The blackboard may be used for writing creative stories based upon the reading lesson or for practicing the form and use of certain words.

The basic reader itself may be used to answer comprehension questions, to take notes, to prepare an outline, or to make a summary. Supplementary books containing stories on a similar topic may be read. Factual and fictional books on topics of interest to individual children may be used in the "free" reading. Reference books may be used in vocabulary study or in the pursuit of information about problems raised in social studies or in connection with stories in the reader.

Frequent protests heard from all parts of the country suggest that kinds of equipment mentioned above are not available, but there are also significant silences

where teachers, also underequipped for the task of teaching reading, are busy preparing materials from resources at hand. Such teachers are cutting pictures and sentences out of their own magazines because there is neither a hectograph nor workbooks; they are helping the class to make a big picture-dictionary because the school hasn't the funds to buy one, and collecting files of other materials.

30. "Reading Levels" Replace Grades in the Non-Graded Plan *

JOHN I. GOODLAD, FRED E. BROOKS, IRENE M. LARSON, AND NEAL NEFF

ALTHOUGH grade classifications have been removed from only a scattered few elementary schools in America, several ungraded plans have been in operation long enough to provide us with some guidelines for further development of what might become a trend. Three of these plans were selected for study with a view to seeing their development in some time perspective.

The original plans studied revealed a good many dissimilarities. Common to a number of them, however, was some attempt to relate children's progress to reading levels, which were determined largely from the basal reading series used. The Nathaniel Hawthorne School in University City, Missouri, the Cabool Elementary School, also in Missouri, and

* From John I. Goodlad, Fred E. Brooks, Irene M. Larson, and Neal Neff, " 'Reading Levels' Replace Grades in the Non-Graded Plan," *Elementary School Journal,* LVII (February, 1957), 253–56. Reprinted by permission of the author and The University of Chicago Press.

most of the schools in Green Bay, Wisconsin, were found not only to be organized without grade levels but also to be cognizant of reading ability in classifying pupils.

It must be emphasized that organization of the elementary school around reading levels is not the only approach to the removal of grades. In fact, some exponents of non-grading maintain that rigorous attention to reading levels actually defeats the original intent of ungraded structure. In the discussion that follows, reading levels serve merely as a device for clarifying some of the problems and procedures that accompany the change to non-grading. They are not intended to prescribe the basis for establishing non-graded plans.

Getting Started

Non-grading apparently grows out of dissatisfaction with some other related aspect of schooling. At Green Bay, for example, first-grade teachers were dissatisfied with making promotion decisions regarding slow starters who were moving along nicely toward the end of the year but who still were not up to "grade" standard. At Cabool the present plan grew out of the demand of parents after a report-card committee of parents and teachers had labored together for months. Teachers and parents at Nathaniel Hawthorne School had difficulty in relating old methods of reporting to a developing concept of individualized, continuous pupil progress.

Apparently teachers want a model when they seek to replace long established practice with something new and, in the eyes of many, radical. Merely intellectualizing the desirability of change, no matter how specifically that change is conceived in the mind's eye, is not enough. Green Bay teachers studied reports of the Milwaukee plan, well established at that time, and also visited schools there and conferred with teachers and supervisors.

Significant change is not a unitary thing, conceived as a whole and transplanted in its totality from conception to implementation. Rather, an idea takes root, grows a little, and perhaps lies dormant for a time. But then, as soon as some outgrowth of the idea becomes operative, new ideas spring forth, and many kinds of changes follow. At Cabool the initial idea of a primary department grew almost immediately into an organization embracing three departments: primary, intermediate, and upper. At Green Bay two schools began with the organization of primary units. Others followed, one after another, until by September, 1955, the plan was in operation in eight of twelve schools. The Nathaniel Hawthorne teachers found the removal of grades to be just an early step in formulating a whole new concept of pupil progress and in effecting accompanying readjustment. The search for a way to trace and report the actual progress of children led to the identification of reading levels.

Reading Levels in Operation

The teachers of the Nathaniel Hawthorne School, in moving to an ungraded primary unit, wanted to maintain some concrete way of determining the actual progress of a given child. It was agreed from the beginning that (1) there should be flexible classification levels; (2) these levels should relate to the length of time a child had been in school; (3) these levels should in some way be related to the basic reading program being used; and (4) the classification system should be related to a standardized testing program.

The teachers soon found that they really had two classification problems: first, grouping to determine the classroom unit to which a child was to be assigned; second, grouping within a given classroom. In seeking answers to the first problem, the teachers developed the following general principles:

1. Pupils should stay with a teacher for a period of at least one year.
2. There should be a normal range of ability in each group.
3. Pupils should be grouped as closely as possible by chronological age.

A classification-index system based on semesters in school was established. Normally a child moves through Semester 6 in completing the primary unit at the end of the third year in school. Slower children, who took as long as four years to complete the classification unit normally completed in three, might be classified as "Semester 7" or "Semester 8."

In answering the second problem, that of grouping within a single classroom, a flexible system of reading levels was adopted. Standardized tests are given frequently to determine present reading performance, but these results are related to other indexes of maturity determined by the teacher. It is conceivable that a child will move through several reading levels in a given year.

At Nathaniel Hawthorne there are nine classification levels through which a child may proceed in completing the three-year primary unit:

Level R.—Pupil not able to read; readiness developed.

Level 1.—Preprimers and primers (testing at a grade level of approximately 1.6).

Level 2.—First readers and many supplementary readers of primer level (testing at a grade level of approximately 2.0).

Level 3.—Second reader with four or five first readers that can be read with fluency and comprehension (testing at approximately 2.6).

Level 4.—Second readers with several easier second readers read with fluency and comprehension (testing at approximately 3.2).

Level 5.—Third readers with many easy high-level second readers read with fluency and good comprehension; child displays good word attack and some independent reading (testing at approximately 3.8).

Level 6.—High-level third-reader material with ability to read with fluency and good comprehension; child does independent reading (testing at approximately 4.2).

Levels 7 and 8.—These levels provide for pupils in the primary school who read well in library books and who read other textbooks, in areas such as social studies and science, with fluency and understanding.

We see, then, that a child classified as 5–7 is in the first semester of his third year at school, reading at the seventh level described above. Such a pupil obviously would go on into an intermediate unit or the fourth grade, whichever existed, at the end of the year. Another child, classified as 5–3, also is in the first semester of his third year at school, but

he probably would continue in the primary school for a seventh or even eighth semester.

Children entering school at Cabool are tested during their second week to determine mental age and reading level. Then, after several weeks of observation, teachers in the primary department determine assignment of pupils to rooms and reading groups. Instructional materials and equipment are centralized and classified in order that teachers may locate quickly what they need in providing for the several levels to be found in a given room at any time.

Teachers in Green Bay schools date the time each reading level is reached. Parents are able to see progress as it occurs, instead of waiting a year and then perhaps being disappointed because actual progress is lost sight of in the face of retarded overall attainment. Changes from group to group, either within classrooms or between classrooms, occur at any time on the basis of social adjustment to a group or of academic progress (mainly reading).

Change Brings Its Own Burdens

Some school practices have been with us a long time and are firmly intrenched. This is certainly true of the grade structure. During the past century, not only have pupils come to be classified by grades, but, in addition, courses of studies and textbooks have been so classified. Teachers have come to think of themselves as second- or fourth- or sixth-grade teachers and to conduct their professional affairs accordingly. *Unfortunately, many proponents of change do not appreciate fully and early enough just how firmly the graded concept is established in the minds of teachers and parents!*

Green Bay brought in the parents just as soon as the teachers were generally agreed on the professional soundness of the suggested plan. Mothers and fathers discussed all aspects of the proposal at evening meetings. But some parents and teachers still have difficulty in seeing that non-grading permits the use of realistic standards for children of widely varying abilities. Non-grading, properly conceived, most certainly is not a first step in the abandonment of standards.

The chief burden shouldered by educators in moving to non-grading is that of continuously educating parents and teachers to the plan. There are always new parents and, too frequently in schools today, new teachers. Few of them come from schools using ungraded schemes. As a result it is constantly necessary to interpret policies to the newcomers.

Initiating Non-Grading: A Word to the Wise

Are you contemplating moving from graded to non-graded structure? If so, those who have walked the road before you have a few words of advice.

1. Develop understanding first. A year or more of study by parents and teachers before any specific change is made will pay rich dividends. Both groups need to understand the wide range of abilities and attainments represented in a first-grade class. Normally, under good teaching the spread increases instead of decreases as children advance. Teachers and parents must come to understand the barriers placed in the way of normal, continuous progress by the grade concept and its concomitants. They need to understand, too, what the removal of grades will and will not do.

2. Move toward non-grading a step at a time. Teachers may first be helped to divorce themselves from their grade stereotypes by moving along with their pupils into the next grade before ungraded units actually are established. In this way the teachers come to understand more readily the tremendous grade-to-grade overlap of abilities and attainments. There seems to be some advantage, also, in removing the grade barriers a year at a time as a first-year entering group begins to advance through the school. In a relatively short time—six to eight years—only transfer pupils will know what it is to deal with grades and the accompanying externally imposed pressures.

3. Try to see an actual model early in the planning. Some persons must see really to believe and understand. If the model is common to the experience of all, it provides a discussion base from which local plans may evolve more readily.

4. Once the step has been taken, go all the way. Removing grades in name only is not enough. Grade signs must be removed from doors and replaced with "Primary—Miss Smith," "Intermediate—Miss Brown." Progress must never be thought of in terms of "promotion and nonpromotion" or "skipping and repeating." The considerations implied by these terms simply do not exist; they have no part in non-grading. This is difficult for some parents and teachers to understand —*very difficult!* Concepts of individuality, heterogeneity, continuous progress with each child moving at the rate that is best for him, must be hammered away at continuously!

5. Rigorous record-keeping and careful, periodic testing are essential. *Continuous* progress does not mean *haphazard* progress. Those persons in charge have a tremendous responsibility for assuring that each child is placed where he can profit most, where his progress in all aspects of development is optimum. Without careful observation, without periodic tests, without occasional shifting—group to group and class to class—children will be misplaced.

6. Stick to the instructional methods

previously assumed to be sound. If the removal of grades suggests new and more appropriate methods, so much the better. But non-grading is an organizational, not an instructional, device.

7. Experiment. Determine what happens when children are moved through a four-year primary unit beginning with kindergarten in three rather than four years. Determine the effects of remaining in such a unit for five rather than four years. Seek to isolate the most significant factors determining satisfactory pupil placement. Find out what areas of instruction can be taken care of best through completely individualized methods, through small groups, and through total group techniques. Non-grading in itself is little more than door-opening. With the door open, look beyond to see what comes next in finding what we need to know and doing what we know to do.

31. Grouping Helps Children Succeed in the Intermediate Grades *

MARIE B. CLARK

SHOW me a child who is happy in school, and I'll show you one who feels that he is an important member of a group, one who is conscious of personal achievement.

Teachers of grades four, five, and six know that in every classroom there is a wide range in the abilities, interests, and experience backgrounds of the many Johns, Marys, Sues, and Pauls who trip hopefully back to school in September. The "new" teacher holds the key to another year of adventure for these children, and she will be held largely responsible for the growth and achievement, the happiness and security which they attain. Because teachers differ as widely as children in amount and kind of training, in energy, in resourcefulness, and in temperament, the effectiveness of any program —and of the reading program in par-

* From Marie B. Clark, "Grouping Helps Children Succeed in the Intermediate Grades," *Teachers Service Bulletin in Reading,* XIV, no. 1 (October, 1952). Reprinted by permission of the author and The Macmillan Co., New York, N.Y.

ticular—depends largely upon the teacher herself. The plan which works well for one may be quite difficult for another.

A plan which does not work at all is to have all children in the grade, be it fourth, fifth, or sixth, reading the same material. We are agreed that these children have widely different interests, abilities, and backgrounds. It follows necessarily that different materials and different approaches must be used to teach them all to read successfully.

Each day, as I face the children in my classroom, I am deeply moved by the conviction that every child has a right to his share of my help; that he not only expects to succeed, but also needs to do so; that he wants to read and read well; and that I am the one who must open the doors of learning to him in such a way that his hopes are realized.

Who is he?

I. He is the average child in the classroom. By average, I mean that his ability, his interest, and his past experience make it possible for him to carry the normal load for his grade level.

II. He is the below-average child. His reading ability may be two or more levels below his grade placement. Because of emotional insecurity, defective eyesight or hearing, prolonged illness, or delayed readiness for the school program, he is not quite able to carry the regular work. He will need much extra help.

III. He is the gifted child—one might call him the neglected child. It has been said that about one percent of the school population have Intelligent Quotients of 130 or above. Approximately half of these gifted children do not go to college. Many of them do not even go successfully through the grades. Too often the gifted child becomes bored or creates a discipline problem because he can read material two to six grades above his average classmate; his ability is not challenged, his interest is not stimulated, and so he develops undesirable study habits. As a result his work begins to lag behind that of his classmates who may actually have less ability. It is time that we did something constructive to develop and use the abilities of this group.

If reading instruction is to be effective for all these children of different abilities, grouping within the classroom is a *MUST*. How it is done depends upon the teacher and her training, the size of the classroom, the size of the enrollment, the materials available, and so forth. There should never be more groups than a teacher can handle at one time. Generally speaking, three is a workable number.

If possible, the furniture in the classroom should be so arranged that it is conducive to groupings. Tables and chairs or movable desks can be easily arranged. Screwed-down desks can be mounted on strips and arranged in a hollow square, double circles, or small groups. Or, the desks can be screwed to the floor after they have been arranged in group situations.

Groupings at the intermediate level may be according to the skills to be developed. These include: reading for information, recalling facts, noting details, predicting outcomes, finding the central idea, proving statements, outlining, summarizing, skimming, drawing conclusions, using the dictionary, developing word analysis (root word, prefixes, suffixes), and using various attacks in word recognition.

The most effective grouping takes into account children's interests. Boys and girls in grades four, five, and six are interested in everything—animals, science, mystery, adventure, biography, fancy, myths, current events, history, home, school, humorous stories—so there is ample choice for groupings. Whatever method is used, the grouping must be flexible so that no child will feel embarrassment because of his placement and so that every child may be an active participant in several groups. A classroom atmosphere which encourages children to ask questions and find out for themselves is conducive to such flexible grouping. Interesting pictures, a library corner, bulletin boards changed often, science tables, display and storage shelves, plants, aquarium, terrarium, a workshop corner all help stimulate interest in various fields.

The teacher should use the results of standardized tests, intelligence tests, diagnostic tests, individual cumulative records passed along by the previous teacher, as well as her own observation of each child's reading behavior in determining the level of instruction for the groups. Systematic reading instruction, based upon a careful analysis of reading habits and using materials within the reading level of the various groups, is necessary for the achievement of good results. Let us assume that we mean good results for every child, not for just a few. Within every group there is need for attention to individual differences which can not be overlooked. Until the child is provided with material he can read, both his time and the teacher's are wasted. Durrell says, "A selection is considered too difficult if the child has difficulty with more than one word in twenty, or if he reads in a slow, labored manner." [1] Therefore, the material on which the group is to start work should be less difficult than this.

The manuals accompanying basal texts have a wealth of research and good teaching techniques behind them, and each particular reading series has a consistent plan of vocabulary and skill development. These make it possible for teachers to shift a child from one group to another as his needs and achievement vary. The manuals list books and selections for extended reading.

Let us presume that for a particular class a basal text is used and that there are three groups. Three short reading periods are not satisfactory, but every teacher can have at least two groups a day for special instruction. The children in the below-average group are a part of the entire class and need to be recognized as such. Those children want the regular text whether they can read it or not. They will be happy, reading in a different book, if they can still take part in the discussion with those of higher reading levels. This can easily be managed if the teacher will use the "each one teach one" method. An above-average child in the sixth grade will enjoy taking one child or a small group over to the reading table and reading the story to them. Then, during the discussion or sharing period, each child will be able to make his contribution.

The superior group does not need as much supervised help from the teacher, but will have more time for extended

reading activities: reference work, extensive reading in relation to the story, perhaps reading the entire book from which a selection is taken, doing recreatory reading, creating dramatizations, illustrating parts of the story, working in clay, developing marionette or puppet shows, making the marionettes and puppets themselves, and helping slower-learning children to get the story. This group, however, does need specific instruction in order to develop further their skills in reading. This is especially necessary in those school systems where systematic reading instructon ends with the sixth grade. In these schools the sixth-grade teacher must be certain that all the children in her class master the essential reading skills before they leave the grade. The average group will need more help from the teacher. The slower group will need intensive daily help.

While the average and above-average groups are given instruction, the slower group will have a study time for work-type lessons or extended reading. While the average group is being aided by the teacher, the upper group may help the lower one. While the average and below-average groups are being guided by the teacher, the superior groups extends its reading in various ways, reads widely in areas related to the story, or does free or recreatory reading. Every third day or so, the three groups meet together, after they have had sufficient preparation for participation. Different groups may present various interpretations of the story; or they may re-create it for school assembly, the sharing period, or another group.

For the enjoyment of poetry, which all children love if it is presented well, all three groups may be taught together. This is particularly good for the listening period. Then grouping may be effected on the basis of collecting poems the children like, creating original ones, or just hearing more read by the teacher or a good

[1] Donald D. Durrell, *Improvement of Basic Reading Abilities* (Yonkers-on-Hudson, New York: World Book Co., 1940).

reader. All creating of poetry should be absolutely voluntary without any fear of threat or failure. The time has passed when children *had* to learn a certain selection or *had* to "make-up" a poem. Every effort should be made to help children feel relaxed and comfortable during the poetry sessions. As they begin to feel the rhythm and the musical quality of what is being read, they will begin to enjoy poetry.

To enrich the basic reading program, it is wise to have not only sets of supplementary readers for group reading, but also one or two copies of many different books varying widely in interest range and level of reading difficulty. It is more fun to share a story or to listen to one if it is different from all the others. Teachers have seen children literally wilt because some child gave the exact story, report, or news that another one had planned to give.

Science and social studies offer excellent opportunities for re-grouping or for committee work. Herein lies the advantage of grouping *within* the classroom rather than *by* classrooms. It's fun to work with John and Harry in reading because they read about as well as George does, but George likes working science experiments with Howard and Guy, and in social studies it's fun to have some girls on the committee, too. These arrangements are possible because there are a dozen books with science experiments, about animals, the new plastics, television, magazine articles about the stars, airplanes, radar, space ships, and so on. Within the group, each child can find material which he can read and interpret and which is different from all the others. One committee from each group goes to the school or public library to get more materials on the area under discussion. With so much available, browsing really is fun.

A class in social studies, for another example, is studying China. Committees are chosen for various sections. "How chosen?" one asks. Therein lies a method many teachers neglect to use. Let the children choose the part on which they want to work; then help them find material they can use. There will be homes, ways of travel, schools, religion, government, the war, ways of making a living, natural resources, games and entertainment, customs, and many other phases. Material may be gathered from social studies books and readers from third-grade level up, through reference books, stories of Chinese life, newspaper articles, magazine stories, movies, filmstrips, and so forth. Globes, maps, pictures are invaluable aids also. The material available is unlimited to the wide-awake teacher who groups children according to interests and finds materials within their abilities. This cannot be done if every child is expected to do what everyone else does; if the slow learner is frustrated because the material is too difficult; if the gifted child is held back to the level of the average because the teacher "can't find enough hours in a day."

Reading is a systematic development of skills, an extension of interests, hobbies, and so on, based upon the needs, abilities, interests, and experience of children, and no one ever "gets through." Reading is not a race nor is it a mold through which all must pass. Reading does make for individual progress and consistent growth.

How to group children depends upon the teacher's training and understanding. Grouping children is just as necessary in grades four, five, and six as it is in the primary grades; it is possible to do whether classes are large or small; it contributes to emotional security better if done within the classroom rather than by classrooms; groups must be flexible to be most effective. Teachers find such grouping a sure way to help every child succeed.

VII

Individualized Reading

There are two extreme points of view concerning individualized reading. One belief is that it can't be done; the other, that all reading instruction should be individualized. The editors' present opinion lies somewhere in between as evidenced by the selections chosen for this chapter.

While contrasting "the basal text program" with individualized reading, Hunt defines individualized reading and briefly discusses its philosophy, organization, and procedures. Daniel follows with a description of how she individualized her fifth-grade reading program, and Fisch offers some procedures for record keeping that might be used in any reading program. Next, noting that inefficiency may be the most serious weakness of individualized reading, Sartain suggests procedures for adding individualized reading to a basic program, and some possibilities for combining the two approaches. In the final article, Sipay attempts to clarify the strengths and limitations of individualized reading.

32. Philosophy of Individualized Reading *

LYMAN C. HUNT, JR.

THE paramount issue is whether our current emphasis on intensive reading instruction can be brought into balance to some extent through a program of extensive reading. A basic characteristic of the

basal text program is that each lesson is developed in a highly structured, comprehensive fashion—an approach best described as intensive reading instruction. Every selection is read and reread in great detail—word by word, line by line, page by page, story by story, and book by book —in a seemingly endless study. There is a great need to balance this intensity of study with a program which builds reading instruction in a broader, more natural fashion.

Certainly a child's mind needs to brush

* From Lyman C. Hunt, Jr., "Philosophy of Individualized Reading," in J. Allen Figurel (ed.), *Reading and Inquiry*, International Reading Association Conference Proceedings, 10 (Newark, Del.: International Reading Association, 1965), 146–48. Reprinted by permission of the International Reading Association and the author.

up against a multitude of ideas; he needs periods of continuous uninterrupted silent reading in order to pursue ideas in larger gulps, in more continuous development. Providing children with opportunities to read widely in the extensive world of literature available for them can best be accomplished through the program most frequently termed Individualized Reading.

What precisely is the individualized reading program and how does it differ from the typical basal textbook program?

Individualized reading is a program organized to give particular attention to the needs and interest of each individual student. Certain aspects of the program may vary considerably among teachers, however. Some basic principles of individualized reading are common to nearly all classroom situations where it is used. Typical common elements are:

1. Literature books for children predominate (rather than textbooks series) as basic instructional materials
2. Each child makes personal choices with regard to his reading material
3. Each child reads at his own rate and sets his own pace of accomplishment
4. Each child confers with his teacher about what he has read and his progress in reading
5. Each child carries his reading into some form of summarizing activity
6. Some kind of record is kept by teacher or child or both
7. Children work in groups for an immediate purpose and leave the group when that purpose is accomplished
8. Word recognition and related skills are taught and vocabulary is accumulated in a natural way at the point of the child's need

Philosophy

This program is markedly different from the textbook program wherein children are assigned to groups according to reading levels. Once grouped, directed reading instruction is presented to all children simultaneously according to a highly defined procedure within the manual. Each child, bound by the pace of this group, must accomplish material according to the teacher's directions. In individualized reading opposite conditions prevail; children spend blocks of time reading extensively. The individualized reading program is based on a premise that a child's pattern of learning cannot be predetermined in either rate or manner and can best be guided within a highly flexible framework allowing for considerable pupil choice and teacher judgment.

With all the materials of wonder, beauty, and breadth of knowledge available to children in the great variety of literature written for them, it is vital that they be given the opportunity, under guidance, to bring their world and the world of books together. They should have time to explore the books that abound and to select those that touch their "growing edges" in terms of what they want to investigate and learn and enjoy.

By contrast most of our reading textbooks are anthologies of short stories or are collections of excerpts from well-known original stories and books, a common and defensible practice. But it does seem advisable to give children opportunities to come to grips with total presentations as they appear in original works rather than always to select a part or the best part of the total selection.

Organization

If each child is permitted to choose his own reading material according to his own interests, development, and proficiency, he must assume certain responsibilities as a member of the class. Each freedom is balanced by a corresponding responsibility to himself—and to others. He cannot behave so as to interfere with the responsible behavior of his classmates.

Each child must sense how he fits into this kind of program. In addition to sustained silent reading, he may be recording his reading, discussing his reading with teacher or classmates, writing creatively about his reading, choosing his next book, and so on.

Procedures

1. *Book Selection:* Varying degrees of guidance are needed in helping children select books. Some children need almost no assistance, others initially need a great deal of teacher direction in choosing books which are appropriate in level of difficulty, value of content, and even in interest-appeal.

2. *Reading:* Children usually read independently in the materials they have chosen. The teacher directs or controls the reading of those not sufficiently independent to pace themselves. Usually the child sets his own purposes and reads silently at his own rate. It is necessary, however, for each child to show through a variety of activities that his reading is being done in a responsible manner.

3. *Recognition vocabulary:* The accumulation of a recognition vocabulary in the textbook program is built on the concept of a controlled vocabulary. Vocabulary control consists of presenting a limited number of carefully selected words which the child is to learn at the time they are introduced. Success or failure is dependent upon whether these preselected words are learned at the time they are presented. In the individual reading, a child meets words naturally within the context of the story he has chosen to read. He learns them usually because he needs them to get the important ideas in his reading.

A teacher who departs from the method of presenting preselected words must be able to discern whether or not a child is accumulating a recognition vocabulary at a reasonable rate and utilizing word study skills effectively. If a child is accumulating a vocabulary at a rapid rate, he can be encouraged to learn many words through wide reading. If a child is stagnated, then careful and organized teaching must take place.

4. *Conference:* The teacher-child conference is central to the individualized program. In the conference the teacher uses all of her talents and knowledge to intensify children's involvement with words and ideas. During this time teacher and child may discuss appealing aspects of the books, ideas presented by the author, and implication of these ideas as guides for living. The teacher determines whether the child knows what is happening and is able to select the important ideas in the book. The child is often requested to read aloud a particular passage of interest or importance. Frequently preparation is made for sharing the book with the class. The teacher may make a note about the need for particular kinds of help or may provide some on-the-spot instruction. The success of the conference depends on the art of questioning developed by the teacher.

5. *Related activities and sharing:* Hearing about books read by others can foster in children a desire to do something on their own with the new ideas, new learnings, and knowledge contained in books being read. Stimulation to reading widely is gained as children learn from others about new books through creative work, panel discussion, dramatizations, etc.

6. *Record-keeping:* Teachers who use individualized reading instruction have found it necessary to devise ways of keeping records of the children's development in reading. Such records serve as a guide for planning and as a basis for reporting to parents on pupil progress.

7. *Skills groupings:* When several children are identified by the teacher as needing help in the same area, they are grouped together temporarily for this specific instruction.

8. *Interest groupings:* Children often like to work together. Frequently, several children decide to read the same book independently and then meet to discuss the important ideas, what the book has meant to them.

9. *Evaluation:* In every instance where individuals are asked to take responsibility for their actions, their own evaluation of accomplishment is of utmost importance. Where children are expected to be developing independence, the need for continuous evaluation cannot be overstressed. The teacher must develop with her children criteria for determining whether or not they are improving their abilities to select books, read independently, use time wisely, and to respond to meanings and implications from what has been read.

The individualized reading program then differs sharply from the basal textbook program; differs in philosophy, in classroom organization, in utilization of printed materials, and, above all, differs in procedures employed by the teacher. Basically, the difference lies between reading instruction conceived as an intensive activity as contrasted to instruction based on broader extensive reading by children.

References

1. HUNT, L. C. "Can Teachers Learn About Individualized Reading Instruction Through Educational Television?" *Changing Concepts of Reading Instruction,* J. Allen Figurel (ed.). International Reading Association Conference Proceedings, 6 (1961), 145–47.
2. LAZAR, M., DRAPER, M., and SCHWIETERT, L. *A Practical Guide to Individualized Reading.* Bureau of Educational Research, Publication No. 40, October 1960. New York: Board of Education of the City of New York, Brooklyn, N. Y.
3. VEATCH, JEANNETTE. *How To Teach Reading With Children's Books.* New York: Teachers College Press, Columbia University, 1964.

33. You Can Individualize Your Reading Program Too *

MARY ANN DANIEL

RECENTLY many articles have been written stressing the effectiveness of individualized reading programs. I became as enthusiastic as anyone else who has read

* From Mary Ann Daniel, "You Can Individualize Your Reading Program Too," *Elementary English,* XXXIII, no. 7 (November, 1956), 444–46. Reprinted by permission of the author and the National Council of Teachers of English.

these articles—here at last was a method which could cope with the wide range of reading abilities within a classroom. The best way to meet individual differences is to deal with them individually. Now, my classroom was going to be different! Reading was going to be fun! All of my pupils were going to read and like it, I hoped.

As I gazed at the 36 faces—some eager, some apprehensive—on the first day of school in September, I wondered if my plan would succeed. It sounded perfect in every article I had read. But 36 fifth-grade youngsters! My school district, in a rather well-to-do suburb of Philadelphia, believes in grouping for reading. Almost every classroom in our eleven elementary schools has three reading groups. This year, a new reading series was purchased which encouraged the ability grouping. The size of my class and the policy of the school district would certainly encourage the "old-fashioned" ability grouping!

I was determined to make an attempt to work out a plan for a combination—group and individualized reading program. The first thing I did was to check the reading ability level of all of the children. This was done for grouping and for my beginning records for the individualized reading. Each child read a paragraph from a story, we talked about it briefly, and we also talked of how they felt about reading in general. It was both amazing and discouraging to discover the number of children who responded, "I hate it; I can't read."

We had our regular reading groups. I gradually worked out the policy, for the top group first, that one day a week they could read any book they selected during a reading period. I checked what they read individually that day. The other two groups responded, just as I hoped they would, by demanding to know why they couldn't read a book of their own choice also. Soon everyone was making his own selection from our room library of approximately 150–200 books.

From there it was easy to guide the children into forming a Book Club. The first undertaking of the club was a book exchange. Books were brought from home—sometimes six or eight at a time by one youngster. The books were all excellent ones! Only one child brought in a comic book, and the youngsters themselves decided they didn't want any more! The first president of the club, who was an extremely capable little girl, planned programs for the care and handling of books, book quizzes, rearranging and classifying the library shelves (the fifth-grade star football player took charge of this task), and getting others interested in reading. From this last topic they decided to present book reviews at least once a week. At first our book reviews were merely short résumés. The more imaginative youngsters later presented drawings, puppet shows, and short plays. These activities took place during a regular reading period or in the afternoon. Much of the time formerly spent on workbooks was being devoted to these creative activities. Our workbook exercises still got done, however!

Reading periods, when we had the individualized program, always ran 40 to 60 minutes. This was never too much time; in fact, the majority of the children requested more time. During that time I called individuals, volunteers first, over to a corner where we talked about what had happened in the book thus far, discussed the characters and their actions, made predictions of what was to come, read a paragraph orally, and discussed how the book had helped them as individuals. Any difficulties the child had were noted, and later they were worked on. If there was a common problem for five or six youngsters, we went over it together. Individual problems were naturally taken care of individually without wasting the time of the entire group. I found that with my weakest students, who had a great deal of difficulty, it was easier to give them individual assistance either before or after school.

The children kept a diary of the books they read. They made a very short comment about each book, told whether they liked it or not, and discussed what they gained from having read the book. I might say the last two items were the most difficult for them. They could not understand, at first, that it was permissible to say they did not like a book. All of the children thought they *had* to say they liked every book they read. Many of them did not understand what was meant by, "How did the book help you become a better individual?" We had several discussions on this, and more and more of them gradually included that item in their diaries. I found that short book reviews of this type were a help in finding books they would like to receive for Christmas. Brief résumés were written about the most appealing books; these were typed and mimeographed and sent home for Christmas suggestions. After reading several books, the children were encouraged to write their own stories. These were put into book form—bound and illustrated—instead of just written on "good penmanship paper." These books were kept in a conspicuous place so that they were available for reading at all times. What could thrill a child more than to see someone pick up his "bound book" to read?

Of course the time for telling about a book read is most valuable. It is amazing to watch the methods of presentation change and improve as the children do more and more of this reporting. At first all of the reports seemed to follow the same pattern: "This book was about. . . . If you want to know what happened read it." I thought to myself, "Where is all the creativity that is supposed to develop in this reading program?" An original presentation by just one youngster was all that was needed to inspire the others. Soon we had radio reporters, plays, pictures, drawings on the blackboard, papier-mâché puppets, string puppets, and book reviews written in our classroom newspaper. The more creative the presentation, the more irresistible the book became to the other youngsters.

As this program was going on, I still had my regular groups about three days a week. The creativeness from the individual program carried over to the groups. We did more dramatization and felt freer to skip around in the book and select stories that had a particular interest at that time instead of reading from the first story to the last in the correct sequence. I have found that all of the children, in the group reading and individually, felt much freer to come to me for assistance. While working in groups, instead of waiting for everyone to finish, those who finished first worked on their book diaries or methods of presenting books read.

As I have watched this reading program develop since September, I have been most pleased with its results. It has enabled me to know more about the level and ability of each child. Thus I have been able to give more worthwhile individual and group assistance. Naturally, as the children read more books, they became more skilled in self-selection of books. They are very capable of selecting books that they understand and that are well written. The weaker pupils are not embarrassed by their selection of easier books, and the superior readers are not held back. Everyone exhibits more enthusiasm and interest in reading. Because the slower readers select books they are able to read, they soon develop confidence in their reading ability, and their whole attitude toward reading is changed. In the individual program the children want to read; the more they read, the greater degree of success they feel in all of their school work.

34. Record Keeping for Individualized Reading *

MURIEL FISCH

INDIVIDUALIZED reading may be used more and more widely as we see that our children profit more from this type of free choice instruction in the elementary schools than from basal reading teaching. The transition from the reader series program to individualized reading, however, requires careful planning on the part of the teacher and the keeping of even more careful records of the progress of each child. Following is a system of record keeping which worked quite satisfactorily in the sixth-grade class with which I used the individualized approach. The child and the teacher each kept records, and we shall consider them separately.

Teacher's Records

Any notebook will do for the teacher's records. Allotting a double page for each child, I arrange the entire class (boys and girls together) alphabetically. Each page is organized as in Diagram I.

In the "Books Read" column, I put the date, title, and author of book taken. I have found it worthwhile to date each entry even when the book was soon discarded by the child. In looking over accumulated notations, a pattern of behavior often begins to show, which guides me in helping a particular child.

The "Interests and Comments" column is a sort of catchall for notations. For ex-

* From Muriel Fisch, "Record Keeping for Individualized Reading," *Grade Teacher*, LXXVI, no. 2 (November, 1958), 90–91, 93. Reprinted by permission of the author and Teachers Publishing Corporation, Darien, Conn.

ample, if the child is a stamp collector I note it here; if he said sometime that he hated school, I put that down.

At the top left-hand corner of the first page, I write the Reading Grade Level and the Vocabulary Grade Level, based on standardized tests.

In this individualized approach to teaching reading, "Skills Needed" is the most difficult part to decide. Which are important and which should wait for later? I make a list at the end of my notebook of those skills which my school system wishes emphasized at each grade level represented by the children in my class. I classify them under "Ideas," "Words," and "Other." Then I further subdivide "Idea Skills" into "Understanding Ideas," "Interpreting Ideas," and "Organizing Ideas." The "Word Skills" column is for recording "Word Meaning," "Word Analysis," and "Dictionary Skills." As I work with each child in individual conferences, I glance at the list and decide which of his needs for his grade level seems most urgent. That need I jot down in the appropriate column.

Under the "Other Skills" column I note such items as "Choppy phrasing in oral reading," "Silent reading: moves lips." Here, too, I write down what the child shared with the class during the "Sharing Period."

When a child has made his book selection, either from the public library or from the school library, I test his ability to read the book without frustration, using the standard of fewer than five errors in a hundred running words. If the book is too hard, then I help him find a

Page 1		Page 2
Tony B.		Tony B.
	Conference Dates	

BOOKS READ	INTERESTS COMMENTS	SKILLS NEEDED		
		Idea	Word	Other

simpler book on the same subject or on an interest I have noted in the "Interests" column.

Library Records

Both children and teacher bring in books for the classroom library from which children may select in the course of the term. The ideal is ten books per child, although I have gotten along with far fewer.

A card is kept inside each on the shelves. Author and title are written across the top, and columns for "Borrower's Name," "Date Borrowed," and "Date Returned" below. A duplicate set on smaller cards, with just author and title, is kept in my files as a record of total number of books in the library. It is convenient to use different colored cards for books belonging in the separate library sections.

The Reading Period

My reading period is forty minutes a day, allocated as follows: thirty minutes for everyone to read silently, except for the child who has an individual conference with me. I see six children for five minutes each in such a period. Then five minutes is used for writing summaries and five minutes for sharing.

During the individual conference I hear the child read, or test some of the other skills at his level. I concentrate on one skill per conference. After a period of two or three weeks there are usually from six to seven children needing help on some particular skill. I take these during the silent reading period and work with them as a group. At the back of my book I note the date, the skill taught, and the children participating.

About once a month I take the reading period to teach to the whole class a skill that is needed by the majority of the children. For this purpose I use a reader because each child needs a copy of a common text.

Child's Notebook

The child's notebook may be arranged in the following way:

SUMMARIES

Date	Title	Author	Pages Read

Summary of day's reading . . . .

The last column contains notation only of pages read during class periods. Gaps therefore indicate home reading. The summary is a sentence or two telling the most important action which took place within the pages read. To assist the child in writing summaries I ask him to answer two or three of the *"W's"*: *Who, What, Why, When, Where.*

The back of the child's notebook is set up as in Diagram 3:

VOCABULARY

Date	Book	Page #	Word in phrase

Word, dictionary meaning, and new phrase with word . . . .

During the individual reading period the child tries to make out any new word from the context. Only if he finds it impossible to continue and make sense of what he is reading does he stop to look up the word in the dictionary, noting the page on which the word occurred. During the summary period he makes the entry on his Vocabulary page, using the phrase from the story and then one of his own.

In the center of the notebook the child keeps suggestions for making summaries, vocabulary notations, and sharing. For example:

Sharing an excerpt:

Introduction: Just enough (one or two sentences) so that the class can understand the part being read.

Excerpt: One or two sentences or a short paragraph which is exciting or mysterious, to share with classmates.

After the sharing of an excerpt, there is a show of hands of all children who, having heard the excerpt, wish to read the book. They can reserve the book by signing on the card for the book, leaving, of course, the "Date Borrowed" column blank.

Sharing vocabulary:

(Choose a word which you think the majority of the children may wish to add to their day-to-day vocabulary.)

Write the word in a phrase on the board.

Underline the word.

Give the meaning and a new sentence orally.

It is necessary for the teacher to go over with the child the item he expects to share with the class. This is done during the individual conference. Shy children need considerable encouragement at first, but the teacher's enthusiasm for a new word or for an especially exciting passage may give the necessary boost. Sharing his contribution alone first with the teacher helps. No comments are made during the brief, five-minute sharing periods.

At the completion of a book, a child may write a review, a character study, a poem about an event or person in the story. He may draw a scene or a portrait of a character. He might make a book jacket—any individually satisfying culmination at his own level.

35. The Place of Individualized Reading in a Well-Planned Program *

HARRY W. SARTAIN

Some Experimental Evidence on Individualized Reading

INDIVIDUALIZED reading has a unique and worthy quality. The personal nature of the conferences between the pupil and the teacher has a highly salutary effect on the child's attitude. He feels that the teacher is interested in him as an individual as well as in what he is reading. He responds to the teacher's encouragement, and, according to most reports, he reads considerably more.

Unfortunately this great strength is offset by a serious weakness in individualized reading—inefficiency. The most conscientious teachers find themselves frustrated in their efforts to schedule as many conferences as the children really need; often they feel that they can take time to teach only a part of the needed skills. They have doubts about the permanence of learnings which are not systematically reviewed. They spend an inordinate amount of time in preparing ten to fifteen individual reading skills lessons each day, and then feel that they are forced to present them somewhat superficially because of time limitations (15).

Some capable teachers who have experimented successfully with a totally individualized program, have preferred to return to basal reading in small groups or

to a combination of procedures. They usually find that their classes can be divided into three to six groups of children, who are able to learn and utilize new skills at approximately the same pace. The planning for six groups can be far more thorough and systematic than that needed for thirty individuals. More important, it permits the teacher to introduce the new words and concepts which the children need in order to read with maximum comprehension and pleasure. The discussion of stories read by *a group* deepens the children's insights, critical reading abilities, appreciation of literary qualities, and ability to express reactions acceptably to others. All these attributes of basal instruction in small groups attest to the greater efficiency of this type of organization over the totally individualized approach.

In brief, it can be said that the individualized system has one outstanding strength—the personal pupil-teacher conference, and one tremendous weakness—inefficiency. Most statistically controlled experiments have revealed that capable pupils with the aid of well-educated, experienced, and dedicated teachers, can learn to read approximately as well in the individualized way as through basic grouping (1,15,21). Since not all children are of good capability and not all teachers organize well the work of thirty children, it would seem unwise to recommend that all classes utilize the individualized plan. It will be much more fruitful to combine the best features of individualized reading

* From Harry W. Sartain, "The Place of Individualized Reading in a Well-Planned Program," in *Contributions in Reading*, no. 28, pp. 3–7. Reprinted by permission of the author and Ginn and Co., Waltham, Mass.

with the proven practices in basal work. Some teachers have been doing this in various ways for years.

Adding Individualized Reading to the Basic Program

When incorporating individual work into standard programs, teachers usually follow these procedures with some variations (23).

1. Divide the class into several small groups for instruction in the basic skills. A minimum of three groups will always be required for adequately differentiated pacing. Five groups will usually accommodate all but the very unusual pupil.

2. If possible, use a "new" basal series for each group. Fresh material for every group greatly improves the children's reading interests, makes basic reading a real thought-getting process, and reduces the stigma associated with grouping. If three basic sets are available, differences in the progress rates of groups will probably be large enough so that books used by the first groups will seem new when read later by the fourth and fifth groups. As each group of children moves into a different classroom for the next school term, *they should continue to work in their own basal series*. Of course, each group should progress through the series at the rate of its capability, regardless of the grade designation.

3. With most groups use only the *one* set of basic materials during the year. This will make it possible to teach a skills program *completely* instead of piecemeal, as is sometimes done when classes race through several series.

4. Utilize the teacher's manual consistently to teach thoroughly the complete skills program for each group. Do not dwell on a specific skill longer than is needed for a group to learn it. However, if the lessons in one manual are not ade-

quate for the group concerned, supplement them from the manuals for other series.

5. Use the basic reader workbooks in the same way to reinforce the skills program and to enrich the study backgrounds. Most children may need most of the pages in their workbooks, but do not hesitate to let a child skip exercises that he does not need. Freely supplement those exercises that are not adequate for some individuals. Do not flood the class with additional workbooks and worksheets which simply keep them busy repeating exercises which they have learned earlier.

6. Collect in the classroom all the additional "basic" readers, supplementary readers, and good trade books that can be obtained. The bibliographies in teachers' manuals can be of invaluable aid in selecting books. One to three copies each of more than a hundred different titles are necessary for an adequate program. They should range in difficulty from approximately four years in the first grade to eight years in the sixth grade. They can be placed on shelves in three or four very general difficulty classifications to simplify selection by pupils. Colored paper slips in each book can direct children in returning them to shelves that are similarly labeled.

7. During all the time when they are not engaged in basic study, the children should enjoy the reading of books and stories of their own choosing from this room library and from other sources. Thus they are introduced to the skills through the basic materials, and they gain proficiency through extensive independent reading. The basic readers may create interests which children will want to follow, or pupils may wish to read along other paths. Now they have something to challenge them in every spare moment during the day, plus homework for those

who want it! The teacher is relieved of the preparation and correction of endless seatwork exercises, and can spend more time with groups and individuals.

8. Arrange to have the children share their independent reading with others in several ways. A few of these are:

—Individual conferences with the teacher as often as possible. These can take place while others are reading silently or during specially scheduled periods. Since skills are taught systematically through the basic program, these conferences need be only long enough to show real interest in the child's work, to motivate further reading, and to provide occasional assistance with individual problems
—Conferences between two pupils about favorite stories
—Storytelling, sometimes to the whole class, but more often to small groups of personal friends
—Oral reading of favorite parts in groups of about four students
—Dramatization of a story enjoyed by several pupils
—Making and displaying dioramas or peep shows that illustrate books
—Designing book jackets that will attract others to read the books
—Making mobiles to stimulate the imagination in respect to certain stories
—"Auctioning" books by telling successively more tantalizing events in the plot, but not reaching the climax
—Having characters in different books meet, either in writing or "in person"
—Making paper doll illustrations
—Giving the story action on the flannelboard

The number of ways in which books can be shared is as unlimited as the imagination of the teacher and the class.

9. Have the children keep records of their independent reading. The satisfaction gained from their accomplishments will spur them on to further reading.

The forms of the records should be changed frequently. Some are:

—Scrapbooks of illustrations and summaries of stories
—Charts showing different types of literary materials read
—"Collection boxes" of "souvenirs" from good stories
—Charts on which stories are evaluated according to criteria set by the class
—Devices to which segments are added for each book read—the "bookworm," the giraffe that "stretches upward" with books, the flowering "garden" of books, the "tower" of books, etc.

10. Keep card records of special learning difficulties of individual pupils. Occasionally bring together several children from various groups for help with a common problem. Schedule at least a couple of fifteen-minute periods a week for this type of corrective teaching in flexible groups.

Organizing Combined Programs

The procedure for dividing instructional time between basal and independent reading will depend upon the wishes of each teacher and the needs of the pupils. A few possibilities are:

Individualized Supplementary Reading

This is the procedure that has been referred to in most of the preceding paragraphs. It is easily managed in both primary and later grades. The basic lessons are taught in small groups. The individualized reading proceeds continuously whenever children are not working on basic assignments. While the teacher is engaged with one group, the others will complete workbook requirements and then spend all remaining time on independent reading. The teacher can relate the sharing activities to language instruction in order to schedule more time. Frequently the "telling time" periods that begin the day can be devoted to telling about books in the interesting ways mentioned earlier. A few brief individual conferences should be scheduled daily in place of the time the teacher would otherwise spend in explaining and correcting needless seatwork. Supplementary individualized reading can be added to all of the additional plans that are suggested.

Alternating Basic and Individual Reading Periods

In primary grades most teachers have long periods for reading instruction twice during the day. In some classrooms the books used in the morning are different from those used in the afternoon. Basic and individualized work can be combined easily by scheduling the sequential skills work in the morning and the self-selected reading during the afternoon period. This is probably the simplest way for the teacher to make a first attempt at individualized reading.

Periodic Reinforcement of Basic Skills with Individualized Reading

At any grade level a group may alternate a few weeks of study in the basic materials with extended periods of individualized reading. In this situation the teacher will keep a group in basic books and workbooks while a new phase of skill building is being introduced. Before the next skill or set of skills is presented, the children may put aside the basic materials and spend a few days or weeks practicing the new skill through individualized reading. Such an organization insures sequential learning and gives specific direction to the instructional emphasis in each phase of the individualized program. In each room some of the groups will be engaged in basal reading while others are reading self-selected materials. Because the skills have already been introduced, the individual conferences can be quite brief, allowing the teacher time to work effectively with the other children in basal groups.

The less capable children should spend a smaller proportion of time on independent than on basic work. One experiment with ten second-grade classes (20) revealed that slower pupils make appreciably less progress when they do not receive direct instruction daily. The plan of alternating extended basic reading with individualized work can be especially well adapted to the needs of slow pupils. Since the reading program of each group is different, the teacher can give slow groups fewer weeks of individualized work without calling this to the attention of other children. Thus the less capable pupils can spend most of the time on sound skills development, which will help them to feel more comfortable in all classroom study situations.

The periodic reinforcement plan is probably the easiest for a teacher who has never scheduled *independent* reading before. Individualized reading can be undertaken with only the most able group while the teacher tries out varied techniques of conferring and record keeping. As one feels secure with the procedures, he can apply them to other groups.

Completion of a Basic Program Before Beginning Individualized Reading

Here each group completes the basic program in its assigned series before the end of the year. The reading periods for the remainder of the year are spent in self-selected reading and individual conferences. Again the brightest children, who complete a basic program fastest, will spend the most time in individual work. This is commendable because they are capable of profiting from self-directed study. Some schools encourage the most able groups to move beyond their grade levels in the basic books. In this case the teacher must judge the point at which the introduction of new skills should cease in favor of more individual practice. Slower children should still have the privilege of independent supplementary reading as a part of their seatwork.

Basic and Individualized Study Combined in the Topical Reading Unit

This is the most complex way to produce this combination, but teachers who have practiced it for several years find the plan to be particularly rewarding. Progress through the basic readers is paced in such a way that two or more groups, preferably the whole class, are reading on approximately the same theme. Examples of such topics are "Imaginative Tales," "Children of Other Lands," or "Stories of Heroes."

Together the pupils and the teacher plan a project which will require extensive independent reading on the topic. The project may be a set of puppet shows, a museum, a radio broadcast, or a program for parents. The children search through all of the room and building library materials to obtain every bit of available information. To aid each other, they evaluate materials; they build a class bibliography; they keep records; and they organize material for sharing. In the process they practice many of the work-study skills that have been introduced.

This instructional organization is especially recommended for the intermediate and upper grades because of the content of their readers. Also there is more possibility of children's being sensitive about grouping as they get older. Under the topical unit plan they work in groups only two or three times a week. The other periods are spent on planning, sharing, and activity work which cuts across group membership.

Summary

Teachers throughout the country have found that there need be no conflict between sequential basic reading in groups and individualized reading. Emphasis on the latter has reawakened teachers to the value of the one-to-one relationship between teacher and pupil. However, there is a heritage of other valuable techniques that has grown through many years of research and practice. By incorporating extensive independent reading and personal conferences into a sound basic program, teachers can take another stride forward in the fruitful teaching of reading.

References

1. Acinapuro, Philip. "A Comparative Study of the Results of Two Instructional Reading Programs—An Individualized and a Three Ability Group Pattern." Unpublished Doctoral Dissertation. New York: Teachers College, Columbia University, 1959.

2. *Adventuring with Books*. Champaign, Ill.: National Council of Teachers of English, 1960. (Supplement, 1963.)

3. Aronow, Miriam S. "A Study of the Effect of Individualized Reading on Children's Reading Test Scores,"

The Reading Teacher, 15 (November, 1961), 86–91.

4. BARBE, WALTER B. *Educator's Guide to Personalized Reading Instruction.* Englewood Cliffs, N.J.: Prentice-Hall, Inc., 1961. 241 pages.

5. CARR, CONSTANCE. "Individualizing Development of Abilities and Skills in Reading: A Description and Critique of Emerging Practices." Unpublished Doctoral Dissertation. New York: Teachers College, Columbia University, 1959.

6. CAVANAUGH, CECELIA L. "Every Child's Reading Needs Are Unique," *Instructor* (March, 1959).

7. DARROW, HELEN M., and HOWES, VIRGIL M. *Approaches to Individualized Reading.* New York: Appleton-Century-Crofts, 1960. 102 pages.

8. EVANS, N. DEAN. "An Individualized Reading Program for the Elementary Teacher," *Elementary English,* 30 (May, 1953), 275–80.

9. ————. "Individualized Reading: Myths and Facts," *Elementary English,* 39 (October, 1962), 580–83.

10. FIGUREL, J. ALLEN (ed.). "Individualized Instruction in the Classroom," *Improvement of Reading through Classroom Practice.* Proceedings of the Annual Convention. (Newark, Del.: International Reading Association, 1964), pp. 92–100.

11. GRAY, WILLIAM S. "Role of Group and Individualized Teaching in a Sound Reading Program," *The Reading Teacher,* 11 (December, 1957), 99–104.

12. GUILFOILE, ELIZABETH. *Books for Beginning Readers.* Champaign, Ill.: National Council of Teachers of English, 1962. (Also a 1963 supplement of *One Hundred More Books for Beginning Readers.*)

13. HARRIS, ALBERT J. (ed.). *Readings on Reading Instruction.* New York:

David McKay Co., Inc., 1963. Chapter VII.

14. KARLIN, ROBERT. "Some Reactions to Individualized Reading," *The Reading Teacher,* 11 (December, 1957), 95–98. (See additional articles in this issue.)

15. LOFTHOUSE, YVONNE M. "Individualized Reading: Significant Research," *The Reading Teacher,* 16 (September, 1962), 35–37, 47.

16. MIEL, ALICE (ed.). *Individualizing Reading Practices,* Practical Suggestions for Teaching, No. 14. New York: Teachers College, Columbia University, 1958.

17. RICHSTONE, MAY. "An Individualized Reading Program," *The Instructor,* 73 (February, 1964), 70–72, 93, 125, 135.

18. ROBINSON, HELEN M. "News and Comment," *Elementary School Journal,* 60 (May, 1950), 411–20.

19. SAFFORD, ALTON L. "Evaluation of an Individualized Reading Program," *The Reading Teacher,* 13 (April, 1960), 266–70.

20. SARTAIN, HARRY W. "The Roseville Experiment with Individualized Reading," *The Reading Teacher,* 13 (April, 1960), 277–81.

21. ————. "Research on Individualized Reading," *Education,* 81 (May, 1961), 515–20.

22. ————. *Individualized Reading, An Annotated Bibliography.* Newark, Del.: International Reading Association, 1964. 8 pages.

23. ————. "Individual or Basal in Second and Third Grades?" *The Instructor,* LXXIV (March, 1965), 69, 96, 100.

24. STAUFFER, RUSSELL G. "Individual and Group Type Directed Reading Instruction," *Elementary English,* 37 (October, 1960), 375–82.

25. VEATCH, JEANETTE. *Individualizing*

Your Reading Program. New York: G. P. Putnam's Sons, 1959. 242 pages.

26. WITTY, PAUL A., with ANN COOMER and ROBERT SIZEMORE. "Individualized Reading—A Summary and Evaluation," *Elementary English,* 36 (October, 1959), 401–12, 450.

27. ———. "Individualized Reading: A Postscript," *Elementary English,* XXXXI (March, 1964), 211–17.

36. Individualized Reading: Theory and Practice *

EDWARD R. SIPAY

INNOVATIONS in education always have met with opinions which have ranged from vigorous enthusiasm to complete denigration. Individualized reading has not proven to be an exception. And just as praise and condemnation were inescapable, it also was inevitable that individualized reading be compared with the more structured basal reader approach. As they say in boxing parlance, it was a natural. A few years ago, emotions ran high and there was no apparent middleground. Battle lines were drawn and research was initiated almost immediately to determine which approach was more effective. The only valid conclusion that could be drawn from much of this "research," however, was that there is a high correlation between the prestudy opinion of the investigator and his findings.

Lately, emotions have subsided and we have begun to take a more objective look at both approaches. Once more we have come to realize that the success or failure

of an approach often is dependent on its proper use; and in turn, that proper usage is based upon a thorough understanding of the approach. Therefore, this paper will be concerned with some of the theories and practices basic to individualized reading, in the hope that a better understanding of what individualized reading actually encompasses and a clarification of its advantages and limitations will result in a more effective use of the approach. . . .

Advantages

There is little doubt that, when properly conducted, individualized reading has certain advantages over other approaches. Articles describing these in detail are common in the current literature. The following list can only hope to summarize a few such advantages:

1. More extensive reading is promoted because self-initiated reading creates interest and enjoyment and because success eliminates undesirable attitudes toward reading.
2. The child strives for self-improvement and makes more rapid progress because he is not compared with others and is therefore neither frustrated nor hindered by group standards.

* From Edward R. Sipay, "Individualized Reading: Theory and Practice," in Coleman Morrison (ed.), *Children Can Learn to Read . . . But How?*, Rhode Island College Reading Conference Proceedings, 1964 (Providence, R.I.: Oxford Press), pp. 82–93. Reprinted by permission of Dr. Coleman Morrison.

3. The reading program is more efficient in that maximum use is made of time because the program is tailored to meet the specific needs of each child.

4. The overall classroom program is strengthened because individualized reading encourages the use of a wide variety of materials in each content subject rather than a single on-grade text.

5. A real audience situation exists for oral reading either during the pupil-teacher conference and/or when the child shares what he has read with his peers.

6. Greater social interaction and growth is fostered because the "caste system of reading groups" (9) is broken down and children are encouraged to share and to discuss their reading with others.

7. The child is assisted in the development of self-direction in that he learns: (a) to select reading materials wisely; (b) to handle individual responsibility; and (c) to set goals for himself.

In addition to these advantages, one of the most valid arguments for individualized reading is the concern shown for the child's mental health. This approach does not pose a threat to the child's ego. When a child competes only with himself, when success is stressed, and when the pressures and tensions created by trying to conform to group standards are eliminated the child feels a sense of security and a stronger self-image emerges.

Limitations

Individualized reading does have many things to recommend it. There is, however, still disagreement concerning the effectiveness of the approach. Many of these debates could be carried on ad infinitum because each side is arguing from a different frame of reference. The opponents frequently condemn the whole approach without making any distinction among its component parts. On the other hand, few advocates will admit to any possible limitations, and rarely is it realized that the main points of disagreement center on the validity of certain assumptions. Hopefully, the ensuing discussion will help to clarify this situation by bringing the points of disagreement and the possible limitations into proper focus and perspective.

Reading Materials

A prime example of the existing confusion involves reading materials. Few would question that the effectiveness of any individualized reading program is influenced by the amount and type of reading materials available to the children; or, that without a wide range of materials from which to choose, seeking and self-selection become meaningless concepts. Rather, disagreement centers on the availability of an adequate supply of materials. Advocates of the approach claim that reading materials are in abundance; the opponents, that there is a paucity. Both are correct to a certain extent. The most recent Harvard-Carnegie study reported that an adequate supply of materials was available where individualized reading was employed; but, it also pointed out that the lack of reading materials in most schools (which used a basal reader approach for the most part) ". . . would drastically curtail, if not preclude, the success of any individualized reading program" (1). So it seems that each faction, like the blind man and the elephant, base their assumptions upon the situation as it exists in their milieus. Once this difference is recognized, the futility of the debate becomes obvious.

One other point needs to be clarified. Granted that most schools do not have a sufficient supply of reading materials, it should be recognized that this is not a weakness in the individualized reading approach itself. One cannot condemn individualized reading for this shortcoming in the schools any more than one could blame the publishing firms for poor reading programs if the schools did not own basal readers. An inadequate supply of reading materials should be recognized as a possible limitation; but one which could be eliminated if boards of finance would loosen their purse strings.

Seeking, Self-selecting, and Pacing

The assumptions concerning seeking and self-selection are more inherent in the approach. As Barbe pointed out, the concept of self-selection ". . . assumes that children have within themselves the ability to select those reading materials which, sometimes for very apparent reasons and other times not so apparent reasons, meet his particular interests and needs" (3). In other words, the assumption is made that the child will seek and select material which is most suitable for him at that particular point in his maturation. The opponents of individualized reading question whether children have the insight to comprehend their needs and suggest that despite the old adage, many books are still judged by their covers or some other eye-approaching factor such as illustrations or size. This is a moot point, however, because there is little, if any, research evidence to substantiate either point of view.

A similar situation exists with pacing. According to Harris, "Advocates of pacing believe that each child's growth pattern is unique and that when he is given freedom the pace he naturally selects will in the long run be wise" (6). Yet, as with self-selection there is little specific evidence that such is or is not the case. What is needed is definitive research in these two aspects of individualized reading.

To digress briefly it should be pointed out that there is also the danger of the concepts being carried to extremes. For example, if the concept of self-selection is followed to its logical conclusion the child has the right not to choose anything at all; or, to put it more bluntly, not to read if he doesn't want to do so. The degree to which a teacher can or should attempt to motivate reading and to guide a child's selection needs to be clarified.

As for pacing, Harris pointed out, "A corollary belief is that if a child does not learn to read the best thing to do is to wait for readiness, even if it takes years; remedial help is considered to be a form of forcing and therefore does violence to the principle of pacing" (6). Such beliefs also appear to stem from the writings of Olson. For example, in his book on child growth and development he proposed that a child should be taught to read only when he indicates his readiness to do so; and seemed to imply that we should wait for the child to display this readiness (10). In my opinion, however, merely to wait and not attempt to develop the factors which can influence reading readiness would be almost as harmful as forcing a child to read when he clearly is not ready to undertake so complex a task.

Regarding remedial instruction, Olson contended:

Psychologists and other workers in reading clinics have made substantial contributions to the understanding of child development, and the writer believes research, mental hygiene for children, and the education of staff members, rather than demonstrated values for stimulation [of growth in reading ability], to be the major long-time justification of such facilities. This conviction stems first from the conclusion that the clinical services are sometimes introduced and used because of unreasonable expectations of accomplishment. For example, about four to nine times as many boys as girls are sent to clinics. There is probably nothing in the difference that time and a good environment in a regular class will not cure equally well for boys as for girls. Unrealistic ideas concerning minimum or average achievement should give way to expectancies that coincide with the full variability of the human material. It seems better in the long run also to work for smaller groups of children in normal grade relationships rather than to confess failure to meet the range of needs in large groups. As teachers increase their professional and technical preparations they should also find it possible to carry into regular classroom procedures some of the clinician's regard for the person.

A more fundamental reservation on the general advocacy of remedial teachers and clinics as agencies for child development in schools arises from the unconvincing nature of the evidence that growth in reading is actually stimulated by tutoring, by special diagnosis and correction of defect, and by specialized instructional techniques (10).

In all candor, it is difficult for me to accept Olson's opinion concerning diagnosis and remediation for to do so would necessitate the seeking of a new profession. He is correct in questioning the scarcity of controlled research which attempted to determine whether children with reading problems who received diagnostic and remedial assistance became better readers than similar children who did not receive such treatment. Yet the wisdom of the apparent admonition to wait for the child to mature and to let time heal "the wounds" is at best questionable. Certainly unattainable goals should not be set for the child; but, we must ask ourselves if it is more harmful to attempt to help the child overcome specific weaknesses which may be preventing him from making progress or to wait and perhaps allow him to flounder. We must be realistic and admit that, be it right or wrong, most of our schools and our society do set certain standards of attainment. And, what hap-

pens to a child's self-image, especially if he is an older intelligent child, when he sees everyone around him achieving and no effort is being made to help him do likewise? He cannot be impervious to this situation no matter how accepting the basic environment. Nor does such a "wait and see" policy consider the possibility of psychological or neurological dysfunctioning.

Another extreme viewpoint also involves the concept of pacing. In some situations, lest she violate the pacing principle, the teacher waits for the child to request a conference rather than schedule conferences for him. The possible dangers in such a practice are so obvious that they need not be enumerated.

Individual Conferences

The debate concerning individual conferences does not involve pupil-teacher conferences *per se* because few would question their worth. Rather, it centers on whether the frequency and duration of these conferences allow a sufficient time to accomplish the desired aims. If, as Veatch contends, "Most teachers, once in the swing of things, can hold six to ten individual conferences and three to five instructional or other kind of group sessions in the average reading period [1–2 hours]" (12), the frequency of conferences would not appear to be any great problem, provided of course that the class enrollment was reasonable. There is some evidence, however, that *most* teachers do not or cannot accomplish such a feat (1). As for the duration of each conference, Harris asserted that:

During these conferences the teacher is expected: (1) to find out what the child has read since his last conference; (2) to have a discussion of what he has read, which includes questioning to evaluate his comprehension and recall and also gives him opportunity to state his personal opinions about the content; (3) to listen to him read orally a small sample from the material he has been reading silently; (4) to give him an opportunity to talk about what he would like to read about next; (5) to make note of any special difficulties or needs that become apparent; (6) to give help with words, teach or reinforce phonic and structural analysis skills, ask questions that stimulate thinking, and in general supply assistance as it is needed; and (7) to write a concise summary in the child's cumulative reading record (6).

Upon reading such a list, three questions immediately come to mind: (1) Are teachers expected to accomplish all of these aims during every conference?; (2) If so, can most teachers satisfactorily accomplish all, or any, of these during a five- to ten-minute conference?; and (3) If not, should the purpose of the conference change with each situation? It is difficult to find definite answers to any of these questions in the available literature. The role of the individual conferences needs to be clarified and understood.

Teacher's Knowledge of Book Content

A factor closely related to the success of a conference is the teacher's knowledge of the content of reading materials. The detractors of individualized reading argue that because there is no limit to what children can select for reading instruction, the teacher's knowledge of book content is not or cannot be sufficient to check comprehension adequately. On the other hand, Frazier maintained that it is unrealistic to expect teachers to know every book as well as the stories in a basal reader which they might have used repeatedly (5). Perhaps we should accept that with the proliferation of children's books it is an almost impossible task to "know" every available trade book

as thoroughly as the basal reader stories. Again certain questions need to be answered: (1) How extensive must a teacher's knowledge of book content be in order to check comprehension adequately? (2) What does adequately mean? and (3) What are the most effective ways of checking comprehension within the limitations imposed by allowing self-selection?

Record Keeping

Adequate record keeping is also essential to a successful individualized reading program. Although the advocates assume that this aspect of the approach is carried out, the assumption does not appear to be a valid one in many cases. According to Austin and Morrison the record keeping of many teachers using an individualized approach was either inadequate or non-existent (1). This should not be misconstrued to indicate the futility of attempting to individualize reading. Realizing that such a situation exists, the proponents should attempt to determine why adequate records are not being kept. Is it because teachers are too busy? Have they found it isn't worth the time and effort? Or, is it due to a lack of knowledge of what to look for, how to record it, and how to make use of this information?

Skill Development

There is also disagreement regarding the development of reading skills. Both groups quote studies which indicate that under their favorite approach children read as well as or better than children exposed to "the other" reading program. Usually, these findings are based upon a comparison of the average scores obtained on standardized tests. But what do grade-equivalent or percentile ranks mean? They do not tell us which specific reading skills the child has mastered. Nor do they indicate which attitudes and habits the child has acquired. The debate is meaningless because both groups speak in generalities not specifics. We really do not know which particular skills or attitudes are best developed through the use of either approach; or, why and under what circumstances particular skills are developed to their fullest. What we need is less petty bickering and more carefully controlled detailed research.

Teacher Competency

Finally, we come to the most important factor in any program—the teacher. There is evidence which indicates some, if not many, teachers may not possess the knowledge necessary to conduct an effective reading program under any approach. For example, Farinella concluded that an alarmingly large number of teachers showed a marked deficiency in their knowledge of phonic and structural analysis (4). And, the Harvard-Carnegie studies found that future teachers received only minimal training in the teaching of reading and that once they entered the profession little help was forthcoming from in-service courses (2,4). Therefore, it seems ludicrous to debate whether or not most teachers could conduct a successful individualized reading program. A teacher cannot design and execute a program tailored for each child if she does not know which basic skills should be developed and how best to teach them. Nor is a great deal of record keeping meaningful if she is unable to diagnose specific reading difficulties and to evaluate progress. In addition, if the teacher does not know the various comprehension skills which should be taught, knowledge of book content is valueless. Any reading program is influenced by the teacher's knowledge and skill; but, in individualized reading a competent teacher is all-important. The teacher is the key to success because she has no planned sequential outline to follow, no manual to clutch faithfully, nor any workbook with which to keep children busy. She has only to rely on her own knowledge and skill. The implications for teacher education are abundantly clear.

Summary

In summary then, individualized reading is based upon sound theoretical and psychological principles. Properly conducted, it has a number of advantages over other approaches. Like other approaches, however, it also has its limitations. Some basic assumptions are open to question and are in need of more specific research and clarification. Before attempting to individualize her reading program, a teacher should not only be aware of the strengths and limitations of the approach itself but of her own as well.

References

1. AUSTIN, MARY C., MORRISON, COLEMAN, et al. The First R. New York: The Macmillan Company, 1963.
2. ———, ———. The Torch Lighters. Cambridge, Mass.: Harvard Graduate School of Education, 1961.
3. BARBE, WALTER D. Personalized Reading Instruction. Englewood

Cliffs, N. J.: Prentice-Hall Inc., 1961.

4. FARINELLA, JOHN T. "An Appraisal of Teacher Knowledge of Phonetic Analysis and Structural Analysis." Unpublished Doctoral Dissertation. University of Connecticut, 1959. (As quoted in Cutts, Warren C. *Research in Reading for the Middle Grades*. Washington, D.C.: U. S. Government Printing Office OE 30009, #31, 1963.)

5. FRASIER, ALEXANDER. "The Individualized Reading Program." *Controversial Issues in Reading and Promising Solutions*. Helen M. Robinson (ed.). Chicago: University of Chicago Press, 1961.

6. HARRIS, ALBERT J. *Effective Teaching of Reading*. New York: David McKay Company, Inc., 1962.

7. HEILMAN, ARTHUR. *Principles and Practices of Teaching Reading*. Columbus, Ohio: Charles E. Merrill Books, Inc., 1961.

8. JACOBS, LELAND. "Individualized Reading Is Not a Thing!" *Individualizing Reading Practices*, Alice Miel (ed.). New York: Bureau of Publications, Teachers College, Columbia University, 1958.

9. LAZAR, MAY. "Individualized Reading: A Program of Seeking, Self-Selection, and Pacing." *Individualizing Your Reading Program*, Jeannette Veatch (ed). New York: G. P. Putnam's Sons, 1959.

10. OLSON, WILLARD C. *Child Development*. Boston: D.C. Heath and Company, 1949.

11. ———. "Seeking, Self-Selection, and Pacing in the Use of Books by Children." *Individualizing Your Reading Program*, Jeannette Veatch (ed.). New York: G.P. Putnam's Sons, 1959.

12. VEATCH, JEANNETTE. *Individualizing Your Reading Program*. New York: G.P. Putnam's Sons, 1959.

VIII

Word Recognition and Word Analysis

In order to be an efficient independent reader, one must amass a vast number of words that are recognized immediately, and be able to decode words that are not in one's sight vocabulary. It is with these two aspects of reading—word recognition and word analysis—that this chapter is concerned.

Word perception is a very complex process. Any doubts of this should be dispelled by Taylor's article. Bagford then discusses the proper role of phonics in a reading program. The next three articles, by Betts, Meighen and Pratt, and Dolch, are concerned with ways of teaching some word analysis skills. These are followed by Burmeister's list of useful phonic generalizations. Lastly, Goodman suggests how oral reading miscues (errors) may be used to improve teaching and learning.

37. Sensation and Perception: The Complexity of Word Perception *

STANFORD E. TAYLOR

WE all live in a world of sensory excitations which we interpret individually, but we must compromise or agree on

* From Stanford E. Taylor, "Sensation and Perception: The Complexity of Word Perception," *Journal of Developmental Reading,* 6 (Spring, 1963), 187, 195–98, 199–202, 204–6. Reprinted by permission of the International Reading Association and the author.

meanings of certain types of excitations in order to understand each other and to communicate. When we analyze the process of reading, we discover that reading, writing, speaking, and listening are common in the thought process involved. Reading, however, differs in that thoughts and reactions are invoked through the presentation of printed symbols. So, the first and most basic stages of reading revolve around the ability to identify and recognize words.

Why the word? Because the word represents our *smallest unit of visual identification and meaningful recognition.* We do identify and recognize letters, but they do not convey meaning. Words, on the other hand, do suggest meaning—sometimes many meanings. Thus we are concerned with words not as concepts, but as building blocks of concepts. . . .

As a result of studying the various factors influencing word identification and recognition, this writer has arrived at the belief that all parts of a word serve some function during word recognition, and that while these parts may be reacted to with varying degrees of attention and scrutiny, the reader must, in some form, respond to all the letters that comprise the total word in order to maintain *consistent accuracy* in word recognition.

When we speak of reacting to the total word, to what aspects are we referring? Specifically, we are reacting to the total structural complex created by the letters, the word's intricate shape, and the grid or pattern caused by the light passing through the letters of the word. That we are dependent on an awareness of the letters is illustrated by the selections below. There is little doubt that the first selection is easier to read and the second more difficult. It is harder to read when only the bottom halves of letters are visible because there are fewer cues to the letters that compose the word.

A good sense of humor requires the ability to

regard things in their proper perspective, and

less well-adjusted individuals tend to be lack-

ing in this department. And their inclination to

take themselves too seriously extends not only

to humor, but to other things as well

A good sense of humor requires the ability to

regard things in their proper perspective, and

less well-adjusted individuals tend to be lack-

ing in this department. And their inclination to

take themselves too seriously extends not only

to humor, but to other things as well.

How dependent we are on the total letter complex for our identification of words is further borne out by this illustration.

scious, and other portions of which register on a more conscious level.

We can conclude, then, that we react to the total word pattern—to its shape,

HOW PICKPOCKETS PICK POCKETS

author of treasure hunting

author of treasure hunting

All three lines present the upper halves of words. The three lines vary, however, in the number of cues they provide as to the component letters. We can read the first line, but not with the same ease with which we read the second line, for capital letters are not as "familiar" as are lower case letters and they present fewer structural "cues." (Our dependence on awareness of the individual letters becomes more evident when we are confronted with different type faces. Some facilitate reading, while others hinder the process of reacting to letter complexes.) The third line is quite difficult to read, for while we have maintained the outlines of the letters, the spaces, which are equally important in distinguishing one letter from another, have been filled in.

Further, let us consider Thurstone's mutilated letters in the Figure on p. 209.

Notice how the words become progressively harder to recognize as more and more of the letter cues are removed. The word *bread* is far easier to recognize than the word *rabbit* (second from the end) because more of the distinguishing characteristics of the letters are retained.

To say that we rely on all the component letters for word recognition does not mean that we are equally conscious of each and every letter. It is undoubtedly true that we react to the letters as parts of a total graphic complex, many portions of which register in the subcon-

to specific dominant elements if they are present, as well as to the total letter complex or "pattern" caused by the particular letter combination of the word. . . . We react less consciously to familiar words or word parts and more consciously to unfamiliar words or word parts. The sensitivity or accuracy with which we react is dependent to a great degree upon our learned visual discrimination ability.

Consider the second major avenue of word identification—that of auditory analysis. Generally, we will have experienced the vast majority of words as auditory sound sequences prior to encountering them in printed form. Exceptions to this might be specific proper nouns, technical words, and other words of very low-frequency usage. Thus our translation of printed symbols into sound can assist in identifying words and word parts.

When a child starts to learn to read, he has a vast auditory stockpile of words and word experiences. He needs only to relate these auditory experiences with their printed counterparts in order to "know" many words. Whether a phonetic or nonphonetic approach is used in teaching reading, the child learns to associate letters and letter complexes with sound equivalents in varying degrees, depending on the instructional stress on sounding out words and the child's auditory discrimination ability.

For a reader to use auditory analysis

bread_____

artist_____

_____

_____

_____

_____

_____

_____

_____

_____

_____

_____

_____

successfully as a means of word recognition, he must first be completely aware of the sounds which compose the words he uses quite glibly in speaking. It is sometimes supposed, mistakenly, that a child hears completely all the sounds which compose the words he speaks. There is accumulating evidence, however, to indicate that this may not be the case —that many children monitor their speech kinesthetically, with a low degree of auditory discrimination. It seems apparent that a reader cannot associate specific sounds with letters or letter complexes unless he has first truly heard them and isolated them as pronounceable entities. Thus, the degree of auditory discrimination would affect a reader's success in using auditory analysis as an assist in identifying and recognizing words.

The true function of auditory analysis should be to introduce the printed words or word parts to the mind so that in later encounters, visual analysis can dominate and call meaning to mind directly. Auditory analysis should be regarded as helpful and desirable when it functions as a conscious act in unlocking unfamiliar words, both in the way it helps the reader to inspect more minutely the components of a word. Should a reader begin to unconsciously translate all words encountered into their sound equivalents, auditory analysis would inhibit fluency in the reading process.

A third means through which the reader might realize a word lies in the suggestion of the content. This, of course, is highly dependent on the reader's ability to understand and use the content in which the word appears, which, in turn, is dependent on the reader's total experiential background, especially his reading experience. The use of context, however, never functions without visual monitoring.

The amount of the monitoring or analysis required is directly dependent on the linguistic probability of the occurrence of certain words in the context. Unknown words that do not complete the meaning of a sentence require the greatest amount of conscious analysis, while more familiar words which quickly and easily complete the thought are responded to with a minimum of conscious monitoring. There are instances in which the content will not suggest any specific word or will suggest many words. When this occurs, visual analysis must be relied upon to a greater extent. There are other instances in which the content may strongly suggest one word, and then present another. When this occurs, visual analysis must instantly correct the perceptual process or inaccuracies of interpretation will occur.

The section below illustrates the relationship of context and visual analysis.

Before skin diving became _____(1) _____, sharks were highly _____(2)_____. The sight of a _____(3)_____ fin _____ (4)_____ the water struck fear in the heart of the _____(5)_____. Then a new

WORD   WITH NO CUES

1. Rapidly and almost unanimously, *popular* is selected.
2. *Feared* is usually selected, but after a certain amount of deliberation, indicating a searching through of probabilities. Sometimes an illogical word, such as "prized" or "scarce" is suggested, showing a certain disregard of content.
3. *Dorsal* is selected only occasionally and by people with more experience with fish. The more common choices, and those more probable, are "triangular" and "black."
4. Numerous choices are made rather quickly: "splitting," "slicing," "skimming," and "cutting" are just a few.
5. There is usually a long delay in the contemplation of this word. Then a few tentative choices will be made: "swimmer," "diver," "fisherman," and "bather."
6. Many times there is no response to this word at all.
7. Those who are familiar with skin diving will hesitantly mention SCUBA. The rest will make no attempt to select a word.

_____(6)_____ emerged, donning equipment called _____(7)_____.

This paragraph has been shown to many groups. They have been asked to call out the words they feel are suggested through their study of the context. Some responses are elicited instantaneously, others after prolonged pondering, while other spaces suggest no words at all. The chart below indicates the responses with no visual clues. The second and third columns indicate those responses when visual clues are progressively added.

It is apparent that the number of struc-

WITH FIRST AND LAST LETTER ADDED

p------r
Popular is immediately reinforced.

f------d
Feared is now confirmed, unanimously and immediately.

d------l
If *dorsal* had been mentioned, this is immediately reinforced.

s------g
"Cutting" is now ruled out, but the other choices still hold.

b------r
"Bather" is now the only choice that is suggested.

c------t
After a great deal of deliberation, *cult* may be suggested by a few.

S------A
SCUBA is confirmed, if it has been mentioned. If it has not yet been mentioned, it is usually guessed by many at this point.

WITH FIRST, SECOND and LAST LETTER ADDED

po-----r
Popular seems quite definite.

fe-----d
Feared is still confirmed.

do-----l
Dorsal is now confirmed.

sp-----g
Hesitantly, the final selection of *splitting* is usually made at this point.

be-----r
Now even "bather" is ruled out. Usually no logical word is selected. Sometimes "believer" and "beginner" are selected. Almost no one guesses the correct choice—beholder.

cu-----t
Cult is now confirmed.

SC-----A
SCUBA is definitely confirmed.

---

tural cues required for word recognition varies with the probability of occurrence inherent in the content and the degree to which words are familiar. It is also evident that once a word has been selected by a reader, he tends to persist in his choice of that word until it is confirmed or invalidated by his visual analysis. As a result of this exercise, in which all words were known words, it becomes evident that the function of the content is to suggest certain words, and that the function of visual analysis is to confirm or reject.

It is likely, then, that we employ several means of identifying words simultaneously, with a stress on visual analysis and context clues. The extent to which each is used in a particular reading situation varies from individual to individual and according to the suggestions of the content, the reader's experiential background, his reading experience, and the degree to which he can discriminate visually.

All stages discussed to this point might be thought of as the "intake" stages in word perception. Beyond this point, however, there is a processing stage during which the initial impression may be strengthened, maintained, or appreciably reduced. . . .

The effect of the context that follows a word was illustrated by the exercise involving context clues. It is sufficient to say that the recognition of a word will either be altered or reinforced in accordance with the meaning of the context that follows.

There are numerous other associations that we have with words that will either alter or reinforce the original impression. Sometimes we are affected by factors completely unrelated to the meaning of the sentence in which they appear. For instance, a student may respond more strongly to one word because of difficulty he had in learning to spell it; or he will associate another word with a family joke or a party game. Still other words may evoke emotional responses, calling forth either negative or positive reactions.

Thus we can see that the process of word identification and recognition is not a simple task and that there can be many pitfalls for the reader. The analysis we have just completed might suggest a reappraisal of some of our procedures for diagnosing and training certain of the abilities upon which effective word recognition rests. A few of these suggestions follow.

1. We need improved visual screening methods that will detect deficiencies in acuity, problems with accommodation or focus—not only of amplitude (the changes required by changing viewing distance), but of rapidity, and the presence or absence of adequate binocular coordination and fusion.

2. We must look for ways of engaging students in learning activities that require higher levels of concentration and attention. Timed exercises, reading activities which require rapid association, and audio-visual techniques can be used to capture students' attention and teach them to concentrate.

3. We must give renewed attention to developing a high degree of visual discrimination. Realizing that not all visual analysis is conscious and that much occurs at a low attention level (or at the level of the subconscious), we need to develop in each child the ability to minutely scrutinize words and word parts

and to discriminate with sensitivity and accuracy, yet with enough ease and rapidity to require little expenditure of energy. The child without these abilities tends to rely too heavily on minimum cues—on a letter or group of letters, the word shape, a prefix, or other small word parts. In doing this, he is subject to inaccuracies of interpretation, particularly when meaning or sound conflicts with the visual interpretation or when attention wanders.

4. We need to find new ways to help students to stabilize and assimilate visual impressions so that each visual impression contributes more toward the reading activity.

5. We need to reappraise the steps we take to develop auditory discrimination ability and insure the fact that students are completely aware of the component sounds they use in oral communication and their relationships to printed symbols.

6. We need to provide students with techniques that will develop efficient functional skills, greater coordination and mobility, and better directional attack in order to reduce the deterioration in initial word impressions and to provide readers with a more organized perceptual activity.

7. We need to strengthen our instruction of comprehension skills, particularly the student's ability to use context clues.

8. We need to continue to try to provide reading experiences that introduce the student to additional meanings and new relationships with old words or known words as well as to acquaint him with new words; again, with a stress on the ability to use context clues in understanding words.

In the final analysis, the end product of word recognition—understanding—can be no better than its beginning.

References

1. TAYLOR, STANFORD E., FRACKENPOHL, HELEN, PETTEE, JAMES L. *Grade Level Norms for the Components of the Fundamental Reading Skill.* Huntington, N. Y.: Educational Developmental Laboratories. Spache, George D. "Is This a Breakthrough in Reading?" *The Reading Teacher,* January, 1962. Walton, H. N. "Vision and Rapid Reading," *American Journal of Optometry,* 1957.

2. KOEHLER, WARREN B. "Phrased Reading: Final Report," *Independent Schools Bulletin,* LX–LXI (November, 1960), 14–18.

3. TAYLOR, EARL A. *Controlled Reading.* Chicago: University of Chicago Press, 1937. P. 183.

4. ROBINSON, HELEN M. "The Findings of Research on Visual Difficulties and Reading," *Reading for Effective Living.* International Reading Association Conference Proceedings, III. New York: Scholastic Magazines, 1958. Pp. 107–11.

5. SCHUBERT, DELWYN G. "Visual Immaturity and Reading Difficulty," *Elementary English,* XVIII (May, 1957), 323–25. Schubert quotes Dr. Louis Jacques, Sr.

6. COLE, LUELLA. *The Improvement of Reading with Special Reference to Remedial Instruction.* New York: Farrar and Rinehart, 1938. P. 282.

7. GRAY, LILLIAN, and REESE, DORA. *Teaching Children to Read.* New York: Ronald Press, 1957. P. 99.

8. FEINBERG, RICHARD. "A Study of Some Aspects of Peripheral Visual Acuity," *American Journal of Optometry* and *Archives of American Academy of Optometry,* LXII (February–March, 1949), 1–23.

9. ROBINSON, HELEN M., *op. cit.*

10. CROSLAND, H. R., and JOHNSON, GEORGIA. "The Range of Apprehension as Affected by Inter-Letter Hair Spacing and by the Characteristics of Individual Letters," *Journal of Applied Psychology,* II (February, 1928), 82–124.

11. WILKINS, MINNA CHEVES. "A Tachistoscopic Experiment in Reading." Unpublished Master's Thesis. New York: Columbia University, 1917. P. 24.

12. HUEY, EDMUND B. "Preliminary Experiments in the Physiology and Psychology of Reading," *American Journal of Psychology,* I (July, 1898), 575–86.

13. GILBERT, LUTHER C. "Speed of Processing Visual Stimuli and Its Relation to Reading," and "Saccadic Movements as a Factor in Visual Perception in Reading," *Journal of Educational Psychology,* LX (February, 1959), 8–19.

38. The Role of Phonics in Teaching Reading *

JACK BAGFORD

. . .

Some Basic Considerations

IN determining the proper role of phonics in a reading program one needs to consider underlying factors which relate to this role. Some of the basic considerations follow.

Children differ in their ability to benefit from a sound-oriented approach to the teaching of reading. It seems plausible to assume that some children learn better from a method which emphasizes a whole-word approach to word recognition while others probably learn better from a method which emphasizes sound-symbol correspondence. To put it another way, some children probably learn better through visual means while others learn better through auditory means. Generally speaking, teaching materials are designed with the underlying assumption that all children learn equally well with all modalities. This assumption may or may not be correct. Thus it seems logical to advise that whenever a child is experiencing difficulty with learning to read, the teacher should investigate the possibility that he may be emphasizing the least effective modality for the child in question.

Research studies that arrive at general-

* From Jack Bagford, "The Role of Phonics in Teaching Reading," in J. Allen Figurel (ed.), *Reading and Realism,* Proceedings of the Thirteenth Annual Convention, 13, Part 1 (Newark, Del.: International Reading Association, 1967), 82–87. Reprinted by permission of the International Reading Association and the author.

izations about which method works best for *large* groups of children miss a very basic point; i.e., methods which produce significantly higher mean scores for the total group do not necessarily work best for each individual student in the group. Certain individuals may profit more from a method which has been shown to produce significantly lower mean scores than another. Teachers should recognize this possibility and adjust their teaching accordingly.

It seems likely that some words are more easily learned by a phonic method than by a sight method, while others are more easily learned by the sight method. High frequency, but irregularly sounded, words probably are more efficiently taught by a sight method while phonetically regular words and words which contain easily learned sounds probably are better taught by a phonic method. Learning the word recognition skills is a step in a developmental process, one of the goals of which is to know a large number of words by sight. Accomplishing this goal by the most efficient method is important. Sometimes the most efficient method is determined by the nature of the word itself.

A given child may be able to utilize a sound-oriented approach better at one age than another. The concept of reading readiness suggests that there is an optimum time in the developmental process for a child to learn any given skill. Presumably, attempts to teach a skill prior to this optimum time will prove unsuccessful and may even cause emotional or psychological problems which seriously retard normal growth. Also, it is assumed that if instruction is postponed until later than this optimum time, the skill involved is not as readily learned as it would have been at the optimum time.

In a like manner, each child may have an optimum time in his total development for learning phonics content. For some, phonic readiness may be achieved relatively early in school while others may take considerably longer. In presenting phonics content, teachers should consider the natural growth patterns of the pupils.

How the teacher feels about the teaching procedure which he is following seems to make a difference in the effectiveness of the teaching method. If children can learn to read by any of several approaches, which apparently they can, then how the teacher feels about the method may well be one of the most important factors in determining its success. If the teacher is philosophically committed to the method he is using, then he is likely to do a good job of teaching reading regardless of how good or how bad the method might be. When selecting a particular phonics program or determining degree of emphasis on content or methodology, one of the key factors to be considered should be what the teachers think about it.

Interest may not be directly related to method. It is doubtful that one method is inherently more interesting than another. Enthusiastic teachers can take very dull content and make an interesting lesson out of it. Other can take what seems to be very interesting material and create pure drudgery for children. Whether a method is interesting is probably less related to method than it is to other factors related to the teaching-learning situation.

Two factors which influence pupil interest are variety of presentation and ap-

propriateness of teaching level. If presentations are varied within a method, interest is not likely to be lacking. Likewise, if a child is given a learning challenge, but at a level where he has a relatively good chance for success, he will seldom lose interest. The important point related to phonics is that approaches probably should not be accepted or rejected because of interest or lack of it. Rather, *effective* approaches should be selected for use and then adjustments made in the teaching situation to maintain a high interest level.

Guidelines for the Reading Teacher

In teaching phonics, the major task which confronts today's reading teacher is how to maintain a proper balance between attention to phonics and attention to other important reading goals. The myriad of research results and the verbal wranglings of reading "experts" are likely to confuse the average teacher about the proper course of action as he performs the daily tasks of teaching reading. The following are suggested as broad guidelines to follow as teachers attempt to determine the role of phonics in the teaching of reading.

Phonics content is taught so that children have a tool to identify words which are known in the spoken form but not in the printed form. All decisions concerning the use of phonics should reflect this purpose. Teachers should regularly ask themselves whether the phonic content being taught and the methods being employed in teaching it contribute to the accomplishment of this major purpose. If not, the teacher should adjust accordingly.

Phonics is but one aspect of word recognition; word recognition is but one goal of the reading program. Phonics is best used in conjunction with other word recognition skills. As a child learns to read, he gradually learns several ways to identify words. Ideally, he learns them in such a manner so that he can coordinate and combine their use as he attacks unknown words. The ability to use sound-symbol relationships is one of the more important reading skills, but it is just one and should be so considered.

The second aspect of this guideline has to do with the relationship of word recognition skills to the total reading program. Word identification techniques should be taught in a manner that facilitates, not hampers, the attainment of other important reading goals. Intensive attention to phonics can seriously impair progress toward goals of speed, interest, and meaning; teachers need to recognize this possibility so that emphasis can be adjusted to best serve the total reading program.

The teacher is the key person in determining the success of a reading program. Whether children learn better by one method than another is largely determined by the skill and enthusiasm of the teacher. In recent years, research has consistently shown that the quality of the teacher in the classroom is the most important variable relating to how well the pupils in a class learn to read. Effective functioning in such a key role requires that a teacher know as much as possible about (1) phonics and research related to phonics, (2) the total reading process, and (3) the pupils' reading abilities and needs.

Acting in terms of the preceding guidelines leads one directly to the next. *Teachers should take an active part in determining the role of phonics in the reading program.* On the whole, modern-day teachers are well-trained, competent people who are capable of determining the reading needs of pupils and adjusting the program to meet these needs. Caring for

individual differences is a constant job, and only teachers are in a position to know these needs well enough to adjust instructional procedures to meet them; teachers should be encouraged to do so.

This guideline means, for example, that teachers should adjust content and method for children who are slow learners or fast learners; for children who have speech and hearing problems; and for those who learn better through visual means than through auditory means. It means that teachers need to recognize and adjust for the fact that some phonic content is learned by all pupils without any direct teaching.

It is recognized that adjusting for individual differences is an age-old problem that has no easy solutions. Nevertheless, with the wide variety of high quality materials available to today's teachers, intensive efforts toward recognizing differences and providing for them can produce rich benefits for the pupils.

Relatively speaking, phonics should be taught fairly early in the reading program. Basically, the two major goals of a reading program are *word recognition* and *comprehension*. These goals can hardly be separated, but for instructional purposes it is probably better to place the heavy emphasis on one and then the other. Early in the process of learning to read, word recognition (including phonics) should receive major attention; and as progress is made, the emphasis should be shifted to comprehension.

Summary

Phonics has an extremely important role to play in the teaching of reading. In this paper it is assumed that phonic analysis is best used in conjunction with other word identification techniques for the purpose of unlocking words which are known in their spoken form but unknown in their written form. It is known that the pupils can learn to read by any of a number of methods. Thus teachers, rather than method, are the most important variable in the teaching process. Teachers are encouraged to know research relating to methods and materials and to utilize their knowledge in adjusting their procedures to the individual needs in their own classrooms. Guidelines for making these adjustments are provided.

References

1. BAGFORD, JACK. *Phonics: Its Role in Teaching Reading.* Iowa City: Sernoll, 1967.
2. BAILEY, MILDRED HART. "The Utility of Phonic Generalizations in Grades One Through Six," *Reading Teacher,* 20 (February, 1967), 413–18.
3. BEAR, DAVID. "Phonics For First Grade: A Comparison of Two Methods," *Elementary School Journal,* 59 (April, 1959), 394–402.
4. BLIESMER, EMERY P., and YARBOROUGH, BETTY H. "A Comparison of Ten Different Beginning Reading Programs in First Grade," *Phi Delta Kappan,* 46 (June, 1965), 500–4.
5. CHALL, JEANNE. *Learning to Read: The Great Debate.* New York: McGraw-Hill, 1967.
6. CLYMER, THEODORE. "The Utility of Phonics Generalizations in the Primary Grades," *Reading Teacher,* 16 (February, 1963), 252–58.
7. DURRELL, DONALD D. (ed.). "Success in First Grade Reading," *Journal of Education,* Boston University, (February, 1958), 1–48.
8. DYKSTRA, ROBERT. *Continuation of the Coordinating Center for First-Grade Reading Instruction Programs.* USOE. Project Number 6-1651. Minneapolis: University of Minnesota, 1967.
9. EMANS, ROBERT. "The Usefulness of Phonic Generalizations Above the Primary Level," *Reading Teacher,* 20 (February, 1967), 419–25.
10. FRY, EDWARD. "A Frequency Approach to Phonics," *Elementary English,* 41 (November, 1964), 759–65.
11. SPARKS, PAUL E., and FAY, LEO C. "An Evaluation of Two Methods of Teaching Reading," *Elementary School Journal,* 57 (April, 1957), 386–90.

39. Phonics: Consonants *

EMMETT ALBERT BETTS

THE story is often told of Amanda and Rebecca, who often spent their afternoons in the parlor knitting and commenting on life in general. One afternoon Rebecca looked up from her knitting and said, "Mandy, do you know that *sugar* is the only word in which the *s* has the *sh* sound?"

Amanda kept to her knitting, lost in serious thought. After a while, she looked up and asked, "Becky, are you sure?"

No, Mandy had not thought of the *sh* sound in *sure!*

Our badly spelled English has many letters for the same sound. The *sh* sound, for example, is spelled *sh* in *shore*, *s* in *sure*, *c* in *ocean*, *ch* in *Chicago*, *t* before *i* in *nation*, *ss* in *passion*.

Then again the sound of *b* is represented by *b* in *bat* and *bb* in *rabbit*. But in *climb* it has no sound!

The letter *c* has no sound of its own, representing *k* in *cat*, *s* in *city*, *sh* in *vicious*, and so forth. Neither does *x* have a sound of its own, representing *ks* in *box*, *g-z* in *examine*, and so on. The letter *q*, of course, has no sound of its own, usually representing the first part of the blend *kw*, as in *queen* and *square*.

In the words *hot* and *hat*, the vowel sound is the cue to the meaning of each spoken word. On the other hand, in the words *race* and *raise*, the consonant sound is the cue to the meaning, the hissing *s*

sound of *c* in *race* and the buzzing sound *z* of *s* in *raise* offering the only clues to the differences in meaning.

Consonant Settings of Vowels

While the key to the syllable is the vowel, its setting usually is a consonant before and/or after it. This consonant setting may be fairly simple, as in *at* or *cat*. Or, it may be made more complex by consonant blends, as in *(gl)ad* or *(spl)ash*. Then, too, the vowel setting may include a number of consonant letters representing no sound at all, as in *(w)rite* and *ni(gh)t*.

Whole-word Approach

One of the first steps in teaching consonant sounds is to help the child tune his hearing to them. He is taught, for example, to hear the simple sound of *m* in *my* and the blend of *st* in *stop*. Then he is taught to hear, for example, the simple sound of *l* in *tail* and the blend of *lt* in *felt*. In teaching both first and last consonants, the child first learns to hear the undistorted consonant sounds in spoken words before he identifies the letters which stand for those sounds.

It is easy for the child to say the sound of long *a*, the sound of *er*, and other vowel sounds in isolation without distorting them. On the other hand, he needs more sophistication in order to say the isolated sounds of *b, v, d*, and other consonants without distorting them. Therefore, it is necessary for him to hear and say consonant sounds in combination

* From Emmett Albert Betts, "Phonics: Consonants." Reprinted from the May 1962 issue of *Education*, pp. 533–36. Copyright © 1962 by The Bobbs-Merrill Co., Inc., Indianapolis, by permission of the publisher and author.

with vowel sounds; that is, in syllables and words.

Confusion results when the child is taught that *buh-erd*, for example, is *bird*. *Bird* is a one-syllable word, but the distortion of the consonant sound produces a two-syllable word. This confusion is compounded when an attempt is made to teach him to hear the syllables in *singing, kindly,* and *happen*.

Sounds of Consonant Phonograms

Pupils are taught how to draw their own conclusions—to make their own rules—regarding the sounds of consonants. As stated before, this approach puts emphasis where it belongs: on understanding rather than the rote memorization of rules.

In learning the sounds represented by the letter *c*, for example, the pupils need (1) to hear the consonant-vowel blend (e.g., *ca* of *cat*) of the spoken word and (2) to examine the written form of the word. In this instance, they might use these words from their reading vocabulary: *cake, call, came, can, cat*. After the study of these words, the pupils may conclude that *c* before *a* usually has the sound of *k*.

Latter they may add to the rule the *k* sound of *c* before *o*, as in *coat, color, come, cookies*. Then they may add the *k* sound of *c* before *u*, as in *cut, cup, cub, cute,* and so forth.

Consonant Blends

When consonants are thoroughly learned, the pupils are well on their way to phonic independence. Before learning the consonant blend *st*, for example, they need to be well grounded in the sounds of *s* and *t*. In short, each element of a consonant blend is learned before blending the sounds.

A consonant blend is a grouping, or a cluster, of sounds. The goal of instruction is to teach the pupils to group letters, as the *st* of *stop*, automatically—to prevent an inefficient letter-by-letter word attack in reading and letter-by-letter spelling. The grouping of the first two consonants of *stop*, for example, cuts the word down to the two parts *st* and *op* or *sto* and *p*, bringing the word under control for the pupils.

This learning to *group* letters into phonograms pays big dividends when they meet in their reading *brook, chair, friend, through,* and other long one-syllable words. But still bigger dividends are paid when they are confronted with *broken, chimney, station,* and other words of more than one syllable.

At this point a word of caution is necessary. The *wh* of *who, whole,* and so on represents the single sound of *h*. However, in *which* it represents the *hw* blend. The phonogram *sh* in *she* represents a single sound and, therefore, is not a blend. Likewise, the *th* and *ng* of *thing* represent single sounds, hence are not blends.

Steps in Teaching Blends

These steps are taken to teach consonant blends:

1. *Listening and saying.* To teach the pupils to hear the *st* blend, for example, have them say *stop* and *story* as they listen to the first sound.

Then, read, in a conversational tone, a list of three or four words and have the pupils raise their hands when they hear a word beginning with the same first sound as *stop*. For example, use *toy, stay, took, stand.* Avoid other consonant blends beginning with the *s* sound, as in (*str*)*eet*.

After the pupils have become fairly sharp in hearing the *st* blend, introduce words beginning with *s* and *sh*. For example, use *soon, star, she, step*. Then have the pupils say each word, listening to the first consonant sounds.

2. *Seeing the consonant phonogram.* For this purpose words from the pupils' reading vocabulary are used. First, the pupils listen to the initial consonant blend and say the *whole* word; for example, *stop* and *story*. Second, the teacher writes the words on the board and has the pupils say the words and identify the *st* letters representing the first sound.

Finally, they may study other words beginning with *s, t,* and *st*. For example, use *see, time, stop*. First, they listen to the initial consonant sound or blend as the teacher says them. Then, they say the words to get the feel of the first consonant. Finally, they identify the letters in whole words that represent the single sounds and the blend.

3. *Blending consonant and vowel.* Additional help may be given by having the pupils study vowel-consonant blends, as the *sto* of *stop* and the *stor* of *story*. By blending the consonant cluster with its vowel, the pupils can say the *sto* of *stop* or the *stor* of *story* without distorting the sound of *st*. After the pupils hear and say the vowel-consonant blend, then they identify the letters representing it in written words.

4. *Blending first consonants.* Some pupils need more help to get the "feel" of consonant blends. For them, these steps to teach the *st* blend, for example, are taken:

a. *Hearing the separate sounds of the blend.* Either using a picture or spoken words, have the pupils tell which words begin with the same sound as *sun: Sue, hen, seven.*

Use the same procedure for reviewing the initial *t* sound. For example, which words begin with the same sound as *toy: red, to, take.*

b. *Hearing the blend.* Then ask, "Which of these words begins with the first sounds of *sun* and *to: soon, story, to?*"

Or, ask, "In which of these words do you hear the sounds of *s* and *t* together at the beginning of the word: *soon, story, to?*"

c. *Seeing the letters of the blend.* Write on the chalkboard: *soon, story, to.*

Have the pupils say each word and listen to the *s* of *soon*, *t* of *to*, and *st* of *story*. In each example, have them identify the letters representing the consonants sounds.

5. *Applying the learning.* These steps are taken to help the pupils apply their skills to first consonant blends:

a. Use the skill to identify new words with the same first consonant blend; for example, apply *st* skill to new words to be introduced in a succeeding reading activity, as *stay, step, still, stood, storm,* and so forth.

b. Blend the first consonant sound with other rhyming parts to make new words; for example, the *st* of *stop* with the *ep* of *step, ill* of *still*, etc.

c. Help the pupils to apply their skill to unknown words in their silent reading. For example, if the pupil needs help on *step*, ask, "What word do you know that begins like *step?*" (*stop*) Or, ask, "What are the first consonant letters?" (*st*) Then, "What word do you know that begins with *st?*" (*stop*) Finally, "What is the word?"

6. *Meaning.* At all points in the development of phonic skills, the meaning of the word is kept uppermost in the minds of the pupils. For example, in silent reading situations, they always check the meaning of the word in its sentence or paragraph setting.

In Summary

Phonic skills are usually taught by beginning with the spoken word and ending with the written word. That is, the pupil is first taught to hear the *kw* sound of *qu* in the spoken word *quick,* for example, before attending to the letters *qu* in the written word *quick* which represent that blend.

On the other hand, when anyone reads he is confronted with the written word and, therefore, must reverse the process. For example, when he sees the *qu* of

quick he recalls the *kw* blend—if he has been taught this skill. Therefore, the pupil is taught how and when to apply his phonic skills to unknown words. If he has not learned his phonic skills, his situation is as hopeless as trying to beat water uphill with a stick. If he has learned them, his success with the systematic examination of written words is always clearly in sight.

40. Development of Vowel Sounds *

MARY MEIGHEN AND MARJORIE PRATT

I. Work Which Precedes Development of Vowel Sounds

THE developmental plan for the teaching of vowels as presented in this bulletin may be preceded by work along the following lines:

A. Auditory Perception

1. Ability to hear and identify initial consonant sounds in words.

Children listen to words pronounced by the teacher and select those which have the same initial consonant as a given word, as: *big.*

  bed· sing *b*asket *b*ake milk

2. Ability to hear and identify final consonant sounds in words.

Children listen to words and select

those which have the same final consonant in a given word, as: *hat.*

  si*t* pan ho*t* tub le*t*

3. Ability to hear and identify consonant blends in words.

Initial blends: *st*ep   *fl*ag   *sm*all
Final blends: fa*st*   wa*sp*   ma*sk*

4. Ability to hear and identify consonant digraphs in words: *ch, sh, th, wh, ng.*

Initial digraphs: *ch*in   *sh*ut   *th*ank   *wh*at
Final digraphs: lun*ch*   wi*sh*   ba*th*   ra*ng*

B. Visual Perception

Ability to associate initial consonants, consonant blends, and digraphs with printed symbols.

Children number their papers to correspond to the number of words to be pronounced by the teacher. They write the initial consonant they hear in each word as it is pronounced.

1. pail   4. happy   7. good
2. took   5. dish   8. money
3. boat   6. face   9. look

* From Mary Meighen and Marjorie Pratt, "Development of Vowel Sounds," PWU Promotional Bulletin 5. Reprinted by permission of Lyons and Carnahan, Chicago, Ill.

Child's paper would show: 1. p 2. t 3. b

This same procedure may be used for reviewing final consonants, initial and final consonant blends, and initial and final digraphs.

C. Practice in the Use of Content Clues and Word Analysis

Meaning clues are of great importance in helping children to attack new words.

1. Example: Children complete sentences, keeping in mind that each word must begin with the initial consonant of a given word, as: *big*.

Baby is asleep in her _____ (buggy)
I can read my new _____ (book)
Father rides in a _____ (bus)

2. Noting likenesses and differences in words, as:
The man walked slowly because he was *lame*.

Children may not know the word *lame*, but they will note the likenesses of the word *lame* to known words such as *came* or *same*.

As children learn to note likenesses and differences in words and to make use of meaning clues, they will develop skill in the ability to identify unknown words accurately.

D. Training in Structural Analysis of Words

1. Finding the root word in the variants of the word, as finding the word *dress* in:

dresses   dresser   dressed   undress

2. Recognition of small words in compound words, as in:

seashore   sunshine   chalkboard

3. Building words from root words through the use of suffixes and prefixes, as in:

folds   unfold   folded   folding

II. Introduction of the *Long A* Sound

A. Oral and Visual Training

As a first step in introducing vowels as an aid in word recognition, give children practice in listening to the vowel sounds in words.

1. The teacher may say, "Listen to these words: *baby, make, table, play*. Sometimes the letter *a* sounds as it does in these words. We call this sound the *long* sound of *a*. It is the same sound as the name of letter *a*."

2. The teacher writes familiar words on the chalkboard for the children to pronounce. In each word the *long a* sound is heard, as in:

gave   may   train   rain
came   paid   make   game

3. The teacher then says, "Now listen to these words. You will hear the *long a* sound in some of the words. Put your hands up when you hear the *long a* sound in a word."

table   pat   may   rain   sad   make

4. Give each child a small card on which he writes the letter *a*. When the *a* vowel cards are ready to use, give the direction: "Listen to the words which I will say. When you hear the *long a* sound in a word, hold up your *a* card."

Teacher pronounces the words:

flat   paid   fat   lake   table   rabbit

As each vowel sound is introduced, the children make a card for it. An envelope should be provided for each child in which he may keep his vowel cards.

5. Select *long a* words from the basic vocabulary in the books which the children are reading. Place these words on the chalkboard along with words in which other vowels are introduced. Children draw a line under each word in which they hear *long a;* then they pronounce the word:

stay   mother   name   way   rake
paper   ate   wish   drop   make

6. The teacher may write *long a* and *short a* words on the chalkboard. Children write the numbers representing the *long a* words.

(1) cake   (3) cap   (5) gave
(2) sat   (4) shake   (6) baby

(7) say   (9) tame
(8) came   (10) cat

7. Using *long a* words in sentences.

Work should be planned so that the child will have experience in applying his knowledge of phonic elements to the recognition of *long a* words. Use types of sentences in which the thought of the sentence is dependent upon the *long a* words.

Introduce *long a* words in sentences. All the words in each sentence should be familiar to the child except the *long a* word. The *long a* word should be a word in which the phonic elements are familiar to the child.

The robin was looking for its *mate.*
Bob and I live on the *same* street.
Mother put my valentine in a *frame.*
I will *wait* here for you.

III. Introduction of the *Short A* Sound

A. Oral and Visual Training

1. Write the following words on the chalkboard:

bake   baby   may   table

Ask children to pronounce the words.

Then say, "We hear the *long a* sound in these words. The letter *a* has another sound known as the *short a* sound. Listen for the *short a* sound in these words." Pronounce the following words:

at   sat   pan   track
cap   cat   man   plan

2. Write the following words on the chalkboard. Children pronounce each word.

man   bag   flag   Dad   thank
apple   back   stand   hat   rabbit

3. Children take out the cards on which the letter *a* has already been written. Say, "Write the letter *a* on the other side of your card. Now, on one side of your card put a short line over the letter *a*, as: ā. We will call this letter *long a.* Now turn the card over. On this side put only the letter *a*, as: **a.** We will call this letter *short a.*" (Some teachers may wish to have the child indicate the *short a* with the curved mark, the breve, though many new dictionaries no longer use this diacritical mark.) Give experience in the use of the card, as:
"Show me *long a.*"   "Show me *short a.*"

4. Pronounce *long a* and *short a* words. Children hold up cards displaying *long a* or *short a* as they listen to the words.

gave am apple hat take game happy

5. When children are familiar with the *long a* and *short a* sounds, place a list of familiar *long a* and *short a* words on the chalkboard, as:

1. baby   4. take   7. ate   10. bag
2. sat   5. rabbit   8. train   11. make
3. black   6. stand   9. man   12. fat

Children underline all the words in which they hear the *short a* sound, pronouncing each word as it is underlined.

IV. Development of the *Long* and *Short* Sounds of the Vowels *E, I, O, U*

Follow the steps outlined for teaching *long a* and *short a* sounds in the development of the vowels *e, i, o, u*.

Do not hurry the work in the development of vowel sounds. Take time to develop the long and short sounds of each vowel, step by step.

V. Review of Vowel Sounds

A. Vowel Cards

After children have learned the *long* and *short* sounds of two or three vowels, they may use their vowel cards in a variety of ways.

1. The teacher pronounces a number of words. Child holds up the vowel card which shows the *long* or *short* vowel sound that he hears in each word.

Teacher may say, "Put the cards showing the short sound of *a, i, u,* on your desks. As I say each word, hold up the card which shows the *short* vowel sound which you hear in the word." Teacher pronounces words, as:

catch   not   trick   fish   step   cut
spin   clap   top   stop   trap   tub

2. The same type of exercise may be used to review the *long* vowel sounds.

B. Chalkboard Lessons in Preparation for Independent Work

1. Children select a *short i* word to complete each sentence.

(a) _____ is a friend of mine. (Jim) (Mike)

(b) Bob is _____ years old. (five) (six)

2. Select a *long o* word to complete each sentence.

(a) Dick likes to play with his _____. (top) (rope)

(b) I saw a _____ in our yard. (crow) (robin)

41. Recognition of Long Words *

E. W. DOLCH

A PRACTICAL schoolman of long experience said some time ago that he did not see why there was so much fuss about reading. "It is all very simple," he said. "You just know the little words, you sound out the big ones, and you know what it says. No one can stop you."

* From E. W. Dolch, "Recognition of Long Words." Reprinted from the May 1955 issue of *Education*, pp. 604–8. Copyright © 1955 by The Bobbs-Merrill Company, Inc., Indianapolis, Ind.

We now know which are the little words that are most useful, and how to teach them, but the problem of the "long words" is still with us. A recent research points out that this is no small problem. Some time ago a list was published combining eleven big studies in vocabulary. This list contains 19,000 words. (It includes the Thorndike 20,000 but leaves out the proper names on that list.) These are probably the 19,000 most common words in reading matter in English. As a check, this list was gone through in order to count the number of one-syllable words, that is, the "little words." In the whole 19,000, there were only 3,000 one-syllable words. That leaves just 16,000 words of more than one syllable. These 16,000 are the most common "long words." But from them on, most of the rest of the words in the 600,000 word dictionary are "long words," that is, words of more than one syllable.

If we think of the three primary grades as the time to learn the common words, that is, the "little words," we can then think of all the rest of schooling as the time for the "big words." This fact is pointed up by a study of the spelling lists used in schools. These lists are obviously common words. But look at the lists for the various school years. It will be found that during the primary years, the great majority of the words are monosyllables, or little words. But these words are "used up" in a few years. Beginning with the fifth-year list (words met with during the fourth year in reading) the lists are about half polysyllables, that is, words of more than one syllable. (We know that the dictionary says a "polysyllable is a word of several syllables, especially of more than three," but let us, for purposes of simplicity call a one-syllable word a monosyllable, and a word of more than one syllable a polysyllable. This is a usage that would help discussion and thinking very much.)

The real point is that, beginning with the new subjects of the fourth grade and for the rest of school and of after life, the problem of every school subject and of every kind of reading is the "long word" or the polysyllable. Monosyllables do still come up at times, but they are few. It is true that we continue to meet *inflections* of monosyllables, such as those with the ending *-ing,* and so on. But these are still monosyllables if we teach the children how to take off the inflectional ending. Inflected or "changed monosyllables" are not what we can properly call "long words."

Attacking the Long Words

A very common method of attack on a long word is to take off prefixes and suffixes. This is a good method, especially when we are emphasizing word meaning. Prefixes and suffixes do alter the meaning of a root or stem, and the way they alter it should be known. Therefore, emphasis should be put on prefixes and suffixes just as soon as the children can discover this alteration of meaning. Obviously, it should not go faster than they can discover it. For instance, the prefix "un-" in "undo," "untie," "uncommon" and the like will easily be discovered, and the effect of the prefix can be understood. But that does not mean that the children should at once take up the meaning of "pre-" and other prefixes. We always tend to try to go too fast with this matter of prefixes and suffixes. If we let the children call them to our attention, then we will have a guide as to when to study them. The study of prefixes and suffixes would naturally begin with the third grade perhaps, and continue on through all the other grades and into high school. But we will not follow the common practice of trying to crowd the subject into a short time, thus doing violence to the children's language by trying to get them to think of unfamiliar roots or unfamiliar changes in those roots.

However, the greatest defect of the approach through prefixes and suffixes is that these concern relatively few words and do not give a general method of attack on all long words. Stauffer found that 24 percent of Thorndike's 20,000 words have prefixes, but this also says that 76 percent of those common words do not. That is, roughly three words out of four in the elementary school do not have prefixes. So let us teach prefixes and suffixes at the proper time, but let us also ask how one should attack other words which do not have prefixes or suffixes.

A second common attack on long words is "finding small words in big words." Here we do not mean the finding of stems in words that have regular endings, such as finding "look" in "looking." That really should be called "identifying the original word." Instead, we mean working out a long word by the aid of groups of letters in them that happen to be little words. An instance is seeing the word "tent" in "contentment," or the word "public" in "publication." We all know that children do use this method of working out big words. We all use it. However, should this method be recommended? One study with this method was made on words in fourth-grade readers. The result showed that, about 40 percent of the time, the correct word resulted, and about 60 percent of the time, the wrong result was found. We all know instances of error, as when one pronounces the word as "*can*-ine" instead of "*ca*-nine" just because the small word is seen at the beginning. Even though the chances of real help are many, we must conclude that this method cannot be fully recommended.

Third, the most common method of teaching attack on long words is just showing children how particular words are actually divided. A child may be sent to the dictionary and asked to write a long list of words divided as done in the dictionary. Or when a child comes to a long word, he may be told what its usual division is. So all we do is just to say, "Well, these words are divided this way." This telling how particular words are divided does not give a method. It does not give rules. It actually leaves it to the child, consciously or unconsciously, to form his own rules or method. Most teachers and most textbooks know only this method. They can say how any particular word is divided, but they cannot say what the rules for division are. The child has to find them for himself if he is to do so at all.

Rules for Recognition of Long Words

There is, however, a definite help that can be given children for the recognition of long words. There are rules that help in *recognition of what word is meant.*

First, however, we must emphasize that these are *not rules for the pronunciation of English.* Rules for that purpose are given at the beginning of the large dictionary in twenty pages of fine print. The pronunciation of English is a very complicated thing. The sounding of different letters, of different syllables, and of different words depends on language origins, on word relationships, on letter relationships, and so on. No school child, not even a school teacher, can know all of these things. The only safe way to find out just how any word is pronounced in English is to get out the dictionary and study the respelling that is given after the word. No simple rules can take the place of such a study.

Second, we are dealing only with the *recognition of words that a child has already heard.* He may or may not know the meaning, but he does know the sound of the word if he could only recognize it. We are definitely not dealing with words which the child has never heard. If he tries to work out a word and does not recognize a familiar sound, he must ask someone what the word is or go to the dictionary and find out just what the sound is. As we have said, no rules can give the correct sounding for English. An attempt to sound out words that have never been heard gives such mistakes as "for*mu*-la," "hypo-*thesis,*" and so on. Instead, we are dealing only with the recognition of long words that the child has heard before. Reading can give him meaning, but it cannot give him the correct sound if he has never heard it.

Third, recognition of long words requires intelligence. Very often, the context suggests what the word might be, and the rules for recognition tell quickly if that is the right word or not. Rules for recognition can never do more than get the reader *near* to the right sound. They can never, as we have said, give the exact sound. Then if the reader gets close to the correct sound, his intelligence, together with the context, will tell him what the word is.

The Three Rules for Recognition of Long Words

1. *Every vowel or vowel combination means a syllable.*

Children are interested to listen to someone and to hear that every syllable means a vowel or vowel combination. They can count the syllables in words heard. They can say words they look at and see that "every vowel or vowel combination means a syllable." Of course "vowel combination" means vowels that go together, such as *oa, ou, oi,* and so on.

In class, the teacher can write long words on the board and ask a child to take the chalk and put a check mark over every vowel or vowel combination. The check marks show the number of syllables.

2. *Divide syllables between two consonants that are between vowels or in front of one consonant that is between vowels.*[1]

Children can understand the reason for this division. If the vowels make the noises or sounds, the consonants show

[1] The second part of this rule holds in only about 6 out of 10 instances. (Eds.)

how the vowel sounds are begun and how they are ended, as in *seen, rich,* and so on. So if we find two consonants between vowels in a long word, the first usually ends the syllable before them, and the second usually begins the syllable after them. But children should look out for the digraphs, such as *th, ch,* and so on. They are never divided.

3. *Usually a syllable that ends in a vowel has the long vowel sound, and a syllable that ends in a consonant has the short sound of the vowel.*

This rule for recognition begins with the word "usually" just because there are many exceptions. For recognition, we recommend that the child try the sound that the rule would give; and if the word is not recognized, try the other sound. It is recognition we are after, and not the exact sounding shown in the dictionary. We must also look out for the vowel with *r,* as the *r* is practically never divided from the vowel, and it has a special sound (*far, her, sir, for, fur*). Of course there are more vowel sounds than the short, the long, and the sound with *r* but again we are only trying to *get close* enough to recognize the word. Only the dictionary gives the fully accurate sound.

Method of Presentation

In teaching these rules for recognition of long words, one should emphasize, as we have, that it is only recognition we are after, not the accurate pronunciation, which can be found only from the respelling in the dictionary.

Then it is advisable to give the children sample words that illustrate the three rules and that can be used to remember them. Proper names are good for this purpose, especially local geographic and other names. In the West, the word *Kansas* illustrates division and the short sound of vowels; the word *Dakota* shows division and the long sound. In the Midwest,

Wisconsin shows the short sound, and *Ohio* the long sound. In the East, *Pennsylvania* illustrates all the rules, but shows more than two consonants between vowels, and an exception to the long sound in the letter *i*. In our rule 3, the word *usually* must be emphasized.

But the best practice with the three rules comes in all the school subjects. In spelling, the children can try the rules to see if they work. "Do the sounds of the letters give the sound of the word?" If they do, they can be used to remember the right spelling; if they do not, the exception can be used to remember the right spelling. In arithmetic, new words can be tried out to see if they follow the rules. In history, science, health, all new words can be checked by the whole class. Classes like to do this. It will help them to give attention to the spelling problem in every word, and will develop skill in use of the Rules for Recognition.

With small children, exceptions to rules discourage. But older children are interested in exceptions. Here the teacher can give added information that will be most interesting. For instance, the word "Philadelphia" does not divide before the single consonant *l,* but there is a reason.

We have a rule that in pronunciation we usually do not divide a root. The root here is "phil" which we see in "philanthropy" and elsewhere. That is why this word does not follow the rules at that point. In the word "helper," the rules would divide into *hel-per,* whereas the rule for not dividing the root would give us *help-er.* Which do we really say? The children will be much interested to try this out. If the class finds a violation of one of the rules and goes to the dictionary, they will often find very interesting information about the meaning or origin or structure of words.

To summarize, beginning with the fourth or fifth grade, long words in reading are the big problem. We can use no rules to tell us the right sound for words we have never heard, but for words we have heard, there are rules for recognition. We will find that the children have much fun in the use of these rules, and they will have a big part of their reading problem solved. To repeat what the schoolman said, "You just know the little words, you sound out the big ones, and you know what it says. No one can stop you."

42. Content of a Phonics Program *

LOU E. BURMEISTER

FOR a long time teachers and children have felt overburdened with vast numbers of phonic generalizations. Often

teachers were aware that many of these "generalizations" had *limited usefulness,* for they applied to only a few words that

* From Lou E. Burmeister, "Content of a Phonics Program," in Nila Banton Smith (ed.), *Reading Methods and Teacher Improvement* (Newark, Del.: International Reading Association, 1971), pp. 27–33. Reprinted by permission of the International Reading Association and the author.

the children read. Other "generalizations" appeared to be *invalid,* in that there seemed to be more exceptions to them than there were instances of application. When being queried by an observant youngster, the teacher too frequently repeated, "That word, Jerome, is an exception to the generalization."

Because of this situation several studies have been made to ascertain both the usefulness and validity of generalizations. Among the reported studies are those done by Oaks in 1952, Clymer in 1963, Fry in 1964, Bailey in 1965, Emans in 1966, and Burmeister (1968a, 1968c).

Purpose

The purpose of this paper is to list particularly useful generalizations. These were found to be valid in the above studies and/or were inductively formulated in newer extensive linguistic studies reported by the present author (Burmeister, 1968b, 1969a, 1969b, 1970).

Findings

Authors of all of the studies agree that there is a need to teach fewer generalizations than were taught in the past. It is possible to classify the particularly useful and valid generalizations into a very few categories: *consonants*—single (b, c, d, f, etc.), blends (bl, cl, dr, sm, spl, etc.), digraphs (ph, sh, ch, th, ng, ck), some silent letters (-mb, -lm; wr-, kn-, etc., and two like consonants); *vowels*—single (a, e, i, o, u, y), clusters (ai, oa, oi, ou, ei, etc.), final *single* vowel-consonant-e (ape, ice, etc.), the *r* control (car, her, hear, care, etc.), and the consonantizing of *i* in the following situations: *tio, tia, cio, cia, sio* (mansion, action, vision, fusion, caution, etc.); *phonic syllabication* in the following graphemic patterns: vowel-

consonant-consonant-vowel, vowel-consonant-vowel, final consonant-l-e.

Particularly useful grapheme (printed symbol) to phoneme (sound) relationships [1]

I. Consonants
  A. Single consonants
    1. Each consonant (except c, g, s, and x) is highly consistent in representing one sound.
    2. When c or g is followed by e, i, or y, it represents its soft sound (city, certain, cycle; gem, agile, gym). When followed by anything else, or nothing, it represents its hard sound (cake, coat, cup, clash, cram, attic; game, goat, gum, glass, grip, flag). Omit *ch* and *gh.*
    3. The letter *s* usually (86 percent of the time) represents its own sound (swim, soft, solo). Its next most frequent sound ($/z/$—11 percent) is found in words such as resort, raisin, music, desire, treason. Omit *sh.* [2]
    4. The letter *x* represents the sounds found in the following words ($/ks/$ or $/k/ + /s/$):

---

[1] A *phoneme* is the smallest unit of sound; a *grapheme* is the symbol we use to represent the sound. The word *cat* has three phonemes and, therefore, three graphemes. The word *main* has three phonemes and, therefore, three graphemes (one grapheme *ai* is spelled with two letters). In this paper grapheme to phoneme relations are described *within* morphemes only (i.e., not between morphemes). Thus syllabication generalizations and grapheme to phoneme relationship dependent upon divisions made because of prefixes, roots, and suffixes are not included

[2] Unless otherwise stated, percentages are taken from the 17,310 words used by Hanna *et al.,* 1966.

ax, box, tax; foxy, taxi, vixen, and (/g/ + /z/): exact, exempt, exist, example.

B. Double consonants (and triple consonants)

1. Consonant blends—When two unlike consonants appear side-by-side, usually the sound represented is a blend of the sounds represented by each (*bl*ock, *cl*own, *dr*own, *gr*ow, *sm*ile, *sp*ook, *spl*ash, etc.).

2. Consonant digraphs — Although spelled with two consonants, consonant digraphs function as single consonants. They are *ch, sh, th, ph, ng,* and *ck. Ch* represents three sounds: /ch/ child, chop—63 percent; /k/ chorus, christen, orchid—30 percent; /sh/ chef, chute, mustache— 7 percent; *sh,* as in should, ship, shed; *th* represents two sounds, voiced, as in this, they, rhythm — 74 percent; and voiceless, as in think, thick, youth—26 percent; *ph* represents an *f* sound, as in elephant, photo; *ng* as in sing, wing, young; *ck* represents a k sound, as in chick, package, cuckoo. (*ck* is really two like consonants together, in which c represents the k sound, and is silent—See 3a.)

3. Silent consonants

a. Like consonants — When two like consonants are side-by-side, they represent only one sound. (This is not true of *cc* or *gg* when followed by e, i, or y— success, suggest.) *E.g.,* ball, egg, guppy, guerilla, tattoo.

b. Unlike consonants—When certain consonants are side-by-side in the same syllable, only one sound is represented. This is true of the following pairs (the only pairs which occur at least once per thousand running words: *initial kn-,* as in kneel, knot; *initial ps-,* as in psalm, pseudo; *initial wr-,* as in wrap, write; *final -dg*(e), as in dodge, bridge; *final -gn,* as in sign, reign, but also *initial gn-,* as in gnat, gnome; *final -lm,* as in calm, palm; *final -mb,* as in bomb, comb; *final -tch,* as in catch, witch.

II. Vowels

A. Definitions: The five vowels (a, e, i, o, u) and two "semivowels" (y and w) are used singly and in pairs and in the final vowel (consonant)e position to represent a variety of sounds. The most common sounds are the vowel's own short sound (h*a*t, p*e*t, h*i*t, h*o*t, h*u*t), the long sound (m*ai*n, m*ea*t, s*i*ze, *oa*k, c*u*te), a schwa (*a*bout, cam*e*l, penc*i*l, lem*o*n, circ*u*s, marriage), an *r* modified sound (c*a*r, c*a*re, h*e*r, h*ea*r, f*o*r), a diphthong (*ou*t, c*ow,* c*oi*n, b*oy*), a *broad a* —or *circumflex o*—*au*to, *aw*ful, b*a*ll; a long and short double o (r*oo*ster, b*oo*k).

B. Single vowel graphemes

1. Closed syllable (syllable that contains a single vowel and ends with a consonant)—A single vowel in a closed syllable represents its own short sound, its r controlled sound when it is followed by an r, or a schwa sound.

2. Open syllable (syllable that contains a single vowel in a final position)—If the single

vowel in an open syllable is an *e, o,* or *u,* it usually represents its own long sound; if the vowel is an *a,* it may represent a schwa—53%, a long a sound—32%, or a short a sound—12%; if the vowel is *i,* it may represent a schwa—49%, a short i sound—37%, a long i sound—14%.

3. Final y—If a word ends with a consonant + y, the y will represent a long i sound if the word is monosyllabic (try, my, thy, cry), but the y will represent a short i (long e) sound if the word is polysyllabic (baby, balcony, century, city).

C. Vowel pairs

There is no generalization that can be taught to cover a majority of instances of vowel pair grapheme to phoneme relationships. A particular generalization, however, may be taught to cover specific vowel pairs. The vowel pairs listed below need description in a phonics program. They are the only pairs that occur at least 50 times in the 17,310 most common English words selected by Hanna, *et al.*

1. First vowel long, second vowel silent—If the vowel pair is *ai, ay, ea, ee, oa,* or *ow,* usually the first vowel represents its own long sound, and the second vowel is silent (main, pay, meat, meet, boat, crow). But *ea* often represents a short e sound (bread), and *ow* often represents a diphthong (cow).

2. Diphthongs—The vowel pairs *oi* and *oy* represent a diphthong (coin, boy). The pairs *ou* and *ow* often represent a diphthong (mouse, cow).

However, when *ou* is in a suffix, it represents a schwa sound (dangerous, wondrous).

3. Broad a (circumflex o)—The pairs *au* and *aw* represent the "broad a" sound (auto, awful), just as does *a* when followed by *ll* (ball, fall).

4. Long and short oo—The pair *oo* represents two sounds (rooster, book).

5. *Ei* and *ie*—The most common sound *ei* represents is *long a* (neighbor, weigh). Otherwise *ei* and *ie* represent the following sounds, in order of frequency: long e (c*ei*ling, f*ie*ld), short i (for*ei*gn, lass*ie*), long i (s*ei*smic, d*ie*).

6. *Ey* represents a short i sound, as in hon*ey,* or a long a, as in th*ey.*

7. *Ew* represents a long u sound, as in n*ew*s, or an ōō sound, as in fl*ew.*

D. Final vowel-consonant-e

1. When a word ends with a *single-vowel,* single consonant, and an e, the e is silent, and the vowel represents its own long sound. The validity level for each vowel is: a—78.9%, e—87%, i—61.1%, o—85.6%, u—78.3%.

2. Exceptions:

   a. There are 68 primary level words which are exceptions to this generalization.

   b. Groups of exceptions are (1) i-e words in which the i represents a short i sound: l*i*ve, g*i*ve, off*i*ce, prom*i*se; (2) i-e words in which the i represents a long e sound: mar*i*ne, magaz*i*ne; (3) a-e words in which the a represents a short i sound, especially *-ace, -age, -ate* words: surf*ace*, pal*ace;* av*erage*, cour*age;* sen*ate*, deli*cate*. (Burmeister, 1969a).

E. Consonatizing of i

When *io* or *ia* follows c, t, or s, the consonant plus the i combine to represent a /sh/ or /zh/ sound: ra*ci*al, so*ci*al; men*ti*on, cau*ti*on; pen*si*on, man*si*on; vi*si*on, fu*si*on.

III. Phonic syllabication

(Phonic syllabication generalizations are used only when morphological syllabication generalizations do not apply—*i.e.,* prefix/root/root/suffix.)

A. Determination of a syllable

1. There is one, and only one, vowel phoneme (sound) in a syllable.

2. There is one, and only one, vowel grapheme (symbol) in a syllable. Vowel graphemes are (a) single vowels—c*a*p, m*e*, b*a*-b*y*, (b) vowel pairs, or clusters—m*ai*n, r*ou*nd, b*eau*tiful, (c) a final vowel (consonant) e—c*a*k*e*, P*e*t*e*, h*o*m*e*.

B. Generalizations

1. Situation: two vowel graphemes separated by two consonants (v c c v)

When two vowel graphemes are separated by two consonants, we divide between the consonants: as-ter, sil-ver, target, but-ler.

It is suggested that words containing two like consonants between two vowel graphemes not be included in this generalization (except cc and gg when followed by e, i, or y) because only one sound is represented by these two consonants. Instead words containing two like consonants

might be included in the v c v generalization (rab(b)-it, car(r)-ot, ba-(l)loon, e-(s)say).

2. Situation: two vowel graphemes separated by a single consonant (v c v)

When two vowel graphemes are separated by a single consonant, the consonant may go with the first or the second vowel. In primary level words, it is more likely to go with the first vowel; in more difficult words, it tends to go with the second vowel. At all levels, there is about a 45–55 percent split. (liz-ard, lem-on, wag-on; ra-zor, spi-der, ti-ger). (Burmeister and Trela, in progress).

3. Situation: word ending in a consonant-l-e—When a word ends in a consonant-l-e, these three letters compose the final syllable (bi-ble, ea-gle, bundle, tur-tle, noo-dle).

Implications for Teaching

The teacher should always keep in mind that phonics deals with relationships between printed symbols and sounds and that phonics will be of no help to the reader interested in getting meaning unless he orally knows the word being attacked. Researchers often talk about paired associates. It might be helpful to think of phonics as part of a *triple associate* skill. The printed symbol triggers the sound (paired level), and the sound triggers the meaning (triple associate level). For example, the reader sees the word *cat;* he responds orally /kat/; he remembers that word to be the oral symbol for a fluffy four-legged animal with a tail—or for a woman who scratches and claws. Unless the triple associate relationship is present, utilizing phonic skills can be busywork.

No longer need a teacher feel confused because of the content of a phonics program. Generalizations which should be taught are few in number. And, as has been noted in the above list, flexibility of approach is often the keynote: the learner should frequently be taught to try one pronunciation, and if that doesn't bring about oral recognition of the word, he should try another in order to reach the paired and triple associate level.

References

1. BAILEY, MILDRED HART. "The Utility of Phonic Generalizations in Grades One Through Six," *The Reading Teacher,* 20 (1967), 413–18.
2. BURMEISTER, LOU E. "The Usefulness of Phonic Generalizations," *The Reading Teacher,* 21 (1968a), 349–56+.
3. ———. "Vowel pairs," *The Reading Teacher,* 21 (1968b), 445–52.
4. ———. "Selected Word Analysis Generalizations for a Group Approach to Corrective Reading in the Secondary School," *Reading Research Quarterly* (1968c), 71–95.
5. ———. "Final Vowel-Consonant-e." A paper delivered at the national conference of the American Educational Research Association in Los Angeles, 1969a. Also *The Reading Teacher,* in press.
6. ———. "The Effect of Syllabic Position and Accent Pattern on the Phonemic Behavior of Single Vowel Graphemes." *Reading and Realism.*

Newark, Del.: IRA, 1969b, 645–49.
7. ———, and TRELA, THADDEUS. "Phonic Syllabication in the V C V Pattern" (in progress).
8. CLYMER, T. L. "The Utility of Phonic Generalizations in the Primary Grades," *The Reading Teacher,* 16 (1963), 252–58.
9. EMANS, R. "The Usefulness of Phonic Generalizations above the Primary Grades," *The Reading Teacher,* 20 (1967), 419–25.
10. FRY, E. "A Frequency Approach to Phonics," *Elementary English* (1964), 759–65+
11. HANNA, P. R., HANNA, JEAN S., HODGES, R. G., and RUDORF, E. H. *Phoneme-Grapheme Correspondences as Cues to Spelling Improvement.* Washington, D.C.: Office of Education, 1966.
12. OAKS, RUTH E. "A Study of the Vowel Situation in a Primary Vocabulary," *Education* (1952), 604–17.

43. Using Children's Reading Miscues for New Teaching Strategies *

YETTA M. GOODMAN

WATCHING and listening to children read orally can give the teacher a great deal of insight into the reading process if he views his role in the classroom as a researcher and diagnostician in addition to the more traditional teaching roles.

When Tony reads "I was a boy" instead of what was on the printed page "I saw a boy," the teacher may respond by thinking "That's wrong; I must do something to correct that behavior" or the teacher might say "That's an interesting problem, I wonder what caused that behavior? . . . what is involved in the learning process and the reading process which caused Tony to do that?"

The innovative strategies for teachers to use in teaching reading in the classroom proposed in this article will examine the major question: "How can teachers make use of children's reading miscues (errors) as a tool to help children learn to read?"

Six children learning to read have been followed since they were in their sixth month of reading instruction (Goodman, 1965). They are now at the end of their fourth year. For each of them, twenty oral reading performances have been recorded during this period. About 2,500 of the children's reading miscues (errors) have been analyzed thus far and at least that many remain to be analyzed. Certain phenomena, supported also by other research,

* From Yetta M. Goodman, "Using Children's Reading Miscues for New Teaching Strategies," *Reading Teacher,* 23 (February, 1970), 455–59. Reprinted by permission of the International Reading Association and the author.

are quite clear and have implications for teachers in the classroom.

Errors Vary

Some reading errors are better than others. The analysis of reading miscues has given a great deal of insight into the development of beginning readers. There is no question that certain types of miscues are of a higher order than others; miscues of low order give way to miscues of higher order as children become more proficient readers. Miscues must be looked at not as mistakes which are bad and should be eradicated but as overt behaviors which may unlock aspects of intellectual processing. In this case, miscues in reading give insight into the reading process. This respectability of mistakes, errors, or miscues has been supported by the vast amount of research done by Jean Piaget. "He found himself becoming increasingly fascinated, not with the psychometric and normative aspects of test data but with the processes by which the child achieved his answers . . . especially his incorrect answers" (Burke, 1969).

Examining the words children omit as they read supplies some evidence of how miscues become qualitatively better miscues as readers become more proficient. One subject omitted words he did not know and could or would not try to figure out, during early oral readings. This was evident because he often paused at these words, looked at the illustration on the page, looked at the word a little longer and then went on. In one story early in the research this subject omitted *fair, going, buy, stay, late.* In the study children were never supplied with assistance or corrections by the researcher. This technique was explained to them prior to their reading and they were encouraged to do the best they could on their own. In a story six months later, the same subject omitted two words only, *a* and *just.* The sentences resulting from the omissions were meaningful language units. The story posed problems for the child, but he had strategies for working out his problems.

When children did substitute one word for another, the substitutions showed finer discrimination of sound-symbol relationships as they became more proficient readers. Early in the study most miscues had initial or medial letters in common with the words as printed but showed little more similarity; *make* for *monkey, man* for *monkey, and* for *can* are some examples. For all subjects, based upon statistical analysis of the miscues, the children developed the ability to produce miscues which showed finer discrimination. This finer discrimination produced more miscues differing by only a single grapheme for example *man* for *men* and *lot* for *let.*

The less proficient readers tended to produce miscues which were responses to the graphic field or to a habit strength association that had been developed. A less proficient reader said *Have a Jimmy* for *What a Jump.* She had read *have* for *what* throughout two stories. *Jimmy* was called after she sounded (j, j) a few times. More proficient readers produced miscues which were more complex, involved more integration of the meaning, grammatical and sound systems of the language with the graphic input and the experience and background of the child than the miscues of the less proficient readers. A more proficient reader read *spot of fur over her nose* for *spot of fur*

above her nose. The miscue made sense in the passage and was the same part of speech as the word which should have been read in the book.

Handling Errors Instructionally

Children learn to correct their own errors. In a previous study of fourth graders, Goodman concluded that "virtually every regression which the children in this study made was for the purpose of correcting previous reading" (Clay, 1967). They were less likely to correct miscues when the resulting passage sounded like language and was meaningful to them. One subject responded with *It's the Big Billy-goat Gruff* for *It's I! The Big Billy-goat Gruff.* The resulting miscue made good sense and resulted in correct sounding syntax to the ear of the child. He made no attempt at correction. The children were more likely to correct when the language prior to and including the miscue was meaningful and sounded like language to them but then conflicted with the remainder of the passage. Another subject said *Very well, he* when it should have been *Very well, be off with you.* He stopped, regressed to the beginning of the sentence again, and read the passage correctly. When the children attempted corrections of their own miscues, they were successful at least 75 percent of the time.

Words should never be introduced out of the context of language. So many things happen when words appear within the context of language. Context changes the grammatical function of words, their syntactic relation to other words, the meaning of words and often their pronunciation and intonation. The word changes depending upon whether it is in the oral language or the written language. Words should be first used with children in the most common grammatical position that the child finds them in his own language. If words appear in less common positions in reading material, teachers may compensate for this. For example, if the word *circus* is to be taught, the child will have a better chance of using more language cues to develop strategies for working it out if it appears to him first as a noun. A prereading story might be developed by the teacher.

> We like to go to the circus.
> There will be clowns in the circus.
> The circus is coming to town.

This would avoid the difficulty that all the children in the author's study had when words were introduced in less common (to the child) grammatical positions in language. When *circus* was introduced as an adjective *circus bear, circus monkey, circus balloon* or when *river* was introduced as part of a noun phrase or as an adjective as in *Singing River* and *river man,* the children had difficulty working out the word, but when it appeared later in the story as a noun, the children often recognized the word.

Concentrate on the concept that words represent rather than on dictionary definitions. It is more important to help the children learn the underlying concept that words represent so that it will have meaning to the child within the context of the story. One subject usually had good comprehension. In one story, the word *globe* appeared eight times and the child sounded it out as /gloh + biy/ the first time he saw it. The second time it appeared, the child called it /glo + b/ and the third time /glohb/. After that he continued to pronounce the word correctly, seemingly knowing the word. However, in the retelling of the story, comprehension was low. A globe had been on the desk in front of the child and in the illustration in the book while he was reading. The researcher pointed to the globe on the desk after the retelling of

the story and asked the child, "What is this?" The child responded, "The earth." It is more important for this child to learn the scientific concept of the word globe than to teach him the sound-symbol correspondence, its graphic identity as a word or its dictionary meaning out of the context of the written language in which it was presented.

Teachers should help children make use of their miscues to provide teaching-learning strategies. Recent research in child language indicates that children have a good deal of control over their own home language when they come to school. The child's mastery of his own language is a strength which he brings to the reading task. Teachers, in an effort to improve children's reading, often work very hard on the weaknesses of beginning readers. It may be that if a child could be shown that he has strengths and if his strengths were encouraged, it might in the long run help him in improving in his areas of weakness as well.

Teachers may help children develop learning strategies by having children keep certain questions in mind as they read. Does it sound like language to you? Does it make sense to you? If not, why not? Have you read it incorrectly? Go back and reread . . . Have you read ahead? Concepts are clarified by reading more of the material. Words are often recognized when they appear a second and third time in the same story. If you still are unable to work out the problem, ask the teacher.

The teacher needs to ask himself questions before he simply gives the child the word when he is asked for help. Are the concepts unknown or partially known to the child? Is the language of the book so different from the child's language that the child needs a translation from book language to his own language rather than know just what one word is? The teacher should avoid giving the word to a child immediately or allowing other children to help when the child first encounters a problem. This will hinder the child's attempt to discover strategies to make the best use of all the language cue systems —the meaning, the sound of the longer strings of language as well as the relationship between letters and sounds. What is important in beginning reading is not the particular word but the development of strategies to use in subsequent situations. The teacher must help the child do the figuring out . . . help the child develop strategies for working out reading problems.

A caution must be kept in mind in making use of these strategies. Oral reading and silent reading are separate processes. However, oral reading provides a continuous window into the reading process and the cognitive processes taking place within children as they read.

So much happens when a child reads. If teachers are able to listen to the child's reading and try to discover why the child makes certain miscues, they will be able to diagnose children's reading problems with greater insight. With greater insight into the complexity of the reading process, the teacher can do a better job of teaching children to read.

References

1. ALLEN, P. D. "A Psycholinguistic Analysis of the Substitution Miscues of Selected Oral Readers in Grades Two, Four, and Six, and the Relationship of These Miscues to the Reading Process: A Descriptive Study." Unpublished Doctoral Dissertation. Wayne State University, 1969.

2. BURKE, CAROLYN L. "A Psycholinguistic Description of Grammatical Restructuring in the Oral Reading of a Selected Group of Middle School Children." Unpublished Doctoral Dissertation. Wayne State University, 1969.

3. CLAY, MARIE M. "The Reading Behaviour of Five-Year-Old Children: A Research Report." New Zealand Journal of Educational Studies, 2 (1967), 11–31.

4. FLAVELL, J. The Developmental Psychology of Jean Piaget. Princeton, N.J.: D. Van Nostrand Company, 1963. P. 3.

5. GOODMAN, K. "A Linguistic Study of Cues and Miscues in Reading," Elementary English, 42 (1965), 641–45.

6. GOODMAN, K. S., and BURKE, CAROLYN. Study of Children's Behavior While Reading Orally. (Contract No. OE -6-10-136) Washington, D.C.: United States Department of Health, Education, and Welfare, Office of Education, 1968.

7. GOODMAN, YETTA M. "A Psycholinguistic Description of Observed Oral Reading Phenomena in Selected Young Beginning Readers." Unpublished Doctoral Dissertation. Wayne State University, 1967.

8. MARTELLOCK, HELEN. "A Psycholinguistic Description of the Oral and Written Language of a Selected Group of Middle School Children." Unpublished Doctoral Dissertation. Wayne State University, 1969.

9. WEBER, ROSEMARIE. A Linguistic Analysis of First Grade Reading Errors. Ithaca, N.Y.: Laboratory for Research on Language Skills, Cornell University, 1967 (preliminary draft).

IX

Development of Vocabulary

Vocabulary development and therefore concept development must be important aspects of a reading program, for, as Langer points out in the first article, reading comprehension problems may stem from difficulty in understanding the words (particularly if they are key words) and the concepts they represent. Because concept formation and language skills are important in developing a reading vocabulary, but often overlooked, they are considered in this chapter.

Langer's paper is concerned with the relationship of vocabulary and concept development, and Bougere's with the development of oral language. Wise then describes a number of activities for increasing hearing and speaking vocabularies, while Lake offers suggestions for developing an interest in words and their meanings. The use and limitations of context in vocabulary development are presented next by Deighton, followed by Miller's description of how a dictionary may be used in vocabulary development.

44. Vocabulary and Concept Development *

JOHN H. LANGER

THE development of vocabulary has a direct and important relationship to the process of conceptualization. Words form the basis for the classification of concepts. Carroll discusses the role of the school in fostering the cognitive de-velopment of children and indicates the need to realize that children bring to school a large number of concepts, but with many gaps in their ability to respond verbally. He urges that schools provide for the development of the child's "verbal-response systems." "This can be done by providing many pertinent experiences and establishing learning conditions which will allow the child to see relevant distinctions in meaning and differential classification of concepts" (3).

* From John H. Langer, "Vocabulary and Concept Development," *Journal of Reading,* 10 (April, 1967), 448, 453, 455–56. Reprinted by permission of the International Reading Association and the author.

Russell and Fea, writing on concept development, cite Heidbreder's 1934 studies with college students (13). Heidbreder found that sometimes correct concepts were applied even though the subject was unable to define the concept verbally, but she required a verbal definition as proof of learning. Unless a child can utilize verbal symbols effectively, he can present little evidence of learning and cannot utilize this learning in new situations.

Definitions of Concepts

It is important for our purposes to give specific definition to the term *concept*. Russell calls it "a sort of shorthand representation of a group of facts such as are symbolized in the words *green leaves* or *pity*. It represents discrimination . . . and generalization . . . and employs symbolization" (9). John Dewey defined a concept as "a meaning sufficiently individualized to be directly grasped and readily used, and thus fixed by a word" (18). Osgood and others in *The Measurement of Meaning* looked into the connotative meanings which are related to a particular word (9). Osgood asked subjects to relate the ideas they associated with a word. He obtained clusters of words which varied widely with individuals. In this approach, peripheral meanings, represented by words, cluster around a central core or main concept. It is possible for any word which represents an important idea to be the primary stimulus for the peripheral clusters. Russell points out that by using the symbol or label the child can himself make one concept central and relate others to it by organizing or reorganizing his past experience (9).

The *Encyclopedia of Educational Research* (*1960*) lists 162 references on concepts (11). This range of research illustrates the diversity and variety of the investigations made regarding the great variety of concepts described in them. Burton, Kimball, and Wing assert that thinking in any field of knowledge is almost impossible without concepts (2). Their definitions of concepts are accepted as valid and are useful for application to this study, in relation to the necessity for symbols, terms, words, and their relationships and associations. A child's progress in reading comprehension is dependent upon possession and development of concepts.

A concept is a defined idea or meaning fixed by, and as extensive as, the term used to designate it. A concept is the amount of meaning a person has for a thing, person, or process.

A concept is a suggested meaning which has been detached from the many specific situations giving rise to it and provided with a name.

A concept is a logical construct capable of interpersonal use.

A concept is a word or other symbol which stands for the common property of a number of objects or situations.

Concept Development

The development of vocabulary is an inextricable part of concept development, and difficulty in reading comprehension stems from difficulty in the understanding of words and the concepts they represent. Communication of ideas depends upon the ability to associate written and oral symbols with the ideas and/or objects represented (symbolized). This association is dependent upon vocabulary development through written and verbal material, using a more or less systematic process of reorganizing concepts already known in the mind and/or integrating new facts and ideas with those known. In this process new terms are searched for and found to accommodate the new concept and/or relationship. The new term more accurately describes the "concept-cluster" or parts of it which are re-associated, and the child integrates the new relationships, which are represented by new symbols (labels), into his store of meanings and their organization. This new construct, or revision of one already existing, makes the relationship communicable and provides the capacity to define and explain, insofar as the individual has labels for the object or ideas associated, or the new relationships.

Concepts involve both discrimination and generalization (12). These generalizations in turn involve a variety of definitions, rules, formulas, and principles as part of any definition of the term *concept*. A concept is a devolping application of thinking to members of a class or group, and is therefore not one specific thing. In addition, a concept discriminates between classes and groups.

The distinction must be made between concepts as they exist in the mind and the terms which represent them. Russell defines a concept as "a symbolic response to the members of one group or class of stimulus patterns" (12). The process of concept formation is not completely understood, although various theories have been proposed. The evidence indicates that concepts develop in stages which are grown into gradually. There is agreement that concepts have symbolic representations and that they become more discriminating in response as they are developed. Concepts are in most instances measured by verbal response. Vinacke indicates the importance of words as related to concepts (18). He points out the role of words in facilitating organization of experience inside the individual by providing labels for systems of that experience. "Words are merely the names of concept systems.

They either evoke concepts or are responses following conceptual processes. When a child reads, the words serve as evokers of concepts—*if the concepts are there to be evoked*."

The approach to concept development that is used most frequently is through words. There are some difficulties. As Serra points out, "Much of the research devoted to determining the most effective means of increasing vocabulary assumes that enlargement of vocabulary is in itself a a virtue, without questioning the dimensions of the concepts with which words are associated. In that direction lies verbalism" (14).

In the abstract one can attempt to describe a concept by pointing out its relationship to other recognized abstractions and generalization, that is, to what is called experience. Serra attemps to describe these relationships:

Concepts exist at all levels of complexity. A concept can be based on one experience with an object or upon a multitude of experiences, and it will increase in complexity with the amount of experience. It can be based on varying degrees of relationships among objects. Concepts of increasing levels of complexity are based on a hierarchy of concepts dealing with objects and their relationships. Concepts are also symbolized and verbalized by the individual, and the symbols or words in themselves become new concepts with a new hierarchy.

What we understand by the words "in themselves" are the ideas represented, for as Vinacke has indicated, words are merely the labels for concepts (22).

It appears that there is an interrelationship among the processes of thought, of conceptualization, and of the use and development of word meaning. In reality, the distinctions may be apparent rather than real, and the mental processes involved may well have a unified function which is dependent upon prior experience, that is, upon already developed concepts. Sutton summarizes the process:

Words and concepts, the raw materials of thinking, are many, but the processes are few. Thinking results from a determined course of ideas, symbolic in character, initiated by a problem or task, leading to a conclusion that is tested in the spectative and participative behavior of the learner (16).

In any subject area there is an obvious problem in the relationships among reading comprehension, meaning vocabulary, and the concepts in the subject area necessary to understanding it. Tinker says, in discussing social studies, that the greatest difficulties in understanding the subject are specialized terms and their accompanying concepts (17). He proposes a solution: "The fact that achievement in a content fields is best reflected by vocabulary knowledge in that field further emphasizes the desirability of teaching pertinent word meanings and clarifying concepts." Lillian Gray points out that "content books often overwhelm the child by presenting too many concepts with too few explanations" (6).

Word-Concept Difficulties

Although word difficulties exist in all areas of the school curriculum, they are more apparent in some than in others. When concepts are developed through direct experiences and the labels for those experiences and their relationships are given, the difficulty is lessened. However, in the social studies especially writers lament the lack of word-concept development. Smith and Dechant quote Horn:

Many of the ideas presented in typical textbooks in geography, history, or other social studies are so intrinsically complicated that they would be difficult to understand even if described in liberal detail, in untechnical language, and in a lucid, attractive style. Ac-

tually, however, they are presented in the form of condensed and abstract statements that are readily understood only by those who have already formed the generalization for which the statements stand (15).

Other writers describe in a similar vein the intrinsic difficulties with words and concepts. Durrell gives Dawson's listing of technical terms, abstract words, multisyllabic words, and concepts, as problems in the social studies (5). Russell makes clear that much research illustrates the wide variance in concept knowledge among children of any one age, and that the ability to give a synonym or repeat a definition does not truly measure understanding (9). A pertinent point in Russell's analysis is that research shows a close relationship between concept development and general vocabulary growth.

Another aspect of concept-word difficulties lies in the very structure of language. Many of the most common words are also the most difficult. These abstract, multiple meaning words indicate relationships, associations, similarities, differences, and analogous relationships among words and their accompanying concepts.

Such structures and schemata, concept constructs, depend upon words which indicate relationships and associations as well as words based on concrete objects and experiences. These abstract, multiple-meaning words make the presentation of idea-relationships effective—that is, they facilitate the process of symbol-manipulation which is the conscious aspect of mental manipulation of concepts.

The Study of Concepts and Their Development

Because the concept is a mental construct, it must be evaluated indirectly, on the basis of some overt response by the subject. Again, because the subject has a choice of response, evaluation of the concept represented by the response is apt to be a function of the ability of the examiner to communicate the stimuli assumed to be capable of evoking a significant response, and the willingness and ability of the subject to utilize verbal or other signs to make a conventional (and thus communicable) response. McCarthy discusses the difficulty of evaluating the specific content of concepts: "Analyses of vocabularies for content or for listing concepts known to children at various ages are of some value at early ages, but at later ages selective factors are probably operative to such an extent that generalizations based on such data are of little value" (7). She also discusses the importance of language in expressing needs, wants, and desires, which illustrates the difficulty of separating the specific concepts to be evaluated from their emotional associative setting.

Few discussions of concepts written in the past few years have omitted mention of Jean Piaget's work. His first book, *The Language and Thought of the Child* (1926), presented a new approach to the functions of language and thought (8). Piaget was most concerned with using the language of the child as a means for determining his thought processes. He distinguished between egocentric and socialized speech, and his experiments provided evidence that children to the age of six use predominantly egocentric speech (a specialized term, in his usage, to emphasize the child's association of outside stimuli to himself). Socialized speech is defined as addressing another for the purpose of getting the other's point of view. McCarthy (7), Russell (10), and others take issue with some of Piaget's findings, but do not minimize the importance of the total value of his insights.

Although Piaget specifically desired his work to be of value to teachers, it is just now evolving as the basis for a specific classroom approach. His research illustrates the difficulty of studying concepts except as functions of speech, and the further difficulty of representing concepts to be anything other than generally similar when communicated.

Russell attempted to measure the *Breadth* (specialized vocabulary and multiple meanings), *Depth* (total understanding vs. synonym recognition), and *Height* (development of vocabulary over nine years) of children's vocabularies. This study also attempted to correlate previous research in the two fields of education and psychology. "Thus it attempts more specific analysis of vocabulary growth than is found in most previous investigations," (12).

This study is most important for its synthesis of the relationships between vocabulary and concepts. Even though there were no unexpected results, the verification of the hypothesis that word meaning has dimensions other than those tested by the usual multiple-choice vocabulary test is significant. It again makes obvious what many researchers have found—present tests of vocabulary are not adequate measures of pupils' understandings of word meanings. Russell summarizes the research:

The sources cited above reveal, by implication, many gaps in the study of vocabulary development. Not all current vocabulary tests are of the same kind, but most of them are alike in giving only a rough measure of miscellaneous knowledge. Further work on explicitness, on breadth, and on power or depth of meaning are needed. The relationships of vocabulary to other behavior are relatively unexplored (12).

Multiple meanings of words are extensively used by the tests constructed for this study. It is evident that Russell considers words to be the key to evaluation of concepts and that measurement of knowledge of concept is dependent upon the words associated with it. Words which cluster around the central or main word are utilized in defining it. Efficiency in categorizing, in generalizing, in making meaningful (that is, communicable) associations is the basis for inferring that a child understands the concepts represented. . . .

The findings of this study point out the difficulties in measuring concepts, in discovering cause-and-effect relationships among the mental processes, and the extreme dependence upon verbal response of the measurement and valuation of these processes.

This discussion of concepts, though by no means comprehensive, should provide a background in which words and their accompanying meanings are viewed. The word-in-itself is devoid of meaning if the user has no concept for it. Conversely, the word for which one has a multitude of associations can be a rich and varied experience. Downey, who studied associations with the word-in-itself using an interview technique, ascribes a fuller meaning to an isolated word than to the word in context. "The 'word' as a detached consciousness has a tendency to blossom into all manner of images, feelings, impulses. It is a focus of association, often exceeding richness. It is haloed with meaning" (4).

Summary

Vocabulary has a direct and essential relationship to concepts and the conceptual processes.

Concepts are general ideas, discriminatory in nature, which must be symbolized to be effectively communicated. Concept development is a gradual process in which concepts develop from simple to complex mental constructs which are evoked and labeled by signs which are most often words and which serve as guides for behavior. A well-developed structure of concept associations is a function of vocabulary-concept relationships. Concepts are extremely difficult to evaluate, study, or even isolate and identify.

References

1. BRAUN, JEAN S. "An Investigation of the Relationship Between Concept Formation Ability and Reading Achievement at Three Developmental Levels." Unpublished Doctoral Dissertation, Department of Psychology. Wayne State University, 1961.

2. BURTON, W. H., KIMBALL, R. B., and WING, R. L. *Education for Effective Thinking.* New York: Appleton-Century-Crofts, Inc., 1960.

3. CARROLL, J. B. "Language Development," *Encyclopedia of Educational Research,* 3rd ed. New York: Macmillan Co., 1960.

4. DOWNEY, JUNE E. "Individual Difference in Reaction to the Word-in-Itself," *The American Journal of Psychology,* 39 (December, 1927), 323–42.

5. DURRELL, D. D. *Improving Reading Instruction.* Yonkers-on-Hudson, N. Y.: World Book Co., 1956.

6. GRAY, LILLIAN. *Teaching Children to Read,* 3rd ed. New York: The Ronald Press Co., 1963.

7. MCCARTHY, D. "Language Development in Children," *Manual of Child Psychology,* 2nd ed. New York: John Wiley and Sons, Inc., 1954. Ch. 9.

8. PIAGET, JEAN. *The Language and Thought of the Child.* Trans. by M. Gagain. New York: Harcourt Brace and Co., 1932.

9. RUSSELL, DAVID H. *Children Learn to Read,* 2nd ed. Boston: Ginn and Co., 1961.

10. ———. *Children's Thinking.* Boston: Ginn and Co., 1956.

11. ———. "Concepts," *Encyclopedia of Educational Research,* 3rd ed. New York: The Macmillan Co., 1960.

12. ———. *The Dimensions of Children's Meaning Vocabularies in Grades Four Through Twelve,* 40, no. 5 (University of California Press, 1954), 315–414.

13. ———, and FEA, HENRY. "Research on Teaching Reading," *Handbook of Research on Teaching.* Chicago: Rand McNally Co., 1963.

14. SERRA, M. C. "How to Develop Concepts and Their Verbal Representations," *Elementary School Journal,* 53 (January, 1953), 275–85.

15. SMITH, H. P., and DECHANT, E. V. *Psychology in Teaching Reading.* Englewood Cliffs, N.J.: Prentice-Hall, Inc., 1961.

16. SUTTON, R. S. "Words vs. Concepts," *Education,* 83 (May, 1963), 537–40.

17. TINKER, M. A. *Teaching Elementary Reading,* New York: Appleton-Century-Crofts, Inc., 1952.

18. VINACKE, W. E. "Concepts and Attitudes in the Perception of Words," *Education,* 75 (May, 1955), 572–76.

45. Vocabulary Development in the Primary Grades *

MARGUERITE B. BOUGERE

THERE is a wryly humorous and revealing story of the first grader who burst into tears on the first day of school when her teacher told the children to "get into line behind each other." Upon being asked why she was crying, the little girl sobbed out: "I don't know where *each other* is!" The story provides a point of departure for a discussion of vocabulary development in the primary grades—a discussion which will focus upon relationships between the spoken and the written language.

In considering means to promote vocabulary development, it should be stressed that such development cannot proceed merely by accretion of isolated words. In speaking and listening, as in reading and writing, individual words have meaning only as they are related to one another and to the ideas expressed. The meaning of the phrase *each other,* for example, is not taught by giving definitions of *each* and *other* separately; it is learned as a whole in the context of meaningful experience. The job of the primary teacher is to help children develop competence in receiving ideas through listening and reading and in expressing

* From Marguerite B. Bougere, "Vocabulary Development in the Primary Grades," in J. Allen Figurel, (ed.), *Forging Ahead in Reading,* Proceedings of the Twelfth Annual Convention, 12, Part 1 (Newark, Del.: International Reading Association, 1968), 75–78. Reprinted by permission of the International Reading Association and the author.

ideas through speaking and writing. Vocabularies grow as children share experiences which broaden their interest in and understanding of their world. In the school setting, the teacher structures experiences in such a way that children are stimulated to use language and to express and receive communication with ever-increasing skill and satisfaction.

In this frame of reference the reading teacher is seen first and always as a language teacher, and vocabulary development is seen as an integral part of total language development in listening, speaking, reading, and writing. Reading is viewed as an extension of the child's previously achieved and still-developing skills in oral language. This view is reflected in some of the well-known series of reading texts which incorporate specific instructional procedures in speaking, listening, and writing as part of a total plan for reading development.

The use of such a frame of reference does not imply that vocabulary develops "just naturally" as maturation and experience bring increasing competence in language abilities. As long ago as 1938, William S. Gray and Eleanor Holmes conducted a series of studies of the development of meaning vocabularies that function in reading. Their findings, which have been corroborated by subsequent investigations, indicate that a close relationship exists between knowledge of word meanings and reading achievement and that direct methods of teaching vocabulary, where the teacher plans for and reinforces the learning of words in context, give pupils greater command of vocabulary than do methods which depend upon incidental learnings only.

Evaluating Language Development

The teacher who wishes to develop in any area is aware that constant evaluation is needed to identify strengths and weaknesses, to chart progress, and to provide guidelines for helpful learning experiences. A pupil language development chart or a notebook with a page for each child can provide a graphic record of each child's language status and development. Marion Monroe and Bernice Rogers, in *Foundations for Reading,* suggest a simple and workable plan for recording and evaluating a pupil's use of language, including his ability to verbalize ideas, his knowledge of word meanings, and his mastery of sentence structure. Time here does not permit a full discussion of this plan, but careful study of this or of the similar suggestions contained in teachers' manuals of language arts series is suggested. Such study will prove rewarding to the teacher interested in fostering language growth.

The special case of the disadvantage child

For those teachers who are working with children from lower socioeconomic backgrounds, it is important to emphasize that evaluation of language use should be made in terms of the child's power to communicate and comprehend rather than merely in terms of middle-class standards of "correct usage." The cataloging of what the teacher considers "errors" does not provide an adequate base for planning situations which will develop greater language competence. Although we do not as yet know enough about the complex process of language learning to pinpoint exact procedures for measuring and increasing language competency, linguistic and educational research strongly suggest that a positive, accepting approach to the child's language is more beneficial than a critical or wholly correction-oriented approach.

English sociolinguist Basil Bernstein

has provided some insights into the school language problems of the disadvantaged child:

The child has to translate and thus mediate middle-class language structure through the logically simpler language structure of his own class to make it personally meaningful. . . . The expressive behavior and immediacy of response that accompany the use of [the child's] language may . . . be wrongfully interpreted by the teacher. This may lead to a situation where pupil and teacher each disvalue each other's world, and communication becomes a way of asserting differences.[1]

I recently observed a first-grade reading lesson, an overview in which children were discussing the pictures. During the lesson the teacher rejected every single verbal offering made by the children. The children's comments were couched in nonstandard but often delightfully colorful language. Sample responses were, "He poppin' the battercakes!" "That's a mighty big icebox!" "She got on her high heels!" The teacher, wearily and grimly correcting every expression, uttered, "He is *tossing the pancakes.*" "The *refrigerator is very* big." "She *is wearing* her *good shoes.*" At the end of the session the teacher was exhausted and discouraged; the children were apathetic and confused. The teacher said to the observer, "It's so hard to teach these children anything— you have to pull everything out of them." Her communication with the children was indeed a way of asserting differences; she was, furthermore, implicitly saying to them, "Of course, you'll never learn to read. You can't even talk."

The teacher might have made an attempt to mediate between the children's

choice of words and that preferred by the school. She might have recognized that they were responding and communicating at the only level they knew. She might have welcomed the opportunity to extend and enrich their vocabularies by discussing alternative expressions pleasantly and positively. For example, she might have said, "Yes, he's having a good time with the battercakes. You know, lots of people call these 'battercakes,' but they have another name, too. Lots of people call them 'pancakes.' Isn't it fun to know two names for something that's so good to eat?"

Personalizing Vocabulary Development

Pupil-made reading materials can help bridge the gap between the child's oral language and the written language. This condition is equally true for the "disadvantaged" child who needs constant reinforcement of the basic notion that reading is "talk written down" and for the verbally able youngster who needs scope for self-expression so that school remains an exciting challenge to his abilities. A good beginning at any primary grade level is a booklet; perhaps entitled "All about Me"; illustrated with snapshots or drawings of the child, his family and friends, including a map of his neighborhood; and containing references to games he plays, books he likes, and activities he enjoys. Such booklets and others based on group experiences, learning from class work, or the child's own creative imagination become part of the class library. They are displayed, read aloud, and discussed in specially planned language periods. The alert teacher uses them for evaluation of individual language growth and selects from them "Mary's new word" and "Joe's interesting sentence" to use in enriching vocabulary development for the entire group.

[1] Basil Bernstein, "Some Sociological Determinants of Perception: An Enquiry into Subcultural Differences," *British Journal of Sociology* (1958), p. 249.

How do teachers find time to help children prepare such booklets? Some teachers plan a few minutes each day in which children can dictate material for their own books. Other teachers, in schools where the concept of the teacher aide is being put into practice, have older children, parent volunteers, or paid aides who can transcribe the children's own language into their booklets.

Using story time to develop vocabulary

The practice of telling and reading stories to children can be an important aid to vocabulary development if the teacher plans for effective listening by actively involving children in such activities as retelling, dramatizing, assisting in, and illustrating the stories heard. Allowing the children to manipulate puppets or place figures on the flannel board to go along with the sequence of the story promotes full involvement. The teacher sets the stage for comprehension and vocabulary development as she clarifies and illustrates the meaning of unfamiliar words before relating the story in which they appear. Asking questions afterwards, such as, "How did the princess show that she was *disappointed*?" or "Why do you think the monkey is called 'Curious George' "? gives opportunities for reusing and further strengthening meaning associations with new words.

Encouraging young children to join in a refrain, such as, "Run, run, run/ As fast as you can/ You can't catch me/ I'm the. Gingerbread Man," promotes unselfconscious oral expression for children who may seldom "speak out" alone. Choral reading by more mature groups serves a similar purpose. Selected words and phrases from favorite storybook passages or refrains can be related to the vocabulary used in school texts. Presenting such words and phrases on the blackboard, charts, flash cards, and sentence strips transfers what has been heard and spoken to the visual realm. The enjoyment of listening and speaking thus motivates meaningful reading experiences.

Capitalizing on enjoyment of songs and rhymes.

The teacher can capitalize on children's love of rhyme and rhythm to develop vocabulary through listening to records and other musical activities. New words learned in songs can become words a child uses frequently and can become part of the reading vocabulary when their printed forms are subsequently introduced on board or chart. The use of familiar folk songs and of the chants and rhymes the children use in games is often helpful in making the culturally different child feel more at home in the classroom. The introduction of these songs and the reuse of their words in other language activities can help build common vocabulary for the entire class.

Developing vocabulary through shared experiences.

Planning and carrying out a class trip or a special event such as a program or holiday celebration can build a background of shared experience which promotes vocabulary development. The planning phase provides a meaningful setting for discussion and interchange of ideas which the teacher may organize by writing out "What We Will See at the Zoo," for example. The trip itself will provide many opportunities for verbal descriptions and discussion of what is seen and done. A recapitulation of the experience through class discussion, dramatization, illustration, and preparation of a story chart or of individual booklets can give further opportunities for use of the newly learned words and concepts which can thus become part of each child's vocabulary.

Developing vocabulary in the content areas.

At one time it was often supposed that "reading in the content areas" was begun at the intermediate level. Today, it is understood that the basis for successful achievement in the content fields must be firmly established in the primary grades. The meaning vocabulary that is needed for reading social studies, science, and other content materials can and should be introduced through oral language activities very early in the child's school life. Beautiful new picture books and easy-to-read science texts and trade books for young children, children's weekly newspapers, discussion and chart presentation of new words and concepts currently in the political or science news, and well-planned class units of study in science and social studies, all provide a basis for learning specialized vocabulary. This vocabulary, comprehended and used in the daily speech of the primary youngster, is the firm foundation for successful reading in the content areas.

Creative book-reporting activities can develop vocabulary.

As children mature in their reading skills, the sharing of stories through a variety of book-reporting activities gives opportunities for vocabulary development. The creative teacher does not limit book reporting to a stereotyped retelling of the story but lets children share their enthusiasm for books through group activities. The youngest children enjoy drawing their favorite characters and mounting them on sticks. They can then, individually or in groups, use the puppets as foils to recount a humorous or exciting scene or bit of dialogue. By third grade some children are socially and linguistically mature enough to take part in panel discussions of books. Book reporting can be particularly useful in helping both reporters and listeners clarify the meanings of abstract words such as *pride, curiosity, danger,* or *courage.* It can further give opportunities for better understanding of figurative language and implied meanings. The alert teacher will capitalize on the children's interest in storybook characters and situations to broaden and deepen their understanding of abstract concepts. Those children who cannot yet read "on their own" need not to be left out of participation in book-reporting activities. They may show pictures from a picture book or occasionally report on a story that has been read aloud to them, and always they are included as active listeners and discussants at book-reporting time, an activity bolstering both their interest in reading and their vocabulary growth.

Conclusion

The foregoing suggestions are but a sampling of the means thoughtful teachers use to foster vocabulary development within the framework of all the language arts. Oral vocabulary development has been viewed as the foundation for and the accompaniment to the development of reading skills. As primary teachers recognize the importance of oral language to growth in reading, they seek throughout the school day to accept, encourage, evaluate, and build upon the children's ability to understand and produce spoken language and thereby promote their ability to perceive, comprehend, and respond to the written language as well.

46. Activities for Increasing Hearing and Speaking Vocabularies *

KATHLEEN WISE

. . . THE ideas for the activities given here have been collected from various sources. The activities have been adapted for fifth-year pupils. Any teacher can make use of the techniques given and apply them to the vocabulary appropriate for the pupils she is teaching.

If one new activity is introduced every second week, interest will be sustained throughout the school year. In the intervening weeks the most popular of the old activities may be reused.

When attention is focused on increasing vocabularies in this or in a similar manner, much interest will be developed and good results will accrue.

Before using most of these activities, the children should have an opportunity to use glossaries and dictionaries or to refresh their memories in some manner. In certain activities, the teacher should suggest a suitable word to the child by a leading question or sentence, a definition, a dramatization, or the like.

Example: *Mumble*—John spoke so no one could understand him even though everyone easily heard his voice; to mutter, to speak with partly closed lips; the teacher (acts out) mumbles a statement.

It is hoped that at least one of these activities will be used long enough to appreciate the value of enlarging the hearing and speaking vocabularies.

* From Kathleen Wise, "Activities for Increasing Hearing and Speaking Vocabularies," *Ideas for Teachers,* Reading Promotion Bulletin, No. 25, pp. 1–4. Reprinted by permission of the author and Lyons and Carnahan, Chicago, Ill.

1. **"Mr. Webster Says."** Some years ago a teacher adapted this popular radio program. Before beginning this activity, five judges are appointed. The remainder of the class is divided into two teams. The leader on the first team announces a word. The leader on the second team must define it and use it in an acceptable sentence, as *decrepit*—old and physically broken down; *His Model T runs but it is very decrepit.* Source of selection for words may well be the glossary of the reading textbook.

The judges decided whether the player on the second team scores a point for his team. The game can continue for a fixed time, each team having the same amount of time or the players from both teams can take turns.

2. **Illustrated Words.** A word such as *pretty* is illustrated. The illustration could be placed across the top of a 8″ x 12″ sheet with the caption *Pretty Words* beneath it. As a child reads or when he hears a descriptive word having a similar, or somewhat similar meaning, it is added to the list with his initials beside it. Example: *comely,* M.Y. *gorgeous,* S.B.

Other captions can be *Said Words,* as *inquired, answered, requested.* (About 350 words can be used in place of *said,* depending upon the mood and meaning of the speaker. They were listed in *Elementary English,* Feb., 1953.) *Wise Words,* as *sagacious, discerning, profound; Healthy Words,* as *robust, hale, vigorous,* and the like may be added. This could easily be a year's project.

3. **The Surprise Box.** If any child hears

a new word used, he writes it on a slip of paper, signs his name, and drops it into the "Surprise Box." During the day, the child who puts the word into the "Surprise Box" familiarizes himself with the word. At the close of the day the box is opened. Each child draws a slip from the box. He pronounces the word and uses it in a sentence to reveal its meaning, as; By his *munching* I knew he had peanut brittle in his mouth. The child who put the word in the "Surprise Box" is responsible for accepting the pronunciation and sentence.

A chart can be made showing each child's name and the days of the week. A check mark in the proper place will show the number of times a child responded correctly.

4. The Minister's Cat. Before this game is begun, a number of words that will be used for each letter of the alphabet is decided upon. At first, five words will be sufficient. Later on this number may be increased. The teacher may begin by saying, "The minister's cat is an *arrogant* cat." A child follows with a statement such as, "The minister's cat is an *acrobatic* cat," and so on, each child in turn. The sixth child might say, "The minister's cat is a *bewildered* cat," or uses some other adjective that begins with *b*. The game continues throughout the alphabet.

Boys can compete against girls. The boys can use the minister's dog. Scores can then be kept to see which team could always supply the number of adjectives designated.

5. A Guessing Game. The child rules or folds a sheet of paper into four sections. In each section he draws a picture and puts the first letter of the word descriptive of the illustration, as a drawing of a cave man and of a dinosaur with *p* written in one corner. Another child guesses the word, *prehistoric*.

6. Adding Words. Later on, sheets from the Guessing Game may be cut up

and the sections jumbled. Each child selects four sections. He gives other words associated with the illustration, as *antiquated, mammoth.*

7. Semantics. A list of words, each of which has a number of different meanings, as *draw, mat, match*, is written on the chalkboard. The child writes a number of sentences showing the different meanings of each word. Each shows a semantic variation of the word. The sentences are read orally.

8. Rhyming Words. A child gives a word, as *please*. His partner responds, for example, with *seize, trees.*

9. Going to Boston. A variation of this game can be used. Each object named must begin with a *b* and must be accompanied by an adjective, as: "I went to Boston and took a *glimmering button* with me." The next player repeats the first player's statement and addes to it, as: "I went to Boston and took a *glimmering button* and *an hysterical bachelor* with me." It is well to arrange the players in teams of about five each. Scores may be kept.

In the next round, instead of going to Boston, go to Cincinnati or Caledonia; then to Dayton or Downingtown.

10. Prefixes. The prefix is announced, as *auto*. Each child gives a word beginning with it, as *automat, autocrat, autograph.*

11. Suffixes. A root word is announced, as *electric*. A child gives as many words as he can that are formed from the root word. Example: *electrical, electrically, electricity, electrified, electrician, electrification, electrifier, electrify.* He scores a point for each word given. If another child can add to the list, one point must be deducted from the original score for each word given by the other members of the class.

12. Dictionary Fun. Each child opens his dictionary at random or to a specified letter. He selects a new word, reads its definitions, selects one meaning, and uses the word in a sentence to show the meaning given in the definition selected. If done correctly he scores for his team.

13. Antonyms. Teams are formed of five or six members each. The teacher announces a word, as: *relinquish;* then uses it in a sentence similar to the way it was used in recent classroom work. Each child on a team, in turn, gives words that are opposite in meaning, as *retain, grasp, maintain, restrain.* A point is scored for each member of the team that supplies an antonym. If a member of another team can supply additional ones, two points for each word may be credited to his team.

14. Synonyms. Conduct this activity in the same way as the one described under Antonyms. The words accepted must mean about the same as the word announced.

15. Association. A child announces a word as: *lawyer.* Each child names a word associated with it, as *will, court, trial.* Teams may be arranged and the activity carried on as described under Antonyms.

16. Classification. A child announces a word, as *time.* Each child names an item that belongs to that category. Examples: *hour, second, century.*

17. Latest Words and Teams. A chart of words in current news may be kept. Examples: *telecast, atom, hydrogen bomb, radioactive, radiophone, space helmet, astronaut.*

18. Crossword Puzzles. The teacher or several of the more advanced pupils can construct puzzles for others to work.

	Across
L o y a l	1. Faithful
H i d e o u s	2. Horribly ugly
P o s t e r i t y	3. Descendants
C o m m u n i c a t e	4. To make known

19. Word Hunt. The teacher writes a word, as *alternate;* then she uses it in a sentence. The children are to listen to what people around them say and notice whether they hear the same word. After twenty-four hours each child relates *when, where,* and *how* he heard or saw the word used. It has been said that a new word will be heard three times in the next twenty-four hours after it is first seen or heard. Some children find pleasure in testing out that statement.

20. Word Collections. For a week, each child collects words that are new to him. He writes a word on a slip of paper, writes the definition of it, the sentence in which he heard it used, the person and the occasion when it was used, as *emulate:* to equal or excel; to rival. *She tries to emulate Marilyn Monroe; Mother used emulate when referring to one of her friends.*

At the end of the week the envelopes are opened. The collected words are shared. The child having the most new words receives the applause of the class.

21. Listings. Select a topic as: *Vehicles.* A child begins by naming all the vehicles he can. The next child adds to the list. In Roget's *Thesaurus of English Words and Phrases* more than two hundred terms are listed under *Vehicles.*

22. Malapropisms. The teacher prepares sentences on slips of oak tag, using the incorrect form of a word. The child reads orally the sentence he draws from the pack. He pronounces the incorrect word and then reads the sentence using the intended word. If approved, a point can be scored for his side. Examples are:

The man that mows my lawn is *obliterate* (illiterate).

My father's *preposition* (proposition) was not pleasing to me.

23. Letter Out. The teacher lists, on the chalkboard, words with one letter omitted. Examples: *inj—red, mild—wed.* The first child tells the letter omitted, pronounces the word and uses it in a sentence to reveal a correct meaning, as *u: injured; The injured man was rushed to the hospital for first-aid treatment.* Scores may be kept.

24. Change a Letter. Write the word *Bride* on the chalkboard. The first child changes one letter in *Bride* so that the word formed will mean just plain salt water, *Brine.* The leader gives each definition in turn. Each player changes only one letter in the last word to form the new word that matches the definition given.

	B r i d e
Just plain salt water	B r i n e
On the edge of things	B r i n k
To wink the eyes	B l i n k
Oblivious to everything	B l i n d
Light-haired	B l o n d
A red-colored fluid	B l o o d
Another name for a flower	B l o o m
Something that makes a clean sweep	B r o o m
Husband of the bride	G r o o m

47. First Aid for Vocabularies *

MARY LOUISE LAKE

ACCORDING to nearly a half-million tests given to individuals from widely varied walks of life, knowledge of the exact meanings of many words correlates with success more often than any other measurable factor. This successful performance matching wide vocabulary holds true not just in business and the professions, among scientists and college students, but in every type of work from the highest to the lowest. Furthermore, the higher the rank of the worker, the wider is his knowledge of words—a definite and surprisingly consistent progression.

It would seem to be logical, then, that every classroom teacher should be vitally

* From Mary Louise Lake, "First Aid for Vocabularies," *Elementary English,* 44 (November, 1967), 783–84, Copyright © 1967 by the National Council of Teachers of English. Reprinted by permission of the author and the National Council of Teachers of English.

interested in establishing a firm base upon which the child might learn to build his vocabulary. Some schools, particularly private institutions, have already shown what can be accomplished when this factor is emphasized.

How can we foster this interest in words in an elementary classroom? First, it is almost axiomatic that much reading leads to a growing knowledge of words, and encouragement along that line is so universally employed by teachers and parents that the point needs no belaboring here. There are children, however, who cannot be lured into wide reading. We cannot afford to write this group off, but how shall we set about broadening their vocabularies?

Interest in words can be taught independently of formal reading and, in the process, the language arts program can be greatly enriched and stimulated. Almost every child responds to games and puzzles, and there are numerous types which can be used to enlarge vocabularies painlessly.

Suppose we start with the pun. Most children's jokes are based upon puns, which in turn are often homonyms. Teach your pupils what a pun is, help them to discover puns in typical jokes in their reading materials, and let this lead into a class collection of homonyms. There are literally hundreds of them in our language and often one of the pair is a new vocabulary word to the elementary child.

Rhyme games cause children to delve deeply into their vague word memories to bring up a proper rhyme. Games such as "Hinky-Pinky" in which a definition must be answered by two rhyming words are a constant delight. Examples: An obese rodent (fat rat); wet hobo (damp tramp); profound slumber (deep sleep). The child who thinks of a rhyming pair he wishes to try on his classmates goes to his dictionary eagerly to find a synonym he can use. Synonym study can also grow from an adaptation of the television program "Password."

Make use of any current fad involving words. "Tom Swifties," for example, are excellent for teaching and expanding the knowledge of adverbs. This game, played by young and old, had its inspiration in Victor Appleton's hero who never just said something, but always said it in an adverbial manner—"firmly," "quietly," "hesitatingly," *etc.* The current fad demands an adverbial pun, as, "I'll never pat another lion," said Tom offhandedly.

All fads may not add so directly to the vocabulary, but I have found that interest in words and enjoyment of what can be done with them is a profitable starting point. In this category would be the periodically recurring "Knock-knock, Who's there?" and word tricks, such as AMNESA ("amnesia" with the "i" forgotten, of course) or C R E A M (which is to be read as "vanishing cream").

Announce a "Challenge" for the class and ask, "Who can give me a four-letter word ending in "eny' without using a pencil?" Other challenges to stimulate the language arts lesson to follow could be: Can you make another word out of the letters in "chesty?" Do you know a word containing double "u" or double "a," double "k," or double "i"? How many words can you think of, with five letters or more, that contain neither A,E,I,O, nor U? Can you think of any English words in which "su" sounds like "shu?" Perhaps you would like to try these yourself. Answers are at the end of the article.

There are endless collections of words children might enjoy adding to as a class project. Palindromes or "mirror words," words spelled the same forward or backward, such as "radar" or "level," are interesting. One Spanish-speaking pupil proudly contributed "reconocer," our longest. The teacher could contribute one of the famous palindrome sentences, such as "Was it a cat I saw?" or "Madam, I'm Adam."

Other collections are: words borrowed from other countries, collective nouns, homographs or heteronyms, words that suggest sounds, words that tell how things feel, or others that the children might suggest themselves.

A dictionary drill will be tackled eagerly, if you make it into a game. Try calling it "Let the Cat Out of the Bag" and list a series of synonyms for words in your class dictionaries which begin with "c-a-t"—a machine for throwing stones (catapult), a mountain lion (catamount), a nasal disorder (catarrh), *etc.* Or list a number of words whose antonyms all begin with "D"—*safety, light, wet, single, lift, etc.* Another letter, as "F" could be used for synonyms for *liberate, end, elf, remote, etc.*

Games already in use can be given a

slight twist to convert them into vocabulary builders. The old "Make as many words as you can from the letters in SCRAPBOOK" allowed the children to make words they already knew. Instead, give definitions to force them to find *your* words which may be new to them, as "a small stream" (brook), "three snakes" (*cobra, asp, boa*), *etc.*

President Kennedy was only one of many famous people who enjoyed word games. His favorite was "Categories" which challenged his wide general knowledge. It can be readily adapted to the classroom, using parts of speech for the categories, for example.

These are only a few suggestions for the upper elementary grades. Materials from schoolbook companies, adult maga-

zines, and puzzle books offer many other possibilities only limited by your own ingenuity in putting them to use. Get a file box in which you can keep your collection to have it readily available. Share with other teachers and exchange ideas. A word project may not be equally successful with every class, but children tend to like the same games year after year. If you can stir their interest, it will be worth any effort you might make, for a fascination with words tends to become a lifetime habit.

(Answers to challenges: Deny. Scythe. Vacuum; bazaar or aardvark; bookkeeper or jackknife; skiing or Hawaii. Myths, gypsy, rhythm, lymph, hymns, *etc.* Sugar or sure.)

48. Vocabulary Development in the Classroom *

LEE C. DEIGHTON

How Context Operates

THERE are four general principles of context operation which can be stated with some exactness. They are stated at this point to permit their being checked against the instances of context which will be quoted later. The *first* general principle has already been stated—context reveals the meaning of unfamiliar words only infrequently. The *second* is that context generally reveals only one of the mean-

* From Lee C. Deighton, *Vocabulary Development in the Classroom,* Bureau of Publications, Teachers College, Columbia University, 1959, pp. 2–6, 15–16. Reprinted by permission of the author and Teachers College Press, Columbia University, New York, N.Y.

ings of an unfamiliar word. Most words in common English usage have more than one meaning recorded in the dictionary. These dictionary entries are only an interpretation by the dictionary editors of the common denominator in a great many instances in which a particular word is used. The dictionary entries are indispensable to us as a point of departure in understanding a word. However, dictionary entries do not limit the use of words. Dictionary entries are shaped, changed, and altered by individual contexts, each of which is different. This in brief is why a single context can illuminate only one phase of a particular word. Which phase is developed will be determined by the demands of the particular context. In presenting this matter to children it is worth repeating over and over again that no word has one fixed and inalterable meaning, that no one context revelation will suffice for all the later uses of the word which may be met.

The *third* principle of context operation is that context seldom clarifies the whole of any meaning. Occasionally, context will provide a synonym, but it must be remembered that synonyms are never exact equivalents. Words are not like coins of even value, to be substituted at random in the exchange of communication. Context more often provides only clues from which the reader may infer the meaning of an unfamiliar word. It is important to make clear to developing readers that the whole meaning of an unfamiliar word can never be gathered in the first encounter with it. Meaning comes from experience, and the wider the experience with a word, the richer will its meaning be for the reader.

From this follows the *fourth* general principle—that vocabulary growth through context revelation is a gradual matter. It is a matter of finding one clue here and another there, of fitting them together, of making tentative judgments and revising them as later experience requires. It is a matter of building meaning into a word over a period of years.

Limiting Factors in Context Operation

In addition to these four general principles, there are certain limitations on the effective use of contexts in classroom study. The first of these follows from what has just been said. *What a context may reveal to a particular reader will depend upon his previous experience.* It is unfortunately true that some words exist for most of us *merely* as words—as spoken sounds or printed symbols having only the vaguest of meanings for us. We have not tied these words into our per-

sonal experience. We have not objectified them. We have not applied them as labels to physical objects or to the observable qualities of physical objects or to the behavior of persons and things. We recognize these words, and we can restate them, perhaps, in other words with more or less success, but we have not attached them to the living experience of our physical world. The degree to which we have objectified the words which compose a context will determine the success with which we use that context to uncover the meaning of an unfamiliar word.

The key words in the context may themselves be unfamiliar to the reader. Although the construction of a context may indicate to the experienced reader that an example or restatement is being given, the inexperienced reader may completely miss the restatement and assume that new material is being added. Inexperienced readers must not be expected to derive as much help from context as experienced readers get. This factor of experience is really a limitation on the effective use of contexts in classroom study.

There are two other limitations worth noting. The first of these is that the portion of context which illuminates an unfamiliar word must be reasonably close to the word if it is to act effectively. It may appear in the same sentence. It may appear in the same paragraph. It may precede or it may follow. If it follows within reasonably close space, it can be used effectively by the average reader in his average haste to cover the material in hand. If it precedes the unfamiliar word by so much as a paragraph, its effectiveness is limited. If it precedes by several pages, it has even less value except to those careful readers who take the time to re-read for understanding. In ordinary adult circumstances, there are few of us who take the time for re-reading. In classroom practice there is always time to re-read; and there could be no more salutary exercise in vocabulary development than to assist and then, as pupils experience grows, to require the pupil to dig out the preceding passages which reveal the meaning of an unfamiliar word.

There is another limiting condition in the effectiveness of context which exists irrespective of experience or reaidng patience. *There must be some clear-cut connection between the unfamiliar word and the context which clarifies it.* This connection may be made by repeating identical sentence structure; by repeating the construction in which the unfamiliar word occurs and by substituting a synonym; by use of pointing words or phrases such as *such as, like, for example, this, that, those,* and many others.

The importance of these constructions and these connecting words is apparent when we examine a context which lacks them. For example,

We were flying at 22,000 feet. M. called for echelon starboard. Our Hurricanes moved into single-file, each plane to the right of the plane in front.

The unfamiliar words are *echelon starboard.* The next sentence describes an echelon starboard, but there is nothing to indicate definitely that it does. How is the reader with no previous knowledge of *starboard* or of *echelon* to know that the next sentence is not a completely new idea?

By contrast note how the parallel construction in the following example reveals what is meant specifically by *moisture.*

The letters they carried were wrapped in oiled silk to protect them *from* moisture, either *from* water in fording streams, or perspiration of the horse.

It is not meant here that the word *moisture* is an unfamiliar word for the

average reader. The example is cited simply to show the operation of context. Similar examples may be found with the same pattern involving words of real difficulty for the most widely read adult. The importance of the example is its illustration of how parallel construction ties context closely to a key word.

To restate: Context reveals the meaning of unfamiliar words only infrequently. A single context reveals only a part of a meaning of a particular word. The building of meaning from context is a gradual process. The effectiveness of context in revealing meaning is limited; it depends on the previous experience of the reader, on the proximity of the enlightening context to the unfamiliar word, and on the clearness of the connection between the context and the word upon which it bears. . . .

Context reveals meaning most simply by outright definition. It reveals meaning by citing examples, and these contexts frequently employ signal words: *such as, such, like, especially, for example, other, this* or *these* (followed by a synonym), *the way* or *in the way that.* Occasionally, when these signal words are not employed, the linking verb is used to show the connection. A third method of explaining an unfamiliar word is the use of modifiers. A fourth method by which context reveals meaning is through restatement in which certain signal words can always be counted upon as introducing a restatement: *in other words, that is, to put it another way, what this means, which is to say,* and all the possible modifications of these. In addition restatement employs two mechanical devices as signals: the dash and the parenthesis.

The classroom study of these four methods of context revelation may reasonably be expected to yield good results for perhaps half of the context situations which will arise in classroom reading.

For the other half, there are no key words and no mechanical devices. The reader must rely on inference. Sometimes these inference contexts show the connection between the unfamiliar word and the explanatory matter by employing repetition of sentence pattern, by repetition of key words, by use of familiar connecting words like *however, yet, therefore, similarly.* Frequently the connection is established only through repetition of thought or statement of its opposite.

There are many instances of inference context which contain none of these connecting devices. They may be dealt with profitably as they arise, in the hope that teacher guidance will encourage the pupil to use his own resources in reading for meaning rather than to pass by all unfamiliar words.

49. Stimulate Reading . . . with a Dictionary *

EDITH F. MILLER

MAKING a dictionary as a class project provides a valuable addition to the reading program and can be adapted to any grade level.

As a first step, in the first grade, I prepare a set of large cards, each with a word on one side and the same word below a picture on the other side. In the lower right-hand corner of the side with the word only, I put the beginning letter of that word. This gives an added means of identifying a word—"dog" will not be called "puppy," "Mother" will not be called "lady" or "woman," "ship" will not be called "boat."

The words on the cards are those with which the children are already familiar from their basic readers, from class activities, from the special weeks and holidays already passed, from writing exercise books or number study—in short, from any source the children have used.

* From Edith F. Miller, "Stimulate Reading with a Dictionary," *Grade Teacher,* 79 (February, 1962), 51–52, 106–7. Reprinted by permission of the author and Teachers Publishing Corporation, Darien, Conn.

Making the Cards

Except for the colors and a few verbs, all of the words are nouns. If the children are familiar with only the singular form or the plural form of a word, it is wise to include the other form, also, as the words are put on cards.

As soon as I start making the cards, I ask the children to help me find the needed pictures. We keep a pile of magazines on hand and the children look for the pictures, colored if possible. These are cut out and mounted. In many cases there will be duplicate pictures which are saved for later use. A good drill in reading is furnished by tacking on the bulletin board the cards which need pictures. As pictures are found, the children tack them under the cards. Later the class helps to decide which pictures shall be used on the cards.

The pack of cards may be used in a variety of ways. The teacher may show the cards, word side only, to the entire class, allowing the children to take turns reading them. The children love to see who can get the most cards. The cards may be used in the same way in a small pupil-led group. Other games may be made up by the class and played by the children in small groups. The cards also provide a good means of developing self-help when a child uses the pack or part of it by himself. Individual children may be tested on the entire pack by teacher or a pupil-partner and the words missed isolated for further drill.

Next Step

After intensive use of the pack of cards, I make a large booklet titled "Our Very Own Picture Dictionary." Each letter of the alphabet appears at the top of a page in the book with several blank pages following each lettered page. When I show the blank booklet to the children, I also show them some published picture dictionaries and picture dictionaries made by previous classes.

The children are most enthusiastic about making their own dictionaries. First their cards are sorted out according to the first letter. We play games with the sorted cards. This proves a good way for them to see, for example, that all "b" words start with the same sound, while the "a" words may have different sounds.

After this activity, we look for the pictures needed for our class picture dictionary. Many of the duplicate pictures which we did not discard are now used. The children do all the cutting and they arrange the pictures in the book in the order of the alphabetically listed words. I check this arrangement before they do any pasting. Then I print the words under the pictures.

As new words are learned, pictures are found and pasted in following the original words; thus the new words cannot be in alphabetical order. New cards are made and, if desired, these are kept in a separate pack so that drill on cards may be centered on the newly introduced words.

Personal Dictionaries

Several months after the beginning of the project, I arrange all the words alphabetically and make duplicate sheets so that each child may make his own copy of "Our Very Own Picture Dictionary." Space is left for illustrations which may be pupil-made but usually are procured from catalogues, old textbooks, gummed seals, conservation stamps, used greeting cards, informals, and magazines.

At the close of the school year, the finished picture dictionaries are taken home. Parents are always impressed with the many words that have been mastered, especially if they realize that only comparatively few words of the children's reading vocabulary can be illustrated. A copy of the dictionary is also sent to each second grade where the pupils go in the fall.

Second Grade and Up

Second-grade pupils who have not made picture dictionaries in the first grade would enjoy the project, following practically the same procedure. Whether they have had the experience in the first grade or not, any second-grade or third-grade group would enjoy adapting the idea by making "A Picture Dictionary of Science Throughout the Year," "A Picture Dictionary of the Seasons," "The Circus," or any topic they study. "A Picture Dictionary of Christmas" is always popular and the number of words added by that one theme alone is amazing.

Third-grade children may use the pack of cards or omit that part of the plan if preferred. If third-grade pupils make dictionaries toward the end of the year, they are mature enough to make up simple definitions for some of the words after studying picture dictionaries carefully. They are happy to make their dictionaries a little more like dictionaries for grownups. Of course, the teacher will have to write many of the definitions with them and for them. Pupils in the third grade and above usually prefer to draw their own pictures rather than to cut them out and paste them.

Fourth-grade pupils can write more of the definitions themselves and should also show how to pronounce each word. Since the fourth grade is the one where dictionary work is usually stressed, making a class dictionary is a natural activity for this grade and provides the needed practice in the use of the pronunciation symbols. Studying glossaries found in their own texts and in sample books helps in all phases of dictionary writing. Thus the transition from a picture dictionary to one with definitions and very few pictures is gradually made.

Pupils in grades above the fourth proceed in the same way. The topic chosen for the dictionary should always be one of real interest to the children. These upper-grade dictionaries will include many words other than nouns.

The dictionary made by a class may be used as a reference or as reading material by other classes, and often inspires creation of their own dictionaries by the other classes.

Transitional Step

As an intermediate step between the picture and name on a card and the "real" dictionary on a given topic, you might like to try this idea, applicable to any grade:

Choose any area where the children need some help in understanding terms—it might be art, music, science, geography, arithmetic, and so forth. Make up a list of terms which you want your children to understand. Give each child one term which can be illustrated. Have each child print his term neatly in red crayon at the top of a sheet of drawing paper. He will then draw an illustration, putting the part which illustrates the specific word in red crayon.

In arithmetic, for example, the term SUM would be lettered in red at the top of the paper and an addition example would be put on the paper in black crayon, with the answer in red. Children can see at a glance that a SUM is the answer to an addition example. However, the definition—"SUM is the answer to an addition example"—will be put on in small letters.

In geography, physical features lend themselves well to this idea; in art, it is possible to illustrate "angles," "vanishing points," "planes," and similar terms; in science, words such as "antenna," "insect," and "larva" may be clearly shown.

Every child may make as many of these sheets as desired. A border of these terms, arranged alphabetically, is a help in spelling when the children are writing on the topic. Understanding of a topic is an outgrowth of such an activity. The pupils sometimes like to make their own booklets of the words in the border, illustrating when possible. This activity could lead very naturally into making a dictionary including terms that cannot be illustrated.

Outcomes

The most important outcome of making dictionaries is that pupils will come to love words and *want* to know more and more of them and their meanings. They will become more articulate in their oral and written reports, in the expression of their thoughts and feelings. Knowledge of words increases the enjoyment of reading and greatly stimulates the desire to read.

Other outcomes include:

1. Picture dictionaries made in the primary grades provide a good foundation for the formal dictionary work of the fourth and later grades.

2. Alphabetizing is introduced sequentially beginning in the first grade and continuing until any list of words can be easily alphabetized by the children. This helps them to find words in a real dictionary easily.

3. The children experience satisfaction through the self-help their systematic study of dictionaries has made possible.

4. The number of words learned thoroughly by this one means is astounding—both words from standard lists and words from special content fields.

5. The finished dictionaries are popular with both children and their parents. The parents can see the progress the children are making in learning.

6. The practice in writing definitions is a real contribution to exact and precise English.

Reading Comprehension

The main aim of reading instruction is to develop readers who comprehend and react to what they read. As Smith indicates in her opening article, there are three levels of comprehension—literal, interpretive, and critical reading. It is with the latter that this chapter is mainly concerned, because there is an obvious need to develop such skills in today's society.

In order to conduct discussions at any of the levels of comprehension illustrated by Smith, the teacher must be able to question wisely. Melnik's discussion of diagnostic and instructional questions should help teachers to do so.

The last three articles deal with critical reading and listening. Lundsteen not only reviews the research in these areas, but also offers specific procedures for teaching such skills. Next Agrast describes one plan for teaching propaganda analysis, and Burrus relates how a newspaper may be used to teach critical and creative thinking skills.

50. Levels of Discussion in Reading *

NILA BANTON SMITH

READING content is one of the most productive mediums to use in developing thinking abilities through discussion. Are we making the fullest use of this medium for this purpose? Are we conducting discussions at a level which is too low, in many instances, to stimulate real thinking on the part of boys and girls? Are we, too often, simply asking them to repeat,

parrot-like, what is said in the book rather than guiding discussion in ways which will encourage them to probe for deeper meanings and to evaluate critically?

We shall present a few examples to illustrate the possibilities of different levels of discussion, as applied to reading content.

Literal Comprehension

Guidance directed toward literal comprehension is the lowest rung on the ladder of discussion possibilities insofar

* From Nila Banton Smith, "Levels of Discussion in Reading." Reprinted from the May 1960 issue of *Education*, pp. 518–21. Copyright © 1960 by The Bobbs-Merrill Company, Inc., Indianapolis, Ind.

261

as stimulation of thinking is concerned.

For example: The children are reading a story about two children and their toys. "With what was Ann playing?" asks the teacher. "Ann was playing with her doll," comes the answer. And this statement is given in so many words in the text. "What was Jack doing?" and the text says quite definitely that "Jack was playing with his rocket."

Questions of this type require only slight mental activity on the part of the teacher and little or no thinking on the part of the pupils. Such questions undoubtedly give children practice in recalling and reproducing statements or facts and have a place in detailed factual reading. It is doubtful, on the other hand, whether this form of questioning helps children to develop the ability to glean the types of meaning from reading that they need to enrich their lives to the fullest extent.

Through continued practice, however, children often become so glib in answering this reproduction type of question that they convey the impression of having achieved a high degree of excellency in "comprehension."

A thirteen-year-old boy named Larry recently was sent to the writer for diagnosis. He had above-average intelligence and was considered a "very good reader," but he was failing in other studies. As a part of the diagnosis, the boy was asked to read the story of Johnny Appleseed. A class of graduate students observed and read the story also. When Larry had finished, he was asked several questions which could be answered by restating what had been said directly in the text:

"How long ago did Johnny Appleseed live?"

"More than a hundred years ago."

"What was his real name?"

"Jonathan Chapman."

"How did he spend his time?"

"He planted apple trees."

These and additional question of the reproduction type were asked, and Larry answered all of them unerringly in the words of the book.

"Do you think Larry needs help in comprehension?" the graduate class was asked.

"No," came the unanimous response, "his comprehension is perfect!"

Interpretation

Larry had been checked on his literal comprehension, but the discussion had been extremely limited. What happened when he was asked some questions at a higher level of comprehension—in other words, questions which called for interpretation of meanings not stated directly in the text?

"Why did Johnny choose to plant his trees deep in the wilderness where the settler had not yet come?"

"He wanted to be alone while he was working," Larry replied.

Larry had missed an important implication in drawing this conclusion. Johnny's real reason for planting the trees before the settlers arrived was, of course, so that the trees would grow and bear fruit by the time the settlers moved in. Larry's reason made Johnny an unsocial person who didn't want anyone around him while he was working.

Several other questions of the thinking type were asked. Larry's replies to all of them were equally faulty, and all of them failed to evoke any give-and-take discussion.

Larry is only one out of hundreds of intelligent pupils who learn the superficial knack of giving back what the text says, but who never tap the significance of meanings which can be gleaned only through the use of mental processes of a higher type.

One of the most productive ways of developing ability to derive meanings in reading is through discussion in which the teacher makes a special contribution by throwing in questions here and there which stimulate cause-and-effect reasoning and which point up the necessity for making comparisons, drawing inferences, arriving at conclusions, and gathering generalizations.

In a third-grade classroom recently, such a discussion took place. The children had read a story about Fred, a boy who visited his Uncle Bill, a sheepherder who lived in a covered wagon in the foothills. During the first few days of his visit, Fred was concerned with his uncle's shepherd dogs, who stayed out with the sheep at night, even in bad weather. One night, Uncle Bill took Fred out to the herd while a storm was raging. He called the dogs. They appeared from the midst of the herd of sheep, but they "did not want to leave their wooly hiding place." Fred said, "All right. I won't worry about them anymore."

The children and the teacher discussed the story as they went along, and also, after they had finished. Everyone entered into the plot with interest and enthusiasm and relived the experiences of the characters. As all of this was taking place, however, the teacher kept uppermost in her mind the importance of stimulating children's thinking in working with meanings derived from their reading. Now and then, at appropriate times, she asked questions to which there were no answers directly in the text—questions which called for inferences, generalizations, comparisons, and reasoning.

"In what part of the country do you think this story took place?"

The children referred to details in the text and pictures and soon concluded that the setting of the story was in the Rocky Mountain region.

"Why do you suppose one of the dogs was called Taffy?"

None of these children ever had seen warm taffy pulled and noted its golden-brown color when it is in this elastic state. The colors they associated with taffy were greens, blues, pinks, and yellows, which they had found in the saltwater-taffy boxes that their parents had brought from Atlantic City. The children lacked the experience necessary for this concept; therefore, the teacher told them about taffy in its natural state and compared its color with Tom's sweater and Jan's hair. The children then easily reasoned why one of the dogs was called Taffy.

"Compare the way that Fred felt at the beginning with the way he felt at the end of the story. Why did he change?"

At no point in the story does the author tell how Fred felt, nor is there any statement in regard to why he changed. The children, however, were able to find telltale words and phrases that indicated how worried Fred was all through the early part of the story, and other words and phrases which revealed his satisfaction and peace of mind toward the end of the story. It simply required one major generalization on their part to uncover the cause of this change in the boy.

Thus a wise teacher can guide discussion fruitfully in connection with children's reading dozens of times every day. And, thus, deeper meanings emerge from the printed page, and the real significance of the printed symbols becomes fully apparent.

Critical Reading

Critical reading is another aspect of the reading-for-meanings area of development—an aspect which requires carefully guided discussion. Critical reading makes use of both literal comprehension and interpretation. It involves both getting the facts and interpreting deeper meanings. In addition, it calls for the personal judgment of the reader in deciding upon the validity of the material. In critical reading, the reader evaluates and passes judgment upon the purpose, the fairmindedness, the bias, and the truthfulness of statements made in the text.

Jean was reading a story in a preprimer about children who made a playhouse by spreading newspapers across the backs of two chairs. Among other things the story said that Furry, the cat, played with them, too, and ran about on top of the playhouse.

Jean stopped in her reading and remarked, "Furry couldn't have run on top of this playhouse, because it was made of newspapers." Jean was doing critical reading.

Tommy, a second-grader, read these statements in some arithmetic material that he was given: "Nancy went to the store to get some milk. Milk was 12 cents a quart. She got two quarts. How much did she pay for it?"

"There's something wrong here," said Tommy. "Milk costs more than 12 cents. I paid 21 cents for a quart at our store yesterday." Tommy also was doing critical reading.

In this age of multitudinous attempts to influence our thinking through the use of printed material, much more emphasis should be placed on critical reading. Youth should be taught to look for slants and biases and tricks of propagandists so that they will be in a position to judge the validity of statements which they read in all printed material.

In the primary grades, we need to rely largely upon guided discussion of books children use in the classroom to develop critical reading. However, more direct work can be done in the upper grades, not only with books used in the classroom but also with materials brought in from the outside.

Ask the children to bring to class newspapers from different publishers; then have them compare several reports of the same event and note the variations. Much worthwhile discussion will ensue. Guide them on the newspaper's reputation for containing "uncolored reports," and on the writer's reputation for presenting facts accurately. Encourage spirited discussion as the children pick out statements which they think are opinions and statements which they think are facts.

Ask the pupils to bring in articles from the various columnists and discuss each one in terms of personal opinion versus facts, biases, radical ideas, and attempts at sensationalism. The same procedure can be used with magazine articles, pamphlets, and books.

In addition to the aforementioned experiences in evaluating, students should become acquainted with methods and tricks used by the propagandists. Each member of the group may bring in a clipping of an advertisement, an excerpt from a speech made during a political campaign, or an article on any topic, in which the writer tries to influence readers in their thinking or actions. Let each child read his selection aloud. Following the reading, encourage free discussion concerning the writer's motive and techniques that he uses to accomplish his purpose.

These are only a few suggestions for developing critical reading through discussion. The teacher who is acutely aware of the significance of critical-reading skills in our current life will find many opportunities each day to help her pupils to grow in this important area of reading achievement.

Summary

We have intended, in this article, to emphasize the urgency of developing children's ability to enter into mental action and reaction with meanings embedded in printed symbols, both those that are immediately apparent and those that lurk between the lines of type. Furthermore, we have tried to point out that on-the-spot discussion, guided by a skillful teacher, is probably one of the best mediums which can be used for this purpose.

The teacher, however, must prepare carefully for any discussion. She must be ready with sagacious questions and remarks; ready to follow and guide discussions into worthwhile channels; ready to "step out" when children are taking over in ways that are truly conducive to growth in their thinking processes; and ready to "step in" when a question will stimulate further mental activity or when a remark will afford subtle guidance in arriving at a sound judgment.

Discussion of reading content under such conditions well may result in the fullest realization of Edward Thorndike's terse but significant definition of some years back: "Reading is thinking."

51. Questions: An Instructional-Diagnostic Tool *

AMELIA MELNIK

A basic concept of reading, which should underlie instruction at all levels, is that reading is a thought-getting process and as a thought-getting process, reading involves comprehension. To comprehend, the reader must judiciously select, organize, and relate the author's pattern of thought. To be selective, the reader must raise significant and appropriate questions relevant to the material as a basis for establishing a purpose for reading. His questions determine what he reads, how he reads, and what he gets out of his reading. In short, questions underlie and guide the reader's quest for understanding as he engages in a dialogue with the author. In this sense, reading is inquiry.

What, then, is the role of questions? And how are they formulated to serve their multiple purposes?

* From Amelia Melnik, "Questions: An Instructional-Diagnostic Tool," *Journal of Reading*, 11 (April, 1968), 509–12, 578–81. Reprinted by permission of the International Reading Association and the author.

The Role of Questions

Questions function in both reading and teaching situations. In reading, questions establish a basis for identifying and clarifying a reader's purpose which influences his method of reading, the degree of comprehension, rate of reading, and the skills employed in reading. More than anything else, a reader's purpose influences what he reads and how he reads.

In instructional situations, the role of questions is by far the most influential single teaching act. According to Taba, "A focus set by the teacher's questions circumscribes the mental operations which students can perform, determine what points they can explore, and what modes of thought they can learn" (7). Moreover, students' concepts of reading are largely influenced by the types of questions asked by teachers. For these reasons questions play a crucial role in affecting the levels of the teaching and the reading process. Yet there is little evidence to suggest that teachers are well prepared in the formulation and analysis of fruitful questions as a diagnostic and instructional tool.

For example, in examining 17 newly published or recently revised professional reading textbooks, only four of them identified the topic of questions in either the table of contents or the index. Even in these four, however, the treatment of questions was rather brief and superficial, with four- or five-paragraph descriptive and prescriptive discussion rather than an analysis with appropriate application. Perhaps in our professional texts too much attention is paid to the content and materials of reading instruction to the neglect of the process of reading instruction.

If teachers are not competently trained in the formulation and use of questions, it is not surprising to find that investigators of teachers' use of questions report that they were found to ask regularly 150 questions per class hour (1). Findings of this kind clearly suggest that the quality of teaching in these situations is at the level of memory of facts and details. Such an emphasis encourages students to read with a mind-set to memorize as many isolated details as possible. Unfortunately, even our most able readers reflect a detail-oriented concept of reading, which reflects the types of questions they have encountered in the classroom. In a study of 1,500 Harvard and Radcliffe Freshmen, Perry (3) made the following observations:

1. The typical approach of 90 percent of these students was to start at the beginning of the chapter and read straight ahead. No attempt was made to survey the chapter, note marginal headings, or first read the recapitulation paragraph in which the whole structure and summary of the chapter was given. Thus, none of the clues and signals provided as a basis for raising questions were used to identify specific purposes for reading.

2. Their performance on a multiple-choice test as far as they were able to read in this manner was impressive. But only one in one hundred—15 in all—were able to write a short statement on what the chapter was about. Perry describes the reading performance of 99 percent of these students "as a demonstration of obedient purposelessness in reading."

Obviously, setting a purpose is a potent influence on reading comprehension. But a purpose for reading can only be defined and established if the reader knows what kinds of questions to ask the author. According to both the Harvard study and the analysis of teachers' questions, it seems evident that students and teachers need to improve the quality of their questions. Perhaps in our teaching we need to shift our emphasis from giving the right answers to raising relevant and significant questions.

The Purposes and Formulation of Questions

As a tool in the teaching of reading, questions have two main functions, diagnostic and instructional:

As a diagnostic tool, they are unstructured, allowing the student to respond in his own fashion, thus giving the teacher opportunity to observe the variety of individual responses in a natural reading situation.

As an instructional tool, questions are more precisely formulated and logically organized to uncover the author's pattern of thought, develop discussion, and clarify meaning.

Questions also serve to evaluate learning, but in these situations, questions are primarily concerned with the content rather than the process of reading, and for that reason will not be considered at this time.

It is the teacher's responsibility to understand these two separate functions of questions so that he may use them independently and concurrently in appropriate situations to stimulate thinking and help the student increase his awareness of the reading process. To do this, it is essential that the teacher first decide for which of these functions he will be using his questions. His purpose will determine what types of questions to ask and how to formulate them. In each situation, students should also be made aware of the purpose of the questions. Otherwise, they perceive all questioning as testing and the classroom atmosphere is charged with tension as the teacher conducts a threatening inquisition instead of a natural discussion.

Diagnostic Questions

As a diagnostic tool, questions are formulated by the teacher to elicit the maximum response from an individual. In analyzing his response, the teacher gains insight into his process of reading, which provides a basis for planning appropriate individual instruction. In obtaining evidence of the student's ability to select, organize, and relate ideas gained from reading, Strang has long advocated the use of the free response (5). In her study of reading interests and patterns, she used as a stimulus the question, "What did the author say?" This question is purposely somewhat vague in order to leave the subject free to express his habitual response to printed material. From analyzing the responses to this question, she concluded that all aspects of reading are involved in answering it, thus giving the most revealing single picture of the individual's reading ability.

While the formulation of the unstructured question poses no difficulty, the analysis of the response does require the teacher to be skillful in identifying which reading skills appropriate to the material should be noted in the response. Among

the insights revealing reading proficiency, the teacher may note evidence of the following:

1. The student's approach to a reading passage;
2. His tendency to relate ideas rather than merely seize on isolated details;
3. His ability to uncover the author's pattern of thought;
4. His ability to organize and show the relation among details;
5 His tendency to let his emotions or prejudices and personal experiences influence his comprehension;
6. His tendency to relate what he reads to other knowledge he has gained;
7. His ability to communicate in writing what he has gained from reading.

Diagnostic questions, then, reveal rather than conceal individual differences.

Instructional Questions

As instructional tools, teachers' questions serve the purpose of guiding the reader to select, organize, and relate the author's pattern of thought during or following the reading experience. In these situations, questions are primarily concerned with identifying the types of thought relationship developed to unify the content. In other words, the central purpose of questions at this time is to focus on the process rather than the content of reading.

How is this accomplished? First of all, the teacher must be able to analyze the author's structure of thought to identify the type of relationships around which he has organized his ideas. For example, ideas that are related through comparison will be identified through signals in the text such as: *some-others; either-or; as-so; one-both; all-none; few-many*. In this instance a question may ask for a comparison in which details are related according to likenesses and differences. If a contrast is stressed, then the questions ask for a response in which just the differences are related. Frequently, details are related in a time sequence, as indicated by signals such as *long ago, later, now*. In this case, the question is formulated so that the response relates details to indicate development and/or change. In other thought patterns, sequence according to process rather than time is significant. Here the student reports details logically organized in a specific series of steps. Other types of relationship are cause-effect; problem-solution; main idea-detail. In each case the type of relationship suggests the formulation of a single question which requires the student to select and relate relevant details in his response rather than a series of specific questions which elicit simple yes-no answers or isolated factual detail.

Profitable instructional questions guide and clarify various types of relationships which influence comprehension. Discussion begins with a global question which focuses on the essence of the selection and serves as a point of departure for evolving further related questions which serve to clarify, modify, or illustrate meaning. Challenging questions stimulate students to report relationships among ideas and lead to fruitful discussion in which more time is spent in listening and in supporting or elaborating answers to questions than in asking them.

The following example is presented to concretely illustrate the process of formulating instructional questions and a method of analyzing responses for diagnostic purposes.

Large machines are moving over some cranberry bogs. The machines are picking a bumper cranberry crop.	INTRODUCTION
Long ago, cranberries were picked one by one. Later, pickers used hand scoops. (Now,) machines pick berries on most bogs. Each machine picks thousands of pounds of berries each day.	MAIN IDEA # 1
After the berries are picked, they are stored in large boxes. Then, they are put in a machine. The machine blows away leaves and twigs. The clean berries then go through another machine. It separates good berries from the bad berries. In the machine good berries bounce like little balls (2).	MAIN IDEA # 2

Analysis of Content	*Author's Pattern of Thought* (4)	
Cranberry Picking	1. *Main Idea*	
hand	detail	SEQUENCE-
scoop	detail	TIME
machine	detail	
Cranberry Processing	2. *Main Idea*	
stored	detail	SEQUENCE-
cleaned	detail	PROCESS
separated	detail	

	Signals:	long ago
		later
		now
		after
		then

I. Instructional Questions: Two types
    A. Isolated Details   B. Integrated Thought Relationships

1. How were cranberries first picked?
2. How were cranberries later picked?
3. How are cranberries picked now?

    1. How has cranberry picking changed?
        (Sequence-Time)

4. Where are cranberries stored after they are picked?
5. What happens to cranberries when they are cleaned?

    2. How are cranberries prepared for market?
        (Sequence-Process)

    3. What is a "bumper crop?"
        (Inference-Context Clues)

    4. How do Machines affect employment?
        (Conclusion)

II. Diagnostic Question: "What did the author say?"
    A. Scale for Rating Adequacy of Responses (6)

1	2	3	4	5
Vague or inaccurate statements	Isolated details	One main idea and some detail	Both main ideas—time and process sequence	A well-organized statement of the author's pattern of thought (both main ideas and relevant details)

    B. Examples of Ratings and Responses:

Rating

1   "It is about berry-picking machines."

2   "The author tells us about machines that pick cranberries."

3   "The author tells about picking cranberries—how they used to be picked by hand and now they are picked by machine."

4   "This section is telling us about the way they used to pick cranberries and how it is done now by machine. It also tells about the cleaning process of cranberries after they are picked."

5   "This selection tells how cranberries have been harvested in the past and how they are now harvested by large machines which do the work of thousands of old-fashioned hand pickers and scoops. The machines also prepare the berries by cleaning them and also separating the good berries from the bad ones."

Concluding Statement

If the effective reader is a questioning reader, more and more opportunity should be given to students to formulate and analyze questions themselves. Perhaps in this changing world of expanding knowledge, it is more important to learn how to formulate significant questions than it is to memorize all the answers.

References

1. BURTON, WILLIAM H. *The Guidance of Learning Activities* (3rd ed.). New York: Appleton-Century-Crofts, 1962. P. 436.
2. *My Weekly Reader.* Columbus, Ohio: American Education Publications, 1965.
3. PERRY, WILLIAM G., JR. "Student's Use and Misuse of Reading Skills: A Report to the Faculty," *Harvard Educational Review,* 29, No. 3 (1959), 193–200.
4. STRANG, RUTH, and BRACKEN, DORO-
THY. *Making Better Readers.* Boston: D. C. Heath, 1957. Pp. 105–56.
5. STRANG, RUTH. *Explorations in Reading Patterns.* Chicago: University of Chicago Press, 1942.
6. ————. *Study-Type of Reading Exercises: High School and College Levels.* (With Manual.) New York: Teachers College Press, 1960.
7. TABA, HILDA. *Thinking in Elementary School Children.* Cooperative Research Project No. 1574. San Francisco State College, 1964. P. 53.

52. Procedures for Teaching Critical Reading and Listening *

SARA W. LUNDSTEEN

IN the school lunchroom Jeannette approached her fifth-grade teacher. "Mrs. Martin, I just wanted you to know that I'm glad you took time last year to teach us about critical reading and critical listening."

"How's that, Jeannette? In what way was it helpful?"

"In class we've been talking about TV and radio programs . . . what we think is good and what's not . . . and why . . . ."

"Seems as if your teacher this year is carrying on where I left off."

"I've used what we learned whenever

I've read advertisements on the back of comic magazines, too. It has kept me from sending off for a lot of expensive, useless stuff. And this summer it helped me when a friend tried that 'everybody-else-is-doing-it' trick on me."

"Yes?"

"But it really came in handy last week in our class meeting."

"How was that?"

"Talk about arguing in a circle! We spotted that error right away and moved to some new ideas. And we were pretty good about judging the difference between a fact and an opinion, too."

As Jeannette waved and started for the playground, Mrs. Martin smiled. It had been difficult teaching children to read and to listen critically. Not all of them had profited as much as Jeannette. But

* From Sara W. Lundsteen, "Procedures for Teaching Critical Reading and Listening," in *Contributions in Reading,* No. 34, pp. 1–7, copyright © 1964. Reprinted by permission of the author and Ginn and Company.

this was just one of many indications that the effort was worthwhile.[1]

It has been said that reading and listening can be dangerous tools if they are used "blindly." Yet how many of us allow our pupils to absorb information at a superficial level? How often do we give them opportunities to read critically in class? Do we expect them to listen critically, or are we satisfied if they just hear? Why is it important to teach critical reading and listening? Just what do these terms mean? What does research tell teachers about critical reading and listening? What does it say about teaching procedures? Some of the answers to these questions are suggested here.

Why Are Critical Reading and Listening Important?

The professional literature on current educational problems makes frequent reference to the need for critical reading and listening. However, the reasons for stressing this important constellation of abilities, though often implied, are not always clearly stated. It is helpful, therefore, to consider the following specific reasons for providing such instruction:

1. The presence of mass media in our culture tends to produce conformity in children, not individuality. Television has been called the giant cookie cutter that shapes the minds of children in the same pattern. According to Everett Dean Martin (12), all tyrannies begin and end in the tyranny of ideas uncritically accepted.

2. Abilities in critical reading and listening are not usually acquired automatically. They do not, as a matter of

course, appear as one aspect of general mental growth; nor do they necessarily accompany high mental ability, high general reading ability, or high general listening ability. Roma Gans (4) says, "Gullibility in reading functioning conjointly with high ability in reading comprehension is an incongruity which should not be tolerated in a process directed toward education." Unless specific provision for suitable instruction is made, children cannot be expected to acquire the critical reading and listening abilities which are essential to good citizenship.

3. If we wait, it may be too late. Studies show that, by the time pupils reach the third grade, many prejudices, misconceptions, and stereotypes have been acquired (21). An experiment conducted at the fourth-grade level showed the great difficulty, if not the impossibility, of correcting misconceptions previously acquired from mass media (6). Postponing instruction in critical abilities until high school or college may be like closing the proverbial barn door.

4. The sheer amount of time spent by children in listening and reading is large and is increasing. Approximately three-fourths of the information an elementary-school child receives through language comes through listening; one-fourth, through reading. Paul Witty (23) makes particular reference to the influence of today's electronic Pied Piper, television. Unless children are taught evaluative and selective techniques, they may, as Witty says, drown in a sea of trivial listening and reading.

5. National committees have stated that critical appraisal should be the central aim of education at all levels. Yet, despite their admonitions, little help has been made available to teachers in the way of procedures and materials for providing effective guidance and training (15 and 16).

[1] The dialogue is taken from actual reports written by children after a recent experiment in teaching critical listening.

What Are Critical Reading and Listening?

In the past, critical thinking, and therefore critical reading and listening, were not clearly defined. Early studies dealing with critical thinking frequently stopped at analysis without proceeding to judgment. For example, pupils might be led to analyze and to detect a propaganda device, such as "name calling," in the use of the term "litter bug" in a clean-up campaign; the label "yellow" applied to a person; or the expression a "steaming, unsavory witches' brew," used by unfriendly critics to describe a social studies program. But no effort would be made to guide the pupil in the next step, namely, the use of standards and an attempt to judge the propaganda, under the specific circumstances, as useful, harmless, or injurious.

More recently, critical thinking while reading and listening has been defined as the process of examining written or spoken materials in the light of related, objective evidence, comparing them with some standard, criterion, or consensus, arriving at a conclusion, and acting upon the judgment made. According to this definition, critical reading and listening are processes of conscious, high-level judgment. Included in the total process are a healthy questioning attitude, knowledge of the problem, and a willingness to suspend judgment until all the available evidence has been examined (17 and 20). . . .

Do Basal Readers Make a Contribution to the Development of Critical Reading?

Teachers need materials and suggestions to help them improve instruction in critical reading. In a valuable research study by Gertrude Williams (22), the teachers' manuals of 10 series of basic readers were checked for materials on teaching critical reading. She concluded that systematic and gradual development of critical reading skills is provided in well-prepared teachers' manuals of several recent basic reading series. For example, the lesson plans in some manuals contain literally hundreds of suggestions for interpreting the materials read. Even first-graders have opportunity to read critically when they are asked to cross out the incorrect response in such statements as "Flip (a dog) can fly."

Many workbooks also give instruction and practice in critical reading. For example, the index of reading skills in one fifth-grade reading workbook has 19 entries for critical reading; while the corresponding workbook for the sixth-grade level has 43 entries. The skills include discrimination between fact and fiction, evaluating information, interpreting ideas, perceiving related ideas, using facts to form opinions, and generalizing.

What Else Does Research Say About Teaching Procedures?

Most teachers may now be asking for evidence to support the assumption that critical abilities can be taught and improved significantly.

Critical reading. Perhaps the most noteworthy experiment in teaching critical reading at the high-school level was Glaser's (5). His experiment resulted in a standardized test of critical thinking, published by World Book Company [1] (the *Watson-Glaser Critical Thinking Appraisal*).

On the elementary level, important studies have been made by Nardelli (14), Maw (13), and Saadeh (19). Nardelli's study indicated that children can improve their analysis of written propaganda.

[1] Now Harcourt Brace Jovanovich. (Eds.)

Maw's study indicated the value of constructing charts of attitudes and using duplicated exercises with children to develop the following skills: (1) selecting relevant facts, (2) judging reliability of data, (3) making generalizations and inferences, (4) recognizing insufficient evidence for a conclusion, (5) determining cause and effect. Saadeh's study used the technique of gaining an abstract concept by noting the similar features of many examples. The skills that the pupils learned and used during the experiment dealt with the judgment of analogies, inferences, and generalizations. His pupils moved successfully from concrete objects, to examples, to the making of examples themselves, to definition, and then to application. All three of these experimenters in the field of critical reading designed tests especially for their studies, and found significant improvement of the scores after training.

Critical listening. Similar findings and significant improvements in critical listening were found by Devine at high-school level (3), and by Lundsteen (14) at elementary-school level. Both investigators constructed experimental tests of critical listening. The students in Devine's experiment appeared to profit from taped practice selections designed to teach recognition of speaker bias, fact and opinion, inferences, emotional language, and the language of report.

The pupils in the Lundsteen study appeared to gain from lessons using programmed learning techniques. For example, pupils were led by small steps involving questions with prompts, clues, and possible back tracking and branching. Moreover, the teaching directed to critical listening abilities, i.e., detection of speaker's purpose, judging of propaganda and arguments, appeared to transfer to other in-school and out-of-school areas.

In both fields, critical reading and critical listening, we must await further controlled experiments evaluating specific teaching procedures. In the meantime, certain specific activities and games appear to have been useful. Several are described at the end of this article.

Conclusion

Mrs. Martin, mentioned in the beginning dialogue, and other teachers have learned that critical reading and listening are of vital importance in the school curriculum. Research seems to indicate that these abilities are best taught by discovery methods in a developmental program.

Furthermore, this judging process is not just a tearing down, but rather a building-up of ideas. Good readers and listeners, as Dale (2) says, are both tender-hearted and tough-minded. They are tender-hearted because they are sensitive, appreciative to mood, feeling, tone. They are tough-minded because they know that blind reading and listening are dangerous tools. They fill up "their extra thinking space" while reading and listening, not with useless odds and ends, but with appropriate questions and standards that build better understandings.

By using such procedures as those suggested here, and by interrelating instruction on critical reading and listening, teachers can give children greater language power. Why not try some of the following procedures today?

Some Specific Procedures for Teaching Critical Reading and Listening

1. JUDGING A BOOK OR STORY. Children can be guided in elevating tastes and setting up standards for judging excellence in literature. From a discussion of classics and other noted books, a checklist such as the following might develop:

a. Does the author show understanding of people and their problems?

b. Is he able to carry you away and show you another time and place? (This ability might include skillful creation of mood, beautiful imagery, convincing dialogue.)

c. Do the facts in the story agree with outside data?

d. Are the author's conclusions or special points of view consistent with the facts he gives?

e. Does he give a fair picture of more than one side?

f. Do the characters seem real, vivid, well motivated?

g. Is the plot masterfully woven, credible? (Evaluation of this ability may require previous understanding of plot patterns and of techniques such as the flashback, change of point of view.)

h. Does the author have the ability to make you forget who and where you are because you are so wrapped up in his story? (Most children who have read *Charlotte's Web* will know what you mean.)

i. Is the end of the story an accident or a credible result of previous conditions?

2. EVALUATING A TELEVISION SHOW. Russell and Russell (18) give a checklist for evaluating a television show. After similar standards are derived by the class, a letter might be written to a television station commending a show that meets the standards. Besides ideas given above under the procedure for judging a book or a story, points to keep in mind in making the evaluation are the program's purpose and presentation, the actors' performances, and the advertising (tasteful, factual, not insulting to reasoning ability).

3. RUMOR CLINIC. Data with which to judge hearsay evidence can be gathered in the classroom, and the fallibility of human observation and listening can be dramatically illustrated. Concepts regarding the quality of a fact can be built, and pupils can begin to evolve rigorous standards by which to judge a fact.

In an activity resembling the game of gossip, all but one of several volunteers are asked to leave the room. The remaining volunteer is allowed to study for a minute a frame depicting one scene from a filmstrip. Neither he nor the other volunteers are allowed to see the frame again. But the rest of the class can observe the picture while the first volunteer describes the scene to the next volunteer, who has just been allowed to enter the room. This pupil, in turn, passes the story or "rumor" on to the third pupil brought into the room, and so on. In a discussion afterward, pupils can note the changes, distortions, additions, and deletions that occurred by the time the "rumor" was fifth hand.

In an alternate activity, a story may be taped on a recorder and replayed after the last of several participants have retold it. Or a little playlet, with a memorized script and carefully rehearsed actions, may be used in a similar fashion.

4. JUDGING FACT AND OPINION. Pupils draw a line down the center of a sheet of paper and label one side Facts and the other side Opinions. They then listen to or read a selection, identify sentences or phrases containing facts or opinions, and enter them in the appropriate columns. For example, on the fact side might be found the sentence, "He did not speak when the girl was there." On the opinion side might be found, "He is bashful." Pupils should be prepared to defend their judgments.

In discussion it can be brought out from comparing many examples that (1) facts may be classed as historical, observable, and experimental; (2) a fact is not true for all time—(It looked as if the world were flat; it looked as if the atom could not be split.); (3) the best quality of opinion is based on the best quality and quantity of facts available so far; (4) in the light of new evidence, this opinion may well need to change; (5) refusal to change opinion may lead to prejudice; (6) opinion should not pretend to be fact. In conclusion, children may enjoy the following rhyme by an unknown author, called *Opinions*.

> Alas, that the strongest
> Are often the wrongest.

Or discussion might end on the note that sometimes all we can have is opinion. "That is the most beautiful sunset I've ever seen!" It would be difficult to construct an accurate test of sunset beauty. Pupils may wish to put their ideas about standards for facts into chart form for reference.

To apply their standard for facts, two pupils of approximately equal oral language ability may describe the same happening (an exciting game, an assembly program, a classroom incident or a story the rest of the class has placed before them for reference). Tape the two reports, if possible, for playback. After the class has listened to both reporters, have the pupils compare the two versions of what happened regarding quality of observation, facts, and opinions.

5. EVALUATING SOURCES OF INFORMATION. After pupils have become familiar with many different references and have acquired skill in locating information, they can begin to weigh and to evaluate several sources on the same topic. Help them learn to be wary of statements such as "Authorities say . . ." or "Informed sources say . . .", by asking "Who says?" or "What informed sources say?" Suggest that speakers can be checked in *Who's Who in America*, in *Science*, in *American Universities*. Pupils can consider the possible bias of a speaker or writer, whether or not his views are supported by facts, whether or not he is an expert in his field, and whether or not other experts agree with him.

To start discussion, the teacher might pose the question, "Which book should we choose for our library, and why?"

One pupil questioned the information in a little book which stated that a spider is an insect. A retelling of this happening, or, better yet, an actual incident experienced by the class or one of its members can initiate this evaluation.

6. A TEST FOR JUDGMENT OF CAUSE-EFFECT STATEMENTS. After examining examples of valid and invalid cause-effect statements, pupils can derive standards such as this one.

Standards for Judging Cause-Effect Statements

a. *Did the happening follow the supposed cause?* Example: "The icy steps caused the old lady's accident." Were the steps icy before the accident? If not, the statement is invalid. But merely coming before is not enough. Example: "Today we had a flat tire because yesterday a black cat crossed my path."

b. *Can the cause be tested?* To illustrate, can you test the statement above that the black cat caused the flat tire? Can you test a certain virus as the cause of polio?

c. *Could there be other causes?* In the example above, could the flat tire have been caused by the nail we see stuck in it, rather than by the cat? Example: "If your turtle is smart enough to turn around when you thump him, mine should be able to do it, too, because I got mine the same place you did." Could there have been other reasons for the turtle's turning performance? (Age, health, teaching technique, individual differences?)

Children can find examples of false cause and superstition in literature (such as in the sixth chapter of *Tom Sawyer*) and in their daily communication. For a description of other logical fallacies which children should learn to recognize, see such books as *Education for Effective Thinking* by Burton, Kimball, and Wing (1). . . .

References

1. BURTON, WILLIAM H., KIMBALL, ROLAND B., WING, RICHARD L. *Education for Effective Thinking.* New York: Appleton-Century-Crofts, 1960.

2. DALE, E. "Why Don't We Listen?" *The News Letter,* Bureau of Educational Research, Ohio State University, 25 (March, 1963), 1–4.

3. DEVINE, THOMAS G. "The Development and Evaluation of a Series of Recordings for Teaching Certain Critical Listening Abilities." Unpublished Doctoral Dissertation. Boston University, 1961.

4. GANS, ROMA. *A Study of Critical Reading Comprehension in the Intermediate Grades,* Contributions to Education, No. 811, New York: Bureau of Publications, Teachers College, Columbia University, 1940.

5. GLASER, E. M. *An Experiment in the Development of Critical Thinking,* Contributions to Education, No. 843, New York: Bureau of Publications, Teachers College, Columbia University, 1941.

6. KLEE, LORETTA E. "Larger Horizons for the Child: A Fourth-Grade Experiment," *Social Education,* 13 (February, 1949), 69–71.

7. LUNDSTEEN, SARA. *Basic Annotated Bibliography on Listening.* NCTE/ERIC, 1969.

8. ———. "Critical Listening Research and Development: Listening-Tests, Curriculum, and Results for the Thinking Improvement Project." *Highlights of the 1968 IRA Preconvention Institute II: Critical Reading and Listening.* Salt Lake City, Utah: Exemplary Center for Reading, 1969. Pp. 43–70.

9. ———. "Language Arts in the Elementary School." *Teaching for Creative Behavior,* W.B. Michael (ed.). Bloomington: Indiana University Press, 1968.

10. ———. "Research in Critical Listening and Thinking: A Recommended Goal for Future Research," *Journal of Research and Development in Education,* 3 (Fall, 1969), 119–33.

11. ———. "Teaching Abilities in Critical Listening in the Fifth and Sixth Grades." Unpublished Doctoral Dissertation. University of California, Berkeley, 1963.

12. MARTIN, EVERETT D. *The Behavior of Crowds.* New York: Harper and Row, Publishers, 1920.

13. MAW, ETHEL W. "An Experiment in Teaching Critical Thinking in the Intermediate Grades." Unpublished Doctoral Dissertation. University of Pennsylvania, 1959.

14. NARDELLI, ROBERT R. "A Study of Some Aspects of Creative Reading." Unpublished Doctoral Dissertation. University of California, Berkeley, 1953.

15. NEA, Educational Policies Commission. *The Central Purpose of American Education.* Washington, D.C.: NEA, 1961.

16. The President's Commission on Higher Education, *Higher Education for American Democracy,* Vol. 1, "Establishing the Goals." Washington: U. S. Government Printing Office, 1947.

17. RUSSELL, DAVID H. "The Prerequisite: Knowing How to Read Critically," *Elementary English,* 40 (October, 1963), 579–82.

18. ———, and RUSSELL, ELIZABETH F. *Listening Aids Through the Grades.* New York: Bureau of Publications, Teachers College, Columbia University, 1959

19. SAADEH, I. Q. "An Evaluation of the Effectiveness of Teaching for Critical Thinking in the Sixth Grade." Unpublished Doctoral Dissertation. University of California, Berkeley, 1962.

20. SMITH, NILA B. "What Is Critical Reading?" *Elementary English,* 40 (April, 1963), 409–10.

21. TRAGER, HELEN C., and YARROW, MARIAN R. *They Learn What They Live: Prejudice in Young Children.* New York: Harper and Row, Publishers, 1952.

22. WILLIAMS, GERTRUDE. "Provisions for Critical Reading in Basic Readers," *Critical Reading,* by E. Elena Socher and others. Champaign, Ill.: National Council of Teachers of English, 1959.

23. WITTY, PAUL A., KINSELLA, PAUL, and COOMER, ANNE. "A Summary of Yearly Studies of Televiewing— 1949–1963," *Elementary English,* 40 October, 1963 (590–97).

53. Teach Them to Read Between the Lines *

CHARLOTTE AGRAST

WITH the Jolly Green Giant ho, ho, ho-ing away, delicate damsels swearing they'd rather fight than switch, and politicians promising panacea, you have to admit, we live in a huckstering world.

So what does all of this have to do with you? Just this: The children in your classroom are not immune. Like the rest of us, they are bombarded everyday with ingenious and crude, sophisticated and unsophisticated, obvious and subtle efforts to sell, persuade and change attitudes and opinions. Isn't it the school's responsibility to supply them with the ammunition to face up to the onslaught intelligently?

At the Coventry School in Cleveland

* From Charlotte Agrast, "Teach Them to Read Between the Lines." Reprinted from the November 1967 issue of *Grade Teacher,* pp. 72–74, with permission of the publisher. Copyright © 1967 by CCM Professional Magazines, Inc. All rights reserved.

Heights, Ohio, we decided to accept this responsibility. All our sixth-graders participate in a unit on propaganda. The aim: To develop some understanding of propaganda—what it is, how it works, when it is bad and when it is good. Our broad goal: To prepare the children to spot and evaluate propaganda wherever they find it, whether in a conservative textbook or in a two-minute TV spot.

Our propaganda unit is based on the seven "reprehensible" techniques cited by the Institute for Propaganda Analysis. It requires seven 45-minute periods from motivation to culmination. And it has four phases: (1) Arousing interest in propaganda. (2) Helping the children realize the importance of understanding it. (3) Getting them involved by "doing." (4) Getting them to master and use ideas advanced. Here's how it worked in our school last year.

Our four sixth-grade classes (about

110 children) met in the auditorium. To generate interest, we used the roving microphone technique.

First, teachers wandered about the auditorium asking children to define the term "propaganda." The answers we got were not surprising. It was clear that the children were familiar with the term, but didn't understand its meaning. In general, they viewed it as a term connoting evil or malicious intent.

Its true meaning came out through discussion. Still using the roving microphone technique, we asked leading questions based on examples of ethical propaganda. Soon the children came to see that propaganda can be bad *or* good. They learned that, whether it's bad or good does not always depend on the content (the person exposed can agree or disagree with the ideas presented). And they came to the conclusion that what really determines the quality of propaganda is the technique used.

By this time, some of the youngsters were able to describe some unethical propaganda techniques to which they had been exposed. This led naturally to the introduction of the IPA list.

The Reprehensible Seven

The IPA's list of "reprehensible" propaganda techniques was flashed on the auditorium screen:

1. Name calling
2. Glittering generalities
3. Plain folks
4. Testimonial
5. Transfer
6. Bandwagon
7. Card-stacking

The children were quick to translate these unfamiliar terms into familiar experiences. There were many volunteers to offer examples of the "reprehensible" seven.

One child mentioned a commercial in which ball players endorse bubble gum. "My kid brother," he said, "is more of a bubble gum expert than they are."

Among other examples cited: Calling a political opponent a "Communist" or "John Bircher" without regard for the facts; the "everybody-with-taste" approach; and ads that try to make every girl feel she can look like a fashion model.

The Reprehensible Seven

Here's a rundown on the Institute for Propaganda Analysis list of unethical propaganda techniques upon which Coventry School bases its search-for-truth unit:

Name calling: Indiscriminate use of such labels as "warmonger," "John Bircher," or "red" to create an unfavorable impression.

Glittering generality: A blanket statement couched in high-sounding words and phrases. The aim: To make people accept a point of view without examining specifics.

Plain folks: Winning public support by promoting oneself as a "common man."

Testimonial: Quoting a popular personality in favor of a product or position.

Transfer: Capitalizing on the respected reputation of an organization by unjustly using its name in support of a program or product.

Bandwagon: The "everybody's-doing-it" approach.

Card-stacking: Selecting and using facts so they give a false or misleading impression.

A Deceptive Dragon

At the second large-group session, the lesson of the first was reinforced. We showed a set of transparencies made from Elsa Bailey's book, *Truth and the Dragon* (American Friends Service Committee). In the book (and the transparencies), Dragon Propaganda—he is the leading character and represents the IPA blacklisted techniques—fights to keep everyone from learning the truth.

The transparencies proved an effective

device for getting the children to appreciate the importance of understanding propaganda techniques. The clever, simple illustrations brought the subject to a level all the children could grasp.

With interest in the unit reaching a peak, we moved to the next phase: Giving the children an assignment we knew they would enjoy. Imagine being ordered to watch TV by your teacher!

Worksheets with instructions were distributed. Pupils were asked to watch a favorite TV commercial, analyze its appeal, identify the propaganda techniques used and to revise the commercial to give it a more honest appeal. Each child also was asked to study a newspaper or magazine account of a political speech and analyze it in the same way.

Brain Storming

Their findings were to be discussed in small-group sessions. In preparation for these brain-stormers, 32 students were trained to serve as discussion leaders and assistants.

The sixth grade was divided into 16 heterogeneous groups for the discussions. Four teachers circulated among the groups to supply help when the children asked for it.

It was obvious that none of the children had shirked their TV homework assignment. It was obvious, too, that they had viewed the commercials with more than 20/20 vision. In a supercharged atmosphere, the children brought up examples of all kinds of bad TV propaganda. Newspaper and magazine clippings were everywhere. The children were really excited.

The Creative Approach

The next assignment was designed to test the ability to apply previous learning creatively. Each of the 16 groups was asked to prepare a simple skit using an actual or invented commercial or political speech to demonstrate the use of propaganda—good and bad. They were given three days to complete the work.

Again, the children were allowed to operate on their own. But this time, conferences were scheduled between the directing teachers and discussion leaders. The conferences were used to review progress, germinate ideas, and work on solutions to problems that arose.

The culmination day provided the opportunity for the children to present their skits before the entire sixth grade. It offered the teachers a chance to see how well the material was getting through.

Each group was allowed up to three minutes for its presentation and analysis. All 16 were finished in less than an hour. The content included political speeches and takeoffs on a variety of TV and newspaper commercials. Many of the groups elaborated on their skits with scenery, props, and costumes. The four evaluating teachers reached the consensus that, in each case, it was a toss-up as to who was enjoying the affair more, the audience or the players. And all agreed that the unit had accomplished its aims.

It was our hope in providing this experience—one that goes way beyond the mere reading of text material—that a small beginning would be made in helping youngsters cope intelligently with the volume of persuasive material to which they are subjected. Undoubtedly, the unit doesn't go far enough. The lessons it offers will need continuous reinforcement until the children learn to recognize propaganda techniques whenever they see them. But, if the project served to reduce gullibility even a little, then it was well worth the effort.

54. Developing Critical and Creative Thinking Skills Using the Newspaper *

DOROTHY BURRUS

IT started one Monday in May when my third graders were preoccupied more with baseball and playing jacks than with school. In searching through my files for ideas to spice up the last month of school I discovered some materials from a workshop held the previous summer on "The Living Textbook." [1] After ordering newspapers (furnished free by Oklahoma Publishing Company) to be delivered to the school each school day for two weeks, I sat back for a couple of days as the children perused their very own newspaper. It was easy to ease into a unit with committees being formed in the following areas: sports, comics, amusements, society, weather, editorials, advertisements, and news (local, state, and national). My objectives were to acquaint the children with the newspaper, to learn the content and arrangement of newspapers, to differentiate between kinds of news, to build a newspaper vocabulary, and to develop the daily habit of reading the newspaper.

The introductory unit was such a success that the children wanted to continue the unit, even though we no longer were receiving the daily paper. The following ideas were attempted and found to be successful at the third-grade level.

Developing a News Article: In order to launch the children on their first newswriting assignment, the five W's were introduced: When? Who? What? Where? Why? Working in pairs the children found news articles and underlined the answers to the five W's in colors: when—blue, who—red, etc. They discovered that the answers to all five W's were usually found in the first paragraph and details were added later. After a cooperative story, it was a simple transition to a news story of their own. These ranged from the simple:

On May 29 David is leaving for Indianapolis to see the car races.

Kim

to the more complex:

Yesterday Denise Allen had a wreck near the high school. She had her friends with her in the car. The guy that she ran into was an old man named Whity. Nobody was hurt in the wreck. She will have to ride the bus to school untill the car is fixed.[2]

Allyn

Using Headlines: Since feature articles often are headed with intriguing headlines, several of these had been discovered, such as "Quiet! Elephant At Work!" and "For Sale: London Bridge." Selecting one which the children had not

* From Dorothy Burrus, "Developing Critical and Creative Thinking Skills Using the Newspaper," *Elementary English,* 47 (November, 1970), 978–81. Copyright © 1970 by the National Council of Teachers of English. Reprinted by permission of the author and the National Council of Teachers of English.

[1] This is an annual workshop on the use of the newspaper in the classroom, held at Oklahoma State University and sponsored by the Oklahoma Publishing Company, Oklahoma City, Oklahoma.

[2] Children's spelling was corrected only when stories were displayed publicly.

read, I placed the following headline on the chalkboard: " 'Dead' Shark Bites Man in Newcastle." Three stories printed here show creative thinking.

A dead shark has bitten a man named Fisherman Ray Ross. The poor man had to have 36 stitches. The shark probably had nearvus reashuns.

Sondra

A shark was shot that weighted 1½ tons. The shark was brought into the Florida coste. The chain reatshon happened while a scientist was overlooking the teeth and a nerve in the jaw loosened up and the jaw fell on his leg. He got 46 stiches.

Sherri

Newcastle, England: Mr. William Brown was killed today while he was fishing on the dock of Petel bay. He got into a boat and was struck by a shark. He was in critical condicun when he arrived at Queen Elizabeth Hospital. He died shortly. The other surrviveors are Mrs. Brown, two children and 18 grandchildren. Church services will be Sunday at St. Mary's Church. He will be buried at Mormireal Park. He was a veteran.

Tammy

Using Want Ads: In studying the want ads, the children's attention was drawn to the pet section. One ad read: "For sale: Dog, well-trained. Must sell. Call WI-9877. Ask for Jimmy." In order to provoke their thinking for a creative writing situation, I asked them the following questions, but did not allow them to answer orally:

What kind of a dog is it?
What does "well-trained" mean?
Why must he sell the dog?
Why should they ask for Jimmy?

The stories produced ten different breeds of dogs, and almost as many reasons for having to sell. "Well-trained" meant dif-ferent things to different children and the reasons for asking for Jimmy personally revealed both compassion and fear.

I have a Pomerenian for sale for $25.00. I am living in an apartment and they will not allow pets in the building.

Mark

I am Jimmy. I have to sell my collie dog named Jip because we are moving. We are going on a airplane and we can't take him on the airplane. Ask for me because my mother wanted to send him to the dog-pound.

Susan

I have a dog for sale. He is house broken and won't bite. He is a dochsun. We live in the country and it is miserable with ticks and flees. P.S. Will not bark at night.

Mike

I want to sell my dog because Momma got a new baby. She sticks her hand in the dog's mouth and he bites her so he has to go! He's a cocker spanial.

Tracy

I have to sell my puddle because I got a allerge. He is well trained. I mean he can sit up, beg, eat from a table, speak, shake hands, won't chase cars and won't bite. Ask for Jimmy because I want a good home for him.

Steven

Analyzing Advertising Appeal: Large advertisements for clothes, cars, furniture and sports items were distributed. The children were asked to circle words or groups of words which they felt would help to sell the article. These were written on the chalkboard. The class was divided into four groups. They were asked to place these words or phrases into categories to determine to whom or to what the advertisers were appealing. Three groups divided the words and phrases into family members:

Father	*Mother*
guaranteed service	wash and wear
dependable	no-iron
easy to maintain	one size fits all
save 16% to 40%	just say charge it
safety features	graceful lines
long mileage	gleaming finish
extra strength	easy to care for
good traction	budget prices
no money down	for the whole family

Girl	*Boy*
right in style	genuine
feel romantic	good fit
groovy	comfortable
spectacular	
newest look	
fashionable	
smartly styled	
the hair color people notice	

The boys were impressed with but few of these appeals, but did report that their older brothers would be impressed with "style," "groovy," "spectacular," etc. as well as the girls.

One group was in a heated discussion because the chairman had expressed the opinion that people bought for only one reason and that was to save money. Since there was some disagreement and since I was not certain if eight- and nine-year-olds could analyze in an abstract manner, I worked with this group to help them categorize. Since money had been mentioned, they listed all the appropriate phrases there. I then asked why the girls wore pretty clothes, and from this came the headings "beauty" and "style." Through a discussion of the value of money and time in relation to purchases, they decided on the term "dependability." The phrases which remained were headed "Hurry," although one child suggested "Be Careful" because something might be wrong with the article.

Money	*Beauty*
easy payment plan	feel romantic
save 16% to 40%	graceful lines
unbelievable savings	gleaming finish
just say charge it	fashionable
budget prices	hair color people notice
save ¼ to ½ and more	spectacular
no money down	
save more than ever before	*Style*
groovy savings	right in style
	newest look
	smartly styled

Dependability	*Hurry* or *Be Careful*
wash and wear	must be sold
must be satisfied	for three days only
good traction	stock up while they last
long mileage	last chance to buy
extra strength	
easy to maintain	
guaranteed in writing	
no-iron	
long-wearing	
washable	
dependable	
genuine	
easy care	
we service what we sell	

I then asked the question, "Do people really read the ads before they buy?" These comments were forthcoming.

"My mother won't buy anything unless it says 'wash and wear.' "
"My dad bought _____ tires because they were guaranteed."
"My mom bought my school clothes at _____ because she could charge them."
"My sis likes groovy clothes."

The question was proposed, "Are the claims that the ads make true?" Several children related instances where money was refunded, where a flat was fixed free since the tire had been purchased there, or where "wash and wear" tags in garments meant just that. However, the discussion produced some skepticism when a few instances were reported which denied guarantees, long wear, etc.

In summation the children decided:

1. You may save money if you read ads from different stores.

2. You may have to pay more if you get long wear, safety, and comfort all in one product.

3. You may save money if you buy when there is a sale.

4. The stores use certain words—groovy, fashionable, spectacular, sturdy, romantic—to reach different kinds of people.

5. Usually the ads are true.

6. You don't save money if you buy something that you don't need.

7. There is a difference between "for sale" and "on sale."

8. Just because the ad claims something, doesn't mean that it isn't that good. It may all be true so the best way is to go see it.

This activity ended with an assignment to write an ad to sell something which they possessed. Added to the advertising appeal were appropriate pictures.

DON'T DELAY— Buy a groovy poke dotted shirt. Save $2.00. Size 10. Buy from Walker Discount store.

Randy

Make it SPLASHY with a new bathing suit.

Ricky

Get the MOST POPULAR book. Doctor Doolittle. See Susan.

For sale: DRUMS. 'DON'T LOSE YOUR COOL.'

Mike

Bicycle. Red and white. New tires. Tuff, no wear. Good condition. Save $30.00. Call Goff's.

Lipstick. Save 15¢. WILDEST colors in town. Sold to first one who asks. Call Cheryl.

FLASHIEST GOWN IN TOWN— Will make boy's eyes POP out! Has 100% gold carrot necklas with it. See Margaret.

The need for students in our schools to have a great deal of accurate information and to use it intelligently in making decisions has never been more obvious. One of the best ways to meet this need is to develop in individuals the ability to read and use the daily newspaper with intelligence and discrimination.

The daily newspaper will never or probably should never replace existing textbooks or be used exclusively, but it can be used as an excellent supplementary teaching tool.

The primary teacher must accept her responsibility in helping a child to develop his ability to communicate. If, in his early years, she can help him to acquire knowledge, form opinions of these facts, and develop an ability to think critically as well as to develop creativity, she will be doing much to contribute to his future scholastic success.

XI

Reading in Content Areas

The *developmental* reading strand of a good reading program is concerned mainly with the teaching and learning of reading skills, with the emphasis on "learning to read." In the *functional* reading strand, the emphasis shifts to "reading to learn." Many new skills must be learned and applied, for successful learning requires reading skills that may be necessary only in a content area. Furthermore, the reader often must locate, read, and organize ideas from more than one source.

Artley's discussion of the nature and development of effective study skills is followed by Dallmann's suggestions for teaching three types of locational skills. In the third article, Miller relates how such skills can be put to use through individual research projects. The last two articles deal with reading skills in specific content areas—Weber's with arithmetic, and the Metropolitan Study School Council's with science.

55. Effective Study—Its Nature and Nurture *

A. STERL ARTLEY

MUCH has been written already about the process of study; but in spite of the attention it has received as a specialized reading activity, major changes in school programs designed to improve study pro-

* From A. Sterl Artley, "Effective Study—Its Nature and Nurture," in J. Allen Figurel, (ed.), *Forging Ahead in Reading,* Proceedings of the Twelfth Annual Convention, 12, Part 1 (Newark, Del.: International Reading Association, 1968), 10–19. Reprinted by permisssion of the International Reading Association and the author.

cedures have not taken place in widespread fashion. A few sporadic and transient programs are the best we can find. Karlin (8) in a paper presented at the Miami meeting of IRA quoted Ruth Strang as saying, "The most discouraging circumstance is that so little has been done to implement sound ideas that were advocated and tried years ago." In the same paper Karlin also refers to a survey made by McGinnis in 1961 in which she reported 61 percent of a total of 1,029 college freshmen said that their high school teachers had not showed them how to improve reading skills. In addition, less than 10 percent of the high school teachers surveyed claimed to have had any training in teaching reading and study procedures.

It is not to be presumed that another paper on study will effect major changes in practice. However, there are several aspects of study that have not been sufficiently emphasized. These I would like to explore with you.

The Nature of Study

First, I should like to discuss the use of the term *study*. Literature uses several terms somewhat synonymous in reference to this subject—*study, study skills, reading-study abilities,* and *reading abilities in the content areas*. All these terms relate to what one uses in terms of skills, abilities, and understandings in the process of study. But study itself, what is it? What does one do or should one do when he studies, whether at the fifth-grade level or the eleventh? . . .

In reading a number of articles and reports dealing with the subject, I have been particularly sensitive to the definition of study that the writer either states or implies. In the majority of cases it seems to be assumed that study is the act in which one engages to accumulate facts, information, or ideas. The end result is a score on a test of factual information or the number of questions that can be answered correctly after one has read a geography or science text. A study-skills course may be devoted to teaching the pupil or student how to locate information or to use a table of contents or to secure data from charts, graphs, diagrams, and the like, after which a study-skills test is administered and progress is noted in the learner's ability to engage in each of these tasks more efficiently, the implication being that he now has at hand a

set of skills that will enable him to acquire facts more expeditiously.

On the other hand, we find statements to the effect that study should be considered as something more than information gathering, or as the dictionary says, "knowledge acquisition." Fay (4) wrote, "Students must be shown that there is more to study than merely reading the pages of an assignment." He contends that study in social studies is an active thinking process of following an author's line of reasoning in relation to a well-defined and clearly understood purpose. In other words, the process of study is engaged in when there exists some purpose or need to be satisfied.

In like manner, Robinson (11) in an article in *The Reading Teacher* said, ". . . a meaningful reading program in social studies or the other content areas will focus on problem-solution as the end, and skill development as the means, not vice versa." He, too, sees study in broader terms than the acquisition of information.

In a paper that I fear has been lost in the welter of literature on reading and study is the one presented by Preston (10) as the keynote speech at the Miami meeting of IRA. In "Reading for What?" Dr. Preston discussed what he called the "low ebb of reading as an intellectual activity." As an intellectual activity, he said, reading was at a low ebb for several reasons, one being that reading people are preoccupied with technical problems, the mechanics of the act, information getting, rather than the end result. He wrote, "We should not take our chief satisfaction in bringing about mere literacy, desirable though literacy is. It is only half the job. We need to conceive of our role in broader terms and not rest content until the learner is eagerly *applying reading to some worthwhile* goal. [italics mine] The real miracle of reading lies less in the process than in what can be accomplished through it." Translating this concept of reading into the language of study, we have the generalization that study is being carried on at its highest level when the reader is doing something with the writer's ideas.

In fact it is almost in these terms that Nila Banton Smith (15) defined study. In differentiating between reading and study she described a housewife perusing a household periodical for entertainment. Later the housewife returned to the magazine and studied an article having a recipe which she wanted to use in preparing the evening meal. In the latter situation she has put information to work and has utilized skills where the intent was "to do something" with the content read.

What we have then are two points of view with regard to the means and the end of the study act. One, that information, knowledge, facts, and ideas are the end; the other, that these are the means to the end of use, application, problem solving, question answering, or issue resolving. One has engaged in the act of study when he has derived information or ideas and has put them to use for some purpose that has relevance and significance to the learner.

Perhaps if we were to look at the study act apart from reading, it might be helpful; for we engage in study many times where no reading as such is involved. Many of us engaged in study when we faced the question as to whether we would attend the Seattle meeting of IRA. For some there were deterrents: it is a long way to Seattle from New York, Florida, and even Missouri, and cost was a major factor. Some were engaged in major projects where time away from the job had to be considered. But at the same time there were reasons why we should come: there were excellent meetings to attend; there was a paper to present;

there were friends that we see only once a year; and the State of Washington is pleasant in May. And so we assembled facts from various sources: we used our past experiences; we talked with friends; we checked to see if there was money in the travel fund; we looked over the program; we may even have read the promotional literature about Seattle, and eventually we came to a decision. Can anyone say that this activity was not the process of study in every sense of the word?

On analysis, what was involved in this act? What were the steps? First, there was a problem, a question, or an issue. Second, there was the securing and marshalling of facts and information needed to solve the problem. Third, there was the evaluting and weighing of the bits of information, since each bit was not necessarily of equal value or merit. Finally, there was a resolution of the problem. All of this together composes the act of study.

Take note, if you will, of the second step in the study act. We called it the securing and marshalling of facts and information. There is no doubt that this was a very important part of the study process; but there would have been very little, if any, reason for it *had there not been a problem to resolve.* Study took place when there was a purpose or motive, and the collection of information was a means to the end of problem solving. Isn't meaning hereby given to Robinson's generalization that study should focus on problem solving as the end and skill development as the means? And in the same way isn't a partial answer provided, at least, to Preston's question, "reading for what?"

I don't wish to labor the place of idea intake in study or in the receptive area, as Herber (7) calls it, yet I do feel that it is in this step that the study act on all levels of instruction—from the elementary grades through college—so frequently begins and ends. It is reflected in the sixth-grade teacher's assignment, "For tomorrow study to the middle of page 126," meaning that tomorrow be prepared to hand the material back in a discussion. It is reflected in the high school teacher's admonition, "Be sure to 'cover' the material carefully, for tomorrow we are going to have a test," which frequently ends up being a series of true-false items measuring little other than factual recall. It is reflected in research in which the researcher matches a control and experimental group to which he gives a series of lessons on the use of the card catalog, use of the dictionary, and map reading. After post-testing the two groups, he enters the data on Hollerith cards, puts them through a computer, and comes out with the fact that the 3.78 points of difference between the two groups is statistically significant at the one percent level. Truly, studying for what?

Facts, knowledge, ideas, all are useful, in fact essential, in the study act because they constitute the raw material in the process of problem solving. But accumulated for their own sake to be regurgitated later, they are no better than the miser's coins which he counts each Saturday night and returns to his sack since they serve neither himself nor society to any useful purpose.

In fact, they represent a kind of pseudo-erudition dramatized in radio days by the Quiz Kids and today in television on the College Bowl program, where for preparation the group dredges up every particle of isolated and undigested information that the questioner might possibly ask. Understanding the process of study would in a dramatic way modify the assignments that we make, the study act in which the students engage, and our teaching methods in general.

The Reading-Study Purpose

The term *purpose* in relation to reading and study also is used in different ways by different writers. Some speak of study as being a purposeful activity when the reader approaches his material with a definite question in mind; such as, "To what extent did Germany's decision to attack the Soviet Union and Japan's decision to attack the United States make possible the defeat of the Axis in World War II?" Others use the term in reference to the reading set or study objective that the reader keeps in mind as he studies, as, for example, to note details, to verify a statement, and to answer a specific question. Still others refer to purpose as adjustments that the reader makes in reading, such as to skim or to recognize devices and words that indicate certain types of idea relationships. Certainly before one can help students establish a purpose for study one needs to know what a purpose is to begin with.

Perhaps the following may help in clarification. The student begins with a study *objective* or study task, which may be a question for which he wants an answer or a problem situation in need of resolution. It is the reader's basic motivation for reading. Examples of these kinds of reading tasks might be: Why does a satellite orbit the earth? What steps are involved in baking a cake? or, What factors made possible the defeat of the Axis in World War II? The reading or study objective, on the one hand, may be met with a minimum amount of reading; or it may require the use of several sources and a prolonged period of study. It may be one that is established by the teacher as part of an assignment. It may be one set by the student himself as something he needs to find out or understand. At any rate it is an essential prerequisite for study. Being without it is like beginning a vacation trip with no idea of where one is going or what one wishes to see.

The study task or objective determines, in turn, the study *purpose*. The purpose may be to determine the main idea, to note details or facts, to trace out the writer's organization, to distinguish between fact and opinion, or to sense idea relationships. The purpose supplies the mental set for the act of study. If the study objective or task calls for tracing out the writer's organization, the student puts his mind to the job of searching for the main ideas being developed and the various levels of subordination used by the writer in developing his ideas. But, of course, a reading purpose cannot be determined until the student clearly has in mind his study objective.

Knowing the study objective and the study purpose, the student now needs to make certain adjustments as he proceeds. An obvious adjustment would be in the area of rate, for some purposes may call for rapid reading while others may call for a slow, study-type reading. The student may need to reread to determine the level of subordination of a given point, or he may need to skim to determine whether a particular bit of information is supplied by the article. The adjustments, then, are those required in order to satisfy the study purpose which in turn is conditioned by the study objective.

The most recent and possibly the most complete piece of research dealing with reading purposes is that of Helen K. Smith (14). She was concerned with student ability to identify appropriate reading purposes from the nature of the content, to comprehend material, and to make necessary reading adjustments in the light of the reading purpose. Using ninth-graders from a suburban Chicago high school, Smith divided them into experimental and control groups, fourteen classes composed of 204 students being experimental and fifteen classes of 307 students being control. From these two sets of classes she matched two groups— an experimental group of 62 students and a control group of like number. All comparisons were between both experimental and control classes and groups. All students were pre- and post-tested with the Cooperative English Test: Reading Comprehension, and a "Test of Purpose" developed by the researcher. This test was made up of two parts: Part I, to assess the ability of students to identify appropriate reading purposes for which a given selection should be read; and Part II, to determine the ability to comprehend passages when given a prestated purpose, as well as to determine the procedures and adjustments used in reading those passages. Over a period of a year the experimental students were given instruction in purposeful reading through work in their regular English classes.

Comparisons made at the end of the experimental period indicated that those between the experimental and control classes were much more significant than those between the smaller groups of experimental and control subjects. As a result of the instruction given in the experimental classes, the students were better able to identify appropriate purposes for reading, to read significantly better for the purposes studied, and to comprehend on a higher level than could the students in the control classes.

As an overall conclusion from this comprehensive study, Smith concluded that well-planned assignments should be made in which students are given reading purposes or are given direct instruction and guidance in setting their own purposes. Moreover, she recommended that instruction in purposeful reading should be given below and above the ninth grade, the grade in which this study was carried out.

Other studies than Smith's confirm the value of study objectives and purposes. Schlesser and Young (13) working with college students found that higher levels of achievement accrued from helping students develop motives for study than from instruction in specific study techniques. They said, ". . . steady, vigorous, highly motivated effort is the outstanding trait of the student whose achievement is high relative to his abilities."

Spache (17) made several pertinent observations concerning study objectives. He pointed out that accurate comprehension assumes clear-cut purposes (reading objectives), established either by the teacher or by the student himself. "Without directions," he wrote, "he is likely to retain neither main ideas, nor details, nor relationships since he knows not what he is seeking." And then he continued discussing the importance of clarifying study objectives for each assignment. He suggested that the instructor ask himself, "What are the reasons for having the pupils read this assignment?" And then he added a statement with which I thoroughly concur, "If the instructor has not a particular purpose in mind, it is doubtful whether the assignment is justifiable."

To my way of thinking, the point Spache made regarding the importance of reading objectives underlies one of the most troublesome problems facing a student in the act of study. When questioned about their study problems, students frequently list as one of the first their inability to concentrate. What they don't know and what we many times don't realize is that unless they are asleep, they are always concentrating on something; but what they are concentrating on may have little relation to the learning task. Rather than thinking about the precipitating causes of the Civil War, the major problem is "How will I ask Susie to go to the spring formal, and what will I do if she says, 'No'?"

It is a well-known principle that one focuses his attention (concentrates) on those things that are of most significance to him. Consequently, if one is to concentrate one must make the learning task preeminent. Granted this is difficult to do when the learning task is in competition with the spring prom, but the principle still remains. If learning tasks are to be competitive with other questions and problems confronting the learner to which his attention might be drawn, two things must be kept in mind. First, the learning task or study objective should be one that focuses on problem solving, issue resolving, or generalization forming rather than memorization of details. Tyler (18) showed, for example, that facts and rote learnings were eroded away by the passage of time while generalizations and principles were retained to a much greater degree. Second, and most important, the learning task must have relevance to the learner. It must be one to which he sees some point, some purpose in doing. Otherwise it becomes another assignment to do, to get out of the way, and to forget. As Spache says, if there is no good purpose for doing it, it is doubtful whether the assignment is justifiable.

When discussing reading-study objectives, the question frequently arises as to whether, to be most effective, the study objectives should have their origin with the teacher or the student. A study reported by Henderson (5) throws some light on this question. Taking 24 good readers and 24 poor readers on the fifth-grade level he subjected them to four different types of purpose-setting behavior. In one of these situations the subjects read the first half of a story and then conjectured and declared a reading purpose. In another the reading objectives were supplied by the teacher. A check of comprehension indicated that the differences between the two treatments were insignificant whether the pupils set their own purposes or were given purposes by the teacher.

Similar findings to those above were reported by Smith (14) in the study to which we have already referred. From her findings, you will recall, she concluded that well-planned assignments should be made in which students either were given reading purposes or were given direct instruction and guidance in setting their own purposes.

It would appear logical to assume that the younger children would profit from study objectives supplied largely by the teacher. Eventually the objectives will be cooperatively derived by teacher and pupils; and still later, as pupils become more mature, they will assume increasing responsibility for formulating their own study objectives.

Skills Involved in Study

In the area of study skills, there is likewise confusion growing out of the inconsistent use of terminology and the overlapping of skills from one learning area to another. Nila Banton Smith (15) helps to clarify the issues here by categorizing skills needed to study effectively as common reading skills, common study skills, and specialized skills and competencies needed for study in the various curricular areas. The common reading competencies utilized in study are those used in any type of reading in any type of content, nontextual as well as textual, and for any type of objective. Important here would be the various word perception abilities, vocabulary, basic comprehension skills, and critical evaluation. To a large degree the comprehension skills are those growing out of the reading purpose we have already discussed—reading for the main

idea, following direction, following a sequence of ideas, forming generalizations, and the like.

One can find almost as many lists of comprehension skills assumed to be important in reading and study as there are writers on the subject. Niles (9) contends, however, that at the heart of the ability to comprehend content of any kind there are three major skill areas. The first is the ability to find and understand thought relationships (comparison-contrast, chronological, cause-effect, etc.). The second is the ability to set specific study objectives and purposes. These we have already discussed at length. The third is the ability to make use of the backlog of real and vicarious experiences that relate to and serve to amplify the new materials. Without a doubt these are essential competencies that would serve well the purpose of reading or study in any area.

The common study skills are those to which frequent reference is made in the literature. They are skills and abilities used in study rather than casual reading and used similarly regardless of the area or subject. Usually these are referred to as location of information with reference to a particular reading task or objective; selecting and evaluating information in the light of the objective; and organizing information (facts, principles, generalizations) in a form or manner demanded by the situation. This task may be in the form of an outline for an oral report, notes for a discussion, an investigative paper, a dramatization, or a cartoon or drawing to illustrate a synthesis of ideas.

Frequently, recall or retention is listed as one of the common study skills. I am omitting it here for it has always seemed to me that recall is inherent to the act of organization. Recall is a by-product of the organization process rather than a separate competency to be developed. In the second place it carries the connotation of memorization for later rote recall or recitation of such things as lists, isolated facts, and statements. These we would hardly accept as the end toward which the study process should be directed.

I am omitting from our discussion anything having to do with the actual teaching procedures for the development of the common study skills, chiefly because the monograph on study skills in the Perspectives in Reading series, prepared under the sponsorship of IRA and compiled and edited by Harold Herber (6), covers this area so completely. This is a monograph that should be in the hands of every classroom teacher, particularly those on the secondary level. Well-written and extremely helpful chapters cover the development of work study skills, the use of book parts, sources of information, and visual aids. I recommend it highly as a source of practical help. Suffice it to say here that there is ample evidence that study abilities can be taught (2) and that the teaching of them contributes to improved learning.

Within the past twenty-five years or so we have become increasingly aware of the fact that efficient reading in the content areas calls for more than the general or common study skills referred to above. A considerable body of research evidence is available that competent reading in one area, literature for example, does not necessarily insure competent reading in science or mathematics. Though there may be skills that overlap one area with another, there are others quite unique to a given area. This is so because each content has its own specialized vocabulary, its method of treating ideas, its pattern of writing, and its own particular objectives which structure the kind of approach required (1).

Further evidence of this is in a study by Smith (16) who made an analysis of 52 texts in science, 60 in social studies, 49 in mathematics, and 45 in literature and arrived at a set of writing patterns used by authors in the development of content in each of these areas. From these writing patterns she derived the various response types demanded of the reader in dealing with the content. For example, social studies requires the reading of pictures, maps, and atlases; the analyzing of content for cause-effect relations, comparisons, sequence of events; and the critical analysis of content where different viewpoints are expressed, where facts are mixed with opinions, and where propaganda is used. This analysis is extremely helpful to teachers in aiding their students to read the subject matter in each of their teaching areas.

Other lists of skills and abilities assumed to be necessary for interpreting content in the various subject areas are found in any text in reading methods. I would want to call particular attention to another monograph in the Perspectives in Reading series titled *Reading Instruction in Secondary Schools* and edited by Margaret J. Early (3). Chapters by Bamman on reading in the science and mathematics areas, Herber in history, and Burton in literature are very comprehensive.

But in the final analysis, as helpful as these sources may be, it is quite difficult to tell Mr. Harris, teaching history in P.S. 46, precisely what study competencies *he* will need to develop. In the first place, the curricular design he follows will determine to a great extent the skills he will need to teach. If he follows a single text, the skills will be quite different from those he would need to develop were he using a problem-centered approach. They will depend on the level of students in his class and to a large extent on their prior instruction. Consequently, Mr. Harris' best guide will come from the answer to a question he asks of himself: "What competencies do my students need in order to study my subject as I teach it?" Following this is the second question: "In which skills and abilities are my students sufficiently competent to deal with in my area?" These remaining skills then become the teaching responsibility of that teacher as they are required, keeping in mind of course that there may be students who will require individual help apart from that given to the group.

Study Skills Programs

The literature contains a number of action studies and a few pieces of well-controlled research attesting to the value of school programs devoted to the development of study skills and abilities. Many of these are described by Catterson (2). She points out that some programs are carried out under the aegis of English classes and others in special reading classes. She notes, however, a trend toward programs handled by classroom teachers in the regular content areas. If content area teachers are involved with content that students use for study purposes, and if study competencies are to a substantial degree specific to each content area, then it must follow, as night the day, that the major responsibility for developing study competencies will be within the context of subject content on all grade levels.

But content area teachers have not been overwhelmingly responsive to this idea. One reason is, they say, that they lack the knowledge to conduct instruction. This, I think, is a rationalization; for if the doing of it is important, as evidence and sheer logic shows, then there are ample resource materials available for help. The two IRA Perspectives monographs to which we have frequently referred, to say nothing about the treat-

ment of study in any reading text, would provide ample help. Moreover, reports of most of the successful reading and study programs on the secondary level have indicated that in-service training of teachers was an essential part of the program. Frequently such instruction was provided by the reading supervisor or coordinator.

Another reason, implied if not actually stated, for letting the task go by default is that the subject matter teacher feels that he hasn't time to develop study procedures along with the teaching of his subject content. The task is assumed to be something extra added to an already overextended course outline. Like selling football tickets on Saturday afternoon, it goes over and beyond the call of duty. But Catterson makes a statement that I think takes away the potency of this as an argument. She says, "The authors of these papers have made it obvious that they think of study skills not as *something* to teach, but as a *way* to teach—a way of teaching which advances not only the student's knowledge of subject matter but his ability to learn other subject matter independently and at will." In other words she was not talking about a unit on study to be added to an already overloaded course outline but something that should be a part of just good teaching.

But if we need to clinch the argument that the teaching of subject content cannot be divorced from the development of study competencies, the following question is offered as the *coup de grace*. What is the teaching of a particular subject such as social studies, science, literature, or home economics other than that of teaching the pupil or student to recognize and face issues, questions, or problems inherent to that body of content; to locate appropriate informative content; and to derive from that content ideas, generalizations, and principles that will help him answer his questions, resolve the issues, or form valid bases for opinions or judgments? It would seem, then, we are saying only in another way that *the teaching of a particular subject is the teaching of the study of that subject;* and that makes inescapable the fact that every teacher is a teacher of reading and study.

References

1. ARTLEY, A. STERL. "Influence of the Field Studied on the Reading Attitudes and Skills Needed." *Improving Reading in Content Fields,* W. S. Gray (ed.). Proceedings of the Annual Conference on Reading. Chicago: University of Chicago Press, 1947.

2. CATTERSON, JANE. "Successful Study Skills Programs." *Developing Study Skills in Secondary Schools,* H. L. Herber (ed.). Perspectives in Reading No. 4. Newark, Del.: International Reading Association, 1965.

3. EARLY, MARGARET J. (ed.). *Reading Instruction in Secondary Schools,* Perspectives in Reading No. 2. Newark, Del.: The International Reading Association, 1964.

4. FAY, LEO. "How Can We Develop Reading-Study Skills for the Different Curriculum Areas?" *The Reading Teacher,* 6 (March, 1953), 12–18.

5. HENDERSON, E. H. "A Study of Individually Formulated Purposes for Reading," *Journal of Educational Research,* 58 (July-August, 1965), 438–41.

6. HERBER, HAROLD (ed.). *Developing Study Skills in Secondary Schools,* Perspectives in Reading No. 4. Newark, Del.: International Reading Association, 1965.

7. ———. "Developing Study Skills in Secondary Schools: An Overview." *Developing Study Skills in Secondary Schools,* H. L. Herber (ed.). Perspectives in Reading No. 4. Newark, Del.: International Reading Association, 1965.

8. KARLIN, ROBERT. "Nature and Scope of Developmental Reading in Secondary Schools." *Reading as an Intellectual Activity,* J. A. Figurel (ed.). Proceedings of the International Reading Association, 8 (1963), 52–56.

9. NILES, OLIVE. "Comprehension Skills," *The Reading Teacher,* 17 (September, 1963), 2–7.

10. PRESTON, RALPH. "Reading for What?" *Reading as an Intellectual Activity,* J. A. Figurel (ed.). Proceedings of the International Association, 8 (1963), 13–20.

11. ROBINSON, H. ALAN. "Reading Skills Employed in Solving Social Studies Problems," *The Reading Teacher,* 18 (January, 1965), 263–69.

12. ROMANO, M. J. "Reading and Science: A Symbiotic Relationship," *Education,* 81 (January, 1961), 273–76.

13. SCHLESSER, G. E., and YOUNG, C. W. "Study and Work Habits," *The School Review,* 53 (February, 1945), 85–89.

14. SMITH, HELEN K. *Instruction of High School Students in Reading for Different Purposes* (Cooperative Research Project No. 1714), Washington, D.C.: Office of Education,

United States Department of Health, Education, and Welfare, 1966.

15. SMITH, NILA BANTON. *Reading Instruction for Today's Children*. Englewood Cliffs, N.J.: Prentice-Hall, 1963. Pp. 307, 312.

16. ————. "Patterns of Writing in Different Subject Areas," *Journal of*

Reading, 8 (October, 1964) 31–37; 8 (November, 1964), 97–108.

17. SPACHE, GEORGE. *Toward Better Reading*. Champaign, Ill.: Garrard, 1963. P. 77.

18. TYLER, RALPH W. "Permanence of Learning," *Journal of Higher Education,* 4 (April, 1933), 203–4.

56. The Development of Locational Skills *

MARTHA DALLMANN

IN this article, suggestions for teaching three types of locational skills are given: (1) developing efficiency in locating information in a nonreference book, (2) acquiring skill in using encyclopedias, and (3) learning to find materials in a library.

Basic Considerations

The teacher should take inventory of what skills her pupils already possess. Even in the beginning of the fourth grade, the teacher will find that many of the pupils have some ability to locate information in print. It is upon this foundation of *what the children already know* that the teacher needs to build, rather than upon some theoretical conceptions of what skills boys and girls should have when they enter her grade.

Develop skills in terms of the resources available. When you are teaching boys and girls to use the index of a book, use

* From Martha Dallmann, "The Development of Locational Skills," *Grade Teacher*, LXXV, no. 5 (January, 1958), 56–57. Reprinted by permission of the author and Teachers Publishing Corporation, Darien, Conn.

the indexes of books that the children already have. Similarly, when teaching encyclopedia usage, use those encyclopedias that are provided in the school or that the boys and girls have in their homes. And again, when teaching how to find materials in the library, let the children learn in terms of the library facilities which are available, either in the room, or the school, or the public library.

The boys and girls should be given a thorough foundation in the techniques and skills needed in locating information. These skills include finding words arranged in alphabetical order, using entry words, locating a page rapidly, and knowing what type of information to look in a given kind of book. Unless, for example, a pupil is efficient in finding words in alphabetical order, he will have trouble when using the dictionary, an index, an encyclopedia, and the card catalogue of a library.

Locating Information in a Nonreference Book

Essential knowledge and skills. Sometime before the pupil leaves the elementary school he should have learned the purpose and location of the parts of a book that serve as aids to finding information in the book: the introduction or preface, the table of contents, the appendix and the index. He should know how to use these divisions of a book to locate information in the book. Furthermore, he should be able to use chapter headings, center heads, and side heads as aids in locating information. He should also know that not all books have these various means for facilitating the location of information, and he should realize in what types of books each is likely to be found—for example, he should not look for an index in a book of fiction.

Since the introduction to a book often gives some clue as to what to expect in it, boys and girls should learn what type of aid they may be able to find in the introduction and how to make use of the information there. They also need to realize that the sole purpose of most introductions is not, however, to help the reader learn to locate information within the book.

The pupils should realize that the table of contents can be very valuable in finding information. They need to know that it contains chapter headings, at times divided into subheadings; that the chapters are listed in the contents in order of appearance in the book; and that the page on which each chapter begins is given. They should acquire efficiency in using the contents to decide, in the case of some books, where to look for information on a given topic.

Important points for children to learn about the index are:

1. If there is an index, it is almost invariably located in the back part of the book.

2. The topics are given in alphabetical order.

3. The main entries in an index are usually subdivided.

4. References indicate on what pages information on main entries and subdivisions can be found.

The following skills in using the index are some of the most significant ones: (1) ability to decide under what key words to look for information on a specified topic or question, (2) speed in finding an entry in an index, (3) skill in interpreting the various types of information given in an index, and (4) ability to make effective use of a reference in an index after it has been located.

The boys and girls should also learn what type of information is likely to be given in appendices to books and how to make use of this information. At times this involves learning how to interpret tables. They should also learn how to use chapter headings, center headings, and side headings in such a way that they do not spend time looking for information in parts of the book where it is not likely to be given.

Methods. In teaching this topic of how to find information in a book, the teacher should utilize meaningful classroom situations as much as seems profitable. Most of the work should not be in the form of exercises; a large part of the needed practice should be obtained as the boys and girls need to find information on some problem or question of significance that confronts them. Frequently, however, some of the pupils will need supplementary practice exercises.

The following are a few of the ways to develop skill in finding information in a nonreference book:

1. Ask the boys and girls to find as quickly as they can, but without haste or tension, the title of a story in one of their basal reading books.

2. Provide incentive for making a table of contents or an index for a notebook that is being made either as a class, a committee, or an individual project.

3. Have some of the children report on the type of information given in the introductions to various books they are using. Ask them to note in particular that which serves as an aid to finding information within the books.

4. Have the boys and girls decide which one of several specified words would probably be the entry word to use when trying to locate information on a specified question.

Using Encyclopedias

Essential knowledge and skills. The boys and girls should learn what types of information can be found in an encyclopedia, how the information is arranged, what aids to the speedy finding of material are given in each set of encyclopedias, and what method each has for giving references to material in addition to that included in the encyclopedia. The pupil should also be helped to develop skill in finding and utilizing material found in the encyclopedia.

Methods. The following are some procedures to help boys and girls use encyclodepias effectively:

1. When introducing the use of the encyclopedia, ask each child to browse through some volume until he can report one fact that he finds particularly interesting or significant.

2. After you have written on the chalkboard a diagram showing the volume guides of an encyclopedia, have the pupils tell the number of the volume in which they would look for information on a topic that you mention, such as George Washington Carver, the Battle of New Orleans, or state flowers.

3. Show the pupils the filmstrip, "How to Use an Encyclopedia," published by the Popular Science Publishing Company (distributed by McGraw-Hill Book Co.,

330 W. 42nd St., New York, N.Y. 10036).

4. Help the boys and girls make arrangements for a "quiz program" in which questions will be asked that are answered in one or more related articles in the encyclopedia. Let a committee of boys and girls, under your guidance, prepare the list of questions. They should inform the rest of the class of the articles on which they will base the questions, but they should not tell their classmates beforehand what the questions will be.

Finding Materials in the Library

Pupils should learn the meaning and use of the following: the card catalogue, its arrangement and value; the three most common types of library cards—the title card, the author card, and the subject card; the arrangement of the books on the shelves; the placement of magazines in the library.

The teacher can do the following to help the boys and girls learn more about the library and how to use it.

1. Help the boys and girls make a card catalogue of books in their room library. Have them include title cards, author cards, subject cards, guide cards, and *See also* cards.

2. Suggest that a committee make a large diagram showing the placement of books in their room or school library.

3. Take the boys and girls to the public library so that the librarian can explain to them the arrangement of books and magazines in their local library.

4. Have the pupils put on a skit showing how to behave when in a library.

Skill in Locating Materials in a Nonreference Book

1. To provide practice in using the table of contents, the boys and girls could

be asked to answer questions based on the table of contents in one of their textbooks.

Directions. Study the table of contents in your science book. Then write the answers on the lines.

_____ a. Into how many main parts is the book divided?

_____ b. On what page does the chapter begin that tells about the sun and other heavenly bodies?

_____ c. In which chapter would you find the answer to the question, "How fast does sound travel?"

2. In order to acquire skill in using the index to a book the pupils could do an exercise like the following.

Directions. Draw a line under the word in parentheses that you would use as entry word in an index under which the answer to each of these questions would be found. When you have finished, use your index in your social studies book to find out whether your answers are correct.

a. What were the provisions of the Missouri Compromise? (provisions, Missouri, Compromise)

b. Why was the transcontinental railroad one of the greatest events in the history of communications in America? (transcontinental, railroad, America)

c. What were the fears of the seamen who were with Christopher Columbus on his first voyage to America? (seamen, Christopher, Columbus)

3. After the boys and girls have learned how to use other than main entries in indexes, they could be given an exercise like the following.

Directions. Find the answers to the following questions by consulting the index in your social studies textbook.

a. Under what main entry and under what subentry in the index do you expect to find information about cranberries in New England?

Main entry _____
Subentry _____

b. On what page is a map given showing the territory included in the Northwest Territory? _____

c. On how many consecutive pages is information given about the Gold Rush of 1849? _____

Skill in Using Encyclopedias

1. In order to develop skill in deciding for what type of information they should turn to an encyclopedia, they could be asked to do an exercise like the following. After they had answered the questions, they could tell orally in what type of book they would look for the answers to questions that are not likely to be answered in an encyclopedia.

Directions. If you think a question will be answered in your encyclopedias, write *yes* on the line. Otherwise write *no*.

_____ a. How many bushels of potatoes were produced last year in the United States?

_____ b. What was the chief contribution of George W. Goethals to the building of the Panama Canal?

_____ c. What was the first message that was sent by telegram, by Samuel Morse?

_____ d. What does the word *compromise* mean?

2. If some of the boys and girls have difficulty in finding the exact sentences in an encyclopedia that give answers to their questions, give them questions like the following. If only one set of encyclopedias is available, only one pupil at a time can answer any one group of questions. In order to encourage the pupils to work as rapidly as possible, yet without haste or tension, tell them to keep a record of when they began the work on the exercise and when they completed it.

Directions. In an article on Niagara Falls in *Compton's Pictured Encyclopedia* (1955 copyright) answers are given to the following questions. When you have found the sentence that answers a question, write the first two words of that sentence. Time yourself as you do this exercise.

_____ a. How many cubic feet of water pours over the falls every minute?

_____ b. Who was the first white man to view the Niagara Falls?

_____ c. How are the falls and rapids illuminated at night?

Skill in Finding Materials in a Library

1. If the boys and girls have visited a local library and had the arrangement of books and magazines in the children's division explained to them, draw a diagram showing the location of the various bookshelves and exhibit tables and exhibit stands. Number in the diagram the places for books and magazines. Then ask the pupils to answer questions like the following, as they indicate the answer by means of the appropriate number listed on the diagram. Tell the pupils that for some of the answers more than one letter is needed.

_____ a. Where are the books for the youngest readers kept?

_____ b. Where are the books on biography shelved?

_____ c. On what shelf (or shelves) would you look for the book

Abraham Lincoln by Ingri and Edgar Parin d'Aulaire?

2. After considerable work on the card catalogue has been done, help the pupils, by means of an exercise like the following, to review some of the important facts learned. In many cases it will be advisable to take time for discussion of the answers after the pupils have completed the written work.

Directions. Write the answers to these questions.

a. In what order are cards in a card catalogue arranged?

_____

b. What kind of card in the card catalogue should be consulted if neither the author nor the exact title of a book is known?

_____

c. If there are books by an author and about an author in a library, which kind of card is filed first in the card catalogue, the books by him or those about him?

_____

d. What is the purpose of a call number?

_____

3. Ask the pupils to write the answers to the following questions concerning periodicals in the public library to which they have access.

a. What are the exact titles of two or three magazines for boys and girls that are ordered by your library which are interesting to you? What is one thing you like in particular about each?

b. What is the name of the reference book that gives information about magazine articles? Where is this reference book kept in your public library?

57. Stimulate Reading with Individual Research Projects *

EDITH F. MILLER

IN my group there were always some children who finished before the others, who I felt would profit by directed reading activities, which at the same time would allow some opportunity for creativeness. A research project aimed at making booklets proved both popular and profitable to the three groups in my class.

Pick a Topic

First of all, each child was asked to choose a topic about which he really wanted to find out more. In our experiment, any topic was accepted, but some teachers may prefer to make a list from which the children may choose.

After the children handed me their choices, I had an individual conference with each child. If a child had chosen a topic which was too broad, such as *Animals,* we narrowed it down to *Woodland Animals* or *Water Animals*. If the topic was too narrow, such as *The Frog,* we changed it to a broader topic such as *Amphibians*. The list of topics was posted so that children could help each other find information and pictures.

When the upper group held its first meeting, I presented each child with a typed slip which had key words and phrases which had to appear somewhere in his finished work. For example, the girl studying *Insects* had to include:

* From Edith F. Miller, "Stimulate Reading with Individual Research Projects," *Grade Teacher,* LXXIX, no. 4 (December, 1961), 28, 29, 84, 85. Reprinted by permission of the author and Teachers Publishing Corporation, Darien, Conn.

1. Definition of an Insect
2. Some Harmful Insects
3. Some Helpful Insects
4. Insect Communities
5. How Nature Protects Insects
6. Metamorphosis

The boy studying *Aviation* had on his list:

1. Lighter-than-air
2. Heavier-than-air
3. How the Airplane Helps Us (Besides transporting people and things)
4. Famous Flights

I tried not to make the list too long for I did not want to discourage anyone. Another year I shall have each child make his own list and add to it if necessary.

The middle group's first meeting was used to make an outline of the subtopics needed in the study of their common topic—*Dogs*. They decided on:

1. The History of Dogs
2. The Care of Dogs
3. The Training of Dogs
4. Working Dogs
5. Dogs as Pets

At their meeting, the children in the slow group helped each other compile about five questions which would be answered in their booklets. The child who had *Pets* as a topic had the following questions on her list:

1. What are the most popular pets in America?
2. Which pets can you train to do tricks?
3. How do you keep your pets well?
4. What are some unusual pets?
5. What pets did early people have?

Sources of Materials

To the first meeting of each group, I brought a number of things which interested the children. They especially liked a large box which had been decorated with pictures of gaily wrapped presents. In this "Present Box" I had put many small pictures, conservation stamps, canceled stamps, some typed poems—in fact any surplus material I had which would later help in illustrating their booklets. As time went on, pupils added "presents," too.

Each child was given a large tension envelope in which all his collected material could be kept safely, and a place was reserved for storing these.

We discussed sources of information. The children realized this was to be primarily a reading project but that other sources would also be used, including firsthand observation, TV, movies, slides, trips, our museum collection, the radio, and talking with people. In our own classroom we had a good set of encyclopedias, many books, and a picture file. We discussed the use that could be made of poems, stories, newspapers, magazines, our own textbooks, pamphlets, and the Public Library.

Organizing Notes

Some children looked up many references and inserted bookmarks with their names on them before doing any reading. Others digested one source at a time. As they read, they took notes. Here, too, they needed help, and we found that stapled sheets of paper with a question or topic at the head of each page seemed the best way to keep the material organized. For example:

What animals are in the woods of New Jersey?

1. Deer
2. Fox
3. Rabbit

How do insects protect themselves?

1. Some look very fierce.
2. Some have a bad smell.
3. Some are born by the thousands.

The notes were reorganized into the children's own stories. When a child had all the information he needed, he would write up the topic. I would then check it and after all revisions and corrections were made, it was ready to go into his booklet.

Children worked on their topics during the reading period whenever their assignments in reading were completed. Occasionally, we spent our entire reading or language period working on the topics so that I could supervise and give help. In addition to the work done in school, many children were so interested in their topics that they voluntarily worked on them at home.

Deadline

Eventually, I set a deadline for the research material to be in, all key words included and all questions answered. Each child worked to complete his work by "Due Date," and I kept a close check on the progress.

As this project was primarily one on reading, all pasting and drawing was postponed till the bulk of the reading was done. This prevented the children from using the reading time to draw pictures.

We used an art period to begin this phase of the project. First we talked about careful selection and arrangement of the pictures to be mounted. We discussed the use of judgment in placing the right pictures with pertinent stories.

For the next two weeks, "Work on your topics" meant drawing, sorting, arranging, cutting, pasting, or copying rather than reading, but books were constantly referred to even in this stage of the project.

Mounting some pictures on colored paper, making decorative borders or end sheets, making pictures in silhouette or all in one color, or using water color illustrations were among the many original ideas which made the finished booklets so attractive.

When all the pages were arranged in order, holes were punched and the booklets were bound with wool or with soft cord that would not tear the holes.

Reading Party

After the booklets were thoroughly checked, they were used as directed reading material for about a week. The children knew that we were to have a "Reading Party" to which guests were to be invited. Each child was to be prepared to read or show anything in his booklet. The children wanted to read the booklets the other children had made, too, so they were placed on a table for easy access and a list of things to look for was put on the board. The list included:

1. A good introduction
2. An index
3. Original poems
4. Some surprising information
5. A good poem
6. A well-copied song
7. An attractive border
8. A well-arranged page
9. Something funny
10. A clearly written article

Each child kept a list of outstanding things he thought should be shown at our Reading Party. For example:

1. Elizabeth's cover
2. Elizabeth's information on How A Jet Flies
3. Cindy's introduction
4. Bill's last page
5. John's cartoons

On the day of the Reading Party, the children showed their covers, most of them gay with cut paper letters. Two children read their Introductions and one read his index. I asked for specific things by saying, "You must see the graph John made"; "Now everyone who made a map will show it"; "Grace made up an original poem." After that, each child showed his favorite pages. Then each child brought out his list and made his request for the display of something unusual in the other children's work.

The Values

After the Reading Party guests left, each child was given a questionnaire. No names were to be put on the papers and it was understood that the class secretary would tally the results and that they were to be perfectly frank in their answers. The results, given below, showed how worthwhile the children felt the project had been.

A Questionnaire on Our Reading Research Project

	Yes	No
1. Did you enjoy the research project?	23	4
2. Did it help you to read more widely?	23	4
3. Would you recommend it for next year's fifth grade?	26	1
4. Are you still interested in your topic?	23	4
5. Did it help you to organize the facts you found?	27	0
6. Did you use many kinds of sources of information?	23	4
7. Will the next research project be easier for you?	24	3
8. Did you add many new words to your vocabulary?	18	9
9. Do you remember much of the information you learned?	25	2
10. Did you enjoy our Reading Party?	27	0

There were many values throughout the project such as sharing, judging, planning, and participating, which are hard to measure but which were natural outgrowths of this experience in research.

One development I had not anticipated as an outgrowth of our study was an interest in new hobbies. For example, I attribute the wave of insect collections largely to the two splendid booklets on that subject which were made as part of our project. And, when one girl phoned me during the summer to ask me to recommend a good book to help her identify insects and another phoned to say, "I'm working more on my topic this vacation just for fun," I knew that the effects of our reading-research project had gone deeper than I had ever dreamed possible.

58. The Demon of Arithmetic—Reading Word Problems *

MARTHA GESLING WEBER

RECENTLY a group of teachers was asked to list some of the troublesome areas in the teaching of arithmetic. "Getting children to read story problems with sufficient understanding to be able to solve them seems to be the *demon* of arithmetic," answered one of the teachers immediately.

"It isn't that we don't teach arithmetic," said another teacher. "We just don't teach reading. My children do all right as long as we work with numbers."

"It must be something more than reading, though," replied a third teacher thoughtfully. "I have children who read very well; yet they have trouble with their word problems in arithmetic."

Perhaps no field of study in arithmetic is more complex than that which deals with the factors involved in solving word problems; so it is not surprising that "getting children to read story problems with

* From Martha Gesling Weber, "The Demon of Arithmetic—Reading Word Problems," *Monograph for Elementary Teachers,* no. 71, pp. 1–3. Reprinted by permission of Martha Gesling Weber and Harper & Row, Publishers, Inc., New York, N.Y.

sufficient understanding to solve them" was classified by the first teacher as being the demon of arithmetic. What is the relationship that exists between the reading of word problems and the solving of them?

What Is a Word Problem?

In arithmetic the pupil is asked to work two kinds of problems: word problems and number problems. Interestingly enough, neither word problems nor number problems may present a matter of doubt or difficulty from a psychological point of view; that is, there may be no doubt in the child's mind as to what is to be done. Problems in arithmetic are "problems" because the pupil must translate the meanings of the symbols into the terms of one of the four fundamental processes: addition, subtraction, multiplication, or division.

Word problems are called word problems because words are used in the writing of them. Number problems are called number problems because they are written with mathematical symbols (number figures and number signs) and according to a prescribed form; for example,

$\frac{115}{-\ 78}$ is a number problem.

Word problems are seldom made up just of words, for number figures are found in almost all word problems. However, since all number figures have number names, it is possible to write a word problem using nothing but words. When the number name is used instead of the number figure, the problem is said to contain a "hidden number."

To understand more fully what a word problem is, let us see several ways in which it is like a number problem and an important way in which it differs.

Number Problem	Word Problem
72	Tom had 72 chickens.
−31	He sold 31 of them.
———	How many chickens did Tom have left?

In both problems the number concepts to be recognized and understood are the same (72 and 31). In both problems the mathematical operation to be performed is the same (subtraction). The difference between the two kinds of problems does not necessarily lie in the number concepts used or in the mathematical operation to be performed. The basic difference lies in the way in which the operation to be performed is indicated.

In the number problem the operation is indicated directly by the number sign minus (−) and by the form in which the number figures are written. In the word problem the operation to be performed is not indicated directly, but must be supplied by the pupil through his understanding of the ideas expressed by the words and number figures. The pupil can be conditioned to respond with the correct computation to the sign minus (−) without understanding the idea which the sign represents, but he cannot solve the verbal problem unless he understands one of the ideas involved in the concept of subtraction. Not even the recognition and understanding of each word and mathematical symbol in a word problem will guarantee that the pupil will understand the idea involved in the fundamental operation to be performed. He must understand the idea or ideas underlying the fundamental operations, and he must be able to recognize those ideas operating in specific quantitative situations when those situations are described in terms of the words and number figures. Lack of understanding of the ideas underlying the fundamental processes is one of the principal reasons why students have trouble with word problems.

For this discussion it can be seen that number problems and word problems are alike in that they both contain (1) number concepts and (2) a mathematical operation to be performed. They differ in the way in which the operation to be performed is indicated. This difference forms the basis for our definition of a word problem. A word problem is an arithmetical situation described symbolically in which the operation to be performed is not indicated directly, but must be supplied by the student from his understanding of the ideas expressed by the words and number figures.

What Is Reading?

Reading is the process by which meaning is put into written symbols. Written symbols may be of different kinds. The following are all symbols which must be read, and they must be reacted to meaningfully if they are to be understood.

Symbol	Kind of Symbol
table	word
95	number figure
XXV	Roman numeral
—	number sign

In teaching the reading of any kind of symbol, the teacher has three major responsibilities:

1. *The development of skill in recognizing the symbols.* Some skills we use in recognizing words are general configuration clues, context clues, phonetic analysis, and structural analysis. What skills do you use in developing recognition of number figures?
2. *The development of a rich background of experiences that will make the symbols meaningful to the child.* Since meanings are not inherent in symbols, the child must first attach meaning to the symbol if he is later to put meaning into it. He will be able to do this only if he has had many experiences with that which the symbol represents.
3. *The development of a positive attitude toward reading.* This is the teacher's most important responsibility. The learning situation in which the understandings and skills are developed must be purposeful to the child and so structured that he will see that symbols, either oral or written, are used to express ideas.

In our schools emphasis is placed on teaching the reading of two kinds of symbols: word and mathematical symbols (number figures and number signs). Because the activity in the classroom centering around the development of the meaning and recognition of words is called the reading period, many teachers do not realize that they are teaching reading when they work with the activities which lead to the recognition and understanding of mathematical symbols.

This column must be read	even as	*This column must be read*

1

3

+

$1 + 2 = 3$

64
−31
‾‾‾

A number figure representing a number concept. The word symbol representing the concept is *one*. All number figures have number names. Although number figures and number names are written differently, they are pronounced the same and mean the same.

Another number figure representing a different number concept. All number figures are a part of a number system and represent concepts that have definite relationships to one another in that system. The child grows in his understanding of arithmetic through his growth in understanding the number system.

A mathematical symbol representing one kind of mathematical operation. Word symbols representing the same process are *and, add,* and *plus.* The four fundamental processes may all be represented by simple signs: $+$, $-$, $\times$, and $)\overline{}$ or $\div$.

A sentence (a statement of an idea) expressed in mathematical symbols. In word form, this sentence would read as follows: One and two are three, or one plus two equals three.

One of the forms (called algorisms) used in writing down mathematical symbols for computation. In this form, these particular symbols represent an incomplete thought which may be expressed verbally as follows: Sixty-four minus thirty-one is . . . .

Did you really read all of the second column? If you did, you will have begun to recognize that the simplicity of representing the number system hides the complexity of the relationships involved and makes the recognition of these symbols far easier than the understanding of them. At the root of much of the trouble which children have in reading word problems is a lack of understanding of the ideas and relationships that make up the number system.

The Relationship Between Reading and Word Problems

If the definitions given for word problems and reading are accepted, it follows that whenever a word problem is presented in written form, a reading situation confronts the child. Usually it is not until the introduction of word problems that teachers begin to consider the reading in arithmetic. Then the emphasis is placed on the recognition of the general and specialized vocabularies often to the exclusion of the mathematical figures appearing in the problem and the mathematical operation to be performed. Why is the language of words stressed in the reading of word problems?

1. Many teachers still think of reading only in terms of words, not in terms of mathematical symbols.
2. There are more words than number figures to be read.
3. Mathematical symbols present far less difficulty insofar as recognition is concerned.

Consider the following problem found in a third-grade text:

One day 29 children went for a hike. There were 3 teachers with them. How many people went for the hike?

There are sixteen different words in this problem and only two number figures.

Many children in the third grade may still be having difficulty in recognizing such words as *with, were,* and *went;* and though they may meet for the first time such words as *people* and *hike* without recognizing them, they will be able to recognize the figures 29 and 3. Since there are more words than figures to be recognized and since children seem to recognize mathematical figures more easily, the emphasis in reading word problems is placed on word recognition.

The concern of many teachers with word recognition skills is a legitimate one. The first phase of any reading activity is apprehending or recognizing the symbols. It stands to reason that if the child cannot recognize the words, he is not going to be able to read a word problem. Further questioning of the teacher who said, "We just don't teach reading," brought out the fact that her pupils were having trouble with the mechanics of word recognition. The comments of the other teachers in this particular group and in other groups indicate that a careful control of the general vocabulary used in writing word problems is essential if the pupil is to center his attention on "thought-getting."

The wide differences in reading ability that are found at any grade level make it difficult to control vocabulary so that the teacher will be safe in assuming that the words will be recognized by every pupil. The teacher will find that difficulties in word recognition will be lessened if the general vocabulary used in word problems is simpler than that being developed in the reading instruction period. Word problems might well be written using a vocabulary *at least one grade level below* the grade placement of the arithmetic symbols and ideas being developed; problems for the fourth grade might be written using only the vocabulary developed through the third grade, problems for the third grade using only vocabulary developed through second grade, and so on.

Since it is generally accepted that all children are not "ready" for reading at the same time and since all children do not grow at the same rate, differences in reading skills become greater rather than smaller with each succeeding grade level. The higher the grade level, the wider should be the lag between the difficulty of the words being developed in the instructional reading program prepared for a given grade level and those included in the word problems.

59. Five Steps to Reading Success in Science *

METROPOLITAN SCHOOL STUDY COUNCIL

Science

MANY reading difficulties faced by pupils studying science arise from the introduction, all at one time, of numerous new concepts, the interpretation of mathematical formulae, and the solving of problems. To read science material successfully, pupils must master certain reading skills:

1. Locating pertinent details
2. Distinguishing between main ideas and supporting details
3. Visualizing
4. Following directions
5. Drawing inferences

To help pupils learn these reading skills, teachers will find the following sample procedures valuable as guides in developing similar lessons in their classes.

Reading skills often essential to science are included in the sample procedures

* From *Five Steps to Reading Success in Science, Social Studies, and Mathematics,* Revised, Metropolitan School Study Council (New York: Teachers College, Columbia University, 1960), pp. 1–7. Reprinted by permission of the Metropolitan School Study Council.

in the Social Studies section of this manual. The teacher may wish especially to refer to the procedures for "Skimming" and "Reading Critically" in that section.

Five-Step Approach in Science

Step One: Readiness

1. Relating the experiences and knowledge of the pupils to the new material
2. Arousing the pupils' interest in the section
   a. The challenge of solving a problem
   b. The desire to satisfy a problem
   c. The practical value of scientific knowledge

Step Two: Concept Development

1. Developing vocabulary
   a. Words and phrases new to the pupils
   b. Familiar words and phrases with new connotations
2. Clarifying ideas of measurement

| Space | Energy |
| Time | Mass |

Step Three: Silent Reading

1. Asking pupils to find answers to specific questions

2. Asking pupils to discover and follow the steps of the experiment or problem

Step Four: Discussion (Oral or Written)

1. Helping pupils to evaluate their answers to questions
2. Helping pupils to discover or to understand principles or theories
3. Helping pupils to see the practical application of principles or theories

Step Five: Rereading (Silent or Oral)

1. Checking accuracy
2. Examining critically

Reading Skill: Locating Pertinent Details

Step One: Readiness

Pupils are aware that green vegetables are a necessary part of a balanced diet. The teacher should stimulate the pupils' curiosity about the reasons for this.

Step Two: Concept Development

The meaning of the following words and concepts should be clarified before the pupils begin the reading. These words and phrases should always be presented in written context.

green plants	*fats*
carbohydrates	*minerals*
proteins	*cellulose*

Step Three: Silent Reading

The pupils then should be asked to read the selection, keeping in mind the questions, "What are green plants made of?" and "What do green plants make?"

"Green plants have been broken down, chemically, to find out what they are made of. They are made of certain *carbohydrates, proteins, fats, minerals,*

and water. But chiefly they are made of a woody material called *cellulose* and contain large amounts of starch and sugar. . . . Sugar is made first. Green plants make starch, cellulose, and even fat and proteins, from the sugar." [1]

Step Four: Discussion

The discussion should stress that green plants, broken down chemically, provide substances for building body tissue and providing energy. Pupils should be able to name the substances.

Step Five: Rereading

Rereading may be necessary to check the number and kind of substances found in green plants.

Reading Skill: Distinguishing Between Main Ideas and Supporting Details

Step One: Readiness

The reading selection that follows concerns the endocrine glands. Before being asked to read this selection, students should be made generally familiar with what the endocrine glands are. The teacher should make clear to students that the purpose of reading about the endocrine glands in this instance is to discover the results of oversecretion of growth hormones in the pituitary gland. To stimulate interest, the readiness lesson might also include a discussion of the following:

1. Why individuals vary in height
2. What causes circus giants

[1] Excerpt from *New World of Science,* by R. Will Burnett, Bernard Jaffee, Herbert S. Zim, Copyright © 1948, 1953 by Silver Burdett Company, p. 136. Reprinted by permission.

Step Two: Concept Development

The meaning and pronunciation of the following words should be clarified before the pupils begin the reading. These words and phrases should always be presented in written context.

pituitary gland	*hormones*
lobes	*somotropic*
anterior	*giantism*
secretes	*acromegaly*

Step Three: Silent Reading

The pupils should locate details about the results of over-secretion of the growth hormone.

"The *pituitary gland* consists of two *lobes*. The *anterior* lobe *secretes* several different *hormones*. One of these, the *somotropic* (so-mo-TROP-ic) or growth hormone, regulates the growth of the skeleton. If an oversecretion of this hormone occurs during the growing years, tremendous height may be attained. This condition is called *giantism*. Circus giants over 7 feet tall, weighing 300 pounds, and wearing size 30 shoes, are examples of this disorder. If the oversecretion occurs during adult life, the bones merely thicken, as they cannot grow in length. However, the organs and soft tissues enlarge tremendously. This condition is known as *acromegaly* (ak-ro-MEG-a-lee). Victims of this disorder have greatly thickened jaw bones, enlarged noses, and greatly enlarged hands and fingers." [2]

Step Four: Purposeful Discussion

The following questions should be on the blackboard while the pupils are read-

[2] Truman J. Moon, Paul O. Mann, and James H. Otto, *Modern Biology* (New York: Henry Holt, 1951), p. 502. Quoted by permission of the publisher.

ing. Such questions aid in giving direction to the reading.

1. What condition is caused by an oversecretion of the pituitary hormone during *the growing years?* Give an example.
2. What condition is caused by an oversecretion of the pituitary gland during *adult life?* Describe the symptoms.

Step Five: Rereading

The rereading may be oral or silent. Pupils may skim through text material seeking the proof of an answer they have given and then read orally to prove the point.

In this particular lesson, pupils may find it necessary to reread to correct errors in spelling or pronunciation of *somotropic* or *acromegaly*. They may want to read to check on the details concerning the circus giant or the symptoms of acromegaly.

Reading Skill: Visualizing Concepts

Step One: Readiness

The teacher should arouse the interest of pupils in the atom by discussing the frequent use of *atom* or *atomic* on the radio, in the newspapers, in the movies, and on television. The pupils should be led to ask what an atom really looks like. The purpose of reading the selection will be to find the answer to that question.

Step Two: Concept Development

The pupils should become familiar with the pronunciations and definitions of the following words and phrases. These words and phrases should always be presented in written context.

atom	*positively charged*
electrons	*protons*
negatively charged	*neutrons*
particles	*electrically neutral*
nucleus	*mass of the atom*
planetary electrons	

Step Three: Silent Reading

The teacher should ask the pupils to try to picture the structure of the atom and to try to compare the size of the nucleus and its electrons.

There is plenty of evidence to show that an *atom* consists of *electrons, negatively charged particles,* whirling about a *nucleus.* These outer electrons, usually called *planetary electrons,* are lightly scattered about the nucleus and at relatively remote distances from it. The nucleus, on the other hand, is *positively charged* and consists of a closely packed group of *protons* and *neutrons.* A proton has a positive electrical charge, whereas a neutron is *electrically* neutral and probably results from the union of a proton and an electron. A proton is almost 2,000 times heavier than an electron so that more than 99.9 percent of the *mass of the atom* is in the nucleus.[3]

Step Four: Discussion

To test visualization powers, students could:
1. Draw the structure of an atom
2. Compare the structure of an atom to our solar system
3. Make a model of an atom from clay and wire

Step Five: Rereading

Some rereading may be necessary to check the accuracy of the proportions of the drawing or model.

Reading Skill: Following Directions

Step One: Readiness

In preparation for an experiment, the pupils have already discussed the use of levers as simple machines. They have learned, by observation, about levers in daily use like the crowbar, scissors, and sugar tongs. They have also learned that levers are used to do work with less effort and with more speed. They are now ready to read the directions for an experiment that will actually demonstrate the scientific principle involved.

Step Two: Concept Development

The meaning of the following words and concepts should be clarified before the pupils begin to read the experiment. These words and phrases should always be presented in written context.

equilibrium	unlike weights
parallel forces	products
balance	vary
fulcrum	sum

Step Three: Silent Reading

Each pupil should be instructed to read each detail carefully and execute each step as stated.

Experiment 33a. Equilibrium of Parallel Forces.—*Balance* a meter stick in a clamp or on a *fulcrum.* Hang or stand two *unlike weights* on the stick and move them until the stick balances. Then measure the distance from each weight to the balancing point, or fulcrum. Multiply each weight by its distance to the fulcrum and compare the *products. Vary* the set-up as much as you like, using different weights . . . or three weights, or many weights. In every case you will find that the product of weight times distance for the left weight equals the product for the right weight (times distance from the fulcrum). When several weights are used, add the products for those on the left and check against the *sum* of products for those on the right.[4]

[3] From *Chemistry: A Course for High Schools* by J. C. Hogg, O. E. Alley, and C. L. Bickel, Copyright © 1948 by Litton Educational Publishing, Inc., p. 274.

[4] From *Elements of Physics* by Robert W. Fuller, Raymond B. Brownlee, and D. Lee Baker, copyright © 1948. Reprinted by permission of Allyn and Bacon, Inc.

Step Four: Discussion

After each pupil has performed the experiment, he should compare the results to determine whether or not the phenomenon is consistent.

Step Five: Rereading

If results indicate that there are some pupils who have not accurately followed directions, the pupils should reread to discover their errors and do the experiment again step by step.

After the lesson has been satisfactorily completed, the class is ready to discuss the scientific principles involved in the experiment.

Reading Skill: Drawing Inferences

Step One: Readiness

The teacher can prepare the class for reading the selection by discussing why many distributors of food prepackage or wrap all foods they display. Pupils will probably mention the danger of contamination from handling by customers or from flies. It should be suggested that there may be another reason why local health suggestions usually require that most perishable foods be packaged or displayed in an enclosed display case.

Step Two: Concept Development

The meanings of the following words and concepts should be clarified before the pupils begin to read. These words and phrases should always be presented in written context.

microscopic	*original formation*
germs	*carbon dioxide*
decay	*minerals*
chemical compounds	*ptomaine poison*

Step Three: Silent Reading

The pupils should be asked to figure out from the facts in the selection the answer to the following question:

What is a third reason for packaging or covering food in stores?

. . . When the *microscopic germs* that float about in the air settle on foods, they start *decay.* The materials in the goods are broken up to form new *chemical compounds.* Some of them are the same as those which entered into the *original formation* of the foods; namely, *carbon dioxide,* water, and *minerals.* When decay takes place, new compounds with bad odors are also produced, and the food changes in taste. The food may even become poisonous. *Ptomaine poison* is an example of this.[5]

Step Four: Discussion

In the ensuing discussion some pupils will probably say that the answer is not stated. Others who have arrived at the correct answer should then explain how they reached the conclusion that food is wrapped as a protection against contact with the air as well as with persons, animals, and insects.

Step Five: Rereading

Those pupils who did not make the correct inference will reread to find the facts from which the inference was drawn.

[5] Ira C. Davis, John Burnett, and E. Wayne Gross, *Science* (New York: Henry Holt, 1952), p. 514. Quoted by permission of the publisher.

XII

Recreational Reading

Most Americans have learned to read with varying degrees of ability. Yet according to studies, not many adults often choose to read in their spare time. One possible factor contributing to this situation may be that little is done in schools to promote a lifetime interest in recreational reading.

Knowledge of which books are likely to interest certain children and where to find such books should aid teachers in helping students develop an interest in reading. Huus' coverage of these topics is followed by Arbuthnot's article that suggests how reading books may help to satisfy some needs of children at various age levels. Larrick next offers ideas for motivating children to read. The final article, by Way, is concerned with the manner in which teachers and librarians can cooperate for the benefit of children.

60. Reading Interests *

HELEN HUUS

TEACHING children *how* to read is one thing; getting them *to read* on their own is another.

Like adults, children read for different

* From Helen Huus, "Reading Interests," in Coleman Morrison (ed.), *Problem Areas in Reading—Some Observations and Recommendations,* Rhode Island College Reading Conference Proceedings (Providence, R.I.: Oxford Press, 1965), pp. 74–81. Reprinted by permission of the author and Dr. Coleman Morrison.

purposes. Sometimes it is to satisfy their curiosity; sometimes it is to check information; other times it is to retreat into a fanciful or exciting world or to escape from the humdrum duties of everyday life; sometimes reading is done just to use time that otherwise would hang heavily; and often reading is purely for enjoyment —of the story, the satisfactory ending, the identification with the characters and their activities, or the beauty of thought and expression.

Unlike adults, children probably read less for prestige, although even youngsters are heard to compare the number of books they have read. Adults may be concerned more with the contents of a recent book club selection or a current article so that they can discuss it, however superficially.

Frank describes purposes of reading this way:

. . . Is it to stimulate the imagination, to delight the heart, to provide a haven of escape from a world "too much with us," to supply information, to broaden the mind, to enrich the spirit, to carry on the culture? Perhaps it is all of these things, but not all at the same time or for the same person. Perhaps reading is for each according to his need. In a magazine, an encyclopedia, a newspaper or even on a cereal box cover one may find a piece of reading which will both delight the heart and inform the mind (2).

If books are selected by children to fulfill needs, then it follows that books which do this will be of interest to them.

"Interest" has been defined as "a disposition or tendency which impels an individual to seek out particular goals for persistent attention" (14). Thus, children who are interested in reading will want to know about the subject, will pursue it consistently, and will usually want to share what they have read.

Knowing which books are likely to capture the interest of children of a given age, which are likely to be of interest to the special reader, and where books can be located for those who have individual hobbies or interests are useful prerequisites for a teacher or librarian who wants children to read and enjoy their reading.

Methods Used

Children's interest in reading as a pastime has been studied by asking children to keep a "log" of their out-of-school activities or by giving them a questionnaire that asks them to indicate the amount of time spent per week on certain types of activities.

One example is a study reported by McCullough, where children kept a log of their out-of-school activities for a week (7). According to their records, recreation, work, and television were the most popular pastimes, with less than one-fourth of them reading books, and even fewer reading newspapers and magazines. In discussing the results, McCullough stressed the importance of the home and family in the cultivation of the reading habit.

Skelton asked the 28 pupils in her sixth-grade class to estimate their outside reading—reading done in addition to school lessons (11). She found an average of 6 hours per week for books, and 3.4 hours per week for other materials. Reading ranked second on the list of activities, and only two pupils indicated a dislike for "reading" as a school subject when they were asked to rank them. The three magazines most frequently read by these sixth graders were the *Saturday Evening Post, Life,* and *Boy's Life,* but Skelton found little interest in television or comic books and less interest in science than she had expected.

Children's reading interests—what they want to read about—have been studied by various means. Questionnaires have been given to children or adults; the number of times a library book has been checked out has been counted; the "wear and tear" on a book has been noted and evaluated; children or adults have been interviewed; recordings of children's spontaneous or guided conversation have been analyzed; observations have been made; and experiments have been conducted.

The studies mentioned in this paper

are but a few of those that have been reported; persons interested in a more complete survey are directed to the summaries by Witty and his associates (14, 15, 16), or to Volume 3 of the IRA Perspectives in Reading Series, entitled *Children, Books and Reading* (4).

Early Studies

As early as 1921, Jordan conducted a survey of children's interests and found that boys preferred adventure stories and that girls liked stories of home and school, love, and history, mild adventure, and fairy stories (5). Boys also liked biography, science, history, and poetry; and humor was less popular with girls than boys. However, if *Tom Sawyer* and *Huckleberry Finn* were omitted from the analysis, then humor would be higher for girls than for boys.

Terman and Lima's study of the reading interests of boys and girls from ages eleven to sixteen, published in 1925, found similar results (12). They noted that from age nine and up, the breach between the reading interests of boys and girls widens, with boys choosing adventure and vigorous action, nonfiction and animal stories, while girls read more than boys and like fairy tales, poetry, sentimental fiction, and animals. The amount of reading was shown to increase from age six until about twelve or thirteen, with a gradual decrease later.

Following these two rather extensive surveys, several other studies of the reading interests of selected age groups or for special purposes were carried out prior to 1935. From that time until the middle of the century, there were relatively fewer studies, with a recurrence of interest following 1950 that has continued until the present.

Reasons for this renewed interest can be attributed, in part at least, to the widespread television viewing by children with the accompanying acquisition of a variety of information and consequent alteration in interest; to the changes in family living following World War II, resulting from mobility, working mothers, and the "affluent society"; to the large number of books available to children, both from increased publication and from the growth of library service that makes the books in print more available than previously; and to the emphasis of the public upon excellence in education, which has focused on the importance of reading as preparation for college. There are doubtless other factors that have influenced individual research workers to devote themselves to a study of children's reading interests. Be that as it may, however, a review of some of the recent studies of post-World War II children yields information regarding the present status.

Studies Since 1950

The most comprehensive of the recent studies, published in 1959, is that by Norvell, who asked 24,000 children in grades three through eight in New York State to indicate their interest in selected works (8). In all, 1576 literary selections were used. His data are similar to those obtained in previous studies, namely: that boys prefer prose and girls poetry; that boys like adventure and action, physical struggle, human characters, animals, humor, courage and heroism, and patriotism; and that girls prefer lively adventure, home and school, human characters, domestic animals and pets, romantic love, sentiment, mystery, supernatural, and patriotism. Neither boys nor girls like description and didacticism; girls did not like violent action, younger boys and girls as characters (except babies), and fierce animals; boys disliked fairies, romantic love, sentiment, girls or women as the leading character, and physical weakness.

Norvell's study also revealed that many Mother Goose rhymes were liked as late as grade six, and that fables and fairy tales were especially interesting to grades three to five. Myths, legends, and hero and folk tales were most popular in grades five to seven.

In 1955, Rudman reported a study of 6313 pupils, 4531 parents, 212 teachers, and 169 librarians in 270 communities (10). His purpose was threefold: (1) to find out what children wanted to read about, (2) what children wanted to find out about, what they were looking up in books, and (3) to see if parents and librarians had the same desires for their children as the children had for themselves. He found the children's "read about" interests included, first of all, science, then mystery, adventure, children, horses, and dogs. From grade four to eight there was an increase in mystery, and a decrease in cowboy and fairy stories, an increase in teenage sports and recreational activities, and throughout a strong interest in animals. There were few sex differences, contrary to other studies, and little difference among rural, urban, and metropolitan centers. Boys more than girls liked astronomy, geology, physical geography, space travel, Indians, science, airplanes, jets and rockets, boats and sports while girls (more than boys) liked animals, literature, fairy tales and mythology, mystery, teenage tales, children, famous people, boy-girl relationships, and school.

Parents wanted children to choose reference books, ethics, and religion, and librarians wanted biography more than children did. The adult preferences were more like each other's choices than they were like the children's, and there were some differences in that rural parents wanted more social studies while urban parents wanted more religion.

In 1956, Vandament and Thalman studied 1034 children in grades six and ten to determine whether social, aggressive, or achievement type fantasy was preferred by different age, socioeconomic, sex, and residential groups (13). They found that sixth-graders preferred storybooks to magazines, while tenth-graders preferred the latter. Girls were more interested in social reading than boys, but boys were more interested in aggressive reading. There was no difference between socioeconomic levels, which led the researchers to question whether this is because children in lower socioeconomic levels are not truly more aggressive than others or because they work out their aggressiveness directly and have no need to read about it. If the latter be true, then a question is raised regarding the relationship between the reading of comics and juvenile delinquency.

From an analysis of 17 hours of recorded discussions of 715 children in grades one through six, McAulay tried to ascertain their interest in social studies (6). He found that the number of concepts increased with age, and that certain topics have "threads" that run through all the grades: "the Westward expansion (cowboys and Indians); the War between the States; the status of the Negro; USSR; Mainland China, and Africa; beginnings and meanings of Communism; underprivileged people; transportation; other people's dress, religion, housing, food, and games; background of social institutions—where the flag comes from or why we are called the 'United States'; and the Cold War." The emphasis on current problems is evident, and though this study was published in 1961, the topics are still very up-to-date. McAulay concluded that the social studies reading "underestimates the interest and information children have secured from TV, radio, movies, and travel, and that the interests seem to be very 'elastic,' in that they move easily from the community to the world scene in any grade."

Studies of Young Children

Several recent studies have dealt with the interests of young children. Cappa used 443 storybooks to get kindergarten children's immediate reaction by observing enjoyment to each story (1). He found the children had a slight preference for fanciful over real. They did not like unrealistic nonsense, and, therefore, storybooks should not be too unrealistic or too far removed from their experiences.

Gunderson found that her 22 seven-years-olds liked the "funny" books most frequently—books containing ridiculous, unbelievable, surprising, imaginative, and absurd incidents (3). The content and story of the 14 books used were chosen in preference to the pictures, and a satisfactory ending, with right triumphant was important. Children found none of the books "too frightening," and they liked "scary" parts, such as the possibility of Bartholomew's head being chopped off and the elephant's child stepping on a crocodile.

Rogers and Robinson gave 275 first-grade children a questionnaire asking if they would "like" or "not like" to read books about certain topics (9). Ninety percent of them would like to read about "a magic ring, George Washington, a happy Christmas day, a friendly giant, and a funny clown." Make-believe was the favorite kind of story, followed by happiness, humor, adventure, history, family, anxiety; today's world was the least-liked category, even though the questionnaire was administered shortly after John Glenn's space flight. The sex differences were marked; boys preferred adventure, history, and make-believe, while girls preferred make-believe, humor, and happiness. Girls were more interested in fantasy, homelife, and romance, than boys, even at first grade, and boys were more interested in adventure, like an exciting airplane ride, what an astronaut does, and exploring a cave. Though there appeared to be a similarity in the reading interests of good and poor readers, the number of poor readers in the study was too small to make any valid generalization.

Summary

In summary, I would make this synthesis of children's interests in reading, based on a study of the research, from a review of child psychology, and from my experience in teaching and working with children and their teachers.

Kindergarten and Grade One. Children of five and six like "pretend" stories, where animals talk and where there is rhythm to the language and where humor consists of exaggeration. Realistic stories of home, little children like themselves, play and daily activities are of interest, and "here and now" stories of cars, trucks, ships (including space ones), and trains are enjoyed.

Second and Third Grades. While seven-year-olds still like magic and fairies, the stories have more plot than those that interest the younger children. Eights, too, like complex fairy stories, especially if there is romance as an added attraction. Second graders are interested in all kinds of transportation, in the world and people, while third graders begin to extend their interests and obtain factual information about far away places and events of long ago, though exactly *how* far away or *how* long ago is not yet of great concern.

Fourth Grade. Fourth grade is a transition in many respects: in the amount of textbook reading required of the pupil, in the physical development of the pupil as he approaches preadolescence, and in the increasing separation of the interests of boys and girls.

Boys show interest in action and aggressiveness, in the affairs of the world, and therefore prefer adventure, science, hero stories, biography, history, and tall tales, while girls still cling to the fanciful stories, myths, stories of chivalry and romance, home life, biography, and accounts of everyday life, though not always in that order. Boys will not choose a book, ordinarily, that has the name of a girl in the title, but girls will choose a boy's book.

Grades Five and Six. Children in grades five and six continue the interests expressed, with hero worship being accentuated among the boys and romance among the girls. Science and mechanics become more interesting to boys, and girls enjoy lively adventure stories, though they prefer their excitement to be less violent than do boys, hence the popularity of Nancy Drew. Both boys and girls react unfavorably to much description and didacticism. Girls are likely to do more reading than boys, and both of them will read only a limited amount in magazines and newspapers.

Humorous stories and animal stories are liked at any age; in fact, adults, too, still enjoy reading such tales.

Conclusion

What do these studies tell the teacher? (1) That a wide variety of materials need to be made available if the interests of all are to be met; (2) that teachers should create interest in books by capitalizing upon the known interests of children; (3) that the home should be encouraged to promote reading as a pastime; (4) that time should be provided in school for sharing books—listening, reading, and discussing; and (5) that grouping books by topics may aid in location and promotion.

Whether children's interests, either those expressed as book preferences or as topics about which they would like to read, are the results of inherent predispositions or of acculturation is difficult to assess. It is true that, in different environments, with different family associations and with different expectations for boys and girls at each age level, there are differences in their approach to reading. In some of the European countries with many men teachers even in the elementary schools, reading comes to be associated as a masculine trait, whereas in our country it tends to be interpreted as feminine and, therefore, not to be emulated by boys who wish to show their masculinity. Such subtle influences are extremely difficult to isolate and study, and yet the fact remains that there are differences among and within groups.

Yet in the long run, if a book has real characters (people, animals, or fanciful creatures) who have curious and sometimes exciting things happen to them and if these events are told with sincerity, with vitality, and with originality, it is interesting to almost any person who can read it for himself or who can understand when it is real to him. Such is the stuff of classics, for these are the perennial favorites that each succeeding generation passes down to the next and that form the solid core of the literary heritage of children.

References

1. CAPPA, DAN. "Types of Story Books Enjoyed by Kindergarten Children," *Journal of Educational Research,* 49 (March, 1956), 555–57.
2. FRANK, JOSETTE. "What Are Children Reading in this TV Age?" *Child Study,* 34 (Spring, 1957), 6.
3. GUNDERSON, AGNES. "What Seven-Year-Olds Like in Books," *Journal of Educational Research,* 50 (March, 1957), 509–20.
4. HUUS, HELEN. "Interpreting Research in Children's Literature." *Children, Books and Reading,* Mildred Dawson (ed.). Perspectives in Reading, Vol. 3. Newark, Del.: International Reading Assiciation, 1964. Pp. 123–44.
5. JORDAN, ARTHUR M. *Children's Interests in Reading,* Contributions to Education, No. 107. New York: Teachers College, Columbia University, 1921.
6. MCAULAY, J. D. "Interests of Elementary School Children," *Social Education,* 25 (December, 1961), 407–9.
7. MCCULLOUGH, CONSTANCE. "A Log of Children's Out-of-School Activities," *Elementary School Journal,* 58 (December, 1957), 157–65.
8. NORVELL, GEORGE W. *What Boys and Girls Like to Read.* Morristown, N. J.: Silver Burdett Company, 1959.
9. ROGERS, HELEN, and ROBINSON, H. ALAN. "Reading Interests of First-Graders," *Elementary English,* 40 (November, 1963), 709.
10. RUDMAN, HERBERT C. "The Informational Needs and Reading Interests of Children in Grades IV through VIII," *Elementary School Journal,* 55 (1955), 502–12.
11. SKELTON, DOROTHY. "Pupils' Interests in Reading," *Elementary English,* 38 (April, 1961), 246–49, 263.
12. TERMAN, L. M., and LIMA, M. *Children's Reading.* New York: D. Appleton and Company, 1925.
13. VANDAMENT, WILLIAM E., and THALMAN, W. A. "An Investigation into the Reading Interests of Children," *Journal of Educational Research,* 49 (February, 1956), 467–70.
14. WITTY, PAUL, and Associates. "Studies of Children's Interests—A Brief Summary," *Elementary English,* 38 (December, 1960), 469.
15. ———. "Studies of Children's Interests—A Brief Summary II," *Elementary English,* 38 (December, 1960), 540–45, 572.
16. ———. "Studies of Children's Interests—A Brief Summary III," *Elementary English,* 39 (January, 1961), 33–36.

61. Developing Life Values Through Reading *

MAY HILL ARBUTHNOT

WHEN Longfellow uttered his portentous warning, "Life is real! Life is carnest!" he neglected to add that life can also be a lot of fun and more full of intriguing people and interesting things to do and see than one lifetime can possibly encompass. The problem is to make the most of life and, as adults, we do have to admit that growing up is also a chancey process. What forces, for instance, made you what you are? And when and where did you begin to grow into the You that is sitting here today? As a group of teachers we may not be in the higher echelon of world shakers, but on the whole we are a fairly competent lot of people. What image of ourselves grown to maturity made us so and prevented us from going in the direction of the unhappy lawbreakers of one kind or another?

As teachers we would be the first to admit that the child's home and the people he is associated with are of paramount importance in forming his ideals of what he himself wants to be. But for the most part these influences are beyond our control. Today we are also concerned about the influence of mass media on the child's developing image of himself. And again his use of these media, outside of school, we can do little about except to know their scope and character. Certainly all forms of mass media—newspapers, pic-

* From May Hill Arbuthnot, "Developing Life Values Through Reading," *Elementary English,* 43 (January, 1966), 10–16. Copyright © 1966 by the National Council of Teachers of English. Reprinted by permission of the National Council of Teachers of English.

torial magazines, moving pictures, radio and television—are very much with today's child. Along with fine documentaries and other substantial offerings, today's child is bombarded daily with closeups of brutality, banality, scandal, and violence. Over the din of the Beatles with their screaming hordes, Western heroes forever fighting, and movie Queens forever misbehaving, what chance to make a deep impression, for instance, has the image of Herbert Hoover's quiet dedicated life? The hopeful element in this mass presentation of savage and silly examples of maturity is their evanescence. Pictures and words come and go with great rapidity and are immediately replaced by something equally brief and easily forgotten. But are they forgotten? We know so little about the image of himself that is gradually forming in that secret, inner world of the child's mind and spirit. But one thing we do know. If we can induct children into a genuine enjoyment of books, we can guide them to stories in which they will discover pictures of noble maturity and of children growing and changing into more competent and lovable human beings at every stage of development.

Reading an absorbing story is a continual process of identification. The child sees himself as the smart, third Little Pig or as Tom Sawyer or Caddie Woodlawn or whoever his current hero may be. Then, because even fluent, rapid reading is a slower, steadier process than the interrupted, piecemeal presentation of television with its station identifications and endless commercials, the hero image in a book has a chance to make a deeper, more lasting impression. Books are a bright hope if we can find the right books for a child at the right time.

For the Youngest—Reassurance and Achievement

The youngest children in our schools, the prereaders and beginners in reading—just because they are small and inexperienced—are uncertain, insecure and generally find themselves in the wrong. Someone is always saying, "Don't do that," or "No, you aren't old enough for that." So, of course, these young pilgrims need lots of reassurance about their place in the world, that they are loved, needed, and capable of doing things on their own. Notice how their first picture stories stress both loving reassurance, and also achievement. For example, these qualities account, in part, for the popularity of *The Happy Lion* series by Louise Fatio with pictures by Roger Duvoisin. The Lion, like small children, is cribbed, confined, and misunderstood. But he has ideas of his own, whether it is going for a walk in the town or getting himself a beautiful lioness, he carries out his plans gently but firmly. And children, after feeling sorry for him, chuckle over his achievements and say, "read it again." Then they pore over those inimitable pictures which are completely one with the text and they triumph again with the Happy Lion.

This autumn has brought one of the most beautiful and satisfying picture stories for the prereaders that we have had. It is called, *Whistle for Willie,* written and illustrated by Ezra Jack Keats who did the Caldecott Medal book *Snowy Day.* This new one is even more beautiful, in luscious pinks against the whole spectrum of colors, and with the same little colored boy in a pink and white shirt trying desperately to whistle for his dog, Willie. Failing, he crawls into a big carton to practice. Then, feeling more grown-up by the addition of his father's hat, he plays father, and all sorts of other things, but always working for a whistle. Suddenly, there is Willie his dog, and suddenly Peter whistles! Wille stops dead in his tracks and then comes flying. Here is a climax and from that point on, sheer triumph! But there is more to this slight story than this briefing indicates. There is the enviable pattern of big boys whose dogs come when they whistle and a little boy struggling to be equally competent. There is an understanding mother, a proud father, love and achievement happily combined to make a small masterpiece.

If you look back over the picture stories that have enjoyed lasting popularity with children, you discover how these two notes—reassuring love and independent achievement—recur over and over again from *Peter Rabbit, Little Black Sambo,* and *Millions of Cats,* through the *Little Tim* and *Madeline* series to last year's splendid and more mature story of *Hans and Peter* by Heidrum Petrides. All of Robert McCloskey's beautiful picture stories stress reassurance. When children identify their own helplessness with the Ducklings or with Sal picking blueberries or losing a tooth or with the family in *Time of Wonder,* they come away from these books feeling that they too, when their time of trial comes, can weather the storm. They are stronger, more confident children for such books. And at an older level, the importance of Alice Dalgliesh's *The Bears of Hemlock Mountain* lies in the fact that Jonathan was genuinely afraid. Nevertheless, he went ahead with his scary undertaking and discovered in himself unexpected resources. A fine achievement tale for the primary.

Certainly, the carefully selected folk tales we use with young children—the fours and fives, sevens and eights—present a lively gallery of up-and-doing heroes and heroines, as, for example, the dauntless Bremen Town Musicians, the Three Pigs, Three Billy Goats, Boots, Beauty, Snow White and their like. These and more complex tales for the older children are saying to the child, "If you show kindness as well as courage, if you beware of silly credulity and use your head as well as your heart, you too can accomplish wonders." These old stories are worthwhile if only to build in children the firm conviction that evil need not be endured; that giants, ogres, and all the other big bullies in the world can be laid low, and meanness, greed, and cruelty exterminated. Our generation may not have finished the job but some progress has been made and maybe the next generation will do better. Anyway, these old tales are good medicine for children to grow on, so don't miss the beautiful new editions of single tales illustrated by such artists as Marcia Brown, Adrienne Adams, Eric Blegvad, and many others. These entrancing editions are bound to revive the popularity of these old tales, and it is about time.

Middle Years—7–10, Curiosity and Zest for Living

Love and achievement continue to motivate stories for all ages, but by the middle school years children seven, eight, and nine should be developing a lively curiosity about an ever expanding world and should have such a gay, coltish zest for living that they seek fun, adventure, and sometimes pure nonsense. Apathy and boredom in these transition years are unthinkable, and yet teachers say there are plenty of both, especially among deprived children in our big cities. Perhaps the bite of frustration and failure has set in. In these years, 7 to 10, the child has taken a giant step. He has learned to read for himself, but alas, not fluently! There's the rub. Learning to read is all very exciting to begin with, but when difficulties pile up, discouragement mounts. These are the years when teachers must try consciously to fill the gap between what the slow learning child can read for himself and what he would like to read. There is often a lag of from one to three years between reading skill and the ability to understand and enjoy. Teachers must fill that gap with plenty of practice in easy-to-read books and by reading aloud to their children books that delight them but are well beyond their reading ability.

There are many lists of easy-to-read books but frequently the content is too immature for the children who need them. Take Else Minarek's *Little Bear* books. They are charming for the fives and sixes, but babyish at seven and eight. Here the books of Clyde Bulla help mightily. He has an easy but never commonplace style and a stepped-up content which the sevens and even the elevens respect and enjoy. He always tells a lively adventure story and his books fit into many subject matter areas as the titles indicate—*Squanto, Friend of the White Men, Down the Mississippi, The Sword in the Tree,* and others. Alice Dalgliesh's *The Courage of Sarah Noble* will balance these boys' stories and give even the mildest little girls a sense of achievement. While we are on historical fiction, these may be good years to read aloud one of William Steele's stories of pioneer boys to introduce children to these books—*Tomahawks and Trouble, Winter Danger,* or any of them. Their importance lies in the fact that besides being exciting adventure stories, these ignorant, wrong-headed boy heroes grow and change in the course of a story, forged into something stronger and better by trials of endurance that call out all their stamina. Such books build up children's self-respect. They are antidotes for discouragement, apathy, and giving up the struggle. It is far too easy for children to accept failure and to downgrade themselves accordingly. Strong stories are energizing. The hero image gives them a clear idea of a competent maturity and the satisfaction of putting up a good fight.

Children also need a sense of fun along the way. The more school or home or personality difficulties increase, the more a child needs the release of laughter or even pure nonsense. Laughter can break tensions and restore balance. Nonsense verse or what children call "funny stories" help. If they can read for themselves those two indestructibles—*Mr. Popper's Penguins* or *Mary Poppins*—they'll chuckle and recover from the doldrums. If they can't, then take time to read one of them aloud. Or if you prefer, choose Oliver Butterworth's *Enormous Egg*, about the hen that hatched out not an Ugly Duckling, but no less than a mammoth dinosaur, amiable but outsize for domesticity. For a group of children to laugh together is to break down hostilities, tensions, and unhappiness. It is well worth the time. And E. B. White's matchless *Charlotte's Web*, which *is* beyond their reading skill but not their enjoyment level, will give them not only the therapy of laughter but the therapy of tears. Children need both. How else can they learn compassion?

These examples of the child's "funny stories" have all been in the field of fantasy, but there is also humorous realism to reassure routine-weary youngsters. If they cannot read Beverly Cleary's *Henry Huggins*, read them the first book, and they'll tackle the next one as soon as possible. The hilarious Huggins' adventures with Ribsey, the dog, and the neighborhood children lead naturally to Keith Robertson's *Henry Reed, Inc.*, one of the funniest books available. Henry, with his complete lack of humor, decides to go in for research. He puts up a sign, "Henry Reed, Inc. Research," to which his pushy girl neighbor adds, "Pure and Applied." He explains that only girls keep diaries "about their dates and different boy friends. But pirates and explorers keep journals." So, in his journal he records their summer adventures in research and these should leave any child a little better able to laugh at himself when he gets into absurd messes of his own making. The second book, *Henry Reed's Journey,* is as amusing as the first. Both are enhanced by some of Robert McCloskey's funniest drawings.

In these years the child's curiosity is boundless, or should be, and so are the informational books written to answer his questions and promote new ones. In any field of science, from dinosaurs to insects, and from stones to stars, there are excellent books at almost any reading level you desire. The same is true in the field of the social studies. But factual books are not the province of this paper which is concerned with literature for children. Fiction may also meet his curiosities about people, places, and ways of living. So his fiction goes back in time to include historical events of long ago and out in space to embrace the diverse regions and peoples of our United States and of other lands. Stories about Amish, Indians, Jewish families, ranchers, farmers, fishermen, migrant workers, city folk, all give a colorful and sympathetic introduction to diverse peoples and customs in this vast country of ours. Young readers get delightful glimpses of life in other countries in such old favorites as Chinese *Little Pear* by Eleanor Lattimore, or Hungarian *The Good Master* by Kate Seredy, or Natalie Carlson's tender and humorous story of Paris *The Family Under the Bridge,* or Harry Behn's Mexican *The*

Two Uncles of Pablo. From all these areas of reading—historical, regional, foreign lands—children get the reiterated truth that peoples of every age or place or country have similar difficulties, suffer deprivations and failures, and are more alike than different in their struggles to achieve a place in the sun.

For these middle years you may have noticed a dearth of recent titles, but there is nevertheless rich treasure in the books available if you are not too dedicated to recency. And why should you be? Just remember, it is the children who are forever recent, the books don't have to be, and a strong book twenty years old is worth a dozen bits of mediocrity just off the press.

Preadolescents—10 to 12 or 14, Compassion and Courage

In the last years of elementary school reading there is such a wide variation in reading abilities and social maturity that placing books by age levels is complete nonsense. A thirteen-year-old who thoroughly enjoyed *The Agony and the Ecstasy* and could discuss it eagerly, play by play, is not going to be satisfied with *Caddie Woodlawn*. Nor will a twelve-year-old, who has a struggle to get through *Henry Huggins,* give more than a passing glance at *Rifles for Watie.* Adults who guide children's reading in the years from ten to twelve or fourteen are pretty much on their own and can let those brashly graded reading lists fall where they may.

Oddly enough there is one area of reading where children and adults frequently meet on common ground and that is the well-written story about animals. By well written we mean authentic, true to the animal species, and neither humanized nor sentimentalized. For instance, *The Incredible Journey* by Sheila Burnford, which meets all these standards, was intended for adults but the children took it over. The same thing happened to Marjorie Rawlings' *The Yearling* and to that poignant little masterpiece by the late James Street, *Good-Bye, My Lady*. And, of course, the values of such books and those by Marguerite Henry, Jim Kjelgaard, Joseph Lippincott, the Georges and others, are manifold. Of first importance, however, is the fact that they stir the readers' compassion for animals. Albert Schweitzer calls this "reverence for life, all life worthy of development." Such reverence is made up of sensitivity to the needs and sufferings of others, compassion and a strong identification that we call empathy. These are all aspects of the same emotion, love. Going out to others selflessly is the most civilizing force in life. Never have we needed it more.

Teachers who have worked in the deprived areas of big cities where children have never been responsible for farm animals or pets, know all too well the horrible acts of sadism practiced by unthinking children against small animals, especially defenseless cats. Only this autumn there have been two such terrible examples of cat-torture that they have made the front pages of the papers. These could not have happened had those children ever cherished a pet cat or a rabbit or a dog of their own. And next to owning or growing up with animals are the vicarious experiences of reading about them. The process of identification that goes on when a child reads about Smoky or Lassie or *King of the Wind* means that he suffers with and for the animal hero. He also senses the nobility and sacrifice of the great gorilla in Lucy Boston's *Stranger at Green Knowe* or the patient endurance of mistreated Smoky or the curious loyalty and first aid the cat gave her two dog companions in *The Incredible Journey*. Perhaps compassion and reverence for life are ambitious terms for the child's emotional response to these books, but certainly they evoke tenderness and the desire to cherish and protect. These are the qualities that make the well-written animal story of great importance to young readers of every age and the reason why a story about animal torture in the bull ring, ballet style, seems regrettable.

The last years between childhood and the budding maturity of youth are hard on children. These preadolescents need almost as much encouragement as the youngest. They try their wings and fall flat on their faces. Failure is bitter and it takes courage to get up and try again. They are acutely aware of their own imperfections—too fat or too skinny or not sufficiently sought after. They are even more critical of the frightful imperfections of their parents. In no book has this ever been more accurately reflected than in those opening paragraphs of Emily Neville's *It's Like This, Cat*. Here they are:

My father is always talking about how a dog can be very educational for a boy. This is one reason I got a cat.

My father talks a lot anyway. Maybe being a lawyer he gets in the habit. Also, he's a small guy with very little gray curly hair, so maybe he thinks he's got to roar a lot to make up for not being a big hairy tough guy. Mom is thin and quiet, and when anything upsets her, she gets asthma. In the apartment—we live right in the middle of New York City—we don't have any heavy drapes or rugs, and mom never fries any food because the doctor's figure dust and smoke make her asthma worse. I don't think it's dust; I think it's Pop's roaring.

The big hassle that led me to getting Cat came when I earned some extra money baby-sitting for a little boy around the corner on Gramercy Park. I spent the money on a Belafonte record about a father telling his son about the birds and the bees. I think it's funny. Pop blows his stack.

By the way, whoever said this book lacked style? It may not have the lyric style of *Wind in the Willows*, but a family conflict is not a lyric. Styles do and should differ, and this is valid for the subject it describes. Incidentally, notice how in these brief paragraphs, the reader gets the theme, problem, and conflict of the entire book, as well as the brash, caustic judgments of youth. The fact that in the course of the story Dave comes to reevaluate his parents and even to see a new image of his own maturity through his father's eyes, makes this a choice book and one of our best big-city stories of a boy growing up.

There are different kinds of courage and it takes a special kind to accept physical handicaps or humiliating failures. That was the special value of the Newbery Medal book by Marguerite de Angeli, *The Door in the Wall*. Young, active, ambitious Robin has to accept the cruel fact of his semi-paralyzed limbs. But thanks to Brother Luke's ministrations and philosophy—"Always remember . . . thou hast only to follow a wall far enough and there will be a door in it. . . ." Robin learned to use his hands again and to get around agilely on crutches. The conclusion is not a cure, but a heart-warming triumph for Robin that should give courage to all permanently handicapped children. The thing is to find a door in every wall.

To come to grips with failure is part and parcel of growing up. Most children's stories grant the hero success in the end. That happened to David in that remarkable book of 1963—*The Loner* by Ester Weir. This is a great book. But there is a recent book that is memorable because in *Skinny* by Robert Burch, the boy's failure to achieve his heart's desire is unalterable. Skinny is an illiterate, eleven-year-old orphan. Miss Bessie has taken him in temporarily to help her in her small town hotel. The work and Miss Bessie suit Skinny fine, and he dreams of adoption. Everyone likes Skinny but at the end of a happy summer the dreaded orphanage is inevitable. The board has refused Miss Bessie's request to adopt Skinny because she is unmarried. Everyone keeps saying, "The orphanage is only forty miles away." To which Skinny replies sadly, "Forty miles is a far piece." And so it is, a far piece from love and a home. But at least he can return to Miss Bessie for vacations and at long last he is going to learn to read and write. It is a sad ending but somehow the right one, for the reader knows that Skinny will make out wherever he lands. He'll put his grief behind him and do with a flourish whatever there is to do.

In Joseph Ullman's older book *Banner in the Sky,* Rudi also saw his bright hope destroyed. This is a new step for children in their reading and in facing life. Things do not always come out happily in the end. Hopes are blasted, struggles are defeated, but the young reader must catch from his reading the image of the hero who picks himself up after defeat to make a new start. That is what reading in these last years of childhood must reiterate, and that is what all of Rosemary Sutcliff's magnificent historical novels are saying over and over . . . get your good readers into these books as soon as they can handle them.

Still another kind of courage, often thankless, is the patient's plodding courage to endure. The recent *Across Five Aprils* by Irene Hunt tells such a story. It is another Civil War book, usual in subject but unusual in treatment. Five years of war are seen through the eyes of Jethro, a farm boy, nine years old when war begins and fourteen when it ends. With his brothers gone off to fight, his father paralyzed, even his beloved school master gone too, all the back breaking toil of maintaining the farm falls on young Jethro. The unusual quality of this book lies in the vivid portrayal of every person in the story, even minor characters. It is a beautifully written chronicle of the enduring courage of one unsung hero, a boy, who did what had to be done.

Another 1964 story of courage at a more mature level is Ann Petry's relentless account of the Salem witch-hunting hysteria, *Tituba of Salem Village.* Tituba was a slave, and from her arrival in Salem, her dark skin and unusual skills made her suspect. There is a grim foreboding and suspense about this story of mounting evil that grips the reader from the first page to the last. Yet with others hanged or burned, Tituba, honest, brave, and patient, miraculously survived. Only mature readers can take this bitter record of white civilization gone wrong. But it has a message for today, not underlined in the book, but there nevertheless. This is probably the most powerful book of the season in the juvenile field, not to be missed by good readers.

Conclusion

In suggesting some of the needs of children at different ages that books can help to satisfy, the list began with reassuring love and independent achievement. It ends with much of the same—compassionate love and the kind of courage that is another phase of achievement. These qualities, by the way, motivate fiction for all ages and help to tie children's books into the whole stream of literature. But in children's books, the quality of love must grow and change as the child matures, until he can begin to see himself vicariously through his book heroes as loved and bestowing love, as dealing compassionately with others and, above all, as picking himself up after failures or shattered hopes or grievous mistakes to try again. These are some of the things strong books can do for children besides giving them keen enjoyment.

Books can show them patterns of compassionate love and courageous achievement of many kinds.

62. Making Books Come Alive for Children *

NANCY LARRICK

WHEN a three-year-old brings you a book to read, don't be surprised if it is about pollution or a man-made satellite. These are hot subjects today, even with the very young; and adults had better take heed.

If you would make books come alive for a child, I know of no better way to begin than with the child. He *is* alive. His interests and concerns will make the book come to life for him. Oddly enough many an adult tries to make books come alive for a child by beginning with his own childhood interests. Frequently they lead to a dismal let-down.

Know Today's Children

Today's children are different from the children we remember we were. They have different interests; they are using different words. Indeed, they are living in a different world. A second grader made this dramatically clear to me when I

* From Nancy Larrick, "Making Books Come Alive for Children," *Childhood Education*, XXXVIII, no. 7 (March, 1962) 311–15. Copyright © 1962 by the Association for Childhood Education International. Reprinted by permission of the author and the Association for Childhood Education International, 3615 Wisconsin Ave., N.W., Washington, D.C. 20016. (Dr. Larrick has made a few changes to bring this paper up to date.)

used the term, "prehistoric times." "Do you mean prehistoric times before television?" he asked.

That stopped me in mid-sentence until I began to think of the shattering changes in our society since television began a new era.

Mass media bombard the modern home with world news. Technical terms are brought from their old hide-out in the laboratory to become the language of the general public, including children. Nowadays children's interests are often as adult as their vocabulary. If you have any doubts, check the toy counter of the nearest five-and-ten. You will see space ships and satellites but few teddy bears and baby dolls. The little red wagon has almost faded away.

Librarians report growing demand for children's books about outer space. Some first-graders are rejecting cowboy stories as too babyish. Instead, they are asking for books about radiation. Fifth and sixth graders often turn to adult books as more appealing than those written for young readers. *The Incredible Journey* (1) and *The Inner City Mother Goose* (2) are favorites with this age level.

Television producers receive quantities of juvenile fan mail about programs created for adults. Apparently children and their parents have the same reading interests and are viewing the same TV programs. Many of these deal with the conflicts and confusions of what we have been calling the adult world. It is small wonder, then, that today's child turns to books with expectations different from those of the child of 1930 or even of 1950. Through television, in particular, a child is likely to establish certain habits which affect his approach to books. For one thing, he is used to making a choice. His TV set permits him to select the program he will view. If one channel does not please him he switches to another. He is used to being part of the adult world, watching the same television programs with his parents and exchanging views on an equal basis.

By Way of Contrast

Imagine a child coming from this kind of world into the traditional classroom. He reads, "Oh! Oh! See. See. Come. Come," in a book selected for him. He meets with a group, also selected for him, to hear others read the same colorless words at a pace that is not his own. And, as one youngster put it, "We read and read, but nothing ever happens in the story."

But something may be happening in the mind and heart of the child himself. He may be deciding that reading is deadly dull and therefore not for him. He may be finding out that this kind of book talks down to him ("Come, children," says Mother. "Come.") while television makes a man out of him, giving him the same straight talk that it gives his parents.

Further, he may rebel against the slow pace of the three-group lock step that means *read, listen, and wait*. He may not register his protest verbally. But, TV-trained as he is, he may tune out that which is not appealing. Daydreaming is one way to do it. Wriggling and squirming and interrupting are other ways.

Let Him Choose the Books

When a child is given the opportunity to choose the book he will read, he begins to see things in a different light. This is what he has done all his life with television. It is the procedure approved by the world outside of school.

If each child is to have a choice, there must be many books from which to select: easy books for the slow reader; more advanced books for the better reader; baseball books; fairy tales; biographies; books about jet planes and outer space, about the moon and deep-sea diving. There must be fiction and nonfiction, poetry and prose.

Unless a child has been used to selecting books for himself, he will need some guidance. He may resent guidance of the "see-see-read-read" variety. But he will welcome guidance that is as straightforward as a newscaster's report.

The second-grader with a yen for monsters will welcome Maurice Sendak's *Where the Wild Things Are* (3). His older brother who is a racing car fan will thank you for suggesting *Chitty-Chitty-Bang-Bang* by Ian Fleming (4). Youngsters who cherish a pet will be keen on *Owls in the Family* by Farley Mowat (5) or *Gentle Ben* by Walt Morey (6).

A book comes alive when it is in the hands of an interested reader. When an interest is already astir in the child, all you have to do is help him find the book which will kindle that interest further. That is the easiest kind of guidance.

To make it even simpler, there are numerous book lists which group favorite children's books by subject and age level. By using the index in the book list and reading the annotations, you have some guidelines by which to aid children in selecting books. Soon fourth- and fifth-graders will be consulting the same book lists when they choose books. Today's children like self-service, even in books.

Make the Introduction Alive and Personal

Beyond this, it is important to introduce children to new interests and to open new vistas which will lead to books. This is where the fun begins—the challenge, if you will—for a child's adventures into new kinds of books and new kinds of subjects depend in large part on the introduction he gets from adults.

A printed list of recommended books won't do it. Certainly, required reading selected by adults won't do it—not today, when children are accustomed to the spoken word of radio and television, to hearing enthusiastic, firsthand reports of world affairs and commercial products.

Take a tip from TV and make your introduction of a new book just as vital, just as personal. First read the book yourself; reread it if there's been a time lapse, letting yourself bask in its humor or pathos or whimsy.

Then while you are still aglow with it, read a chapter or two to children. Your delight in the book will show in the way you read it, and children will sense your enthusiasm. Soon they will want to be a part of it and ask for more.

Some of the real gems of children's literature need this kind of read-aloud introduction. Tell a ten-year-old that *Charlotte's Web,* by E. B. White (7), is about a talking spider, and he may shy away. But read aloud part of that remarkable book, and Charlotte will have another devotee. The interest and sympathy in your voice and the magic of Charlotte's personality will do the trick.

Sam, Bangs and Moonshine by Evaline Ness (8) and *Zeely* by Virginia Hamilton (9) profit from the same kind of introduction. Indeed, any book does. Read aloud a few chapters of a book you have already read and are sold on, and a listener's indifference is likely to vanish.

This is true for poetry, too. But you will have to read and reread before you meet your audience. The misreading of poetry can be as discordant as a soloist off key, and a dull listless voice will deaden interest from the start.

If your children have not been hearing poetry lately, begin with something light such as the poems in *A Little Laughter,* an anthology compiled by Katherine Love (10). Or try *The Arrow Book of Poetry,* a paperback collecton of poems for every mood (11). There is gentle humor and pathos in the exquisite poems of *Prayers from the Ark* by Carmen Bernos de Gasztold (12).

Remember, too, that children today are used to seeing as well as hearing, so share the pictures as you read. In *Charlotte's Web,* Garth Williams' pictures of Wilbur the pig are irresistible. Even the most hard-bitten fifth-grade missile expert will soften before Wilbur's contented smile as he stands under Charlotte's Web.

When you read *The Snowy Day* by Ezra Jack Keats (13) or *Where the Wild Things Are* by Maurice Sendak (3), hold the pages so that children can see the pictures as you read. Here, as in many of the best children's books, the illustrations add information, charm, and even suspense to the words.

Young and Old Alike

The best books for children have a quality which appeals to young and old alike. Try *Crictor* (14) on some of your contemporaries, for example, and I think you will find them as charmed as the children. Or read *The Fiddler of High Lonesome* (15) or *A Certain Small Shepherd* (16) and watch the reaction. Such books have a subtlety, a sophistication if you wish, that lifts them above grade-level limitations.

Watch for this as you search for books to introduce to today's children. Before you bring a book to a class, give it the read-aloud test. If it flows rhythmically to your adult ears, the chances are it will appeal to readers atune to adult oral-language media. If it speaks in the straightforward manner accorded grown-ups, children will be pleased.

If you are intrigued by the information in a book of nonfiction or glowing with satisfaction over a book of fiction, you can be sure that most children will do likewise.

It's up to you!

References

1. BURNFORD, SHEILA. *The Incredible Journey*. Boston: Little, Brown, 1961.
2. MERRIAM, EVE. *The Inner City Mother Goose*. Bloomfield, N.J.: Simon and Schuster, 1969.
3. SENDAK, MAURICE. *Where the Wild Things Are*. New York: Harper, 1963.
4. FLEMING, IAN. *Chitty-Chitty-Bang-Bang*. New York: Random House, 1964.
5. MOWAT, FARLEY. *Owls in the Family*. Boston: Little, Brown, 1961.
6. MOREY, WALT. *Gentle Ben*. New York: Dutton, 1965.
7. WHITE, E. B. *Charlotte's Web*. New York: Harper, 1952.
8. NESS, EVALINE. *Sam, Bangs and Moonshine*. New York: Holt, 1966.
9. HAMILTON, VIRGINIA. *Zeeley*. New York: Macmillan, 1967.
10. LOVE, KATHERINE. *A Little Laughter*. New York: Crowell, 1957.
11. McGOVERN, ANN. *Arrow Book of Poetry*. New York: Scholastic, 1965.
12. BERNOS DE GASZTOLD, CARMEN. *Prayers from the Ark*. New York: Viking, 1962.
13. KEATS, EZRA JACK. *The Snowy Day*. New York: Viking, 1962.
14. UNGERER, TOMI. *Crictor*. New York: Harper, 1958.
15. TURKLE, BRINTON. *The Fiddler of High Lonesome*. New York: Viking, 1968.
16. CAUDILL, REBECCA. *A Certain Small Shepherd*. New York: Holt, 1965.

63. How Elementary School Teachers and Librarians Work Together *

OLIVIA R. WAY

ONLY in recent years has the school library been recognized as a fundamental part of the elementary school program. As school systems throughout the country develop, enlarge, and enrich their library programs, teachers are discovering, and indeed are promoting, the library as a vital aid to their classroom teaching and are drawing more constantly on its resources and the help of the librarian.

Throughout the Ridgewood schools, as our library facilities are improved and our staff is increased, there are more opportunities for teachers and librarians to work closely together to give the children the full benefit of the library resources. Much of the librarian's time is spent in reading guidance. Since knowing the child is often essential to the success of finding the right book for him, the librarian turns to the teacher for help in knowing more about him. Numerous and varied techniques involving the library are used to aid in the teaching of reading. They may be changed or modified, or new ones devised to fit a particular need. They are most successful when there is understanding and careful planning between the classroom teacher and the librarian— the teacher giving the librarian insight into the children's needs, and the teacher and the librarian working together to find ways to meet these needs.

* From Olivia R. Way, "How Elementary School Teachers and Librarians Work Together," *Rading Teacher,* 17 (December, 1963), 159–63, 169. Reprinted by permission of the International Reading Association and the author.

Only a few of the specific practices which have proved effective in Ridgewood elementary schools can be described here.

It has been the general practice throughout the primary grades (kindergarten through second) to have the children themselves choose books from the library for their classroom collection (teachers choose books also, of course), and from this collection each child may borrow one book at a time to take home. This means, if he wishes, he may take a different book every day. The teacher keeps a very simple record of each book a child borrows, making sure one book is returned before another is taken.

Occasionally, there are variations of this plan. For example, one small kindergarten class borrowed books in their own names directly from the library for a while. In another kindergarten a little boy had been reading with real skill for some time before he came to school. After the teacher and the librarian had talked with his parents he was invited to come to the library to choose three or four books to take home. These were loaned to him directly. He read them to himself, read them aloud to his little sister, and shared them with his parents. He was permitted to change the books whenever he had finished them and was ready for a fresh collection, usually in about a week.

Occasionally, after the librarian has shared a book with a primary grade in the library and the book has been taken to the classroom, the teacher has used it as a central theme around which she has planned classroom activities. A first-grade teacher used such a book as stimulation for a creative art lesson, for rhythms, for word recognition; she then developed a little choral speaking program around it, which was shared with the librarian during one of their library visits. The art work was displayed in the library.

A second-grade teacher had an advanced reading group. As the first half of the year progressed, it was apparent that these children needed more books, and books with higher reading level and wider interest range than those they had been using. The teacher and the librarian decided that the children together should choose library books for their reading group. They planned in advance for the group's first visit to the library. The teacher shared with the librarian her knowledge of each child. Before the group came to the library the teacher and the children talked about the plan and listed some ideas about choosing their books. They discussed the kinds of books they might like to read and the importance of sampling the books when choosing, to try to select one that appeals and one that is not too easy or too difficult. Each child was permitted to choose two or three books. The books were a part of the classroom collection. They were read in the reading group and outside the reading group; they were taken home to be read; they were discussed, exchanged, and sometimes shared in original ways with the entire class and with the librarian. As the group finished with the books they were returned to the library and the children chose a fresh collection. This procedure continued throughout the school year.

There was no concrete evidence as to whether or not this little project contributed directly to the improvement shown in the children's reading scores. However, there were other positive and worthwhile results that were easily discernible. En-thusiasm for reading increased and continued at a high level. The range of interests widened. The ability to choose books improved. In their enjoyment of discussing and sharing books the children gained poise and confidence. Of course, this kind of activity need not be confined to an advanced group of second graders, but might be used, with variations according to the need, for any group at any grade level.

Reading aloud to little children is an accepted practice, but all too many teachers of upper elementary grades do not read aloud to their children. Reading aloud should be considered an essential part of the classroom program, no matter what the grade. Reading aloud is enjoyment shared. It provides pleasure for the children and the teacher. It is a source of stimulation to a child's own reading. It is important that what the teacher chooses to read aloud has quality and purpose. The selection should be made with great care. There may be an occasion, of course, when a teacher will choose to read a brief portion of a book to encourage the children to read alone. But, particularly in the upper grades, it is the reading of a full-length book, chapter by chapter, or section by section, that gives the children the joy of looking forward from one day's reading to the next. The choice should be something unusual, a book the children might not choose to read themselves, but one that in the sharing comes alive, opens up new worlds, and suggests new ideas. The librarian can help by suggesting several books from which the teacher may choose the one that seems most suitable for his class. A variety of books—biography, travel, mythology, folk literature, poetry, nature study, and science, as well as fiction— might be tried throughout the year. The children will probably go back to some of these books that are pleasantly remembered, and read them for themselves with renewed enjoyment. The elementary school librarians in Ridgewood are now preparing a suggested bibliography of books that seem especially suitable for reading aloud. The titles will be grouped for primary, middle, and upper elementary grades, and each title will have a brief annotation. The list will go to the teachers for their comments and suggestions before it is put into its final form.

An imaginative teacher with a class of bright third graders devised a scheme for vocabulary building that involved the library and proved to be great fun for the class. Each time the class returned to their room after a visit to the library they were permitted to read their library books, and were asked to list on a piece of paper any words they found in their reading that they did not know. They could do this whenever they read, if they wished to. These papers were given to the teacher. She transposed each word onto a single card, using the primary typewriter. The next day she gave each child his own cards. The children then found the dictionary definition for each word and wrote it on the card. The new words and definitions were shared with the class. Each child arranged his cards in alphabetical order. As the year progressed each one had his own set of vocabulary cards. The words were used for the spelling lessons and for any vocabulary study that was done. The children devised games that they played in groups and in pairs, and sometimes they exchanged their sets of cards. This scheme could be used in any upper grade group, and the children themselves would discover ways and means to make it their own.

One day the librarian handed a fourth-grade teacher a new collection of poems which she thought would appeal to her and her class. In a few weeks the class gave an assembly program of choral speaking using some of the poems from the collection. At the end of the program, in a rather intriguing way, they announced that the book could be found in the library. Of course, there were numerous requests for the book.

Book discussions have been carried on in the upper grades with considerable success. Patterns of procedure vary according to the librarian and the class group that is participating. A first essential is the teacher's interest and enthusiasm for the idea and his continued support.

In one school the librarian has used a panel discussion. The librarian suggests a book to be discussed, and the panel members are chosen by the teacher from volunteers in the class. As many children as possible are given an opportunity to participate on a panel during the year. The panel members read the book, choose a moderator, and plan the discussion with the advice of the teacher and the librarian, who, of course, have read the book. In his planning the teacher allows as much time as is necessary for preparation. A few broad general questions are formulated so that when the real discussion takes place, the panel will have a lively, extemporaneous exchange of ideas which will be fresh and original. Several copies of the book have been made available to the class in advance so that all who wished to read it have done so. They are encouraged to react to what the panel says, or express their own opinions and ideas. With multiple copies of the book available, ten days to two weeks seems to be ample time to allow for the preparation.

Some panels do well in expressing ideas and giving their reactions to the book, but their organization is weak. Other panels are well organized but miss some pertinent points that should be brought out. "Sometimes," to quote the librarian, "a panel combines the two to an extent that awes me with their maturity and ability."

In another school the group discussion plan is used and the entire class participates. In this school, the library has a collection of paperbacks (about ten or fifteen copies of each of forty books) which is used specifically for this purpose. The teacher and the librarian together decide which book or books the class will read, and set a date for the discussion. Ten days to two weeks is the usual time allotted to read the books, so that everyone will have read them before the class comes to the library to discuss them. When two books are related in some way, they are read and discussed together: for example, Enid Meadowcroft's *Silver for General Washington* (4) and Marie McSwigan's *Snow Treasure* (3). Both are about children courageously serving their country in time of war. Although they take place in different periods of history and in different countries, they have much in common. This contributes to good discussion.

The discussion begins with a résumé of the book given by a child who has volunteered. Then the discussion grows, guided, but allowed to run freely, depending on what is of most interest to the children. This leads into an evaluation of content, characters, and ideas. The classroom teacher participates in the discussion also, because he too has read the book.

One advanced group of fifth and sixth graders (a combination class) read and discussed separately *The Incredible Journey* by Sheila Burnford, *Wind in the Willows* by Kenneth Grahame (2), and *Charlotte's Web* and *Stuart Little* by E. B. White (5,6). Finally they had a kind of summary discussion of the four books. Some of the questions which brought forth good ideas and opinions were:

What is fantasy?
Are any or all of these books fantasy?
Give a reason to support your opinion.
Which character in each book did you like the most and why?
Was there any character you disliked, and why?

The answers to these and other questions made it quite evident that these children had read with perception and insight, had enjoyed the reading, and were eager to express their opinions.

Essential to the success of this activity are the positive attitudes the classroom teacher establishes as the idea is first introduced and the flexibility of the daily program in the classroom to provide many opportunities for the children to read. Basic to the entire idea is the constant communication between the teacher and the librarian. Each must know what the other is doing and what has happened in their contacts with the children.

This kind of book discussion may be used successfully with slow reluctant readers as well as with average and above average enthusiastic readers. Titles used for the slow groups are different from those used for the advanced groups. To quote one enthusiastic teacher whose class of reluctant readers showed real interest in this kind of reading project, "Whether the standardized tests have shown improvement or not, the teacher, the librarian, and a good number of the parents are willing to testify that no matter what this reading program did for the children in their school work, it has taught them that reading is fun. It has given them a pleasure that was not heretofore available to them."

The book discussion in whatever form has some valuable outcomes:

1. Group discussion of one or two books is very stimulating.

2. There is an exchange of ideas which may be new to some in the group.

3. The informal, relaxed atmosphere of the discussion encourages some to participate who might otherwise be reluctant to make an oral contribution before the class.

4. Group discussion provides opportunity for the organization of ideas expressed orally.

5. Each child is encouraged to express his opinion (pro or con) freely, but sound reasons for his opinion must be given.

6. Discussion of characters and important incidents in the book aid in developing sound and critical judgment.

In all our efforts, experience seems to underline the importance of teacher-librarian communication and understanding if good results are to be achieved.

References

1. BURNFORD, SHEILA. *The Incredible Journey.* New York: Bantam Books, 1961.

2. GRAHAME, KENNETH. *Wind In the Willows.* New York: Scribners, 1961.

3. McSWIGAN, MARIE. *Snow Treasure.* New York: Scholastic Book Services, 1942.

4. MEADOWCROFT, ENID. *Silver for General Washington.* New York: Scholastic Book Services. 1957.

5. WHITE, E. B. *Charlotte's Web.* New York: Harper, 1952.

6. ————. *Stuart Little.* New York: Harper, 1945.

Dept. of Curric. & Instruction
College of Education
University of Wyoming
Laramie, Wyoming 82070

XIII

Materials for the Reading Program

A vast amount of material is now available for teaching reading. The purpose of this chapter is to present ideas as to how some materials that have long been available and more recent innovations might be employed to develop a more effective reading program.

O'Leary opens by explaining the reasons she feels use of a basal reader series provides for the best instructional (developmental) reading program. Next Thompson relates the "whys and hows" of workbooks and teachers' manuals. Sucher's article suggests how to set up three types of classroom reading centers and the purposes for each; and the use of audio-visual aids in teaching reading is discussed by DeBernardis. Finally, Calvin tells how to use programmed textbooks.

64. Preserve the Basic Reading Program *

HELEN F. O'LEARY

So many adverse criticisms and so many provocative questions are being voiced about the limitations, the regimentation, the lock-step tendencies, and the alleged monotony of the basic reading program technique that a comprehensive review of its possibilities and an evaluation of its

* From Helen F. O'Leary, "Preserve the Basic Reading Program." Reprinted from the September 1963 issue of *Education,* pp. 12–16. Copyright © 1963 by The Bobbs-Merrill Company, Inc., Indianapolis, Ind.

recommended procedures deserve to be presented and evaluated.

Moreover, despite the introduction of many versions of individualized reading instruction plans which tend to displace and discourage the use of basic reader series, and despite the increasing use of multi-level reading kits, this basic reading series program still continues to maintain its status as the most widely used and the most popularly known equipment for one important part of an effective reading program—namely, the developmental phase wherein sequential aspects of reading growth are analyzed, recognized, planned for, and carefully paced through a series of graded readers arranged in levels of reading difficulty.

Obviously, teaching materials are enriched or impoverished by those who administer them, and a teaching tool without a good teacher becomes a weak and barren instrument. Therefore, it is my opinion that in the hands of a competent and imaginative teacher the basic reading series can contribute most effectively to the so-called developmental phase of the reading program.

In fact, the features which comprise the essential steps in the teaching procedure of a basic reading series correspond to the principal steps in an effective lesson plan for any type of subject-matter presentation.

What are these steps which are common both to a basic reading setup and a good lesson plan?

Readiness for Reading

Introduction of Vocabulary

First, there is readiness or preparation for reading. In this vital introductory program the teacher sets the stage with the introduction of all necessary vocabulary, development of concepts, establishment of reading purpose, and building of adequate background. In this part of the reading plan the richness or paucity of the teacher's skill becomes the potent and deciding factor.

Since reading lessons form such a major part of a day's work, oftentimes dull routine and take-it-for-granted attitudes characterize stilted reading lessons which become meaningless, uninspiring, and nonproductive. But imagine the contrast when a teacher realizes and utilizes countless ways for introducing words!

For the teacher who possesses knowl-edge, ingenuity, and skill in presentation of vocabulary a reading lesson gets off to a stimulating and interesting start:

1. Using *concrete objects* which are readily available, such as a darning needle, an abacus, a compass, an avocado, a jigsaw puzzle.
2. Showing *pictures* to depict native costumes, a seashore, a horizon, types of animals, colors, types of homes.
3. Running *filmstrips* to develop concepts of irrigation, conservation, the solar system, the making of honey, etc.
4. Utilizing *moving pictures* to give enough information about sheep shearing, wheat farming, lumbering, the meat packing industry, a rodeo, and other activities not a part of the community scene.
5. Telling *stories* to exemplify the meaning of greatness, poverty, humility, heroism, or some other abstract quality.
6. Taking *field trips* to have direct contact with such areas as an airport, papermaking, samples of erosion, kinds of trees, moss, a silo, a state capitol.
7. Holding *conversations* to build gradually such appreciations and understandings as the work of pilots, postmen, or scientists or conversing to gauge the scope of knowledge possessed by the class.
8. Arranging *display tables* to present objects and symbols characteristic of any central theme of a unit of stories such as pioneer life, inventors, reference books.
9. Analyzing by *structural analysis* to discover how words have been built, such as *discouragement, unhappy, mislaid,* or *refreshment.*
10. Relating *word histories* which reveal how words originated such as *boycott, bonfire, fallout.*
11. Illustrating by diagramming words which lend themselves to this technique such as a *perpendicular line,* a *cataract,* a *plateau.*
12. Suggesting by *clues* which encourage students to guess or analyze the mysterious word which can be concealed until

a successful solution is reached—words like *cotton, cellophane, brick, petrified wood, memento.*

13. Displaying *a series of three or four pictures* which suggest one common adjective such as *enthusiastic, anxious, young,* or *daring.*

Naturally such preparation for vocabulary presentation cannot represent any spur-of-the-moment preparation. However, neither is it a mammoth undertaking, for it is almost a point of view about the importance of this step that matters. A teacher who is aware of varieties of techniques in word presentation will know how to combine methods, motivate challenging word reviews, prepare classes interestingly for vocabulary tests, and in general add spark and vitality to a lesson.

This mode of word introduction truly represents a far cry from the too-common method in which a teacher puts a word on the board in one context situation, acquaints the children with the fact that this is the new word, and admonishes them to remember it. Such a teacher, who may be pressuring to get to the reading book, will need time to be converted comfortably to this point of view about word presentation, but she will soon recognize that more challenging learning situations are paying dividends.

Building Background

Building background, the second part of the preparation for reading, is, of course, very closely related to the previous task of vocabulary development. This phase also imposes tremendous responsibility upon the teacher, who must appraise the environment in which the children live, the first-hand and vicarious experiences they have had, and the background required for full comprehension of the story.

For example, children who live in a dairy-farm community contribute rather than require knowledge about such a farm. However, these same children might associate an erroneous concept with the elevator in the big city or evince absolute ignorance concerning the "dumb waiter" in the apartment block or the escalator in the department store. A class in Pennsylvania can be a resource expert about mining and greatly supplement a teacher's knowledge.

Definitely the teacher must realize that many children in the class are experts and resource persons in various areas. It should be her privilege and pleasure not only to discover the stamp collector, the expert fisherman, the skillful golfer, the clever dressmaker, and the budding cook, but also to arrange situations for children to reveal their expertness. Rarely will the child forget the teacher who arranged for him to have a "red-letter" day, and fortunate is the class led by a teacher who releases all channels of learning whether from pupils or teacher.

Establishing a Purpose

Establishing a purpose for reading the story is the last step in preparation for reading. Allowing a reader to have some question that needs to be answered is a stimulus to thoughtful and intelligent inquiry.

Thus, this first major part of the plan preparation consists of presentation of vocabulary, building of necessary background, and establishment of reading purpose.

Interpreting the Story

The second major step, interpreting the story, concerns itself with the actual reading and takes in both silent and oral aspects, with silent reading always preceding oral reading.

In the primary grades silent reading takes the form of so-called "guided reading" in which the teacher with pertinent questions motivates the silent reading of a short section which may be a paragraph or a page. The answers to these questions and the resultant discussion aid considerably in developing fuller comprehension and preparing for later interpretative reading.

For children with limited reading skill guided reading is a most valuable aid, for questions asked by the teacher often clear up misconceptions, errors in pronunciation, and stir up waning interest. Then comes the oral reading, which in the beginning stages of reading growth should merit careful supervision and evaluation.

Teachers in primary grades should establish criteria for good reading and guard against their students' becoming accustomed to poor reading. Good oral reading, for instance, should simulate a child's normal conversational tone and pace. Any artificial speech inflection, a marked difference in pace between reading and speaking, difficulties in word perception, and signs of uneasiness and fidgeting should be recognized as symptoms of reading difficulty.

At this stage in the reading plan teachers should improvise reasons for rereading such as, "Mary, how would you read that page?" or "Remember, Father was a little puzzled about what was happening. Can you read that page so that you will sound like Father?" Or, reassign the same lesson for dramatization or audience reading for another day. Let a pair of children try to reread the entire story to each other without a mistake.

In the intermediate grade levels the lesson either in parts or in entirety is read silently without the direct guidance of the teacher but always in response to a definite pre-established purpose or purposes. This is followed by a discussion directed by the teacher's questions, which again aids comprehension, tests for reactions and inferences, and stimulates interest. Oral reading at intermediate grade levels occurs only when specific purposes can be established and can be justified.

In some stories only vocabulary may be stressed—for example words which express action or denote color. In other stories sequential elements may be emphasized. In still other selections parts of the stories may be reread in order to answer specific questions, and in exciting and interesting stories rereading or dramatization may be suggested.

Thus, in the second major phase of the plan, silent and oral reading characterize the activities.

Development of Word Analysis

In the third major phase comes the area most often neglected but vitally needed, the development of word analysis skills. Actually, the stories have been selected, written, and arranged to provide a frame of reference, as background of understanding for the presentation of these skills. And it is in this part of the basic reading series that the teacher realizes that reading is a sequential skill, for one glance at the index of skills, listed in the basic reader, reveals the vast number of separate abilities which the good reader must possess.

In this stage of the plan the teacher's manual is most helpful in supplying specific sentences, word lists, questions, and seatwork necessary to promote proficiency and to provide variety. The workbooks, also, are specifically geared to supplement the lesson.

However, even though these workbooks are regarded as independent activities, they are independent only in the final analysis. Enough help and direction should be presented in an actual reading period so that when children are on their own, these activities can be performed with a high degree of accuracy and assurance. Moreover, they should be corrected carefully and thoroughly in another reading period with each child having an opportunity to evaluate and inspect his own results.

Thus, the third phase of the basic reading plan, the teaching of word analysis, is an essential step requiring an extensive knowledge on the part of the teacher.

Extension of Interests

The final phase of the basic reading program, referred to as the extension of interests or related enrichment activities, can prove to be very enjoyable, but again it often represents one aspect of the plan which is entirely omitted.

What prompts a teacher to minimize this phase of the program? First of all, many teachers do not see the relation between these activities and the teaching of reading. However, the enrichment offered by suggesting stories to be read either by the teacher to the children, or by the children independently, the rhythmic activities which emphasize the tone of the story, the suggested art activities, the records, films, and filmstrips all strongly indicate that a basic reading program does not have to be a stilted monotonous routine. The program will be as alive as the teacher who directs it.

In this phase of the program reading really joins hands with the other aspects of the language arts—poetry, choral reading, storytelling, independent reading suggestions, vocabulary illustration, outlines through scenes in a mural, original stories, and other enrichment activities.

Oftentimes a teacher can even in a three-group situation turn these activities into entire class activities. The storytelling, the independent reading, the poetry activities, the rhythmic interpretations can furnish life to the daily language lessons. However, the teacher must not favor any one group but must introduce a book by some reference such as the following:

"Jim's group enjoyed the story about *Red Flame.*"

"This story of *Black Beauty* is a story about a horse that children have enjoyed. I'll read you the introductory chapter, and then I'll put it on the library table."

"Mary's group has finished its unit on pioneer stories. Let's imagine what activities children had then and let us compare them with your activities."

"Who are our modern pioneers?"

With a superior group a teacher can read from the manual the suggested activities and let each member of the group choose one for class or group presentation.

Conclusion

In this review of the typical plan in the basic reading series it becomes quite evident that there are ample opportunities for originality, ingenuity, variety, and imagination for the teacher who utilizes all phases of the basic series program.

Moreover, instead of disregarding entirely the philosophy behind individualized or personal selection plans for reading, the resourceful teacher incorporates these ideas into a strong recreational or free reading program, another important phase of the total reading program. With the further addition of a functional reading phase, an effective reading program is being planned for and utilized to develop readers for all purposes.

65. The Purposes of Workbooks and Teachers' Guides *

MARTHA THOMPSON ORR

THEY didn't just happen. We realize this when we look at the open pages of a complete series of reading workbooks and teachers' guides which are used in our schools today. What refinement has taken place in these tools, which enable teachers to guide boys and girls to successful experiences in understanding the printed page!

How Workbooks Developed

The child of yesteryear used a slate on which to practice the learnings that his teacher thought basic to his reading program. Today's child moves from reading level to reading level with the aid of scientifically planned workbooks. Between the time of the slate and today's workbook, there came a period of worksheets that were planned by the teacher to accompany the reading stories of the textbook in use at the particular grade level. Planning and duplicating the worksheet took much of the teacher's time and energy. Often the children were unable to read that which they saw before them. The inability to read the assignment might have been due to the teacher's lack of knowledge of worksheet preparation. The vocabulary in the lesson may have been unrelated to that of the reader. The print

* From Martha Thompson, "The Purposes of Workbooks and Teachers' Guides," in *Materials for Reading,* Supplementary Education Monographs, No. 86, compiled and edited by Helen M. Robinson (December, 1957), pp. 71–74. Reprinted by permission of the author and The University of Chicago Press.

may have been too light, or the teacher's printing may not have even resembled the type on the printed page. Sometimes teachers used cursive writing instead of manuscript, and then the children were really lost. Beyond all of this, perhaps the teacher thought of only two or three basic skills that were being taught in reading and therefore prepared worksheets that were much the same day after day. Materials were wasted; the teacher's and the pupils' time was wasted; and learning moved at a slow pace compared with the potential rate of development.

Two teaching aids were developed to upgrade the program. Duplicating machines appeared and brought results—if the teacher was not in too big a hurry or too tired to produce master sheets which were definitely related to the reading text and to the child's and the group's needs and, most important of all, which provided for developmental growth in basic skills and abilities. Then too, workbooks appeared, but they were unrelated to the reading textbook and therefore failed to contribute to the growth potential which was awaiting development.

Modern Workbooks

The modern teacher knows, just as the teacher of yesteryear knew, that children need an opportunity to extend their basic learnings through practice. Today's teacher knows that the workbook which the child uses with his basic textbook is planned by skilled educators who have the knowledge of how best to develop specific skills and abilities from level to level in a sequential and systematic pattern of growth. The teacher knows that this "doing book" parallels the reader, complements it, and adds a variety of extending and enriching experiences. He knows, too, that there are workbooks which are textbooks in themselves (such as prereading workbooks for developing readiness) and review workbooks (such as those for use between the elementary and the junior high school grades). As the teacher is a member of a staff of instructors in reading, he takes in the entire "doing" program in order to help the child at his own level of learning. The teacher knows best the grade levels below and above his own grade. He realizes that workbooks should be used at every level to build toward independence.

A step-by-step procedure for using workbooks might be as follows: (1) The teacher works with the group, from the reading of the directions to the doing of the exercises, checking for and correcting any misunderstandings. (2) Without pencils, the teacher and the group work through the workbook page. The teacher then releases the children to print or write and finally evaluates, with each pupil, his strengths and his weaknesses. (3) The teacher and group, without pencils, work halfway through a page together, and the pupils are then released to work the entire page to the point of completion and correction. (4) The teacher and group work one sample together, and then each pupil works alone. (5) The children interpret to the teacher what they are to do, and they go on from there independently until the results are checked by the teacher. This procedure calls for teacher-pupil planning, as well as the use of class time to develop the plans and to evaluate the outcomes.

The workbook can be used as a diagnostic tool. As the teacher works with the children in evaluating (finding their errors and correcting them), he can list, on the particular page in his own workbook, the names of the pupils who will need more guidance when the basic skill is reviewed. If the workbook carries an index of basic skills, the child's name can be recorded on the very page presenting the same skill. (This is an excellent way to account for absentees and to make sure that they receive the lessons for developing skills.) Because they mark their own workbook pages, the children, too, can see where they are in error and can correct the mistakes immediately. Won't they cheat? No child cheats when the atmosphere of the classroom is conducive to honesty and when he understands the purpose of the lesson.

The workbook is used for learning and not as a grading device. To grade workbook pages alerts the child to look for a grade instead of realizing the value of the lesson. Teachers who trudge home with shopping bags full of workbooks or stay long hours after school to grade or even to mark errors in workbooks are missing the real advantage of the use of a modern tool of education.

At teacher-parent conferences, workbooks may be used to indicate to the parents where the child's strengths and weaknesses are. The parents will be pleased to see successful pages, for, if the child is working at his ability level, such pages will be numerous. Parents will be pleased to see errors corrected because they will know the child has seen his mistakes and learned from them. Parents will find out that today's workbooks are planned not to keep the child quiet by merely keeping him busy but to increase his ability to read through purposeful activities.

The Teacher's Guide

The guide for today's workbook and today's reader is the teacher's guidebook.

It, too, has been improved through a series of changes. The first teacher's guide was probably the teacher's own plan of how to teach the reading lesson of the day. Then the author of the reading book probably thought that some teachers were missing the point, and he decided to tell them a little bit about how he would like to have his book used. Today's guidebook (thank goodness, it is no longer called a "manual") really does what it says! It guides the teacher so that teacher and pupils have successful experiences when using the reading books and the workbooks. Good guidebooks develop master teachers, who, through creative and thorough teaching, develop pupils who read up to, and beyond, their mental abilities.

A good guidebook reviews for the teacher the psychological development of the child who will be using the reader at a particular level. It requires the instructor to think of the mental, physical, and emotional development of the child in relation to the stories which are to be read and enjoyed while basic skills and abilities are being taught. The philosophy of the author of the particular series of books is presented, along with the objectives or goals to be reached. A basic or fundamental plan for developing and enriching the skills which are to be achieved is found in the guide. It may be a three-step or a four-step plan, but it has been established upon scientific findings to produce results.

Bibliographies have been added, listing titles of (1) supplementary readers which present stories related to those in the particular reader being used, (2) library books which are also related, (3) reference books, and (4) books for the teacher's own development. Lists of films and records are suggested to add to the extension and enrichment of the child's outside-the-book experiences. An index of the basic skills and abilities has been mentioned previously in connection with the workbook. Such a list is found again in the guidebook, and indications of the appropriate pages of the reader and workbook save the time of the teacher in planning for individual and group needs.

Additional assistance for teachers of the upper elementary grades may be found in an appendix, which lists exercises for constructive help. Suggestions for charts and record cards are made in the guidebook. Tests, to find out at what level a child is reading before beginning to work with him and then to find out how far he has come, are printed for duplication. A teacher who avoids the guidebook is like the cook who shuns the new, easy, efficient ways to arrive at a dish "fit to set before the king"; or the businessman who fails to read the bulletins which come in the mail to tell him how to produce better products with less waste of time, energy, and materials; or the doctor who stacks his medical journals on the side of his desk and misses the new and better ways to help his patients. Both the newcomer to the teaching profession and the teacher of experience need to know the contents of the guidebook peculiar to their respective grade levels and, to assure a stronger schoolwide program, those of the complete series as well.

Guidebooks must be used properly and faithfully, in sequence, if the program is to be successful. The teacher should always use them in planning the unit and then in planning the daily lesson. Day-to-day planning, month-to-month building, and year-to-year achievement will help boys and girls to acquire security through successful experiences assured by their strength in skills which have been developed by teacher after teacher. The teacher who is found using the guide is to be praised.

The guidebook, since it includes questions which arouse the children to think constructively and which set their imaginations on fire, is helping future citizens to share and compare in discussions that will lay the foundations for tomorrow's thinking adults. The teacher should be careful to state the questions exactly as they appear in the guide to insure responses which go beyond the usual replies to factual questions. Also, enough time should be allowed to let the children really express their feelings. Too often we rush over this wonderful opportunity to share and compare because we or someone else thinks we are wasting time.

Teachers, especially those who are experienced, should feel that, even when using the guidebooks, they can add their own ideas and use their own initiative in their work with individuals and groups. As long as the results of the teaching contribute to the growth of the child's ability to read, there can be no complaint. Child, classroom, and total school behavior can be improved by *how* reading is taught and *what* reading is done.

Concluding Statement

No, workbooks and guidebooks didn't just happen, and they shouldn't just happen to be chosen for use by the children whom we instruct in our classrooms of today. A good reading program should mean careful selection of guidebooks, readers, and workbooks to insure the development of basic skills and abilities so that our boys and girls may continue to thrill to the printed page.

66. Developing Classroom Reading Centers *

FLOYD SUCHER

THE idea of classroom reading centers is neither new nor original. Many classroom teachers have provided interest centers of various types. (Roach Van Allen has suggested many such types of centers in his lectures and publications.) Others have provided comfortable pieces of lounging furniture in nooks and corners of their classrooms where children could relax and enjoy a reading experience.

* From Floyd Sucher, "Developing Classroom Reading Centers," in William K. Durr (ed.), *Reading Difficulties: Diagnosis, Correction, and Remediation* (Newark, Del.: International Reading Association, 1970), pp. 180–87. Reprinted by permission of the International Reading Association and the author.

The classroom reading center brings stimulating points of interest and an abundance of reading materials to a comfortable setting where children can browse or read during free or directed periods of time.

The Purpose of a Classroom Reading Center

Every teacher has the challenge of helping children accomplish two major objectives in reading: (1) to learn how to read and (2) to develop a habit of and a love for reading. Classroom reading centers can help a teacher accomplish both of these objectives. By establishing and using a pleasant, comfortable reading atmosphere displaying many stimulating reading materials, a teacher can develop within children a love for reading, and, at the same time, provide practices in reading skills of the most meaningful nature.

Developing a Habit of and a Love for Reading

Where do adults do their free reading? In a straight, hard chair sitting at the kitchen table? Generally not. More than likely it is in a comfortable chair, lying on a couch, propped up on a pillow in bed, or perhaps lying on the floor. Most adults seek a comfortable, relaxed position in a warm, quiet atmosphere.

When do adults do their free reading? Most adults read on one of two occasions. One is when they have acquired a particular book, magazine, or reading material that has caught their interest. Under this condition they will plan to set aside a period (and a comfortable place) for reading it. On other occasions they will just move to a comfortable setting and the most available and stimulating activity will capture their attention. It may be the TV or it may be an interesting magazine, book, or pamphlet. It often depends on which is closest at hand.

A reading center should encourage both of the needs described in the above paragraphs. It will provide children with an inviting, comfortable setting and stimulating, interest-catching materials.

A well-prepared reading center can be one of the most valuable aspects of the classroom for setting a "reading mood" and for establishing a positive attitude toward school within children. Children who have had positive experiences with reading within the classroom will have "warm" feelings toward reading and school. Whether or not children will learn to enjoy reading through the use of a classroom reading center is dependent upon the degree to which their interest is captured by the materials in the center, the availability of reading materials at their reading levels, and the amount of time they are allowed to use the center. If these three conditions are met, children will spend much time browsing, playing, investigating, and reading in the center. Interest can be expanded in a very "painless" and natural way and children will begin to establish a satisfying reading habit—a habit that will bring pleasure and success throughout childhood and adult life.

Providing Application and Practice in Reading Skills

Since extensive reading often is the direct result of good attitudes toward reading, providing application and practice in reading skills might be one of the most important things a classroom teacher can do in order to develop reading skills. One of the best ways to teach children to read is to get them *to* read. A good reading center can be an invaluable aid in achieving this objective. Once a teacher has introduced phonics, structural analysis, comprehension, or other skills in reading, it is possible for children to practice and learn many of the skills independently. The teacher, by placing well-chosen books, magazines, pamphlets, charts, games, puzzles, and manipulative devices in the reading center, can introduce children to the use of the materials and then permit these materials to be used during free time and selected periods during the day. This is another condition under which learning takes place "painlessly." The teacher, having introduced a skill, now uses the reading center as a means of having the students practice the skill under satisfying and enjoyable conditions.

Kinds of Reading Centers

Primarily, there are three kinds of reading centers: (1) the special interest center, (2) the diversified center, and (3) the combination center. Each center has special appeal and because a teacher will want to vary his centers during the year, a more detailed description of each follows.

The Special Interest Center

The special interest reading center features a specific topic or subject for a specific length of time: for example, Indians, pioneers, sea life, other lands, or an area of literature. It will often be built around a unit of study in social studies, science, music, art, or other curriculum areas. Bulletin boards, charts, realia, and an abundance of reading materials on a single subject are displayed in an intriguing manner. Small placards with brief accounts of information or motivating questions are posted in easily viewed places. The reading material will include library books, special collections of subject-centered books, magazines, pamphlets, filmstrips, literary readers, poetry, songs, and charts relating to the chosen theme. In addition, tape recordings and records on the selected theme are very appropriate.

The Diversified Reading Center

The diversified center has global appeal and contains a wide variety of reading materials which cover many interest areas, levels of reading difficulties, and forms of literature. No central theme is featured. It relies more heavily on comfort and high interest materials as the motivating force for its use. This center, again, will contain the many types of reading materials described in special interest centers, but with unlimited topics selection. This center becomes somewhat permanent and even though reading materials are added and revolved, many elements will remain unchanged.

The Combination Center

The combination center includes features of both of the above. In it are found materials that are somewhat permanent such as word games, encyclopedias, dictionaries, or maps; but there is also provision for emphasis of specific topics. Children who use this center may desire to play skill development games, refer to and read materials with which they are familiar already, or they may be enticed into reading materials to which they are exposed through theme presentation.

Contents of Reading Centers

Three major types of materials should be considered in setting up centers: furnishings, reading materials, and realia.

Furnishings

The main emphasis of furnishings should be *comfort*. Soft, cushioned couches and chairs are especially good. Rocking chairs both large and small are comfortable and inviting. While not imperative, carpeting or a large rug is very desirable. Children can sit or lie on pillows or cushions on a covered floor area remaining clean and comfortable in a home-like atmosphere. Small tables, book cases, and magazine display racks are important for effective display of materials. Where large window areas exist, drapes add warmth and atmosphere as well as control excessive direct light. In some centers, table or floor lamps are necessary for adequate lighting. Globes, aquariums, terrariums, animal cages, and chart racks are examples of other furnishings that add much to the success of a center.

Reading Materials

Materials are probably the single most important factor in a successful center. In selecting materials the teacher should keep in mind (1) multiple reading levels, (2) a wide variety of subject interest areas, and (3) variety in literary forms.

The differing levels of reading progress within a classroom make it necessary to provide reading materials at several levels. The lower grades will require materials ranging in difficulty from simple picture books to books at least two grades above grade level. The intermediate grades will need materials from three to four grade levels below to three to four grade levels above the actual grade level to stimulate the abilities of every child.

A multitude of interest areas should be represented at as many reading levels as possible. Science, social studies, art, music, animal stories, mysteries, fables, sports, romance, travel, and biographies are only a few of the possible interest areas.

In addition, as many literary forms as possible should be represented. These would include short stories, novels, plays, poetry, letters, editorials, factual discourses, jokes, anecdotes, comics, and many others.

The sources of such information are plentiful. Library books of both fiction and nonfiction should be available in groups of 50 to 200 in a center. Many companies now produce collections of appropriate books; for example, the Macmillan *Reading Spectrum* or Scott, Foresman's *Invitation to Personal Reading.* The *Little Owl Series* by Holt, Rinehart and Winston is another example of such a collection.

Large collections of literary readers containing a variety of the best in children's literature are a must for a good center. At least twelve companies now produce good sets of these readers. Books of plays and books of poetry should also be displayed and reading games should be available. (For a detailed listing and review of suggested library books, literary readers, and reading games consult *Recreational Reading for the Classroom,* Central Utah Reading Council, Rice House, Brigham Young University, Provo, Utah, 84601.)

Realia refers to real objects, artifacts, and other three-dimensional items which children can observe and handle. In most cases realia used in a reading center will be inanimate objects, but on occasion they may be animals or plants. Included in this vast area would be globes, aquariums, terrariums, rocks, models, industrial or agricultural products, clothing, tools—in short, any artifact or object relating to subject or special-interest areas (science, social studies, health, etc.) that will be of interest to children. These realia should be attractively displayed, with interest-catching placards which give a small amount of information or invite further reading. Such realia and placards serve as eye-catchers which draw attention to the reading center and its contents.

Experience charts and informational charts are valuable reading materials to include in a reading center. Pamphlets and travel brochures or folders are often stimulating because of the many color pictures and small amounts of reading. Magazines and newspapers are materials of high frequency use in a center. Sets of encyclopedias, science collections, atlases, and almanacs have appeal to many children and should be easily accessible in a center. Filmstrips with viewers can provide very stimulating reading experiences for children. Likewise, available listening stations with tapes and records of interesting stories can motivate children to read the stories, either along with the recording or separately.

Setting Up a Classroom Reading Center

A classroom reading center can be arranged by the teacher alone or by the teacher and children working together. In either case, it is essential for the teacher to have clearly in mind the purpose of the particular kind of center that is to be established. He also must be acquainted with the location, space, furniture, equipment, and materials that are required and available for the desired center.

The primary dictate of location of a reading center is control of noise and movement. It should be set up on an area generally free from noise and heavy flow of traffic, yet easily accessible to the students and easily observable by the teacher. The size will be dictated by classroom size and student enrollment. Some centers may be as small as six feet by eight feet; others as large as fifteen feet by twenty feet. A comfortable size would be approximately ten feet by fifteen feet. Naturally the size will have an effect on furniture and equipment. Small centers may rely on a rug and cushions for seating and bookshelves for partitions. Once these factors, along with the type of center and the materials needed, are determined, the center can be developed.

Perhaps the most effective classroom reading center is the combination center in which the teacher provides and prepares certain permanent aspects of the center, and then guides children as they select and prepare the specific interest part of the center. Given proper guidance and sources of materials, children often develop centers that have more appeal to other children than a center prepared by the teacher.

In order to locate and supply appropriate reading materials for the center, children must read and classify the materials. This reading and classifying not only creates interest, but also helps children develop reading skills. In addition, the enthusiasm of children is often infectious, and they inspire and motivate other children to read materials that have been placed in the center.

Use of a Reading Center

Like any other device, a reading center's potential value is not realized unless it is fully used. Maximum benefits are derived from a center when children are permitted to use it by choice during free periods of time or at other times when the teacher schedules their use of it. If it were used only during free time when his work was completed, the child needing it most would never get to use the center. For this and other reasons, some scheduled periods are necessary.

Self-Directed Free Periods

The reading center materials are used most effectively when they are available to children during most of the school day. Materials might be accessible to students before the formal beginning of school each day, during the recess and noon hours, and at times during the day when children have completed assigned work.

During free choice periods the students are encouraged to browse in the center to select something of interest to read. They may then remain there to read or take the material with them to their seats. They may choose to play a game with someone else, view a filmstrip, or listen to a tape or record. Two or three students may choose to share stories with one another, either by reading them orally or telling and discussing them. They may decide to do puzzles or writing activities in conjunction with an article in a magazine or storybook. The interesting atmosphere may stimulate some to create stories, poetry, or charts that all can share.

Scheduled Periods

Scheduled periods are provided to ensure every child's use of the center regularly and to introduce special activities. During these scheduled periods in the center the teacher provides many sharing activities and opportunities to explore new areas. A knowledge of student interests, needs, and available materials will be most helpful to a teacher here.

Possible sharing activities are innumerable. They may be discussion oriented to a particular subject, such as animals, with each child sharing a part of something he has read. They may be oral reading experiences with children shar-ing an exciting part of a good book. Pantomime dramatizations and radio plays are other ways of exchanging good material. Art projects, such as posters or diagrams can be used for conveying something of interest.

In addition to sharing, students should explore the materials available. This may be stimulated by effective displays of realia, interest-catching placards, or through puzzle sheets or treasure hunt sheets. The latter items supply questions that can be answered through exploring the available materials.

Conclusion

Classroom reading centers are not new, nor are they a panacea for solving reading problems. Experience, however, seems to substantiate that the establishment and proper utilization of an effective classroom reading center can be one of the most productive methods a teacher uses to develop within children a love for reading and, at the same time, provide practice in necessary reading skills.

67. Audio-Visual Reading Tools *

AMO DE BERNARDIS

WE hear a great deal of criticism today about the unfortunate influence which the commercial motion picture, the radio, and now television may be exerting upon

* From Amo De Bernardis, "Audio-Visual Reading Tools," *Grade Teacher,* LXXII, no. 8 (April, 1955), 33, 79, 80. Reprinted by permission of the author and Teachers Publishing Corporation, Darien, Conn.

the development of the child—particularly in relation to his reading habits. There is a growing fear that the child listening to radio or watching the TV screen may have little time for books. But no such criticism can be made over the value which a school can derive from these audio-visual materials in promoting a better education for the child, and this includes more and better reading. When properly selected and used, the motion picture, the various types of recordings, the radio and television programs can become some of the best tools available to the classroom teacher, and can contribute a great deal to the school's reading program.

Too many people look upon reading merely as the ability to recognize words on a printed page and to repeat them aloud. They measure the child's skill in reading by his fluency, and are more concerned over the fact that some children find it difficult to recognize the printed symbol than the fact that many are unable to understand what they do recognize.

Consequently, unless the child has accumulated a background of experience, of contact with real objects or people, or their visual representation, he cannot hope to understand the printed word even if he can say it correctly. The audio-visual tools now available for the classroom teacher help the child acquire this essential background.

In the early grades the problem is simple. The symbols on the page refer to father, mother, baby, dog, house, or common action words—all of which are part of every child's environment, and therefore universally understood. However, even here audio-visual aids can be helpful, and the beautifully illustrated primers in the modern school are excellent examples of this merging of picture and word.

Once the child gets away from these simple elements in his home or his neighborhood, the problem is no longer as simple. He must find other means of acquiring the understanding of things not in his immediate environment. He must acquire new knowledge. For this purpose audio-visual tools, and to these we may add field trips, are important, even essential.

Field Trips

The field trip is rapidly becoming a standard audio-visual practice in almost all school systems. To conduct one involves a number of administrative problems: securing permission, arranging for transportation, and working out a proper time schedule. But the results of a successful field trip make the effort worthwhile. Each child who takes part has acquired a rich and vital experience which not only advances his education but can be made to develop a growing interest in oral and written communication, and eventually in the reading of print.

A trip to a factory, a farm, or a fire station has been a learning experience which then and thereafter seeks expression in language. After each field trip, children are eager to describe what they saw and reproduce the event in various forms. One is the reading chart which the teacher builds out of what the children relate. This helps to develop word recognition and, what is more important, to give real meaning to an abstract symbol. The class has turned the field trip into a reading exercise which is both interesting and readable.

Motion and Still Pictures

One of the best substitutes for actual experience is the motion picture, and next to it, the filmstrip and the photograph. As in the case of the field trip, the full educational possibilities in them can be achieved only if the experience itself is followed by interpretation and criticism from the children. The pictures merely furnish facts and situations. The learning takes place when these presentations provoke discussion and debate. The film or filmstrip should really be regarded as motivation for further learning activity, not as mere enjoyment. Pictures stimulate the imagination, and the wise teacher encourages the full play of this imagination and its expression in a variety of ways—in speech, in writing, in art, and above all, in further reading.

Mounting and Arranging Flat Pictures

In addition to the motion picture, the filmstrip, and the slide set, there is the vast field of the flat printed picture. The professional photographer has covered the world with his camera—its people, its institutions, its occupations, its customs, its human relations. The result of his efforts may be found in every illustrated book, and especially in the numerous magazines devoted to science and travel—foreign places, foreign people, and all the scenes of American life and work.

Many of these pictures are available to the classroom teacher, but to make the best use of them, they should be mounted and systematically filed.

One device used by many teachers for displaying pictures is the flannel board. Its simplicity, ease of construction, and flexibility makes this a valuable teaching tool. Words, phrases, sentences, and pictures can be displayed on it, and it is especially excellent in storytelling, since, with its aid, the story can be developed step by step and visualized.

Opaque Projectors

One of the most versatile tools in the reading program is the opaque projector. With its help, an infinite variety of materials from books, pictures, photographs, students' written or printed work, and even objects themselves may be projected on the screen for examination and discussion by the whole class.

Projection of a child's work so that all the class may see it at the same time and discuss it presents an excellent teaching and learning situation. The projected picture centers attention on material being discussed. Individual children may be called upon to read or interpret what is on the screen. Errors may be pointed out and corrections agreed upon, and the whole exercise made an opportunity for motivating further reading.

Audio Aids

A wise teacher has said that children should be grouped in their classrooms for instruction in reading not on their reading level, but on their *thinking* level. It is useless for a child to be able to recognize words he cannot understand or use in his own mental processes. Too much of this "parrot reading" has existed in the past and much of it is still to be found in many places in the present.

It is here that audio materials such as recording tapes and radio programs find their relationship to better reading. They motivate attentive listening; they provoke comment and discussion; they improve understanding. There are available for the classroom today recordings of almost infinite variety—speeches, narratives, descriptions, dramatizations, poetry, and almost anything that can be made through sound.

The tape recorder has made it possible for any classroom teacher to create his own audio aids. The mechanics of operation have been so simplified that even the pupils can operate the machine. The tape itself can be kept intact for repeated use in the future or erased and then re-used.

All these audio-visual devices and classroom methods must be used properly if they are to promote the cause of good reading. In themselves they are only tools, but in the hands of a good craftsman they can be made to create worthwhile education provided he doesn't forget the real purpose for which they are being used. If his objective is to increase the child's interest and ability in reading, then the teacher must keep this continuously in mind, and use every opportunity created by the field trip, the motion or still picture, the tape recorder, and every other device to advance the cause of reading. There is no such thing as an automatic tool for teaching. No matter how dramatic or exciting the visual, the auditory, or the actual experience may be, it takes the skilled teacher to turn it into an effective learning situation. In the last analysis, the teacher himself is the chief miracle worker. But the right tools will help him accomplish the miracle we call education.

References

1. DALE, EDGAR. *Audio Visual Methods in Teaching* (rev. ed.), "English and Reading," Ch. 26. New York: The Dryden Press, 1959.
2. DAVIS, HUBERT J. "Teaching Reading the A–V Way" *Educational Screen,* 31 (December, 1952), 417–19.
3. GORMAN, HARRIET. "Adventure with Film-Readers; How Motion Pictures plus Correlated Film-Storybooks Help Young Readers Read, *Educational Screen,* 30 (January, 1951), 13–15.
4. JACKSON, E. B. "More About the Flannelgraph in Teaching Reading Readiness," *The Grade Teacher,* 65 (February, 1948), 26–27.
5. LEESTMA, ROBERT. *Audio Visual Materials for Teaching Reading.* Ann Arbor, Michigan: University of Michigan Press, 1954.
6. RUSSELL, D. H., and KARP, E. E. *Reading Aids Through the Grades.* New York: Teachers College, Bureau of Publications, Columbia University 1951.
7. SULLIVAN, L. H. "Using the Radio in Developing Reading," *The Elementary School Journal,* 27 (June, 1946), 53–57.
8. WILLEY, ROY DE VERL. "Using Audio-Visual Methods in Teaching Communications," *Elementary English* (May, 1954), pp. 276–83.
9. Filmstrips that correlate with *Alice and Jerry* series of books, available through Society for Visual Education, 1345 Diversey Parkway, Chicago 14, Illinois.
10. Filmstrips, supplemented by study guides, for *Better Reading Series* (Pasadena, California: Stillfilms Inc.).
11. Wilmette, Illinois: Encyclopaedia Britannica Films, Inc. and Boston: D. C. Heath Co. have made available a series including such titles as *Three Little Kittens, Shep the Farm Dog, Farm Animals.*
12. A set of books to correlate with the Encyclopaedia Britannica Films series *Children of Many Lands* has been published by Row, Peterson and Company, 1911 Ridge Avenue, Evanston, Illinois.

68. How to Teach with Programmed Textbooks *

ALLEN D. CALVIN

THIS year, more than one million pupils will be using programmed materials. While programmed textbooks can be used successfully in a number of different ways, certain patterns of use have been found by teachers to be the most effective. These patterns, revealed in a recent study of 200 school systems using programmed materials, can be of help to teachers planning to use such materials in their classrooms for the first time.

The single most important factor bearing on the success of the programmed approach is the teacher. The teacher working with programmed textbooks is even more important to the success of his class than is the teacher in the traditional setting. It is essential, at the outset, for you to recognize that your role as a teacher will be expanded when you work with programmed materials.

When introducing a class to programmed textbooks for the first time, here are some important points to bear in mind:

1. First, read through the program carefully. You needn't write the answers, but it is important that you go through the program in detail, just as your students will.

2. After your usual introduction to the students, tell them that they are being given the opportunity to use a new and more effective kind of textbook because it is arranged in such a fashion that the

subject is made readily understandable. Explain that each student will understand more and remember more because he will be able to learn at his own pace— neither pushed faster than he can comfortably work nor held back if he happens to work rapidly.

3. Explain that although the programmed textbook is cast in a question/answer format, *it is not a test.* Point out that the questions help the student make certain he truly understands earlier information before he proceeds to new information. Let your class know that, as a result of this new approach, you will have more time to work with each of them individually. Make it especially clear to each student that, should he have any questions about the material, he is to raise his hand immediately, and you will be glad to answer his question.

4. Explain to the class that the programmed textbook has been carefully tested on students comparable to themselves and that, because of this, they generally will be able to proceed without any difficulty. Emphasize that you welcome a chance to work with each student individually.

5. Explain to your students that they will not only be working with the programmed textbooks, but that there will be lectures, specific discussion periods, projects, and so forth.

6. In your own words, explain the mechanics of using the programmed textbook. Be sure you make clear whether pupils should say the answers to themselves, write them in the book, or write them on a piece of paper beside the

* From Allen D. Calvin, "How to Teach with Programmed Textbooks." Reprinted from the February 1967 issue of *Grade Teacher.* Copyright © 1967 by CCM Professional Magazines, Inc. All rights reserved.

book. In most cases, pupils will not be able to mark the books directly.

Whether it is more desirable for students to write their responses has been the subject of considerable research. Some studies indicate that the type of response makes no appreciable difference, while other studies indicate that written responses are more desirable for maximum retention.

One study indicates that for hard-to-remember materials it is better to write the responses, while for easy material it makes no difference whether the responses are written or not. This finding seems to have a certain amount of face validity since, if the response required were the word "red," it would not seem to make any difference whether a pupil wrote it or said it to himself. However, if the response were "$x^4 - 2x^2 + 4ab - 7$," a written response would probably be desirable in order to allow accurate comparison with the correct answer.

Unless there is pressure for speed, it is probably best to stay on the safe side of this question by requiring your students to write their answers on a piece of scratch paper kept alongside the book.

7. Explain that looking ahead at the answers and copying a response without reading the material will obviously hinder their learning. Reemphasize the fact that it will be those students who follow the simple procedure you are outlining who will learn readily and perform extremely well on examinations.

Explain that if a student cheats by not reading the material and simply copies the answers, he hurts no one but himself because he will, as a consequence, not learn and his examinations will make this clear. Teachers report, incidentally, that although there is initially a small amount of "looking ahead," within a few days such behavior tends to disappear as the students find they can understand

the material without difficulty. Students who do look ahead during the first few days of class, despite your warnings, usually do so because in the past they found they simply could not understand the material being presented. When such students find they can understand the material in the programmed textbook, the need for "looking ahead" disappears.

8. After you have demonstrated the mechanics of the programmed textbook, inform the class of your testing procedures, homework requirements, and the like.

9. At this point, ask the students if they have any questions. After answering any questions that arise, let them read the instructions to the program to themselves. Allow ample time for each student to finish reading the instructions, ask once more for questions, and then have the class begin the program.

10. A steady diet of programmed materials is not nearly so stimulating for the student as an approach that involves a variety of educational experiences. Suppose you prefer steak to any other food. If we gave you steak morning, noon, and night, day after day, you would soon reach the point where your preference for steak would drop considerably. Don't let pupils' initial preference for programmed material override the importance of bringing them into contact with a number of different educational stimuli.

Structuring the Classroom

In the higher grades, from five on up, most schools schedule daily classroom periods. These classes meet a specified number of days each week, and the teacher must cover a minimum amount of designated subject matter during a particular time period.

To meet the requirements of this framework and still achieve the full benefits of the individualized instruction offered by programmed textbooks, most teachers suggest that a specific portion of the class time be set aside for work on the programmed textbook—the exact amount of time allotted to depend on the intellectual level of the class and the material to be covered. Some teachers recommend a specific amount of time each class period, say 25 minutes. Others suggest using the programmed textbook for the entire period on specific days, say Monday and Wednesday of each week. Both methods have their advocates, and both work effectively.

For the purpose of illustration, let's assume that the following conditions exist. The class meets five periods a week for 50 minutes a period. On Mondays and Wednesdays, the first half of the period is spent with the students working on the programmed textbooks. On Tuesdays and Thursdays, the students spend the second half of the period working on the program.

On Friday, during the first half of the period, either a student/teacher discussion is held or a student panel is presented, and the last half of the period is given over to an examination. Obviously, the examination will not always come on Friday. When an examination should be given will depend on the amount of time you wish to spend on a particular section of the program.

The experiences of teachers who have used an approach similar to this indicates that the response of your students will surpass your expectations. Students who have shown a lack of motivation in the traditional setup, often respond enthusiastically.

What to Watch Out For

Certain aspects of this plan need more thorough discussion. What do you do, for example, about the slow reader who has not completed the necessary material by examination time? If a student cannot read fast enough to cover the assigned material in time, and if he is forced to do so anyway, he will simply turn pages and later report that he has completed the assigned work. Therefore, *under no circumstances should a student be assigned a minimum amount of material to be covered in class.*

Because the teacher in the traditional classroom must cover a prescribed amount of material in a specified time period, he has a difficult time giving individual attention to slower students. Even with the best intentions, the teacher must balance the needs of the slower students against those of the majority of the class. If the class is halted to take time to deal with the slower students' questions, the rest of the class will be slighted. Yet any action on the part of a teacher that forces a student to go faster than he is capable of going causes severe problems. This "forcing" action probably is the foremost cause of failure in today's classrooms.

How does the classroom using programmed textbooks accommodate the needs of the slower student as well as the needs of his more capable colleagues? Note that under the plan just described the students are fully aware at the beginning of the week that an examination will take place at the end of the week. Moreover, they know precisely what material will be covered in the weekly examination. They also know that each class period will be divided into specific activities on a regular basis.

The Slow Can Keep Up

Above all, the teacher will have made clear that students who do not complete the assigned material by the end of a

period will be free to work on the programmed material at home or in study
hall in order to complete the assignment.
This framework permits the slower student to move along at his own pace
during class and yet maintain pace with
the class at the beginning of each period.
The responsibility of maintaining pace
with the class belongs to the slower student, and he is provided a fair opportunity for doing so.

Now how about the student who finishes his work ahead of the rest of the
class and who performs well on his examinations? Such a student should be
encouraged to undertake extra-credit enrichment work in the topic under study
or perhaps in other topics.

It is worth noting, however, that the
student who can proceed more rapidly
at one stage of the presentation may very
well move more slowly at another stage.
Logarithms, for example, may strike a particular student as easy material, whereas
factoring may not. Another student may
find just the reverse.

In the lower grades, from one through
four, programmed materials are used in
such a fashion that each student is allowed to proceed at his own pace, free
of the requirement that a predetermined
amount of material be covered in a
predetermined amount of time. Such an
approach is also particulary effective in
an ungraded school or in a school whose
curriculum has been deliberately designed
to emphasize individualized instruction.

This is also the approach best suited
to a remedial situation, such as remedial
reading. The student uses the programmed textbook as a means of acquiring core information in the subject
matter under study. The programmed textbook is used only in the classroom and
according to a schedule somewhat along
the lines of the plan described earlier.

Since the students proceed through the
material at varied rates of speed, tests
are administered on the basis of the reviews that appear in most contemporary
programmed textbooks. These reviews are
placed strategically throughout the text,
indicating to the student that he should
request a progress test from his teacher
whenever his performance on the review
is satisfactory.

The student's test is returned to him as
rapidly as possible so that he is given
immediate feedback on his performance
and is thus able to proceed without delay.
As a result, a considerable proportion
of the teacher's time is spent using the
examinations in a diagnostic fashion and
discussing the results with students in
individual conferences.

Regardless of the classroom setting,
no single factor will have a more profound influence on a student's success
than the encouragement and reward of
his teacher.

Give Constant Encouragement

Don't just give your approval to the
superior student. He needs encouragement, of course, but so does the slower
student as well as those who are most
often neglected—the so-called average
students. Make it a point to give as much
encouragement as you can to *each* student. This approach not only brings about
dramatic results in learning, but it also
brings about a marked improvement in
the climate of the class—which sharply
decreases disciplinary problems.

Most programmed textbooks are accompanied by a series of objective tests.
These tests are often prepared in two
alternate forms. In some situations, you
may want to use the questions as a pre-
test. In other situations, you may wish
to use them for a final examination.

It is essential that the examination be

graded and the results reported *at the earliest possible opportunity.* The teacher should never allow a week or more to elapse between testing and reporting. Immediate grading of progress tests lets you apply their results diagnostically—that is, in time to offer appropriate recommendations and guidance before the student with deficiencies has progressed beyond the point where your assistance would be most helpful.

Study the results of progress tests carefully, noting in which areas individual students are having problems. Do not permit a student to proceed with the material until his difficulties have been resolved. Such students should be given individual help and then redirected to that section of the program where they encountered difficulty.

At the beginning of the course there will occasionally be a few students who have difficulties that are not cleared up during the classroom period. These difficulties will not be discovered until the examination. Thus, when you give your first test, you may find several students whose performance is not adequate.

As soon as you discover these inadequacies on the first examination, you should attempt to assist these students. Many students who have a history of failure have learned not to ask questions.

Ways to Help

Teachers using programmed materials have reported a number of approaches that have been effective in working with such students. Local conditions will, of course, determine which of these approaches are the most effective for you. Some teachers work with the pupils individually during the class period. Others offer an opportunity for individual help before and after school. Still others allow the brighter student an opportunity for extra credit if he works with a student having difficulty, either in a separate area during class or outside the regular class period.

Don't feel you must always use the tests provided with the programmed textbook. Some of you may feel that a particular test is too hard or too easy. By all means, make up your own test questions whenever you wish. Just remember to make sure the questions cover the material that is actually in the textbook.

Don't overlook the opportunity to use audio-visual materials wherever appropriate. The occasional use of a filmstrip or motion picture will add variety to classroom activities. As you go through the program yourself, it will be helpful if you note places in the text where appropriate enrichment material should be presented.

CHAPTER

XIV

Some Special Issues in Reading Instruction

Three of the sometimes controversial issues of the reading program that warrant special attention are oral reading, speed of reading, and the role of parents.

Gray presents six characteristics of effective oral reading and Bleismer offers suggestions for making oral reading more purposeful. Next the research dealing with the relationship of rate, flexibility, and study skills to comprehension is reviewed by Harris. This is followed by Tinker's evaluation of devices to improve reading speed. In the final article, Larrick states that teachers and parents should work cooperatively in a good reading program, and indicates how teachers may help parents to contribute to the growth of their children's reading ability.

69. Characteristics of Effective Oral Reading *

WILLIAM S. GRAY

THE fact that the role of oral reading has expanded rapidly during recent years emphasizes the urgent need of training boys and girls to read well to others. To achieve effective results, we need a clear understanding of the attitudes and

* From William S. Gray, "Characteristics of Effective Oral Reading," in *Oral Aspects of Reading,* Supplementary Education Monographs, No. 82 (December, 1955), pp. 5–10. Reprinted by permission of Mrs. William S. Gray and the University of Chicago Press.

skills that characterize a competent oral reader. . . .

We are emerging today into a highly significant period with respect to oral reading. Its importance as a useful art is clearly recognized. The large emphasis given to silent reading has provided new techniques for use in mastering basic reading skills and in grasping the ideas and feelings intended by the writer. Furthermore, oral reading has been freed from many of the formal practices which prevailed when it was taught chiefly as an instructional aid. We are now in a position to focus attention specifically upon the development of those attitudes and skills that characterize efficient oral reading.

The Current Scene

Today oral reading is considered to be (1) an instructional and diagnostic instrument, (2) a useful art in communicating ideas to others, and (3) a fine art which conforms to certain aesthetic standards. In the discussion that follows, we shall be concerned primarily with oral reading as a useful art and to some extent with oral reading as a fine art.

In the effort to identify the characteristics of effective oral reading, an analysis was made of recent discussions by specialists in this field. The impressive fact revealed was that, in the judgment of all, and independent of the maturity level of the reader, four significant tasks are involved: grasping the author's intended meaning, sensing the mood and emotional reactions which the author intended to produce, conveying the author's meaning to the listener, and conveying mood and feeling. Although reading specialists discuss these tasks either separately or in varying combinations, all maintain that a high degree of skill should be developed in each of them.

Securing the ideas and feelings intended. Without exception, the fact was emphasized vigorously that a reader must secure a clear grasp of the thoughts and feelings intended by the author before he can convey them to others. The steps involved have been likened to the charging of a battery prior to its use for an important service. The ideas and feelings acquired supply the inner drive and condition both the mind and the body of the reader to the challenging task of reading well to others. Time and again the

fact was pointed out that, without adequate impression, there can be only ineffective expression. As essential requisites in securing adequate impressions, three characteristics of an efficient reader were discussed.

The first is ability to secure a clear grasp of the author's meaning. The attitudes and skills involved are similar to those required in any reading situation where full understanding is essential. As implied earlier, the reading specialists of previous generations directed attention largely to such items as the major point in a selection, coordinate and subordinate ideas, and the grouping of words and their sequence. Valuable as are these clues to meaning, they are based largely on an analysis of the structural elements of the passages read.

Current writers have adopted a far broader and more dynamic concept of the steps involved in securing the meaning of a passage. Of major importance is the need of a unified grasp of the story as a whole, of the message intended, or of the information presented. As a necessary background the reader should often know the kind of material he is reading, why the author wrote it, and, to some extent, the author's background.

As the reader gains a broad grasp of the author's meaning, he tries to identify its central theme, idea, or contribution. He studies the way in which the various ideas presented reinforce and expand the central idea. He examines the words and figures of speech used in their contextual setting and identifies the way in which they delimit, qualify, or enrich the meaning of the passage. As his search for meaning continues, he recalls parallel experiences in his own life, the geographic setting of the incidents related, their historical background, and everything he knows that makes clear the meaning of the passage. He also searches for meanings that are intended but not stated, for example, the kind of person a story character is as revealed by what he does or says. At every step in reading, vivid memory images are recalled or the reader reconstructs in imagination mental pictures of the things, scenes, and activities described.

A second requisite is ability to sense the mood and emotional tone which the author intended to create. Oral reading which fails to develop appropriate feeling responses falls far short of its goal. In order to produce desired effects, a good writer selects and organizes with great care the ideas to be presented. He also uses words and forms of expression purposefully and creatively in presenting specific ideas, in describing scenes and events, and in depicting character. Furthermore, he tries to build up vivid mental pictures that elicit emotional responses, and he uses such devices as repetition, rhyme, and sound to produce appropriate effects. His aim may be to convince his readers; to modify their attitudes; or to develop certain moods or feelings, such as joy, sorrow, hatred, fear. No matter what they may be, a good oral reader is able to identify and interpret all clues to the mood and emotional responses which the author intends to develop.

A third requisite is ability to react thoughtfully to both the ideas presented and the effects that the author is seeking to develop. A favorable reaction by the reader influences in a positive manner the vigor and effectiveness of his oral interpretation. If his reactions are unfavorable, they are more or less unconsciously reflected in his attitude, facial expression, or tone of voice while reading to others.

Conveying ideas and feelings to others.
The task of conveying ideas and arousing feelings through oral reading is no less challenging than that of grasping the meanings and sensing the feelings to be conveyed. As preconditions for this step, three personal qualifications are discussed repeatedly in the literature.

In the first place, a good reader is eager to share with his listeners something to which he attaches real importance. It may be valuable information, a unique point of view, a vivid description, an interesting character sketch, a bit of humor, or the musical effects produced through the choice and arrangement of words. Without a compelling motive, oral reading rarely rises above the commonplace.

In the second place, a good oral reader knows his audience and adapts his interpretation to their interests and needs. He is aware, for example, that they are receptive and eager for the message or that their interest must be aroused, favorable attitudes developed, and desirable response elicited. In the light of such facts, he plans his approach to the reading and develops the kind of presentation that will arouse maximum interest and convey effectively the ideas and feeling intended.

In the third place, the good reader has mastered the basic skills of perception so well that he recognizes words quickly and accurately and pronounces them clearly and distinctly. Equally important is ability to group words together in thought units and to read aloud smoothly and without evidence of effort or difficulty. To achieve the level of mastery desired, long periods of basic training in reading are often necessary. Not infrequently the help of a speech specialist is desirable in overcoming specific difficulties.

In helping his listeners grasp the author's meaning, the good reader uses various devices. He highlights, through the use of emphasis, new or important ideas; he makes clear the transition from one idea to another; he indicates by proper phrasing the units of thought within a sentence; he relates the ideas of a series by keeping his voice up until the end is reached; he indicates climax by the force and vigor of expression; he brings out similarities and contrasts by emphasizing the items compared. He varies his rate of reading, modulates his voice, and uses facial and bodily expressions in the effort to convey meanings.

The training of pupils to convey meanings effectively is an insightful but subtle art. The teacher should have a good understanding of the techniques or skills involved. However, he does not center attention up them as such. If, for example, a pupil emphasizes the wrong word in reading, the teacher helps him to identify the right one. If a pupil fails to bring out a difference, the teacher directs his attention to the things to be contrasted and suggests that he re-read the passage to make clear the difference between them. The teacher relies far more on helping the child to grasp clearly the idea to be presented than on formal directions concerning modes of expression. On occasion, however, he may read a passage to help the pupil identify an improved way of expressing an idea, or he may ask other pupils to do so.

The imparting of mood and feeling is an equally challenging task. If it is achieved effectively, it greatly heightens interest and appreciation on the part of the listeners. As indicated earlier, a first requisite of a good reader in this connection is a vivid sensing of the mood and feeling intended by the author. The techniques for helping the listener acquire the mood and feeling are many and varied. For example, changes in rate of reading often reveal action or excitement. A rising inflection indicates doubt; a falling inflection, certainty; a rising and falling inflection, indecision. The spontaneous use of facial expressions, and bodily activity aids materially in imparting mood, such as joy, sorrow, excitement. The belief prevails, however, that, if the reader senses mood and feeling vividly and appropriately and is eager to read to others, he will need little guidance in these techniques. When he is unsuccessful, the teacher attempts to aid him, primarily through a discussion of the meanings and feelings he wishes to convey.

The comments thus far have related chiefly to oral reading as a useful art. One of the most valuable sources of help now available for teachers is Ogilvie's chapter on oral reading in her recent book entitled *Speech in the Elementary School*.[1] Other chapters give needed help in related fields, such as informal speaking, speech, voice, diction, dramatics, and choral speaking. The authors [2] of textbooks on speech and expression for use at the high school and college levels think of oral reading much more largely as a fine art. Accordingly, they analyze in great detail the basic elements of expression, the various aspects of voice, and the nature of the various speech sounds. Independent of the level for which a textbook is intended, the suggestions made are concerned with the four major tasks in oral reading, to which reference was made earlier. The chief differences, as far as age groups are concerned, relate to

[1] Mardel Ogilvie, *Speech in the Elementary School* (New York: McGraw-Hill Book Co., Inc., 1954).

[2] *a*) Argus Tresidder, *Reading to Others* (Chicago: Scott Foresman & Co., 1940).

b) W. M. Parrish, *Reading Aloud* (New York: Ronald Press Co., 1953).

c) Charles Woolbert and Severina E. Nelson, *The Art of Interpretative Speech* (rev. ed.; New York: F. S. Crofts & Co., 1946).

choice of materials, the specific methods used, and the intensity of the training provided.

Concluding Statement

As an appropriate conclusion to this discussion, may I summarize briefly six characteristics of effective oral reading as currently conceived:

1. It is motivated by a keen desire on the part of the reader to share with others something to which he attaches real significance.

2. It is prepared and presented in the light of a careful study of the purposes to be achieved and the interests, needs, and probable attitudes of the listeners.

3. It is based on both a penetrating grasp of the meaning and a vivid sensing of the mood and feeling intended by the author. The great importance attached to this requirement is one of the distinguish-

ing features of the current effort to improve oral reading.

4. Effective oral reading is preceded by such a thorough mastering of word recognition that the reader, while reading to others, is free to focus attention entirely on the act of transmitting the author's message to them.

5. A good oral reader makes use of varied techniques in conveying both meaning and feeling to his audience. The prevailing view today is that this should be done within the framework of the reader's natural modes of expression and his normal pattern of conversation. As pupils advance, however, increasing attention should be given to the more technical aspects of expression and speech.

6. A good measure of the quality of oral reading is its effectiveness in conveying the desired understandings and in producing the intended effects on the listener.

70. Toward More Purposeful Oral Reading *

EMERY P. BLIESMER

THE last few years have seen what is supposedly a recurrence of, or an increase in, emphasis on oral reading. There frequently seems to be implied the notion that our children are not having enough oral reading in school and that this is the reason some children are poor readers. This perhaps explains why we frequently still find, with some degree of prevalence,

* From Emery P. Bliesmer, "Toward More Purposeful Oral Reading." Reprinted from the May 1959 issue of *Education,* pp. 547–50. Copyright © 1959 by The Bobbs-Merrill Company, Inc., Indianapolis, Ind.

the practice of consistently having children read aloud, in a group, materials or selections which all have already read silently (some more than once) and have discussed and rehashed, both before and after the silent reading. If some children have prepared for the reading lesson by "studying" at home, chances are good that a number will already have read given selections orally a number of times also.

Under the above conditions, the purpose of giving information or pleasure to, or of sharing it with, others tends to be obviated. Further obviation ensues when all the "listeners" (??) in the group are following the selection silently (more or less) while someone is reading it orally. Consequently, oral reading in this type of situation is relatively purposeless. Where such practices or situations exist, there is little incentive for listening—except for children to see who can be the first to pounce upon the mistakes a reader might make. While there might possibly be some merit in helping children develop skill in quickly detecting errors made by someone while reading aloud, this can hardly be justified as a major purpose for oral reading; and certainly little security or self-confidence is promoted in the poor readers who are the consistent targets for such practice in pouncing.

Need for More Purposeful Oral Reading

"But," teachers might say, "my children want to read orally. If we don't let them take turns reading aloud in a group they complain." Or teachers might even have had the experience of having parents complain because their children were not having their daily stints at reading orally, in turn, during the reading class. Perhaps this might sometimes be a reflection of teaching method or practice. If reading a selection aloud, in turn, after the selection has already been read, studied, and discussed has been the regular reading lesson experience for children, they might well have "learned" that this is what "reading" is mainly.

Another seemingly strange observation frequently noted is that even the poorest readers will usually clamor or insist that they also be given their turns to read aloud. If a teacher tries to avoid embarrassing a child with his poor reading performance by skipping him (seemingly accidentally), she usually does not get by with it. The child will call attention to

the omission and insist upon his turn. Perhaps he regards putting on a public display of his reading inadequacies as less humiliating or degrading, or being made to seem less different, then being singled out by omission or skipping.

Should we then omit oral reading entirely? Certainly not! While oral reading is not the major type of reading which is required and used most often (and we sometimes seem to forget this), oral reading skill is of importance. However, oral reading needs to be more than a means of showing that one can detect errors rapidly or that one is skillful in making all the right noises associated with given graphic symbols. It needs to be more purposeful than that. The oral reading practices or situations described previously, and often decried, are ones in which the oral reading is relatively purposeless. How, then, can provisions be made for more purposeful oral reading?

Modifying Reading Lesson Procedures

Frequently, slight adaptations or modifications of some typical reading lesson procedures can accomplish more purposeful oral reading. Must a reading selection always be read aloud in entirety, from beginning to end, and consecutively paragraph by paragraph? Why cannot parts of a selection be read aloud in other than a consecutive order? Why cannot some parts be skipped? The writer has had these suggestions be received in aghast fashion at times. "What about continuity of thought? What about omission of some important ideas or details? Won't the children miss a part of the story?" These have been some of the reactions. Certainly a selection or story needs to be read in entirety and in the order in which written if this is the only exposure to, or contact with, the material involved. However, in a reading class all the children will usually already have read the material silently (more or less) in (supposedly) a continuous, consecutive, and orderly fashion; so oral reading is not the major means by which such reading is, or should be, accomplished. Reading it again in this way, but orally rather than silently, would often make the reading somewhat purposeless.

Would it not be more purposeful for each of various children to read aloud for example, a part he especially liked or a part which might be particularly effective in evoking imagery? The discussion which should usually follow the silent reading of a selection can also provide some very good purposes for oral reading. If two children should disagree on a certain point, each can read aloud the part which he used as a basis for his opinion. If the class seems to have missed some pertinent details relative to a given point, another good reason for having a part, or parts, be read aloud is afforded.

Children's responses on worksheets or workbook exercises also offer good opportunities for meaningful oral reading. Rather than merely marking responses as "right" or "wrong" and giving a score or "grade," it would be much better to have a child read the parts of a selection which he used as bases for his answers to some given items or exercises—and, thus, perhaps lead him to see or understand better why some of his answers might not be the best or the right ones. (Some right, as well as wrong, responses should be utilized in this way; otherwise a child may be apt to view any request to read a part of a selection aloud as an indication of a mistake or failure.)

If the teacher customarily reads the directions for worksheets or other activities to a class, some pupil might be given the opportunity to do this instead, at times. Attention might also be given to modifying or varying directions at

times so that there is a real need to read directions before proceeding with given tasks; and such directions might be read to the class by a child before the other pupils have a chance to read the directions silently. After the silent reading of material, individual children might also be guided to the oral reading of parts not covered by specific guide questions for silent reading.

Situations Outside the Reading Class

Thus far, mainly oral reading during the reading lesson or class has been dealt with. But we need to keep in mind that oral reading, as well as silent reading, is usually most functional and meaningful outside the reading class. We need to help our children become aware of, and direct their attention toward, this. There are many opportunities for purposeful oral reading outside the reading class. We need to look for such opportunities and, in some instances, modify or adapt our teaching procedures so that additional opportunities are afforded. Quite often certain materials the teacher is in the habit of reading to the class might just as well be read by some of the children, keeping in mind, however, that a child should be given a chance to prepare before he reads to a group. An announcement concerning a PTA meeting might be read to the class by a child before children are given these announcements to take home to their parents (and might be better insurance, in some cases, that the information will actually reach parents). A note of instructions or directives from the principal's office might be read by a pupil. A child who has received a letter from a former member of the class might be prevailed upon to read the letter aloud to the group. A reply to a class request to visit some local place can give one child some good oral reading experience. A particularly funny joke or a part of a story which has caused an individual to chuckle unusually might be shared with the class. If the teacher is reading a story aloud to a class (Why do we do so much less of this above the primary grades?), why could not several children, chosen from among the better readers, participate in this reading also?

Opportunities in Content Areas

Numerous opportunities for purposeful oral reading are to be found in the content areas also. If some point in arithmetic seems confusing or a particular arithmetic problem appears to be stumping some pupils, a class might listen and concentrate on understanding while one pupil reads the problem or other pertinent material aloud. An erroneous concept in science or social studies might be clarified better by having children listen while a child reads a relevant part of a chapter than by having the teacher tell or "explain." A whole class can benefit from listening to one of its members read material which is pertinent to a topic being studied but which has not been generally available to the whole class. Various modifications of procedures suggested for the regular reading class might also be readily used in content area classes.

Criteria for Purposeful Oral Reading Situations

The foregoing suggests some of the situations which might well be used in providing for purposeful oral reading. If they are consciously and consistently on the watch for such, teachers will be able to find many other meaningful opportunities. Relatively purposeless types of oral reading might be avoided more readily if the chief purpose or function of oral reading is kept in mind: to convey ideas to listeners, to tell them something. Obviously, if what is being read aloud is already general information for the supposed listeners, there is then no really good reason for listening—or no really good reason for oral reading in the first place. Another obvious, and frequently made, point to be kept in mind is that if what is being read orally can be read silently by supposed listeners at the same time, there, again, is no reason for listening. These points should perhaps be among the chief criteria used in the selection of situations which offer opportunities for purposeful oral reading; and constant and consistent application of these should aid in eliminating much of the oral-reading-for-its-own-sake practice—and make oral reading be more than a matter of making the right noises in response to given visual stimuli.

Increasing the opportunities for children to read aloud in functional and meaningful situations should aid in making the reading act or process more meaningful to children also. However, it may take a little time for some children (and some parents and teachers also) to accept and become acclimated to this more meaningful and functional approach, if they have become somewhat habituated to a more ritualistic and mechanistic type of oral reading practice. Some teachers may even find themselves in the situation experienced by a friend of the writer. One night early in the school year this teacher received a phone call from a rather disturbed mother who wanted to know why the teacher was discriminating against her Geraldine. The little girl had complained to her mother that the teacher was not letting her read very much in school. Actually, Geraldine had been given frequent daily opportunities to read, but in situations other than the "now-let's-read-around-the-circle-in-turn" one. On succeeding days after the phone call the teacher made it a point to comment favorably upon Geraldine's reading every time she read orally and to call her attention, indirectly, to the fact that she was reading. At the end of each day the teacher called the child aside, helped her recall all the various times she had read orally during the day and suggested (for further insurance, perhaps), "Don't you think your mother would be pleased to hear about all the times you read for us today?"

71. Research on Some Aspects of Comprehension: Rate, Flexibility, and Study Skills *

ALBERT J. HARRIS

THERE is a voluminous literature on the relation between rate of reading and comprehension, much of which was completed before 1940. The degree of correlation was found to range all the way from low negative to high positive. The results varied with the age of the readers, with the kinds of materials employed, with the methods used in measuring the two characteristics, and with the purpose for reading. At the secondary and college level most of the correlations tended to be positive but quite low, around .30 (20). Among bright pupils fast readers tended to comprehend better than slow readers, while at lower intelligence levels there was some evidence that the slower readers tended to comprehend better (13). In mathematics and science the correlations tended to be low and negative; with many exceptions, the faster the pupil read, the less he tended to understand (1).

* From Albert J. Harris, "Research on Some Aspects of Comprehension: Rate, Flexibility, and Study Skills," *Journal of Reading,* 12 (December, 1968), 205–10, 258–60. Reprinted by permission of the International Reading Association.

Flexibility in Reading

Out of early recognition of the complexity of the relationship between rate and comprehension grew the point of view that pupils should learn to vary their rates of reading according to their purposes for reading and the nature of the reading material. In 1928, Yoakam (22) distinguished four main rates of reading: skimming, for a quick survey or for locating a specific item; rapid reading, for very easy material, for reading superficially just to get the main ideas, and for rereading; normal reading, for getting both main ideas and some supporting details; and slow, careful reading, for difficult material, for grasping nearly all of the content, for high accuracy, or for critical evaluation. Since then, hardly anyone has questioned the idea that an efficient reader should vary his rate of reading according to his purposes and the kinds of material he reads.

Research findings indicate, however, that most readers are rigid rather than flexible in their rates of reading. McDonald (7), for example, studied over 6,000 readers at elementary, secondary, college and adult levels, and found that more than 90 percent of them tended to maintain a characteristic approach and a relatively invariant rate with all of the types of reading tested, despite instructions for differentiation of purpose and in spite of variations in difficulty, style, and content of the materials.

To some extent this individually characteristic and relatively invariant rate of reading may be constitutional; Buswell (3) found that there is a substantial correlation between rate of reading and rate of thinking on nonreading tasks. To some extent, this inflexibility is learned; many professional men complain that the habit of slow, careful reading that they employ in their occupational reading carries over into their recreational reading. Lack of flexibility in rate may simply be the result of lack of appropriate training (9). Although lip service in favor of flexibility has been given for many years, not much effective teaching to develop flexibility has taken place.

That flexibility in rate can be developed has been shown by Braam (2). High school seniors starting a six-week summer reading program intended to improve their chances for success in college were tested on five different kinds of content and showed an average difference of only 19 words per minute between highest rate and lowest rate. By the end of the program, not only was their average rate higher on all five kinds of material, but also the difference between highest and lowest average rate had increased to 159 words per minute. It seems safe to conclude, therefore, that flexibility in rate can be substantially improved with appropriate instruction.

Recent writers on flexibility or versatility in reading have emphasized that rate is only one of the characteristics of reading which expert readers should vary according to circumstances. McDonald (8) has expressed this very well:

Continued research has led us to conclude that reading flexibility consists of the ability to utilize those reading processes and techniques which are particularly appropriate for the style, difficulty level, and theme of the reading material while, at the same time, being consonant with achieving the reader's purpose at the optimum level of performance. Thus, the flexible reader possesses those reading skills, techniques, and methods of attack which enable him to achieve as complete an understanding of the author's meaning as is dictated by the reader's purpose. The flexible reader also has a psychological set toward the reading process which leads him to differentiate his reading approach to suit the difficulty of the article's content and style, the amount of background knowledge he possesses as well as the urgency of his need to satisfy his purpose through reading the article. The flexible reader, as the result of his attention to purpose, difficulty of material, complexity of theme, and background knowledge, makes many adjustments of reading approaches and specific techniques. These adjustments may be made within a single section or even a single paragraph of an article. Such adjustments are, of course, reflected in measurement of rate. Variability in rate, however, is *not* the *cause* of flexible reading. Rather, rate variability is the *result* of flexible reading approaches.

Effect of Rate Improvement on Comprehension

Since World War II there has been a tendency in the United States to place a great deal of stress on training to increase rate of reading in reading improvement programs at the secondary school and college levels and in reading programs for adults, such as those sponsored by industrial concerns and the armed services. The manufacturers of instruments that are usable in speed-reading programs, and some private businesses that offer training in rapid reading, have maintained advertising campaigns that make fast reading seem to be a very important objective. For example, in *The New York Times,* Sunday, June 23, 1968 (Section E, pages 7 and 8), there are large display advertisements by two organizations, each of which guarantees to triple reading efficiency without loss in comprehension, or refund the student's money. The tremendous volume of reading material which a typical student or business executive needs to cover has made such training seem very attractive. We may well ask, what effect does speeding up reading have on comprehension?

Reports of fairly conventional programs to increase rate of reading generally state that comprehension averaged nearly 70 percent at the beginning of the program. Gains of 20 to 40 percent in average rate are usual, with no significant change up or down in comprehension.

At the elementary school level there is some evidence that practices designed primarily to stress rate do not produce as much growth in comprehension as developmental reading programs in which rate is not stressed. For example, Skarbeck (15), in a doctoral thesis, compared the effects of an experimental program designed to improve rate of comprehension with a control conventional developmental reading program, using pupils in the sixth grade. The experimental group made greater gains in rate, but the control group made greater gains in the comprehension of study-type exercises. Witham (21) compared the gains made by eighth-grade students in three programs: a controlled reader group using a machine which required them to read at a given rate; a materials group using the same content as the controlled reader group, but in normal printed format without the machine presentation; and a con-

trol group following the regular curriculum in English language arts, with little or no attention to reading skills. In this doctoral study both experimental groups gained more in reading than the control group. The machine group made slightly greater gains in rate than the materials group, while the materials group made slightly greater gains in comprehension. One is tempted to repeat the old generalization that we learn what we practice; when greater stress is on rate, that is the area of greater gain; and when greater stress is on comprehension, greater gains are made in comprehension.

The commercial organizations which guarantee to produce tremendous gains in rate without harm to comprehension do not publish research results, and as yet there is little evidence of a research nature concerning the real outcomes of such programs. Spache (16) has pointed out that while rates of several thousand words per minute can be attained by rapid skimming or scanning in which large portions of the printed matter are not perceived, genuine reading in which most of the printed words are perceived cannot proceed faster than 800 to 900 words per minute. Tinker (19) has also concluded that 800 words per minute is about the fastest rate possible for genuine reading, and that rates faster than that are based on skimming. These calculations are based on the assumption that ten-word lines are read with an average of three fixations per line, of approximately one-quarter of a second each, plus the very brief times required for moving the eyes from one fixation to the next, and from the end of one line to the beginning of the next line. This would be truly superior reading, for average college students read at 280 words per minute with nine fixations for a ten-word line (17,18). Thus, genuine reading is possible at a rate about three times the rate used by average college students. It is open to serious question whether turning pages at rates of over a thousand words per minute is really reading, or a form of skimming.

Spache (16) also reported eye-movement studies of some graduates of one of the commercial speed reading organizations. In reading test selections for the eye-movement camera their rates tended to fall between 400 and 600 words per minute, with about 70 percent comprehension; these are representative results for superior readers at the college level. In reading a book in the way they had been taught, group average rates ranged from 1800 to 2400 words per minute, with about 50 percent comprehension. While there are some reading situations in which 50 percent comprehension may satisfy the reader's purpose, such a low comprehension score can hardly be recommended as satisfactory in typical reading situations.

Liddle (6), in a doctoral thesis, compared 25 college students taught by the Wood Reading Dynamics Method with a control group. The experimental group increased their rates of reading tremendously—6.1 times in fiction and 5.6 times in nonfiction. However, the experimental group after training, did not do as well on comprehension tests either as they themselves had done before training, or as the control group did. This study reinforces the conclusion that present techniques for achieving extremely high reading rates are somewhat injurious to comprehension.

Development of Study-Type Reading Skills

For students, and for professional, scientific, and occupational reading, the most important applications of reading skills are in those activities we call study-

ing. Study-type reading may be divided into two main kinds. The first, the most common, is *assimilative reading,* in which the purpose is to absorb and remember the content of a reference work such as a textbook. The second kind is *research reading,* in which one starts with a problem, locates sources of information, selects what is relevant to the problem, analyzes and compares information from different sources, and organizes one's findings into an oral or written report. This paper, for example, is based on research-type reading.

Assimilative Reading

A systematic study procedure first published by Francis P. Robinson (11), called the SQ3R system, has been very widely used. This system involves five steps: (1) survey—make a quick overview of the material; (2) question—turn each heading and sub-heading into a question; (3) read—to find answers to the questions; (4) recite—state the answers and evidence found to yourself, subvocally, orally, or in the form of written notes; and (5) review—at appropriate intervals for permanent retention. This system seems to be well grounded in the experimental psychology of learning, but has not been subjected to much experimentation.

One recent report (14) indicates that the SQ3R system can be successfully taught to pupils in the seventh grade. Two comparable classes were taught social studies with the same materials; one class was taught the SQ3R plan and guided in applying it in studying the textbook, while the other class was given no special guidance in how to study their assignments. The experimental class finished the year significantly ahead on teacher-made tests, although there were no significant differences on standardized social studies tests. Although this was a small-scale study and lacked some desirable experimental controls, it does show that the SQ3R plan can be successfully taught as early as the seventh grade.

The most stimulating paper on study skills in higher education to come to my attention in recent years was written by Walter Pauk (10), who is director of the Reading-Study Center at Cornell University. Pauk believes that combining training for increasing rate with training in study skills within one program sets up a conflict which diminishes the value of the training in study procedures, and he recommends that effort should be concentrated on training in various forms of careful, close reading. As evidence, he cites results from two different kinds of college reading programs. One was a six-session study skills course in which the students were advised to ignore rate and to concentrate on developing study skills. The other was a fourteen-session course in which the first two sessions were on speed reading, then six sessions on study skills similar to those in the six-session course, and finally six sessions on various aspects of comprehension. During the fourteen-session course the students were given the opportunity to practice rate improvement individually. Both programs were followed by some improvement in average grades the next semester, but the six-session program was followed by a gain in grade point average which was three times the gain made in the fourteen-session course. Pauk attributes the lesser gain in the fourteen-session course to the preoccupation of some of the students with rate rather than with careful study. Thus he challenges the widely prevalent idea that improving rate of reading, without loss in comprehension, should be a major objective in reading programs for students. Pauk advocates full commitment to the teaching of a study pattern, the taking of lecture notes and reading notes, and other study skills.

The rather startling results reported by Pauk should be checked by repeating the essentials of his study in other institutions. If it can be verified that a six-session course concentrating on study skills can produce more improvement in students' grades than most current college reading improvement programs, a major change in the nature of such programs may be desirable. There would naturally follow a corresponding change of emphasis from rate improvement to study techniques in secondary school and adult reading programs. Training in rate might then be reserved for the minority whose rate is unusually and unnecessarily slow, and for those whose reading needs require the rather sketchy coverage of large amounts of reading material. The newer programs would concentrate on teaching the student how to study, how to extract what he needs from what he reads, how to organize this knowledge, and how to remember what he has read.

Research Reading

Although problem-centered or project-centered reading has been employed in schools to some extent since the beginning of the Progressive Education movement (5), very little research has been done on this important kind of reading. Nearly thirty years ago, Gans (4) studied the ability of superior readers in grades four through six to distinguish between paragraphs that are helpful in providing information on a specific question and paragraphs that are somewhat related but provide no information on that question. Although these children scored well on standardized tests, they had considerable difficulty in selecting the relevant paragraphs. It seems probable that unless specific skills of research reading are taught, many children will not develop them.

A necessary preliminary to the formulation of sound research in this area is a satisfactory classification of the behaviors involved in research reading. H. Alan Robinson (12) has developed such a classification, based on the use of interviews, introspection, and written reports on the procedures used by bright fourth-grade pupils. The resulting categories include seven types of location skills and eight types of comprehension skills, and closely resemble the classifications to be found in several textbooks on how to teach reading. The comprehension headings Robinson used are: using experience and/or knowledge; defining the problem; grasping main ideas; reading for details; making inferences; drawing conclusions; comparing ideas; and understanding vocabulary.

This area of reading is one in which considerable new research is needed.

Summary

The relationship of rate to comprehension has been a subject of research interest for several decades. It has become evident that correlations between the two vary according to the group tested, the kinds of reading matter used, the measuring instruments, and the purpose for reading; most correlations have been positive but quite low. Although flexibility in reading has been stated as a desirable objective for many years, research shows that most people are relatively inflexible in their ways of reading. Flexibility can, however, be improved when reading practice is directed toward it. Conventional programs which aim at improving rate generally produce moderate gains in rate with no significant changes in comprehension. New techniques can produce extremely large gains in rate of reading or skimming, but do so at the expense of a significant loss in comprehension. A recent study suggests that exclusive attention to study skills with no attention to rate may produce greater gains in scholarship than combining some training in study skills with some rate improvement practice. Studies on research-type reading have demonstrated that good basic reading skills do not guarantee effective research-type reading, and have provided confirmation of the categories usually employed in describing research reading skills.

References

1. BLOMMERS, PAUL J., and LINDQUIST, E. F. "Rate of Comprehension of Reading: Its Measurement and Its Relationship to Comprehension," *Journal of Educational Psychology,* 35 (November, 1944), 449–73.

2. BRAAM, LEONARD. "Developing and Measuring Flexibility in Reading," *The Reading Teacher, 16* (January, 1963), 247–54.

3. BUSWELL, GUY T. "Relationship Between Rate of Thinking and Rate of Reading," *School Review,* 49 (September, 1951), 339–46.

4. GANS, ROMA. *A Study of Critical Reading Comprehension in the Intermediate Grades.* Contribution to Education, No. 811. New York: Bureau of Publications, Teachers College, Columbia University, 1940.

5. HARRIS, ALBERT J. "Progressive Education and Reading Instruction,"

The Reading Teacher, 18 (November, 1964), 128–38.

6. LIDDLE, WILLIAM. "An Initial Investigation of the Wood Reading Dynamics Method." Unpublished Doctoral Dissertation. School of Education, University of Delaware, 1965.

7. McDONALD, ARTHUR S. "Factors Affecting Reading Test Performance," *Ninth Yearbook of the National Reading Conference,* 1960, 29–35.

8. ———. "Flexibility in Reading." *Reading as an Intellectual Activity,* J. Allen Figurel (ed.). International Reading Association Conference Proceedings, 8 (1963), 81–84.

9. ———. "Research for the Classroom: Rate and Flexibility," *Journal of Reading,* 8 (January, 1965), 187–91.

10. PAUK, WALTER. "Scholarly Skills as Gadgets," *Journal of Reading,* 8 (March, 1965), 234–39.

11. ROBINSON, FRANCIS P. *Effective Study.* New York: Harper & Row, 1946.

12. ROBINSON, H. ALAN. "Reading Skills Employed in Solving Social Studies Problems," *The Reading Teacher,* 18 (January, 1965), 263–69.

13. SHORES, HARLAN J., and HUSBANDS, KENNETH L. "Are Fast Readers the Best Readers?" *Elementary English,* 27 (1950), 52–57.

14. SISTER MARY DONALD. "The SQ3R Method in Grade Seven," *Journal of Reading,* 11 (October, 1967), 33–35, 43.

15. SKARBECK, JAMES F. "The Effect of a Program Emphasizing Rate of Comprehension Upon Rate of Reading and Comprehension at the Sixth-Grade Level." Unpublished Doctoral Dissertation. School of Education, University of Maryland, 1965.

16. SPACHE, GEORGE D. "Is This a Breakthrough in Reading?" *The Reading Teacher,* 15 (1962), 258–63.

17. TAYLOR, SANFORD E. "Eye Movements in Reading: Facts and Fallacies," *American Educational Research Journal,* 2 (1965), 187–202.

18. ———, FRANCKENPOHL, HELEN, and PETTE, JAMES L. *Grade Level Norms for the Components of the Fundamental Reading Skill.* Research Information Bulletin, No. 3. Huntington, New York: Educational Development Laboratories, 1960.

19. TINKER, MILES A. "Recent Studies of Eye Movements in Reading," *Psychological Bulletin,* 55 (1950), 4.

20. ———. "Speed Versus Comprehension in Reading as Affected by Level of Difficulty," *Journal of Educational Psychology,* 30 (1939), 81–94.

21. WITHAM, ANTHONY P. "An Investigation of a Controlled Reading Technique with Eighth Grade Students." Unpublished Doctoral Dissertation. School of Education, Wayne State University, 1966.

22. YOAKAM, GERALD A. *Reading and Study.* New York: Macmillan, 1928. Pp. 64–68.

72. Devices to Improve Speed of Reading *

MILES A. TINKER

EXAMINATION of the book and materials exhibits at the national meetings of the International Reading Association reveals a bewildering array of gadgets promoted to improve the speed of reading. In addition are the advertisements in both scientific and popular magazines, plus the visits of persuasive salesmen. The claims made for these devices are enticing and more often than not appear valid to the teachers and others who want to improve the reading speed of pupils or of themselves. It is high time to make an objective evaluation of the usefulness of these devices or machines or gadgets.

All or most of these devices have their origins in attempts to improve reading speed by training (i.e., pacing) eye movements. In these attempts stress was placed upon the difference between the eye movements during reading of poor and good readers. The good readers tended to make few fixations and regressions per line of print, while poor readers usually made many fixations and regressions in their reading. This observation eventually led to the practice of attempting to improve rate of reading by training eye movements. Early procedures "trained" a reader to fixate three times on vertical marks equally spaced across lines of the length of ordinary printed lines. Presumably, after this habit was perfected, the reader would use only three fixations for

* From Miles A. Tinker, "Devices to Improve Speed of Reading," *Reading Teacher,* 20 (April, 1967), 605–9. Reprinted by the permission of the International Reading Association and the author.

each line of print in reading. Another variation was to print or type phrases separated by extra spaces and to encourage the reader to make one fixation on each phrase. But individuals vary greatly in the number of fixations employed in reading a line of print, even after training such as described above. Any statements that superior readers make only three or four fixations per line are misleading generalizations of the facts. When a line of twenty-four to twenty-six picas (commonly used in printing books) is used, six to eight fixations per line are employed by good readers, according to data cited by Anderson and Dearborn (1). In fact, it has been shown that after the training described above readers continue to make more than three fixations per line. Buswell (4) also notes that few subjects ever achieve three fixations per line.

Soon gadgets or devices appeared on the market designed to pace eye movements so that only three fixations would be employed to read a line of print. One of these machines is the metron-o-scope, a triple-action electrically operated tachistoscope (short exposure apparatus) which exposes successive thirds of a line of printed matter. (Although this apparatus is no longer on the market, hundreds of them are owned by schools and clinics.) After the first line of a selection has been exposed in this manner, the second line is exposed similarly. This continues with successive lines until the whole selection has been read.

Using the metron-o-scope gives rather uniform results in promoting faster reading. The question arises as to whether the use of the apparatus is necessary to achieve speedier reading. Whether dealing with children or adults, the answer is no. Cason (5), working with third-grade children, found significant gains: (a) by use of the metron-o-scope, (b) by well-motivated reading in the library, and (c) by use of special phrases marked up into phrase units. The gains proved to be just as good by one method as by any other. Her analysis indicated no special benefit from use of the machine. And Westover (11) found that college students who used ordinary materials and methods in a well-motivated speedup program made just as good gains in speed of reading as students using a modified metron-o-scope.

Another device which has found wide usage is the Harvard Reading Films or modification of the principle such as the High School Reading Training Films (State University of Iowa). These are motion picture techniques in which phrases, grouped in thought units, appear on a screen in boldface type on a faint printing of the whole page of connected material. The rate at which the phrases succeed one another can be varied by adjusting the speed control of the projector. The alleged values of the films are that they (a) give a mechanical stimulus which focuses attention and aids concentration and the rapid association of meanings without verbalization, (b) provide practice in reading by thought units, and (c) give students objective evidence that improvement is possible.

Glock (6) evaluated the film technique by studying the effect upon eye movements and reading rate of three methods of training: (a) using the Harvard films, (b) employing a new film which exposed two successive lines simultaneously, and (c) reading printed material while motivated to read fast and comprehend. Four weeks of training was given to six sections of college students.

The students made significant improvements in eye movements and thus in rate of reading under all three methods of training. But there were no significant differences between results of the three methods, i.e., the technique that paced eye movements (Harvard Films) was no more effective than either of the others in increasing speed of reading.

Other pacing machines are in common use. Some devices pace the reader by moving a shutter, line by line, over the material being read. The reader is expected to keep ahead of the shutter. The rate of moving the shutter may be varied from slow to fast. In one variety of this type of machine, a shadow from a wire moves down the page of printed material. The reader tries to keep ahead of the shadow. The trade names of some of these machines are: Controlled Reader, Reading Accelerator, Reading Rate Controller, Rate Reader, and Reading Board. The same end may be accomplished by a push-card method. The teacher pushes a large card from top to bottom of a page while the reader is supposed to keep ahead of the card. The rate of moving the card can be varied to suit the needs of the particular pupil.

Reading speed is increased for many but not for all pupils by use of pacers just described. But there is no assurance that the gains are lasting after the pacing is stopped. Also, the improved rate is not transferred to other types of reading material without special training. Proponents argue that the machines improve rate of reading because of the increased motivation of the reader while using the gadget. Spache (9) states: "The answer that research gives to this question is that gains in reading rate or speed of word recognition can be achieved equally as well by ordinary motivated practice or carefully planned classroom activities." He also states that the use of these pacers when other methods fail to provide sufficient motivation or impetus will help some students to read faster. And he notes that the pacers are not successful with all students and cannot be used indiscriminately.

Should the teacher use the reading accelerator type of pacer to improve the speed of reading? One argument usually advanced for use of pacers is that pupils are tremendously interested in the use of the device and thus highly motivated. This is true. But even so, such children make no greater gains than do those taught by regular methods. Any skilled teacher should be able to provide the incentives that promote good motivation. There is always a possibility that some child will improve with machine training but not by good classroom methods. However, no investigation has shown this to be so.

Another difficulty is that, when speed per se is taught by machine, the pupil may be prevented from becoming a versatile user of rates of reading, i.e., from becoming flexible in the use of different rates according to the kind and difficulty of the material to be read and the purpose for which the reading is done. Too frequently, a teacher may consider that a machine will solve all her problems, and will use it not as a supplement but to the exclusion of proper emphasis on more fundamental aspects of reading instruction.

The Flashmeter, the Tach-X, and other short exposure devices known by the general name tachistoscopes are employed to flash number series and words upon a screen for a brief interval. The aim of this technique is to develop quick perception and increase the span of recognition, and hence speed of reading. Flash cards may be used instead of a tachistoscope. However, Anderson and Dearborn (1) are doubtful that tachistoscopic training has value in increasing the speed of reading. They conclude that the time might

be better spent on promoting growth in comprehension. But Brown (3), on the other hand, describes and supports the alleged advantages of using the tachistoscope to improve reading, including rate. His report, and others like it, apparently fail to take into account the role played by other factors in an experimental program, such as motivation to improve vocabulary, comprehension training, etc. In a carefully controlled experiment Manolakes (8) checked the influence of tachistoscopic training on improvement of eye movements and hence on speed of reading. When the effects of other factors were isolated, he found that the use of the tachistoscope had no effect upon reading performance. In a more recent study Bormuth and Aker (2), using sixth-grade pupils, investigated the influence of tachistoscopic training on reading performance. All other factors in the experiment were carefully controlled. They found that the tachistoscopic training over a period of twenty weeks was ineffective in improving rate of reading, comprehension, or vocabulary. Jones and Van Why (7) also found that tachistoscopic training over a period of three months had no effect on reading rate and comprehension with fourth- and fifth-grade pupils. An evaluation of the entire body of relevant literature by Tinker (10) suggests that tachistoscopic training to improve rate of reading is of no, or at least of questionable, value.

A summary for the evaluation of machines, gadgets, and devices used to improve speed of reading follows:

1. Many so-called procedures for training eye movements or for controlled reading result in improved speed.

2. The improvement obtained by eye-movement training, with or without elaborate apparatus, is no greater than that resulting from motivated reading alone.

3. Experiments concerned with pacing

eye movements and controlled reading usually involve other techniques and are never divorced from increased motivation. Buswell (4) flatly states that "training eye movements does not increase reading ability."

4. The use of pacing devices too often becomes a ritual tending toward an over-emphasis upon the mechanics of reading to the sacrifice of adequate attention to the more important processes of perception, apprehension, and assimilation. This mechanical training may result in a decrease in the flexibility and adaptability of reading habits that characterize good readers. According to Buswell (4), "The exploiting of machines and gadgets" to

control reading "by persons who do not understand the psychology of reading seems at present to be adding greatly to this mechanistic folly."

5. The tachistoscope is without value for increasing speed of reading. And the tachistoscope and rate controller devices are relatively expensive equipment. The money might be better used for books and other more worthwhile supplies.

6. It is the view of this writer that as long as gadgets and comparable devices are used by those with an inadequate understanding of the psychology of reading we shall continue to have the undesirable emphasis upon oculomotor mechanics.

References

1. ANDERSON, I. H., and DEARBORN, W. F. *The Psychology and Teaching of Reading.* New York: Ronald Press, 1952.

2. BORMUTH, J. R., and AKER, C. C. "Is the Tachistoscope a Worthwhile Teaching Tool," *Reading Teacher,* 14 (1961), 172–76.

3. BROWN, J. I. "Teaching Reading with the Tachistoscope," *Journal of Developmental Psychology,* 1, no. 2 (1958), 8–18.

4. BUSWELL, G. T. *Remedial Reading at the College and Adult Levels.* Supplementary Educational Monographs, No. 50, 1939.

5. CASON, E. B. *Mechanical Methods for Increasing the Speed of Reading.* New York: Bureau of Publications, Teachers College, Columbia University, 1943. No. 878.

6. GLOCK, M. D. "Effect Upon Eye Movements and Reading Rate at the College Level of Three Methods of Training," *Journal of Educational Psychology,* 40 (1949), 93–106.

7. JONES, R., and VAN WHY, E. "Tachistoscopic Training in the Fourth and Fifth Grades," *Journal of Developmental Reading,* 6 (1963), 177–85.

8. MANOLAKES, G. "The Effects of Tachistoscopic Training in an Adult Reading Program," *Journal of Applied Psychology,* 36 (1952), 410–12.

9. SPACHE, G. D. *Toward Better Reading.* Champaign, Ill.: Garrard Publishing Company, 1963.

10. TINKER, M. A. "The Study of Eye Movements in Reading," *Psychological Bulletin,* 43 (1946), 93–120.

11. WESTOVER, F. L. *Controlled Eye Movements versus Practice Exercises in Reading.* New York: Bureau of Publications, Teachers College, Columbia University, 1946. No. 917.

73. Parents Are Needed in a Good Reading Program *

NANCY LARRICK

A child's success in reading depends in large part on his parents. If they are interested in reading, he grows up with the positive attitude that reading is something to be cultivated. If they have read to him and provided books even in early childhood, he comes to school ready for many new experiences with books and stories.

"I can always tell when a child has been read to," said one teacher, "because he enters first grade eager to read himself."

Whether the parent realizes it or not, he has guided the child's education for five to six years before formal schooling begins. It may have been very stimulating guidance that has contributed to the child's language development, interest in reading, and intellectual maturity. In some cases, it may have been a negative sort of guidance that insisted the child be seen and not heard.

Consciously or unconsciously, the parent's influence continues after schooling begins. By probing questions and invidious comparisons, the overanxious parent may have a paralyzing influence on the child. At the other extreme is the parent whose apathy may be deadening. Somewhere in between is the well-informed parent who is the teacher's mainstay in developing the child's interest in reading and through this interest his skill in reading.

* From Nancy Larrick, "Parents Are Needed in a Good Reading Program," in *Contributions in Reading,* no. 23, pp. 1–7. Copyright © 1959. Reprinted by permission of the author and Ginn and Co., Waltham, Mass.

In most cases, a child's reading is more completely related to his out-of-school life than any other segment of the school program. His facility with language depends in large measure on the experiences he has before and after the school day. His vocabulary, his enunciation, his ability to interpret language often develop according to his language opportunities outside of school. If his use of English has been limited in a foreign-language home, he begins first-grade reading with a handicap. If he has been nurtured on baby talk, he is poorly qualified to begin the first lessons in word-attack skills.

Few parents realize that such factors influence a child's reading. All too often they think of reading in terms of special books, special word lists, and special teaching procedures from which they are excluded. Occasionally a parent is heard to say, "All I can do is keep hands off." What such a parent does not realize is that his influence continues, even under the hands-off policy. It may be a positive influence or a negative influence, but it is there just the same.

Teachers and Parents Need Help from Each Other

One of the great responsibilities of teachers and school administrators is to enlist parents' support so that the home influence is helpful, not hindering. Teachers need parental backing and daily cooperation if classroom reading lessons are to be fully effective. Parents need information and guidance if they are to influence a child's reading positively. For best results, there should be a two-way exchange of information.

What Teachers Can Learn from Parents

To teach reading effectively, you need to know the child well. From the parent you can get first-hand information that will be helpful. What things is he most interested in? What is his favorite free-time activity? What stories does he prefer? What school events does he talk about with pleasure? How does he get along with children in the neighborhood? Is he silent and retiring with them? Or does he talk easily and naturally? Does he raise questions about unusual things he sees on a family outing or trip? Does he get plenty of rest and outdoor exercise? Does he have time to talk things over in a relaxed setting at home? Is he learning to think critically, raising doubts and making comparisons in order to reach his own conclusions? What books does he have access to, either at home or through the public library? Is he given an opportunity to use reading as an everyday tool —hunting up numbers in the telephone directory, checking timetables, reading directions on the can of frozen fruit juice, or searching the TV guide?

Of course, not all these questions should be hurled at a parent at one sitting. But they are the kinds of questions that parents can answer more easily than the teacher, and all have bearing on the child's reading. Even one or two such questions may bring valuable clues to the child's interests and personality. And in answering such questions, parents may begin to realize that reading is much more than systematic word drill.

What Parents Want to Know

Some of the most articulate parents ask immediately about the way reading is taught today. Often they plunge right in with questions and comments about modern methods and older methods.

When parents come loaded with questions, they are entitled to prompt and direct answers. Postponing the answers serves only to increase blood pressure. If your explanation is simple and your suggestions are specific, your chances of winning the parent as a helping teacher are much greater.

Those parents concerned with teaching methods usually begin with queries about the sight method and the phonic method. Frequently they assume that teachers use one or the other and that reading difficulty stems from selecting the wrong method. Yet the best teachers are helping children to read by sight and to use phonics along with other word-attack skills.

If parents stop to analyze their own reading habits, they recognize the place of sight reading. They read hundreds of words by sight every day—their names, stop-and-go signals, TV commercials, newspaper banners, familiar billboards, and such connecting words as *in, for, by, to, with.*

They use phonics to figure out unfamiliar words. But even so, phonics will give only the sound, not the meaning. Sometimes they use word parts or structure but the meaning is still not clear. So they may have to turn to a dictionary to find the definition of *anticlinorium.* Furthermore, no rule of phonics will work with such irregular words as *bough, cough, enough,* and *through.*

In one survey, parents were asked to name the questions about children's reading which troubled them most. The following were mentioned most frequently:

1. What is the sight method?
2. What about phonics?
3. Why teach more than phonics?
4. How does a child learn to read?

5. When should he start to read?
6. What is meant by "reading readiness"?
7. When do children learn the alphabet?
8. Why do children in the same class use different books?
9. How does the teacher handle so many reading levels in one class?
10. How does she check reading progress?
11. Why promote a child who isn't reading up to grade standard?
12. Shouldn't the superior reader skip a grade?
13. What reading materials are recommended for different grade levels?

Such questions show that parents are eager to get at the reasons back of the are more interested in this sort of thing than others. But most of them want to school reading program. Some parents know why reading is taught as it is today. Once their questions are answered, such parents are eager for specifics of how they can help the child outside of school.

Other parents will skip the reasons and move into the how-to-do-it stage at once. At some point they all want to know how to help.

This is a do-it-yourself age, and parents are geared to that philosophy. They can get exact directions for laying linoleum in the kitchen, so they expect equally specific directions for giving help in reading. Department stores and mail-order catalogues capitalize on this situation by offering how-to-do-it kits "guaranteed to teach your child to read." Games and gadgets galore are available for word drill and word analysis.

Frequently parents think this is the only way they can help a child with reading. Yet, except in special cases, isolated word drill is probably the least effective way.

Far more promising is parental aid in creating a desire to read and in developing lifetime reading habits. To translate this into specific recommendations, cer-

tain basic principles of learning must be kept in mind:

1. *We learn by doing.* Children's reading improves with their use of language in conversation, listening to stories being read, and eventually through reading to themselves and sometimes to others.

2. *We usually learn best the things we like to do.* Children who have enjoyed stories read aloud to them and who have an opportunity to read about their greatest interests are more apt to grow rapidly in their reading skills. In general, reading skills increase with reading pleasure.

3. *We comprehend more readily the information and ideas that have immediate relevance and use for us.* Children who have a rich background of experience are more likely to understand what they read and to evaluate and criticize.

Few parents will be receptive to a 1-2-3 list of "basic principles of learning"; but they will welcome suggestions for activities that are backed by reasons which are logical and within their grasp. They have heard their babies learn to talk and understand words. They have watched their children learn to jump rope and roller-skate. They have observed many differences among children. They know the driving power of a child's interests. Yet few of them have been aware that the same principles of learning affect the way a child learns to read.

The parents' role in the reading program will be much clearer if they learn to think of the child's reading in relation to his total life and personality.

Three Major Areas for Parent Help

Since parents are with the child far more than the teacher is, their influence can be more far-reaching. It takes time to develop understanding, yet reading is understanding the printed word. Equally important, it takes time to develop appreciation and satisfaction, yet the lifetime habit of reading grows out of pleasure in reading.

Further, the relaxed atmosphere of the home can be more conducive to leisurely reading aloud, two-way conversation, and really personal evaluation than the more formal and crowded classroom. And the intimate association of parent and child can result in making reading more personal and hence more significant to the youngster.

Reading Aloud at Home

Reading aloud at home is one of the most effective ways by which a parent can help with his child's reading. This is an activity that should begin in playpen days if the child is to grow up with the conviction that reading is a pleasure worth his time and effort. Even a two-year-old will be able to chime in on the refrain of familiar nursery rhymes. He learns where the story begins, how to turn pages, how to get meaning from pictures, and how to follow the sequence of events that brings suspense to the simplest of stories. Woe betide the adult who makes a slip in reading a familiar story!

Even when the child is in school, reading aloud at home should continue. The beginning reader has limited skills and needs to hear the rhythmic language of an experienced reader. This will sharpen his determination to perfect his own skills so that he can undertake more advanced stories himself. Equally important, it will give him an opportunity to talk over what has been read, perhaps criticizing the effectiveness of the story or the accuracy of the information.

What about reading aloud to the child who can read to himself? Won't it spoil him if he is read to? Doesn't he need practice in reading, rather than more practice in listening? Of course he needs practice in reading to himself. But he also needs to make the acquaintance of new stories which the parent can introduce. And he needs the warm, reassuring experience of talking over what has been read.

The independent reader will want to take his turn at reading aloud while parents and younger children listen. And that is good, for he is beginning to assume a more mature role in the family reading hour. But he should not be deprived of the pleasure of listening simply because he can read on his own.

Relating Reading to Interests

Relating a child's reading to the things he is interested in is the second big area in which parents can make a great contribution. Once he stops to think, any parent will acknowledge that little or nothing can sidetrack the child who is interested in what he is doing. The third-grader interested in dinosaurs will stretch his skills to read a LIFE article on his favorite subject. And his sixth-grade brother, fascinated by news of outer space, will read a technical article that would stump many an adult. Both boys would have spurned a story about children at play in a sand pile. They will make an extraordinary effort over a longer period when the subject is close to their hearts.

What does this mean for parents? It means a three-step program at home·

1. Encourage a child to pursue his interests
2. Help him to develop new interests through new experiences and new horizons
3. Help him find reading matter that will whet the curiousity and answer the questions that stem from his interests

Every home is full of potential interests for a child: a pet, a TV weather report, the recipe on a package of hot dogs, observance of holidays, family history, the oil burner repairman's visit, family experiences related at the supper table. Beyond his home, the opportunities are limitless: historical landmarks in the community, the airport or railroad yard, a foreign-language family down the street, an approaching hurricane, unidentified rocks or snakes, a new sports car in the neighborhood, a television program, announcement of a new moon shot.

These are subjects that intrigue boys and girls today. But what do these subjects have to do with reading? Once the fact is pointed out, every parent will see that each of these interests can become a springboard to reading. The moon shot can raise the question of the distance to the moon, a direct lead to the family dictionary or encyclopedia. If interest is great enough, it can lead to interesting and authentic books about the moon and the stars.

A television program can send children to the library in droves.

Sea shells collected on vacation can lead to fascinating reading about marine life, the pull of the tides, and our changing earth.

In many families, however, vacation souvenirs gather dust until they are relegated to the trash the following season. And a child's repeated "Why?" is often squelched by adults who fail to recognize this as a springboard to reading.

Most parents need to be alerted to the value of children's questions and interests. If they cultivate an attitude of "Let's look it up," they may lead children to home reference books that give immediate information. These, in turn, can lead to more extended reading of magazine articles and books. But the bridge from curious question to extended reading isn't built by itself. Parents need to lead the way, to help in the selection of books, and sometimes to read aloud the introductory chapters that will sell the book to the child.

Equally important, parents need to introduce new interests. One possibility is through family trips and outings. An expedition to a nearby battlefield or historical shrine might lead to reading of many kinds: road maps that show the way, historical markers and folders, encyclopedia articles that give further explanation, biographies, history, stories laid in the same setting or period.

For children too young to be reading themselves, a trip to a turkey farm or dairy will give the impetus for questions, conversation, and information. Further, such trips will add meaning to the printed words read to the child or which he will read by himself later on.

Providing Many Books in the Home

Surrounding the child with books at home will increase his interest in reading and provide the practice that he needs to become a fluent reader. Without attractive reading material, many a child turns to comic books and TV as his favorite entertainment. Usually he has never had a comparable array of books from which to select. Access to an interesting book should be as easy to access to an interesting TV program.

Parents can help provide this extensive reading fare by patronizing the public library. Even tiny tots will benefit from a visit to the children's room or corner. The weekly story hour for boys and girls is the perfect introduction to the library and many favorite books to be read aloud at home or read independently by the child. Public library lists help with book selection, and the children's librarian is usually full of suggestions for books that will appeal to a child's special interests.

Certainly, regular visits to the public library—with plenty of time to pick and choose—are just as important as visits to the supermarket. The child who is at home in the public library is likely to remain a frequent library visitor and borrower.

The school library is another excellent source of books and information about children's reading. Often the school librarian can go one step further because she is able to suggest books that relate directly to classroom projects and interests.

Borrowed books are just right for some kinds of reading. But a child needs books he can go back to again and again. They will make reading seem a more intimate part of his life, and with books of his own around him he is more likely to read and reread. A small bookrack on a child's bureau will give a fixed place for his first books of Mother Goose and nursery stories. Later, bricks and boards can make a convenient bookcase for his expanding library.

Every home should have a dictionary, almanac, and atlas to which children can turn for quick answers to their questions. Once a family establishes the habit of raising questions and seeking answers, a family encyclopedia will prove invaluable. Collections of stories and of poetry add richness and delight for all ages.

Beyond these, each child should have some books that fit into his particular interests—horse stories, adventure stories, Indian legends, and so on.

Parents who shy away from book buying as too expensive may feel differently when they compare book prices with the tags on "ten-cent-store" plastic toys of doubtful value.

The possibility of book-club membership will interest many parents as a way of buying children's books regularly. In most cases, book-club selections are made by experienced people who know children and books. Added to this is the child's keen interest in anything that comes by mail addressed to him.

How to Reach Parents

Teachers should start early if they want to be of greatest help to parents and get their greatest support. As soon as a child comes under school guidance, arrange to meet the father and mother. At that early stage it is easy to approach a parent and win his friendship.

Remember that co-operation is mutual aid—you need the parents' help just as they need yours. So be ready to meet them at the time and place most convenient to them. Be prepared with questions that show you seek their guidance and help. Give the parents a chance to present their own questions and problems.

Much can be gained in a face-to-face conference with the parents of just one child.

With small groups of parents—the mothers of your class, for example, try the following:

1. Arrange a series of discussion groups to explore such questions as these: How can parents help the beginning reader? How can a child's interests and hobbies help with his reading? How can read-aloud time at home help with school reading? What can be done about the comic book craze?

2. Set up special displays and demonstrations: Favorite books of children in the class. An exhibit of book lists that will help in selecting books for children (*see* p. 381). An exhibit of books and pamphlets about children's reading (*see* p. 382).

3. Compile and distribute a TV guide to children's reading, listing popular TV

programs and the titles of related children's books.

With an auditorium group, sometimes in co-operation with the PTA, many kinds of programs can be set up to explain how children learn to read and how parents can help. For example:

A panel discussion by parents, teachers, and librarians is an excellent way to provide a lively exchange of information on such topics as:

How reading is taught today
How to select books that appeal to children
How to help children enjoy reading
How to select and use reference books in the home
How library facilities in the school and community can be improved as an aid to children's reading

A panel discussion by older children with a good adult leader can bring out important issues about children's reading with suggestions for improving procedures. Popular topics are:

What has helped us most with reading
How we learned to read
Favorite books and why we like them
What would encourage us to read more

Any program—whether with a small or a large group—will be more effective if parents assume the lead in planning and performing. The teacher should help, too, but each person who participates will learn a great deal and develop more intense interest.

Most Important

Nothing encourages a person to read as much as the vivid, first-hand recommendation of others who love reading. In a classroom, one child's enthusiasm for a book can sweep the group like wildfire.

If a teacher has read the book he recommends, children quickly sense the authenticity of the report and are easily persuaded that it is one they would enjoy. Even the teacher's enthusiastic comment about an adult book he is reading on the side may influence a child to value reading more highly.

Similarly, the influence of the parent is greater if he enjoys reading himself. The very fact that he borrows adult books from the library may encourage his children to enjoy the library too. And if parents themselves read, they are demonstrating to children that reading gives continuing satisfaction. With such an example in the home, youngsters soon begin to make reading pleasure a lifetime pleasure.

Book Lists for Family Reference

Adventuring with Books (National Council of Teachers of English, 1111 Kenyon Rd., Urbana, Ill. 61801). Over 1250 outstanding children's books grouped by subject.

Best Books for Children (R. R. Bowker Co., 1180 Avenue of the Americas, New York 10036). Annotated list of over 4,000 current books, grouped by grade level and by subject, with extensive indexes and cross references.

Books for Beginning Readers by Elizabeth Guilfoile. (National Council of Teachers of English, 1111 Kenyon Rd., Urbana, Ill., 61801). Detailed comments about 300 books easy enough for second graders. Revised in 1964.

Children's Books Too Good to Miss compiled by May Hill Arbuthnot and others. (Press of Case Western Reserve University, 11000 Cedar Rd., Cleveland, Ohio 44106). Annotations for 230 choice books for children, with illustrations.

Growing Up with Books (R. R. Bowker Co., 1180 Avenue of the Americas, New York 10036). A list of 250 favorites in a small illlustrated booklet revised annually. Excellent for quantity distribution through PTA, women's clubs, and discussion groups. Also *Growing Up with Science Books* (same publisher).

Let's Read Together: Books for Family Enjoyment, selected and annotated by a special committee of the National Congress of Parents and Teachers and the Children's Services Division, American Library Association. (American Library Association, 50 E. Huron Street, Chicago, Ill. 60611). About 750 books are annotated and arranged in subject areas. A splendid guide for parents.

Books and Pamphlets About Children's Reading

Before the Child Reads by James L. Hymes, Jr. (Harper and Row). Practical suggestions given in a warm and convincing manner.

"Bequest of Wings": A Family's Pleasure with Books by Annis Duff (Viking). How the Duffs introduced books and reading to their children, with anecdotes and suggestions.

Books, Children & Men by Paul Hazard, translated by Marguerite Mitchell (The Horn Book, Inc.) The pertinent comments of a member of the French Academy on children's book choices as opposed to those of adults.

Children and Books by May Hill Arbuthnot (Scott, Foresman). Intended primarily for teachers, this book tells of the reading interests of children from two to fourteen, suggests hundreds of good books, and advises how to introduce children and books.

Common Sense in Teaching Reading by Roma Gans (Bobbs-Merrill). An inspired teacher gives her down-to-earth suggestions.

A Parent's Guide to Children's Reading by Nancy Larrick (Hardbound—Doubleday, Garden City, N.Y. 11530; Paperback—Pocket Books, 620 Fifth Ave., New York, N.Y. 10020). An easy-to-read handbook that gives detailed answers to parents' questions about how reading is taught and how they can help. It includes booklists, book club information, and suggestions for a home library.

Recipe for a Magic Childhood by Mary Ellen Chase (Macmillan). In this tiny book, first published as a magazine article, a beloved author recalls how her parents introduced her to reading.

This Is Reading by Frank G. Jennings (Bureau of Publications, Teachers College, Columbia University; Paperback—Dell Publishing Co.). A provocative book about the nature, the uses, the teaching, and the value of reading. For parents and teachers.

Using Literature with Young Children, edited by Leland Jacobs (Teachers College Press, Teachers College, Columbia University). Twelve chapters about ways to introduce children and books through reading aloud, storytelling, choral speaking, dramatization., etc.

Your Child's Reading Today by Josette Frank (Doubleday, Garden City, N.Y. 11530). An interesting report on children's reading, their interests and choices, with suggestions to help parents, plus annotated lists of books for various needs.

XV

Reading for the Gifted

Approximately three percent of the school population are endowed with superior intellect. A number of these children learn to read before entering school and most of them far surpass the level of reading ability possessed by the rest of their age group. Unfortunately, often little is done to help gifted children in the area of reading. Because of their superior achievement, these children are often overlooked when it comes to developing reading skills and interests.

In the first article, Witty notes major characteristics of the gifted and outlines what he considers to be a balanced reading program for them. Martin follows with a discussion of their needs, the roles of the school personnel, and enrichment practices that may be used with superior children. The last two articles are more specific: Merryman's dealing with the use of trade books, and McCracken's with developing reading speed.

74. A Balanced Reading Program for the Gifted *

PAUL A. WITTY

ON the opening day of the school year six-year-old Bill arrived carrying under his arm a book—*All About Electricity*. At recess the principal of the school, who had noticed the book on Bill's desk, commented to the boy: "That's a good book. Are you enjoying the pictures?"

* From Paul A. Witty, "A Balanced Reading Program for the Gifted," *Reading Teacher,* 16 (May, 1963), 418–24. Reprinted by permission of the International Reading Association and the author.

"Yes, it is a good book," Bill answered. "I've read about two-thirds of it. I like the pictures too."

Bill's language devolpment was really exceptional. Although he was barely six years of age, his vocabulary was outstanding. He was able to read and comprehend third- or fourth-grade materials readily. He had already completed a rather large number of children's books, and he was presently finding out all he could about electricity.

Bill could read before coming to

school. He was not *taught* to read. He had learned, his mother said, by asking the names of the words he saw on signs and in newspapers, magazines, and books. Soon he was able to read phrases and short sentences.

There is a considerable number of such very intelligent children. In Bill's own classroom in a suburban area there were two other pupils who on entering school were able to read primary-grade materials successfully. In the second grade of the same school, there was Mary, who exceeded the average of pupils in the sixth grade on tests of reading ability.

These children are clearly to be classified as "gifted." There is of course no clear-cut line of distinction between the gifted and others, although educators have for many years been inclined to refer to children as gifted if their I.Q.'s were 130 or higher (12). At one time, such children were thought to comprise about 1 percent of the elementary school population. Today, estimates are usually somewhat higher. For example, J. J. Gallagher indicates that 2–4 percent of the general school population will have I.Q.'s of 132 and over and may be referred to as "gifted." In favorable socioeconomic communities the percentage may be 6–12 (6).

Characteristics of the Gifted

One of the most noticeable characteristics of the gifted child is his remarkable language development. Thus, C. C. Miles states: "Approximately half of the California gifted children learned to read before starting to school. In Witty's group 38 percent learned to read before the age of five; and of Terman's children, 20 percent learned at this age, 6 percent before three" (8).

Early precocity in vocabulary development continues in the typical gifted child.

For example, one ten-year-old child studied by the writer said that *flaunt* meant "to show or display with intent to show"; *Mars* was defined as "a planet, God of War, also a verb."

Another characteristic of gifted children is the rapidity of their learning. They usually complete assignments in less than half the time allotted to them. On examinations such as the Stanford-Binet, they sometimes finish in a few seconds tests for which a minute is permitted.

By the time the typical child in the writer's early study was in the fourth grade, he had displayed knowledge and skills on tests which equalled the norms for children two grades above him (15). Many were the equals of pupils in grades three or four years above them.

The verbally superior child can be identified readily by the use of intelligence tests. There are other children, however, whose ability and promise are also outstanding who cannot be discovered in this way. These children, too, should be found and encouraged to make full use of their abilities. Perhaps it would be desirable to consider the gifted child as one whose performance in a potentially valuable line of human activity is consistently or repeatedly remarkable.

Educators must be concerned about all types of gifted and talented children, but attention will be given in the first part of this article to pupils of high abstract intelligence. There is evidence that this group is frequently neglected. Moreover, such pupils are found in almost all classrooms, and every teacher can do much to enrich their experience and to encourage their full development. Perhaps the greatest possibility for enrichment lies in the field of reading and language development.

It is evident that guidance of gifted children should begin at home. Parents should read aloud to them and answer their numerous questions about the names of letters and words and phrases they see. Under such conditions and without formal instruction, some gifted children learn to read. Books on various topics should be made available to them, and they should be encouraged to read, without exploitation (1,16).

It is important that the gifted child's ability and rate of learning be fully recognized when he starts school. Teachers, therefore, should have knowledge of the results of intelligence and aptitude tests. They should make an appraisal, too, of the child's reading status at the time he enters the first grade. If a gifted child who already can read is required to follow routine textbooks assignments and is forced to "read" highly repetitious and largely meaningless materials, he will often develop unfortunate attitudes and habits. From the first, reading materials should be made avaliable which will challenge the gifted child's abilities, extend his interests, and present context in a meaningful way (17).

Although some gifted children learn to read before they start school, many others require instruction. In these cases it is essential for the teacher to recognize the rapidity of their learning. With such children it is usually desirable to begin with experience charts and then move rapidly into the reading of primers such as *Friskey the Goat* or *Peanuts the Pony* from Our Animal Story Book Series. There should be a correlated use of reading materials from such series as The True Books, I Want to Be Books, and others (10). Children's literature should be a part of a balanced reading program (7).

The provision of valuable experiences perhaps proceeds with fewer obstacles when grouping is practiced, as in Cleveland's Major Work Classes. Partial segre-gation, as followed in the Colfax Elementary School of Pittsburgh, is also highly successful in enabling the gifted child to advance rapidly in accord with his ability and interests. But how is the teacher in the typical heterogeneous class of the primary grades to offer such children appropriate opportunities and motivation? In the first grade the problem is especially perplexing and difficult. A crucial factor in determining the success of such a program resides in the availability of sufficient materials of instruction to satisfy the pupils' varied needs. Since a few gifted children will be able to read upon entering school, a wide assortment of books encompassing various topics and levels of difficulty should be provided. Children's encyclopedias, dictionaries, magazines, and weekly papers are also desirable. Plans should be made by the teacher for individual conferences with each child to offer the guidance many superior pupils require to gain skills in reading and develop resourcefulness and self-direction in selecting and using books.

To provide for skill development, standard tests of oral and silent reading may be administered to an entire class of primary-grade pupils. Then the pupils may be assigned to small groups for the acquisition of needed skills. Appropriate practice materials or devices such as the Reading Laboratory may be used to offer the specific help some individuals may need, while the teacher gives additional help to other individuals encountering difficulties. If the gifted pupil needs little or no help in skill building, he may employ his time in independent reading or in other types of suitable, constructive endeavor to be shared later with his classmates (2, 5).

There are several kinds of group endeavor which are especially suitable for entire classes of pupils who vary widely in ability. Through suitable group endeavor the gifted pupil may receive appropriate attention. The writer has stressed the value of using certain films and their accompanying books in such efforts. For example, the film "Shep the Farm Dog" and others in the It's Fun to Find Out Series were shown and the books were read by pupils in second-grade classes (18). Discussion followed, and opportunities were made for the pupils to explore each topic further in children's books.

The results of testing showed that under these conditions gifted pupils as well as others made significant gains in the acquisition of reading skills. Similar results have also been obtained in classrooms in which filmstrips such as "The Little House" have been shown and the text on the filmstrip has been followed in books.

The following type of grouping has also been employed successfully in attempts to meet the needs of the gifted in classes enrolling pupils of widely varying ability. Interest inventories are administered and the results are used to set up small flexible groups to explore each area of interest considered to be worthwhile and appealing. Reading materials related to each topic are then made available on varied levels of difficulty. In these interest groups the gifted child is able to participate and contribute from his own individually challenging reading. Such opportunities are not only profitable for the gifted pupil; they have been found of value in motivating other children to read books of greater difficulty than they ordinarily might be expected to read. This type of grouping is often effective in science and social studies.

As has already been indicated, the importance of interests should be fully recognized (4). Studies have shown that most gifted children have rich and varied

interests. They often have a few strong interests, but usually are versatile. They may collect stamps or specimens of various kinds. They are often enthusiastic observers of birds, flowers, the stars, and animal life. But there are some whose home backgrounds are impoverished and in whom wholesome interests are few. To ascertain the extent and nature of the pupil's background and interests, it is desirable for the teacher to administer an interest inventory informally to each child. Worthy interests should then be identified and associated with reading materials whenever possible. In case interests are few or are deemed unsuitable, efforts should be made to create new patterns through direct experience, the use of films and filmstrips, and other activities. One of the chief responsibilities of the school is to provide for the gifted learner wide and suitable reading experience throughout the primary grades.

In the middle grades an effort should be made to provide a balanced program of reading according to the unique nature and needs of each child. Extensive reading in the subject fields is desirable for the gifted child, who should be encouraged to adjust his rate of reading according to his purposes and the type of subject matter.

Despite this promising picture, there are many gifted pupils who need greater help and guidance. In fact, each gifted child requires careful study to determine his particular nature and his needs. As L. M. Terman and M. H. Oden (13) have pointed out:

Gifted children do not fall into a single pattern but into an infinite variety of patterns. One can find within the group individual examples of almost every type of personality defect, social maladjustment, behavior problem, and physical handicap; the only difference is that among gifted children the incidence of these deviations is, in varying degrees, lower than in the general population.

One problem teachers encounter in dealing with some gifted children is their tendency to concentrate too much reading in a single area, to become too specialized in their reading interests. This tendency sometimes appears in an area such as science, in which a gifted child may want to read to such an extent that his pattern of reading lacks balance. In this case, encouragement of wide reading is especially desirable, although special interests should be recognized. In many instances balance in reading is achieved when the teacher and the librarian work together in efforts to help gifted pupils become increasingly proficient in selecting and using books independently.

Some gifted pupils require assistance and guidance in acquiring reading skills. They should receive appropriate instruction geared to their needs. These children are sometimes regarded as "underachievers" and may display personality irregularities and emotional problems traceable to factors such as unfavorable home conditions and unfortunate previous school experience. Attention to these conditions should accompany reading instruction.

To engage successfully in encouraging the gifted child's reading, the teacher should have information about each child's ability and his status in silent and oral reading. The results of standard tests will be helpful, but the teacher should be able to employ other techniques of child study to obtain additional information. It has been pointed out that from interest inventories clues may be obtained which will help the teacher understand pupils' attitudes, problems, and needs (9). Similarly, anecdotal records and other forms of observation may yield data of value. Occasionally, such study will simply make it clear that the teacher's major problem is to help pupils develop more varied or worthwhile patterns of interest.

A balanced program provides the gifted pupil with opportunities to satisfy some of his personal and social needs through reading. An identification with a character in a story is sometimes beneficial. Thus, a gifted boy recovering from rheumatic fever experienced great personal satisfaction by reading Marguerite De Angeli's *Door in the Wall,* a narrative laid in seventeenth-century England, which portrays the ways in which Robin, the son of a nobleman, stricken on the eve of departure for the contest, overcame his affliction and won the king's recognition. Similarly, Eleanor Estes' *The Hundred Dresses* proved of value to an insecure girl through her discovery of the successful course followed by another girl in obtaining group sanction. Elizabeth Yates' *Amos Fortune: Free Man,* a story of a boy's rise above his environment, tells of the problems faced and overcome by an African prince sold into slavery. His devotion to the needy and his many sacrifices proved a heartening picture of what man can be at his best. This book has proved a source of inspiration to many boys.

In the excellent biographical literature now available gifted pupils may find additional inspiration as well as a sound basis for the formation of an ideal of self that is in keeping with their outstanding abilities and promise. Regional books like Lois Lenski's *Strawberry Girl* and *Cotton in My Sack* and family stories such as Eleanor Estes' *Ginger Pye* may also help some gifted children understand people better. Many other books contain materials suitable for fulfilling varied needs.

Muriel Crosby has described a number of situations in which books have served admirably in enabling pupils to make wholesome identifications (3). She states:

All children, like all adults, have problems. Books will not by themselves solve children's problems or adults' problems. But books may help. Books often tell of the problems children may sense but not fully recognize as their own. Books often bring to light a problem which a child cannot bring himself to talk about.

Reading for the Creative Student

Many of the foregoing suggestions concerning reading guidance apply not only to the verbally gifted, but also to pupils of outstanding promise in art, music, creative writing, and other fields. Such pupils may also be superior verbally. We cannot anticipate, however, that all gifted pupils will be located through the use of intelligence tests. In fact, E. P. Torrance states that "about 70 percent of the top 20 percent on measures of creativity would have been excluded from gifted groups which were selected on the basis of intelligence only" (14).

Since the coefficients of correlation between measures of verbal ability and proficiency in art, music, and other creative pursuits are relatively low, there will probably be found a considerably larger number of poor readers among creative pupils than among the verbally gifted. It is desirable, therefore, that creative students be identified and that a thorough appraisal be made of their reading ability and needs. Necessary skills should then be cultivated through the use of appropriate materials.[1]

In some talented children we may find reading limited to a narrow specialization, while in others there may be only a meager interest shown in reading. In still others, reading may be seldom en-

[1] The Reading Laboratories of Science Research Associates and other skill-building materials may often be used independently by many of these pupils.

gaged in because of unfortunate attitudes concerning its value. Attention to interest and motivation is essential if unfortunate habits and attitudes are to be altered. In this effort inventories may be employed to disclose interests that may often be profitably associated with reading experience. There is also the possibility of helping the creative child find suitable reading in the area of his talent.

That the need for guidance of the creative student is great may be seen by reference to the work of E. P. Torrance, who has pioneered in making suggestions for rewarding creative activity. In a provocative article on creative thinking (14) he states:

Many of the highly creative individuals are disturbing students in classroom groups in elementary schools. The problem of teachers and guidance workers resolves itself into one of helping highly creative individuals maintain those characteristics which seem essential to the development of creative talent and, at the same time, helping them acquire skills for avoiding, or reducing to a tolerable level, the peer sanctions.

Like the verbally gifted, the creative child often has a need for experience in reading that will enable him to meet personal and social problems and help him build an appropriate and individually suitable ideal of self. Reading for these purposes may prove even more effective for creative pupils, whose need for assistance appears to be so great. Of course, reading alone is not enough. But reading related to experience and accompanied by discussion may prove quite rewarding.

It will be noted that in this paper the suggested program in reading is essentially developmental in nature and may be recommended for all pupils. One of the great values of such an approach is the pleasure to be found by pupils in "the wonderful world of books." This statement certainly applies to gifted children who, when they have an opportunity to read materials of interest to them, turn joyfully to reading for information and recreation. Their lives will be enriched greatly as their satisfactions are enhanced through books.

References

1. ABRAHAM, WILLARD. *Common Sense about Gifted Children.* New York: Harper, 1958.
2. BARBE, WALTER. *Educator's Guide to Personalized Reading Instruction.* Englewood Cliffs, N.J.: Prentice-Hall, 1961.
3. CROSBY, MURIEL. "Reading for Human Relations," *The Packet,* 16 (Winter, 1961–62), 13.
4. DARROW, HELEN F., and HOWES, VIRGIL M. *Approaches to Individualized Reading.* New York: Appleton-Century-Crofts, 1960.
5. DRAPER, MARCELLA K., and SCHWIETERT, LOUISE H., revised and edited by MAY LAZAR. *A Practical Guide to Individualized Reading.* New York: Board of Education, Publication No. 40, October, 1960.
6. GALLAGHER, JAMES J. *Analysis of Research in the Education of Gifted Children.* State of Illinois: Office of the Superintendent of Public Instruction, 1960.
7. LARRICK, NANCY. *A Teacher's Guide to Children's Books.* Columbus, Ohio: Charles E. Merrill, 1960.
8. MILES, CATHERINE COX. "Gifted Children." *Manual of Child Psychology* (2nd edition) Leonard Carmichael (ed.). New York: John Wiley, 1954.
9. *Northwestern University Interest Inventories.* Evanston, Ill.: Northwestern University.
10. *Our Animal Story Books.* Boston: D. C. Heath. *The True Book Series.* Chicago: Children's Press. *I Want to Be Books.* Chicago: Children's Press. *The Walt Disney Story Books.* Boston: D. C. Heath.
11. STAUFFER, RUSSELL G. "Individualized and Group Directed Reading Instruction," *Elementary English,* 37 (October, 1960).
12. TERMAN, LEWIS M. and ODEN, MELITA H. *The Gifted Child Grows Up.* Stanford, Calif.: Stanford University Press, 1947.
13. ———. "The Stanford Studies of the Gifted," *The Gifted Child,* PAUL WITTY (ed.). Boston: D. C. Heath, 1951. P. 25.
14. TORRANCE, E. P. "Exploration in Creative Thinking," *Education,* 81 (December, 1960).
15. WITTY, PAUL A. *A Study of 100 Gifted Children.* Lawrence, Kansas: University of Kansas Press, 1930.
16. ———. *Helping the Gifted Child.* Chicago: Science Research Associates, 1952.
17. ———. "Reading Instruction—A Forward Look," *Elementary English,* 38 (March, 1961).
18. ———, and FITZWATER, JAMES P. "An Experiment with Films, Film Readers, and the Magnetic Sound Track," *Elementary English,* 32 (April, 1955).

75. Enrichment Activities for the Superior Child in the Reading Program *

RUTH MARTIN

. . .

What Are the Needs of Gifted Children?

THE basic needs of gifted children are the same as those of all children. Acceptance, achievement, and affection are just as necessary to them as to the slowest students in the classroom. Therefore, the teacher cannot merely identify the bright children and leave them to their own devices. These children must have, in addition to help with their personal needs, aid in understanding other peoples of the world, tolerance of their political and religious beliefs, and appreciation of their cultures.

Gifted children also need help in understanding themselves. They need help in becoming well-adjusted people in their homes and classrooms. The bright child has to learn to show his ability without fear at the same time that he learns to demonstrate his leadership without arousing antagonism.

One of the primary goals in working with these children is to develop critical thinking and the ability to solve problems in an intelligent manner. The challenging teacher realizes the necessity of presenting materials with varying points of view, such as different political leanings, in

* From Ruth Martin, "Enrichment Activities for the Superior Child in the Reading Program," in *Contributions in Reading*, no. 22, pp. 2–4, copyright 1958. Reprinted by permission of the author and Ginn and Co., Waltham, Mass.

order to aid these students in forming opinions based on facts rather than emotions. Similarly, the understanding teacher is aware of the importance of raising a variety of problems in science, social studies, mathematics, health, and other areas and of encouraging careful and comprehensive attacks on these problems.

Another aim in working with gifted children should be to broaden their interests in all fields of knowledge. An appreciation of art, music, drama, and good literature aids in the broad cultural development that we wish to give to our potential leaders.

Some other objectives in challenging the gifted child are:

To promote the enrichment of a human life that has shown great capacity for appreciation.

To help the gifted child to recognize and appreciate excellence.

To help him gain confidence in his abilities and to learn the extent of his own abilities.

To help him to know what he wants out of life.

To develop in him a strong sense of social responsibility.

To help him explore the potentialities of life and discover the rich resources of interest, enjoyment, service, and insight which await the alert mind.

To give him the basic tools and the disciplines of self-education.

Reading is without doubt the greatest single skill to which the teacher can turn to aid in meeting these aims.

The Administrator's Role

The administrator can assist the classroom teacher who has gifted students in his care. He can establish a well-planned testing program for identifying students with high intellectual ability and with high achievement records. This gives the teacher an objective means of verifying or refuting his judgment of each child. It also gives him a way of recognizing talents in students who have not been achieving well in class. These students who have potential ability and have developed lazy habits need to be recognized as early as possible and encouraged to work more nearly to capacity.

The hiring of special teachers to work with gifted children can come about only through the encouragement and support of school boards and administrators. Many school districts are now realizing that this group of children has been the "neglected" group and are making special arrangements for their instruction. The two commonest methods in such provisions have been homogeneous grouping of students and partial segregation. With this latter method the students leave their regular classroom teacher some time during the week to have additional enriched work with a special teacher. The newest surveys indicate that this method is becoming more widely accepted as school districts study ways of developing programs of the gifted.

The administrator must assume the leadership in helping the school and community decide what kind of special provisions should be made for more able children. In addition to special classes or part-time arrangements, some schools are attempting enrichment in regular classrooms. Perhaps no classroom in the country today has all the instructional materials a teacher desires. A good teacher, faced with the responsibility of a large class enrollment and the necessity to enrich the program for some gifted students, must have a great variety of books, magazines, and reference materials to assist him. For this equipment he is dependent on his administrator and the budget.

The administrator must also allow freedom with the curriculum to the teacher who works with these children. A creative teacher can find himself completely defeated if the curriculum is so rigid that no leeway is permitted. No matter what method is followed, the teacher who attempts to work with the gifted student needs the support and understanding of the administrator.

The Librarian's Role

The school librarian can become the teacher's most important assistant in working with gifted children. The typical teacher does not have the time to keep himself informed of the wonderful variety of books published each year for children of school age, nor does he have the knowledge to evaluate the age level for which the books are most suited. This is the place where the librarian can play an exceedingly helpful role.

Gifted children need the books of the proper level for their age and grade but also other books that are geared to pupils who are two to three years above their level. These are the books that will be a real challenge to them, and they should be available in large numbers.

Supplying teachers with annotated lists of library books that are available in the school library or are recommended for reading from the city, town, or county libraries is very helpful. In some cases the able students can become library assistants and help the classroom teachers select, arrange, and distribute books that are on loan.

Librarians can also be useful in giving specific training in library work to a group of gifted students. These boys and girls can be taught the Dewey Decimal System, the method of cataloguing and classifying books, of circulating and distributing them, and can soon become classroom librarians. Although not all gifted children are bookish in their interests, all can profit from skills in locating and using varied library materials.

Qualities of the Teacher

Valuable as help from administrators and librarians can be, if our gifted children are to be encouraged to work at their intellectual capacity, it is the classroom teachers who must help them. All outside assistance is of little avail unless the teacher has the ability and the personal qualities that are necessary for working with these children. What are these qualities?

A group of gifted students gathered together on a panel at a teachers' institute agreed that a teacher should be patient, nonexcitable, understanding, strict, helpful, and that he should have a sense of humor. The teachers who were the most helpful to these students were, according to them, the ones who set goals other than grades, who took an individual interest in them and challenged them to improve, who offered them opportunities to do independent research apart from the regular work, who asked questions rather than stated cold facts, and who were strict and gave them plenty to do. When asked if they felt they had been well prepared for college, these same students answered that they felt the lack of a background of wide reading and wished they had been made to do much more reading in the earlier grades.

Creativeness is contagious. Just the opportunity to be with a creative teacher every day may do much toward instilling creativeness. Teachers of the gifted should also be well read and acquainted with the world's great literature. Creative uses of books and other materials may encourage children to see what they can do.

Reading as an Enrichment Activity

Basic to any discussion of reading as an enrichment activity is the assumption that all gifted children must learn the skills of reading. There is danger that children who learn to read easily and speedily may miss out on some of the basic developmental skills. Let us assume that the teacher will make certain that this does not happen and that all children will be given a solid background in the basic abilities as well as opportunity to read widely among the great wealth and variety of books for children.

Since reading will be the chief method used by many gifted children to achieve their desired goals or fulfill their needs, it is essential that they receive special attention in developing ability to locate information by gaining skill in the use of table of contents, dictionary, encyclopedia, card-file index, maps, and charts; the ability to evaluate the information they obtain; the ability to gain insights and apply ideas. In addition to developing these skills, the teacher of the gifted will want to sample the enrichment activies suggested in the next sections.

Enrichment Practices for Use at Any Level

Children should be supplied with a wide variety of books and allowed to read widely.

Children should be allowed to progress at their own rate and should not be held back in learning to read until others are ready.

Children should be allowed freedom in selecting books from an ungraded library.

Children should be allowed time for free reading at school and at home.

Teachers could enrich the reading program by using some of the following techniques:

Make use of radio, television, movies, and all of the other diversions which beguile children away from reading, to promote interest in related reading materials.

Use storytelling to get children interested in reading certain desirable books.

Read an outstanding chapter or two from a book children should know in order to motivate their desire to read it.

Form a literature club and have the students set up aims and rules.

Introduce book-length stories which have some connection with stories in the basic reader.

Allow a child to tell something that identifies him with the story or that he associates with it.

Encourage pupils to dramatize stories they read and to present them as TV productions.

Have children find new words in the next story. Print these words on the chalkboard and discuss the important ones.

Use community resources and bring real authors to the class.

Establish a "Story Hour," allowing students to read an interesting story or play to their own class or others over the intercommunication system. Use suitable background music and sound effects. . . .

76. Using Trade Books with Superior Children *

DONALD MERRYMAN

ALTHOUGH we will always have children in our schools who do not have the ability to do grade-level work, we also have children at the other extreme who are reading several years above grade level. Far too many schools are still giving these superior children a reading program geared to the average child, when their reading ability and reading interests are at least one or two years above their

* From Donald Merryman, "Using Trade Books with Superior Children," *Elementary English*, 40 (March, 1963), 248–50. Copyright © 1963 by the National Council of Teachers of English. Reprinted by permission of the author and the National Council of Teachers of English.

chronological age. Because superior children learn more and learn it faster than most children, they are able to acquire the basic skills earlier than their peers. Therefore, they need to move into new experiences and new ideas more rapidly than most children and need a broader program of enrichment.

They need scope and materials on which their imagination can feed and opportunities to exercise this imagination. Using trade books with children in a variety of ways is one way of providing for their needs. These children also need access to museums, instruments, paints, resource people, ideas, visual aids, and the host of other media that will give them the opportunity to feed themselves with the heritage that is theirs—both past and present.

What are some activities, then, which teachers can plan with superior children that are not particularly suitable for other elementary school children? All the items included in the following list may not be limited to just the superior children but most of them seem to be more suitable for children of high ability than for average pupils.

1. Read a number of science fiction books and review them critically in light of facts gathered from reading informational science trade books on the same subject.

2. Read several biographies of the same famous person and compare them. Be sensitive to each author's point of view, noting the different approaches each might use. Bring out any discrepancies which you might note. By using other books see if you can find which are factually true.

3. Plan and conduct a panel discussion on books about a certain theme such as Modern Talking Animal Stories. The teacher should provide the pupils with a suggested book list so all have a common basis for intelligent discussions.

4. Arrange a display of creative paintings inspired by particularly beautiful passages from a favorite book. Under each picture quote the passage in bold black print, noting the author and title of the book. (This need not be limited to superior children, but they may use this as a planned exhibit to foster appreciation in others of beautiful passages from good literature and possibly motivate others to read books that might otherwise be by-passed.)

5. Adapt a story for dramatization. Design and plan stage settings, select recordings for background music to fit the mood of the story, design costumes, and develop original dances. These are all related activities which might be considered. A radio script of the same story would eliminate some of these activities and would not involve as much time in preparation.

6. Develop a good up-to-date book list relating to your favorite hobby. With different people working on different hobbies, you may pool your findings and develop a rather complete bibliography on many varied hobbies and duplicate it for other children in the school. Check with the librarian to see if the bibliographies can be placed in the library for students who wish a copy.

7. Develop a list of new words in our American language you have come across in your reading, which have been coined over the past ten years or just since you've been born. List the title and author of the book where the words were used and comment on the origin of each word.

8. Form a group to work with the school librarian in making preparations for the book fair, and assist her in carrying out the details. Help in the selection of books to be purchased, plan and carry out the publicity work, help arrange the display using original and unique ideas, assist in selling the books. Select a new book at the fair and take it to a classroom to introduce it to the class. Be familiar enough with it that you can create some interest in the book.

9. Write letters of appreciation to authors and illustrators of your favorite trade books.

10. Study a number of books written by the same author. Note any similarities in style of writing, themes or ideas repeated, etc.

11. Compare one book read with another of a similar theme. Contrast the authors' viewpoints. (This will be a good experience in critical thinking and evaluation.)

12. Read widely about a topic of per-

sonal interest and share your findings with the class. Think of unique ways of making your presentation that will interest your audience.

13. Select a trade book that would appeal to children of the primary grades. Become so well acquainted with the book that you will be able to tell the story well to some of the primary classes at a suitable time for both you and the teacher.

14. Find out as much as you can about the life of your favorite writer or illustrator by using a variety of sources. Present a biography of that person in written or oral form noting style of writing, similar threads which may run through a number of his books, background of experiences which may have influenced him to write certain stories, etc.

15. Use trade books in developing a social studies project which requires authenticity in facts and details. E.g.,—Hold a man-on-the-street interview with a man from one of the critical periods of our history such as the Revolutionary War or Civil War. This may be tape recorded.

16. By using trade books, trace the origin and development of a number of things that we take for granted such as tools, shoes, cars, etc. You may work individually or in small groups. Include not only the history of the object in your reading and research, but how the object might be improved, or what it might look like by the year 2000 A.D.

17. Develop a list and short history of origin of words met in reading such as johnnycake, willy-nilly, etc.

E.g., *Bonfire*—at one time meant a fire of bones and referred to a method of disposing of carcasses.

18. Arrange if possible to have an author or illustrator visit your class. Make arrangements for the visit and preparations for using to best advantage the time the person will be with the group. (The children in our school were thrilled to have two of their favorite authors and one illustrator visit the school during their celebration of Book Week.)

19. Take a character out of a book such as *Robin Hood* or *Cinderella* and transport them to the twentieth century. Write a story about their reactions to modern life. What scrapes might they get in if they were living in our times?

20. From a suggested list, read stories of children from a markedly different social group. Note the differences between their lives and ours. What in their culture brought about these differences? (This should help children gain an understanding of human relationships. By seeing deeply into people they may become more sensitive of problems that exist in America as well as in other countries.)

21. Become familiar with the common culture of people from various parts of the world through reading trade books about people of these countries. What contributions have been made by these people to enrich our lives in such fields as art, music, science, etc.?

22. Through appropriate reading lists work toward building better attitudes such as tolerance, kindness, and consideration for all people. (This is worded as direction to teacher instead of student.)

23. Contrast humor in comic books with genuine humor in good trade books.

24. Teachers could organize a Junior Great Books Club where small groups of approximately eight children read and discuss the same book. Teachers or librarians can guide the discussion. Often children are eager to talk with someone who has read the same book they have read. A plan such as this offers opportunity to compare ideas, interpretations, and analysis of the book. (We have begun this in our school this year and found it

to be a rewarding experience for both children and leaders.)

25. Choose a book from a selected list of historical fiction. Read from other sources to gather information about historical events of the same period. See if you can find any incidents in the fictional story that are historically inaccurate.

These twenty-five items are merely suggestions from which teachers may gain ideas of ways of using trade books with their children. The list may be modified to fit the needs of a particular group of pupils, for a school program forms *after* the teacher has greeted the children who will make up the class for the year. This may act as a springboard for teachers to dive into new and better ideas of their own.

77. Accelerating the Reading Speed of Sixth-Grade Gifted Children *

ROBERT A. MC CRACKEN

Purpose

IN determining the reading needs of two sixth-grade classes by the use of an informal reading inventory, it became apparent that silent reading skills were underdeveloped. Of the 56 pupils examined in the two classes only one pupil exceeded the speed of 250 words per minute when reading silently. The purpose of this study is to evaluate a three-week training program for eight gifted children who performed well in all areas of reading except silent speed.

The Subjects

Pupils were selected by three criteria:

1. They rated above 120 IQ on the *California Test of Mental Maturity, Ele-*

* From Robert A. McCracken, "Accelerating the Reading Speed of Sixth-Grade Gifted Children," *Exceptional Children,* XXVII (Spring, 1960), 27–28. Reprinted by permission of the author and *Exceptional Children.*

mentary S-Form, given six months earlier.

2. They rated above sixth-grade level in both reading vocabulary and comprehension on the *Iowa Test of Basic Skills, Form I,* administered two weeks prior to the beginning of the reading instruction.

3. They exhibited no reading deficiency on the informal reading inventory except the inability to read rapidly silently.

The eight pupils who met these criteria were girls. Table 1 presents their chronological ages, the mental ages, the CTMM IQ scores, and the ITBS grade level scores for reading comprehension and vocabulary.

The Teaching Procedures

The procedures were similar to those used in adult and college reading programs. No mechanical devices were used. The pupils met for nine lessons of 45 minutes each.

<table>
<tr><td colspan="5">Table 1.</td><td></td></tr>
</table>

TABLE 1.

Identifying Data for Girls Receiving Reading Instruction

Pu-pil	Chrono-logical age	CTMM MA	IQ	ITBS grade levels compre-hension	vocab-ulary
A	11–9	15–2	129	8.2	8.7
B	11–1	14–6	131	8.0	8.2
C	11–4	15–0	133	9.0	8.1
D	11–8	14–2	121	10.6	9.0
E	11–0	16–5	149	10.6	absent
F	11–2	16–6	148	8.0	8.5
G	10–9	15–4	143	7.9	8.6
H	11–5	14–6	127	7.5	9.0

During each session at least one practice exercise was read, speed measured, and comprehension checked. All comprehension was done without reference to the text. The *Reader's Digest Skill Builder* for grade four, part one,[1] was used at the beginning of the program and the *Skill Builder* for grade six, part two, was used for the last two sessions.

The following ideas were discussed with the group:

1. Speed is related to the difficulty of the material being read.
2. Speed should be shifted to suit the reader's purpose.
3. Rapid reading is an active search for answers (answering the purpose).
4. Rapid reading depends upon what the reader brings to the text.
5. Formulating questions from text clues, recalling known information stimulated by the title and text clues, and reading questions before reading the text speed comprehension.
6. The paragraph is the basic unit of thought.

[1] *The Reader's Digest Reading Skill Builders,* Education Division, Reader's Digest Services, Inc., Pleasantville, N. Y., 1958.

7. Most paragraphs contain a topic sentence.

The Results

Table 2 gives the result of the rate exercises.

TABLE 2

Mean, Minimum, and Maximum Words per Minute, and Average Percentage Comprehension for Representative Lessons

Lesson	1	3	5	8	9
Maximum	244	414	540	1260	1200
Mean	202	280	450	966	792
Minimum	160	210	360	470	524
Comprehension	89	92	96	81	95

Several reactions were noted as the pupils participated:

1. They were reluctant to accept the belief that word meanings and ideas come from within the reader, that the reader rearranges his understandings from the stimulus of an author's words.
2. On essay questions the pupils did not like to consider more than one answer correct, even when different answers could both be supported by the text.
3. At first they were reluctant to accept reading as the getting of meaning. They said, "I answered all the questions, but I really didn't read it."
4. At the end they were worried about going too fast. They wanted to know how fast they should read.
5. At the beginning they did not feel that they could read much more rapidly, and at the end they did not understand why they had ever read so slowly.

Discussion

The author inferred that these pupils did not want to accept the responsibility required of a mature reader, the responsibility for determining what is worth reading, why it should be read, how it should be read, and when it has been read satisfactorily. This may be a result of their educational environment which does not encourage greater independence.

The nine lessons possibly did little except disinter the latent achievement of these pupils. Probably much latent achievement is still buried. Even these gifted children could benefit from instruction to this end.

Generally the concern for speed reading and mature reading-study habits is reserved for college reading classes or high school classes for college-bound students. Apparently these skills could be taught much earlier; the gifted children in this study were well ready at the beginning of sixth grade. It seems a tremendous waste to wait until college to help these pupils to exploit themselves. The increased amount of reading that sixth-grade pupils could be freed to do in junior and senior high school is yet to be realized.

XVI

Helping the Retarded Reader

Children with reading problems are a common concern of teachers. In almost every classroom there are some children whose reading ability is significantly below their grade level. Once identified, their specific strengths and weaknesses should be determined and a remedial program, based upon their findings, conducted and evaluated.

Harris first defines reading diagnosis and discusses its who, what, where, how, and why. Five suggestions for identifying and helping children with learning disabilities are then presented by Frankel, and Reich reminds us that there is more to overcoming reading problems than simply attempting to teach skills. These articles are followed by Frostig's in which a number of clinical teaching procedures that may be adapted for use in the classroom are described. Lieben closes the chapter by stressing the importance of teachers' and parents' attitudes and interactions in helping children with reading problems.

78. The Diagnosis of Reading Disabilities *

ALBERT J. HARRIS

SOMETIMES names that we use to label certain things or objects or events are very impressive, but when we look more carefully into the meaning we find that

* From Albert J. Harris, "The Diagnosis of Reading Disabilities," in *Corrective and Remedial Reading,* A Report of the Sixteenth Annual Conference and Course on Reading (Pittsburgh: University of Pittsburgh Press, 1960), pp. 31–37. Reprinted by permission of Donald L. Cleland, Director of the Reading Laboratory at the University of Pittsburgh.

the label does not really tell us any more than a much simpler term would convey. Medical specialists, for example, have devised quite a number of special terms to describe difficulties in learning to read. For example, the term *alexia* simply means inability to read. This can be subdivided into *acquired alexia* (loss of ability to read as a result of damage to the brain), *congenital alexia* (the person has never been able to read), or *developmental alexia* (the person has not developed any reading ability). Another favorite medical term is *dyslexia,* which simply means *that there is something wrong with the person's reading.* The term *strephosymbolia* simply means twisted symbols, or in other words, the individual has a reversal tendency.

The term *diagnosis* also seems formidable to some teachers. It is derived from Greek roots which mean "to know through" or "to know thoroughly." Taking this word out of the medical setting and applying it educationally, it refers to what is really a straightforward process. When we are diagnosing a difficulty, what we want to do is to find out what is wrong, what caused it, and what can be done for it. That is what diagnosis means as applied to reading disability.

Continuing the effort to explain diagnosis in plain and simple English, we may regard the diagnostic process as one that consists of asking five kinds of questions. These questions are summarized by the well-known little words: who, what, where, how, and why.

The first of these, *who,* means: who are the children who need special help? All children whose reading seems to be significantly below grade level need some special attention. Within this large group, usually consisting of one-quarter to one-third of all the children, we have to make some differentiations. We need to distinguish, first of all, between those whose reading problem is just one aspect of generally slow mental development and those who have the potentiality of making considerable improvement. The generally slow child, who is usually reading close to his mental ability level and sometimes manages to read somewhat above it, does not need a remedial program, but rather a total curriculum which is adapted to his limited learning abilities. He needs to be recognized and appreciated for doing the best that he can, and relieved of the pressure of trying desperately and vainly to

come up to the normal group. The other children, who are below both the standards for age and grade and their general level of intellectual functioning, are children with reading disabilities, ranging from slight to severe.

Children who have slight to moderate reading disabilities are generally able to be helped considerably by the classroom teacher, working with them either in groups and helping them in the areas of their greatest difficulty, or providing them with some highly individualized help in the general classroom setting. The remainder, the severely disabled readers, need a much more careful diagnostic study and need to be given remedial help individually or in quite small groups, and usually outside of the classroom setting.

The task of estimating the mental ability of a retarded reader is not an easy one to solve. In the primary grades, the group intelligence tests in common use do not require any reading, and therefore are less likely to underestimate seriously the intelligence of a poor reader than the tests used above the third grade. The majority of the group intelligence tests now in use in schools at the fourth-grade level and above present most of their questions in printed form, so that the child who cannot read the question is automatically low. For this reason, group intelligence test results must be interpreted with caution when trying to establish the mental ability of a poor reader. Individual testing by a trained psychologist is generally much more accurate in indicating what the child is able to do.

Assuming that one has a dependable measure of the child's mental age or level of mental development, it is simple to determine his average level of reading performance, express it in terms of an age score, and compare it with his mental age. If the mental age is significantly higher, there is a disability, and the greater the discrepancy, the more serious the disability.

The second question, *what,* asks: at what level can the child read? In answering this question, we find that teachers and school administrators tend to place too much reliance on the scores obtained from standardized reading tests. While average and good readers tend to get most of their scores on such tests by actually reading and answering the questions, the scores of poor readers are often based largely on guess-work and so they frequently overestimate the level at which the child can really read. Standardized reading tests are very good instruments for comparing groups and for measuring rate of progress of groups. They are somewhat less satisfactory as measures of the status or progress of an individual child.

Increasing emphasis has been given in the past few years to the actual tryout of a child in a book to see if the book fits him. Usually we try to distinguish between the instructional level, at which the child can read fairly well when given instructional assistance of the usual sort, and the independent level, at which he can read for pleasure and without any assistance. Determining these levels for the disabled reader is extremely important, since we find over and over again that one of the reasons that certain children do not improve is that the materials with which they are being taught are just too hard for them.

With disabled readers, it is unsafe to rely on silent reading alone. It is necessary to listen to the child's unrehearsed oral reading in material of varying levels of difficulty, and to test his sight vocabulary and word analysis skills.

The next question, *where,* is an inquiry into the specific reading skill or skills that are central to the child's difficulties with reading. For example, let us assume that a sixth-grade child scores at fourth-grade level in a standardized silent reading test. Presumably his reading comprehension is quite inferior. But if we test his word recognition skills, we find that they are even more limited, since he has a small sight vocabulary and cannot read many words of greater than second-grade difficulty. Under these conditions, it seems evident that the word recognition problem is more central than the comprehension problem, or, in other words, he cannot understand the material primarily because there are too many words that he cannot recognize. The special help that he would need would have to concentrate more on word recognition skills than on comprehension. Similarly, many children who are very slow readers are slow readers because they have to hesitate and pause to puzzle out words, and again the central difficulty would not be the rate problem but rather a word recognition problem.

The next question, *how,* signifies: how does the child proceed in reading? What is he trying to do? What goes on in his mind? Here we can ask a number of questions, all of which are highly significant.

First, how does he attack words? Does he read only the words that he knows and wait to be told the others, or does he make some effort to figure them out? If so, does he try to sound words letter by letter, or by phonograms, or does he try spelling the word, or some other technique? In order to be able to answer these questions it is helpful to try the child on words presented individually rather than in continuous material, because some children have become such expert guessers that many of their shortcomings in word recognition pass unnoticed when they are allowed to guess from context. Furthermore, it is very helpful, when the child does not recognize the word immediately, to ask him to do his thinking out loud so that you can find out what he is trying to do and why it works or doesn't work. This is perhaps the most helpful single technique in reading diagnosis that I know. Sometimes more can be learned by listening to a child as he tries to figure out two or three words than can be gained from hours of other kinds of testing in terms of providing insight and understanding about the child's difficulties.

A second question is, how does the child approach the reading material? With what intentions, expectations, or mental set? Is he reading to try to find out something, or is he just trying to say the words? In oral reading is he reading to himself out loud, or is he trying to read with expression so as to communicate to others?

A third area of inquiry is, how does the child feel about reading? Many children who have difficulties in reading approach printed material with fear and trepidation. They may anticipate that they will make many mistakes and that somebody will laugh at them. They assume it is going to be difficult and frustrating. If this is true about a child, then obviously helping him to change these feelings to more constructive ones would have to become a major objective in trying to help him. Answers to this kind of question are sometimes not easy to obtain, but once the child trusts you he will very frequently be able to tell you frankly just how he does feel about reading.

A fourth area of inquiry is, how does the child respond to instructional help? Does he seem indifferent, resistive, passively accepting, or gratefully enthusiastic? If he is already enthusastic, perhaps one can concentrate on *what* to teach him; but if he displays very little responsiveness, perhaps major attention will have to be given to motivation for a considerable length of time, and skills development may have to be kept at a minor level of importance. It is desirable to inquire not only into his response to instruction in general, but whether he responds differently to different kinds of activities or different kinds of material. Sometimes finding a book that appeals greatly to a child's special interest may provide a magic key to getting him started. Sometimes a child who is a slow learner with one method of instruction may respond ever so much faster to a different method. Experimental tryout of a variety of materials and a variety of teaching approaches may play a very important and practical part in the total diagnostic program.

The final question, *why,* is an attempt to get to the heart of causation. The causation of reading difficulties is very complex and frequently there are more causal handicaps for a particular child than we need in order to account for the difficulties that he is experiencing. Sometimes even in an intensive study by a group of specialists in a clinic it is difficult to do more than conjecture as to what the causes really were when the difficulty started several years ago. Nevertheless, the effort to find out what causal handicaps have interfered with the child's learning is very worthwhile, and even if we do not find full and complete answers, we often discover contributing factors or handicaps about which something can be done.

It would be a mistake to assume that it is always necessary to understand the causes in order to help the condition. From a practical standpoint, it is useful to make a diagnostic distinction only when there is a difference in treatment involved. For example, if there are half a dozen kinds of organisms that can cause a sore throat and they can all be treated with the same antibiotic, a sensible physician does not bother to make laboratory tests to decide which particular organism is the cause this time. Instead, he prescribes the antibiotic and the sore throat gets cured. On the other hand, if there is an abdominal pain and he does not know whether it is a digestive disturbance or an inflamed appendix, it is very important for him to make a diagnostic differentiation because the treatment of these conditions has to be so different.

In reading diagnosis, the first differentiation that has to be made is between those children whose problems are specific to reading and those who are generally slow. In this way we narrow our range of special inquiry to those children who can really profit from special attention. We look through the accumulated school records for any information that they can throw on how long he has had trouble in reading, what previous teachers have recorded about him, recorded intelligence and achievement test results, attendance, physical factors, conduct and personality rating, and so on. A talk with his mother is desirable. This search may or may not cast light upon the causation. We should then proceed to a straightforward analysis of his reading problems, leading to the formulation of a teaching plan. If the parents are cooperative and interested, it may be helpful to suggest that the possibility of a significant visual or other physical defect be checked by comprehensive private examinations.

At this point it is proper to proceed with a remedial program, even though several areas of causation have not been explored at all deeply. If the child responds well to remedial help, it is an academic question whether or not we ever get answers to those questions. If after a reasonable period of tryout the child is making very disappointing progress, it is wise to try to get additional diagnosis in those areas that have not previously been covered. For example, it may be desirable to find out, through referral to a psychologist, psychiatrist, or mental hygiene clinic, whether the child's emotional problems are such that he cannot at present profit from remedial instruction. Proceeding one step at a time, in this way, we are able to avoid wasting our precious resources of psychological and psychiatric examinations, which are usually limited in availability, and use them for those cases that really need them, rather than giving every child a thorough diagnostic study.

In summary, diagnosis is nothing more than the application of a straightforward, common sense, problem-solving approach to the study of children who have difficulties in reading. We try to find out what is wrong, what caused the difficulty, and what can be done for it. We do it by intelligent use of our common question words—who, what, where, how, and why? We first single out those children who require special attention to their reading, and then we try to find out the level at which they can profitably be taught, specific reading skills that need to be tackled first, the incorrect procedures that the child is using so that we can correct them, and, finally, we try within the limitations of the study procedures available to us to find the causes of the child's poor reading and what handicaps may still be preventing him from effective learning.

79. Five Suggestions: An Approach to the Identification and Management of Children with Learning Disabilities *

HERMAN M. FRANKEL, M.D.

THIS conference is concerned with meeting the needs of a large group of children not succeeding, or even surviving, in the regular classroom. The precise size of this group depends upon the broadness of the definition of "Learning Disabilities." Without becoming involved in word-splitting or hair-splitting, I propose to use the definition of Barbara Bateman (Associate Professor of Education at the University of Oregon) and include all "those children whose rates of learning various skills are very uneven." This will give us the flexibility to include children who are excluded by certain more rigid definitions due to low overall level of functioning, membership in a "culturally deprived" segment of the population or lack of definite evidence of "cerebral dysfunction." This definition will, by its very broadness, constantly remind us that these children do not make up a homogeneous group.

My own interest in these youngsters stems in part from contact, as a pediatrician, with children referred by schools because of "learning problems" or "slow progress." This presentation, in the form of five suggestions to classroom teachers, is intended to provide a point of departure for the actions of other educators, of health workers, and of other concerned adults.

Don't panic or overreact to the child

* From Herman M. Frankel, "Five Suggestions: An Approach to the Identification and Management of Children with Learning Disabilities," *Journal of Learning Disabilities,* 1 (December, 1968), 750–55. Reprinted by permission of the author and *The Journal of Learning Disabilities.*

with a learning disorder. The children aren't new. It's only the massive professional interest that's new.

Make good use of your consultants. Every child should get the best medical care that we can possibly deliver to him, whether he is thought to have a medical problem or not. I would like to talk about the referrals that you are in a position to make when acting in your capacity as a professional educator, rather than those which you make simply as an intelligent adult who has noticed something wrong with a child.

A professional referral should occur when the referring professional has encountered difficulty in doing his job, and believes that someone in another profession or specialty will be able to offer some help.

As this applies to the classroom teacher, there is one implication that needs to be made explicit: *the principle job of the elementary school teacher is to teach children.* Her primary job is not the categorizing of children, the labeling of children, the ordering of laboratory tests on children, the neurological diagnosis of children, nor the transferring of children out of her classroom. Her initiation of or participation in these activities in her professional role as a teacher should occur only as part of, or in direct support of, her efforts to teach.

This point is not being made to discourage referrals. Quite the contrary. Teachers can get more help from their consultants than they are getting today.

It is certainly appropriate to call for help from other professions in planning a teaching program for many problem children; however, the requests should be precise if the help is to be of any value to you as a classroom teacher. By all means, contact the physician if you suspect that Billy is having paroxysmal lapses of consciousness; but don't request an "EEG and neurological evaluation" when you wonder whether medication could possibly help keep Tyrone from calling out or getting up out of his seat 12 times an hour.

If you've just noticed that Johnny is quite clumsy, or that he has a tremor, or that these signs are getting worse, his physician should be the one called upon to rule out a degenerative disease or tumor of the brain. If his doctor returns Johnny to you with a diagnosis of "minimal brain damage," understand that this has no definite implications for you as a classroom teacher other than that it is safe for Johnny to be taught in your classroom instead of being treated in the hospital. It does not tell you what things he needs to be taught, nor how to teach them, nor in what order they should be taught.

Don't hesitate about taking advantage of the physician's position and prestige, and calling upon him to help with the interpretation of Kenny's overall problem to his parents. Be honest and explicit in stating the referral question.

It is appropriate to ask the school psychologist whether Eddie's auditory perceptual skills are adequately developed for you to be able to begin ordinary phonics instruction. Of course the audiologist can help you decide whether Marilyn's· unresponsiveness to spoken questions and instructions is due to a hearing loss. Your consultants can help you if you ask specific questions of them.

Don't be overly concerned about why a particular child's learning progress is atypical.

Our present techniques usually cannot reveal with any certainty why any particular child has a learning disability. Of even greater importance is the fact that a knowledge of etiology rarely tells the teacher how to teach or what to teach.

While extensive research into the etiologies of learning disorders is being done in many parts of the country, this is primarily for the purpose of teaching us how to prevent children from developing such disorders. There is today little reason to think that knowing that Ellen was anoxic at birth, had Hemophilus influenza meningitis at one month or a head injury at six weeks, or dehydration and a single convulsion at two months, will help her teacher decide how to deal with her present inability to comprehend what she is reading.

Most children make what we usually consider satisfactory progress in the classroom. At last year's conference on "Medical Aspects of Learning Disorders" at the University of Washington, a panel of teachers and doctors observed that most "intact, well-adjusted children can learn in spite of poor teaching." Frank Hewett (Assistant Professor of Educaton and Medical Psychology at UCLA) has estimated that 85 percent to 90 percent of school children learn "by anything you do."

But some children don't make the progress expected of them in school. Their satisfactory achievements in some areas lead us to expect adequate progress in others, but they do not fulfill expectations.

Tempting as it has been to approach such a child's problem by asking "What is wrong with him and why is he this way?", this approach has not produced answers that have proven to be of direct help to the classroom teacher. For her, and for those who would help her, there is a different kind of question that needs to be asked.

Focus on the right question: What does this child need to learn?

The teacher's professional training and

experience prepare her to teach. The principal question to be asked about a child who is not surviving in the classroom is, "What does he need to learn?" It is crucial in all stages of planning and therapy that we keep our minds on this question, and that we not become overly concerned with matters of professional territoriality (Which department does he belong to?), nomenclature (Is he a true dyslexic after he has been taught to do fair word-calling but can display no comprehension?), or perceptuomotor and psychological correlates (Shall we postpone his reading instruction until after his scores improve on his sensorimotor tests? Must we work with beads and geometric figures to improve his visual memory or may we use letters and number symbols?). Find out what he needs to know and then teach it to him!

In general, the "things" a child needs to know to survive in school may be categorized as academic skills and academic behaviors. Frank Hewett has formulated a hierarchy of academic behaviors which may be described in objective, observable terms and which form the conceptual framework of his strikingly successful "engineered classrooms," one in each elementary school in the Santa Monica Unified School District. Although the sequence should not be thought of as a rigid, one-step-at-a-time staircase, the various levels do represent successively higher attainments. Students are likely to demonstrate at least some behaviors on levels higher than the ones on which they are consistently functioning.

The first task level is the Attention Level. Does the child fail to pay attention to learning tasks? (Always? Sometimes? Never?) Does he daydream (How often?) Is he preoccupied with repetitive behavior (such as self-stimulation, rituals, neatness, cleanliness) which interferes with learning? (How often?)

The next level is called the Response Level. In addition to paying attention, the child must do something. Does he refuse to undertake a learning task? to volunteer an answer? to respond when called upon? (Always? Sometimes? Rarely?) Is he controlled and rigid with learning tasks? (How often?) Does he avoid contact with teacher and peers? (How often?)

The third level is called the Order Level. In addition to noticing and doing something, the child must function in an orderly routine and follow directions. Does he fail to follow directions when doing learning tasks? (How often?) Does he fail to finish learning tasks? (How often?)

The fourth level is the Exploratory Level. Once he is attending, responding, following directions and ordering his behavior, the child can be an efficient explorer of his environment through multisensory experience. Is his exploration of his environment limited? (How severely?) Is he dependent on others for choice of interests and activities? (To what degree?)

The child not only has to attend, respond, follow directions, and explore in learning, but he must be able to operate and do these things in a world of people. He must learn to gain the approval of others and to avoid their disapproval, without being overly dependent on their attention and praise. This becomes the fifth level, the Social Level of the hierarchy.

The sixth level is called the Mastery Level. It is on this level that work is undertaken in such intellectual skills as speech, writing, spelling, reading, and arithmetic.

Most children arrive in school the first day of kindergarten able to function fairly well on the attention, response, order, exploratory, and social levels. The teacher's job is mainly one on the mastery level where the building of self-care and intellectual skills is undertaken. The normal child's experiences at home and elsewhere have helped to get him up to the mastery level before he enter school. But the child with an emotional or severe learning problem is often a casualty in kindergarten or preschool. He is often a "kindergarten dropout" and stopped learning very early in his school career or perhaps was never ready to learn in the first place. At the top of the hierarchy is the Achievement Level, the highest goal in education. On this level, the child functions in learning situations without needing overt external reward.[1]

A word about "how to" teach would be appropriate, as the principles involved are the same for teaching academic skills as academic behaviors. The strategy used by Dr. Hewett in teaching academic behaviors is one which can be applied to the use of almost any "method" in the teaching of almost any skill. The basic principles, presently called "behavior modification," have been understood and described in the literature for more than 30 years; however, they have been used by teachers for centuries with varying degrees of sophistication and efficiency. At one formal presentation, a prominent educator who was oriented as far from formal behavior modification as possible reacted to one of Dr. Hewett's films by saying, "Why, you aren't talking about conditioning at all. You are just talking about good teaching!"

The "good teaching" inherent in the behavior modification strategy involves

[1] This description is adapted from Hewett, Frank M., "Institutional and Public School Application of Behavior Modification Theory in Programs for Children with Learning Disorders," in *Proceedings of the 1967 International Convocation on Children and Young Adults with Learning Disabilities,* Home for Crippled Children, Pittsburgh, 1967.

efficient application of three essentials in learning. These are: (1) a suitable educational task (which must often be a thimbleful rather than a bucketful, especially with the children we are considering here), (2) a meaningful learner reward, and (3) an appropriate degree of teacher control or structure. This third element, teacher control, is especially critical. We must know what we want the student to be able to do that he was not able to do well or at all before the lesson. We are responsible for determining the rate at which rewards, tangible, social, or intrinsic to the task, are to be administered in the course of his participation in the lesson.

When each of you must make the decision of what to teach for any particular student, I would suggest that you focus your attention on the question, "Exactly what is the next thing that he needs to learn that he hasn't been successfully taught?" I further suggest that you be prepared to work on Dr. Hewett's thimbleful instead of a bucketful. In this connection, I recommend Robert F. Mager's paperbound volume called *Preparing Instructional Objectives* (Fearon Press). It is an excellent programmed text on how to formulate teaching goals with precision and in such a way that you will be able to tell exactly how successful your teaching has been.

Continue your efforts to get useful and worthwhile training. You are professionals, and you must demand the best possible education for yourselves. You are in a position to influence the schools of education of which you are alumni. You know better than anyone else what competencies they should be developing in their students and how well they succeeded when you were in school. You are in a position to demand useful and worthwhile continuing education through your professional organizations, through the schools or school systems in which you teach, via in-service programs and summer workshops.

What skills should you want from your training programs? You need diagnostic skills: you want to be able to tell, for example, by having a child read to you, whether he is having trouble with the mechanics of reading (converting the visual stimulus into sounds) or with comprehension (attaching meaning to the sounds produced). You want to be able to tell, in the case of a child who is having trouble with the former, whether he is not using the word attack skills he has mastered or whether he needs to be taught word-attack skills. Is he relying too heavily on context cues? on pictures? on the gross appearance of the word? on the first letter? What word-attack skills does he lack?

You want to be able to derive a therapeutic prescription directly from diagnostic findings and to be able to give appropriate therapy. You want to be able to use, when needed, a good phonics method, a good multisensory method, programmed materials, books for developmental teaching or for remedial work or for comprehension work and study skills in the intermediate grades.

You want to be able to organize your classroom, when appropriate, so that different children will be involved in different activities at the same time, not only each working at his own pace, but each working on the skills he needs.

You want to be able to use efficient techniques for assessing the progress your children are making and the effectiveness of your teaching. How many new words did Susie learn this week, compared to last week? How many arithmetic problems does Robert complete in a half-hour now compared to last month? How many are right? How many times does Martin poke his neighbor in an hour now, compared to his behavior in October?

All these classroom skills can be taught to teachers. All classroom teachers have the right to be taught how to use them.

Continue your efforts to get useful and worthwhile training. Much of the material that appears in current scientific and professional literature, para-educational as well as educational, can be applied directly to your own classroom work. Can groups of you, not necessarily classroom teachers only, meet one evening a month or once a week, to discuss papers that each member has chosen from the journals he reads? Can the group maintain correspondence with authorities of its own choosing, asking for continuing suggestions about articles relevant to its interests?

These, then are my five suggestions: don't panic about the child who is having particular difficulty in certain areas of learning, make good use of your consultants, don't be overly concerned about *why* the child is atypical, spend your energy deciding exactly what he needs to learn and then teaching it to him, and continue your efforts to get useful and worthwhile training.

We are still searching for the answers to many general and specific questions about youngsters with learning disabilities, but there is a great deal that can be done in the classroom right now to help them.

80. More Than Remedial Reading *

RIVA R. REICH

JUST as there is no "typical" or "normal" third grader, just as we cannot speak of a typical or normal situation in any phase of classroom or small group work—so there is no "typical" or "normal" remedial reading "case" or remedial reading situation. And yet, those of us who have watched how they function, or do not function, in their classrooms, do find that there are certain characteristics or attitudes common to all or to most.

Poor Reader Is Discouraged

A child who comes for remedial help is a discouraged child. He has failed in an area that he can conceal neither from himself nor his parents, and worst of all, not from his peers. He has failed in an area that, in our culture, has tremendous status-giving power, and the lack of reading, by the same token, results in serious feelings of inadequacy. In our society everybody is expected to know how to read—this is the burden that is carried into the school by every child who enters first grade. You have only to see the apprehensive look in the eyes of first graders—a look that often says, "I'm glad to be in First Grade. I'm going to learn to read." Just as often that look says, "Will I learn to read? Will I be able to please my mother? She expects me to

learn to read. What if I fail?" This burden and this fear of failure becomes aggravated as the child grows older, so that our third grader or fifth grader who comes to us for help has been carrying this emotional load for years.

Poor Reader Is Frustrated

A child who comes for remedial help is a frustrated child. He has tried to learn to read; his teacher has tried to teach him; his mother (sometimes also father, grandmother, and the "aunt who teaches") has pressured him, and he has not learned. He is bored with the "easy" books. He says he "doesn't like to read," or "hates books" or "school." Many times he feels he's just "dumb" and will never learn, so what's the use?

A child who comes for remedial help is a child who has lost his self-respect. He has lost status with his peers, with his parents and last, but not least, with himself.

It is our job, then, to restore confidence, to build up self-esteem just as much as to teach these children to read. Scars will remain, we cannot remove them. But we can so build the child's acceptance of and belief in himself so that he can begin to learn and meet success.

Our first duty is to face the child with his problem, not to minimize it. Thus, to a younger child we might say, "Yes, you have a hard time with reading, but now that I've heard you read, I can tell what's wrong. It's my job to help children like you, and I've been able to help many, many children. I'd like to help you, too."

Or, to an older child we might say, "Yes, you have a reading difficulty, but I think I can help you. I know others have tried, but perhaps you weren't ready to be helped at that time." Often, with a little encouragement and friendly interest, the older child will be able to analyze his own reading problem. "I don't know how to sound out big words," or "I can read and I know all the words, but I don't know what I'm reading." Sometimes a child's own diagnosis is even more revealing: "I can read here for you, but when I read in class in my reading group, I stumble over the words." Enlisting the child's help in verbalizing his problem is often a good beginning. An eighth grader said, after one session with the remedial reading teacher, "I never read so well in my life." What he is really saying to us is, "I now have hope. There is someone who cares and wants to help me."

Inform Child of Progress

Informing the child of the diagnosis of his reading difficulty seems to have real value in most cases. Even second graders seem to gain assurance from knowing that they point with their fingers too much, or do not move smoothly enough from line to line, or do not know their consonant or vowel sounds. This is even truer of older children who seem to find relief from knowing that they need work on word-attack skills, or that their phrasing is poor, or that syllabication is weak. You almost hear the sigh of relief as if they were saying to themselves, "Whew! So that's all it is! And I thought there was something wrong with me, that I was stupid, that I was just a failure at reading, and would never learn."

Materials of instruction need to be selected wisely and subtly. Finding the right book is not always easy. Sometimes it seems almost impossible: a book about a veterinarian for a sixth-grade boy who is reading on second-grade level; or a book on nursing for the fifth-grade girl whose reading ability is third grade. Even the First-Book-Of series is too difficult, and some of the I-Want-To-Be series are too juvenile and therefore insulting to the child. Here the teacher's judgment and, better still, intuition is the best guide. If the child can wait, then a substitute book can be found which the child will accept as "next best" until the "best" turns up. If the need seems urgent, then the teacher and child together can write a book of their own, hunt for pictures together or make their illustrations. This book may be dictated to the teacher, may be written by the child, bound and decorated and "dedicated," too. For her book on Nursing, the fifth grader interviewed her pediatrician and his nurse and made a visit to the local hopsital where she collected pictures, folders, and valuable information.

"What if the child wants a book that is too easy or too hard?" the perplexed teacher often asks. Again, we must try to find out what this choice means to the child. Why does he want a book that is "too hard" or "too easy"? If it seems very important psychologically, then perhaps the "hard book" can be read through quickly with the teacher's help. Here a bargain, an honest legitimate bargain, can be made: "The next book will be one I recommend to you," says the teacher, and the pact is sealed. There should be no feeling of condescension in granting permission to the child to read an "easy" book. It is more honest and realistic, not just comforting to the child to say, "I know how you feel. Once in a while I like to read an easy book" (or relax with a crossword puzzle). Again a bargain between friendly understanding partners is easily understood and honored and the next time the child will accept the teacher's suggestion easily and gracefully.

An accepting attitude on the part of the adult breaks down the resistance and creates a good give-and-take relationship. The child becomes more amenable to suggestions and begins to feel that the teacher is working for and with rather than against him. A simple, concrete illustration sometimes helps a child who refuses to face his weakness or inadequacy in reading and persists in choosing work that is beyond him. Elicit from the child an answer to the question: "If you were going to build a house, where would you start?" Depending on the age and experience background of the child, the answers may be "from the ground," "from the bottom," "from the basement," or "first you dig a foundation." Then you ask, "After you have the bottom or basement what would you build?" The answer always is "The first floor." "If you were going to build a tall building, with many floors, could you build the fifth floor after the first one?" The child never fails to see the humor and the impracticality of this suggestion. "It's the same way," the teacher says, "with reading. I cannot start with you from the fifth floor or the sixth floor—we must start with a good foundation and build up. And I'm sure you'll get to the top floor in good time."

Poor Reader Is Easily Bored

The child who comes for remedial help is easily bored and has a short span of attention. To meet this, there must be a variety of materials, a flexibility in approach and a sensitivity to children's moods. Attractive books (not necessarily those on the "latest list"), games, puzzles are indispensable. In addition, paper, oak tag, crayons (and what would we do without the Magic Marker?) should be available so that materials for drill can be made by the teacher and/or child which answer an immediate need. One boy worked out an ingenious chart for suffixes and prefixes by backing these with magnets and then matching them to his "base" words on a chart. This chart later was put up in his classroom, and the recognition he received helped greatly in giving him status he sorely needed.

Over every remedial reading case hovers an anxious parent. At times this is a kindly, overprotective attitude. More often it is charged with deep feelings of disappointment, failure, and guilt. Whether expressed or not, these feelings come through to the child, and he reacts either with resistance or rebellion and flatly refuses to read and says so; or he resists inwardly and blocks himself so that it looks as if he "just can't read." Parents try to help him but in their anxiety and frustration they become impatient and strike out at the child, wounding him in his most vulnerable area. "Why don't you remember that word? You had it on the other page." Or, "How many times have I told you the difference between 'went' and 'want'?" Also, "Why do you bring home such baby books? When I was your age, I was reading The Classics." Or, worse still, "You have to read with me every day for half an hour, even if it means giving up play or TV."

To help this situation, a close relationship must exist between the parent and the remedial reading teacher. The parent should be advised about the nature of the difficulty. If possible, the parent should observe so that the attitude, methods, and materials can be explained and demonstrated. Parents must have a role, but they should have a clear conception of what that role is. An arrangement like this has proven effective. Say to the parent, "Yes, methods and materials have changed since your schooldays, so why not leave the teaching to us. We are especially trained and prepared. We will look after the phonics, speed, etc. You read with your child and make it a mutually enjoyable experience. If he stumbles or hesitates over a word, tell it to him, and let him go on. Perhaps you can read a page and have your child read one to you." Thus reading becomes a happily shared experience. The parent ceases to be the censor, the child is gradually freed from this feeling of pressure, and both parent and child become more relaxed. In turn, reading is helped.

Cross Grade Lines

Crossing grade lines in planning remedial reading groups has many advantages. It gives an older child an opportunity to help a younger one. For the older child this is often the first time he has been called on to help another child. It is an agreeable change of roles for him. In his own group he was always in the "third" group, the lowest, or among the nameless ones who are not even part of a group. Someone has always been assigned to help him with reading, with arithmetic. Here, for the first time, he is in a position where he can help another. "I feel like a teacher," was the way a sixth grader articulated his obvious pleasure. Perry, a fifth grader, asks if he can listen to Elliot who is very anxious to finish *Something New at the Zoo*. The teacher, who is busy with someone else, nods assent. About ten minutes later both boys run over and announce proudly (together), "He's finished the book!" "I've finished the book!" Both boys have accomplished something. "Can I help him find another book?" asks Perry, for whom this is an entirely new experience. After some deliberation and selection, Perry is heard to advise, "Elliot, take *Nobody Listens to Andrew*. Is it ever funny! It's about this boy who says there's a—no, I won't tell you any more, because I'll give away the whole story." We have no way of measuring quantitatively the positive effects these situations have on our Perrys

and Elliots, but the change in attitude toward work and self are sufficient proof.

Teacher Cooperation Necessary

A close relationship must exist, too, between the remedial teacher and the classroom teacher. It is important sometimes for the remedial teacher to watch the child in his classroom. It can also benefit the classroom teacher to see how he functions in the remedial situation. The classroom teacher can be helpful by supplying information about background and general behavior, relationship to peers; the remedial reading teacher is often in a better position to contribute personal, intimate remarks and attitudes which the small group or one-to-one relationship can foster. When there is mutual understanding and trust, the remedial reading person can offer suggestions as to materials, procedures, and so on. A classroom teacher with 25 or 30 children, with a reading range of five years or more, beset with all kinds of problems, plus extra duties such as collecting Red Cross money and putting on a play for Christmas and participating on a panel for PTA—cannot always find the time to help a child who does not fit in any group.

"I have never written a book report," confides the sixth grader to the remedial reading teacher. "My class is studying the American Revolutionary period," announces a fifth grader, "but I can't make a report because all the books are too hard." In the first case, it was easier for the remedial reading teacher to help this boy find the right book and help him write a book report, a small accomplishment, perhaps, but a step forward toward making the boy feel a part of the group. In the second case, the remedial reading teacher helped the classroom teacher find some books relating to that period in American history on first- and second-reading level, so that all the children could participate and contribute something. When there is easy, trustful communication among all the parties concerned, these things will happen. But before they can happen, the child, the remedial reading teacher, the classroom teacher, the parent must be able to speak to each other.

Last, but not least, the child must be able to observe his own progress. Assurance from the teacher that he "is reading better" is necessary, but not enough. The child who has met failure over a long period is not convinced. He'd like to believe it, but he's not sure. He needs concrete proof, proof in terms that he can see and measure. Playing a recording of the child's reading made early in the year and comparing it with a later recording; comparing a "before and after" score of the same type of reading test —these are concrete proof. Plotting a day-by-day graph of reading speed or reading success; keeping a list of words "I Do Not Know" and seeing them checked off; using short, timed paragraphs —these proofs the child can follow, analyze and evaluate himself.

Younger children, for example, seem to thrive on this simple, word-learning device: Any word that is missed during the reading session is written on a small piece of paper (2 x 4). If the child knows the word at the next session, the teacher or the child puts a small star in pencil on the corner of the paper. If the child knows the word at the second session, he gets another star. On the third day, if he knows the word (that insures repetition) he may throw it in the basket. It is both revealing and amusing to watch the variety of ways in which this paper goes to its last resting place. Some crumple it fiercely, some first tear it to bits almost with venom, others hurl it with great passion into the wastebasket. A picturesque name was given to this whole operation by a third grader who came back after summer vacation and said, "Why don't we play that good game where you can throw words in the garbage?"

In summing up what "more than remedial reading" implies, perhaps the best that can be said was uttered by Gerhart, a fourth-grade boy who, after a year of remedial reading, poked his head in the door and said, "I'm not coming here any more. I don't need you any more. Thank you!" That was indeed a compliment!

81. Corrective Reading in the Classroom *

MARIANNE FROSTIG

THREE major approaches to the teaching of reading may be distinguished, principally on the basis of the materials commonly used. With the so-called basic ap-

* From Marianne Frostig, "Corrective Reading in the Classroom," *Reading Teacher*, 18 (April, 1965), 573–80. Reprinted by permission of the International Reading Association and the author.

proach the teacher uses the familiar basic readers, and the children are usually grouped according to reading achievement. During the reading lesson the children are told about the material they will read, and new words are introduced before they read. The individualized reading approach permits each child to make his own selection from a great variety of books, magazines, and pamphlets. The teacher gives asistance as needed. Each of these approaches has advantages and disadvantaged for a total communication program. The language experience approach meets many of the disadvantages of the other two since in this approach the reading material is mainly composed by the children themselves. They tell their experiences in class and the teacher writes them down for later reading.

All of these approaches to the teaching of reading are valuable and each supplements the others. They are the three major lines of approach, and none can be neglected. Nevertheless, in teaching reading to children who have learning difficulties, whether the cause is emotional disturbance, brain damage or a developmental language disorder, it is necessary to modify and augment these approaches. This paper is devoted to an account of a variety of ancillary methods which should be used to supplement these approaches when teaching children with learning difficulties. But I should like to state most emphatically that these additional techniques can be used very effectively in the regular classroom as well as with exceptional children. They can speed up the process of learning to read for all children and help eliminate nagging difficulties that might impede even a relatively proficient learner.

Labeling

During World War I, Kurt Goldstein developed methods to rehabilitate soldiers who had suffered brain damage because of gunshot or shrapnel wounds. He found that some of those who had lost their reading ability were unable to regain the skill when taught by the regular methods because the symbolic functions of their brains had been impaired. Reading involves a double symbolic process, for not only are the spoken words symbols, representing real things or events (the word *chair* stands for a real chair, *house* for a real house, *running* for a certain type of locomotion), but the printed words are symbols also, standing for the combination of sounds that make up the words.

To help soldiers whose ability to master symbols had been impaired by cerebral dysfunction, Goldstein introduced a method of matching words to pictures. Kindergarten teachers now often use a similar method by putting labels on objects or pictures in the room. When a child first sees the configuration of the word *chair,* it is meaningless to him, but when he sees it paired with either a real or pictured chair he can understand what it means. The child at this stage is only labeling, however; he cannot be said to be reading until he is able to recognize and understand the word alone, unsupported by the object or picture.

In teaching children with reading difficulties by this method, we usually start with just two words. The two words, cut out from an old workbook, and their matching pictures are put in an envelope fastened to the back of a page, ready to be matched with either the word or pictures pasted on the front of the page. When the child can match the words and pictures well, the identical two words are used again on the next page, but with a new word added, and this system is maintained. All three words are used on the third page, plus a fourth word. The matching can be repeated indefinitely, since the material to be matched is always available. The child should switch frequently between matching words with pictures and matching pictures with words. The words should be joined in as many ways as possible to form simple phrases or sentences. The words *run* and *Billy* can be written "Run, Billy" or "Billy, run," or "Billy, Billy run!" for instance.

This method is, of course, limited by the fact that only words for concrete objects or depictable actions can be matched with pictures. Conjunctions and other parts of speech which exist for the purpose of organizing language cannot be illustrated. Such words as *the, to,* and *and* have to be added gradually to the illustrated words so as to make phrases and sentences. These words have to be learned by repetition, but only in the context of phrases or sentences in which their function is clear.

The labeling method has been found of particular value in teaching children suffering from specific dyslexia or more pervasive defects, such as mental retardation, who fail to learn by any other method. The process requires careful use and preparation by the teacher, but usually need not be maintained for an extended period. When the child has learned to match from nine to twelve words, he will very likely indicate that he has developed the ability to visualize words and will no longer need the help of pictures.

The Highly Controlled Vocabulary

All books designed for children just learning to read employ a vocabulary which is controlled to some degree, with new words being introduced slowly and with frequent repetition. But in teaching children who have learning difficulties, this process needs to be intensified. In preparing such children for reading a preprimer, for instance, it is advisable for the teacher to first compile original books for them, using the same vocabulary that is used in the preprimer. The teacher thus has control over the pace at which vocabulary is accumulated and can eventually provide each child with encouraging success when he tackles the printed book.

The teacher should write in the right upper corner of each page of each child's book the words that the child has learned in the order of their original presentation. In the middle of the page the same words are presented in story form. As soon as the child knows a few words, this presentation is made in as lengthy units as possible—phrases, sentences, and finally paragraphs—rather than in the individual words or two-word phrases which necessarily characterize learning by the matching method. Emphasizing larger word units avoids chopped and relatively meaningless learning, which lessens interest and fails to instill a feeling for the structure of language.

One or two new words should be introduced daily, and repeated daily for a sufficient period of time to insure overlearning. The list of words in the upper corner constitutes a record of the sequence. If a word is missed, the teacher can go back to the page on which this word was first introduced and review the succeeding pages. When necessary, a page is prepared without new vocabulary for the purpose of review. It is helpful to give the children familiarity with reading different kinds of print by composing the reading matter in the book from words cut from old textbooks, newspapers, and magazines, as well as from words written by hand in both articulated and cursive writing. Illustrations can be gathered similarly from a variety of sources or can be made by the children themselves.

Proper names which occur at this stage in most preprimers are best omitted, because they are not common vocabulary and because it is best to teach the children to think in a less specific way at first than by reading stories about a single family. The appropriate proper names can be introduced when the rest of the vocabulary has been learned and the child is about to read the book itself. When the child has learned to read one book in this way, he should learn to read others in a different series at a similar level before progressing to the vocabulary and stories of the next level.

Other commercially available books may be used in addition to primers and preprimers in such a way as to insure sufficient repetition of each word. For instance, the series called Easy Readers, published by Wonder Books, New York, has a highly controlled vocabulary and a great deal of repetition, but as with all commercial books, some words are repeated as many as thirty times and other words only a few times. Before giving these books to the children, therefore, all words which are likely to cause difficulty should be written on flash cards and learned beforehand. Words which are missed by the child in reading the book should also be written on flash cards or listed on a chart and taken home by the child for review.

The Easy Readers may also be used to develop other reading skills. A list of printed questions concerning the text can be prepared, glued to cardboard, and inserted in a pocket on the last page of the book. These questions help the child in developing certain areas of reading comprehension or reading skills, such as finding a certain bit of information on a particular page, finding the main idea of the story, finding a word which rhymes with a given word, and so on.

Teaching reading by the use of a highly controlled vocabulary can be adapted to work with both the usual basic readers and individualized reading programs. Insuring adequate mastery of the vocabulary beforehand greatly enhances the probability that the child will enjoy what he reads and will acquire increased motivation.

The Child's Own Book

A third auxiliary method consists of constructing a book based on each child's own experiences and using it according to the principles of the language experience approach, in which reading, writing, and oral language are integrated. The fact that the child's own experiences constitute the subject matter does much to assure his interest and cooperation.

The child is presented with a booklet made from newsprint stapled between sheets of construction paper, and he is told that the teacher is going to help him to make his own book. The teacher will necessarily have to steer the child closely to make sure that the vocabulary is appropriate to the child's level and is augmented sufficiently slowly. On the first page is pasted a photograph of the child, or a picture of any boy or girl, and the name of the child is written beneath it. Then one or two more words may be added so that a simple sentence can be written: for example, "I am Billy," or "See Billy." In writing the next page, the child can be asked what he saw recently that interested him, and the sentence constructed accordingly. It might read, "Billy, Billy, see the car," or "I see a dog." The incident to which this new word, car or dog, refers is discussed, and the simple sentence may have all the qualities of a real adventure for the child.

I recall how successful this method was with Jim, a little boy from Alaska who had been sent to us because he had not been able to learn to read. He was at first very homesick for Alaska. His teacher talked with him about what he liked best there, and he told how he went out in a boat to fish with his father. For the first page of Jim's book, the teacher put a picture of a father standing by a boat, and the words were, "Jim, see the boat." Jim and his teacher talked about the construction of the boat, how it would be launched, and so on. For the second page, the teacher wrote under a picture of a father beckoning his son: "Jim, ride in the boat. See the boat, Jim. Jim, ride in the boat. See, Jim, see! See the boat." Jim told how the first time he went out in the boat he was so excited that he could not sit still and his father told him not to jump in the boat. So his third page read: "Jim, ride in the boat. See Jim ride. See Jim jump. Jim, Jim, jump not in the boat. Jump not in the boat, Jim." In the upper right corner of the first page the words used were written: *see, Jim, the, boat*. On the second page, the words used were written in the same order in the right hand corner: *see, Jim, the, boat, ride, in*. The words on the third page were: *see, Jim, the, boat, ride, in, jump, not*.

In this way the story was developed, and the entire preprimer vocabulary introduced with sufficient repetition. For the adult the story may seem somewhat inane, but for the child it represented a series of most pleasurable experiences.

Besides learning to read the words, the child should be taught to write them as soon as possible, and he should be encouraged to read his book to other children and discuss with them the contents of his book and theirs.

The Child's Own Book method need not be restricted to young children. It was found to be equally effective for teaching a group of nonreading adolescent girls between thirteen and seventeen years of age in a camp for juvenile delinquents near Los Angeles. These youngsters had not even mastered the preprimer vocabulary, and an attempt to teach them from a printed book would have evoked only a scornful refusal to work. The idea of making books of their own, however, caught their interest. Surprisingly, they did not choose as their subjects the lives of film stars or stories of crime or romance, as might be expected, but cooking, travel, and flowers.[1] When they had learned a basic vocabulary in the man-

---

[1] A catalog is often a most helpful source for illustrations. In this instance a Sears-Roebuck catalog and a National Park brochure were used.

ner described above, they were told that they were now equipped to read a preprimer. They were at first reluctant to try, until it was suggested that they should imagine they were mothers wanting to read a story to their children, or older sisters reading to the younger members of the family. This imaginative touch stimulated them to read aloud in turn from a preprimer, and they were delighted with their accomplishment.

Phonics

The purpose of teaching phonics is to help the child to recognize the association between the phoneme and the grapheme —between the auditory stimulus, the sound, and the printed word or symbol. It is often possible to teach reading without the aid of phonics by using the whole-word method, but in our experience, the latter method is difficult, if not impossible, for children with certain disabilities in visual perception, nor does it give a child a tool with which to attack new words. It seems, therefore, that the whole-word method should be augmented by instruction based on phonics.

Teaching a child to associate the sounds of the language with the written symbols is especially difficult in English, because of the great disparity between many of the spelling and phonetic rules. Even the greatest admirers and promoters of the phonic methods, such as the author of *Why Johnny Can't Read*, cannot claim that more than 80 percent of the words in the English language are phonetically written, and many maintain that the proportion is less. It is even difficult to teach rules of exception, since there are exceptions to the exceptions. For instance, when the letter *i* appears in short syllables, it is pronounced as in the word *bit, except* when it appears before the letters *nd*, when it is pronounced with a long sound (as in *kind*), *except* in the word *wind,* referring to air in motion.

For this reason, we place greater emphasis upon a functional approach to phonics than upon a systematic teaching of phonetic rules, but it must be acknowledged that opinion on this question is divided. Sabaroff (5), for instance, found that an experimental group of low achievers made progress with systematic instruction in the rules of phonics.

Color Cues

Our usual method is to associate phonemes with graphemes from the beginning, writing each distinct sound in a word in different color. The first words to be introduced are, of course, phonetically "pure," and it is best to introduce words containing short vowels first, then words with long vowels, and finally more complex sounds, such as diphthongs and digraphs. Where letter groups are pronounced uniformly, as, for example, the combination *ur* in the words *hurt, curtain, turn,* the letters in the group are written in the same color, to help the child learn the pronunciation of that particular combination. Sometimes it is necessary to teach a child to read only the initial letter in a word, at first, then the last letter, and finally the middle letter or letters. In these cases, the appropriate letter only is colored. Colors can also be used to teach syllabification, each syllable of a word being written in one color. Silent letters, such as the *e* in *those,* can be indicated by an appropriately insubstantial stippled effect so that the letter does not stand out from the background. We have not generally found it necessary to use the same color for one sound consistently, except in a few instances in which a child shows a particular difficulty which he can be helped to overcome by receiving a consistent cue, but we have found it useful to use consistently one color for *all* of the long vowels, and one other color for all of the short vowels.[2]

Kinesthetic Methods

The sense modality basic to the reading process is of course vision. Accurate space and form perception are essential. But when a child has disturbances in visual perception, the visual modality can be supported by the auditory even at the beginning of reading (as with the phonic instruction described above) and also by the kinesthetic modality. As kinesthetic activities are largely a matter of tracing, they not only provide training in reading but serve also to further writing and spelling skills.

Kinesthetic methods have other advantages as well. They form a bridge between the experience of an act extended in time, which occurs when we hear, and the experience of an act extended in space, which occurs when we see. Whenever we say a word or read it aloud, we experience an act which is extended in time. The *v* at the beginning of the word *visual,* for instance, is heard before the *l* at the end of the word. But when we read silently, we usually take the word in at a glance, and all of the letters seem to be perceived at the same time. The word is no longer perceived as extended in time, but as extended in space. It may be that it is just this translation from a spatial dimension to a temporal one, and vice versa, which makes it difficult for a child to associate words which he hears with the printed word. The kinesthetic method helps overcome the prob-

[2] We have not discussed the use of the Augmented Roman Alphabet in teaching reading because we have had no experience with it. It would seem to be a very worthwhile method, however.

lem by forming a bridge between the auditory stimulus and the visual one. When we write or trace a word, it takes *time* to write it; we perceive that a time span elapses while we are writing. We also experience a spatial dimension as we see the word "grow" from left to right on the page. When a word is presented kinesthetically, therefore, it has both a temporal and a spatial dimension, which makes it easier for the child to connect the two experiences of seeing and hearing.

There are many modifications of the kinesthetic method. Pulliam (3) has suggested that children write in grooves, experiencing in this way the movement of the word and learning its kinesthetic pattern. For children with severe motor defects, it is helpful to write in clay or on some similarly resistant surface. Many clinics advocate the Fernald method (2) of first tracing words with the fingers and then writing them.

Blind Writing

The blind writing kinesthetic method deserves a detailed account because of its effectiveness with children whose visual perception is inadequate, as is often the case with children who have minimal brain damage.

Recent research (1, 4) has shown that even in small children the visual experience is stronger than the haptic one. ("Haptic" means the dual experience of touch and kinesthesia, which are combined, for instance, in taking an object in one's hand and feeling it totally while moving a finger over it to experience its shape.) When the children were first shown something which they experienced visually, and then felt the same object without looking at it, their final description of the object was in visual terms rather than in terms of touch. Because of

this natural predominance of the visual modality, a child with a severely distorted visual perceptual sense is very seriously handicapped. It is necessary in these cases to train the child's less effective, but at least unimpaired, kinesthetic abilities so that he can perceive accurately by movement, as blind children can do. The kinesthetic modality can then be used to guide the visual one.

To teach the child to write and read by the blind writing method, the teacher first writes the letter or word on the chalkboard at a height which can easily be reached by the child. Then the teacher guides the child's hand while he traces the word with closed eyes. The elimination of visual stimuli enables him to concentrate entirely upon the kinesthetic experience. While the teacher guides the child's hand, she pronounces the word slowly, trying to use as much time for saying the word as the child takes in tracing it. With repetition, the teacher will feel the child's hand begin to follow the lines of the word independently. She can then remove her hand while he continues to trace, without opening his eyes and without her assistance. The next step is to have him make the connection between the kinesthetic and the visual modality by looking at the word as he traces it, and then as he writes it. The child is finally asked to find the word on a page in his book, to read the sentences in which it appears, and then to write it again. The use of cursive writing is a great advantage because of the uninterrupted flow of the kinesthetic pattern the child perceives, even though he has to make the association between the written and printed forms of the word.

Causes of reading difficulties. Difficulties in reading occur not only because of a specific difficulty with the reading process itself. They may be due to disabilities in comprehension or to a lag in any other area of development, such as in perception, motor skills (especially eye movements), language, and social and emotional development. The possible difficulties in any one of these areas are

legion. But the corrective methods described above can be used with all children in the regular classroom during corrective reading.

References

1. BIRCH, HERBERT G., and LEFFORD, A. "Intersensory Development in Children," *Society for Research in Child Development Monographs,* vol. 28 (1963).
2. FERNALD, GRACE M. *Remedial Techniques in Basic School Subjects.* New York: McGraw-Hill, 1943. P. 349.
3. PULLIAM, ROY A. "Invented Word Cards as a Sensori-Motor Aid in Vocabulary Development," *Peabody*

Journal of Education, 23 (July, 1945), 38–42.
4. ROCK, I., and VICTOR, J. "Vision and Touch: An Experimentally Created Conflict Between the Two Senses," *Science,* 43 (February, 1964), 3606.
5. SABAROFF, ROSE. "A Comparative Investigation of Two Methods of Teaching Phonics in a Modern Reading Program: A Pilot Study," *Journal of Experimental Education,* 31 (March, 1963), 249–56.

82. Attitudes, Platitudes, and Conferences in Teacher-Parent Relations Involving the Child with a Reading Problem *

BEATRICE LIEBEN

"I told the mother not to worry. Johnny is in the slowest reading group, but he is moving along at his own pace. Leave him alone."

Students enrolled in a graduate course on "Diagnosis and Treatment of Reading Disabilities" were asked at their first class session to comment freely on the

* From Beatrice Lieben, "Attitudes, Platitudes, and Conferences in Teacher-Parent Relations Involving the Child with a Reading Problem," *Elementary School Journal,* 58 (February, 1958), 279–86. Reprinted by permission of the author and The University of Chicago Press.

statement quoted above. The purpose of this project was to discover students' attitudes toward the parents of children with reading disabilities so that the course work could be meaningfully designed to meet the training needs of the students.

In the class were seventeen teachers, with experience of from one to twenty or more years, and five psychologists in training, three of whom had had some teaching experience. All were mature and intelligent, were dedicated to their work, and deeply interested in the content of the course. Thus the responses may be considered characteristic of the attitudes held by experienced teachers now practicing in our school systems.

An average response given by a student at the end of the semester should cover some of the following points:

1. If Johnny is in the slowest reading group, then we must recognize that the mother has a right to her anxiety. Anxiety is to be expected of the interested and concerned parent if Johnny is failing to keep up with his peers.

2. If the mother is worried and anxious, then the admonition "Don't worry" is of little value, particularly when Johnny's "own pace" is extremely slow. The reasons for the delay may not be profound, but it suggests to the uninformed parent the frightening possibility of gross stupidity, physiological impairment, or deep emotional disturbance. The mother needs to know what "moving along at his own pace" means specifically for Johnny. Supplying this information involves helping the mother to understand the possible causes for reading delay as it relates to Johnny and how his learning needs are being met in the classroom.

3. If the child is badly delayed in reading, then the statement "Leave him alone" is ineffective advice for both the teacher and the parent. The teacher needs to teach; the parent who is filled with anxiety, whether rightly or otherwise, needs to help the child through difficulties. The problem is how each can supplement the other's efforts. To solve the problem requires. that the mother be involved in the treatment plans for the child and that she and the teacher identify the possible things she may do to help.

The Kinds of Responses Obtained from Students

Of course responses like those above were not fully expected of students just beginning their work in this course, but it seemed reasonable to expect that many

of the responses would approach these in attitude. Let us examine the results.

Of the twenty-two students, only one, a young teacher of several years' experience, was truly uneasy with the given quotation. She felt that full recognition should have been given to parental anxiety, that "moving along at his own pace" was an insufficient explanation, and that the "mother should have been helped to understand the problem and have been given clues as to how she might help." Fifteen students stated that they felt exactly as did the teacher making the remark. Four felt the teacher's remark reflected good and appropriate attitudes but that his approach was "too tactless." Two students—one teacher and one psychologist—missed the issues entirely and went off into other areas.

In the case of nineteen students who supported the teacher attitude revealed in the quotation, the responses of fifteen clearly reflected hostile, negative attitudes toward the parents of the poor achiever. A response made by an experienced male teacher in a training program for psychologists was typical: "Her Johnny is in the slowest group . . . what a disgrace! It reflects back on her. She will really get him to move along but fast." Mothers were seen as doing more harm than good; they were seen as more or less directly responsible for the problem in the first place, and hence a "hands-off" attitude for mother is best. These opinions were implicit in statements such as: "Too much parental pressure often leads to reading trouble. The child is being pushed beyond his ability." "[The mother] is pushing him on to greater things, ignoring the child's own pace. This is to satisfy her own desires rather than to help the child." "Certainly leave him alone." "[The child] needs less interference from the parent." "He should not be pushed."

Four of the nineteen students showed some recognition of the feelings of parents. While the "mother should be told off," the telling-off should be done in "more tactful ways."

On the whole, the responses reflected hostility toward the parents of the child with a reading problem. There was little recognition of the feelings that parents might be experiencing when children consistently performed below the norm. It was taken for granted that parents were the most likely cause for the difficulty, particularly in their destructive "push" for achievement. "Hands off" was clearly the best policy for parents, with the "teacher-knows-best" attitude flaunted accordingly. With few exceptions, the parents were excluded in the treatment plans for the child. However, despite all the attitudes thus shown, every response in the group revealed genuine concern for the child.

Effects of Teachers' Negative Attitudes

We might paraphrase Bettelheim and say "concern is not enough." However great the teacher's concern for his pupil, such negative attitudes toward the troubled parent can only have a more depressing effect upon the child who is already in difficulty. When the teacher operates from such assumptions as those seen in the students' responses (and our experience suggests that many do), the teacher-parent conferences can only leave the mother feeling more anxious, frustrated, and guilty. She now knows something is wrong, and she must be to blame. She is given only the vaguest of generalities about possible causes and is told there is little she can do to help. She gazes at her child with sad, helpless eyes, seeking for signs to verify her worst fears, or she looses her anger by railing at him for not trying hard enough. Either reaction can only result in increasing the child's fears about himself and in arousing feelings of

guilt about his failure to meet the expectations of parent and teacher.

Undoubtedly a teacher's attitude is shaped in part by the kinds of assumptions he makes about his teaching role and the kinds of hidden needs and motivations he brings to his job. One teacher may feel his responsibility is to be all things to all pupils—loving parent, trained psychologist, character-molder, teacher of all skills. Such a teacher may make such unrealistic demands upon himself that he is overwhelmed by all he must accomplish. His frustrations may result in resentment against parents, particularly the parents of those children who "fail" despite his excessive zeal.

Another teacher may measure his success against the yardstick of "love." Thus he is warm and responsive to the children who respond to him, bothered and resentful toward those who do not. In the classroom the unresponsive pupils may move to the periphery of the teacher's awareness so that, in a sense, they almost do not exist for him. To meet with the parents of such children is an uneasy, disturbing situation for the teacher, with the result that his actions at the conference are detached and uninvolved.

Unquestionably, hidden needs and unrecognized assumptions have consequences for the teacher-child relationship as they must have for the teacher-parent relationship. But these hidden forces elude our awareness. It requires specialized techniques to open them for examination and to effect changes. We recognize that teacher-education programs must eventually include more individual-oriented procedures through which a teacher may gain awareness of his own hidden promptings and the ways in which they are reflected in his professional relationships. Meanwhile, there is much that can be done on other levels to improve teacher-parent relationships and thus to effect more therapeutic results which will work for the benefit of the child.

Cause and Effect in Reading Retardation

Basic to the teacher-parent relationship and effecting its outcomes are the teacher's implicit assumptions about the role of the mother in academic delay. In discussions of reading disability, teachers continue to express a feeling that parental attitudes are the most likely determinant in reading disability. Causation, when not obviously related to mental retardation or to physical factors (poor hearing, vision, and the like), is sought in whatever attitude the mother assumes. Whether she shows concern or nonchalance, whether she helps the child with his homework or "leaves him alone," these actions are seen equally by teachers as reflections of a negative parental attitude which must have acted as a distorting factor in the expected developmental pattern. *Ad nauseum*, we hear, "Find the disturbed child, and you find the disturbed parent." "Overanxious," "overambitious," and "rejecting" are terms too loosely used to describe parents of children who are failing to progress academically in expected ways.

Of course the mother plays a fundamental role in a child's development, but the relationship is extremely complex, particularly in reading difficulties. Here causation is frequently so unclear that we cannot separate the causes or even cause and effect. We must avoid the pitfalls of oversimplification.

A mother acts upon her child but, at the same time, is acted upon by the child. The child, from the beginning, comes to the situation with certain potentialities, limitations, and experiences, which, in part, help to determine how he acts, and how he is acted upon, in a situation. For example, in delayed readiness we may have an intellectually average or even superior child who was developmentally slow in speech or in motor-perceptual coordination or in both. At our present stage of knowledge, these delays can be ascribed to an innate or an individualized developmental pattern, which is "normal" for this child, or they may be referred to as "symptoms" of "disturbance." In any case, the preschool child becomes aware that he does not speak or ride his "bike" or catch a ball as well as other children do, that he lacks certain important competencies. This awareness may have negative effects on his image of himself. He also experiences the effect of his incompetencies in the attitudes of his age mates toward him.

The mother, too, has become aware that the child does not seem to talk or to do things as well as other children of his age. The resulting concerns must be reflected in her attitudes toward Johnny. The relationship between the two, their mode of interaction, must, in part, be determined by how Johnny experiences himself and the ways in which his feelings are expressed; by the mother's concerns and the ways these are expressed; by the effects that the expressions of the hidden concerns of each have upon the other. Here the mother is not the villain. She is merely one facet of a total situation; her actions and attitudes are partly determined by the actions and attitudes which Johnny brings to the relationship.

This developmentally "delayed" child may well come to the school-learning situation with hindering emotional attitudes. He carries the consequences not only of his own awareness of his incompetence but also of his awareness of the effects that his incompetence has on the attitudes of others toward him. The teacher may see an uncertain, passive, noncurious child who daydreams or doodles when faced with new challenges. Or the effects of his experience may be expressed in more disruptive ways. It is not necessary, or even helpful, to assume that there must be a "rejecting" or "overprotective" mother in the background. There are other assumptions which hold greater promise for positive outcomes in the teacher-parent relationship.

Those of us who have worked extensively with children with reading disabilities have been struck with the fact that parents, so far as they are able, desire to do the very best for their children. We can assume, with little fear of negative effects, that the mother of a child delayed in reading does the very best she can within the limits of her understanding, capacities, and the exigencies of everyday living. Few parents fail their children willingly, and most parents suffer pangs of guilt over their real or imagined failures. No parent can be perfect in meeting basic needs; all fail their children in one way or another. Luckily, children bring with them varying reserves of strength, resiliency, and thrust toward good adjustment.

The degree to which children are endowed with the necessary resources may determine, in the long run, the degree to which they can deal successfully with psychic hurt. What may prove traumatic to one child may be taken in stride by another. A parent does not affect the child as do pellets bombarding an inert system. The parent and the child in their relationship are each an individual, dynamic system, seeking to maintain an equilibrium and stability in the face of the effects one has on the other. Without full and exhaustive exploration, the teacher or the psychologist cannot, in good conscience, place the blame on the parent for the problems of the child.

The Conference

When a child is of particular concern to a teacher, one of the most important resources for working through problems is the parent-teacher conference. An informal survey recently undertaken by the writer revealed that current textbooks on the teaching of reading contain little or no reference to parent-teacher conferences per se. Yet we all recognize that the results of such conferences may play a decisive role in a remedial program. Teachers see parents in any case. How may these meetings prove more effective?

Parent Attitudes Toward the Conference

According to the teachers responding to the statement quoted at the beginning of this article, the attitudes that parents bring to the parent-teacher conference are among the chief reasons for the ineffectiveness of the conference. "Haughtiness," "chip on the shoulder," "annoyance," "not giving," and "disinterest" are some of the ways teachers describe the parent attitudes which most anger and frustrate them. What are such attitudes expressing? There is a tendency in all of us to react negatively to such behavior, but the professional person must be listening with all senses alerted, not to the behavior itself, but to that which is being expressed through the behavior.

What kinds of feelings may be aroused in the mother of a poor achiever by a request for a conference with the teacher? There are the feelings related to the present problem, such as fear of what she may hear about the child, fear of how this may reflect upon her as a parent, shame or guilt that she has failed the child in some irrevocable way, and the like. Then there may be feelings related to the school. Many parents carry to the conference their own childhood attitudes toward school as a place of fearful authority; they again become children, who are being kept after school for some dreadful failure or fearful infraction of rules.

A parent of an academically delayed child may approach the conference armed with mighty defenses against further hurt and inner turmoil. There is little value in responding blindly to the attitudes which guard these inner feelings. It is more than likely that, if the teacher responds to the underlying feelings and to the needs they imply, the defensive attitudes will dissolve like sand castles in water.

Teacher Anxiety About the Conference

Often the teacher's own concerns about his competency will hamper his ability to respond to the parent's underlying feelings. For example, a child who is doing inferior work in school may prove a threat to the teacher's self-esteem just as, for different reasons, his failures are a threat to the mother's self-esteem. The teacher may have all kinds of self-doubts because the child has not responded well to his teaching and has failed to meet the goals he has set for the pupil. He may feel himself vulnerable to the charge of incompetence, and, although this fear is usually unrealistic, he may come to the conference prepared to meet this challenge and to deal effectively with it. Armed with defenses against his own inner uncertainty and insecurity, the teacher becomes less free to respond with full sensitivity to what is really present in the situation; he can deal with only limited aspects of it.

When the teacher approaches the conference with an openness concerning the parent's role in the difficulty and with an attitude free of blame, then other things can happen. The teacher can be truly accepting of the mother; that is, he can accept the parent as she is, with her faults, weaknesses, limitations, and problems. He can be reassuring in that he can recognize with the mother that she has been a "good" parent; that her intentions were of the best; that her fears, her

uncertainties, even her angers and harshnesses, are human and understandable in view of the pressures with which she must deal. Even if the troubled mother gains nothing else in contacts with the teacher, this reassurance will reflect in positive ways on her relations with Johnny.

The Teacher's Role in the Conference

Initially, parent attitudes may present a barrier to good teacher-parent communication, but the professional responsibility of the teacher demands that he move through these attitudes to establish the kind of relationship that will work for the benefit of Johnny. It is also the teacher's responsibility to structure the conference so that he, at least, is perfectly clear about the reasons for the conference and the outcomes he hopes to achieve through it.

Why Call a Conference?

A conference concerning a child with a reading disability may be called for a variety of reasons. Since the reasons lend structure to the discussion and help to shape outcomes, the teacher must be clear in his own mind as to why he is seeing this particular parent at this particular time. For example, a child may be giving the teacher specific concern, and the teacher may feel the need for supplementary information not supplied by the school records. He may wish to share his concern with the parent and, through this sharing, to gain the kinds of information which will help him deal with the child in the classroom. He may seek for specific data, such as developmental history, home situation, medical facts; or he may seek for the less tangible, but possibly more important, kinds of information relating to parental attitudes and expectancies or the kinds of environmental pressures to which the child is subject. Such data could be valuable in helping the teacher to formulate his own attitudes toward the child and to determine what he can reasonably demand of him. This is essentially a conference for clarification, called by the teacher for his own teaching purposes.

When the teacher feels that he understands certain aspects of the child's behavior and that, through conferences, certain environmental changes can be effected which will help Johnny, he may call a conference for the purpose of helping the mother bring about these changes. While the teacher cannot expect to, nor should he attempt to, deal with and effect changes on the more profound levels, there is much he can do on another, and perhaps as meaningful, a level.

Suppose Johnny's reading behavior and latest visual examination reveal a need for glasses. Johnny claims he does not own a pair. In conference the teacher, as he expected, finds the mother much concerned about this. "But," says the mother helplessly, "he's already had five pairs. He breaks or loses them as fast as he gets them." The teacher recognizes with the mother that here is a problem: Johnny needs glasses, he does not have them, and he cannot seem to keep them when he gets them. The teacher agrees with the mother that she has been a "good," "efficient" parent, who has spent time and money trying to do what is right for Johnny. It is understandable that she does not know what to do next. Well, what can one do? The teacher does not know, but, by discussing the possibilities, the teacher and the mother together may evolve a plan which will help Johnny to keep and to wear his glasses when he gets a new pair.

Or suppose that the teacher suspects that underachieving, oversized, eight-year-old Mary shoulders too many adult responsibilities within the home. During the conference the teacher gains some understanding of the nature of, and the rationale for, the mother's demands upon the child. He can then discuss, from the vantage point of the mother's actual situation, how she and others, including the teacher, may be blinded by Mary's size so that expectancies for her are in terms of her eleven-year-old appearance rather than her actual age of eight years. From this, the conversation may turn to a discussion of the affectional needs of an eight-year-old child, which the mother, as well as the teacher, may be overlooking because of Mary's seeming maturity. Many changes can be effected through such a conference, which could prove of surprising importance in the life of the young child.

Teacher Use of Information

How sensible or appropriate a goal will be and how likely it is to be implemented through a conference depend, in large measure, on the teacher's overall competence and skill and his understanding of the learning and emotional needs of the child with reading problems. A conference must of necessity be short. A teacher cannot afford to spend time gathering information that will have little or no direct bearing on the present problem. Also, from all the child's problems, the teacher must be able to evaluate those which are most crucial and are amenable to remedial treatment. It is felt that among the most important responsibilities of the classroom teacher are those of evaluating the nature of the child's difficulty and of evolving appropriate ways to deal with it.

Our experience, particularly in field work with experienced teachers, suggests that teachers often fail to recognize that they have all the evidence needed to evaluate, *for their own teaching purposes,* the nature of the learning difficulty and ways of dealing with it. Record cards and observation alone supply a wealth of information: a history of intelligence-test results; achievement-test results; medical facts, such as information concerning the child's hearing, vision, nutrition, and illnesses; records of absences; school changes; family constellations; economic conditions; personality comments; and the results of the teacher's own usually perceptive observations. How does the teacher relate and evaluate the discrete bits of information for the bearing they may have on the present problem? How can he use this information in the role of teacher?

We all agree that teachers are not expected to be clinical psychologists. Nevertheless, they should know something about factors which may hinder reading progress, the bearing that the information already in their possession may have on the problem, and the implications of the information for teaching. One teacher requested diagnostic and treatment service for a problem reader when he himself could have noted that the child held his book up close to his face when reading. In his concern for more profound causation, the teacher also overlooked the record-card notation of severe visual impairment and a recommendation that the child be fitted with glasses, which had not been followed through. Another teacher, when given the opportunity, did not request special services for a retarded reader because he equated poor reading achievement with low intelligence. The teacher accepted as valid the last recorded intelligent quotient of 77 and ignored, as incidental data, the initially recorded intelligence quotient of 122.

Careful and skilled evaluation of the available evidence, assessment of needs and how they may be met in class, referral through appropriate channels for specialized diagnostic and treatment service when indicated—all are part of the teacher's repertory of skills. Certainly, when he meets with the parent of a child with a reading problem, the teacher's overall ability to deal with this aspect of his work lends substance and depth to the conference and allows for a relevance and specificity in discussing the particular child. When the teacher communicates to the parent his understanding of reading delay in general, and its meaning for this child in particular, the terms "don't worry" and "moving along at his own pace" acquire real meaning. In light of this understanding, the mother can then be helped to recognize in what ways she can "leave Johnny alone" and in what ways she can provide him with real and necessary help.

Concluding Remarks

In most teacher-parent conferences concerning reading disabilities, outcomes can be more meaningful if we start with the assumption that the mother, as does the teacher, attempts to fulfil her role as well as her own limitations and the situation allow. Implied in this assumption is the attitude, "How can we work together to help Johnny." The teacher, as does the parent, recognizes that he cannot, nor is he required to, come to the conference equipped with all the answers. Each must evolve for himself the ways that are appropriate for him to use in dealing with the problem. However, through the conference, through sharing the difficulties and exploring together the various possibilities for dealing with them, and by respecting one another's competence and good intentions, the parent and the teacher may each help the other to discover courses of action which each can use to bring about more positive outcomes for Johnny.

XVII

Reading Instruction for the Disadvantaged

In the past few years there has come to be an intense awareness that a long overlooked segment of our school population is in need of special assistance in learning to read. Despite the many different opinions as to how best to help these disadvantaged children, the teacher should have some understanding of the psychological, linguistic, and cultural factors that contribute to their problems.

After describing who are the disadvantaged, Harris summarizes their psychological and sociological characteristics and outlines the implications of these factors for teaching reading. Laffey summarizes pertinent language research that may have implications for teaching reading to the disadvantaged. These are followed by Baratz's article, which emphasizes that the language of the disadvantaged is "different," not "deficient." Based upon her beliefs she offers one *possible* reading program for the ghetto child. York and Ebert discuss the implications the previously described factors have for teaching primary-grade children. Finally, Feeley treats the problem of teaching non-English speaking first graders how to read.

83. Reading and Disadvantaged Children: Psychological and Sociological Factors *

ALBERT J. HARRIS

Introduction

THE term "disadvantaged" has come into favor to refer to those boys and girls whose environment outside of school does not equip them well to meet the requirements of the educational and economic

* From Albert J. Harris, "Reading and Disadvantaged Children: Psychological and Sociological Factors," *New England Reading Association Journal,* 3 (Fall, 1967), 11–18. Reprinted by permission of the New England Reading Association.

systems of our culture. A few years ago the term "culturally deprived" was popular. This was subject to the criticism that the groups with whom we are concerned have rich cultures of their own, cultures which are not necessarily inferior. The term "disadvantaged," or its near synonym "underprivileged," indicates that, in terms of what our school systems expect, these children are handicapped by the circumstances of their lives outside of school.

Although there has been a tendency recently to equate "disadvantage" with the Negro inhabitants of urban slum ghettos, they are by no means the only large disadvantaged group in the United States. Among the main varieties of disadvantage, different facets may be distinguished. Extreme poverty, with accompanying malnutrition, disease, and inadequate meeting of basic needs for food, clothing, and shelter is true of some. Parental and community attitudes indifferent to education or actually hostile to school aims are true of some. Impoverishment of experience is true of some. Speech in a local dialect different from the speech patterns of teachers is true of some. Insufficient mastery of English because parents speak a foreign language is true of some. Many children, unfortunately, experience more than one form of disadvantage; the educational adjustment of some children is impeded by all, or nearly all, of the factors just mentioned.

There are several large groups of disadvantaged people in the United States. Among them are the Indians on the reservations; the poor whites of the Appalachian hills and hollows; the Mexican-Americans of the Southwest; the Puerto Ricans in the northeastern cities; the French-Canadians in northern New England. The most numerous group, and currently the main focus of concern, are the Negro children, many of them recent immigrants from the South or children of parents educated in the South, who dwell in thickly populated slum sections of most Northern cities, large and small. The designation "disadvantaged" should not be equated with membership in an ethnic group, but should be defined in terms of environmental characteristics and the characteristics of the individual.

Sociological Factors

Any attempt to depict the characteristics of the disadvantaged, or of the conditions in which they grow up, runs into the problem that for every generalization there are notable and important exceptions. Robert Weaver has emphasized the diversity to be found in slum dwellers:

Slums in American cities today house families which hold a wide range of values and evidence a variety of behavior patterns. Some are households with female heads and are stable none-the-less; others may be ungrammatical but adhere to high moral standards; still others evidence all the attributes of middle-class behavior and are dedicated to its values, if not recipients of its rewards. All three groups have ambition and talent, but fight an uphill battle in maintaining respectability and achievement for themselves and their children . . . (16).

The Family

The family in which the disadvantaged child grows up is, first of all, an "extended" family; it contains not only parents and children, but often grandparents and uncles and aunts. In most disadvantaged cultures the men are dominant, while among Negroes the family tends to be matriarchal. Common-law marriages and fatherless homes are relatively frequent. But when parents are missing or incapable, other relatives tend to assume responsibility for the child.

Lower-class parents tend to be authoritarian in their child-rearing practices. Corporal punishment is usual, and is sometimes quite harsh. At the same time discipline is often casual and inconsistent. The male role is chiefly that of the punisher.

The home is likely to be crowded, busy, and noisy, with little or no opportunity for privacy. Partly because of limited space, partly because of working mothers, young children are out on the street at an early age, cared for by an older brother or sister. Lower-class children tend to be free to roam the neighborhood and join in unsupervised play at an age when suburban children are in nursery school or confined to their own backyards. Thus the peer group of other children plays a dominant part as a socializing agent and a source of values much earlier for the lower-class child. Precocious independence from the family is less common among Puerto Rican children than among poor white and Negro children because family ties are close and warm and the Puerto Rican mother tries to be protective.

The working-class mother tends both to rely heavily on punishment and to show little overt affection for her children. Often the main wage-earner, she often transfers major child-rearing responsibility to the grandmother or an older daughter. When the father is missing, the mother may be bitter in her attitude toward men and may show an open preference for daughters over sons.

Opportunities for educationally useful learning experiences are limited in the lower-class home. In a study of lower-class Negro and white children, Deutsch found that 65 percent of the Negro children had never been more than twenty-five blocks away from home. Half of them reported no pen or pencil at home. The majority of their homes contained no books, although the majority had tele-

vision sets. Toys and other playthings were scarce and soon broken. Many of the children had to fix their own meals and a large number went to school without breakfast (8).

Employment

A generation ago jobs for semiskilled and unskilled workers comprised a major share of the total job market. Indeed, guidance counselors were taught that there were more feebleminded jobs than there were feebleminded people. On the farm, in the factory, and in the construction industry, there were millions of jobs requiring little more than physical stamina and a willingness to work.

Since World War II this situation has changed radically. Complicated machinery has progressively taken over more and more of the repetitive work that used to be done by human hands. One mechanical cotton-picker can displace a score of plantation workers; one mechanical brick hoist can eliminate jobs for two dozen hod carriers. The computer, which can govern the sequencing and control of many mechanical operations, has made severe inroads into semiskilled factory jobs.

This has brought about a drastic curtailment of employment opportunities for people who are lacking in education and in specialized work skills. As a result, unemployment is closely related to educational level. The dropout, the person who hasn't finished high school, faces a steadily shrinking job market in which the available jobs are likely to be distasteful, low paid, and temporary. Unemployment is as high as 25 percent among teenage school dropouts. Partly because of prejudice, partly because he tends to be a comparatively recent arrival and to lack job seniority, the Negro unskilled worker is likely to be the last hired and the first laid off. Chronic unemployment is one of the major factors underlying the riots that have occurred in many cities this past summer.

Mobility

Families which lack financial stability are likely to move. A desire for economic betterment has been a major factor in the widespread migration of rural Negroes to the cities of the North. Similar motivation accounts for the increase in Puerto Rican populations in urban centers. Several studies have documented the fact that the newly arrived Negro or Puerto Rican child does not score as well on achievement tests or IQ tests as locally born children of similar parentage. In New York City, Negro and Puerto Rican children born in the city average 5 points higher in IQ and about a half-year higher in achievement than in-migrant children (12).

Mobility within the city is also high among the disadvantaged. Many families move when they cannot pay the rent and for other reasons related to marginal economic status. In a third-grade follow-up of Negro children tested early in the first grade, only about one-third of the original 1,350 were still in the same schools. In 1960 there were 41 schools in New York City which had a turnover rate of 70 percent or more per year; nearly all were in Negro or Puerto Rican neighborhoods. The movement of pupils in and out of classes disrupts continuity of schooling and is one of the factors that lower achievement levels.

The Effects of Discrimination

According to Riessman, discrimination is pervasive in school systems and is unwittingly practiced even by the best-intentioned people. He lists as forms of discrimination:

The reading texts used in classrooms which typically contain materials far less attuned to the interests of the disadvantaged; the Parent-Teacher Associations which often patronize or ignore underprivileged parents; the intelligence tests, the applicability of which to lower socioeconomic groups is increasingly being questioned; the school psychologists and guidance counselors, who frequently underestimate the possibility of the economically underprivileged child; the friendship cliques and clubs which favor less the child from a poor neighborhood; the teacher's unfavorable images and expectations which militate against the respect and encouragement so needed by the child (14).

Health as a Sociological Problem

Health problems tend to be more frequent and more severe among disadvantaged children than among middle-class children. All kinds of communicable diseases tend to be more prevalent because of overcrowded and often unsanitary conditions. Late hours and crowded beds may induce fatigue due to insufficient sleep. Hunger due to poverty is now rare in this country, but poorly balanced diets and qualitative malnutrition are common. Deficiency diseases, like pellagra, exist in some areas and debilitating infestations, like hookworm, are widespread in other sections. Visits to health clinics may be postponed and medical recommendations may not be followed. Special difficulty is often reported by school nurses in getting disadvantaged children who need eyeglasses to get them and wear them; the implications of this for reading are obvious.

There is also some evidence that neurological problems interfering with reading are more common among disadvantaged children. Such children may show not only severe learning difficulties but also highly impulsive behavior than can disrupt the classroom.

Psychological Factors

Intellectual Development

In recent years psychologists have moved away from the concept of the IQ as determined primarily by heredity and as remaining constant throughout childhood. While hereditary influences are not denied, substantial influence is now attributed to opportunities for learning. Piaget's theories have been quite influential in this change. One of Piaget's principles has been stated by Hunt as follows:

. . . the rate of development is in substantial part, but certainly not wholly, a function of environmental circumstances. . . . Thus, the greater the variety of situations to which the child must accommodate his behavioral structures, the more differentiated and mobile they become. Thus, the more new things a child has seen and the more he has heard, the more things he is interested in seeing and hearing. Moreover, the more variation in reality with which he has coped, the greater is his capacity for coping (11).

Martin Deutsch has described how the environment of the disadvantaged offers a restricted range of experience and therefore inhibits intellectual development. He points out that, visually, the slum and its overcrowded flats offer a minimal range of stimuli. Furniture and toys are sparse and lacking in form and color variations. Verbal interaction between parents and children involves a minimum of conversation and is largely limited to orders and directions. While there is considerable sound, most of it is noise which is not meaningful to the child and tends to be ignored or "tuned out." By not being asked to talk about his experiences, the child is not encouraged to remember. Rewards for successfully completing tasks are few. Questions are not encouraged and are often not answered, discouraging curiosity. Thus, in many ways, the dis-

advantaged child is not stimulated to achieve the maximum mental growth of which he may be capable (13).

Efforts to stimulate the mental growth of young disadvantaged children are getting a great deal of attention at present. Preliminary reports on Head Start programs, which only started in the summer of 1965, have encouraged the continuation and expansion of such programs. Many other ways to foster mental development and readiness for learning have been tried. One study, for example, has reported an average gain of 8 points in IQ for first-grade disadvantaged children exposed to a carefully structured language development program (10).

Conventional intelligence tests assume equality of opportunity to learn. For disadvantaged children such tests may function more as measures of present readiness to learn than as measures of improvability.

Perceptual Development

On tests of visual perception of the kinds used in tests of reading readiness, disadvantaged children tend to score about as well, or as poorly, as they do on the test as a whole. Usually the average score for the disadvantaged group falls near the 20th to 25th percentile of the national norms. Expectations that verbally handicapped children would compensate by doing well on nonverbal tasks are true of some disadvantaged children, but not of the group as a whole.

Disadvantaged children, and particularly Negro children, do very poorly on tests of auditory discrimination of word sounds. For example, our first-grade population of 1350 Negro children in New York City made an average score at the lowest percentile of the Phonemes Test of the *Murphy-Durrell Diagnostic Reading Readiness Tests*. This seems in part due to speech patterns; the speech they hear at home tends to understress consonant sounds, elide word endings, and use variant vowel sounds. Cynthia Deutsch has suggested that the habit of ignoring or disregarding background noise leads to a general inattention to auditory stimulation. Thus the child may "tune out" what the teacher is saying on the basis of a habit developed at home (7).

Although the group as a whole scores low, variations within the group are about as predictive of success in beginning reading as with representative groups.

Language Development

There is general agreement that disadvantaged children tend to be retarded in nearly all aspects of mastery of standard English, and that this retardation does not diminish but actually increases during the elementary school years (8). Among the aspects of language in which they tend to lag are: sentence length, use of complete sentences, use of compound and complex sentences, agreement of subject and verb, use of present for past tense, inflectional endings, range and accuracy of vocabulary, and clarity of enunciation. For many disadvantaged children, the teacher's speech is so different from neighborhood speech as to be very difficult to understand. Similarly, the language of books is for many almost a foreign tongue.

A great deal of exposure to language is necessary for good language development. This involves training, experimenting with naming objects and receiving corrective feedback, listening to a variety of verbal material, and observing the language usage of adults and older children. In lower-class homes the adults tend to use short speech sequences with poor syntax. There is also considerably less conversation between adult and child than in mid-dle-class homes. Thus the disadvantaged child's language-learning opportunities outside of school are drastically limited.

Cognition

Much of the factual information which teachers tend to assume is lacking in many disadvantaged children. First graders may not know their last names, home addresses, or names of parents. They often have rudimentary or missing ideas regarding number, or such concepts as near and far, above and below, big and small. Even at junior high school level the gaps in informational background may astound the teacher who questions carefully.

A slower tempo of thinking is characteristic of disadvantaged children. They require more examples and illustrations before forming a concept or coming to a conclusion. They tend to be slow in settling down to work, in taking tests, in solving problems, and in reading. In a culture which seems to value speed as an end in itself, this slower tempo is sometimes mistaken for inability to learn.

Riessman summarizes these aspects of cognitive style as being typical of disadvantaged children: physical and visual rather than auditory; emphasis on content rather than on form; practical and specific rather than abstract and general; inductive rather than deductive; spatial rather than temporal; slow and persevering rather than quick and flexible.

He points out that the parents of underprivileged children value structure, rules, discipline, authority, rote, order, organization, and strong external demands for achievement. He suggests that when this kind of firm structure can be combined with motivation, learning by doing, an appropriate pace, and drawing examples from the child's experience, the disadvantaged child can learn effectively (14).

Ego Development

Ego development refers to the ideas and feelings one has about himself, and the motives, values, aspirations, and key personality traits related to his self-concept.

Lower-class children, who are weaned from dependence on parents at an early age, come to value the goodwill of their companions above that of adults. By middle childhood the peer group attitudes tend to discourage them from accepting the teacher's authority, seeking teacher approval, or using the teacher as a model for emulation. Being a good student means running the risk of social ostracism for many a bright, disadvantaged child (13).

The parents of these children generally did not experience much success or satisfaction in school, and they do not expect their children to do so. While lip service to the value of education is increasing, and more lower-class parents have come to see schooling as an avenue to upward mobility, the preponderant attitude is probably still one in which school success does not really seem possible and parental help is not often forthcoming either for motivating school work or in providing help in meeting the school's expectations.

Lack-of-success experience is a third factor weighing against strong motivation for school success. The majority of disadvantaged children are below average in reading readiness when they enter first grade, but they are bright enough to appraise their own progress, in part through sensitivity to the teacher's disappointment with their performance. Thus, many think of themselves as slow learners from the first grade on. Acceptance of this derogatory self-rating militates against the exertion of real effort; for, why try when success is impossible?

Thus, the lower-class child usually fails to develop middle-class attitudes which support effort in school that can be maintained over long periods of time. The so-called middle-class "deferred gratification pattern" involves renunciation of immediate pleasure in favor of long-range goals, willingness to work hard, high tolerance for frustration, impulse control, orderliness, punctuality, thrift, and long-range planning for future educational and vocational goals. Relatively few disadvantaged children can govern today's conduct by expected future success.

For Negro children, the fact of skin color remains an additional burden about which they can do nothing. Although discrimination is not supported by law, it continues in informal social practices. Until recently a common kind of response involved submission, apathy, and lethargy; a pattern some older movie goers will recognize as the Stepin Fetchit pattern. Recently, submerged resentment has been breaking out more frequently in explosions of hostility. Both lethargy and hostility represent attempts to cope with deep feelings of worthlessness and hopelessness, feelings which result from living in what is perceived as an unaccepting and unfriendly society. Negro girls seem to have less difficulty in adapting to the social structure and academic expectations of the school than their brothers.

Implications for Reading Instruction

A first implication stems from the massive size of the reading retardation of disadvantaged children. Remedial facilities for a few children are not of much value when the majority of children are seriously below grade in reading. Solutions must aim at meeting the needs of the many.

Improvement of Readiness

In view of the inadequacies of disadvantaged homes in preparing their children for success in school, it seems reasonable that much effort should go into improving the readiness of the disadvantaged child for beginning reading instruction. The current emphasis on pre-kindergarten and kindergarten programs seems wise. To the extent that such programs include specific, carefully planned and structured reading readiness activities, they may lessen the present high proportion of failure in first-grade disadvantaged classrooms.

Positive Approach to Learning

The teacher of the disadvantaged must have the conviction that her children can learn and must insist on order and the exertion of effort.

Slower Pace of Learning

In view of the disadvantaged child's slower tempo, an instructional pace that employs ample review and repetition and does not go too fast for children seems desirable.

Immediate Reward

The disadvantaged child's need for immediate rather than deferred rewards suggests a generous use of praise and some use of concrete, material rewards or prizes.

Realistically Designed Reading Materials

Reading instruction should respect the disadvantaged child's need that things should be, as a dear colleague of mine used to say, "for real." He does not want to be patronized nor talked down to. He wants his reading materials to be appropriate for his age, even when he has great difficulty with them. Materials should combine mature interest appeal with difficulty below the frustration level.

Wide Variety

While at the beginning levels content that emphasizes the familiar seems desirable, the disadvantaged child needs exposure to the full range and variety of reading materials.

Opportunity for "Identification"

It helps to raise the self-image of the disadvantaged child when he can find characters that resemble himself, his family, and his friends in at least some of the stories he reads. This also enhances the interest appeal of the materials. The kinds of interaction among characters of different ethnic backgrounds should be of kinds that can happen in our society, although they may not happen as often as they should.

Short Assignments

Reading assignments should be capable of completion within the attention span of the child. They should be short, clear, and carefully structured.

Related Activities

The physical and motoric strengths of the disadvantaged child can be utilized in reading. Stories can be dramatized. Drill procedures that involve physical activity can be employed. Construction and art activities can be related to the reading program.

Adjusted Speech Patterns

The teacher must be aware of the differences between her speech and that of the children. The teacher should speak slowly and clearly. The colloquial language of the children should be accepted, and later revised into standard English; the desire to communicate should be encouraged even when the form is imperfect.

Supplementary Helpers

The school should provide the equivalents of the kinds of help in reading that middle-class parents give their children. Help with homework, and time and place for independent reading, belong within the disadvantaged child's school day. Wider use of school aids and volunteers can assist the school in these responsibilities.

Method and Materials

Most disadvantaged children can learn by the same methods and from the same materials as middle-class children. Recent experimentation has not discovered any particular reading method that is especially suited to the disadvantaged.

In-service Help

There is ample evidence that the inexperienced teacher, assigned to teach reading to disadvantaged children, needs expert guidance and help. In-service programs in reading instruction need to be improved and expanded, and consultative services need to be enlarged.

References

1. AUSUBEL, DAVID, and AUSUBEL, PEARL. "Ego Development among Segregated Negro Children." *Education in Depressed Areas,* A. H. Passow (ed.). New York: Bureau of Publications, Teachers College, Columbia University, 1963.

2. BARTON, ALLEN H. "Reading Research and Its Communication: The Columbia-Carnegie Project." *Reading as an Intellectual Activity,* J. Allen Figurel (ed.). International Reading Association Conference Proceedings, 8 (1963), 246–50.

3. BECK, JOHN M., and SAXE, RICHARD W. *Teaching the Culturally Disadvantaged Pupil.* Springfield, Ill.: Charles C Thomas, 1965.

4. BLOOM, BENJAMIN S., DAVIS, ALLISON, and HESS, ROBERT. *Compensatory Education for Cultural Deprivation.* New York: Holt, Rinehart and Winston, Inc., 1965.

5. BLOOM, BENJAMIN S. *Stability and Change in Human Characteristics.* New York: Wiley, 1964. Pp. xiv & 237.

6. DAVIDSON, HELEN, and LANG, GERHARD. "Children's Perceptions of Their Teachers' Feelings Toward Them Related to Self-Perception, School Achievement and Behavior," *Journal of Experimental Education,* 29 (1960), 107–18.

7. DEUTSCH, CYNTHIA P. "Auditory Discrimination and Learning: Social Factors," *Merrill-Palmer Quarterly of Behavior and Development,* 10 (July, 1964), 277–96.

8. DEUTSCH, MARTIN. "The Role of Social Class in Language Development and Cognition," *American Journal of Orthopsychiatry* (1965), pp. 35, 78–88.

9. ———. "Minority Group and Class Status as Related to Social and Per-

sonality Factors in School Achievement." Monograph No. 2. Ithaca, New York: Society for Applied Anthropology, 1960.

10. DUNN, LLOYD M., and MUELLER, MAX W. *The Effectiveness of the Peabody Language Development Kits and The Initial Teaching Alphabet with Disadvantaged Children in the Primary Grades: After One Year.* IMRID Behavioral Science Monograph No. 2. Nashville: George Peabody College for Teachers, 1966.

11. HUNT, J. MCVICKER. *Intelligence and Experience.* New York: Ronald Press Co., 1961. P. 363.

12. MORIBER, LEONARD. "School Functioning of Pupils Born in Other Areas and in New York City." Pamphlet No. 168, Board of Education of the City of New York, Bureau of Edu-

cational Program Research and Statistics, May, 1961.

13. PASSOW, A. HARRY (ed.). *Education in Depressed Areas.* New York: Bureau of Publications, Teachers College, Columbia University, 1963.

14. RIESSMAN, FRANK. *The Culturally Deprived Child.* New York: Harper, 1962.

15. SEXTON, PATRICIA. *Education and Income.* New York: Viking Press, 1961.

16. WEAVER, ROBERT. "Human Values of Urban Life." *Proceedings of the Academy of Political Science* (1960), pp. 33–34.

17. WHIPPLE, GERTRUDE, and BLACK, MILLARD, compilers. *Reading for Children Without—Our Disadvantaged Youth.* Newark, Del.: International Reading Association, 1966.

84. Selected Language Research and Its Implications for Teaching Reading to the Disadvantaged *

JAMES L. LAFFEY

SINCE the late 1950s when the plight of the educationally disadvantaged became widely known, special education programs for the disadvantaged learner have increased in number. Professional literature has reflected the interest and concerns of the educator. Many articles

* From James L. Laffey, "Selected Language Research and Its Implications for Teaching Reading to the Disadvantaged," in J. Allen Figurel (ed.), *Reading Goals for the Disadvantaged* (Newark, Del.: International Reading Association, 1970), pp. 55–62. Reprinted with permission of the author and the International Reading Association.

have reviewed and described major innovative projects, such as *The Great Cities Improvement Program.* Because of the attention given to these types of innovative efforts, I would like to discuss a specific area of language research which appears to show some promise of making a significant contribution to instructional programs for the educationally disadvantaged.

During the past two decades, language research concerning disadvantaged youths has been focused on prerequisite skills to language learning, extent of vocabulary, and grammatical usage of standard English. Bloom, Davis, and Hess (3) indicate that the disadvantaged child comes to school from a home background in which language use is different from that of the middle-class child. In middle-class homes, language is used in a variety of ways. Some uses include discussions to explore ideas, to analyze feelings, and to clarify individual interpretations. In the deprived home, language is used in a much more limited way. Communication often takes place through gestures and other nonverbal means. Also, the language used is often grammatically incorrect and likely to be limited to a small number of grammatical forms.

Language differences between socioeconomic classes, in terms of classroom performance, were summarized by Gordon (6). Middle-class children mastered a higher number of speech sounds, articulated better, demonstrated a greater frequency of mature-sentence types, constructed more complex sentences, verbally built better-elaborated concepts, and showed a higher incidence of words. On the other hand, lower-class children's language behavior was found to be characterized as "restricted," i.e., communicated signals and direction with thinking confined to a relatively low repetitive level. Generally, there was a delay in language acquisition which very likely resulted in some difficulty in making the language transition necessary for dealing with abstract modes of thought. While these research findings demonstrated the profound and complex problems faced by the culturally disadvantaged in the school setting, the findings also established a research base for a different kind of language research. This research began to ask a new set of questions. The questions placed a new perspective on the language of the disadvantaged. Much of the earlier research appeared to place the language of the disadvantaged as an inferior version of standard English. The

new research considered the language behavior of the disadvantaged as a different point on the language continuum that ranges from the most formal to the most free. It also viewed nonstandard English as a separate mode of expression. Nonstandard and standard English were viewed as different approaches to formal English, each having its own use. This view of the language acted as a springboard to an entirely new series of sociolinguistic studies on the language of the disadvantaged. Linguists conducting these studies were concerned with (1) examining the language differences in the black and white populations; (2) relating the language of the socially and educationally disadvantaged to school-related problems; and (3) exploring the possibility of developing instructional materials based on the culturally different language systems of students.

What have the researchers found concerning the language systems of these different cultural groups? How do the findings of this research relate to school problems?

To provide an answer to the first question, one need only review the studies of Bailey (1), Dillard (4), Labov (7) and Shuy, Wolfram, and Riley (12). These researchers have described the techniques and linguistic parameters of Negro nonstandard English. Labov, however, points out that even though there are distinct features in the nonstandard Negro dialect, these distinctive features also occur in the speech of Northern and Southern whites.

What are some of the features of the nonstandard English dialect? Essentially the dialectical differences occur in the sound system, grammar, and vocabulary. Some of the more obvious differences in the sound system or phonological patterns are described by Labov (7). He categorizes the phonological differences into three classes: *r*-lessness, *l*-lessness, and consonant clusters simplification. The *r*-less pronunciation refers to extending the vowel sound in certain words so that the vowel sound obscures the *r*-sound. For example, a lengthened vowel sound in either *car* or *guard* obscures the *r*-sound. Other examples which Labov uses to illustrate the *r*-less pronunciation are the centering glide sound or [schwa] in place of the *r* in *fear, feared, care, cared, bore,* and *bored.*

The *l*-less sounds found in the Negro dialect are illustrated in the following examples, Labov (7). Homonyms are formed by the following words: *toll = toe, help = hep, tool = too, all = awe, Saul = saw,* and *faught = fought.*

In the class of consonant clusters, the most general tendency is toward the simplification of consonant clusters at the end of words. Labov points out that there are two distinct tendencies among Negro speakers: (1) to reduce clusters at the end of words to single consonants, (*past-pass*), (*rift-riff*) and (2) a more general process of reducing the amount of information provided after stressed vowels, so that individual final consonants are affected as well. (She wow! = She wild!)

The grammatical differences between standard English and the nonstandard dialect of Negroes have been summarized by Baratz (1969). Some examples of these differences relate to verb in number, form, tense, subject expression, and use of the pronoun and indefinite articles. In the Negro dialect, the speaker often neglects to use a linking verb. For *"He is going,"* the speaker of nonstandard English says *"He—goin!"* In the nonstandard dialect there is often a lack of verb agreement. For *"He runs home,"* "He ru*n* home." The verb form is also different. "I *drank* the milk" becomes "I *drunk* the milk." In expressing the subject, the nonstandard dialect speaker often inserts a pronoun immediately after the subject. "Joe *he* live in Pittsburgh." In using the pronoun, the nonstandard dialect speaker often uses the third person pronoun in place of the first person pronoun. Instead of *"We* have to do it," it is *"Us* got to do it." When the nonstandard speaker uses the indefinite article, the *a* is not replaced by *an* in front of words beginning with a vowel. "I want an apple" is stated as *"I want a apple."* There are other examples of the grammatical differences in the language systems of the speakers of non-standard and standard English. (For a complete listing of these differences see Baratz, 1969.)

Another facet of the nonstandard dialect of the Negro speaker which has received some research attention is vocabulary. Shuy (11) reports that teachers hold the erroneous concept that because they lack school vocabulary disadvantaged children also lack overall vocabulary. Contradicting Shuy's assertion that the disadvantaged students do not lack general vocabulary is the research of Figurel (5) and Loban (9). Figurel compared culturally disadvantaged students' vocabulary with estimates from the Thorndike word list and found the students to be below the Thorndike estimates at all grade levels included in the study. Loban suggests that the disadvantaged were inferior on "language fluency measures" reported in his eight-year longitudinal study. One measure used to determine "language fluency" was the extent of the student's vocabulary. Possibly, the difference in viewpoints of these writers is a difference in research methodology. Shuy (11) hints at this when he states, "The notion that children in disadvantaged homes are products of language deprivation seems to mean only that the investigators proved to be such a cultural barrier to the interviewee that informants were too frightened and awed to talk freely, or that the investigators simply asked the wrong questions." While this statement is an oversimplification of the varieties of complex research problems an investigator might encounter, it does provide some insight into the mehodological problems that could be involved with research in this area.

While these are some of the current research findings concerning the differences in the language systems of a selected population of standard and nonstandard speakers of English, it is important to stress that these are differences and not deficiencies. Linguists studying the Negro nonstandard English agree that the differences are systematized rules within the vernacular. The linguists agree also, as Baratz (1969) points out, that these differences can interfere with learning standard English.

A second question generated by the findings of linguistic researchers is "How do these research findings relate to school problems?" Shuy (11) suggests these findings concerning the language systems of the disadvantaged indicate that these students "speak another language." Shuy suggests also that since the linguistic system of the ghetto student is different from that of standard English, it (linguistic system) does interfere with learning reading skills taught in standard English. Labov (8), however, differs with Shuy's view of the effect of linguistic differences on learning. Labov states, "Practically nothing has been done in examining the vocabulary of instruction to see when speakers of nonstandard dialects might be at a disadvantage." He supports his viewpoint by pointing out that only two kinds of nonstandard dialects have been carried out to date: ". . . those carried out by linguists outside of school, and those carried out by psychologists and educational researchers within school." He states further, "The teaching process

itself has not yet been observed through the lenses provided by systematic sociolinguistic analysis" (p. 41).

Although Labov's views on the lack of research in this area were valid at the time the statements were printed, more recent research has considered the questions of teacher and pupil language differences. This research makes Labov's viewpoint less valid. A preliminary survey was reported in the *Reading Newsreport* (10) of a language project conducted by Marie Marcus at Louisiana State University. She found that teachers of lower-class children in her project use nonstandard English while instructing children. She found also that lower-class children had difficulty in understanding questions stated in standard English. One conclusion drawn by Marcus was ". . . without exception, that the teachers of the lower-class children serve as poor language models." Even though some of the data may suggest this conclusion, it appears pertinent to raise at least one question. Do the teachers in the project without exception serve as poor language models, or do some teachers imitate the language of the children in order to communicate effectively with the children?

Stewart (13) offers another point of view. He maintains that beginning reading materials should be adapted to the linguistic patterns of nonstandard Negro dialect. This author supports his viewpoint by anticipating and refuting four possible arguments against the development and use of such materials.

In summary then, while there does not appear to be unanimity of opinion among the linguists concerning the educational implications of sociolinguistic research, two of the three authors quoted above offer specific suggestions for making changes in school practice. Shuy (11) notes that educators have two options concerning how to make adjustments for the dialectical differences between textbook materials and student dialect— "One is to adjust the child to suit the materials. The other is to adjust the materials to suit the child." On the one hand, to adjust the child to the materials implies that the child should learn standard English before learning to read. Because of the complex problems in teaching a child a new language and the questionable value of teaching students the standard English, Shuy recommends that materials be adjusted to the child. He offers three specific suggestions for adjusting text materials to the social dialect of the culturally disadvantaged:

1. Include in the beginning reading materials the grammatical forms which occur in nonstandard, even though they may be absent in standard English.
2. Exclude from the beginning reading materials the grammatical forms which occur in standard but do not occur in nonstandard.
3. Write beginning reading material in such a way that the syntactic structures of the written text reflect the syntactic structures of the reader's oral language experience in a way that is consistent with the task at hand—learning to read.

These suggestions have direct application to beginning reading. However, the suggestions also have implications for the culturally disadvantaged disabled reader at higher grade levels.

Stewart (13) proposes a third alternative to alleviate the problems associated with the nonstandard dialect. He suggests that some adjustment to both the materials and student be made. Initially, it would seem necessary to adjust the materials to fit the student's needs. After some initial instruction, materials could be designed as transition material, in which the student would have an opportunity to modify his responses to match the standard dialect or to modify the materials to match his dialect. The value of such a system would be the gradual recognition of the standard dialect—a prerequisite to academic success.

This brief review of selected language research clearly suggests new ways of thinking about nonstandard English dialects and new directions for research on language and instructional materials. The research suggests that educators need to be sensitive to the stigma of value judgments often associated with nonstandard English. Nonstandard English needs to be discussed as a difference model of English and not a deficit model. In addition, linguistic scholars need to delineate clearly the differences between standard and nonstandard rules and suggest applications for classroom instruction. Once the rules are clearly defined it will be possible for teachers to learn and apply the rules in the classroom. It will also be possible for publishers to consider developing instructional classroom materials which would incorporate the rules and discussions of their implications.

References

1. BAILEY, B. "Linguistics and Nonstandard Language Patterns." Paper presented at the National Conference of Teachers of English, 1965.
2. BARATZ, J. C. "Teaching Reading in an Urban Negro School System." *Teaching Black Children to Read,* R. W. Shuy and J. C. Baratz (eds.).

Washington, D.C.: Center for Applied Linguistics, 1969. Pp. 93–115.

3. BLOOM, B. S., DAVIS, ALLISON, and HESS, R. *Compensatory Education for Cultural Deprivation.* New York: Holt, Rinehart and Winston, 1965. Pp. 70–71.

4. DILLARD, J. "Negro Children's Dialect in the Inner-City," *Florida FL Reporter,* 5 (1967).

5. FIGUREL, J. A. "Limitations in the Vocabulary of Disadvantaged Children: A Cause of Poor Reading," *Improvement of Reading through Classroom Practice,* Proceedings, 9. Newark, Del.: International Reading Association, 1964. Pp. 164–65.

6. GORDON, EDMUND. "Programs of Compensatory Education." *Social Class Race and Psychological Development,* Martin Deutsch, Irwin Katz, and Arthur Jensen (eds.). New York: Holt, Rinehart and Winston, 1968. P. 381.

7. LABOV, W. "Some Sources of Reading Problems for Negro Speakers of Nonstandard English." *New Directions in Elementary English,* A. Frazier (ed.). Champaign, Ill.: National Council of Teachers of English, 1967.

8. ———. *The Study of Nonstandard English.* Washington, D.C.: ERIC Clearinghouse for Linguistics, Center for Applied Linguistics, 1969. P. 71.

9. LOBAN, W. D. *The Language of Elementary School Children.* Champaign, Ill.: National Council of Teachers of English, 1963.

10. MARCUS, M. "Why Can't They Understand?" *Reading Newsreport,* 3 (April, 1969), 33–35.

11. SHUY, R. W. "A Linguistic Background for Developing Beginning Reading Materials for Black Children." *Teaching Black Children to Read,* R. Shuy and J. Baratz (eds.). Washington, D.C.: Center for Applied Linguistics, 1969. P. 117–37.

12. ———, WOLFRAM, W., and RILEY, W. *Field Techniques in an Urban Language Study.* Washington, D.C.: Center for Applied Linguistics, 1968.

13. STEWART, W. "On the Use of Negro Dialect in the Teaching of Reading." *Teaching Black Children to Read,* J. C. Baratz and R. W. Shuy (eds.). Washington, D.C.: Center for Applied Linguistics, 1969. P. 156.

85. Linguistic and Cultural Factors in Teaching Reading to Ghetto Children *

JOAN C. BARATZ

THE low-income, urban Negro child is failing in our schools. His inability to read is a major challenge to contemporary educators because of its relationship to the child's self-esteem and his ultimate social effectivness.

Failure to acquire functionally adequate reading skills not only contributes to alienation from the school as a social institution (and therefore encourages dropping out), but it goes on to insure failure in mainstream job success. There is certainly a relationship between reading success or failure on the one hand, and receptivity to or alienation from the society in which those reading skills are highly valued (Labov and Robins, 1967). It is almost impossible to underestimate the chain of reactions which can be touched off by early and continued educational failure which so many disadvantaged Negro children experience in even the most well-intentioned school systems. Because the educational system has been ineffective in coping with teaching inner city children to read, the system treats the reading failure (in terms of grading, ranking, etc.) as if the failure were due to intellectual deficits of the child rather than to methodological inadequacies in the teaching procedures. Thus the system

* From Joan C. Baratz, "Linguistic and Cultural Factors in Teaching Reading to Ghetto Children," *Elementary English,* 46 (February, 1969), 199–203. Copyright © 1969 by the National Council of Teachers of English. Reprinted by permission of the author and the National Council of Teachers of English.

is unable to teach the child to read, but very quickly teaches him to regard himself as intellectually inadequate, and, therefore, of low self-worth and low social value.

Despite the enormous expenditure of energy in remedial reading programs, children in the ghetto are still not learning to read (National Advisory Council on Education of the Disadvantaged, 1966). Although the difficulties of teaching reading to a portion of the population is a unique problem for the United States, the problem itself is not unique. The parallels are quite clear between the difficulty we are experiencing in teaching reading to the disadvantaged Negro child with those of emergent countries which are attempting to make a multicultured population literate in a single national tongue.

In his recent report on the Washington, D.C., School System, Passow (1967) indicated that the central question that must be answered is: "What are the educationally relevant differences which the District's pupils bring into the classroom and what kinds of varied educational experiences must be provided by the schools to accommodate these differences?" One major educationally relevant difference for Washington, D.C., as for ghettos across the nation, is that of language. The Negro ghetto child is speaking a significantly different language from that of his middle-class teachers. Most of his middle-class teachers have wrongly viewed his language as pathological, disordered, "lazy speech." This failure to recognize the interference from the child's different linguistic system, and consequent negative teacher attitudes toward the child and his language, leads directly to reading difficulties and subsequent school failure.

The differences between Negro nonstandard and standard English have been described in some detail by Stewart (1965, 1967, 1968), Labov (1967), Bailey (1965) and others (Dillard, 1967, Baratz and Povich, 1967). Some of these differences were concerned primarily with distributions and patterning and others focused in greater detail upon syntactic differences between the Negro nonstandard system and standard English. It is possible to compile a list of some of the differences between the two systems such as the following:

different rules. This leads to varied disagreements as to why a particular feature exists (i.e., phoneme deletion versus creolization), but it does not dispute the fact that the linguistic feature is present. No one would disagree that standard English has a grammatical structure and uniqueness and many descriptions of that structure have been written. Yet it is probably true that no two linguists would agree in all details on how to write that grammar. This equally explains the current controversy of the linguists as to how one writes the grammar of the vernacular. Controversy as to the exact nature of the vernacular does not negate the fact that the vernacular is there.

This language *difference*, not deficiency, must be considered in the educational

VARIABLE	STANDARD ENGLISH	NEGRO NONSTANDARD
Linking verb	He *is* going.	He_goin'.
Possessive marker	John*'s* cousin	John___cousin.
Plural marker	I have five cent*s*.	I got five cent__.
Subject expression	John_lives in New York.	John *he* live in New York.
Verb form	I *drank* the milk.	I *drunk* the milk.
Past marker	Yesterday he walk*ed* home.	Yesterday he walk_home.
Verb agreement	He run*s* home.	He run_home.
	She *has* a bicycle.	She *have* a bicycle.
Future form	I *will go* home.	I'*ma go* home.
"If" construction	I asked *if he did it*.	I aks *did he do it*.
Negation	I *don't* have *any*.	I *don't* got *none*.
	He *didn't* go.	He *ain't* go.
Indefinite article	I want *an* apple.	I want *a* apple.
Pronoun form	*We* have to do it.	*Us* got to do it.
	His book	*He* book
Preposition	He is over *at* his friend's house.	He over *to* his friend house.
	He teaches *at* Francis Pool.	He teach_ Francis Pool.
Be	Statement: He *is here all the time*.	Statement: He *be* here.
Do	Contradiction: No he *isn't*.	Contradiction: No he *don't*.

But what of these differences? All the linguists studying Negro nonstandard English agree that these differences are systematized structured rules within the vernacular; they agree that these differences can interfere with the learning of standard English, but they do not always agree as to the precise nature of these

process of the Negro ghetto child. In 1953, the UNESCO report regarding the role of language in education stated that: "It is axiomatic that the best medium for teaching a child is his mother tongue. Psychologically, it is the system of meaningful signs that in his mind works automatically for expression and understanding. Sociologically, it is a means of identification among the members of the community to which he belongs. Educationally he learns more quickly through it than through an unfamiliar medium."

Since 1953 studies employing the recommendations of the UNESCO report have clearly illustrated the importance of considering the vernacular in teaching reading in the national language (Modiano, 1965). It is clear that structural knowledge of nonstandard vernacular and the ways it can interfere with learning to speak and read standard English is indispensable to teaching ghetto Negro children. Goodman (1965) and Bailey along with Stewart have all indicated the existence of interference from the dialect on ability to read. Labov (1967) has also stressed that the "ignorance of standard English rules on the part of the speakers of standard English" and the "ignorance of nonstandard English rules on the part of teachers and text writers" may well be the cause for the reading failures that occur in the schools. In addition, Wiener and Cromer (1967) in their article on reading and reading difficulty discussed the need to determine the relationship between language differences and reading problems because a failure to be explicit about the relationship between reading and previously acquired auditory language often leads to ambiguities as to whether a particular difficulty is a reading problem, language problem, or both.

If the disadvantaged Negro child, like the Indian having to learn Spanish in Mexico, or the African having to learn French in Guinea, has to contend with the interference from his vernacular in learning to read how does his task of learning to read differ from that of the middle-class "mainstream American" child? When the middle-class child starts the process of learning to read, his is primarily a problem of decoding the graphic representation of a language which he already speaks. The disadvantaged Negro must not only decode the written words, he must also translate them into his own language. This presents an almost insurmountable obstacle, since the words often do not go together in any pattern that is familiar or meaningful to him. He is baffled by this confrontation with (1) a new language with its new syntax; (2) a necessity to learn the meaning of graphic symbols, and, (3) a vague, or not so vague, depending upon the cultural and linguistic sophistication of the teacher, sense that there is something terribly wrong with his language.

Although both the middle-class child and the disadvantaged Negro child are first faced with the task of relating their speech to a graphic representation that is arbitrary and without a direct one-to-one correspondence to their speech (i.e., the "silent e" in *love,* the "silent k" in *knife,* the "k" as represented in *cut* and *kite,* and the "s" as represented in *Sue* and in *cement,* etc.) the cards are stacked against the inner-city Negro child because his particular phoneme patterning is not considered in the curriculum at this early phase so that when he reads *hep* for "help," *men'* for "mend," *boil* for "ball," the teacher presumes that he cannot read the word. Hep and help, men and mend and boil and ball are homonyms in the inner-city child's vernacular. Similarly during the initial stages of learning to read, the disadvantaged child is confused and presumed ignorant and unable to comprehend concepts if when he is taught the rhyming concept in reading he responds that *han'* (hand) rhymes with *man.* When told he is wrong he becomes confused for he is right: *han'* and *man* do in fact rhyme in his speech. In instructing these children it is necessary for the teacher to separate the concepts to be learned from the details of standard

English. Until we do this, Negro children will continue to be confused and will continue to have great difficulty in learning to read standard English.

Despite the obvious mismatching of the "teachers and text writers" phoneme system and that of the inner-city child, the difficulties of the disadvantaged Negro child cannot be simplified solely to the pronunciation and phoneme differences that exist in the two systems. There is an even more serious problem facing the inner-city child which concerns his unfamiliarity with the syntax of the classroom texts. Although the middle-income child also must read texts that are at times stilted in terms of his own usage, there is no question that the language of the texts is potentially comparable to his system. That is to say, although he does not speak in the style of his reading text, he has the rules within his grammar to account for the occurrence of the textbook sentences. However, the textbook style is more deviant to the ghetto child than it is to his middle-class standard speaking agemate because much of the reading text is not a part of his potential syntactic system.

Because of the mismatch between the child's system and that of the standard English textbook, because of the psychological consequences of denying the existence and legitimacy of the child's linguistic system, and because of the success of vernacular teaching around the world, it appears imperative that we teach the inner-city Negro child to read using his language as the basis for initial readers. In other words, first teach the child to read, and then teach him to read in standard English. Such a reading program would not only require accurate vernacular texts for the dialect speaker, but also necessitate the creation of a series of "transition readers" that would move the child, once he had mastered reading in the vernacular, from vernacular texts to standard English texts. Of course, success of such a reading program would be dependent upon the child's ultimate ability to read standard English.

The advantages of such a program are threefold. First, success in teaching the ghetto child to read. Second, the powerful ego-supports of giving credence to the child's language system and therefore to himself, and giving him the opportunity to experience success in school. And third, with the use of transitional readers, the child has the opportunity of being taught standard English (which cannot occur by "linguistic swamping" since his school mates are all vernacular speakers) so that he can learn where his language system and that of standard English are similar and where they are different. Such an opportunity may well lead to generalized learning and the ability to use standard English more proficiently in other schoolwork.

The continued failure of programs of reading to ghetto children that offer more of the same (i.e., more phonics, more word drills, etc.) have indicated the need for a new orientation toward teaching inner-city children to read. Any such program must take into account what is unique about the ghetto child that is impairing his ability to learn within the present system. This paper has suggested that one of the essential differences to be dealt with in teaching inner-city Negro children is that of language. The overwhelming evidence of the role that language interference can play in reading failure indicates that perhaps one of the most effective ways to deal with the literacy problems of Negro ghetto youth is to teach them using vernacular texts that systematically move from the syntactic structures of the ghetto community to those of the standard English speaking community.

References

1. BAILEY, B. "Linguistics in Nonstandard Language Patterns." Unpublished paper. NCTE meetings, 1965.
2. BARATZ, J., and POVICH, E., "Grammatical Constructions in the Language of the Negro Preschool Child." Unpublished Paper. ASHA, 1967.
3. DILLARD, J. "The English Teacher and the Language of the Newly Integrated Student," *Teachers College Record*, 69, 2 (1967), 115–20.
4. GOODMAN, K. "Barriers to Reading Comprehension," *Elementary English* (1965), pp. 853–60.
5. LABOV, W. "Some Sources of Reading Problems for Negro Speakers of Nonstandard English, in *New Directions in Elementary English,* National Council of Teachers of English, Champaign, Ill., 1967.
6. ――――, and ROBINS, C. "A Note on the Relation of Reading Failure to Peer-Group Status in Urban Ghettos." Unpublished Paper, 1967.
7. MODIANO, N. "A Comparative Study of Two Approaches to the Teaching of Reading in the National Language," U.S.O.E., Final Report, 1965.
8. PASSOW, A. H. *Toward Creating a Model Urban School System: A Study of the District of Columbia Public Schools.* New York: Teachers College, Columbia University, 1967.
9. STEWART, W. A. "Foreign Language Teaching Methods in Quasi-Foreign Language Situations," *Non-standard Speech and the Teaching of English.* Washington, D. C.: Center for Applied Linguistics, 1965.
10. ――――. "Urban Negro Speech: Sociolinguistic Factors Affecting English Teaching." *Social Dialects and Language Learning,* R. Shuy (ed.), Champaign, Ill.: National Council of Teachers of English, 1964.
11. ――――. "Sociolinguistic Factors in the History of American Negro Dialects." *The Florida Foreign Language Reporter,* 5 (1967), 4–5.
12. ――――. "Continuity and Change in American Negro Dialects," *The Florida Foreign Language Reporter,* 6 (1968), 3–14.
13. WIENER, M., and CROMER, C. "Reading and Reading Difficulty: A Conceptual Analysis," *Harvard Educational Review,* 37 (1967), 620–43.

86. Implications for Teachers—Primary Level: Grades 1–3 *

L. JEAN YORK AND DOROTHY EBERT

Changing Social Values

COMPETITION, individual excellence, and material wealth are less valued by certain other cultures than by the American middle class. For example, Indians and Latin Americans value group membership more than personal competition. It is important that teachers help children to understand the strengths of their respective cultures rather than simply stressing the superiority of middle-class culture.

Many disadvantaged children are not competitive about grades nor about excelling in their class; they tend to accept little responsibility for their own learning. Yet, learning is one of the most important means for the child to become self-realizing, to become mobile in society, and to become a member of a different economic group. Therefore, it should be organized in such a way that children can pursue some of their own real interests. It needs to be organized in such a way that they feel free enough to experiment yet secure enough to fail on an occasional attempt at learning without being punished (Bruner, 1960). The learning environment must provide outlets for frustration and good-natured exuberance, for children thrive on movement, activity, and projects. Disadvantaged children are accus-

tomed to the physical expression of emotions and ideas. Indeed, they are "action oriented" and often express what they are unable to verbalize by bodily movements or by acting out. Teachers who stifle this natural outlet for self-expression risk not only the pupil's loss of enthusiasm for learning but also the loss of an extremely valuable vehicle for language development.

Reading satisfies many of the requirements of an effective school program, since literature abounds with tales of excitement and adventure, stories of humorous events, stories containing funny, make-believe language, and stories about a young child's desire for a better future. The creative teacher who makes good children's literature come alive in the classroom can encourage disadvantaged children to expand their world of experience and imagination. As they identify with fictional or real characters from the world of books, they may increase their range of possibilities for living and learning.

Building a Positive Self-Concept

Warm acceptance of disadvantaged children and identification of their strengths are especially important in the primary grades. Such acceptance should include whatever language the children bring to school. Typically, a disadvantaged child comes to school with a positive self-concept (Soares and Soares, 1969). If from the outset the teacher focuses on his lack of knowledge in the areas related to middle-class experiences and pointedly rejects his language, the pattern of defeat and alienation is fairly well assured, for the child is very likely to develop a poor self-concept.

A highly motivated, concerned teacher, able to see past the "problems" to the "potential" of such children, refuses to despair of them. Instead, she sets about providing the intensive oral-language foundation that must precede success in most academic tasks and takes pains to provide these experiences in a creative, flexible, and happy classroom situation where the children can feel accepted and worthwhile.

The home language of the children should be respected and might be used as a basis for extended and expanded language learning. Some of the most exciting and rewarding language experiences, both oral and written, occur in the classroom where these children and an appreciative and sensitive teacher meet. Kohl, in his excellent book entitled *Teaching the "Unteachable"* (1967), provides many rich examples of what can happen when the life experiences and language of disadvantaged children are treated with respect and appreciation in the classroom. Some exciting and promising experiments with bilingual teaching in the primary grades with populations of disadvantaged Mexican-American, black, and white children indicate how easily most young children take to language learning and point the way to building bridges of understanding between cultural groups (Arnold, 1968a).

There are so many rich possibilities for using children's life experiences to promote language growth that it would be impossible to list them here. One enthusiastic and perceptive young teacher constructed an eye-level, freestanding bulletin board for her classroom and labeled it simply "Class News." Each morning simple one- or two-sentence news items supplied by the children were quickly printed and placed on the newsboard. A typical day's headlines might include: Dan has a brown puppy; Mary wore a new yellow slicker; Tommy is eight today; Angela skinned her knee; Manuel's father has a new blue truck; today we will visit the bakery. Many primary teachers have found that the use of a large-print typewriter in the classroom to type out what the children say right before their eyes is a very satisfying experience for children just beginning to discover the magic of communication. Often a holiday, field trip, or class project can lead to a pupil-made book that can be read so that the experience can be shared by the class over and over again. Using the children's own language and common experience to produce teacher-pupil-made reading material has a number of obvious advantages. Not only does it promote a desire to read, but it also bolsters the child's self-image and sense of worth, since it is his *own* language that is being recorded for the class to read.

It is especially important in the primary grades that disadvantaged children be met with respect and acceptance. Riessman (1962) states repeatedly that the disadvantaged child does not so much need love as he needs *respect* in the classroom. As Havighurst and others point out . . . the mere fact that a child lives in a slum, belongs to a minority group, or comes from a home where the income is below the poverty level does not mean that this child, even though suffering some language and concept deficiencies, is necessarily seriously disadvantaged if family ties are strong and there is emotional security and ethnic pride. If middle-class teachers can meet such children with genuine respect, assess objectively both their strengths and weaknesses, and then create a learning atmosphere in which they can find repeated, steady success, the primary years will be rewarding for them. Building a positive self-concept and a feeling of "it is fun" and "I can do it" are crucial ingredients in the primary years. An atmosphere of positive expectation must permeate the school if disadvantaged children are to overcome their handicaps to learning. . . .

Paucity of Verbal and Cognitive Skills

For a long time educators and others concerned with education have given at least lip service to the close association between language development and academic success. One obstacle, lack of skill in the use of standard American English, has increasingly been recognized as a major contributing factor to the success of a child beginning his formal education. Furthermore, many years of research in reading have underscored the necessity for adequate oral language development prior to success in reading. Loban (1966) points out that children who do not possess adequate language simply do not learn to read, to comprehend, or to enjoy and appreciate what the school is trying to teach.

Linguistically different learners, even if not seriously handicapped in other ways, still present primary teachers with a formidable task; for as long as their speech remains stunted or nonstandard, they will be socially and educationally marked and will generally find academic achievement to be limited. It would seem obvious, then, that particularly in the primary years children should be given every opportunity to overcome their language deficiencies and to learn to use standard American English with ease and agility. It is not enough for them to acquire an enriched vocabulary in a socially unmarked dialect alone. They must learn to manipulate language in meaningful and efficient ways. In other words, the structure of language, the use of movables and subordinate elements, is of equal impor-

tance. Children should constantly be encouraged to listen for and to respond in sentences with increasing elaboration and variety. Reading success for disadvantaged children must entail the cognitive uses of language.

Special attention, moreover, should be given to special words that give precise meaning to language. Prepositions, conjunctions, modifiers—the words that make language "hang together" and give it precise and subtle meanings—these usually need to be taught to children who use restricted language. For example, an enterprising first-grade teacher of Mexican-American children (who typically have great difficulty with prepositions) spends a few minutes each day playing the preposition game. She simply uses some common classroom object, such as a book or pencil, and lets the children check to see if the child who is "it" can correctly place the book *behind* the record player, *under* the round table, *beside* the aquarium, *over* the sink, *between* two yellow books, and so on.

Making a game of language learning in this manner provides spontaneous, informal motivation and at the same time gives concrete illustration to expression and word meanings. Once the game is understood and several of the prepositions learned, letting a child give the verbal directions provides a further reinforcement of language learning.

The school curriculum is usually planned for children who are ready for reading, who, for example, have more verbal skills in standard English than disadvantaged children have. Most teachers teach reading to children in the primary grades by utilizing a good basal series that includes a teacher's guide and accompanying materials. Some educators say that disadvantaged children cannot learn to read from traditional books because they cannot relate the activities of the children in the books to their own lives. This may or may not be true. Loban's study (1966) indicates a correlation between a child's general language ability at the kindergarten level, as determined by vocabulary scores and by language ratings by his teacher, and his reading ability in the primary grades. He concludes that language ability is necessary for competence in reading. Thus the problem may well be the children's paucity of verbal skills rather than the content of the reading book. In this situation, language skills should be established before the reading program commences. Furthermore, speaking and listening should be an integral part of the whole language-arts curriculum.

Teachers might evaluate the content and format of the reading book and select another vehicle for instruction for children who cannot meet success with the traditional material. For example, teachers might develop oral language and reading by using content-based experiences presented in the classroom (Arnold, 1968b). Today when publishers have provided teachers with a wide variety of excellent tools for teaching reading, teachers must decide which combination of materials will best help their pupils.

It seems rather imprudent to discard a sequential reading program that is successful with twenty-five children because five children cannot relate to the story or are having difficulty with phonic analysis skills. The twenty-five children making satisfactory progress might continue in their reading program, and other materials and methods might be selected for the five children who are not succeeding. A good many instances of children making little progress in reading can be related to the fact that the teacher was trying to take children with little language experience and motivation for learning to read through a fixed number of books at each grade level.

Since disadvantaged children generally have had a minimal range of stimuli at home, teachers should expand their knowledge by using a wide variety of tradiional and innovative materials in the classroom. Children can expand their knowledge by listening to tapes of favorite stories, by listening to records, and by manipulating objects. Language is learned as it is heard and used to express thought; furthermore, language is facilitated as the learner has an opportunity to see a relationship between a concrete object and its label or its function. An example of this is the primary-grade child who plays with a bar magnet, a scrap of paper, a number of pins and paper clips, iron filings, a piece of cotton, and a pair of scissors. During the process of manipulation he needs to be able both to name the objects and to communicate the function or classification of the objects. Through such processes he is learning both the phonology and grammatical structure of language as it relates to reading, or content. He is also extending his critical thinking skills.

A second example is the child who plays "store" with objects in the classroom. The presence of empty boxes and containers for items commonly purchased by more advantaged families may provide an opportunity for the child to learn about such vegetables as asparagus, Brussels sprouts, broccoli, and avocados; about such fruits as pineapples, pomegranates, and grapefruit; or about such household supplies as floor wax, fly spray, and paper napkins. These experiences, once again, expand language and thinking skills necessary for competence in reading, mathematics, and other areas of the curriculum.

Reading requires that children bring meaning to the written symbols on the page. Part of the task of teaching the disadvantaged is expanding the number and quality of experiences these children have. Teachers can assist in this process by providing a curriculum filled with exciting learning experiences, such as field trips, motion pictures, filmstrips, and interesting experiences in the classroom in which the children are actively involved. Teachers must expand the vocabulary and understanding of the children beyond what they have learned at home.

During instructional activities in the classroom the teacher can extend the child's understanding by the use of thoughtful questions. As Havighurst points out, parents of disadvantaged children tend to speak to their children in a restricted language, whereas middle-class parents use an elaborated language. Consequently, disadvantaged children need help in seeing relationships, in recognizing causal factors, in comparing, in classifying, contrasting, and categorizing, and in sequencing and generalizing. Teachers must teach thinking skills that are of a higher order than rote recall of fact.

Teachers should also help disadvantaged children correlate concepts learned in language arts, mathematics, science, health, music, and art. Some common vocabulary appears in each of the content fields; in other instances, a child can unlock the familiar word using his reading skills but must be taught an expanded or different meaning for the word in the new content area. Such words as *set, bridge, regroup,* and *observe* have a variety of different and appropriate meanings in the various disciplines. Jacobs (1964) explained that a word is a label: "It is not the experience itself, but it is an identification tag for an experience. It is a verbal sign, signal or symbol . . . the label is useful only to the extent that it 'calls up' an experience for both the speaker and listener or writer and reader. . . ." The teacher can help children to expand their knowledge by providing instructional experiences with words where alternate meanings for words are clarified.

In order to achieve the objective of expanding vocabulary meaning, primary teachers must carefully and prudently plan prior to the class period. It is necessary that they know what specific skills they are going to teach each child, what activities they are going to use, what learning materials are needed, and how they will evaluate the child's changed behavior, since learning is evidenced in changed behavior. They should make frequent written anecdotal records of each child's performance as he reads, for no teacher can remember precisely the numerous correct and incorrect responses made by each child if she waits until the end of the day to make such an evaluation.

Jackson (1967) states that a teacher may have as many as one thousand interactions with children per day that are unrelated to her teaching plans. The implication is that anecdotal recording—of reading errors, for example—should be done while the child is reading. Recording such data may seem unimportant to some teachers until they realize that the diagnosis of today's errors provides the basis for the next day's diagnostic teaching techniques. Teachers should take prompt action specific to their diagnoses rather than merely reiterating the time-honored phrase "meeting individual needs."

This process will enable teachers to provide an individualized sequential task for the child that is related to his present needs for learning. An analysis of the daily errors of each child gives teachers an opportunity to structure their teaching or reteaching of a concept or skill. This analysis also affords teachers an objective tool for a dialogue or meaningful discussion with the pupil concerning his personal progress. Like all children, disadvantaged pupils benefit from the teacher's personal interest in their problems. Many teachers have compassion and sympathy for the social and economic needs of the child, but are unaware that, by itself, this empathy is insufficient to help the child. When teachers complement their empathy and understanding with improved diagnostic teaching procedures for each child, they are effectively assisting their pupils. . . .

References

1. ARNOLD, RICHARD D. "Retention in Reading of Disadvantaged Mexican-American Children During the Summer Months." Paper presented at the International Reading Association Convention, Boston, April, 1968a.

2. ———. "Teaching English as a Second Language," The Reading Teacher, 21 (April, 1968b), 634–39.

3. BRUNER, JEROME. The Process of Education. Cambridge, Mass.: Harvard University Press, 1960.

4. CHING, DORIS C. "Methods for the Bilingual Child," Elementary English, 42 (January, 1965), 22–27.

5. EDMAN, MARION. "Literature for Children Without," Library Quarterly, 37 (January, 1967), 32–45.

6. JACKSON, PHILLIP W. "The Way Teaching Is," The Way Teaching Is, report of the Seminar on Teaching, Association for Curriculum Development, Center for Study of Instruction of the National Education Association,.1967. Pp. 7–28.

7. JACOBS, LELAND B. "Teaching Children More About Words and Their Ways," Elementary English, 41 (January, 1964), 30–34.

8. KANE, PETER E. "Role Playing for Educational Use," Speech Teacher, 13 (November, 1964), 320–23.

9. KOHL, HERBERT. Teaching the "Unteachable." New York: A New York Review Book, 1967.

10. LOBAN, WALTER. "Oral Language Proficiency Affects Reading and Writing," Instructor, 75 (March, 1966).

11. MANNING, JOHN. "Assessing Pupil Growth in Language." Elementary School Language Arts: Selected Readings. PAUL C. BURNS and LEO M. SCHELL, (eds). Chicago: Rand McNally, 1969. Pp. 471–74.

12. PEYTON, JIM. Nonpromotion. Bulletin of the Bureau of School Service, College of Education, University of Kentucky, Lexington, 40 (March, 1968).

13. RIESSMAN, FRANK. The Culturally Deprived Child. New York: Harper & Row, 1962.

14. RUDDELL, ROBERT B. "Oral Language and Development of Other Language Skills," Elementary English, 43 (May, 1966), 489–98.

15. SMITH, DORA V. "Developmental Language Patterns of Children." Elementary School Language Arts: Selected Readings. Paul C. Burns and Leo M. Schell, (eds.), Chicago: Rand McNally, 1969. Pp. 65–75.

16. SOARES, ANTHONY T., and SOARES, LOUISE M. "Self-Perceptions of Culturally Disadvantaged Children," American Educational Research Journal, 6 (January, 1969), 31–43.

17. STRICKLAND, RUTH G. "Implications of Research in Linguistics for Elementary Teaching," Elementary English, 40 (February, 1963), 168–71.

18. ———. The Language Arts in the Elementary School. Boston: D.C. Heath, 1957.

87. Teaching Non-English Speaking First-Graders to Read *

JOAN T. FEELEY

Part I

The Problem and the Historical Response

I think we have been teaching reading, and teaching teachers to teach reading, from the top down instead of from the bottom up. I think we've failed, particularly with environmentally handicapped children and with children of a foreign language background from home or abroad, because they hear and speak one language and we teach them to read another. . . .

Reading facility is a kind of quintessence, a distillate produced by the communication process. The search for the almost magic formula for success in reading must, therefore, go beyond the crucibles of the resultant broth into the cauldrons of the language potions and ingredients from which it springs.[1]

The Problem

AMERICAN schools are faced with the tremendous problem of educating great numbers of non-English speaking children. There are pockets of bilinguals throughout the United States—French in New England, Scandinavians in the north-

ern middle states, and large Spanish-speaking populations in the Southwest, Florida, and in the ever-spreading cities of the East. Of the 1,100,000 pupils in New York City, more than 200,000 are Puerto Rican and foreign born.[2] Since reading is considered a major tool for our educative process, it receives prime concern in the beginning school years.

The Historical Response

Historical Thinking. Tireman says, "The educational pattern is largely fixed in this country. All children in the continental part of the U. S. who speak another language must learn English."[3] Historically, we have followed a pattern of supersaturating the non-English speaking child with our national language. We "turn off" his preschool means of communication in order to quickly teach him to understand, speak, and *read* English. Over the last twenty years our research has centered on the finding of the best methods and materials for teaching English as a second language. The *Miami Linguistic Readers* and Faye Bumpass' *We Learn English,* an audio-lingual approach, are examples of recent developmental programs.

Back in 1948 Tireman described his San Jose Experimental School near Albuquerque, New Mexico. It had a pre-first grade in which the learning of English was the chief objective. A 500 to 700 English word vocabulary was developed

* From Joan T. Feeley, "Teaching Non-English Speaking First-Graders to Read," *Elementary English,* 47 (February, 1970), 199–208. Copyright © 1970 by the National Council of Teachers of English. Reprinted by permission of the author and the National Council of Teachers of English.

[1] John B. King, "The Most Powerful Educational Weapon in Our War on Poverty: Teaching English as a Second Language to Environmentally Handicapped Pupils and as a Third Language to Pupils of Foreign Language Background," *Public Schools of New York City Staff Bulletin* (April 25, 1966), pp. I, II.

[2] *Ibid.,* p. II.

[3] L. S. Tireman, *Teaching Spanish-Speaking Children* (Albuquerque: University of New Mexico Press, 1948), p. 38.

by games, activities, songs, and conversations. English was taught by the Direct Method—speaking English.[4]

New York City's "English as a Second Language" program runs along traditional lines. Daily thirty-minute language emphasis lessons are scheduled by class teachers for non-English speaking pupils. These children are usually placed in regular classes to achieve the advantages of an English speaking environment.[5]

Manuel writes, "At present in the Southwest, it is the policy of the public schools to use English as the language of instruction throughout the school grades. . . . It is the general practice to minimize its [Spanish] use and to use English exclusively. In fact, many teachers have little or no knowledge of Spanish." [6]

*Recent Studies Concerning the
Historical Response*

McCanne studied three approaches to teaching first-grade English reading to children from Spanish-speaking homes in Colorado: a basal reader (BR) group, a "teaching English as a second language" (TESL) group, and a language experience approach (LEA). The BR approach developed the highest achievement in reading skills. This may be because of ". . . certain culturally determined thinking and behavior patterns, such as an unwillingness to initiate original expression in a formal school setting. . . ." [7] A combination of TESL and LEA was recommended for preschool and kindergarten levels since these approaches were shown to have particular strengths in oral vocabulary and writing fluency.

James Cooper had conducted a somewhat parallel study in the U.S. Territory of Guam.[8] The majority of Guam's pupils enter first grade speaking only Chamorro, a native language influenced by Spanish, Filipino, Micronesian, Japanese, and American English. The school program is traditionally conducted in English, reading being taught from the Scott-Foresman readers.

The experiment compared two oral English approaches of different amounts of time, one year (Conversational) and one half year (Revised Readiness) with two sets of control classes which used their usual basal readers. At the end of one year both experimental groups excelled in the ability to speak English. At the end of four years, the control basal reader groups showed a small, but not educationally significant, lead in reading ability as measured by the California Reading Tests.

In questioning the negative results of his study, Cooper theorized that what was needed was a reevaluation of the content of the oral English instruction. He called for a careful linguistic analysis of the Chamorro and English patterns to point out similarities and differences so that a more suitable content in oral-aural English might be further tested.

Thus we can see from the above research that the historical approach to teaching non-English speaking children to read through varying types of total-English School environments is still

---

[4] *Ibid.,* pp. 27–29.

[5] Board of Education, City of New York, *Educating Children For Whom English Is a Second Language* (New York: Board of Education, 1965), p. 7.

[6] Herschel T. Manuel, *Spanish-Speaking Children of the Southwest* (Austin: University of Texas Press, 1965), p. 119.

[7] Roy McCanne, "Approaches to First-Grade English Reading Instruction for Children from Spanish-speaking Homes," *The Reading Teacher,* 19 (May, 1966), 674.

[8] James G. Cooper, "Effects of Different Amounts of First Grade Oral English Instruction upon Later Reading Progress with Chamorro-Speaking Children," *The Journal of Educational Research,* 58, pp. 123–26.

receiving much attention and acceptance.

The Effectiveness of the Historical Response

The picture is none too rosy. Despite the search for the best methods and materials, the work of linguists in analyzing the phonological, syntactical, and morphological units of English and other languages, and the work of social anthropologists and behaviorists in studying the culturally disadvantaged, large blocks of non-English speaking children continue to fail in reading.

Tireman's San Jose School, with its specially selected teachers, pre-first grade program, and enriched curriculum produced better results than the regular local programs. Children in San Jose's first and second grades tested slightly above national norms on the Gates Reading Tests and the New Stanford Achievement Tests, but beginning with the third grade there was a steady downward divergence from the national norms of about one and one half years. The control groups in local programs showed similar directions of achievement but were three to four years below national norms in third grade and up.[9]

New York City's Special Service Schools and More Effective Schools, designed to offer a language-enriched curriculum, apppropriate materials, and smaller classes to linguistically handicapped and disadvantaged pupils have not had notable successes in teaching reading. Last year, they reported median reading scores that were two or more years below national norms.[10]

The Chamorro project showed the oral English readiness programs to be no more effective than Guam's traditional basal reader approach under which Guamian pupils were trailing up to three years behind their mainland counterparts.[11]

Anne Stemmler sums up the situation in the Southwest:

The annual reports filed by all school districts with the Texas Education Agency reveal that approximately 80 per cent of all beginning first graders from a non-English speaking background fail the first grade because of their inability to read. . . . The Texas Education Agency estimates that between 40 and 60 per cent of the approximately 100,000 entering non-English speaking first graders each year will have dropped out of school permanently by the end of the elementary grades.[12]

Manuel H. Guerra writes about the Mexican-American child who fails in reading in California. He feels that Juanito's problems are multifaceted—linguistic, environmental, and emotional. "Juanito's mind must deal with a basic conflict of loyalties between the English-speaking culture of his school and the Spanish-speaking heritage of his home. What confuses him—and in his juvenile immaturity this seems irreconcilable—is that the differences of language and culture must be incompatible with the American way of life to which he emotionally yearns to belong." [13]

It seems as though our historical response of a totally English approach to teaching reading to non-English speaking children has been largely ineffective and unsatisfactory.

[9] Tireman, op. cit., p. 29.

[10] "Reading Scores of Pupils in the City's Elementary and Jr. High Schools," The New York Times, January 25, 1967, pp. 44.

[11] Cooper, op. cit., p. 125.

[12] Anne O. Stemmler, "An Experimental Approach to the Teaching of Oral Language and Reading," Harvard Educational Review 36 (Winter, 1966), 43.

[13] Manuel H. Guerra, "Why Juanito Doesn't Read," California Teachers Association Journal (October, 1965), p. 19.

Part II

A New Approach—Reading First in the Native Language

Strands of Thinking

Through the years those concerned with the education of non-English speaking children have theorized and speculated about the chances for success if the mother tongue were used in the initial stages of teaching language skills, and specifically in beginning reading. Twenty years ago Tireman wrote, "Whether they [Spanish-speaking children] could make greater advancement by using the mother tongue during the beginning year is a question that cannot now be settled." [14] "Many people hold that if all instruction began in Spanish and gradually changed over to English the children would learn more rapidly. They point out that this is a common practice in such bilingual areas as Wales, Luxembourg, and Puerto Rico." [15]

More recently, William R. Holland,[16] who had tested Spanish-speaking elementary school children bilingually with a Spanish-English adaptation of WISC to analyze language barrier as an educational problem, concluded the generally low verbal development in both Spanish and English is more likely the consequence of bilingualism in an underprivileged ethnic group. He hypothesized, "Bilingual education for bilingual children might prove to be a worthwhile experiment. Teachers who could supplement the language of the classroom with that of the home and neighborhood might achieve more optimal results than are presently realized with all classroom instruction exclusively in English." [17]

Research about the relationship of oral language to beginning reading supports the aforementioned thinking of Tireman, Holland, and John B. King (see quote page 454). Fries says, "From the evidence available, we believe that we can assume that any child can learn to read within a year after he has learned to 'talk' his native language satisfactorily . . . we would always measure the child's reading performance against the background of that language control." [18]

We know that children come to school with a large stock of oral-aural vocabulary—from 2,000 to 6,000 words and higher depending upon the investigator and methods used.[19] Phrases, sentences, and grammatical structure of the oral native language are learned in varying degrees in the pre-school years. We try to use these familiar words and patterns (with some editing) in our experience charts and primer materials so that children can come to see that print is just "talk written down"; we proceed to lead him from talking and listening to reading —if he is an English-speaking child. All of this thinking seems to be forgotten when dealing with the non-English speaking youngster. By our "English only" atmosphere we negate his preschool language learnings instead of improving them and building upon them. He enters a new and strange world of "school language." Is it any wonder that so many fail?

[14] Tireman, *op. cit.,* p. 35.

[15] *Ibid.,* p. 60.

[16] William R. Holland, "Language Barrier as an Educational Problem of Spanish-Speaking Children," *The Disadvantaged Learner,* Staten W. Webster (ed.). (San Francisco: Chandler Co., 1966), p. 348.

[17] Holland. *loc. cit.*

[18] Charles C. Fries, *Linguistics and Reading* (New York: Holt, Rinehart and Winston, 1965), p. 187.

[19] Gladys Natchez, "From Talking to Reading Without Really Trying," *The Reading Teacher,* 20 (January, 1967), 339.

Research Concerning the Native Language Approach

Reading Comprehension in the National Language. Modiano compared two approaches to teaching reading in the national language (Spanish) to children of linguistic minorities (Indian) in three tribal settings in southern Mexico. One approach, found in schools administered by the National Indian Institute, taught oral Spanish in the first year, but reading was begun in the mother tongue, via the "global method," using primers in this language. Reading in Spanish and the regular state-prescribed curriculum was introduced the second year. The other approach was found in schools operated by the Federal Secretariat of Education. This was monolingual, with all instruction, including beginning reading, proceeding in Spanish.[20]

The thirteen groups literate in the mother tongue prior to reading in Spanish scored significantly higher than the thirteen monolingual groups on a Spanish language instrument specifically developed for the sample. When the proportions of students deemed by their teachers to be able to read with comprehension in Spanish were compared by approaches to reading instruction, the proportion of students who had first learned to read in their mother tongue was significantly higher.

Modiano concluded that children of linguistic minorities learn to read with greater comprehension in the national language when they first become literate in their mother tongue. They learn one new skill, reading, through materials which have meaning instead of memorizing strange symbols and sounds.[21]

The Horn Study. An extensive study of the effects of intensive oral-aural English, oral-aural Spanish, and non-oral-aural instruction on beginning reading readiness is under way in San Antonio, Texas, under the direction of Thomas D. Horn.

Initially the Horn team was concerned with three elements in their experimental approach—the audio-lingual technique, science content, and comparative phonology. The audio-lingual dialogues relating to objects present in the classrooms were to be the major teaching methods. Science-based content was used because it was thought to be "culture-fair," not reflecting the value system of any social group or ethnic group and being as difficult for one group as for another. The introduction of those phonological elements in English which are not paralleled in Spanish was carefully controlled.[22]

Nine classes of oral-aural English (OAE), ten classes of oral-aural Spanish (OAS), and nine classes using a non-oral-aural approach (NOA) represented the research sample, 735 Spanish-speaking children in all. Each of these three groups used the "culture-fair" science content, but the OAE and OAS groups used the content with audio-lingual techniques in their specific languages, replacing the usual readiness instruction of one hour per day.[23]

[20] Nancy Modiano, "Reading Comprehension in the National Language: A Comparative Study of Bilingual and All Spanish Approaches to Reading Instruction in Selected Indian Schools in the Highlands of Chiapas, Mexico." (Unpublished Doctor's thesis, New York University, 1966), pp. 9, 59.

[21] Modiano, *op. cit.,* pp. 105–7.
[22] Stemmler, *op. cit.,* pp. 43, 44.
[23] Thomas D. Horn, "A Study of the Effects of Intensive Oral-Aural English Language Instruction, Oral-Aural Spanish Language Instruction on Reading Readiness in Grade One," Cooperative Research Project No. 2648 (Austin: University of Texas, 1966). pp. 10–12.

Many limitations were recognized as the study progressed. Most serious was that of instrumentation. The usual readiness tests, e.g., Metropolitan and Murphy-Durrell, used initially, produced a pile-up of scores at the zero-plus level. The Goodenough-Harris DAM caused sufficient doubt for the examiners to use the Inter-American Test of General Ability with questionable results. "The primary foci of the study, i.e., the development of oral language, cognition, and experiential backgrounds as preludes to reading, are still largely unmeasured." [24]

Socioeconomic factors were limiting also. Children were described as inadequately clothed, fed, and cared-for, coming from impoverished and broken homes. The negative self-image, characteristic of the disadvantaged, was more ingrained in these children because of their additional handicap—a language which was different from the school language. Even their native language was underdeveloped; they were "alingual" rather than bilingual. The teachers' command of the audio-lingual method, teacher-pupil interactions, appropriate instructional materials, and adequate linguistic analyses round out the galaxy of limitations to this first phase of the Horn Study. [25]

In view of the above, it was decided to extend the study for three more years; it is still in progress. The following were some major conclusions and implications based on the first year: There was no significant difference between the posttest mean scores of the three groups on the criterion instrument, The Metropolitan Readiness Test; the large number of zero scores in the pretesting showed the inappropriateness of most available standardized tests for this population.

The staff observed that regardless of the language level of the entering child, he spoke Spanish, usually considered a low status symbol. In ignoring Spanish, the school cuts off communication and rejects an important part of the child's makeup. They also categorized these children as disadvantaged, displaying lacks in all physical, social, perceptual, and emotional development. The science-based materials seemed a good, new approach to the problems of language and disadvantagedness, but these materials did not help in the all-important development of the "self-image." [26]

The above observations of the research team seem valid and understandable; however, the kinds of materials that were developed may have influenced the findings. Inductively, the concepts of "circle," "ellipse," "rectangle," etc., were introduced before the general concept of "shape." Then, "shape" would be applied to other instances deductively.[27] The dialogues were built around these concepts. How much interest can these learnings elicit from first graders from impoverished homes? Would there be any carry-over of the patterns and vocabulary into their everyday lives—play, home, neighborhood? In either Spanish or English the content doesn't seem to fit the situation.

Certainly, there can be no identification of self with these kinds of concepts or the labels that are attached to them. The researchers plan to write (or have now written) primers and easy readers to parallel the concepts and patterns taught in the initial oral-aural approach. Will the children want to read this kind of material? Can they identify with an "ellipse," a "rectangle?" Perhaps judgment should be reserved until the finished products are seen, but they seem destined to be, at best, highly structured, dialogue-

[24] Horn, *op. cit.,* p. 49.
[25] *Ibid.,* pp. 50–52.

[26] Horn, *op. cit.,* pp. 52–8.
[27] Stemmler, *op. cit.,* p. 48.

type, linguistic, concept books which will not evoke the child's interest or his need to identify.

The content in the Texas Education Agency's Bulletin Number 642 seems more appropriate.[28] These English language lessons were given to all the Horn groups since they are included in the regular Texas first-grade curriculum for Spanish-speaking children. One dialogue was about pets. This type of content certainly would appeal to six-year-olds; perhaps similar content could be developed in Spanish to improve the child's control of his native language.

The Horn Study, carried over the projected four years, should supply more insight into the best approach to teaching beginning reading to these Spanish-speaking children in Texas, with implications for teaching non-English speaking children everywhere.

Dade County, Florida. Since 1963 Dade County has been experimenting with bilingual education. Dr. Paul Bell, Coordinator of Bilingual Education for the county, describes the pilot school, Coral Way School, as "a school in which all pupils have the opportunity to become completely bilingual." [29]

Located in a neighborhood which is 50 percent English-speaking and 50 percent Spanish-speaking, Coral Way offers its pupils a program in which one-half of the school day is conducted in Spanish and one-half in English. In the beginning stages the basic skills and concepts are always introduced in the first language of the child. These are later incorporated into the second language as part of a language learning experience, thus rein-

forcing concepts and skills and simultaneously advancing the mastery of the second language.

Teachers work as teams; each team, having one Spanish-speaking and one English-speaking teacher, handles about sixty children. Each teacher is responsible for developing the usual curriculum in his native language with his native language pupils and the second language learnings for the other group. Basal readers, science books, health texts, and modern math texts are provided in Spanish; state-adopted texts are used for the English program. Social studies units were being planned with a mixed language content, e.g., the early history of Florida in Spanish and modern Florida in English.[30]

Although statistical data were not available, the following evaluations were reported after two years. The pupils were making progress comparable to monolingual programs. Some parents who had requested that their children be placed in regular programs prior to the new approach were asking to have their children changed to the bilingual program. The teachers reported that they were planning better and found the students more highly motivated than usual groups.[31]

The Coral Way Project represents only one school, located in a middle-class community; therefore, the application of its program may not be universal. It would be interesting to see some statistical evaluation and to review some of the materials being developed. It is indeed a unique situation that bears watching.

Hoboken, New Jersey. The Thomas G. Connors School in Hoboken has a first grade of thirty-three Spanish-speaking children being taught in Spanish by a native-speaking teacher. Spanish primers,

---

[28] Horn, *op. cit.,* Appendix V.
[29] Paul W. Bell, "The Bilingual School." (Paper read at a meeting of the International Reading Association, Detroit, Michigan, May 3–4, 1965), p. 2. (Mimeographed.)

[30] *Ibid.,* pp. 3–8.
[31] Bell, *op. cit.,* p. 7.

arithmetic books, and other texts have been provided. Forty children, distributed throughout three other heterogeneous groups are to be the control sample. Started in Sepember, 1967, evaluation is planned at this year's end and again after three years. Oral-aural English is included incidentally this first year; reading instruction in English is to begin in second grade.[32]

New York City. Announcement was made last spring that New York City will open its first bilingual school this fall in the southeast Bronx, an area with a heavy concentration of Puerto Ricans. The children will be taught English as a second language, but content in such subjects as science, social studies, and mathematics will be taught in Spanish until the children have mastered enough English to learn and read content in it.[33]

It is interesting to note that this New York City project was spurred by community protests against the all-English school. Puerto Rican parents and community groups in the area have been requesting bilingual education for some time, desiring that their children grow in knowledge and appreciation of their Spanish language and heritage, as well as in general education and English. A contrastive attitude was met in San Antonio when the Horn program was announced. At first, the parents regarded the Spanish oral-aural approach suspiciously; they wanted their children to learn English, the local high-status language. This home-community attitude may have been an-

other factor in the rather inconclusive results of the first year of the study.

New York City has been experimenting with other bilingual programs. One is a bilingual kindergarten, started in 1965. Its aims are to develop:

(1) Bilingual readiness in both English-speaking and Spanish-speaking children.

(2) Positive attitudes toward and respect for one's native language and culture as well as the culture and language of other groups.[34]

Formal evaluation is scheduled at the end of three years.

Another project has been a bilingual science program in eighteen selected city junior high schools. In a report issued on March 4th, the Board of Education stated that after three years the experimental students (bilingual) did better in science than a selected control sample (regular approach), their mastery of English was not impeded, and they scored higher in subsequent citywide reading tests. Also, the students appeared less anxious, had a more positive attitude toward self and cultural background, and were rated better in effort and reliability.[35]

Thus, New York City, in response to community demands, has been moving forward on three levels in the field of bilingual education.

The above completed research of Modiano and the in-progress studies of Horn in Texas, Bell in Florida, and the New York City Board of Education, plus several scattered smaller projects point to the interest in a new look at an old problem—teaching non-English speaking children to read.

---

[32] Conversation with Mr. Peter Vecchio, Director of Title Three Bilingual Program for Beginning Reading, Hoboken, New Jersey, Public Schools.

[33] Leonard Bruder, "City Plans Spanish School in Bronx for Next Fall," *The New York Times,* March 15, 1968, p. 41.

[34] Board of Education, City of New York, *op. cit.,* p. 2.

[35] Olive Evans, "Now the Bilingual Course," *The New York Sunday Times,* March 17, 1968, p. E9.

References

1. BELL, PAUL W. "The Bilingual School." Paper read at a meeting of the International Reading Association, Detroit, Michigan, May 3–4, 1965.

2. Board of Education, City of New York. *Educating Students For Whom English Is a Second Language.* New York: Board of Education, 1965.

3. BRUDER, LEONARD. "City Plans Spanish School in Bronx Next Fall," *The New York Times,* March 15, 1968.

4. COOPER, JAMES G. "Effects of Different Amounts of First-Grade Oral English Instruction upon Later Reading Progress with Chamorro-Speaking Children," *The Journal of Educational Research,* 58: 123–27.

5. EVANS, OLIVE. "Now the Bilingual Course," *The New York Sunday Times,* March 17, 1968.

6. FRIES, CHARLES C. *Linguistics and Reading.* New York: Holt, Rinehart and Winston, 1965.

7. GUERRA, MANUEL H. "Why Juanito Doesn't Read," *California Teachers Association Journal* (October, 1965), 17–19.

8. HOLLAND, WILLIAM R. "Language Barrier as an Educational Problem of Spanish-speaking Children." *The Disadvantaged Learner,* Staten W. Webster (ed.). San Francisco: Chandler Publishing Company, 1966. Pp. 338–49.

9. HORN, THOMAS D. "A Study of the Effects of Intensive Oral-Aural English Language Instruction, Oral-Aural Spanish Language Instruction and Non-Oral-Aural Instruction in Grade One," Cooperative Research Project No. 2648. Austin: University of Texas, 1966.

10. HUGHES, MARIE M., and SANCHEZ, GEORGE I. *Learning a New Language.* Association for Childhood Educa-

tion International, Bulletin No. 101. Washington: Association for Childhood Education International, 1958.

11. KING, JOHN B. "The Most Powerful Educational Weapon in Our War on Poverty: Teaching English as a Second Language to Environmentally Handicapped Pupils and as a Third Language to Pupils of Foreign Language Background," *The Public Schools of New York City Staff Bulletin,* April 26, 1966.

12. MANUEL, HERSCHEL T. *Spanish-Speaking Children of the Southwest.* Austin: University of Texas Press, 1965.

13. McCANNE, ROY. "Approaches to First-Grade English Reading Instruction for Children from Spanish-speaking Homes," *The Reading Teacher,* 19, pp. 670–75.

14. MODIANO, NANCY. "Reading Comprehension in the National Language: A Comparative Study of Bilingual and All Spanish Approaches to Reading Instruction in Selected Indian Schools in the Highlands of Chiapas, Mexico." Unpublished Doctoral Thesis. New York University, 1966.

15. NATCHEZ, GLADYS. "From Talking to Reading Without Really Trying," *The Reading Teacher,* 20, pp. 339–44.

16. "Reading Scores of Pupils in the City's Elementary and Junior High Schools," *The New York Times,* January 25, 1967.

17. STEMMLER, ANNE O. "An Experimental Approach to the Teaching of Oral Language and Reading," *Harvard Educational Review,* 36 (Winter, 1966), 42–59.

18. TIREMAN, LLOYD S. *Teaching Spanish-Speaking Children.* Albuquerque: University of New Mexico Press, 1948.

Index

Agnew, D. C., 17, 18
Agrast, C., 277
Aker, C. C., 373
Allen, R., 106
Allen, R. V., 108, 342
Allen, V., 106
Ames, W. S., 43
Andersen, I. H., 371, 373
Arbuthnot, M. H., 318
Arithmetic, reading problems
  in, 302ff.
Arnold, R. D., 449, 451
Artley, A. S., 21, 284
Association, learning by, 38;
  in phonics, 232
Attitudes, 40, 420ff.
Audio-visual aids, 10, 11, 347ff.
Auditory discrimination, 44,
  212
Auditory factors, and reading
  readiness, 77
Auditory perception, 44
Austin, M. C., 203

Badal, A. W., 140
Bagford, J., 214, 217
Bailey, B., 438, 444, 445
Bailey, M. H., 63, 229
Balow, I. H., 21, 87
Baratz, J. C., 439, 440, 443,
  444
Barbe, W. B., 201
Barnhart, C. L., 63, 105, 114
Barrett, T. C., 21, 151
Barton, A. H., 44
Basal reader approach, 96ff.,
  148, 160, 334ff.
Beginning reading, 9, 20, 42,
  78, 88ff., 96ff., 102ff., 110ff.
Bell, P. W., 460
Bernstein, B., 245, 246
Betts, E. A., 4, 55, 60, 63, 147,
  156, 157, 218
Blending, 44, 125
Blends, 220, 229, 230
Bliesmer, E. P., 368
Blind writing, 419
Bloom, B. S., 42, 436
Bloomfield, L., 4, 63, 64, 104,
  105, 114
Bond, G. L., 20, 21, 110, 112,
  114, 117, 118, 120
Bormuth, J. R., 156, 373
Botel, M., 157
Bougere, M. B., 244
Braam, L., 365

Brooks, F. E., 176
Brown, J. I., 373
Bruder, L., 461
Bruner, J. S., 41, 448
Burke, C. L., 234
Burmeister, L., 228, 229
Burrus, D., 280
Burton, W. H., 239, 275
Buswell, G. T., 15, 18, 21, 29,
  365, 371, 374

Caluin, A. D., 351
Cappa, D., 315
Carden, M., 104
Caroline, Sister Mary, 103
Carroll, J. B., 47, 62, 64, 238
Cason, E. B., 372
Cattell, J. M., 21
Catterson, J., 292
Chall, J. S., 20, 21, 22, 44, 49,
  97, 102, 110, 114, 115, 117,
  119
Chase, N. C., 12
Child development, and read-
  ing, 41ff.
Chomsky, N., 57, 58, 65
Clark, M. B., 180
Clay, M. M., 234
Cleland, D., 399
Clymer, T., 1, 63, 159, 229
Color cues, 418
Comprehension, 18, 19ff., 36ff.,
  53, 66ff., 101, 127, 261ff.,
  364ff.
Conant, J., 97
Concepts, of reading, 1ff.;
  development of, 238ff.
Conferences, individual, 202;
  parent-teacher, 420ff.
Configuration cues, 21, 51
Consonants, 124, 218ff., 229ff.
Content areas, reading in, 248,
  284ff., 294ff., 302ff., 306ff.
Context clues, 52, 211, 254ff.
Contributors, list of, vff.
Cooper, J. G., 455
Cooper, J. L., 156
Cooperative Research Program
  in First-grade Instruction,
  20, 110ff., 116ff., 123
Cordts, A. D., 63
Corrective reading, 14, 413ff.
Critical reading, 263, 270ff.,
  277ff., 280ff.
Cromer, W. C., 445
Cronin, S., 23

Crosby, M., 387

Dahms, P., 21
Dale, E., 5, 273
Dallmann, M., 294
Daniel, J. E., 156
Daniel, M. A., 187
Daniels, J. C., 104
Danielson, A., 50
Davis, A., 437
Davis, M. C., Sr., 156
Dearborn, W. F., 371, 373
De Bernardis, A., 347
Dechant, E. V., 241
Definitions of reading, 1ff, 48,
  54
Deighton, L. C., 254
Delacato, C. H., 22, 92
Determining reading needs,
  130ff., 164, 399ff.
Deutsch, C. P., 433
Deutsch, M., 43, 45, 430, 432
Devine, T. G., 63, 273
Dewey, J., 239
Diack, M., 104
Diagnosis, 11, 130ff., 139, 267,
  399ff.
Dialects, 49, 68
Dictionary, use of, 257ff.
Dietrich, D. M., 12
Digraphs, 229, 230
Dillard, J., 438, 444
Disadvantaged children, 9, 43,
  44, 45, 245, 428ff., 437ff.,
  443ff., 448ff.
Dodge, R., 21
Dolch, E. W., 224
Downey, J. E., 243
Durken, D., 20, 22, 41, 42, 88
Durrell, D. D., 156, 182, 241
Dykstra, R., 20, 110, 112, 113,
  114, 117, 118, 119, 120

Early, M. J., 291
Ebert, D., 448
Emans, R., 63, 229
Emotions, 40
Encyclopedia, using, 296ff.
Erdmann, B., 21
Evaluation of reading, 13,
  130ff.
Evans, O., 461
Experience charts, 29, 124
Experiential background, 37,
  42, 61, 77
Eye movements, 21, 22, 23

Farinella, J. T., 204
Fay, L. C., 285
Fea, H., 239
Feeley, J. T., 454
Fernald, G. M., 30, 419
Figurel, J. A., 184, 245, 284
Fisch, M., 190
Flesch, R., 2, 103, 105
Flexibility, in reading, 364ff.
Fodor, J. A., 67
Frank, J., 312
Frankel, H. M., 404
Frasier, A., 203
Fries, C. C., 3, 63, 64, 105, 114, 124, 457
Frostig, M., 22, 44, 92, 413
Fry, E., 118, 229

Gallagher, J. J., 384
Gans, R., 271, 368
Gates, A. I., 15, 16, 17, 18, 20, 21, 29, 90, 91
Gattegno, C., 103
Gessell, A. L., 89
Gibson, E., 106
Gibson, E. J., 4, 50
Gibson, J. J., 50
Gifted children, 383ff., 390ff., 393ff., 396ff.
Gilbert, L. C., 22, 23
Glaser, E. M., 272
Glock, M. D., 372
Goins, J. T., 44
Gold, L. A., 9
Goldstein, K., 414
Goodlad, J. I., 176
Goodman, K., 54, 234, 445
Goodman, Y., 59, 234
Gordon, E., 438
Gray, C. T., 29
Gray, L., 241
Gray, W. S., 5, 6, 7, 16, 17, 18, 28, 29, 97, 356
Grouping, 159ff. 180ff.
Guerra, M. H., 456
Guidebooks, 98, 339ff.
Gunderson, A., 315

Habits, reading, 12
Hall, G. S., 89
Hammond, M., 50
Hanna, P. R., 229
Harris, A. J., 7, 9, 41, 82, 119, 130, 201, 202, 364, 399, 428
Harrison, M. L.. 76
Hayes, R. B., 114
Hayes, W. D., 55
Heilman, A., 63
Hempstead, R. R., 19
Henderson, E. H., 289
Herber, H., 286, 291
Herbert, A. P., 99
Hess, R., 437
Hewett, F., 405, 406, 407
Higginbottom, E. M., 50
Hildreth, G., 35

History of reading, 27ff.
Hoggard, J. K., 71
Holland, W. R., 457
Holmes, J. A., 22, 41
Home school relationships, 72ff., 420ff.
Horn, T. D., 119, 448, 458, 459, 460
Horne, D., 22
Huey, E. B., 27
Hunt, J. M., 42, 46, 432
Hunt, L. C., Jr., 184
Huus, H., 76, 311

Independent reading, 11, 172ff.
Individual differences, 11, 40ff.
Individualized reading, 107, 184ff., 187ff., 190ff., 193ff., 199ff.
Informal inventories, 147ff., 151ff., 156ff.
Informal testing, 13, 145ff., 147ff., 151ff., 156ff.
Intelligence, and reading, 42; development of, 42ff.; and reading disability, 400
Interests, reading, 16, 311ff.
i/t/a, 27, 106, 107

Jackson, P. W., 452
Jacobs, L. B., 452
Jenkinson, M. D., 41
Jones, R., 373
Jordan, A. M., 313
Judd, C. H., 15, 18, 29

Karlin, R., 284
Katz, J. J., 67
Kender, J. P., 156
Kerfoot, J. F., 96
Kilgallon, P. A., 156
Kimball, R. B., 239, 275
Kinesthetic methods, 30, 418
King, J. B., 454, 457
Kohl, H., 449
Kriege, J. W., 164

Labov, W., 68, 438, 439, 440, 443, 444, 445
Laffey, J. L., 437
Lake, M. L., 252
Langer, J. H., 238
Language-experience approach, 108ff.
Language, and reading, 37, 48, 437ff.; development of, 43ff., 125, 433ff.
La Pray, M., 145
Larrick, N., 325, 375
Larsen, E. P., 140
Larsen, I. M., 176
Learning disabilities, 404ff.
Learning, principles of, 35ff.
Leary, B., 16, 18

Lefevre, C. A., 65, 106
Letter names, 52, 92
Levin, H., 4
Librarians, and teachers, 329ff., 391
Library, 11, 296, 298
Liddle, W., 367
Lieben, B., 420
Life values, developing through reading, 318ff.
Lima, M., 16, 18, 313
Linguistic reading programs, 104
Linguistics, and reading, 62ff.
Listening, 23, 270ff.
Literature for children, 318ff., 325ff.
Loban, W. D., 439, 450, 451
Locational skills, 294ff.
Lorge, I., 49
Lundsteen, S. W., 270, 273

Mager, R. F., 407
Malinquist, E., 44
Manolakes, G., 373
Manuals, 98, 160, 339ff.
Manuel, H. T., 455
Marcus. M., 440
Martin, E. D., 271
Martin, R., 390
Mason, G. E., 117
Materials, for the reading program, 334ff.; assigning appropriate, 164
Mathews, V. H., 12
Maw, E. W., 272, 273
Mazurkiewicz, A. J., 107, 120
McAulay, J. D., 314
McCanne, R., 455
McCarthy, D., 242
McCracken, G., 54, 104
McCracken, R., 151, 157, 396
McCullough, C. M., 3, 19, 122, 172, 312
McDavid, R. I., Jr., 68
McDonald, A. S., 364, 365
McGinnis, C., 284
Measuring reading outcomes, 130ff.
Meighen, M., 221
Melnik, A., 265
Merryman, D., 393
Metropolitan School Study Council, 306
Miles, C. C., 384
Miller, E. F., 257, 299
Miller, G. A., 61
Miscues, reading, 56ff., 234ff.
Modiano, N. A., 458
Monroe, M., 21, 78
Montessori, M., 108
Moore, O. K., 41, 107
Morphett, M., 20, 90
Morrell, K., 120
Morrison, C., 9, 82, 203, 311
Motivation, 36

Motivating reading, 11, 12, 325ff., 343ff.
Moynihan, D. P., 22

Nardelli, R. R., 272
Natchez, G., 457
Neff, N., 176
Nelson, S. E., 359
Newspaper, using, 280ff.
Nida, E. A., 67
Niles, O., 290
Non-English speakers, teaching to read, 454ff.
Non-graded plan, 176ff.
Norvell, G. W., 313, 314

Oaks, R. E., 229
Oden, M., 386
Ogilvie, M., 359
O'Leary, H. F., 334
Olson, W. C., 201, 202
Oral reading, 23, 29, 57, 58, 356ff., 368ff.
Orme, L., 79
Orton, S. T., 30
Osgood, C., 239
Osser, H., 50

Packman, L. A., 156
Parents, 375ff., 420ff.
Parrish, W. M., 359
Passow, A. H., 443
Pauk, W., 368
Perception, 21, 22, 39, 43ff., 58, 206ff., 432
Perry, W. G., Jr., 266
Personality development and reading, 45ff.
Phonics, 8ff., 17ff., 49ff., 63ff., 103ff., 124, 209, 214ff., 218ff., 221ff., 228ff., 417
Piaget, J., 234, 242
Pitman, J., 106
Poetry, language of, 68
Polysyllables, 224ff.
Povich, E., 444
Practice, role of, 39
Pratt, M., 221
Preston, R., 285
Programmed learning, 108; textbooks, 351ff.
Propaganda, teaching to detect, 277ff.
Psycholinguistics and reading, 47ff., 54ff.
Psychology of reading, 35ff., 41ff.
Psychotherapy and reading, 46, 47

Questions, using as a tool, 265ff.

Rabinowitz, R., 46
Rate, reading, 365ff., 371ff.
Readability, 12, 16

Readiness for reading, 41, 42, 71ff., 76ff., 79ff., 88ff.
Reading capacity, 14, 400
Reading centers, 342ff.
Reading, definitions of, 1ff., 48; future of, 32ff.; history of, 27ff.; psychology of, 36ff., 41ff.
Reading disability, 27ff., 404ff.
Reading groups, 159ff., 180ff.
Reading interests, 311ff.
Reading lesson plan, 335ff.
Reading levels, 148, 176ff.
Reading programs, effectiveness of, 110ff.; key factors in, 7ff.; systematizing, 164ff.
Reading readiness, 8ff., 30, 41ff., 71ff., 76ff., 79ff., 82ff., 88ff.
Reading speed, 364ff., 371ff.
Record keeping, 190ff., 203
Recreational reading, 11, 12, 311ff.
Reed, D. W., 3
Reed, M. M., 30
Reich, R. R., 409
Reid, H. C., 119, 120
Remedial reading, 14, 29, 30, 409ff., 420ff.
Research projects, 299ff.
Research, reading, 15ff., 18ff., 28ff., 41ff., 88ff., 110ff., 193ff., 272ff., 364ff.
Retarded readers, 13ff., 399ff., 423ff.
Richards, I. A., 12, 106
Riessman, F., 431, 433, 449
Riley, W., 438
Robins, C., 443
Robinson, F. P., 367
Robinson, H. A., 11, 285, 315, 369, 370
Robinson, H. M., 1, 4, 5, 6, 7, 159, 339
Rogers, H., 315
Rosner, S. A., 156
Ross, R., 145
Ruddell, R. B., 114, 120
Rudman, H. C., 314
Russell, D. H., 15, 18, 20, 21, 239, 240, 241, 242, 274
Russell, E. F., 15, 274

Saadeh, I. Q., 272, 273
Sabaroff, R., 418
Sapir, E., 64
Sartain, H. W., 193
Schlesser, G. E., 289
Schmidt, W. A., 29
Schneyer, J. W., 114, 120
Schutz, R. E., 21
Science, reading in, 306ff.
Semantics, 61, 67ff.
Serra, M. C., 240
Serwer, B. L., 9
Sheldon, W., 96, 114

Shuy, R. W., 438, 439, 440
Silent letters, 229, 230
Silent reading, 29, 59
Singer, M., 18, 19, 21, 22
Sipay, E. R., 116, 156, 199
Skarbeck, J. F., 366
Sketton, D., 312
Smith, M. K., 288, 290
Smith, H. L., 105
Smith, H. P., 241
Smith, N. B., 16, 18, 27, 261, 286, 290, 291, 356
Soares, A. T., 448
Soares, L. M., 448
Socio-cultural factors and reading, 44ff., 428ff.
Spacke, G. D., 2, 23, 42, 44, 45, 54, 289, 366, 367, 372
Spalding, R., 103
Speech, and reading, 48, 359ff., performance, 65
Speed of reading, 18, 19, 22, 59, 365ff., 371ff.
Spencer, D. U., 119, 120
Staats, A. W., 21
Staats, C. K., 21
Standardized tests, reading, 13, 131ff., 140ff.
Stauffer, R. G., 117, 119
Stemmler, A. O., 456
Stewart, W., 68, 440, 441, 444, 445
Stone, J. C., 19
Strang, R., 17, 18, 267, 284
Stratemeyer, F., 105
Strickland, R. G., 43
Structured reading program, 159ff.
Study skills, 137, 284ff., 367ff.
Sucker, F., 342
Superior readers, 383ff., 390ff., 393ff., 396ff.
Sutton, R. S., 241
Syllabication, 52, 227, 232ff.
Syntax, 61, 66ff., 126

Taba, H., 265
Tanyzer, H. J., 107, 114, 119
Taylor, S. E., 206
Teacher-parent relations, 420ff.
Teacher's manual, 98, 160
Terman, L. M., 16, 17, 18, 313, 384, 386
Testing, informal, 145ff., 147ff., 151ff., 156ff.
Test scores, understanding, 140ff.
Tests, 82ff., 131ff., 140ff.
Thalman, W. A., 314
Thompson, M., 339
Thorndike, E. L., 15, 17, 18, 28, 156
Tinker, M. A., 3, 241, 366, 371, 373
Tireman, L. S., 454, 456, 457
Torrance, E. P., 388

Tressider, A., 359
Tyler, R. W., 289

Values, developing through reading, 318ff.
Vandament, W. E., 314
Van Why, E., 373
Veatch, J., 202
Vecchio, P., 461
Vernon, M. D., 43
Vilscek, E., 120
Vinacke, W. E., 240

Visual analysis, 209, 211
Visual discrimination, 21, 22, 212
Visual perception, 22, 43, 44, 58
Vocabulary, in basal readers, 100; development of, 9, 10, 238ff., 244ff., 249ff., 252ff., 254ff., 257ff.; size of, 49, 224
Vowels, 124, 221ff., 229, 230, 231

Walcutt, C. C., 3, 54, 104
Wardhaugh, R., 62
Washburne, C., 20, 90
Watsen, J., 4
Way, O. R., 329
Weaver, R., 429
Weber, M. G., 302
Wechsler, D., 42
Welch, C. M., 55, 60
Westover, F. L., 372
Wiener, M., 445